So lernst du mit Green Line

Introduction

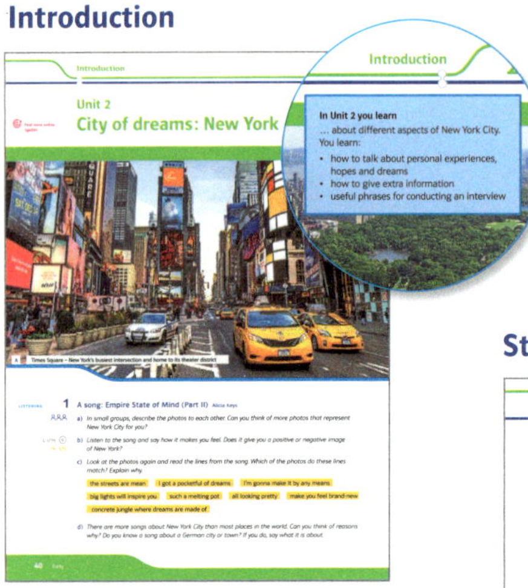

Die ersten beiden Seiten stimmen dich auf das Thema der Unit ein. In der blauen Kompetenzbox siehst du, was du in dieser Unit lernen wirst.

Die roten Dreiecke zeigen dir, dass du hinten im Diff pool z. B. Hilfen und leichtere oder weiterführende Aufgaben findest.

Stations

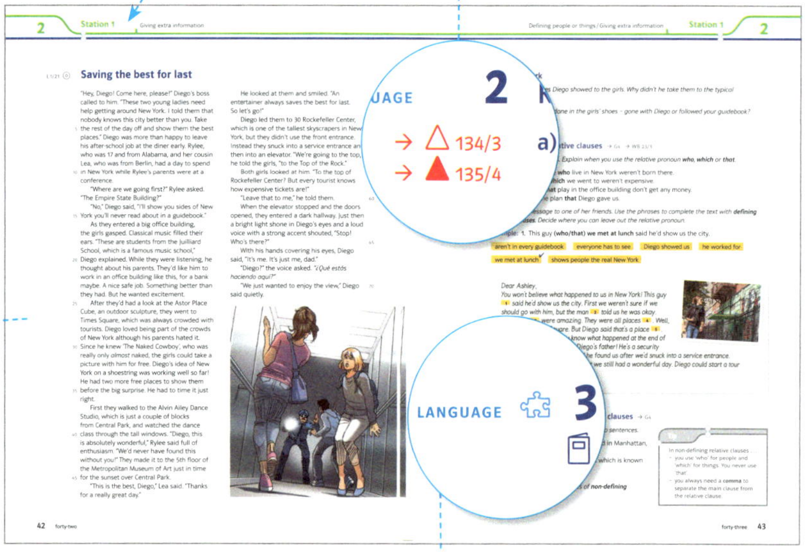

In den beiden Stations jeder Unit findest du deinen neuen Lernstoff, tolle Texte und passende Aufgaben.

Die Aufgaben mit dem Puzzle-Symbol unterstützen dich besonders dabei, deine Lernziele zu erreichen und helfen dir bei der Vorbereitung der Unit task.

Unit task

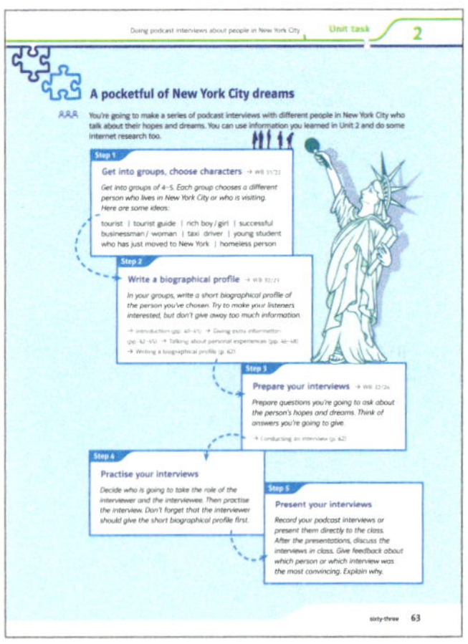

Und so kommt zum Schluss alles zusammen. Anhand dieser großen Unit-Aufgabe kannst du deine neu erworbenen Fähigkeiten schrittweise überprüfen und festigen und dabei auf kreative Weise zeigen, was du nun kannst.

Story

Hier findest du lustige und spannende Geschichten mit interessanten Aufgaben.

Action USA!

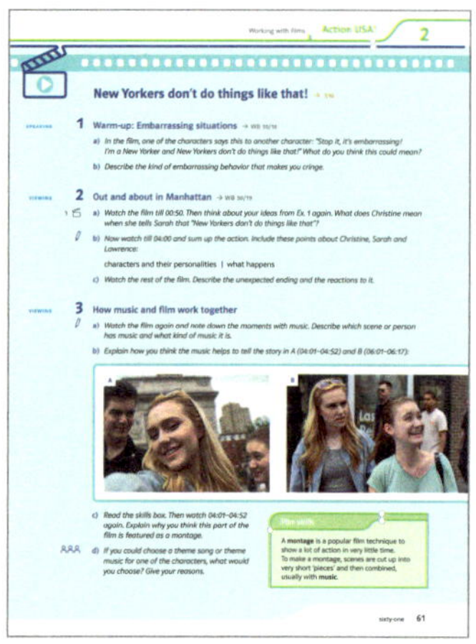

Und auf diesen Seiten gibt es tolle Filme aus den USA!

Text smart

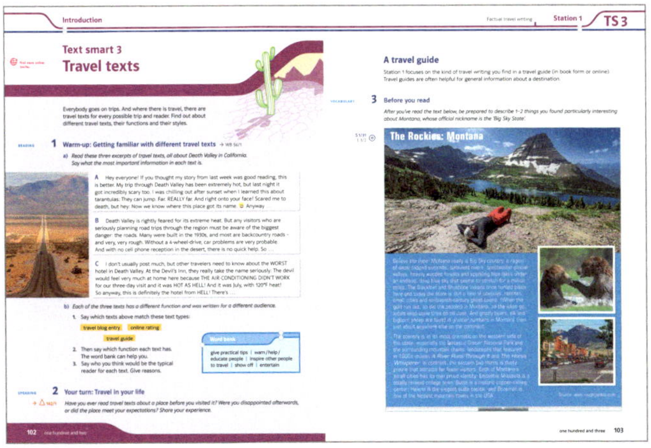

Auf den *Text smart*-Seiten lernst du, wie du mit authentischen Texten (z. B. Sachtexten, Werbetexten) umgehst und sie im Anschluss für deine eigenen Arbeiten nutzen kannst.

Across cultures

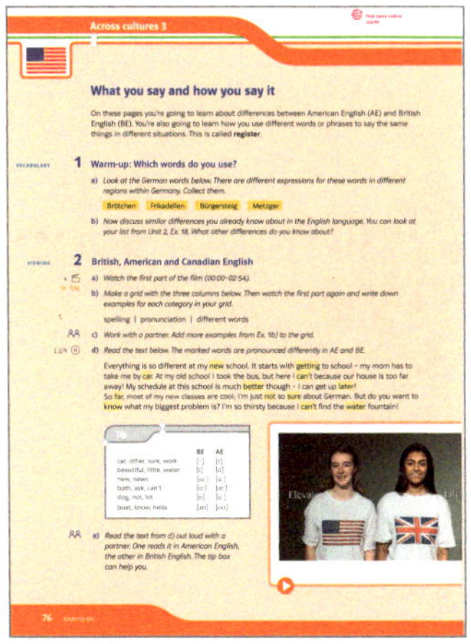

Vergleiche auf diesen Seiten deinen Alltag mit der Alltagskultur den USA und lerne, mit verschiedenen Begegnungssituationen umzugehen.

Diff pool

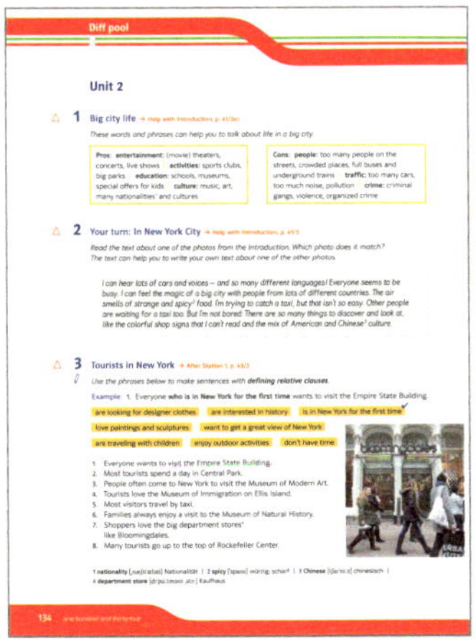

Skills

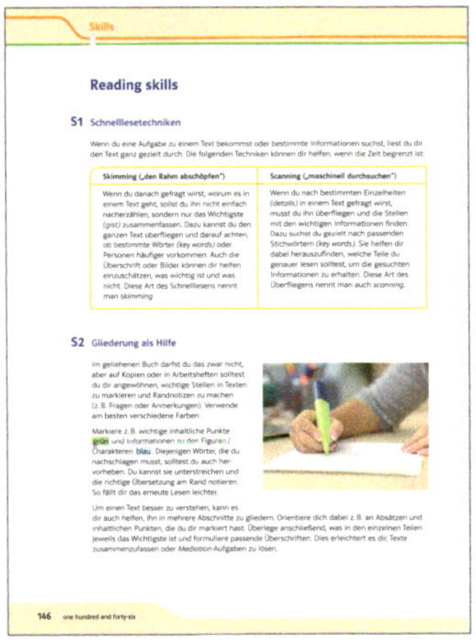

Grammar, Vocabulary

Im hinteren Buchteil stehen dir hilfreiche Anhänge zur Verfügung. Achte auf die Verweise in den Units, die dir sagen, in welchem Anhang du nachschlagen kannst.

Symbole

- → △ 134/3 Verweis auf leichtere Aufgaben / Hilfen im Diff pool
- → ▲ 135/4 Verweis auf anspruchsvollere Aufgaben im Diff pool
- → WB 7/4 Verweis auf eine Übung im Workbook
- → G2 Verweis auf die Grammatik im Anhang
- → S2 Verweis auf die Skills im Anhang
- Partnerarbeit
- Gruppenarbeit
- Hier entsteht ein Produkt für dein Portfolio.
- Schreiben (geschlossen / einfach)
- Schreiben (offen / kreativ)
- S1/14 Verweis auf die Schüler-CDs im Workbook (Audio)
- L1/19 Verweis auf die Lehrer-CDs (Audio)
- Verweis auf die Lehrer-DVD (Film)
- Code auf www.klett.de eingeben und Zusatzmaterial nutzen
- Übungen, die die Unit task besonders vorbereiten
- Across cultures

Green Line 4 für Klasse 8 an Gymnasien

Herausgeber: Prof. Harald Weisshaar, Bisingen

Autorinnen und Autoren: Jennifer Baer-Engel, Göppingen; Carolyn Jones, Beckenham; Jon Marks, Ventnor; Prof. Harald Weisshaar, Bisingen; Alison Wooder, Ventnor sowie Cornelia Kaminski, Fulda; Elise Köhler-Davidson, Exeter; Katja Krey, Reutlingen; Friderike Ulmer, Tübingen; Bernd Wick, Neckartenzlingen

Beratung: Paul Dennis, Lahnstein; Cornelia Kaminski, Fulda; Nilgül Karabulut, Aachen; Hartmut Klose, Seevetal; Antje Körber, Merseburg; Jörg Nieswand, Berlin; Jörg Schulze, Dresden

Zusatzmaterial für Schülerinnen und Schüler zu diesem Band:

Workbook + Audio-CD + Übungssoftware	978-3-12-834248-1
Workbook + Audio-CD	978-3-12-834245-0
Fit für Tests und Klassenarbeiten mit Lösungsheft und CD-ROM	978-3-12-834247-4
Trainingsbuch mit Audio-CD	978-3-12-834304-4
Vokabellernheft	978-3-12-834284-9
Vokabeltraining aktiv	978-3-12-834334-1

1. Auflage 1 8 7 6 5 | 2024 23 22 21

Redaktion: Michael Mattison; Anette Mohamud; Martina Reckart; Lektorat editoria: Cornelia Schaller, Fellbach
Herstellung: Anita Bauch; Anne Leibbrand

Gestaltung: Petra Michel, Essen
Umschlaggestaltung: know idea, Freiburg; Koma Amok, Stuttgart
Illustrationen: Peer Kramer, Düsseldorf; jani lunablau, Barcelona
sowie Christian Dekelver, Weinstadt *(Karten)*; Denise Drews, Zürich *(Time line)*
Satz: Satzkiste GmbH, Stuttgart
Reproduktion: Schwaben-Repro, Stuttgart
Druck: PASSAVIA Druckservice GmbH & Co. KG, Passau

Printed in Germany
ISBN 978-3-12-834240-5 (fester Einband)
ISBN 978-3-12-834241-2 (flexibler Einband)

Green Line 4

von
Jennifer Baer-Engel
Carolyn Jones
Jon Marks
Harald Weisshaar
Alison Wooder
Cornelia Kaminski
Elise Köhler-Davidson
Katja Krey
Friderike Ulmer
Bernd Wick

herausgegeben von
Harald Weisshaar

Ernst Klett Verlag
Stuttgart · Leipzig

Inhalt

GRAND CANYON

Inhalt

Legende

- Kompetenzaufgabe
- *Across cultures*
- 〈 〉 fakultativ
- [ ] Diese Aufgaben sind in Baden-Württemberg nicht verpflichtend zu behandeln.

Die in diesem Band aufbereiteten Inhalte stellen ein Angebot dar, sie sind nicht obligatorisch durchzunehmen. Maßgeblich für die Auswahl der Texte und Aufgaben ist der Lehrplan Ihres Bundeslandes bzw. Ihr schulinternes Curriculum.

Find more online: 9d69uv

The USA: Country of contrasts

How many contrasts can a country have? If you're talking about the United States of America (or 'the US'), the answer is: Lots! Find out for yourself on these pages and in the rest of this book.

A In New York City, the 'city that never sleeps', there are more than 13,600 taxis. But outside the big urban centers, in the endless, sparsely populated rural areas of the US, you can drive for hours and hours and not see a single car. (Well, maybe a tractor.)

B In Arizona the summers are hot – and the winters too. In the desert Southwest, temperatures often climb to 110°F or more. No problem for a cactus! But if you fly about two hours to the northwest, you'll be in a much cooler climate zone: The Pacific Northwest has green forests and huge mountains, like Mt. Rainier in Washington State.

C The country which started as a British colony and later became the United States was built on immigration. In the 19th and 20th centuries, immigrants were usually Europeans and arrived by ship at Ellis Island in New York. Today, most immigrants come from Asia and Latin America. Together, all the immigrants have created a country rich in cultural contrasts.

D The biggest, the best, the fastest: You can find lots of superlatives in the US!

For example, the world's tallest trees are found in California, like this huge redwood here. They can be 250 ft., 300 ft. tall or even taller!

In the early 20th century, Chicago and New York gave the world the first really tall skyscrapers. In 1931, the Empire State Building in New York became the world's tallest building at 1,454 ft. It isn't the tallest anymore, but it's probably still the world's most *famous* skyscraper.

E You can see American flags all over the country – at sports events, at schools, in front of homes, in big cities and in small towns. Each state also has its own flag.

People fly flags to show who or what they identify with. For some first-time visitors to the US, all the flags are a contrast to their own countries, where you don't see as many.

F Lifestyles can be hugely different in the US. More than 45 million Americans are poor: This means a family of four has only about $24,000 a year. At the same time, there are about 10 million millionaires in America – that's more than the population of Austria or Sweden. And billionaires? There are more of them in the US than in all of China, India and Russia together.

SPEAKING

1 Getting to know the US → WB 2/1

a) *Describe the scenery or the situation in each photo on pages 8–9. What can you see? These words and phrases can help:*

Word bank

crowded | sparsely / densely populated | urban | rural | out in the country | landscape | region | scenery | distances | open spaces | dry | wet | hot | cool | rain | water | climate | desert | mountainous | flat | tall | high | low | gigantic | tiny | rich | wealthy | poor | wasteful | luxury | lifestyle | love your country | leave your old life behind | start a new / better life | refugee | immigrant

Tip

Americans usually call their country 'the United States', 'the US' or simply 'America'. They don't often say 'the USA'.

Useful phrases

- The picture on the left shows … while the picture on the right is an example of …
- The picture of … shows / represents / symbolizes …
- The picture is a way to say that people in America …

b) *Now describe how the four photo pairs (A, B, D, F) show contrast in the US.*

c) *Write a heading for the four photo pairs and for the two single photos.*

d) *If **you** had chosen the photos to show the US as a 'country of contrasts', would you've chosen other ones? Which? Based on what information? Explain your reasons.*

VOCABULARY

2 Word-building: Adjective + noun collocations

→ S17

a) *Lots of the words that you see on these pages are used in typical **adjective** + **noun** collocations: **rural area**, **hot climate** etc. These collocations are useful for describing people and places. With your partner, make as many collocations as you can with the words below.*

Adjectives:
high | low | dry | wet | hot | cool | harsh | mountainous | flat | extreme | open | crowded | sparsely / densely populated | rural | urban | cultural | wealthy | healthy | beautiful | interesting

Nouns:
region | landscape | climate | climate zone | area | scenery | lifestyle | standard of living | temperature | space

b) *Once you have your collocations, arrange them in **categories** that interest you (climates, landscapes, regions). As you learn more information and vocabulary about the US in this book, add on to your list / lists to make a mini-dictionary.*

Example: **Rural areas:** sparsely populated; open spaces; beautiful scenery; …

WRITING

3 Your turn: Contrasts in your country → WB 2/2

What photos would you choose to show contrasts in Germany? Choose one topic (nature, food, buildings etc.) and find two photos for that topic which represent it well. Write a short text (5–6 sentences) for your topic and photos. Share your results with the class.

READING

4 Do you know how big everything is here?!

L1/1

Tristan and Callum's families became friends on vacation in Cornwall some years ago. Tristan lives in San Diego; Callum in London. Right now they're chatting online.

Dude, our summer vacation starts on June 10. When will you get to San Diego?

We're going to leave London on 12 June and stay in America for 5 (!) weeks.

5 weeks of surfing. AWESOME!

Sorry, first NYC and a Broadway play for Mum. Then surfing.

So 2–3 days in NYC and then a 6-hour flight to SD. CU on the 15th?

Wait, how many US states are there?

50. Why?

My mum and dad want to see half. Do you think we can see that many?

Hey, your mom and dad have no clue! Do you know how big everything is here?!

It isn't like it would take YEARS to see it all. And hey, we've got 5 whole weeks.

Not enough. My route planner says NYC to SD is 2,800 miles! 41 hours by car!!! And that's just time in the car. NO STOPS.

Wow, that IS far. So besides SD, what should we see? Boston?

Brits in Boston? Ever heard of the Boston Tea Party? American colonists who threw all the British tea into the harbour?

Oh, sounds like history. Don't tell my dad, he'll want to go. What about the South?

Callum, wrong direction! California is out WEST. Hello!

There are lots of states in the middle there. What could we see in the Midwest?

Endless corn and wheat fields. Some mountains too. The Rockies.

Sounds like lots of open space. Cool! Not like England. Good for riding horses?

Maybe, but not for riding WAVES. Get to Cali, man. Surfing! Fun in the sun!

Mum says we'll be in SD on the 4th of July. Isn't that the day with all the fireworks?

Epic, that's Independence Day! HUGE beach party on the 4th of July every year.

Massive! But wait: I'm going to celebrate how you guys became independent from us Brits?! I don't know about that …

Chill out. That was a long time ago. JUST GET HERE!

a) *Look at the map of the US at the back of your book and find all the places that are mentioned in the chat. Which place would you be most interested in? Explain why.*

b) *Understanding the text:*

1. Point out the moments in which Tristan could have given Callum more or better information about his country, for a more complete picture of the US.
2. Explain why you think Tristan doesn't offer more information. Isn't he interested?

c) *Your turn: Which places could you visit about 2,000 miles from where you live? Do some internet research on one place. In a short text with photos, describe how you could travel there and what you could do and see when you get there.*

Unit 1
Kids in America

Find more online: 7b66mg

A

B

VOCABULARY

1 Teen life in the US: First impressions

a) *Describe what you see in each picture. You can look at the word bank on the next page for ideas.*

b) *If you wanted to find out more about the topic 'Kids in America' on the internet, which words from the word bank (or other words) would you use as key words for search engines? Which of the photos give you ideas for your research? Explain why.*

SPEAKING

2 Preparing to live in America

On p. 13, you'll hear about a group of European teenagers who have just arrived in America for a year. Their families have moved to the US for work reasons.

Think-pair-share: What aspects of the three topics on the right would you want to know about if you moved to the US? On your own, think of 1–2 questions you might have. Exchange ideas with your partner before you both share your ideas with the class.

- family life
- school life
- free time activities

In Unit 1 you learn

... how to talk and write about everyday life in the United States. You learn:

- about school life, family life and free time
- how to describe and analyze pictures
- what goes into a school yearbook
- [how to use gerund and infinitive constructions to express your ideas]

C

LISTENING **3** **Orientation weekend: Welcome to America!** → WB 3/1–2

L 1/2–3

→ 128/1
→ S15

a) *Josh, an American teenager, is giving a talk for European teenagers at an orientation weekend in New York. What information does he start with? Listen to the first part and then sum it up. The word bank can help here too.*

b) *Listen to the rest of Josh's talk. Take notes and sum up what he says about* ***neighborhood / family life, school life*** *and* ***free time activities****.*

c) *Which of your questions from Ex. 2 does Josh answer? What else would you have asked him about?*

Word bank

urban / city life | rural / country life | suburb | suburban | lots of / not enough space | long / short distances | apartment | front yard | backyard | swimming pool | lifestyle | shopping mall | rich | poor | quiet | noisy | safe | dangerous | middle school | high school | hallway | hall pass | dress code | restroom | locker | have fun | make friends | be the new boy / girl

d) *Your turn: Talk about what you find surprising / interesting / strange / different about life in America. Think of what you know from Across cultures 1 and from these pages.*

L1/4

Living here isn't bad

Matt (from Cambridge) and Lena (a German-American from Hamburg) are two of the teenagers from the New York orientation weekend.

Hi Matt! I can't believe it's only been a week since we met in New York. So much has happened! Living here in rural Pennsylvania isn't bad – but it sure isn't like in the movies. Our house is huge – I love having a big bedroom. You should see my huge walk-in closet! There are a few young people around and I like hanging out with Madison, the girl down the road. They have a swimming pool in their backyard! But there isn't much to do here where the suburbs end and the country begins. Madison has talked about organizing a party for Thanksgiving, but that's not until NOVEMBER! There's a huge shopping mall with 400 stores on the other side of Pittsburgh, but getting there is difficult; it's a long drive. Madison's 16-year-old brother has a car (!), but he doesn't always want his little sister and her friends along for the ride. ☹☹☹ And all the families around here have strict curfews for their kids – Madison has to be home very early each night. ☹☹☹ Same in your neighborhood? – Anyway, I'm homesick for Germany! I miss seeing my old friends and I'm scared of changing too much so they won't like me anymore when I go back. I enjoyed meeting you in New York; how about meeting up in Pittsburgh soon? Lena

Hey Lena. Sounds like our experiences here are quite different. I don't miss my life in England at all! Being in a city is cool – Pittsburgh is big and we live in an apartment close to downtown. I'm still getting used to living on the 22nd floor – the elevator is a BIG part of my life! Can you imagine walking up 22 floors if it stopped working? I miss having a garden (= yard!) so I go out a lot. I take the bus everywhere; the buses are cheap. And luckily we've got shops, cafés, parks and cinemas (or 'movie theaters', as the Americans say) super close to where we live. I'm looking forward to starting school and making new friends next week. I'm good at swimming and football (= soccer!); maybe that will help at Birchview Middle School. But stop worrying about losing your old friends or your identity – just jump in and enjoy the experience. – Hey, I'm afraid I'm very busy right now; meeting up isn't easy. Do you remember Sophie from orientation? She's going to move to Pittsburgh soon – it'll be cool to see her again! Well, keep in touch. CU! ☺ Matt (PS: I keep forgetting your dad is American; no wonder your English is so good!)

READING

1 Two different experiences in America → WB 4/3

→ S1

a) *Sum up Lena's and Matt's situation in America. Whose situation sounds better to you? Say why.*

b) *Compare how Lena and Matt have been experiencing the US. What's the same, what's different?*

c) *Write another message from Matt to Lena to cheer her up with advice.*

READING

2 Thanksgiving: A very American holiday → WB 4/4

a) *Lena mentioned an important American holiday: Thanksgiving. Read the box and talk to your partner about festivals and holidays that are celebrated in Germany.*

Across cultures

Thanksgiving is one of the most important national holidays in the United States – and a very important day for families too. On the fourth Thursday in November each year, families all over the country get together for a big, wonderful meal. The meal is a symbol of everything one should be thankful for. This tradition started nearly 400 years ago …

In late 1620, the Pilgrims left England for America so they could practice their religion freely. The first American winter was very hard; the Pilgrims had to build houses and they had to find food. By spring more than half of them had died. The survivors then asked the Native Americans for help with planting food. With that help, the harvest in 1621 was a success. The colonists gave thanks with a big meal which they enjoyed together with the Indians. **What was on the menu?** Roast turkey, cranberry sauce, sweet potatoes and pumpkin pie – the same dishes you'll still find on lots of Thanksgiving tables today.

The first Thanksgiving, 1621

A typical Thanksgiving meal

b) *Your turn: What do you have to be very thankful for? Write about it in 5–6 sentences.*

c) *Why do you think Lena can't wait for Thanksgiving?*

LANGUAGE

3 [Different categories of gerunds] → G1

*Each of the left-hand sentences below features a **noun**. To the right of each sentence you see a sentence which is almost the same, but with a **gerund** instead of a 'normal' noun. This shows you how gerunds are really verbs which work as nouns:*

1. Homework isn't bad.	→ Living here isn't bad.
2. I like burgers.	→ I like hanging out with Madison.
3. I'm good at football.	→ I'm good at swimming.
4. I'm looking forward to our trip to New York.	→ I'm looking forward to starting school.

a) *The sentences above are examples of the four gerund categories you see on the right. Match each category to one of the four gerund sentences above.*

b) *Go back to Lena's and Matt's messages. Find four different gerund examples which work in the same way as the four examples above. Make a grid.*

→ △ 128/2

a) gerund after adjective + preposition
b) gerund after verb + preposition
c) gerund as sentence subject
d) gerund as sentence object

LANGUAGE **4** **[Gerunds as subject or object]** → WB 5/5

→ △ 129/3

Sophie was another girl at orientation in New York. She has posted her first thoughts about the US on a social media page for the others who were there. Use the words on the right to complete her post with gerunds as ***subject*** *or* ***object****.*

travel | move ✓ | live | hang out | be | share | cycle (2x) | have

Help! I didn't mind **moving** from Germany to America, but I never imagined 1 in the middle of nowhere! Luckily, we're only staying here with my aunt and uncle until our apartment in Pittsburgh is ready. 2 a bedroom with my messy cousin really gets on my nerves! I just can't get used to 3 such a messy room. Anyway, Dad always says how beautiful it is out here in the country, but where's the *action*?! 4 bored is no fun! I miss 5 with my friends. And, can you believe this? 6 to the next mall takes TWO HOURS by car! My cousin has just suggested 7 somewhere this afternoon – but I don't feel like 8 anywhere. I mean, where to anyway? We're in the middle of nowhere!

LANGUAGE **5** **[Gerunds in phrases]**

Now read Matt's reply to Sophie's post. Put in the missing ***verb + preposition*** *or* ***adjective + preposition*** *to make complete gerund phrases.*

Don't 1 feeling bored. When you get to Pittsburgh, you'll soon have to 2 being busy all the time! It's a great place, with lots to do. I'll never be 3 living here! I'm already very 4 finding my way around the city and I'm not at all 5 getting lost. I'm 6 going to my first baseball match soon. Do you 7 meeting up and going together? I'm 8 seeing you when you get here. Can't wait!

looking forward to | worry about | feel like | thinking of | tired of | good at | scared of | get used to

SPEAKING **6** **[Gerunds to talk about likes and dislikes]** → WB 5/6

→ △ 129/4

Gerunds are often helpful when you want to talk about likes and dislikes. Here, Lena is talking to her new friend, Madison. Rewrite their sentences with the phrases on the right and with ***gerunds****. Don't change the meaning!*

keep | look forward to | start | don't mind ✓ | stop | think of | be interested in | love

Lena

1. I'm a bit shy when I meet new people, but it's OK.
   → I **don't mind meeting** new people.
2. Maybe I'll go to the mall; I'm not sure yet.
3. Mom tells me to unpack every day!
4. There's a dress code so I don't wear crazy T-shirts to school anymore.

Madison

5. My brother learned to drive when he was 16.
6. Would you like to meet some more people in the area?
7. I can't wait to plan our Thanksgiving party!
8. I listen to music all the time!

SPEAKING

7 Your turn: Likes and dislikes

→ △ 129/5

a) *With the words on the right, tell your partner about things you like and dislike. (Tip: It might help to write out some of your ideas first. Also, the vocabulary box on p. 188 can help.)*

love | hate | enjoy | dislike | dream of | be tired of | be interested in | be scared of | be worried about | be good at | be crazy about

Example:

A: I'm never crazy about being the 'new person'. It always makes me feel so insecure. What about you?

B: For me, trying new things is great! You'll never know you're good at something until you try.

b) *Go back to p. 13 and 'climb into' photo C. Imagine* **you** *are there in the hallway on your first day at school. In 5–6 sentences, describe what's going through your mind.*

SPEAKING

8 How to: Describe pictures → WB 6/7–9

→ S5

What does America look / feel like for teens in rural areas? And in the city? After you read the skills box, work with a partner and answer the questions below. He / She chooses one of the pictures; you choose the other. The useful phrases box can help you too.

1. Describe your picture. Who's in it? What's happening?
2. Do you think your picture is a good example for showing what America might look like for Americans the same age as you? Why do you think so? Explain your ideas.

Speaking skills

When you talk about pictures (photos, cartoons), do it in steps:

1. First, **describe** what is happening. For this, you use the **present progressive**. It's also important to talk about what you can see in the foreground, middle and background.
2. After that, you can **analyze** a picture: You can give your opinion about it or explain what you think it means. For this you use the **simple present**.

Look at the phrases box below for examples.

A

Useful phrases

Describing pictures:

- In picture X, a person is talking / running / having fun with … / asking … | Somebody else is laughing / shouting / …
- In the foreground, there's a/an … / there's some …
- In the background, you see a/an … / lots of …

Analyzing pictures:

- In my opinion, the picture is a typical example of … because it shows …
- The picture represents … / shows …
- The picture tries to show … but I think a picture with … instead of … would work better because …

B

L1/6 That's the worst thing to do!

Matt is on Birchview's yearbook committee. They decide what goes into the yearbook - and what doesn't. Matt is sitting with two of the most popular 8th-graders, Scott and Eva.

Scott, Eva and Matt were looking at different layouts in second period when Scott stopped to say something in Matt's direction. "Hey, let's go for lunch together."

"Yeah, with us this time, Matt. You don't want to sit with Henry and Tyler again, do you?" Eva added with a funny look on her face. "Stop talking to them. They're geeks."

"If you want to be popular, that's the worst thing to do!" Scott agreed.

Matt went on looking at the different layouts in front of him; he needed time to think - what a dilemma! "So, they want me to be friends with them," he thought to himself. "But why are they so mean about the boys I had lunch with yesterday, the 'geeks'?"

"The geeks are no fun to hang out with because they never *have* fun."

"Yeah, I mean, who wants to be around people whose idea of fun is to go to the mall and shout at the shoppers?"

Matt was confused. "I don't understand."

"They keep on talking about changing the world. So whenever there's a protest against child labor and sweatshops, the geeks are always the first to shout at the people who buy cheap sweatshop clothes."

"I mean, I agree: Child labor is awful," Eva went on. "But now the geeks want us to write about it in the yearbook. That isn't what it's for. A yearbook should be for fun things, for the highlights of our year!"

Another girl in the room had a different opinion: "Sorry Eva, but demonstrating for children's rights *is* a highlight of the year!"

Matt agreed. But all he could say was, "Well, I guess it isn't so easy to decide what goes into the yearbook!" He was smiling, but inside he didn't know what to think. "Do Scott and Eva expect me to drop my new friends just because they're different? I was looking forward to hanging out with them again," he thought. "Should I go to lunch with the in-crowd?" He didn't know. Yesterday had been his first day at this school, with two surprises: The day started with the Pledge of Allegiance - very different to the UK! And then in the cafeteria came another surprise: He was looking for a place to sit when two boys invited him to their table. They seemed a bit different and at first they talked a lot about their protests, but then they went on to talk about other things too. Matt liked them. Did he really need to choose between them and the others?

READING

9 Matt's dilemma → WB 7/10

a) *Eva and Scott are part of the popular in-crowd, and they talk about Henry and Tyler as 'the geeks'. What do you think of cliques like this at school?*

b) *What is Matt's dilemma? Describe it in your own words.*

c) *How would you react in Matt's situation? Write him an e-mail with your advice.*

→ 130/6

READING 10

Everyday life in American schools → WB 7/11

L1/7

Across cultures

Most American students take the **Pledge of Allegiance** every morning. They stand, face the American flag, put their right hand over their heart and say:

"I pledge allegiance to the Flag of the United States of America, and to the Republic for which it stands, one Nation under God, indivisible, with liberty and justice for all."

a) *What do you think of the Pledge of Allegiance?*

b) *With your partner, talk about other ways people show that they belong to a country/group/school/club/...*

LANGUAGE 11

[Find the rule: Infinitives with question words] → G2

→ △ 130/7–8
→ ▲ 131/9

a) *When you talk about what people ask themselves, you often use **infinitive constructions**. Look at these examples. Make a rule for questions with and without question words.*

Matt asked himself, "What should I think?" → Matt didn't know **what to think**.
He thought, "Should I go for lunch with the in-crowd?" → He wasn't sure **whether to go** for lunch with the in-crowd.

b) *Matt had a lot of questions during his first days at school. Make sentences about him.*

Start: He wanted to know **where to go** for a drink of water.

- Where can I go for a drink of water? ✔
- Should I use my own laptop?
- Should I buy lunch or bring my own?
- How much money must I bring for lunch?
- When can I use my locker?
- What do I have to wear for PE?

LANGUAGE 12

[Infinitives after superlatives]

***Superlative phrases** with **infinitives** are easy to use. Look at the example below. Then use the words on the right to complete what some students in the school café are saying to each other.*

1. You eat so quickly. You're always **the first to finish**!
2. You take so long to choose your food! You're always ...
3. You're having salads?! I want a burger! Am I ...?
4. We shouldn't eat too much before swimming. That's ...
5. The pizza here is fantastic. I always think it's ...
6. If you don't have much money, soup is ...
7. I like having lunch with you guys. You're ...

the only one / eat meat
the cheapest thing / have
the first / finish ✔
the funniest people / sit with
the worst thing / do
the last / sit down and eat
the best thing / order

LANGUAGE **13** [Object + infinitive: Expressing wishes and expectations]

a) *Change the sentences below into German. Then compare the German and English constructions:*

1. Scott: Come on, Matt. Sit at our table today!
   ↓
2. Scott wants Matt to sit at their table today.

→ △ 131/10
→ ▲ 131/11

b) *What do these people want or expect others to do? Look at the example and rewrite the other sentences in the same way. The yellow grid below can help too:*

Example: Scott: Don't sit with Henry and Tyler, Matt.
→ Scott doesn't **want Matt** to sit with Henry and Tyler.

1. Eva: No, sit with us instead. → Eva **would prefer** …
2. Matt to himself: They don't think that I should be friends with Henry and Tyler.
   → They **don't want** …
3. Tyler: We're happy when people think we're different. → We'**d like** …
4. Henry: We hope they'll start thinking about where their clothes are made.
5. Tyler to Matt: The teachers say we can't work on our protest events during class.
6. Matt to himself: Scott and Eva always think that everybody should agree with them.

want / would like would prefer would expect		object (noun or pronoun)		infinitive with *to*
I (don't) want I expect I'd like I'd prefer	+	me you him / her / it us them	+	to …

Tip

Be careful! It's a typical mistake not to use an **infinitive with *to*** in sentences with *want you to …* or *expect you to …* because the sentence structure is different in German.

LANGUAGE **14** [Infinitives with and without *to*] → WB 8/12

Read this e-mail from Sophie to Matt. Complete it with the verbs below. Use the infinitive form, with or without ***to****.*

get | meet up | take | come | have | keep | do (2x) | control | calm down

Tip

The Grammar will help you to decide where to use ***to***. (→ G2)

Hi Matt – You know we wanted 1 in Pittsburgh next week? Well, sorry but I can't. My parents have been worried about me all the time since we moved to the big city and they don't let me 2 anything. They're crazy! They've decided 3 everything I do! Today, I had planned 4 a coffee with friends after school but they made me 5 straight home. I think it's probably better just 6 as they say – but soon I'll make my escape! They should 7 and relax – but it might 8 a while! I promise 9 in touch – let's 10 together soon. xo 🙂 Sophie

LANGUAGE

15 [Gerund or infinitive: It depends on the meaning] → G3 → WB 8/13

a) *Some verbs (begin, like, prefer etc.) can be followed by an infinitive or a gerund with no difference in meaning. But with a few verbs, the meaning changes. It's important to learn by heart when you need a gerund and when you need an infinitive. First, write these two sentences in German to find out how the meaning of* ***remember*** *changes:*

1. He **remembered** saying goodbye to his friends back home; it made him feel sad.
2. She **remembered** to tell her parents what time she was coming home.

→ △ 132/12

b) *In the text on page 18, the verbs* ***go on*** *and* ***stop*** *are each used with an infinitive and with a gerund. Talk about how the meaning changes for each verb. Then write the sentences in German; this will help you to see the difference more clearly.*

c) *Read these sentences from an argument Sophie had with her mother and complete them with a* ***gerund*** *or an* ***infinitive****.*

Sophie: I'll never forget [1] (hear) that you were taking me away from all my friends in Germany!
Mom: Don't forget [2] (call) me when you arrive at your friend's house!
Sophie: Please stop [3] (give) me rules and curfews all the time!
Mom: Can't you stop [4] (have) some lunch? I'm tired of arguing with you!
Sophie: Try [5] (listen) to me sometimes. I just want to make friends and fit in! Why don't you try [6] (understand) how I feel?
Mom: Playing sport is a good way to meet friends.
Sophie: Sure, but it means [7] (stay) after school – and you won't let me!
Mom: I don't mean [8] (upset) you. But America is new for all of us and I worry.

MEDIATION

16 Clean out your attics for the clothing drive! → WB 9/14–15

→ △ 132/13
→ S13

Birchview Middle School is having a clothing drive for a homeless shelter. The committee for the project has written a flyer for it. On video chat, Lena wants to tell some students at her old school in Hamburg about it. One of you plays Lena and describes the main ideas in the flyer; 2–3 others play students who ask Lena questions about it.

HELP THE HOMELESS!
Birchview Middle School Clothing Drive

Are you tired of looking at all the old clothes in your closet? Worried about what your next new outfit will be? Well, some people wish they had problems like that. The Lakeview Homeless Shelter needs our help, and Birchview has ALWAYS been good at helping.
So … **Donate as many old clothes as you can!**
(We'll accept clothing for kids and adults, and also shoes, belts, toys and bikes.) **The benefits:** Our school will get 15 cents a pound for all of the items we donate. And YOU'LL get a great feeling of knowing you helped homeless people, your school *and* your parents! (Remember, cleaning out the attic and garage is something they really expect you to do!) 🙂 THANK YOU!

(Clothing drop-offs: Mo–Fr this week in the cafeteria, before or after school)

S 1/3–10
L 1/9–16

Nightmare at the mall!

SPEAKING

1 Before you read

What teen films have you seen that felt believable at first, but then went in a direction that didn't seem believable at all? What was that moment? Use the words and phrases below to help you explain your ideas.

exaggerated actions / feelings / …

unrealistic situation / language / coincidence

actions which didn't match the character / the role

A Lena was excited. Madison's mom was finally driving them to the big mall on the other side of Pittsburgh. It was a long drive through lots of suburbs. After three weeks of waiting far outside the city, where the suburbs end, she was going to see the *real* America and have an afternoon away from her boring life. She could still hear her own mom's voice in her ears: "If you lose your friends, call me – and don't do anything silly!"

In the car, Madison's older brother Josh explained to Lena what was happening at the mall that day. "We're going to see a really famous baseball player, Wayne Larson," he explained. "He's going to open a new sports store, so expect big crowds. He might even sign a T-shirt for you!"

B When they finally arrived, Lena was amazed. So many stores, so many people, so much noise! For a moment she felt scared – but only for a moment. "This will be fun!" she thought. "Mom will come back later," said Madison. "If we lose each other, we need to meet here at these benches at 5 o'clock."

"Don't worry. I'm going to stay right next to you!" said Lena. But exactly at that moment, there was a huge cheer and she was suddenly pushed into a big crowd of hundreds of people; everyone was trying to get a look at Wayne Larson. Lena tried to grab Madison's arm, but the crowd was moving too fast and she soon realized that she had lost her friends – after only five minutes at the mall!

C Lena tried to turn around as the crowd pressed against her but she couldn't move at all. She started to feel sick and dizzy. The voices all around her were getting louder, then some voices became even louder than the rest …

"Down with child labor!" …
"What if they were YOUR children?!"

What was going on? Wayne Larson was looking very worried as his bodyguards helped him to escape from the crowd. Who were the protesters? Lena was just able to see a group of young people who were all carrying signs and shouting. Then the crowd started pushing again. This time, her feet didn't touch the ground and she flew through the air. She landed very close to the protesters. Then she felt a very strong pair of hands which then took her away.

D "I've got one of the troublemakers right here!" a man shouted. "So what do you have to say for yourself, young lady?"

Lena couldn't believe it! Now the police were arresting her! She tried to speak but nothing came out. "I …, I …,"

"Well, you'd better think of some good answers to our questions quickly or you'll find yourself in big trouble!" said the police officer. Lena could easily imagine spending a night in prison and she was starting to panic when a voice shouted from behind her.
"LEAVE HER ALONE!" Who was that?

E "She isn't doing anything wrong! She isn't from here. Let her go!" the voice continued. She tried again to speak "I …, I …"

"Sshh," whispered the voice. Pretend you don't speak English!"

She turned around and came face to face with … Matt?! From the New York weekend?! "What are YOU doing here?!" she asked.

"Er, rescuing you!" he answered. "Now, don't say anything else. I'll get you out of here." Lena waited while Matt spoke to the police officer and soon she was free to go.

F "What are you really doing here?" she asked Matt as they pushed through the crowds.
"Oh, I've come to support the protesters – they're my friends, from my new school in Pittsburgh."

Lena wanted to ask more questions, but then she remembered. What was she thinking? Matt had clearly told her that he didn't want to meet up with her – while he had made it very obvious that he wanted to meet *Sophie!* Lena found a small gap in the crowd and hurried away from Matt.

G What a nightmare! Lena wasn't enjoying her afternoon at the mall at all. Where were Madison and the others in this sea of people? Lena was going up and down escalator after escalator; she looked everywhere and just couldn't find them. She needed to call her mom and felt silly about it – surely she was old enough to look after herself better than this? But Lena accepted that it was time to give up and call her mom, so she opened her bag to get her phone and – it wasn't there.

H As Lena moved down *another* escalator, still looking all around her for Madison, she was trying so hard not to cry that she almost didn't notice the boy in front of her – Josh!

"Lena!" he shouted when he saw her. "We couldn't find you! Madison has already gone home with Mom – but don't worry. My friend, Nick, has a car. Come on!"

Lena didn't think twice: "Yeah, sure!"

"Cool, I'll drive you!" smiled Nick. But then Lena knew she really shouldn't go. She didn't know Nick and she didn't like his smile. And, her mom would go crazy … But really, she was too tired to care. She was just walking along slowly with the boys when from behind her she suddenly heard a voice she knew. "Lena! Here you are. I lost you! Look, here's your phone. You dropped it!" Matt was all smiles.

"He's just saved my life – for the *second* time today!" Lena thought. "I can't forgive him yet for liking Sophie more than me …" But then she said: "Let's have a coffee before I call my mom." They both smiled.

READING

2 Understanding the story → WB 10/16

a) *Match one of these headings to each of the eight parts of the story.*

1. Next stop: Prison?!
2. I can't be his friend
3. Alone already?!
4. Too old to be in this mess
5. Rescued again!
6. Escaping from home – finally!
7. Protests and shopping don't mix!
8. A friend to the rescue

b) *The title of the story is 'Nightmare at the mall'. Can you think of a title which would work better? Write it down and tell the class why you chose it.*

READING

3 Believe it or not?

Which of these events in the story did you find believable – or not? Explain your reasons.

1. Lena lost her friends at the mall.
2. Matt was at the same mall as Lena.
3. Lena was stopped by the police.
4. Matt found Lena's phone.
5. Lena agreed to get into Nick's car.
6. Matt found Lena twice.
7. Lena invited Matt for a coffee.
8. The mall was so crowded.

WRITING

4 An exaggerated storyline: Make it more realistic → WB 10/17

→ S7–9

Writing skills

Storylines are often exaggerated for more action and excitement. Examples:

- **coincidence:** *She turned around and came face to face with Matt.* (lines 70–71)
- **exaggerated language:** *He's just saved my life!* (line 118); *What a nightmare!* (line 89)
- **unrealistic situation:** *She felt a very strong pair of hands which then took her away.* (lines 49–51)
- **extreme action:** *Her feet didn't touch the ground; she flew through the air.* (lines 47–48)
- **extreme reaction:** *Pretend you don't speak English!* (lines 68–69)
- **out-of-character actions:** *Lena didn't think twice.* (line 108)

a) *Collect all the coincidences and unrealistic situations in the story.*

b) *Decide which situations in a) you would have left out of the story. Explain why.*

→ △ 132/14

c) *Creative writing: Choose one part of the story to rewrite so that it's more believable.*

SPEAKING

5 <Your turn: Are you telling the truth?>

a) *What **true stories** can you think of which are exaggerated and almost impossible to believe? Which stories can you think of which would be fun to tell but **didn't really happen**? Make notes about a story you can tell in b).*

b) *Play a game: Now tell your stories to the class. Everyone can show if they believe your story or not: A **green** card means "I believe it" and a **red** card means "No way, I don't believe it!" Each person needs to explain his/her green or red card.*

Go on, text her! → S16

SPEAKING

1 Warm-up: What do you look for in others? → WB 11/18

Share your ideas in your group about what you find attractive in others. The words / phrases in the boxes can help you.

Useful phrases

- I look for … in a friend / boyfriend / girlfriend.
- The person should have / be …
- The most important thing to me is …
- It's attractive if the person is / has …

nouns:
positive attitude | nice smile | good looks | sense of humor | sense of style | good listener | lots of the same interests

adjectives:
honest | fair | funny | attractive | smart | popular | outgoing | laid-back

VIEWING

2 The characters

1 **a)** *Watch the two scenes with Wesley and Jessica (till 04:09). Then describe each character in the story so far: Wesley, Jessica and also Leanne. What are their roles in the storyline?*

b) *Now watch again and answer these questions:*

1. Describe what Jessica means at these moments with her advice for Wesley:

Don't you think that's overdoing it? It's not really you. | Just relax and be yourself. | Remember not to eat anything with garlic. | Clothes aren't everything.

2. Explain why it's good advice – or not. 3. What advice would you give Wesley?

VIEWING

3 The date

a) *How does Wesley change between the scene on the left (03:34) and the scene on the right (05:25)? Describe what happens (in 5–6 sentences) and how these two stills show the difference. Think of how Wesley acts, talks and looks.*

b) *Do you think Wesley and Leanne have a chance together? Go back to Ex. 1. Think of what Wesley and Leanne might find attractive and interesting in each other.*

How to write in the appropriate style

This page can help you to find the right style and tone when you write different kinds of texts.

1 Listening: Students on the yearbook committee

L1/17

→ S15

a) *Listen to two students who are discussing yearbook pages. Take notes about these points:*

the three main sections in yearbooks | typical content for each section | the appropriate language for each section

b) *Listen again. Which of these photos and texts are good and which ones need to be changed? What changes do the students suggest?*

OMG, how cute is Austin Ford's smile?! No surprise that he won 'Boy with the Best Smile'! (What toothpaste does he use?)

((Dear yearbook team – we still need a text here!))

Why does Janie ALWAYS have to be in the middle of EVERY photo? Here she is again! She'll never learn, will she?

2 Find the right writing style → WB 12/20

In pairs, make a grid with three columns for ***Student Superlatives, Highlights of the Year*** *and* ***Clubs and Sports****. What language tone do you need for each category? What style of photos? What phrases are typical? Fill in your grid with ideas and phrases from the boxes below.*

3 Write a short yearbook text

→ S9

Now go back to Ex. 1b). Write the text for photo 2 and improve the text for photo 3. Peer-edit each other's texts. Are the tone and the language appropriate?

Word bank

Language tone:
funny | serious | ironic | simple | informative

Style of photos:
silly | natural | serious | individual / group | a silly / serious / … pose

Useful phrases

The swim / soccer / … team had their best season ever. | Being in / Participating in the Drama Club / the Yearbook Committee was … special / different / interesting this year because … | The Art Club started the year with … | Wasn't the Spring Dance / the championship basketball game the best ever? | We'll always remember the day when … | Here he / she is again with … | He / She will never learn! | We wanted you to see THIS! | How could we ever forget …?

An American-style yearbook

Here you get the chance to create some typical double pages in English for an American-style yearbook about your own school.

Step 1
Form groups

*Divide up into six groups. There should be **two groups** for each of the **three categories** of typical yearbook content you see on the right.*

- Student Superlatives
- Highlights of the Year
- Clubs and Sports

Step 2
Think about typical content for your pages → WB 13/21

*Each group is going to plan **a model double page** for its category. First you need to think about what kind of content is typical for your category. Think about these points as you brainstorm your ideas:*

- What kind of **texts** will you need: short / long; factual / funny?
- What kind of **photos**: individual / group; serious / funny; several / few / just one?
- What kind of a **design** would look best for your pages?
- What **examples** of school and free time activities from this unit can give you ideas for your own pages? What funny / strange / interesting things are there to report?
- What **vocabulary** and **language** from the unit could help you?

Tip

For the category 'Highlights of the Year', many yearbook commitees feature **free time** activities and events too (e.g. something that happened at the mall / a concert / at a party / …)

→ Vocabulary about teenage life (Introduction) → Likes / dislikes (Station 1) → Describing pictures (p. 17) → Questions and superlative phrases (Station 2) → Using the appropriate style and tone / Yearbook phrases (p. 26)

Step 3
Make a poster for your plan → WB 13/22

On a poster, make a plan that shows what your double page could look like. Then trade posters with the other group that has your category. Make sure you aren't doing the same things!

Step 4
Create your pages

Now divide up the work in your group: Collect photos, write texts, peer-edit each other's work. Also, somebody will need to present your pages to the class.

Step 5
Present your pages

Present your pages to the class. Explain why the topics, photos and texts are good examples. Other groups will say which parts of your pages they liked best, and give their reasons.

LISTENING

1 Moving

L 1/18

a) *Listen to the conversation between Kim and her best friend Tina. What is Kim's problem? What does Tina tell her?*

b) *Listen again and find examples of exaggerated language and extreme reaction. How does this match the turning point in the girls' conversation?*

c) *Partner A: You're going to move to another town / country with your family and you're really sad to leave your friends. Partner B: One of your best friends is going to move to another town / country. What do you tell him / her to make him / her feel better? Collect ideas and act out your conversations first together and then for the class.*

VOCABULARY

2 Urban vs. rural → WB 16/2

a) *Replace[1] the words and phrases in **bold** with the adjectives below to make the text more interesting. Sometimes you have to add the verb **be**.*

awesome | wealthy | dizzy | endless | flat | amazed | insecure | natural | gigantic | homeless

When I first saw New York City, I was **very surprised** by all the lights in the city. They seemed to be everywhere and to be on 24 hours a day! Sometimes when I looked up, I felt **like everything was spinning**[2] because all the buildings were **very, very big**. New York is a city of contrasts too. I saw people who were **very rich** and people who **didn't have a home**.

After three days in New York, I was ready to leave the city, but out in the country I felt small too because the landscape **had no mountains** and the sky **never stopped**. Everywhere I went people were **really, really great**. At first I **didn't feel very sure of myself**, but the Americans I met were all so friendly that soon it was **completely normal** for me to speak English with everybody!

b) *Use five of the adjectives from a) to write your own sentences.*

LANGUAGE

3 I'm looking forward to ...

*Use the words and phrases to rewrite the conversation with **gerunds**.*

Start like this: A: I'**m looking forward to seeing** you on Friday!

be good at | keep | look forward to ✔ | stop | be used to | be worried about

A: I can't wait to see you on Friday! ✔
B: Me too! I'm counting the days.
A: I'm not so sure if I should take the train.
B: Don't worry! It's easy to use the train.
A: Yeah, for you it's easy. You take the train all the time.
B: Yes, I do. But when I'm late, I have a problem. I can't run like you can!

1 **to replace (by/with)** [rɪˈpleɪs] ersetzen (durch) | 2 **to spin** [spɪn] sich drehen

LANGUAGE

4 Sophie's bedroom → WB 16/3

a) *What do the things in Sophie's bedroom and her telephone conversation say about her? Use the words and phrases to make sentences with* ***gerunds****.*

Example: Sophie **loves buying** new shoes.

decide against | dream of | be crazy about | be excited about | be good at | love ✔

dance | watch | go | listen | travel | buy ✔

I want to buy new shoes …

b) *Think about things in your room. What do they say about you? Write three sentences with* ***gerunds****.*

WRITING

5 America is different

a) *Imagine you've spent some time in America. Think of three things that are different there. Write down tips for someone who is visiting America for the first time.*

Start like this:
If you have to use the toilet in America, don't ask where the 'toilet' is. Instead …

b) *Your turn: What is different in Germany? Work with a partner and write down three tips for people who are visiting Germany for the first time.*

LANGUAGE

6 Too many rules

Put the words in the right order to make sentences with ***gerunds as subject or object****.*

1. the rules | isn't | following | cool
2. what everyone else | I | don't like | does | doing
3. with my parents | arguing | is awful | about my curfew
4. isn't | with a troublemaker | a good idea | being friends
5. don't mind | with the popular kids | I | hanging out
6. but | having | I | my own ideas | love

LANGUAGE

7 Celebrating Thanksgiving

a) *Use the verbs to complete the text with* ***gerunds as subject or object****.*

be | bother | celebrate | eat (2x) | play | talk | wait | watch

1 Thanksgiving is good and bad. I don't mind **2** turkey every year because my mom makes the best turkey ever. **3** polite and **4** my grandma's potatoes although I don't like them is hard. One of the worst parts is **5** with my annoying little cousins. They never know when to stop **6** me. **7** for dessert is probably the worst part. The adults spend so much time **8** before we get our pie. There's another big Thanksgiving tradition. I love **9** football on TV with all my uncles.

b) *What do you like / don't you like about holidays with your family? Make sentences with* ***gerunds*** *and share them with your partner. These ideas can help you:*

Celebrating holidays with my family is … | On holidays I really like / don't like … | … is the best part of holidays. | I always look forward to …

MEDIATION

8 Fair for everyone → WB 15/1

Lena is showing Matt a website about a fair trade group in Germany. Answer Matt's questions.

1. Why are they showing the picture of a clothes store? 2. What do they say about being fair?
3. The children in the picture are wearing school uniforms. What is said about this in the text?

FAIR FÜR ALLE – Wir setzen uns ein, damit alle fair handeln können.

Immer mehr Leute wollen Produkte kaufen, die „fair" hergestellt wurden, egal ob es sich um Lebensmittel oder Kleidung handelt. Oft wissen sie aber nicht, welche Produkte sie kaufen sollen und was „fair" genau bedeutet. Unser Ziel ist es, dass mehr Menschen sich für das Thema „fairer Handel" interessieren.

Und „fair" hat viele verschiedene Aspekte. Einer davon ist die Kinderarbeit, denn in manchen Ländern müssen die Kinder arbeiten, um zum Familienunterhalt beizutragen. Wir sind der Meinung, dass etwas dagegen getan werden muss. Alle Kinder sollten die Chance haben, eine Schule zu besuchen.

LANGUAGE

9 In the yearbook office

*Use **infinitive constructions** to rewrite the sentences.*

Example: 1. Tom loves the yearbook. He is always **the first to arrive** at the office.

1. Tom loves the yearbook. He is always the first person who arrives at the office. ✔
2. Julie has a good camera. So she is the only one who takes pictures.
3. Sue is very careful. She is always the first person who finds mistakes in the captions.
4. David is responsible. He is the last person who looks at the yearbook.
5. The last yearbook was amazing. It was the only one that won a prize.

SPEAKING

10 Student superlatives

In some yearbooks students are asked to vote in different categories, e.g. 'Most likely[1] to succeed', 'Most likely to become president[2]'.

a) *Describe the cartoon. If you need help, go back to the skills box on p. 17.*

b) *Explain the message of the cartoon. The useful phrases in the box can help you.*

Useful phrases

In my opinion, the cartoon's message is … | I think the cartoon wants to show / tell us that … | The cartoonist wants us to think about … / wants to make fun of[3] …

Talk about Snooty. She was listed as 'most likely to be googled' in the class yearbook.

LANGUAGE

11 Pocket money

a) *Use the prompts to make sentences with **object + infinitive**.*

Example: 1. Jill doesn't have any money. She **wants her father to lend** her some.

1. Jill doesn't have any money. her father | lend her some | she | want ✔
2. Her father thinks Jill is lazy. get an after-school job | he | her | would like
3. Jill says she doesn't have enough time. give her more pocket money | her parents | expect | she
4. Jill's father believes there is an easy solution. tell | he | her | to get a calendar
5. Jill gets angry. her father | her | to be polite | warn
6. Suddenly Jill is very sweet again. her father | remind | she | to give her her pocket money. Today is the first of the month!

b) *What do your parents like or expect you to do? And what do you like or expect your parents to do? Make a list and share your ideas in class.*

1 **likely** ['laɪkli] wahrscheinlich | 2 **president** ['prezɪdnt] Präsident/-in | 3 **to make fun of** [ˌmeɪk 'fʌn‿əv] sich lustig machen über

VOCABULARY

12 English in Britain and America

a) *Look at these words in American English. Find British English words which have the same meaning.*

vacation | yard | restroom | movie | downtown | elevator | movie theater | soccer | apartment | period | store

b) *Answer the following questions about American English.*

1. What do the Americans mean when they talk about a 'holiday'? 2. Where's the first floor in America? 3. Why do the Americans use the word 'soccer'? 4. Why is the temperature in America always so high?

LANGUAGE

13 At the shopping mall

*Change the infinitive constructions back into **questions**.*

Example: There were so many entrances to the mall. Lena didn't know which to use.
→ Lena: Which entrance should I use?

1. She wanted to know where to buy a new winter jacket.
2. She didn't know which store to go to first.
3. She wasn't sure whether to buy a jacket now or wait.
4. She asked herself what to do.
5. She didn't know who to ask about a restroom.
6. She wasn't sure when to take the bus home.

LANGUAGE

14 How to get around → WB 17/4–5

a) *Change the verbs into **gerunds** or **infinitives**.*

I'd always dreamed of **1** (travel) across America, but I wasn't sure how **2** (do) it. By bus? By train? By plane? I decided **3** (use) all different kinds of transportation[1]. I don't really like **4** (fly) so I did that first and flew to New York City. The next morning I went to the train station and was the first one **5** (buy) a ticket. My mother wants me **6** (take) lots of pictures on my trip so my first photos were of the train that arrived at the station. **7** (ride) on the train to Florida was nice, but I was tired of just **8** (sit) so next I rented a car and drove myself all the way to Chicago. **9** (drive) in America is easy because the roads are flat and wide and I'm good at **10** (concentrate). In Chicago I was really excited about **11** (get) a motorcycle, but I took the bus to the Grand Canyon instead. That's where I got a horse. At first I was worried about **12** (fall) off, but **13** (ride) it was so great that I rode it all the way to California!

b) *Think of places you'd like to visit in the US. Share your ideas with a partner. Tell him / her why you'd like to go there. Then present your partner's ideas in class.*

1 **transportation (*AE*)** [ˌtrænspɔːˈteɪʃn] Verkehrsmittel; Transport

SPEAKING

15 Who do you want to help?

a) *Look at the pictures. Say what the people are doing. Can you think of more ways to help other people? Collect ideas and share them in class.*

b) *Which of the three people or groups would you like to help? Explain why. Discuss your ideas with a partner.*

OCABULARY

16 Across the USA

Complete the text with the words in the box.

attitude | colonists | European | harvest | populated | population | rights | rural | symbolizes | temperatures | tractors | vacation | wealthiest | attractive | demonstrated | skyscrapers | religion | urban | shopping malls

If you want to spend your **1** in the United States, there are many different destinations to choose from. Let's start on the East Coast. Many people say that this is the most **2** region in America; maybe because that's where most of the **3** in the 1600s were from. The East Coast is also densely **4** and has many big cities such as Boston, Washington, D.C., New York and Philadelphia. If you want to see **5**, you should start in New York City. In contrast, the rest of New York State is quite **6**.

States in the South are known for their warm **7**. That's one of the reasons these states have an older **8**. In the South many people practice a **9** so there are a lot of churches, and this is also where, in the past, many people **10** so that black and white people could have the same **11**.

In the middle of the US there are a lot of farms. People here enjoy living in the country and far away from cities. It's normal here for teenagers to drive **12** and to help with the **13**. But they also enjoy spending time at **14** just like **15** teens.

For some people the West Coast **16** an easy-going lifestyle and a relaxed[1] **17**. But the West Coast is more than Hollywood and beaches. It is also a very **18** location for the computer industry and some of the **19** Americans have started their companies here.

1 relaxed [rɪˈlækst] entspannt; locker

Find more online: 8f2ug3

Text smart 1
Advertisements

You can see advertisements for products just about anywhere you look. How and why do advertisers try to win customers over? What are key features of most print ads? Find out here!

VOCABULARY

1 Warm-up: Are you a dream customer?

→ S17

a) *Describe what you think of when you hear the word 'advertisement'. Explain why you think that way.*

b) *Are you an advertiser's dream customer? Take the test and find out!* Yes ↓ No ↓

Start here

On the radio, they mention a big sale at a clothes store in the mall. They're offering two T-shirts for the price of one. And it's your favorite brand!

If you can avoid it, you don't pay attention to ads on the radio, on TV or anywhere.

You decide to go to the mall immediately to look for the T-shirts from the radio ad.

You're going to go to the mall anyway, so you'll have a look at them while you're there.

At the mall, they don't have any T-shirts in your favorite color. But you love a bargain, so you decide to buy two anyway.

You don't need one new T-shirt, so why would you need *two*? Forget it!

You don't like the T-shirts in the sale. But you see another T-shirt that looks really great. Maybe you'll buy it.

They're giving away free samples of a new chocolate bar, but you walk away; you'd feel guilty about not buying one.

They're giving away free samples of a new chocolate bar. You take one. Mmm, good! Then you decide to buy one.

They're giving away free samples of a new chocolate bar. You take one but won't buy one later. You never fall for *that* trick!

You see your favorite movie star on a new shampoo. You buy it because he / she has *perfect* hair.

You see your favorite movie star on a new shampoo. You aren't really happy with the product you're using now. Maybe you'll try this one; maybe not.

You never buy products that are advertised by celebrities. They earn enough money already.

You seem to be an advertiser's dream customer! You're receptive to ads and interested in buying new products.

You're interested in new things but you don't react immediately to every new temptation the advertisers try to sell you.

You seem to be sceptical about advertising and having new things. Ad people won't have an easy time with you!

c) 1. Say why you agree or disagree with your test results.
2. Give a short definition of what you think an advertiser's dream customer is.
3. Explain which *one* situation above comes closest to describing how *you* typically react.

d) *Your turn: Give an example of how an ad has succeeded in making you buy something.*

Did you see that new ad?

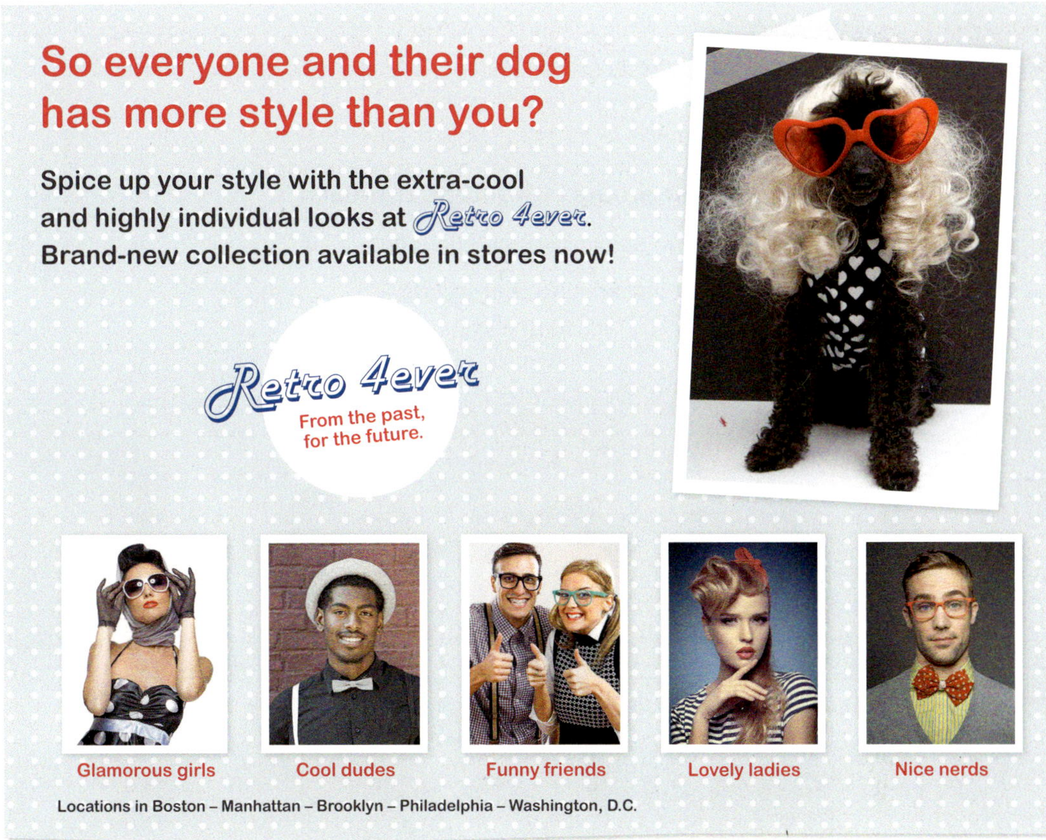

READING

2 The features of print ads → WB 18/1–2

→ S7

a) *Study the ad above.*

1. Describe what product the advertisers are trying to sell to their customers.
2. Say who you think the target group of customers is.

→ △ 133/1

b) *How is the ad above put together to sell the product? Point out the different features. (The skills box can help you.)*

c) *Now think about the language of the ad. Give examples of how these features work in the ad copy:*

humor adjectives

Reading skills

With print advertisements, be aware of the **typical building blocks** that work together to sell the product:

- an **eye-catcher** (a visual and / or a text)
- a **slogan**
- the **ad copy** (the text parts of an ad)
- one or more **images** of the product
- **contact** and **location** information

d) *Your turn: If you were the customer and saw the ad above in a magazine, on a poster or on a billboard, would you be interested? Explain your opinion.*

SPEAKING

3 Slogans: A closer look

a) *'From the past, for the future' is the slogan for the* **Retro 4ever** *ad. In your group of 4–6, discuss reasons why you think it fits – or doesn't fit – the product.*

b) *Go back to the Retro 4ever ad. Together, think up a better slogan for the product. Why is it better? Compare your slogan with another group's.*

READING

4 Print ads: Similar product, different approach → WB 19/3

→ △ 133/2

a) *Study the ad below and answer these questions:*

1. Describe what product the advertisers are trying to sell.
2. Say who you think the target group is.

b) *Point out which features of print ads you can find in this ad and describe them.*

c) *Give your opinion on the quality of the ad:*

1. Explain how effective it is for the target group the advertisers are trying to attract.
2. Explain what 'fabulous' means here.

WRITING

5 Comparing the two ads

a) *Think – pair – share: Use the headings below to make a grid for each ad. On your own, write down key words for your opinion of the different features. Then talk about your ideas with a partner from your group in Ex. 3. In a classroom discussion, point out the differences and similarities between the two ads.*

visuals | slogan / ad copy | humor | product | target group | effectiveness

→ △ 133/3

b) *With your partner, use your ideas from a) to improve the two ads. You choose ad 1, your partner chooses ad 2. Make changes that you feel would be improvements. Then swap ads. Afterwards, explain to each other why you made your changes.*

WRITING

6 Options: Create your own ads → WB 19/4

Option A: Trash to treasure

→ S7–9

a) *Each of you finds an object at home you think is useless / ugly / awful / too old. It should be something you think nobody would buy!*

b) *Now slip into the role of the advertiser: What kind of an ad could make one of your objects sound like a great product? Together, write and design an ad for it.*

c) *Present your product to the class. How many classmates think your ad is convincing?*

Option B: Create an ad around the visual

→ S7–9

a) *Choose one of the photos below. What kind of a product could a print ad be about with a photo like that? Think of how you could combine the typical features of print ads to make your product sound wonderful for your target group! Together, write and design your ad.*

b) *Present your product to the class. How many classmates would buy your product?*

Find more online: jt8g3w

School life – dos and don'ts

SPEAKING

1 Your turn

Talk about rules at your school. Look at the different situations below and the phrases on the right.

corridor | cafeteria | gym | laboratory | classroom | computer room | library | outside

Useful phrases

We can / can't | are / aren't allowed to | have to / don't have to
be late | eat / drink water | use our cell phones | shout | wear a uniform | be there without a teacher | skip classes | cheat | leave bags on the floor | …

If we break the rules / get caught …
- we have to stay after school | do extra work | stand outside | see the principal | …
- we are suspended | sent home
- we get detention
- our parents get a letter / phone call

VIEWING

2 A look at a US school

a) *Look at the film still. What do you think the problem is?*

2 → S16

b) *Watch the film. Describe the situation. What's the problem with Ruby?*

Tip

If you break a rule in a US school, your teacher might give you **detention**.
This means that you have to stay in the classroom with a teacher in your free time – at lunchtime or after school. The teacher will give you some work to do and you have to do it in silence. You must complete all the work before you can leave the room.

Useful phrases

- If she …, she'll …
- If she doesn't …, her teacher might …
- She shouldn't … because …
- It's a bad idea for her to … because …
- If I were Ruby, I'd …
- Otherwise, she'll …

c) *Watch the film again. What are the consequences for Ruby? The phrases in the box can help you.*

d) *Give your opinion: What do you think about the way Ruby is acting? Does she deserve the consequences? Why / Why not?*

OCABULARY

3 A further look at rules → WB 21/1

a) *Match the verbs with the phrases. Then write down the correct rule (positive or negative!).*

Example: Don't bring stuff into the classroom!

get | use | bring ✔ | skip | stand in line (*AE*) | be (2x) | stand

1. stuff into the classroom ✔
2. late
3. in the hallway
4. for lunch
5. in the corridor without a hall pass
6. classes
7. detention
8. your cell phones

b) *Look at what the teacher is saying to her students. What do you think the student has or hasn't done in each situation?*

1. The class started 10 minutes ago!
2. Please put your bag into the locker!
3. Where were you this morning?
4. Switch it off right now, please!
5. You call this 'homework'?!

WRITING

4 Reasons behind the rules

Look at the rules from Ex. 3 again. Take turns to write a rule and to explain the reasons behind that rule.

Example:
A: 'No texting friends during class' means that they want students to listen to the teacher and focus on their work.

SPEAKING

5 Role play

→ S11

a) *Your friend doesn't agree with a school rule and is about to break it. You don't want your friend to get into trouble so you try to persuade him / her not to break the rule. Choose from one of the situations below and write the conversation. The phrases in the box can help you.*

fake hall pass so that he / she can skip classes

cheat in a test / use a cheat sheet

b) *Act out your conversation in class.*

Useful phrases

Persuading someone to change their behavior
- You're going to get into so much trouble!
- You're so going to get detention!
- You'll be suspended if you …
- They have that rule because …
- I see your point but …
- You might be right but …
- You'd better … / You should … / Why don't you …?
- If I were you, I'd …

Expressing an attitude
- No risk, no fun!
- They want me to …
- They make me so mad!
- Why can't I …?
- They can't stop me …!
- I can't see the point of …
- It's a waste of time telling him / her …
- I don't understand why …

Unit 2
City of dreams: New York

Find more online: 5ge3kh

A Times Square – New York's busiest intersection and home to its theater district

LISTENING

1 A song: Empire State of Mind (Part II) Alicia Keys

a) *In small groups, describe the photos to each other. Can you think of more photos that represent New York City for you?*

L1/19 → S15

b) *Listen to the song and say how it makes you feel. Does it give you a positive or negative image of New York?*

c) *Look at the photos again and read the lines from the song. Which of the photos do these lines match? Explain why.*

the streets are mean | I got a pocketful of dreams | I'm gonna make it by any means | big lights will inspire you | such a melting pot | all looking pretty | make you feel brand-new | concrete jungle where dreams are made of

d) *There are more songs about New York City than most places in the world. Can you think of reasons why? Do you know a song about a German city or town? If you do, say what it is about.*

In Unit 2 you learn

… about different aspects of New York City. You learn:

- how to talk about personal experiences, hopes and dreams
- how to give extra information
- useful phrases for conducting an interview

B The Chrysler Building in Midtown Manhattan

C Central Park – New York's big green lung

D In Chinatown

E Homeless people in the streets

LISTENING 2 Big city life

→ △ 134/1

a) *Think – pair – share: Imagine you lived in a big city like New York with your family. What do you think you'd enjoy most? What wouldn't be so great about it? Exchange ideas with a partner before you both share your ideas in class. Here are some topics to start with:*

people | entertainment | activities | education | culture | traffic | crime

L 1/20

b) *Listen to the interview with David, a teenager from New York. What does he or doesn't he like about life in the city? Take notes.*

→ S15

c) *Compare your ideas from a) with David's answers. What's the same, what's different?*

WRITING 3 Your turn: In New York City → WB 22/1–2

→ △ 134/2

Look at the photos again. Which photo could you imagine yourself in? Write a short text about what you're doing in the photo and what you can feel (see, hear, smell, taste).

L 1/21

Saving the best for last

"Hey, Diego! Come here, please!" Diego's boss called to him. "These two young ladies need help getting around New York. I told them that nobody knows this city better than you. Take the rest of the day off and show them the best places." Diego was more than happy to leave his after-school job at the diner early. Rylee, who was 17 and from Alabama, and her cousin Lea, who was from Berlin, had a day to spend in New York while Rylee's parents were at a conference.

"Where are we going first?" Rylee asked. "The Empire State Building?"

"No," Diego said, "I'll show you sides of New York you'll never read about in a guidebook."

As they entered a big office building, the girls gasped. Classical music filled their ears. "These are students from the Juilliard School, which is a famous music school," Diego explained. While they were listening, he thought about his parents. They'd like him to work in an office building like this, for a bank maybe. A nice safe job. Something better than they had. But he wanted excitement.

After they'd had a look at the Astor Place Cube, an outdoor sculpture, they went to Times Square, which was always crowded with tourists. Diego loved being part of the crowds of New York although his parents hated it. Since he knew 'The Naked Cowboy', who was really only *almost* naked, the girls could take a picture with him for free. Diego's idea of New York on a shoestring was working well so far! He had two more free places to show them before the big surprise. He had to time it just right.

First they walked to the Alvin Ailey Dance Studio, which is just a couple of blocks from Central Park, and watched the dance class through the tall windows. "Diego, this is absolutely wonderful," Rylee said full of enthusiasm. "We'd never have found this without you!" They made it to the 5th floor of the Metropolitan Museum of Art just in time for the sunset over Central Park.

"This is the best, Diego," Lea said. "Thanks for a really great day."

He looked at them and smiled. "An entertainer always saves the best for last. So let's go!"

Diego led them to 30 Rockefeller Center, which is one of the tallest skyscrapers in New York, but they didn't use the front entrance. Instead they snuck into a service entrance and then into an elevator. "We're going to the top," he told the girls, "to the Top of the Rock."

Both girls looked at him. "To the top of Rockefeller Center? But every tourist knows how expensive tickets are!"

"Leave that to me," he told them.

When the elevator stopped and the doors opened, they entered a dark hallway. Just then a bright light shone in Diego's eyes and a loud voice with a strong accent shouted, "Stop! Who's there?"

With his hands covering his eyes, Diego said, "It's me. It's just me, dad."

"Diego?" the voice asked. *"¿Qué estás haciendo aquí?"*

"We just wanted to enjoy the view," Diego said quietly.

READING

1 Diego's New York

→ S1 a) *Sum up which places Diego showed to the girls. Why didn't he take them to the typical New York sights?*

b) *What would you have done in the girls' shoes – gone with Diego or followed your guidebook? Explain why.*

LANGUAGE

2 Revision: Defining relative clauses → G4 → WB 23/3

→ △ 134/3
→ ▲ 135/4

a) *Look at these sentences. Explain when you use the relative pronoun* ***who, which*** *or* ***that****.*

1. Most of the people **who** live in New York weren't born there.
2. The restaurants **which** we went to weren't expensive.
3. The musicians **that** play in the office building don't get any money.
4. We followed the plan **that** Diego gave us.

b) *Read Rylee's message to one of her friends. Use the phrases to complete the text with* ***defining relative clauses****. Decide where you can leave out the relative pronoun.*

Example: 1. This guy **(who/that) we met at lunch** said he'd show us the city.

aren't in every guidebook | everyone has to see | Diego showed us | he worked for | we met at lunch ✔ | shows people the real New York

Dear Ashley,
You won't believe what happened to us in New York! This guy 1 *said he'd show us the city. First we weren't sure if we should go with him, but the man* 2 *told us he was okay. The things* 3 *were amazing. They were all places* 4 *. Well, except for Times Square. But Diego said that's a place* 5 *. It was amazing! And you know what happened at the end of our tour: We got caught by Diego's father! He's a security man at Rockefeller Center and he found us after we'd snuck into a service entrance. That was a bit embarrassing, but we still had a wonderful day. Diego could start a tour company* 6 *.*
Miss you! xoxo – Rylee

LANGUAGE

3 Find the rule: Non-defining relative clauses → G4

a) *Explain the difference between these two sentences.*

1. The Juilliard School, which is located in Manhattan, is known around the world.
2. My cousin goes to a music school which is known around the world.

b) *Find at least five more examples of* ***non-defining relative clauses*** *in the text.*

Tip

In non-defining relative clauses …
- you use 'who' for people and 'which' for things. You never use 'that'.
- you always need a **comma** to separate the main clause from the relative clause.

LANGUAGE

4 What happened before

*Read what happened before Rylee and Lea met Diego. Decide if the sentences have **defining** or **non-defining relative clauses**. Put in commas where you need them.*

After the girls had said goodbye to Rylee's parents, Rylee who had never been to New York before decided to give her cousin a tour of the city. Rylee lived in a city that was home to only 10,000 people, but she wasn't worried at all. She told herself that she was a person who never got lost. The two girls took the subway to Lower Manhattan. Rylee planned to follow their guidebook which suggested a walking tour through Chinatown. 20 minutes later, the two girls were back at Wall Street Subway Station which is where they'd started. "So that's what you call an amazing tour," Lea groaned.

LANGUAGE

5 Flying to New York

*Combine the two sentences into one. Use **non-defining relative clauses**.*

Example: 1. Our plane is going to leave from Stuttgart Airport, which is close to our house.

1. Our plane is going to leave from Stuttgart Airport. This is close to our house. ✔
2. We're going to fly to JFK International. This is one of the busiest airports in the US.
3. We're going to visit my Aunt Nancy. She works in the Empire State Building.
4. Aunt Nancy speaks six languages. She gives tours of the building.
5. The Empire State Building was built in 1931. It has 102 floors.
6. The elevator is really fast. It only takes one minute to get to the 80th floor.

LANGUAGE

6 Make the text more interesting → WB 23/4

→ △ 135/5

*Use **non-defining relative clauses** to add the extra information below.*

The Statue of Liberty is one of New York's most famous sights. But did you know that this symbol of freedom was a present from France? It was designed by the French artist Auguste Bartholdi. The statue was completed in France in 1884 and then brought to America. There it was rebuilt on Bedloe Island. In her right hand, 'Lady Liberty' is holding a torch, and in her left, a tablet with the date July 4th, 1776. The seven spikes on her crown stand for the seven seas and the seven continents of the world. Today the Statue of Liberty is a popular tourist attraction. You can even go up to the Statue's crown!

1. The Statue of Liberty stands in New York harbor.
2. This symbol of freedom has become so important for American culture.
3. Bartholdi based his figure on the Roman Goddess of Liberty.
4. The statue took nine years to build.
5. Bedloe Island is now known as 'Liberty Island'.
6. The torch stands for 'enlightenment'.
7. July 4th, 1776 is the date of America's independence from Britain.
8. The Statue of Liberty is visited by millions of people each year.

SPEAKING

7 Your turn: Give extra information

*Get into two teams. One team gives the main clause and the other team has to add a **non-defining relative clause**. Take turns.*

Example: My friend Ben has a dog. → My friend Ben, who is sitting next to me, has a dog.

READING

8 Food in New York City

Read the box about different food in New York. Then talk to your partner about food and places to eat where you live.

Across cultures

Life in New York City has been strongly influenced by its millions of immigrants from all over the world. You can best experience this when you start looking for New York **ethnic food**. From the outside, some restaurants look like just a hole in the wall, but inside you can find delicious Indian food like samosa, which is a fried pastry with a vegetarian filling. Another famous New York dish is bagel and lox – typical Jewish food.

Walking down the street is a great way to find delicious food too. New York has hundreds of **food trucks and carts** around the city which sell everything from hot dogs – New York's most famous snack – to schnitzel or tacos. New Yorkers are still combining flavors and specialities to create new dishes, e.g. the cronut – a combination of croissant and doughnut.

MEDIATION

9 What do you eat? → WB 24/5

→ △ 135/6
→ S13

On their tour of New York City, Lea told Diego about some typical German food. A few days later, Diego sends her an e-mail and asks about more typical food from her region. Lea finds this article on the internet. In their next video chat she tells Diego about it.

Say what Lea tells Diego. Use ***non-defining relative clauses*** *to give extra information.*

Ein weiteres beliebtes Gericht aus der Mitte Deutschlands ist „Himmel und Erde". Hinter dem Wort „Himmel" versteckt sich der Apfel, der am Baum in den Himmel ragt. „Erde" bezieht sich auf die Kartoffel, die bekanntlich in der Erde wächst. Das sind die Hauptzutaten für dieses vegetarische Gericht. In manchen Regionen werden die gekochten, zerkleinerten Äpfel und Kartoffeln vermischt und mit Brot serviert. Häufig isst man dazu auch Blutwurst, Speck oder Leberwurst. Und bitte die Röstzwiebeln nicht vergessen …

WRITING

10 Your turn: Your city on a shoestring → WB 24/6, 25/7–9

a) *You're helping to write a guidebook about your hometown or region. In small groups, choose 3–4 interesting facts you want to include. These ideas can help you:*

the best view | the best thing for free | the best lunch under €10 | the highest spot | …

b) *Write short texts for each of the points you chose in a). Remember to give extra information.*

Example: The highest spot in our town, which is in a castle, is easy to get to. It's …

L1/23

Life is a trip

Diego's father, Emilio, had been waiting in his taxi for just 20 minutes before his first passenger came. He lifted the young man's big suitcase into the trunk and then asked him where he wanted to go. "To the airport," the man groaned, "I'm done with this city." He'd come to New York when he was 19 and had been hoping for his big break for five years. All this time he'd gone to hundreds of auditions and had sung thousands of songs, but nobody had wanted him. He'd been thinking about his decision for quite some time and that morning, when he got another rejection e-mail, he'd decided the time had come. Now he was going home to Wisconsin, where he had an offer to teach music at a high school. "My dream just didn't come true here," he explained. "At least as a teacher I can make music every day."

Emilio wished the young man good luck and thought of his own dreams. They hadn't been as big when he'd come to America, but he still understood what it meant to get disappointed.

When Emilio got back in his car, another passenger was waiting on the sidewalk. Emilio knew the type – successful businessman but not necessarily happy. The man gave Emilio an address on Wall Street. And then something surprising happened. The man started talking to him, asking him questions. Emilio told him about his son, Diego, and how he and his wife had such big hopes for him. They'd been saving for his education since he was born, working two jobs each and now Diego said he wanted to be an entertainer. Emilio was sure this rich businessman would understand how disappointed Emilio felt. However, when they arrived in Manhattan, the man said something completely different. "Let your son follow his dreams. It's better to have a son with dreams you aren't happy about than not to have your son at all." He pressed a large bill into Emilio's hand and quickly got out of the taxi without his change.

Emilio's taxi wasn't empty for long. Two teenage girls and about 20 shopping bags got in. The girls didn't say hello; they just gave him an address on Park Avenue. Emilio listened to them as they talked about a life so different from his and yet so typical of New York. They'd been walking around Manhattan since 10 o'clock and now they were tired after all the shopping. They complained that today it was hard to find any good clothes in New York. Obviously they'd been shopping at the same stores for hours when they realized that London might be the better place to shop. Needless to say, they didn't give Emilio a tip. And needless to say, they didn't give the homeless woman on the sidewalk a single look as they got out of the taxi.

READING

11 A day in the life of Emilio → WB 26/10

→ S1

a) *Collect information about Emilio's passengers. Think of what is said about them in the text, but also about what they say or how they act. Make a mind map.*

b) *Use your mind map from a) to compare the different passengers.*

c) *Role play: Choose one of Emilio's passengers – the musician, the businessman or one of the rich girls. With your partner, write down five questions you'd like to ask this person and the answers this person might give. Then act out the dialogue.*

LANGUAGE

12 Revision: Present perfect progressive

→ △ 135/7

*Remember: You can use the present perfect progressive for activities which began in the past and have been going on until now. Use the prompts to make sentences with the **present perfect progressive** and **since** or **for**.*

Example: 1. It's already 10 o'clock. We**'ve been waiting** for our taxi since 9:30.

1. It's already 10 o'clock. We | wait for our taxi | 9:30. ✔
2. Can we leave? We | listen to the piano player | one hour.
3. We'll never get to the show on time. We | walk | hours.
4. Look how tall the skyscraper is already. They | not build | long.
5. I got a part in a play! I | dream about this | I arrived in New York.
6. It's so sad. He | live on the streets | he was 16.

LANGUAGE

13 Find the rule: Past perfect progressive → G5 → WB 26/11

a) *Look at these two sentences. Say which verb forms you need to form the **past perfect progressive**.*

1. Emilio **had been waiting** for 20 minutes.
2. They **had been walking** around Manhattan since 10 o'clock.

b) *Find more examples of the **past perfect progressive** in the text.*

c) *Look at the tip box and the sentences from a) and b). Write down the rule of how the **past perfect progressive** is used. Compare it to the use of **present perfect progressive**.*

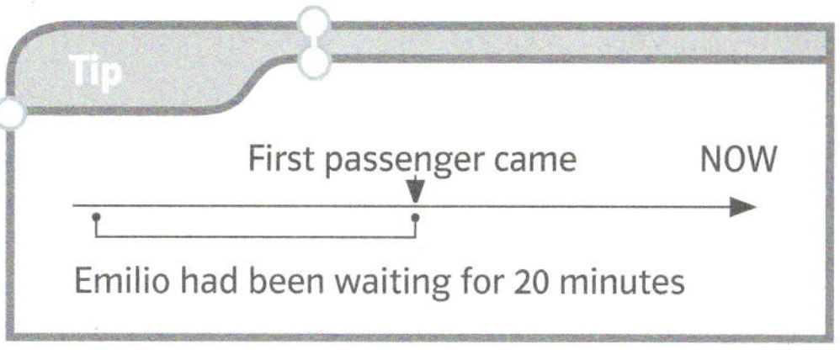

LANGUAGE

14 What had Meredith been doing?

*Complete the sentences with the **past perfect progressive**.*

1. Meredith (talk) about becoming an actor even before she saw her first Broadway play.
2. She (plan) to move to New York for eight years before she finally arrived there.
3. When she went to her first audition, she (not live) in New York for very long.
4. She was very tired that day because she (practice) all night long.
5. She (wait) for two hours when they told her that they didn't need any more people.
6. Her friends didn't know how long she (walk) around the city before she came home at midnight.
7. They knew she (hope) for a part in the play, but they told her that tomorrow was another day!

LANGUAGE

15 Why were they tired when Emilio's taxi arrived? → WB 27/12

→ △ 136/8
→ ▲ 136/9

When Emilio arrived in Central Park at 11 o'clock yesterday, he saw different people who needed a taxi. Why were they tired? Make sentences with the ***past perfect progressive*** *and* ***since*** *or* ***for****.*

Example: 1. The young girl **had been running** for one hour / **since** 10 o'clock.

LANGUAGE

16 What had been happening before?

→ △ 136/10

Complete these sentences with your own ideas. Use the ***past perfect progressive*** *and an* ***expression of time*** *(since / for …, all morning / day / week / night / year etc.).*

Example: When I looked out of the window this morning, the ground was all wet.
It **had been raining all night**.

1. I was very tired when I got home after school because I'd been …
2. Dave got the best grade on the test because he …
3. We … when there was a heavy storm and we had to go back.
4. When Kelly arrived at the café, her friends …
5. Our dog was very dirty. He …
6. Lisa thought her friend would never call. She …
7. Mary's eyes were very red. She …

SPEAKING

17 Your turn: Your experiences in a new place

Do you remember the last time you were in a foreign city / a new place? What kind of people did you meet? What did you experience, see, hear, feel, smell? Tell your partner about it and ask each other about your experiences.

LISTENING

18 Differences between British and American English → WB 27/13

L 1/24 → S15

a) *Listen to a conversation between a British and an American student. What are they talking about? What differences do you notice in the way they speak?*

b) *Listen to the conversation again. Then look at these sentences. Change the British words to American and the American words to British.*

1. Buskers perform on the street to make a living.
2. It is easiest to take the subway when you want to explore the city.
3. Traffic is so slow here, let's use the freeway instead.
4. If you want to transport something that is big and heavy, you'll need a lorry.

c) *Can you think of more words that are different between British and American English? Start a list.*

READING

19 Living in New York City → WB 28/14–15

a) *In her song about New York Alicia Keys sings: "If I can make it here, I can make it anywhere." What does this tell us about how people see New York?*

b) *Read the box about life in New York. Have you seen huge contrasts like this where you live?*

Across cultures

As a city of superlatives, New York attracts people from all different social backgrounds – rich and poor, young and old, from the US and from abroad. They all come to New York with their **hopes and dreams**. A lot of them live their own 'rags to riches' success story, but others fail to make their living.

Today New York is one of the cities with the widest **gap between rich and poor** in the US. There are one-bedroom apartments for $5 million, and in New York's most expensive apartment building a penthouse was sold for $100 million. On the other hand, there are almost 60,000 homeless people who live on the streets or in poor conditions.

c) *Imagine you're either very rich or homeless. What would be different compared to your real life? Share your ideas with a partner.*

SPEAKING

20 Before you read

a) *You're going to read a graphic novel which is set in New York City. Read the quotation below from OG, one of the main characters in the story. Think about what he could mean.*

"Here is where you are. There is where you want to be. But you can't get there from here." (Harrison Blanchard aka OG)

b) *What might the graphic novel be about? Keep in mind what you've read in the Across cultures box.*

Asphalt Tribe by Stefani Kampmann

Our city was as hectic and busy as usual.
MADAME TUSSAUDS
AMSTERDAM
ONE WAY
7 AV
CHASE
QUICKSILVER
MARY POPPINS

This is where we lived.
This was our home.
Hey!
Thieves! Stop!

Faster, Maybe!
They can't catch us.
Idiots.
They're just too stupid.
Come on, show me what's in there!

Just a bunch of junk. No cash.
Shit!
What do those chicks need all this stuff for?
Maybe! Rainbow!
Hey, Tears!
Where have you been?
ROCK

Behind the deli.
Cool!
Fast food from the dumpster.
There's enough for everyone.
Come on, let's look for the others. This will be a feast.

Aw, Maggot!
Your spray is ruining my manicure.
DON'T WORRY DIE HAPPY!
SMASH
Come off it, Jewel.
You could learn a lesson or two from 2Moro. Look how she's using her delicate fingers.
Hey guys! Supper is ready!

Mmmm, delicious. Cold with mayo.
Aren't you going to bitch about the capitalistic throw-away society?
Never! Viva el capital!
Shit! The police!

When the cops came with their van, we had to run.
Otherwise they'd stick us in a juvenile home.

SPEAKING

1 Your reaction

What do you think of the graphic novel? With a partner, agree on three aspects you like or don't like about it. Explain why.

READING

2 Understanding the story → WB 29/16

a) *Divide the excerpt from the graphic novel into scenes. Sum up each scene in 2–3 sentences.*

b) *Compare your summaries with a partner's. Explain how you found out about what is happening in each scene.*

READING

3 How a graphic novel works

a) *Look at the first panel of the graphic novel (p. 50). Describe the picture and the atmosphere. Why do you think the artist used this picture as a lead-in to her story?*

b) *Now have a closer look at pages 54 and 58. What are the differences between them? Make a grid and fill in the information for both pages. Use these headings:*

content | sizes and shapes of panels | sequence of panels | shots

Reading skills

Graphic novels are divided into **panels** (the individual pictures) which can be different sizes and shapes. Some of the panels have **speech** or **thought bubbles** and / or **captions**. The short caption texts tell part of the story from the perspective of a first- or third-person narrator.

The **sequence** (or order) of the panels can play an important role. Sometimes panels are not arranged consecutively, but they overlap. This means that some smaller panels are laid over a larger one.

Just like in films, graphic novels make use of different kinds of **shots**. There can be **long** or **medium shots** (the camera is at a great or medium distance from the object that is being filmed) and **close-ups** (the camera is very close to the object).

→ △ 137/11

c) *Look at your grid from b) and the two pages from the graphic novel again. Describe the effects the stylistic elements have. How does that match the content? The useful phrases in the box can help you.*

d) *Explain how the choice of black and white matches the story. Do you know any other graphic novels? If you do, does the artist's choice / style of visuals match the story?*

Useful phrases

create suspense / a quiet atmosphere | make the reader live through / experience the story | show reactions / feelings of characters | introduce fast action / speed | create a distance

WRITING

4 What happens next?

What do you think happens when the kids run away from the police? Make a plan for the next two pages of the graphic novel. Think of content, sizes and shapes of panels, sequence of panels and shots. If you like being creative, you can even draw the panels.

READING

5 ‹ Comparing the genres › → WB 29/17

a) *The graphic novel* Asphalt Tribe *is based on the novel* Can't Get There from Here *by Todd Strasser. Read this short excerpt. Think about how the artist might convert the scene into panels.*

Chapter One: New Year's Eve

It was one of those nights when there wasn't much traffic on the streets of New York. Most people were done with their stupid New Year's celebrations and back in the four-walled cells they called apartments. Prisoners of the system, Maggot said. Out here in the cold where we weren't walled in, we were free to go where we wanted to.

"Guess the cops have the night off," Maggot said, his brown dreadlocks stringy from the mist.

"The rest of the world too," muttered 2Moro. She was wearing a red-and-orange patchwork jacket, a tight black skirt, and high black boots. The piercings in her ears and eyebrow and nose glinted in the streetlight. Tattooed around her neck was a circle of black barbed wire.

I drank cold coffee from a paper cup. At night we drank coffee to stay awake. It was safer to sleep during the day.

A man and a woman came around the corner wearing raincoats and sharing a red umbrella. They slowed down when they saw us. The woman slid her arm through the man's and said something in his ear. Probably wanted him to turn around and go another way. But the man shook his head.

When they got near, the woman wrinkled her nose like something smelled bad.

"Have fun tonight?" Maggot asked, kind of menacing.

The couple stopped. "Yes, we did," the man answered.

"No work tomorrow, huh?" Maggot said.

"That's right."

"Day after that it's back to the old nine-to-five routine," Maggot said.

"You could say that," answered the man.

"Happy New Year," said 2Moro, not in a friendly way.

"Same to you," said the man. He and the woman hurried past. She kept glancing over her shoulder at us until they reached the next corner.

"Robots," Maggot said. "Just following the rules. Work till they die. Then new robots replace them."

b) *Give a summary of the excerpt in 2–3 sentences.*

c) *With your partner, make a list of the differences between a graphic novel and a novel. How are they effective in different ways?*

d) *What would you prefer to read – the graphic novel or the novel? Give reasons for your choice.*

WRITING

6 ‹ Writing the novel version of a scene ›

→ △ 137/12

a) *Look back at the scenes you were working with in Ex. 2a). Divide up the scenes among the class. Then write a short novel text for your scene. Keep in mind the differences between a graphic novel and a novel which you collected in Ex. 5c).*

b) *With a partner, peer-edit each other's texts.*

New Yorkers don't do things like that! → S16

SPEAKING

1 Warm-up: Embarrassing situations → WB 30/18

a) *In the film, one of the characters says this to another character: "Stop it, it's embarrassing! I'm a New Yorker and New Yorkers don't do things like that!" What do you think this could mean?*

b) *Describe the kind of embarrassing behavior that makes you cringe.*

VIEWING

2 Out and about in Manhattan → WB 30/19

3 **a)** *Watch the film till 00:50. Then think about your ideas from Ex. 1 again. What does Christine mean when she tells Sarah that "New Yorkers don't do things like that"?*

b) *Now watch till 04:00 and sum up the action. Include these points about Christine, Sarah and Lawrence:*

characters and their personalities | what happens

c) *Watch the rest of the film. Describe the unexpected ending and the reactions to it.*

VIEWING

3 How music and film work together

a) *Watch the film again and note down the moments with music. Describe which scene or person has music and what kind of music it is.*

b) *Explain how you think the music helps to tell the story in A (04:01–04:52) and B (06:01–06:17):*

A

B

c) *Read the skills box. Then watch 04:01–04:52 again. Explain why you think this part of the film is featured as a montage.*

d) *If you could choose a theme song or theme music for one of the characters, what would you choose? Give your reasons.*

Film skills

A **montage** is a popular film technique to show a lot of action in very little time.
To make a montage, scenes are cut up into very short 'pieces' and then combined, usually with **music**.

How to conduct a podcast interview

For the unit task you're going to do podcast interviews about different people in New York City. This page will give you some useful phrases and a model for your interview.

1 Before the interview: A short biographical profile → WB 31/21

a) *In a podcast interview, the interviewer often gives his/her listeners a short profile of the person he/she is going to interview. With a partner, think of general kinds of biographical information that listeners might like to know before the actual interview. Make a list.*

b) *Read the biographical profile about Rita Moreno, an immigrant from Cuba who lives in New York. Compare the information with your list from a).*

Rita Moreno came to New York from Cuba when she was 16 years old. Her aunt and uncle, who had already been living there for three years, gave Rita a bedroom, but she had to work hard for everything else. Her dream was to become a dancer. In Cuba she'd already been going to a dance school for ten years, but she and her family saw no future for her there; the country was just too poor. Rita's path to success was very long and hard. She cleaned offices, sold tickets in a theater and always went to auditions. It took her almost three years before she got her first dancing job. Today she makes her living by dancing on stages around New York and the world, but she also helps young dancers who have their own hopes and dreams.

c) *You want to find out more about what Rita likes or doesn't like about her life in New York. Write down five questions you'd ask her in an interview.*

2 Conducting an interview: Daniel's Do-it-yourself Diner

L 2/5 → S15

a) *Listen to the interview. Then sum up what you've found out about Daniel and his New York City dreams. Why is his diner called 'Do-it-yourself'?*

b) *Listen to the interview again. Note down which phrases from the box you hear in the interview.*

c) *What's important for a good interview? Make a list of criteria with your partner.*

Useful phrases

Small talk: This is a beautiful office / area / room. | How long have you been living / working here? | Where did you grow up?

Follow-up: Can you tell me more about …? | That's interesting. Tell me a little more about that. | But don't you think that …? | Can you explain that to me? | Sorry, I didn't catch that.

Getting specific: How long have you …? | How many …? | When did you …? | How often …? | How long had you been … (+-ing) before you became … / went … / found …

Open questions: What are your feelings about …? | What do you think about …? | What are your goals?

At the end: Thanks, I enjoyed talking to you. | Thank you very much for this interesting talk.

d) *Write a short biographical profile about Daniel. Keep in mind the points you collected in Ex. 1.*

A pocketful of New York City dreams

You're going to make a series of podcast interviews with different people in New York City who talk about their hopes and dreams. You can use information you learned in Unit 2 and do some internet research too.

Step 1

Get into groups, choose characters → WB 31/22

Get into groups of 4–5. Each group chooses a different person who lives in New York City or who is visiting. Here are some ideas:

tourist | tourist guide | rich boy / girl | successful businessman / -woman | taxi driver | young student who has just moved to New York | homeless person

Step 2

Write a biographical profile → WB 32/23

In your groups, write a short biographical profile of the person you've chosen. Try to make your listeners interested, but don't give away too much information.

→ Introduction (pp. 40–41) → Giving extra information (pp. 42–45) → Talking about personal experiences (pp. 46–48) → Writing a biographical profile (p. 62)

Step 3

Prepare your interviews → WB 32/24

Prepare questions you're going to ask about the person's hopes and dreams. Think of answers you're going to give.

→ Conducting an interview (p. 62)

Step 4

Practise your interviews

Decide who is going to take the role of the interviewer and the interviewee. Then practise the interview. Don't forget that the interviewer should give the short biographical profile first.

Step 5

Present your interviews

Record your podcast interviews or present them directly to the class. After the presentations, discuss the interviews in class. Give feedback about which person or which interview was the most convincing. Explain why.

LISTENING

1 I ♥ NYC

L 2/6

a) *Listen to Makenna as she talks about her hometown New York. What does she say about these topics? Take notes.*

Stuyvesant High School | crime | people in New York | activities

b) *Make notes about your school and your hometown. Use your ideas to write a short text like Makenna's.*

MEDIATION

2 Getting around in New York → WB 34/1

You're spending a year as an exchange student in New York and your parents are visiting you for five days. They want to do some sightseeing on their own and ask you which subway ticket you think is best for them. You find this information about the MetroCard on a website. Tell them about the different options. Then say which ticket you think is best and why. Use a dictionary to look up new words.

To find out about the different ticket options, press 'Start', then 'MetroCard' and next 'Get new card'. Now you have to decide between an 'unlimited' and a 'regular' card. An unlimited MetroCard for seven days costs $31. This card is good if you want to use the subway a lot – even if you're going to be in New York for less than seven days. It's the best deal if you're going to use the subway at least 12 times, or do six round trips. Then each ride costs $2.38. The more you ride, the cheaper each ride is! If you ride 25 times, it's only $1.24 per ride. But remember – only one person can use the card! If you don't want to use the subway that often, you can buy a pay-per-ride or regular MetroCard. Up to four people can share the same card. You choose the amount that you want to put onto your card. The more you put on it, the more you save because you get an 11% bonus for every $5.50 you purchase. You can pay at the machines with cash, an ATM card or a credit card. If you pay in cash, your change will be all in coins.

LANGUAGE

3 Who is who?

You're new in New York and you don't know the people who live next door – Mr. Singh, Mr. Masengi and Mr. Nelson – very well, but you need a ride to the airport. Find out who the taxi driver is. Read the clues and make a grid in your exercise book.

The neighbor who lives in the yellow house doesn't drive a taxi.

Mr. Masengi, who is a security man, doesn't like the color red.

The actor, who doesn't live in a yellow house, is Mr. Nelson.

The house that Mr. Singh has been living in for five years isn't red.

LANGUAGE

4 More facts about New York → WB 35/2

Write 2–3 sentences about each topic below. Use ***non-defining relative clauses*** *where possible.*

Example: New York, **which is the largest city in the US**, is located on the East Coast.

New York	New York taxis
– largest city in the US – located on the East Coast – about 8 million live here; 1.6 million on island of Manhattan – Manhattan: most famous of NY's five boroughs[1]	– bright yellow in color – can be seen all around the city – many of the taxi drivers born outside the US – transport about 241 million passengers each year
The Brooklyn Bridge	**The Staten Island Ferry**

– connects[2] Manhattan and Brooklyn – designed by John A. Roebling in 1869 – completed after Roebling's death by his son – one of NY's top tourist attractions – cost $15 million to build	– in service[3] since 1817 – operates[4] 24 hours a day, 7 days a week – transports about 21 million passengers each year – free of charge[5]

LANGUAGE

5 Moving to NYC

a) *Put in a* ***gerund*** *or an* ***infinitive with to****.*

1. ___ (move) to New York City was the best decision I've ever made!
2. I was the first one in my family ___ (leave) our town.
3. At first my parents were afraid of ___ (let) me go on my own.
4. But I've always been crazy about ___ (try) new things.
5. I decided ___ (leave) as soon as I was done with high school.
6. My family didn't expect me ___ (stay) in New York for more than a year.
7. But I keep ___ (surprise) them with new dreams and ideas.
8. Now my brother is thinking of ___ (follow) me to NYC!

b) *What's the best decision that you've ever made? What happened because of this decision? Tell your partner about it.*

1 **borough** [ˈbʌrə] Stadtteil | 2 **to connect** [kəˈnekt] verbinden | 3 **to be in service** [ɪn ˈsɜːvɪs] in Betrieb sein | 4 **to operate** [ˈɒpreɪt] in Betrieb sein | 5 **free of charge** [ˌfriː əv ˈtʃɑːdʒ] kostenlos

READING

6 New York in a poem

Untitled by Jasbel
In this city
full of buildings
big, small, brown, orange
tiny windows
1 out of 1000
small and black
but still you and I
look outside
see the bridge
or the trees
mostly cars
and yellow taxis
cheese buses
and MTA buses
But where am I
If I go downtown alone
no one knows me
If I go to Brooklyn
no one knows me
alone in the middle of the big apple
places unexplored unknown to me
clueless[1], lost
In the middle of this jungle

a) *Read the poem. Find lines that show how Jasbel feels about New York City.*

b) *Discuss if this poem gives a good description of New York in your opinion. Explain why, why not.*

LANGUAGE

7 Defining or non-defining? → WB 35/3

Decide if these sentences have ***defining*** *or* ***non-defining relative clauses****. Put in commas where you need them.*

1. Diego who we met at a diner showed us some fantastic sights.
2. Some of the sights that Diego showed us were fantastic.
3. Rockefeller Center which is located in the heart of Manhattan is a huge shopping and entertainment center.
4. Rockefeller Center is a huge shopping and entertainment center that is located in the heart of Manhattan.
5. The Chinese dumplings[2] which we bought for lunch from a food truck on 14th Street tasted delicious.
6. The best restaurant for falafels is in Greenwich Village which is on the west side of Lower Manhattan.
7. In Times Square we saw the Naked Cowboy who is a famous street artist.
8. In Times Square we saw a street artist who was almost completely naked.

LANGUAGE

8 New in New York → WB 36/4–5

Put the verbs into the ***past perfect progressive****. Use* ***since*** *or* ***for*** *where it is needed.*

In August, Tyler and Missy finally left for New York City. They **1** (save) their money for the trip ever **2** they finished high school. They took the bus from Idaho to New York, and when they finally arrived in Manhattan, they **3** (already travel) **4** 24 hours. They **5** (hope) to stay with Missy's sister, but when they called, nobody answered the phone. Missy's sister **6** (not expect) them until the week after, and now they didn't know where to go! They **7** (look) at their map **8** a long time when a man asked if they needed help. He told them it was their lucky day. He **9** (help) people to find rooms in New York **10** 2005. That's when he had first arrived in New York without a room and someone had helped him!

1 **clueless** ['klu:ləs] ahnungslos | 2 **dumpling** ['dʌmplɪŋ] Kloß

SPEAKING

9 New York's nicknames[1]

a) *There are many different names for New York. Which one do you think describes the city best? Exchange ideas with your partner.*

The melting pot | The center of the universe[2] | The city that never sleeps | The Big Apple | The city so nice they named it twice

b) *Think of nicknames for your hometown. They can be realistic or funny.*

LANGUAGE

10 What had people been doing?

a) *Use the prompts to write sentences with the* ***past perfect progressive****.*

Example: 1. Meredith came home late for dinner. She **had been shopping** since 10 o'clock.

1. Meredith came home late for dinner. She | shop | 10 o'clock.
2. Sam was feeling very tired. He | wait to get into the Empire State Building | two hours.
3. When Maisie came back to the hotel, she looked very red from the sun. She | walk | in the sun | all day.
4. Alex didn't know which subway station was next. He | sleep | 15 minutes.
5. Joe left the diner at 8 o'clock. He was very upset with his friends. He | wait | for them | 7 o'clock.
6. When Julie's mom arrived home at 10 p.m., the TV was still on. Julie | watch videos | all evening.

b) *Your turn: Partner A asks a question, Partner B answers. Use the* ***past perfect progressive****.*

Example: A: Why were you so tired last night?
B: I**'d been playing** football with my friends for three hours.

VOCABULARY

11 Avoiding mistakes

a) *Look at these three words. Explain their different meanings.*

my cousins | my cousin's | my cousins'

b) *Complete the sentences with the correct form of the nouns.*

1. When I first came to New York, I lived in my ___ (sister) apartment.
2. She had crazy ___ (ideas) and we had lots of fun together.
3. One day we went to a party at her ___ (friends) place.
4. They lived in one of ___ (New York) tallest skyscrapers.
5. It was amazing to see the ___ (city) lights from up there.
6. And guess what? My best ___ (friend) brother came to the party.
7. He and his sister lived near my ___ (grandparents) house when we were kids.
8. He is one of the most attractive ___ (guys) I've ever met!

1 **nickname** ['nɪkneɪm] Spitzname | 2 **universe** ['juːnɪvɜːs] Universum

LANGUAGE

12 An interview with Colin

a) *A reporter from TeenMusicMag interviewed Colin, a young musician who plays his piano in Washington Square Park. Complete the interview. Decide if you need the* ***present perfect progressive*** *or* ***past perfect progressive****.*

TMM: Were you born in New York, Colin?
Colin: No, I'm originally from Tennessee, but I **1** (live) here for five years.
TMM: And why did you come here?
Colin: I **2** (dream) about it forever! And then one day I was finally brave enough to do it.
TMM: Colin, why did you decide to play your piano outside?
Colin: Well, I **3** (work) in a bar as a musician for two years, but I didn't like working every night.
TMM: Did you look for a new job then?
Colin: Yes, but I **4** (not look) for long when I decided to play in the park.
TMM: And do you make enough money with that?
Colin: I **5** (not expect) that before I started, but I do make enough.

TMM: How long **6** (perform) in Washington Square Park?
Colin: I **7** (do) it for two years now.
TMM: What do you do if the weather is bad?
Colin: I stay home! But one day I **8** (play) for only half an hour when it suddenly started to rain.
TMM: What did you do? Your poor piano!
Colin: The people who **9** (listen) helped me to cover it and then I quickly pushed it home.
TMM: And how long **10** (play) the piano altogether[1]?
Colin: I **11** (take) lessons since I was five.
TMM: Are you still taking lessons?
Colin: Well, not at the moment. My audience is my teacher!

b) *Write down questions you'd like to ask your partner. Then take turns to interview each other. Use the* ***present perfect progressive*** *and* ***past perfect progressive****.*

Example: A: How long **had you been playing** basketball before you joined our team?
B: I**'d been playing** basketball for one year.
A: And how long **have you been playing** basketball altogether?
B: I**'ve been playing** basketball since I was 12.

VOCABULARY

13 New York collocations

a) *Combine the words from the two boxes to make collocations you've learned in Unit 2.*

classical | melting | brand | follow | social | make | ethnic | food | city | office | concrete

a living | background | building | jungle | life | music | new | pot | a dream | cart | food

b) *Write a sentence for each of the phrases from a), but leave a gap where the phrase should go. Then exchange sentences. Your partner needs to find out which phrase goes in which sentence. Take turns.*

1 **altogether** [ˌɔːltəˈgeðə] insgesamt

WRITING

14 I want to go to New York!

If you want to go on a student exchange, you usually have to fill out an online application[1] form. Answer the following questions about yourself in full sentences.

1. Which foreign languages have you studied, and for how many years?
2. What are your favorite school subjects?
3. Are you active in sports? If yes, which sports?
4. Which (if any) foreign countries have you visited?
5. What are your favorite hobbies, interests etc.?
6. Use one adjective to describe yourself. Explain why you have chosen it.

LANGUAGE

15 9/11 – New York had to rebuild

a) *As you've already learned, you can only use the modal verbs in the simple present. With other tenses, you use their substitute forms:* ***be allowed to****,* ***be able to*** *and* ***have to****. Rewrite these sentences in the simple past. Use the right substitute form.*

1. I can't call us a taxi because my phone is broken. We must take the subway.
2. We needn't buy tickets for the museum. Our class can go in for free.

b) *Complete the text with the verbs and the right substitute form:* ***be allowed to****,* ***be able to*** *or* ***have to****.*

On September 11, 2001, several terrorists **1** (hijack[2]) two planes and fly them into the twin towers of the World Trade Center in New York. At first nobody knew what had happened. One survivor said, "All I knew was that I **2** (get) out of the building." Of course the people in the World Trade Center **3** (not use) the elevators because of the fires. Firefighters[3] from all over New York came to help, but they **4** (not rescue) a lot of the people and at some point they **5** (leave) the scene because the buildings collapsed[4]. More than 3,000 people died. Until several months later, people who had lived near the World Trade Center **6** (not move) back into their apartments. Soon after 9/11, however, New Yorkers decided that they **7** (find) hope again. In 2014, One World Trade Center was opened as a new office building. At the place where the twin towers once stood there is now a memorial[5] and a museum, which tells the story of 9/11.

1 **application** [ˌæplɪˈkeɪʃn] Bewerbung | 2 **to hijack** [ˈhaɪdʒæk] entführen | 3 **firefighter** [ˈfaɪəˌfaɪtə] Feuerwehrmann/-frau | 4 **to collapse** [kəˈlæps] einstürzen | 5 **memorial** [məˈmɔːriəl] Denkmal

Find more online: b8bg7s

Text smart 2
Internet texts

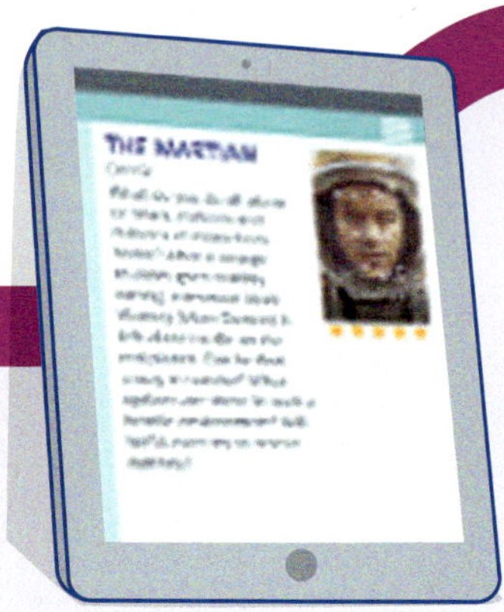

In Text smart 2 you're going to take a look at typical kinds of online texts. Who writes them, what are their typical features, how reliable is the information you get online?

VOCABULARY

1 Warm up: The internet in everyday life

a) *How would you finish this sentence: "If I had to spend a whole Saturday without my smartphone / my tablet, it would be so inconvenient because …"*

L 2/7–8 → S15

b) *Part 1: Tim and Marlon meet each other on the bus.*

1. Describe what Tim's problem is and how Marlon can help.
2. Then sum up what both boys say about the internet. The words below can help you.

Word bank

get quick information with apps | stay up-to-date on social media | watch tutorials | do research for school projects | follow / read blogs | follow social media profiles | post an opinion / comment on blogs / social media websites / …

c) *Now listen to part 2.*

1. Describe the problems Tim and Marlon mention.
2. Discuss how you feel about those problems.

SPEAKING

2 Your turn: Your reasons for using the internet

What were your main reasons for using the internet during the last 2–3 days? Compare your experiences with your partner's.

SPEAKING

3 America and the moon landing

On the following pages, you're going to work with internet texts about the first moon landing.

Read the box. Then say what other great moments or inventions in science and technology you can think of. Describe one for your partner.

Across cultures

On July 20, 1969, NASA astronaut Neil Armstrong became the first human on the moon. The **moon landing** is considered one of the greatest moments in the history of science and technology.

An online wiki text

The moon landing

The first moon landing took place on July 20, 1969, as the climax of NASA's Apollo 11 mission. Hundreds of millions of TV viewers watched on live TV as the landing module Eagle touched down on the moon's surface. Astronaut and Apollo 11 commander Neil Armstrong announced to mission control in Houston: "The Eagle has landed," words which soon became famous. More famous words followed six hours later when Armstrong stepped out of the Eagle and onto the moon: "That's one small step for (a) man, one giant leap for mankind." Armstrong was then joined by astronaut Buzz Aldrin. Together they took pictures to document the historic event and collected 46 pounds of moon rocks. After 21 hours, Armstrong and Aldrin returned to the command module Columbia, where astronaut Michael Collins had been waiting in orbit.

Years before, in 1961, the moon landing had become one of President John F. Kennedy's top priorities. He challenged the engineers and scientists at NASA to put a man on the moon by the end of 1969. It was clear to all that this would be the biggest challenge ever. It was also clear that it would be very political: During the Cold War, a triumph like the first moon landing was a prize that both the US and the Soviet Union wanted very much.

READING

4 Understanding the text → WB 37/1

→ S1–3 **a)** *Read the wiki text above. Sum up what happened in your own words.*

b) *Find phrases in the text that make the style factual and convincing. This box can help you:*

Reading skills

- A **factual text** should concentrate on **facts**. Opinions don't belong here.
- Factual texts about history focus on **times, dates, places** and **people**. Information like this can be easily checked at other text sources.

Tip

- **Wiki texts** are written to give information in the style of an encyclopedia. But wiki texts can be written or changed by any reader.
- Wikis try to be as **factual** as possible. But with so many authors, the regulators of wiki websites can't always keep their content completely free of opinions. So it is important to always look for **other reliable sources of information**. Don't rely only on wiki texts.

A blog post

READING

5 Hoaxes and conspiracy theories

→ △ 138/1

Across cultures

In the English-speaking world, there have been some famous hoaxes and conspiracy theories. The internet is full of such stories.

- When somebody stages a **hoax**, the person is playing a trick on the public. A typical hoax often features realistic photos that show something unbelievable like a UFO, or a monster.
- A **conspiracy theory** often involves an event or situation that a group of people would like to keep secret in a cover-up. The conspiracy theorists often see governments at the center of cover-ups. A famous example: Is the US government trying to keep real aliens a secret at the Area 51 air-force base?

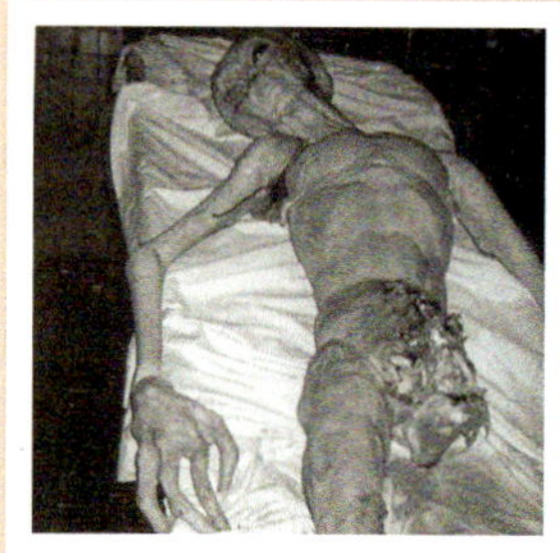

Read the box. Then talk about these questions in class:

1. Think of reasons why people would want to stage a hoax.
2. Explain why people often believe in conspiracy theories.

READING

6 A blog post on the moon landing: Was it all just a hoax?!

a) *Pre-reading: Some conspiracy theorists say the moon landing was just a hoax! But who could stage something so big? Share your ideas. The phrases below can help you.*

b) *Now read the blog post. Point out the main argument the blogger uses to claim that the moon landing never happened.*

c) *Give your opinion about the blogger's argument.*

Was it all just a hoax?! YES!

If this was possible then (with all that ANCIENT technology) why is nobody flying to the moon TODAY?! The way I see it, this argument is still one of the strongest. It makes sense. I mean, my smartphone has more computing power than the Eagle had, and that was the height of engineering at the time. So a small computer would be enough to run all the software you'd need to control the landing module.

If that is correct (and it IS correct), why haven't we been there since 1972? NASA doesn't want to go? Of course they want to go! Did our tech improve? Of course it improved! Do we know more about the moon today than we did 40 years ago? Of course we do! So WHY, WHY, WHY?! It must have been a conspiracy. There's NO WAY we could have been there in 1969.

POSTED BY MR_WISEGUY ON NOV. 7 AT 8:43 PM

Useful phrases

You can't believe everything you read / see / … | With enough money / power, you can stage / fake / … | I bet a powerful company / the government / Hollywood could … | Something that big / complicated would be easy / impossible / … to fake.

Tip

A **blog** is a website which the blogger uses as a platform for his / her **blog posts** on a personal-interest subject. There are blogs for just about any topic. The word 'blog' is made up from the words *web* + *logbook*.

WRITING

7 Characteristics of a blog post

a) *Read the skills box. What key points would you add; what would you leave out?*

b) *Go back to the blog post in Ex. 6. Which key points from the list can you find there? Write down as many examples as you can find.*

Writing skills

Blog posts are written for others, not just for the blogger. These are **key points** many bloggers follow:

1. **Opinions** can be strong, but they should be fair too.
2. A blogger who is **honest** with his / her readers will probably enjoy the most respect.
3. **Clear, simple writing** and **short paragraphs** are easier to read.
4. **Spelling** is important online too, not just on paper.
5. Bloggers often have their own special **writing style**.
6. Readers will probably leave more **comments** if the blogger asks questions in his / her posts.
7. Headings and visuals **grab the reader's attention**.
8. People like **entertaining** posts, not boring ones.

READING

8 Comparing wiki and blog texts → WB 37/2

a) *Have a closer look at the wiki text and the blog post. Compare them in the three categories below. Then discuss them in class.*

function | language | reader interest

b) *Which of the two texts seems more reliable to you? Explain your choice. The words in the box can help you.*

Word bank

lie | fake sth | play a trick on sb / trick sb | stage a hoax | claim | be based on facts | estimate | make sth sound convincing | question somebody's motivations | think critically | informative | reliable | believable

WRITING

→ △ 138/2
→ S7–9

9 Your turn: Write your own blog response

Would you support the writer's conspiracy theory in Ex. 6 or would you argue against it? Write your own blog response.

Start like this:

- This is a comment on the … / on what you said about … | I'd like to comment on …
- I agree / disagree with you about … / with the idea that …
- In my opinion … | The way I see it, you …
- You might be right about …, but I don't think you're right about …

Tip

When you write a response, make sure you make it clear **what you're referring to**:

- the whole blog post?
- just one part of it?

Online ratings

SPEAKING

10 Reasons for rating things

Give reasons why so many people go online to rate things, e.g. films or restaurants.

READING

11 Films about space: Two film summaries

Read the two summaries below. Talk about them with a partner to make sure you both understand the plots. You need this information to deal with online ratings in Ex. 12.

Capricorn One (1978)
Imagine that the greatest moment in space exploration never happened! The NASA engineers on the Mars space program are unable to land their astronauts on the red planet. So they decide to fake the first Mars landing before the US government ends the expensive Mars program. Will NASA be able to stage the greatest hoax of all time?

The Martian (2015)
What do you do all alone on Mars, millions and millions of miles from home? After a voyage to Mars goes terribly wrong, astronaut Mark Watney (Matt Damon) is left alone to die on the red planet. Can he find a way to survive? What options are there in such a hostile environment? Will NASA even try to rescue Watney?

READING

12 Ratings on a website for film fans

a) *Read the two ratings. Describe how positive or negative each one is for its film.*

A Overall, this is a pretty good film. The plot and the acting are convincing, in my opinion. There's well-written dialogue too. But to be honest, it's a bit disappointing. I think I would have enjoyed the movie much more if I'd seen it when it was new. Back then, there weren't that many movies about space or conspiracy theories. But now there are so many great space movies. ★★★

B This is about as good as a film can get, if you ask me! As if the breathtaking visuals weren't already enough, Matt Damon has given one of his very best performances. Best of all: It's a strong, believable plot; a perfect combination of science, suspense, the power of friendship and BIG emotions. You really feel how lost and lonely a person can be. Excellent! ★★★★★

b) *Explain which rating motivates you more to watch the film. Give reasons.*

c) *Can you trust ratings? Give and explain your opinion about how reliable they are or aren't.*

READING

13 < Internet research >

→ S18

Find out as much as you can about the film above that interests you the most. Write down possible search terms before you start your search.

WRITING

14 Characteristics of ratings

→ WB 38/3–4

Writing skills

When you rate a film (or book), think about these points:

1. Structure your rating in **categories**. This helps you to concentrate on **what is important**, e.g. the acting | the plot | the special effects.
2. You don't need to write a summary for the film's plot; this is almost always included on the rating website already. Concentrate on **your opinion**.
3. Explain what you like or don't like, but **always be fair**. It isn't necessary to use bad language or make rude comments.
4. **Words and phrases** from other people's ratings can be very useful to help you to express your ideas. Examples from Ex. 12: *breathtaking visuals; well-written dialogue.*
5. Use the **simple present** to describe action and scenes (*When the story begins …; The main character never knows …* etc.).

→ △ 138/3

a) *Read the points in the skills box above. Then go back to the two ratings in Ex. 12. Find examples of points 1–4 and put them in a grid. (For point 4, you might find phrases in the box on the right to add to your grid.)*

b) *Your turn: In a group of 3–4, choose a film that three of you have recently seen. You each write a short rating (6–8 sentences) for it. Then peer-edit each other's texts. Say whose rating you like best and why!*

Useful phrases

well-developed / undeveloped / convincing characters | well-written / badly-written dialogue | a good performance / one of his / her very best performances | great / disappointing actors / acting | silly / weak / creative / believable / … plot | In my opinion … | If you ask me …

WRITING

15 Options: Create wall displays

→ S7–9

Option A: Internet research for your own wiki text

Some people believe that aliens have really landed on Earth, e.g. in Roswell, New Mexico!

a) *As a group, find one example of a UFO sighting and do research on different websites about it. Which are the most helpful and reliable?*

b) *In your group, write your own wiki text about your subject. Decide what sections your wiki text will need and divide the work up so that everyone has the same amount of work.*

c) *Arrange your wiki text as a wall display for your classroom.*

Option B: Watch a film together and rate it

You've talked about the films on p. 74, now it's time to watch one together and then rate it.

a) *Form a group of classmates who would like to watch one of the movies you read about on p. 74.*

b) *Find the film on DVD or online.*

c) *After you've watched it, each person in your group will write a rating of the film. Don't forget to give each rating a number of stars from 1 to 5! Then peer-edit each other's texts.*

d) *When the ratings are finished, arrange them as a wall display for your classroom.*

Find more online: t42r99

What you say and how you say it

On these pages you're going to learn about differences between American English (AE) and British English (BE). You're also going to learn how you use different words or phrases to say the same things in different situations. This is called **register**.

VOCABULARY

1 Warm-up: Which words do you use?

a) *Look at the German words below. There are different expressions for these words in different regions within Germany. Collect them.*

Brötchen | Frikadellen | Bürgersteig | Metzger

b) *Now discuss similar differences you already know about in the English language. You can look at your list from Unit 2, Ex. 18. What other differences do you know about?*

VIEWING

2 British, American and Canadian English

4

a) *Watch the first part of the film (00:00–02:54).*

→ S16

b) *Make a grid with the three columns below. Then watch the first part again and write down examples for each category in your grid.*

spelling | pronunciation | different words

c) *Work with a partner. Add more examples from Ex. 1b) to the grid.*

L 2/9

d) *Read the text below. The marked words are pronounced differently in AE and BE.*

Everything is so different at my new school. It starts with getting to school – my mom has to take me by car. At my old school I took the bus, but here I can't because our house is too far away! My schedule at this school is much better though – I can get up later!
So far, most of my new classes are cool; I'm just not so sure about German. But do you want to know what my biggest problem is? I'm so thirsty because I can't find the water fountain!

Tip

	BE	AE
car, other, sure, work	[–]	[r]
beautiful, little, water	[t]	[d]
new, news	[juː]	[uː]
bath, ask, can't	[ɑː]	[æː]
dog, not, lot	[ɒ]	[ɑː]
boat, know, hello	[əʊ]	[oʊ]

e) *Read the text from d) out loud with a partner. One reads it in American English, the other in British English. The tip box can help you.*

VIEWING

3 Register differences

a) *Watch the second part of the film (02:55–end). What happens in the two scenes?*

A

B

b) *Describe how register plays a role in the scenes. Explain why it is important to speak in different registers.*

c) *Your turn: In what situations do you change the way you talk? Say why and how you change it.*

OCABULARY

4 Changing register → WB 40/1–2

a) *Match the words and phrases to the correct category:*

formal register | informal register

Hey! | How are you? | anymore | I really don't like it much. | child | Nope. | It really sucks. | Sorry, but I don't think so. | It's, like, so wild to … | I ain't … | I'm, like, … | Hello. | Totally! | Whatever! | kid | What's up? | No, I'm not. | How nice to … | no more | It's really boring. | I'm sorry. | Yes, I have. | Not in a million years! | I'm not … | It's totally not my thing.

b) *Change the register of this conversation between Brodie and his aunt June to make Brodie's words more formal and polite.*

Brodie: Whoa, sorry dude! Didn't mean to … – Oh! Hey, Auntie June! It's you! What's up?
June: Brodie! How nice to see you again. Happy Thanksgiving!
Brodie: Thanks! Same to you. It's, like, so wild to see you again.
June: How are you? You look like you've really grown in the last year.
Brodie: Totally! I'm, like, 6 feet tall now. I ain't no little kid no more!
June: How's school? Are you enjoying it?
Brodie: Nope. It's, like, so totally not my thing.
June: Well, I guess I didn't always enjoy school either.
Brodie: No. It really sucks!
June: I'm sorry you feel that way. But please mind your language!
Brodie: Whatever! The only parts I like are lunch and the final bell.
June: Maybe you can talk to one of your teachers.
Brodie: Not in a million years!

Unit 3
A nation invents itself

Find more online: 27yb5b

A

B

C

SPEAKING

1 America: A country of innovation → WB 41/1

a) *Describe pictures A–C. Explain why they represent aspects of modern-day America.*

b) *What else comes to your mind when you think of America today? Get into groups of 3–4. Copy the grid and write down your ideas.*

Technology	Music and film	Transportation	Food

→ △ 139/1

c) *America is known as a country of innovation. What does a country need in order to be innovative? Think of the points you collected in b). Then discuss the question in your groups.*

d) *Your turn: What kinds of pictures would you use to illustrate modern-day Germany? Find pictures on the internet or in magazines and make a collage. Then present it in class. Give reasons for your choice of pictures.*

In Unit 3 you learn

… about different periods of American history. You learn:

- how the present and the past are connected
- how to improve your written style with adjectives and linking words
- how to work with statistics
- how to write a short report

D

LISTENING **2** **The face of America today**

a) *How would you describe a 'typical American'? Collect ideas with a partner. Say where you got your ideas from.*

b) *Picture D shows people who live in America today. What do you notice about them? Explain what the pictures tell you about the modern face of America.*

L 2/10 **c)** *Listen to three American teenagers – Tony, Carlos and Eileen – who talk about their families. Take notes about the following points:*

→ S15

where their families came from and when | why their families left their home countries | what languages the teenagers speak at home | what they say about their identity

⟨d)⟩ *Your turn: Do a quick survey in your class. How many of you have parents or grandparents who came to Germany from other countries to start a new life here? Get into pairs or small groups and interview your classmates about their family history. The key points in c) can help you with your interviews. Think of a good way to present your results. Then give a short presentation in class.*

Soon after Christopher Columbus had reached America in 1492, European powers began to explore and colonize it. The first permanent English settlement was founded in 1607 in Jamestown, Virginia. By the time of American independence in the 1770s, there were 13 British colonies on the eastern coast of what is now the US America.

A

On July 4, 1776, the 13 British colonies declared independence from Britain because they weren't happy about the way the mother country had been treating them. With French help, the American army under General George Washington won the Revolutionary War against Britain. Washington later became the first president of the US.

B

SPEAKING

3 Key points in American history

a) *In order to understand modern-day America it can help you to know more about American history. Read the four texts A–D about different historic periods. Then think back to what you learned on pages 78–79. Explain how past and present are connected.*

b) *Think-pair-share: Now read the quotations and sayings below. Say how they go with the different periods in American history. Share your ideas with a partner and then with the class.*

United we stand, divided we fall.
Popular saying

Our beautiful America was built by a nation of strangers.
President Lyndon B. Johnson

Remember, remember always, that all of us, and you and I especially, are descended from immigrants.
President Franklin D. Roosevelt

Go West young man, and grow up with the country.
Popular saying

E pluribus unum ('One from many')
From the seal of the United States of America

After President Jefferson had bought large parts of North America from France in 1803, more and more settlers arrived to start a new life in the wide, open spaces of the West, and the Native Americans suffered badly: Many were killed, while many others lost all or large parts of their traditional land.

D

In the peak immigration period from 1880 to 1930, a total of 28 million people arrived in the US. Most of them came by ship from Europe and passed through the famous immigration center at Ellis Island, which was open from 1892 to 1954. Other immigrants came by land through Mexico in the South and Canada in the North.

SPEAKING

4 Your turn: Past and present → WB 41/2

a) *Get into groups of 3–4. Choose one of the pictures C or D above. Go 'back in time' and try to imagine life during the period of American history that the picture represents:*

Picture C: I feel so small! We've only got a few belongings with us in this tiny covered wagon! And when I look outside, the landscape just goes on forever. We've got three more days in this wagon and then …

Picture D: Well, here we are in New York City! But I had no idea there would be so many other people from so many different countries! What language are they speaking over there? Wow, this is really …

Think about how you feel. What is most important / exciting / difficult for you when you arrive at your new home or in your new country? Write a short text.

b) *Now come back to the present. Imagine that you have to leave Germany with your family to live in another country. Answer the questions about how you feel in a). Discuss how the experience of starting a new life has changed between past and present. What's the same, what's different?*

L 2/11

This story sounds great!

Lee picks up his best friend Tim to go to baseball training for the first time. Tim has sent him a text before he arrives because he can't find his father's old baseball bat.

Lee: Did you find the baseball bat?

Tim: Yeah, it was up in the attic. It took me forever to find it, and that's not all I found. Look at this book. My dad kept it separate from the other books.

Lee: It looks old.

Tim: Super old. It's a diary by someone called Johan Förstner. Look, here's his name, and the date: 1901. It tells the story of his first few years here. He was 21 when he arrived from Germany. The entries for the first couple of years are in German, then they're in English.

Lee: Who was he?

Tim: My parents and I had no idea, so we asked my grandma. She told us that he was her grandfather. He came to America around that time.

Lee: Förstner … your last name is Forester.

Tim: Johan changed his name in the 1920s. Some people here found 'Förstner' difficult to pronounce.

Lee: Have you read the diary yet?

Tim: Yeah, some of it. The most interesting part is the German section. It's about his journey here, and starting a new life in America.

Lee: I didn't know you spoke German.

Tim: I don't, but my grandma speaks it well. She spoke German at home to make her grandparents happy. She translated some of it for me. Look, in this part here, Johan said he was looking forward to going to America, but he was feeling scared too.

Lee: I'm not surprised. It took several days to get here, didn't it?

Tim: Yeah, and on a really crowded ship. Johan describes how you had to pass a medical examination after you'd finally arrived. If you got sick on the way, you had to go back.

Lee: That sounds awful!

Tim: But Johan was lucky. He got in, and then he came here to Wisconsin.

Lee: Why here?

Tim: There were already other Germans here. I guess he wanted some people around who spoke the same language.

Lee: Yeah, that makes sense.

Tim: But something seems weird to me. He keeps talking about his sister Ursula and he says that it's his greatest wish to see her happy again. Then there are a couple of pages missing, and after that Ursula has just disappeared.

Lee: Does your grandma know what happened to her?

Tim: No. She didn't even know her grandfather *had* a sister. Oh look, a piece of paper just fell out of the book. I'll get it …

READING

1 Understanding the text

→ ▲ 139/2
→ S1

a) *Sum up what you learn about Tim's great-great-grandfather and his journey to America.*

b) *Explain why immigrants would want to live close to people from their own country.*

LANGUAGE

2 Revision: Adjective or adverb? → WB 42/3

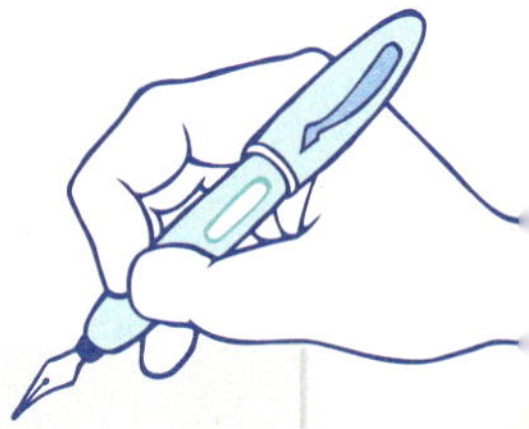

a) *The piece of paper that fell out of Johan's diary is a letter from his sister Ursula. Complete the text. Decide if you need an* ***adjective*** *or an* ***adverb****.*

Dear Johan,

I can't believe that I've found you again! I've thought about you every day and I've missed you 1 *(terrible). The last time we saw each other was at Ellis Island in 1901. That's 17 years ago now but I remember it as* 2 *(clear) as if it was yesterday. I'd caught an eye infection on the journey over. It wasn't* 3 *(serious), but they sent me back anyway. I'll never understand how they could be so* 4 *(cruel) and treat me so* 5 *(bad). Of course my English wasn't* 6 *(good) at that time. That's why I studied* 7 *(hard) and learned to speak it as* 8 *(good) as possible before I came back two years later. I live in Milwaukee now with my husband Jack and our* 9 *(beautiful) son John, who is 12. He looks just like you and he sings as* 10 *(beautiful) as you too! I hope that one day very soon we'll be able to meet again.*

Your sister,
Ursula

b) *How do you think Johan felt when he read Ursula's letter? Write a letter from Johan to his sister in which he expresses his feelings and talks about what he did after he'd arrived in Wisconsin. Use* ***adjectives*** *and* ***adverbs*** *to make your writing more interesting.*

LANGUAGE

3 Verbs with adjectives → G6 → WB 42/4

a) *You already know that adverbs describe the verbs they follow. Sometimes there's an adjective after the verb or after a verb and an object. Copy the grid and find more examples in the text on p. 82.*

Verb + adjective	Verb + object + adjective
The book that Tim found smells very old. During the examination Johan stayed calm.	Many people found the journey terrible. Tim's grandmother kept Johan's story secret.

b) *Your turn: Finish these sentences with your own* ***adjectives****.*

1. I like my music …
2. I find the internet …
3. When I get up in the morning, I look …
4. I don't like it when people call me …
5. When we do tests, I feel …
6. In my dreams I imagine myself …

WRITING

4 The journey to America → WB 43/5

→ △ 139/3
→ ▲ 140/4

Imagine you're sailing to America in the year 1901, a journey which takes several days. The ship is really crowded and many of the people are scared. Write about your experience. Use the verbs ***taste****,* ***smell****,* ***sound****,* ***look****,* ***feel****,* ***seem*** *and your own* ***adjectives****.*

Start like this: The drinking water tastes strange … | I feel scared / sad / excited because … | Some of the other passengers seem … | The sea makes me happy / sad because …

READING

5 The first Americans → WB 43/6

Across cultures

Before the European settlers arrived, between 10 and 15 million people had already lived in what is now the US. The first European visitors called these people 'Indians' because they thought they had arrived in a part of south Asia. Today the term **Native American** is used more often than **Indian** – but both are correct. In fact, the Native Americans often call themselves 'Indians'.

When the European settlers moved out West, some Native American tribes managed to keep at least parts of their land, which are called **reservations**. Today there are more than 560 officially recognized tribes, and about 330 of them have their own reservation. The largest tribes are the Navajo in the Southwest and the Cherokee in the Southeast. Many Native Americans speak their tribal language in addition to English.

a) *Do you think the European settlers had the right to take the land away from the Native American tribes? Give reasons for your opinion.*

<b)> *In small groups, choose one of the tasks and do some research on the internet. Think of a good way to present your results, e.g. a poster, a mind map etc.*

→ S18

- Collect information about a Native American tribe that interests you.
- Find out more about what happens on Native American reservations. Where are the biggest ones? Why do some tribes have no reservations?

LANGUAGE

6 Participles as adjectives → WB 44/7

a) *Look at the two sentences below. Explain how **present participles** and **past participles** are formed and how they're used here. It might help you to translate the sentences into German.*

Many things were **surprising** for the immigrants when they arrived in America.
The others on the boat tried to comfort me when they saw how **frightened** I was.

→ △ 140/5

b) *Read the story of an Italian woman who arrived in the US in the early 1920s. Find more examples of **present participles** and **past participles** in the text.*

"We were so relieved when we finally arrived in New York after an exhausting journey. I went to the front of the ship, and in the distance I could see the Statue of Liberty. After we had gotten off, we had to stand in line with our belongings. I had just one small, broken suitcase. There were hundreds of people around us. We went past a group of scared children who were crying and calling for their parents. First we had a medical examination and then we had to join another long line to show our money and our immigration papers. We were worried because we only had about a hundred dollars. Finally we got onto a crowded boat to take us over to the city. It was so exciting! Everything was different from home …"

c) *Think-pair-share: What do you think might have been different for the immigrants in America? Collect ideas with your partner before you share them in class.*

LANGUAGE

7 Starting a new life

*Complete the sentences with **present participles** or **past participles**.*

1. When I found my grandma's diary, I was very ___ (excite). 2. It was ___ (hide) in an old cupboard under some ___ (break) toys. 3. In her diary she told some ___ (frighten) stories about her journey to America. 4. So you can imagine how ___ (thrill) she felt when she finally arrived in her new home. 5. It must have been ___ (excite) to start all over again. 6. Now I'd like to travel to her home country, but my parents are ___ (worry) and don't want to let me go.

SPEAKING

8 How to: Work with statistics → WB 44/8, 45/9

L 2/13 → S15

a) *Listen to another conversation between Lee and his friend Tim. What do they say about immigration to America? Take notes and share your results in class.*

→ S6

b) *Choose one of the diagrams below. What does it tell you about the immigrants who came to America between 1880 and 1930? Make notes. Read the skills box and the useful phrases if you need help.*

Immigration into the United States 1880–1930	
Italy	4,600,000
Austro-Hungarian Empire	4,000,000
Russian Empire	3,300,000
German Empire	2,800,000
Great Britain	2,300,000
Canada	2,300,000
Ireland	1,700,000
Sweden	1,100,000

Source: The Statue of Liberty – Ellis Island Foundation, 2016

Immigration into the United States 1880–1930

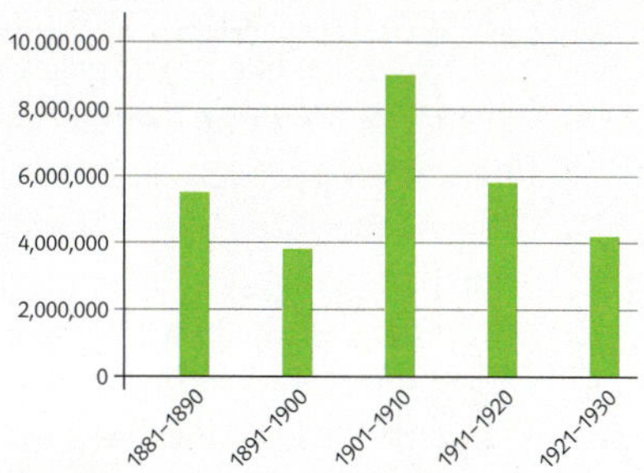

Source: United States Census Bureau, 2012

Speaking skills

When you talk about a **diagram**, you can follow these steps:

1. Begin with what type of diagram it is and what it is about. Don't forget to mention the source and the year of its publication.
2. Describe what you can see in the diagram.
3. Summarize the gist of what the diagram tells you in 1–2 sentences.

Useful phrases

- The table / bar graph / line graph / pie chart / … was published by … in …
- It is about … / deals with … / …
- The (next) largest group of … | The majority / minority of … | Half of … | Most of … | 30 percent of the immigrants come from … / are …
- The number of … goes up / grows by … / drops / goes down / doesn't change.
- The numbers / figures show / suggest that …
- We can draw the conclusion that …

c) *Work with a partner who chose the same diagram. Compare your results. Then present them to the class.*

d) *With your partner, find statistics about immigration to Germany after World War II. When did most people come here, and from which countries? Give a short presentation in class.*

L 2/14

Necessity is the mother of invention

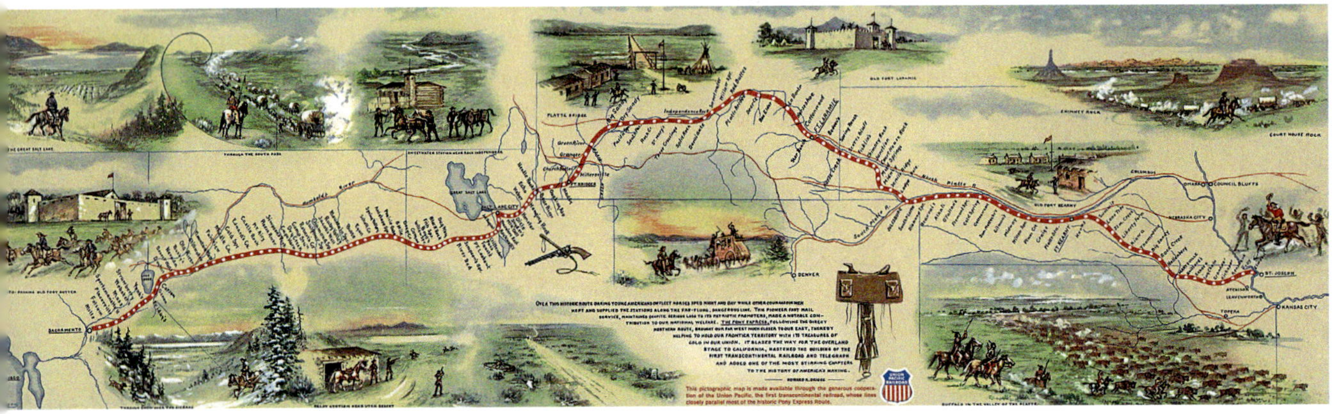

Today, the US has a very good transportation and communications network. When a New Yorker and a person from Los Angeles need to meet face-to-face instead of by video link, one of them can get on a flight at lunchtime and be with the other in time for dinner. Of course, it hasn't always been so easy …

Around the beginning of the 19th century, large numbers of people started migrating from the towns and cities of the East to start new lives in the huge areas of land out West. These pioneers founded settlements in areas which are now the central and western US states. After the discovery of gold in California in 1848, many more settlers began to move there in the hope of becoming rich. Many of them didn't find gold, but stayed in California and became farmers.

This mass migration to the West created a new problem. How would people in this expanding nation stay in touch with each other? It could take weeks or even months for a letter to get from one side of the country to the other. Then in 1860, this advertisement for an innovative new service was published in newspapers:

> WANTED!
> Young, skinny fellows not over eighteen.
> Must be expert riders, ready to risk death.

The Pony Express was looking for horse riders who would carry mail between Missouri in the central part of the US and California on the West Coast – a distance of more than 1,800 miles. Horses were kept at about 190 stations along the route. As soon as a rider arrived at a station, he'd change horses and then continue quickly on his way. Each rider rode for about 70 miles before he gave his bag of mail to the next one. All riders had to be skinny so that the horses could go faster. For that reason only boys were employed, some as young as 14. As the journey was completed by about 20 riders in this way, it only took around ten days. Even though there were many dangers, and a number of horses and riders died, the Pony Express only ever lost one bag of mail.

However, like many great innovations before it, the Pony Express was soon replaced by something even better. Back in the 1830s, three Americans named Morse, Henry and Vail had developed the electric telegraph. Morse had invented a code that used long and short sounds to represent each letter of the alphabet, and in 1844 he sent his first message from Washington, D.C., to Baltimore, Maryland. Telegraph lines had already been laid across much of the country before the Pony Express started in 1860. When these lines finally connected the East and West Coasts in 1861, it became possible to send messages across the continent almost instantly. The Pony Express then was no longer needed.

READING

9 Understanding the text

→ S1 a) *Sum up what you learn about the Pony Express.*

b) *Imagine it's 1860 and one of your best friends wants to join the Pony Express. There are a lot of questions you want to ask him. Do a dialogue together and present it in class.*

c) *Explain the title of the text. Can you think of other examples which show that 'necessity is the mother of invention'?*

LANGUAGE

10 Linking words → G7

a) *Use the words to complete the sentences. Sometimes there's more than one correct answer.*

although | as | as soon as | because | even though | since | when | and

1. Millions of pioneers migrated to the West ___ they hoped for a better life there.
2. The journey was hard and dangerous ___ many pioneers never arrived.
3. ___ it was a great innovation, the Pony Express came too late to be a long-lasting success.
4. ___ the US is a young country, it has produced many important inventions and innovations.
5. ___ almost everybody speaks English, you'll find travelling in the US is easy.
6. Call me ___ you arrive in New York tomorrow morning.

b) *Find more sentences with **linking words** in the text on p. 86.*

c) *A game: One of you thinks of a main clause. Then the other adds an **adverbial clause**. Take turns. Make sure to use all the linking words you collected in a) and b).*

Example: A: I didn't go to football training … – B: … **because** we had a Math test the next day. | … **although** we had an important match on Saturday.

LANGUAGE

11 New nation, new ideas → WB 45/10, 46/11

→ △ 140/6

*Choose the correct **linking words** to complete the text.*

The history of the US has always been linked with innovation. **1** (When | Since) the first colonists arrived in the New World in the 17th century, they had to be innovative in order to survive in the harsh, new environment. Later, **2** (after | before) America had won its independence from Britain, large waves of immigrants from different parts of the world brought new skills and new ideas with them. The beginnings of modern communication started off in the US **3** (even though | because) the first working computer and the internet were invented here. **4** (When | While) not all important inventions were made in America, it has often been Americans who have made them great with further inventions. Think of the motor car, for example. **5** (As soon as | Although) it was invented by the German Carl Benz, it was the American Henry Ford who made it a 'mass market' product **6** (so that | before) millions of people could buy one. The World Wide Web, the system used by websites, is another example. In 1989 it was the British scientist Berners-Lee who created the web, **7** (but | and) if you look at the most popular websites, you will find that many of them are American: Google, Facebook, YouTube, Wikipedia or Twitter.

SPEAKING

12 Important American inventions → WB 46/12

a) *Get into groups of 3–4. Discuss which of these American inventions are most important in your opinion. Present your 'Top 3' in class. Explain why you chose them.*

Start like this: We think … is most important because … | Although … is important too, I think …

1891: Thomas Edison invents the motion picture camera

1903: The Wright Brothers build and fly the world's first plane

1908: The Ford Model T is the world's first 'mass market' car

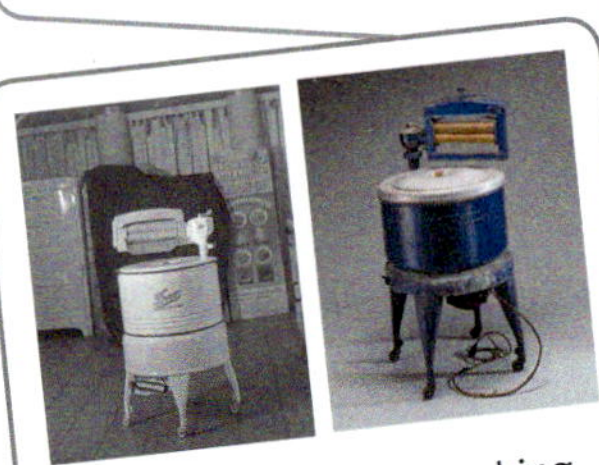

1908: The first electric washing machine is invented

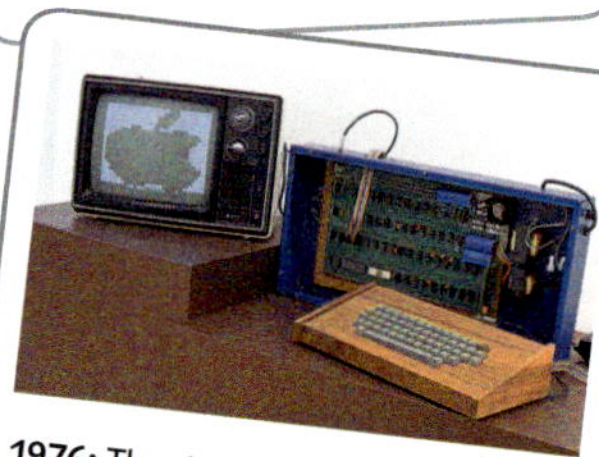

1976: The Apple-1 is the first Apple computer

2004: Mark Zuckerberg creates Facebook

b) *Find out about some German inventions. Sort them according to their importance.*

LANGUAGE

13 < If these things hadn't been invented … >

→ 141/7
→ 141/8

When you want to say what would be different today if something in the past had or hadn't happened, you can use the ***past perfect*** *in the if-clause and* ***would(n't) / could(n't) + infinitive*** *in the main clause. Finish the sentences to make conditional clauses.*

Example: If the first plane **hadn't been built**, we **couldn't fly** to the other end of the world.

1. If Mark Zuckerberg hadn't created Facebook, I … 2. If the Americans hadn't invented the internet, … 3. If the first electric washing machine hadn't been produced, we … 4. If nobody had invented the car, … 5. If Levi Strauss hadn't produced the first jeans, … 6. If the fridge hadn't been invented, …

WRITING

14 Your turn: Your own invention → WB 46/13

a) *Be a pioneer: In small groups, think of an invention that would change the world. Write a short text to present your invention. Use adjectives and linking words to make your text more interesting. If you want to be creative, you can draw a picture of your invention.*

b) *Present your invention to the rest of the class in a* ***gallery walk****. Be prepared to answer questions your classmates might have.*

READING

15 American identity
→ WB 47/14–15

Across cultures

The Americans' **fight for freedom** in the colonial days and the settlers' **pioneer spirit** have shaped the American identity. This can still be felt today, especially on the Fourth of July when the Americans celebrate the day they declared their independence from Britain in 1776. Independence Day, as it is also known, is a huge national holiday with barbecues and fireworks all over the country. The **American flag** plays an important role in everyday life, not only on Independence Day. The 50 stars stand for the number of states in the US, while the stripes represent the 13 original colonies.

Can you think of symbols that represent German identity? Collect ideas and share them with a partner.

LISTENING

16 ‹ A song: Firework › Katy Perry

L 2/19
→ S15

Do you ever feel
Like a plastic bag
Drifting through the wind
Wanting to start again

Do you ever feel
Feel so paper-thin
Like a house of cards
One blow from caving in

Do you ever feel
Already buried deep
Six feet under
Screams but no one seems to hear a thing

Do you know that there's
Still a chance for you
Cause there's a spark in you
You just gotta

Ignite the light
And let it shine
Just own the night
Like the Fourth of July

a) *Listen to the song. Explain why it refers to the Fourth of July.*

b) *With your partner, collect ideas about what has made you the person you are. Think of your family and friends, your school and the country or countries you have grown up in.*

SPEAKING

17 ‹ Your turn: Looking back at the unit ›

a) *Imagine you had the chance to go back in American history. Which of the historic periods from this unit would you choose? Discuss it with your partner.*

b) *Together you can take five things with you on your time travel. First work alone. Write down things that you absolutely want to take with you. Then show each other your ideas. Discuss all the suggestions and decide on the five things you're going to take. Explain why they are so important to you.*

How to write a report

This page can help you to write a report about what another person has told you.

1 My grandmother's story

At a family event, Laura and her grandmother talk about the life of Laura's great-grandmother. Some days later, Laura is asked by her exchange partner Kelly to send her a short written report about their conversation for a history project she's taking part in at her school.

L 2/20 → S15

a) *Listen to the first part of the conversation between Laura and her grandmother. Sum up what they're talking about in 2–3 sentences.*

b) *Laura writes two versions of the report for Kelly and she isn't sure which one to send her. Read the two reports. Say which one you find better and why.*

Writing skills

When you have to decide which **information** to choose for your report, the following questions can help you:
- What do you think the reader already knows about the topic?
- What information will he / she need to know in order to understand your report?
- What parts of the story will he / she find the most interesting?

A: I asked my grandmother about her mother. That's my great-grandmother. I don't remember her at all because she died when I was four or five years old. My grandmother told me some interesting things about my great-grandmother which I didn't know. When she was 14 or 15 her parents took her and her brother Dieter and her sister Ingrid to America. I think they went there by ship. Then they went to Chicago. Her father probably worked in an insurance office and her mother probably worked for a bank. They had enough money and a nice house. After a few years my great-grandmother decided to come back to Germany. I thought that was a very interesting story and I found it really interesting to find out more about my family. I wish I'd have known my great-grandmother.

B: I asked my grandmother about her mother Anna, my great-grandmother. She died when I was about five years old. I found out that when she was about my age, she went to America with her family to start a new life. This was just after World War I. Life was very hard in Germany back then and many people didn't even have enough to eat. Her family sold everything they had and bought the tickets for the journey to America. As soon as they arrived, they went to Chicago. Anna's parents got good jobs and soon they had enough money and a nice house. Anna had a natural talent for languages and she was able to learn English quickly. Even though everything was going well, she didn't feel at home there. When she was about 19, she decided to come back to Germany.

2 Write a short report

L 2/21

Listen to the second part of the conversation between Laura and her grandmother. Note down the most important information and write a short report in English. Keep in mind the points you collected in Ex. 1b). Then exchange texts with a partner and give each other feedback.

Oral historian for a day

Oral historians ask people about their personal experiences. They want to collect information that you won't necessarily find in history books. Here you get the chance to be an oral historian for one day. You're going to do an interview with a person of your choice. Then you're going to write a short report about him / her, together with some historical background information.

Step 1

Choose an interview partner

Get into groups of 3–4. Think of a person you know who has come to live in Germany in the past. Ask the person if he / she would agree to answer your questions.

Step 2

Do the interview → WB 48/16

Write questions for your interview. Focus on the following points:

his / her reasons for coming to Germany | feelings about leaving his / her home country | how he / she came here | his / her first experiences in Germany

Discuss the questions in your group. Choose the ones you definitely want to ask. Then do the interview.

Step 3

Write your report → WB 48/17, 49/18

Now write a short report about what you've found out in the interview. Make sure you use adjectives and adverbs as well as linking words to make your text more interesting. If you like, you can use pictures to illustrate your report.

→ Improving your style with adjectives (pp. 82–85) → Improving your style with linking words (pp. 86–88) → Using the right information and style for a report (p. 90)

Step 4

Find background information

In order to make it easier for the reader to understand your report, it is important to give some historical background information. Find facts and statistics on the internet about this particular period of immigration and group of immigrants.

→ Working with statistics (p. 85)

Step 5

Present your results → WB 49/19

Think of a good way to present your results in a gallery walk. Read the presentations of the other groups and give feedback.

S1/21–30
L2/22–31

A journey into the unknown

SPEAKING

1 Before you read

What might have been difficult on a trip across the US in 1848? Collect ideas with your partner.

March 11th, 1848
This afternoon Ma came up to me, holding a book in her hands. "Now you're the oldest, Lilly, I think you should continue writing Abbie's diary," she said. "It's what she would have wanted."

She was talking about my older sister. Abbie had kept a diary about everything that happened to our family. But then last summer she and my two older brothers, Moses and Clayton, all died from swamp fever. First Moses, then four days later Abbie and Clayton, just a few hours apart. I still find it hard to think about that terrible, terrible week. But as Pa says, "Life goes on."

I'm writing this upstairs in the light of my candle. Downstairs, Ma and Pa are whispering excitedly. It's good to hear them talking again. They have both been very quiet since we lost Abbie and the boys.

March 12th, 1848
At breakfast, Pa and Ma had some big news for us. Pa's cousin Jake is organizing a party to join the Oregon Trail, and we're going to be part of it! We're going to sell the house and some of our belongings to buy a wagon and some horses to pull it. There'll be five or six wagons, with some people we know from Pittsfield and some we don't.

The rest of the morning was spent talking about all the preparations we'll have to make. Pa seems very excited about heading West, but I'm not so sure about Ma.

"There's space and lots of land to farm. Everything will be better there," said Pa. "No bad memories."

"What will we eat while we wait for our first crops?" Ma asked.

"It says here you can catch fish just by putting your hand in the river," Pa said, waving a pamphlet.

"Your Pa sure has got the Oregon Fever," Ma said in a serious voice, when he was out of the room. "2,000 miles! I just hope ..." but she didn't finish her sentence.

I'm still so shocked I don't know what I feel. My best friend Myra went last year. Maybe I will get to see her again.

March 27th, 1848
No time for the diary these last two weeks, as we were so busy with packing. It was hard to decide what to take and what to leave, and Ma and Pa kept arguing about it. Now we've stopped for the first night of our journey, at a small town called Black Lake. I've never been this far from Pittsfield before. In front of us there's nothing but open prairie, just miles and miles of grass and some mountains in the distance.

Next to us are the Jamesons. They have eleven children and two wagons. It makes our family seem very small. Now it's just Ma, Pa, me, Harriet and the twins.

April 3rd, 1848
We passed some furniture, abandoned in the long grass. There were three good chairs, a wardrobe and a piano. It was almost time to stop for the night anyway, so we decided to camp there. I realized I hadn't sat on a proper chair for a whole week.

Mrs. Jameson started playing the piano, but it was very out of tune.

"It was a good piano, before it got rained on," she said. "Must have been rich folks who owned it. I wonder why rich folks were out here on the Trail."

April 6th, 1848
There's a ferry downriver, but we would have had to wait three days to use it. Instead we crossed at a place where the river is shallow

enough for a tall man to walk across, up to his chest in the water. First we all joined in painting the bottoms and sides of the wagons with something to keep the water out.

"Make sure to cover everything," said Jake, "Or your wagon will sink and everything in it will be ruined."

Then one by one, my Pa, Jake and two of the other men floated the wagons across the river, while the rest of us were sitting in them. Just like boats! I couldn't believe my eyes when I saw our horses swimming across the river!

April 10th, 1848

Cornbread and a little bacon again for dinner today. I sure miss the food back home. I was washing the plates in the river when I found a pretty blue bead. I showed it to Pa.

"I reckon that's an Indian bead," he said. "A few years ago, this was Indian country. Till they got pushed out by our boys."

I looked for more beads so I could make an Indian necklace, but all I found was an old arrowhead.

April 13th, 1848

It's raining too hard to drive the wagons through the mud. Another party of about ten wagons and a couple of families traveling alone are camped here too, now. We're all just waiting for the rain to stop and the ground to get firm enough for our wagon wheels.

April 15th, 1848

The rain has finally stopped. The big party of wagons has gone, and so has one of our bags of flour, some coffee and the last of our eggs.

"Easy enough to reach into a wagon when everybody's asleep," said Mr. Jameson. They lost supplies too.

I think to cheer us up, one of the single families (they're from Russia, and don't speak much English) made a kind of spicy tea and shared it with everybody. Then the father took out an instrument I'd never seen before and played some Russian songs. The rest of us clapped along. In spite of our recent troubles, it felt good to be alive!

April 24th, 1848

I'm so scared of what will happen next, it's all I can do to write this. This morning Ma sent me and the twins to fetch water from the river. The water was muddy, so Ma put in a handful of flour to make most of the mud fall to the bottom. Then she used the clearer part to make soup. Now Ma, Pa and the twins are all so sick, they can hardly move. Harriet and I'll have to do our best to look after them.

May 2nd, 1848

Pa got better quite quickly but Ma and the twins were too sick to travel for more than a week. We are so lucky none of us died. We couldn't ask the others to wait for us. Pa told Jake that we would catch up with them soon, but I think they both knew that wasn't going to happen.

Now we're on our own. Ma and the twins are still weak from being sick, our supplies are getting low and the next part of the Trail is even more dangerous, as there's trouble with Indians there. Last night Ma and Pa decided we should turn back, but this morning they'd changed their minds.

"What would we go back to?" said Pa, while Ma started crying again.

SPEAKING

2 Your reaction

a) *What's the first adjective that comes to your mind after you've read Lilly's diary? Give reasons for your choice.*

b) *Have you read any other stories or seen films about this historical period? Compare them with what you've heard from the diary.*

READING

3 Understanding the story → WB 50/20

a) *Explain how Lilly's parents feel differently about leaving Pittsfield.*

b) *What difficulties are the settlers scared of? Compare them with what you talked about in Ex. 1.*

c) *Hot seat: One of you takes the role of Lilly. The others think of questions you want to ask her about how she feels about their journey and how she experienced the first few weeks after they'd left their old home. Take turns to ask your questions.*

READING

4 The purpose of a text

→ △ 141/9

a) *Explain why the author wrote her story in the form of diary entries. What's the purpose of choosing this text type? Share your ideas with a partner. The skills box can help you.*

b) *Have a closer look at the language the author uses for her story. Find examples in the text. Explain why this kind of language fits the purpose of the text.*

Reading skills

When you read a text, it is important to think about the effect it wants to have on the reader. Each text type has a specific **purpose**, and for this it uses a particular kind of **language**.

Examples: A news report wants to inform the reader. It focuses on facts and doesn't use emotional language. A print advertisement tries to persuade the reader to buy a certain product. It addresses the reader directly and makes use of emotional language.

WRITING

5 Group writing: How the story continues → WB 50/21

a) *Get into groups of 3–4. You're going to write more entries for Lilly's diary. Think about how the story might continue. Discuss your ideas and agree on who will write each diary entry. The following ideas can help you:*

a broken wagon wheel | a large herd of bison |
a group of Native Americans that is coming towards the settlers

b) *Write your diary entries. Think about what you found out about Lilly's feelings in Ex. 3c). Use adjectives and adverbs to express her feelings and thoughts.*

c) *Exchange your diary entries and give each other feedback. Then present your diary entries in class.*

d) *Imagine smartphones were available in the 19th century. Read Lilly's diary entries again and think of tweets she might have posted on Twitter. Compare the effect of both text types.*

Examples: Just done the first 1,000 miles. Only 1,000 more to go!
Another broken wheel! We'll be stuck here for the rest of the day.

America: A big salad bowl? → S16

You already know Jessica, Wesley and Christine. Now they're with another classmate, Emilio, on a class trip to Ellis Island.

VIEWING

1 In New York Harbor

5 *Watch the first scene (till 02:08). Sum up the action. Write a heading for the scene.*

VIEWING

2 Different ethnic backgrounds → WB 51/22

a) *Watch the film till 03:05. Take notes about the students' different ethnic backgrounds. What do you learn about them?*

b) *Explain why you think the Americans have built a huge 'Wall of Honor' for immigrants.*

c) *Answer these questions:*

1. Describe the argument in this scene. Who caused it? Whose feelings were hurt?
2. Explain the meaning behind the statements in the two speech bubbles below.
3. Your turn: Say whose comments can you identify with the most so far, and why.

> All Americans are equal, no matter how they came here or where they're from.

> Everyone in this country has a chance to make the best of their life.

Looking for family names at the American Immigrant Wall of Honor on Ellis Island

VIEWING

3 Melting pots and salad bowls

a) *Now watch the rest of the film. Sum up the main theme of the students' conversation.*

b) *Describe the difficulties newly-arrived immigrants to Ellis Island could face.*

c) *In your own words, describe what these two concepts of immigration in the US mean: **melting pot** and **salad bowl**.*

d) *Is Germany more of a melting pot or a salad bowl? Explain your opinion.*

LISTENING

1 Leaving your country

L 3/1

a) *Listen to the story of an emigrant who left his country and his family. Take notes to answer the following questions:*

1. Why did he leave his country? 2. What does he say about his journey?

b) *Now imagine yourself in the same situation. How would you react? What would you do? Talk about it with your partner.*

c) *Think of other reasons for leaving your country. Collect ideas and share them in class.*

MEDIATION

2 Hamburg's emigration museum

a) *Your aunt from America is going to come for a visit. Her German isn't very good; she left Germany when she was very young. You tell her about your plans to visit BallinStadt – an emigration museum in Hamburg. On video chat, she wants to know what you can see and do there. Read the website of the emigration museum. Then write down in English what you tell your aunt about the museum.*

In Haus 1 – dem „Hafen der Träume" – tauchen Besucher in die Welt vor 120 Jahren ein, als Albert Ballin den Entschluss fasste, eine Zufluchtsstätte für die Millionen Auswanderer aus Europa zu schaffen, bevor ihre Reise in die Neue Welt begann. Seine faszinierende Geschichte wird ebenso gezeigt wie auch die historische Bedeutung des Ortes für die Welt.

Unter dem Motto „Welt in Bewegung" präsentiert die BallinStadt in ihrer Hauptausstellung in Haus 2 die Ein- und Auswanderungsgeschichte aus vier Epochen. Los geht es mit der Eroberung Amerikas und der Kolonialisierung durch die Auswanderer. Die 2. Epoche konzentriert sich auf das „lange" 19. Jahrhundert (1789–1914), als die europäische Auswanderung in verschiedene Teile der Welt explodierte. Der Erste und Zweite Weltkrieg (die 3. Epoche) bedeuteten das große Aus für die europäische Überseewanderung. Stattdessen bestimmten Flucht, Vertreibung und Massenausweisung das Schicksal von Millionen von Menschen weltweit. Die 4. Epoche thematisiert die Zeit nach 1945, als die Welt nach dem Ende des Krieges im Wandel war.

Bewegende Geschichten voller Aktualität berühren die Besucher anschließend in der „Lebenslinien"-Ausstellung in Haus 3. Briefe, Fotos, Andenken und persönliche Erinnerungen dokumentieren hier eindrücklich, dass hinter jeder Zahl in der Statistik ein einzigartiger Lebensweg steckt. Am Ende erleben die Besucher einen Abschluss ihrer Reise durch die Geschichte, den sie so nicht erwartet hätten.

b) *Would you like to visit the emigration museum? Give reasons for your opinion.*

LANGUAGE

3 Adjective or adverb? → WB 54/3

*Decide if you need an **adjective** or **adverb** in these sentences.*

1. The food on the ship tasted ▬ (awful).
2. That's why I tasted everything ▬ (careful).
3. I felt ▬ (terrible) for most of the trip.
4. When I saw the Statue of Liberty, I ▬ (quick) felt much better.
5. Suddenly everyone around me looked ▬ (happy) too.
6. When we arrived, I looked around ▬ (excited).

VOCABULARY

4 Word families

*Look at the words in brackets. Find another word of the **same word family** to complete the sentences.*

Example: 1. Many new **innovations** were developed because something was needed.

1. Many new ▬ (innovative) were developed because something was needed. ✔
2. One reason European countries wanted ▬ (colony) America was to get richer.
3. Although the new country was huge, most of the first ▬ (settler) were on the East Coast.
4. In a covered wagon, there wasn't much room for personal ▬ (to belong).
5. Some pioneer women got scared when their husbands ▬ (suggestion) that they should go West.
6. Often it was the poor job situation in their home country which made people ▬ (migration) to America.
7. Since ▬ (history) can't travel back in time, they have to rely on other sources and eyewitness reports.

b) *Find other words in the same word family. Use a dictionary.*

immigrant | to declare | nation | important

WRITING

5 The Wild West

a) *Describe the situation and the atmosphere in the picture.*

b) *Imagine you're one of the people in the picture – the man who is driving the stagecoach[1], one of the passengers or one of the Native Americans. Write about the scene in the picture from your point of view. Remember to use adjectives and adverbs to make your text more interesting.*

1 **stagecoach** ['steɪdʒkəʊtʃ] Postkutsche

LANGUAGE

6 Life in the New World

a) *Add the objects to these sentences.*

the Europeans' hunting[1] methods | the first white people | the Native Americans | the new lands | their traditions

1. The Native Americans called ___ scary because they looked like ghosts.
2. Both groups kept ___ alive and celebrated in their own way.
3. The Native Americans found ___ wasteful because they didn't use all parts of the animals.
4. The Pilgrims called ___ violent even though they were often peaceful[2] people.
5. Wars between the Native Americans and the Europeans made ___ in the West dangerous.

b) *Write three more sentences like in a). Use the verbs and objects and your own adjectives.*

Verbs:
call | find | see | keep | make | like

Objects:
your reaction | my story | the music | her friends | the internet | our trip

LANGUAGE

7 Excited about the Pony Express

→ WB 53/1, 54/2, 55/4

a) *Decide if you need a **present participle** or a **past participle**.*

One of the most **1** (excite) days of the week is when the Pony Express arrives in town. The **2** (cheer) crowds welcome the rider and hope that he's got a letter in his bag for them. My favorite rider is William Cody, who also has the **3** (thrill) name Buffalo Bill. One day Bill rode his horse into Three Crossings, but there was no one there to ride the next part of the trip! The **4** (miss) rider had been killed in a fight the night before. Bill made up for[3] the **5** (lose) time by riding even faster. He arrived at the next station on time but he was really **6** (exhaust). Another time Bill had a **7** (frighten) experience when he was attacked by Native Americans near Horse Creek. I was **8** (amaze) when I heard this story, but also **9** (scare). Still I hope that one day I can have the same job. This **10** (come) year I'll be 14 – the perfect age for a Pony Express rider!

b) *Imagine you're a Pony Express rider and you're on your way to the next station. Complete these sentences with interesting adjectives.*

1. The sky looks … 2. My legs feel … 3. The air smells … 4. The mail bag seems …

1 **to hunt** [hʌnt] jagen | 2 **peaceful** ['pi:sfl] friedlich | 3 **to make up for** [ˌmeɪk‿'ʌp fɔ:] wiedergutmachen

LANGUAGE

8 I should have gone West! → WB 55/6

a) *Read this short dialogue between two American settlers. The verb forms in bold are* ***modal verbs*** *with the* ***perfect infinitive****. You can use this construction to say that something probably happened or that things might have been different in the past.*

Charles: I've got fantastic news! I harvested[1] my first crop[2] of corn yesterday!
Frank: Amazing! That **must have felt** really good.
Charles: It did! It **could have been** even better, but I didn't plant all of my fields.
Frank: Well, now you know the soil[3] is good and that you **should have planted** more.

b) *Complete these sentences. Use* ***modal verbs*** *with the* ***perfect infinitive****.*

Example: 1. We might get snow tomorrow. We **should have left** earlier.

1. We might get snow tomorrow. (should | leave earlier)
2. This woman's husband left for Oregon eight months ago and she hasn't heard from him since then. (must | die)
3. There's no more room in the wagon for our clothes. (shouldn't | pack so many things)
4. It's too bad there wasn't a doctor on the trip with us. (could | save many lives)
5. The weather was perfect on the trail last year – not like now. (might | make it then)
6. All the Native Americans we've met have been helpful. (needn't | worry)
7. I think this is the wrong trail. (should | turn left an hour ago)

LANGUAGE

9 Everything would be different if …

a) *Complete the text with the correct verb forms.*

Dear Elisabeth,

Just imagine – if I **1** *(not come) to America on the ship last year, I wouldn't know you now. How empty my life would be! And if you'd stayed in Germany, you* **2** *(not be) as happy as you are today. Our lives have definitely changed – they've become much better. If I* **3** *(listen) to my mother and stayed in Italy, I'd still have no work. But now I'm so happy that I can go to work every morning. And I earn enough to send money back to my family.*
We could still be together if you **4** *(not find) a new job in Milwaukee. It's so far away, but I know it's for the best. If we hadn't made that decision, we* **5** *(not be) happier. As soon as I can, I will follow you to Milwaukee. Perhaps there is work for me there too. I keep reminding myself – if we hadn't met, I* **6** *(not have) such a wonderful person to think about.*

Love,
Giuseppe

b) *What decisions did you make in the past that are important for your life today? Write three sentences about yourself.*

Start like this: If I hadn't studied for the test … | If I'd listened to my parents …

1 **to harvest** ['hɑːvɪst] ernten | 2 **crop** [krɒp] Ernte | 3 **soil** [sɔɪl] Boden; Erde

VOCABULARY

10 Prefixes and suffixes

You can use prefixes[1] and suffixes[2] to make new words from the same word family.

Example:
You already know the word **to attract**. If you add the suffix **-ion**, you get the noun **attraction**. If you want to form an adjective, you add the suffix **-ive**: **attractive**. You can make the opposite[3] of the adjective when you add the prefix **un-**: **unattractive**. Or you can make the adjective into another noun with the suffix **-ness**: **attractiveness**. (→ Vocabulary box p. 202)

a) *Add the suffixes **-ment** or **-ion** to make these verbs into nouns. Be careful with the spelling!*

collect | connect | announce | excite | educate | communicate
describe | enlighten | act | state | entertain

b) *There are a lot of suffixes and prefixes that mean 'not' in English. Choose the right **prefix** or **suffix** and add them to the words in the text. You need some of them more than once.*

il- | im- | in- | mis- | un- | -less

A few days ago, I had an interesting experience while I was walking into town. The road seemed end **1**, and I was feeling nervous and very **2** secure because everything was **3** familiar to me. My biggest problem is that I'm what they call an **4** legal immigrant. So when I saw a man who looked very **5** friendly and who was walking quickly towards me, I was very **6** sure what to do. For a moment I felt quite help **7** and just wished I was **8** visible. But in situations like this, wishing is use **9**. The truth was I couldn't get away. It was **10** possible for me to escape. Then the man suddenly started to wave his arms wildly, and I just panicked. I turned around and ran away as quickly as I could. When he caught up with me, he asked why I'd been so **11** polite. So I told him that I'd been scared. Then he laughed and said that I'd **12** understood. "Waving your arms wildly is just the way people say hello here," he explained.

LANGUAGE

11 Stars and stripes

*Use **non-defining relative clauses** to join the sentences. Don't forget the commas!*

1. A legend says that Betsy Ross sewed[4] the first American flag in 1776.
   She is famous in her hometown Philadelphia.
2. The stripes on the American flag are red and white.
   They represent the original 13 colonies.
3. The first official American flag has been changed 26 times since 1777.
   It was designed by Francis Hopkinson.
4. In 1818 the US Congress decided that each state gets a star on the flag.
   Congress makes the laws[5] in America.
5. In 1885 B. J. Cigrand started the first Flag Day. It is still celebrated on June 14.

1 **prefix** ['pri:fɪks] Vorsilbe | 2 **suffix** ['sʌfɪks] Nachsilbe | 3 **opposite** ['ɒpəzɪt] Gegenteil | 4 **to sew** [səʊ] nähen | 5 **law** [lɔ:] Gesetz

SPEAKING

12 Talking about statistics

Look at the line graph on the right. What does it tell you about the numbers of patented US inventions in the 19th century? Make notes to give a short presentation. The useful phrases on p. 85 can help you.

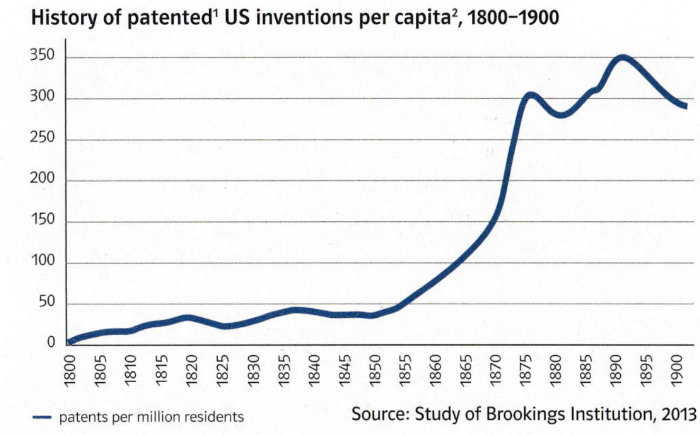

LANGUAGE

13 Linking inventions → WB 55/5

Use the linking words to join the two parts of each sentence.

Example: 1. The Ford Model T was important for poorer people **because** it didn't cost a lot of money.

1. The Ford Model T was important for poorer people … (because) ✔
2. Today Hollywood is the center of the movie industry … (although)
3. The Wright brothers had published a newspaper in Ohio … (before)
4. John Pemberton invented Coca-Cola … (when)
5. Many social media networks were created … (after)
6. People had washed all their clothes by hand … (before)

a) the first movies were made in New Jersey.
b) he was really trying to make medicine.
c) Friendster had started in 2002.
d) the first electric washing machine was invented in 1908.
e) it didn't cost a lot of money.
f) they flew the world's first plane.

LANGUAGE

14 Celebrating in Milwaukee

*Write sentences about different ethnic festivals in Milwaukee. Use the **past perfect progressive**.*

Example: The organizers of Bastille Days **had been making** crepes since the early morning when they didn't have anymore eggs.

1. Tony Blazonczyk's band ___ (practice) for three hours before their concert at the Polish[3] festival started.
2. The salsa dancers at the Mexican Fiesta ___ (dance) for an hour before a winner was chosen.
3. The band 'We Banjo 3' from Galway ___ (perform) at the Irish festival for two hours when it started to rain.
4. The Festa Italiana committee ___ (plan) a concert since December so they were sad when the singer couldn't come.
5. The visitors of the German Fest ___ (play) Schafskopf for three hours and there was still no winner.
6. At the Indian Summer Festival members of the Ojibwe tribe ___ (teach) people how to build wigwams before the dancing began.

1 **patented** [ˈpætntɪd] patentiert | 2 **per capita** [pə ˈkæpɪtə] pro Person / Kopf | 3 **Polish** [ˈpəʊlɪʃ] polnisch

Find more online: 34v74u

Text smart 3
Travel texts

Everybody goes on trips. And where there is travel, there are travel texts for every possible trip and reader. Find out about different travel texts, their functions and their styles.

READING

1 Warm-up: Getting familiar with different travel texts → WB 56/1

a) *Read these three excerpts of travel texts, all about Death Valley in California. Say what the most important information in each text is.*

A Hey everyone! If you thought my story from last week was good reading, this is better. My trip through Death Valley has been extremely hot, but last night it got incredibly scary too. I was chilling out after sunset when I learned this about tarantulas: They can jump. Far. REALLY far. And right onto your face! Scared me to death, but hey: Now we know where this place got its name. 🙂 Anyway …

B Death Valley is rightly feared for its extreme heat. But any visitors who are seriously planning road trips through the region must be aware of the biggest danger: the roads. Many were built in the 1930s, and most are backcountry roads – and very, very rough. Without a 4-wheel-drive, car problems are very probable. And with no cell phone reception in the desert, there is no quick help. So …

C I don't usually post much, but other travelers need to know about the WORST hotel in Death Valley. At the Devil's Inn, they really take the name seriously: The devil would feel very much at home here because THE AIR-CONDITIONING DIDN'T WORK for our three-day visit and it was HOT AS HELL! And it was July, with 120°F heat! So anyway, this is definitely the hotel from HELL! There's …

b) *Each of the three texts has a different function and was written for a different audience.*

1. Say which texts above match these text types:

   travel blog entry | online rating | travel guide

2. Then say which function each text has. The word bank can help you.
3. Say who you think would be the typical reader for each text. Give reasons.

Word bank

give practical tips | warn / help / educate people | inspire other people to travel | show off | entertain

SPEAKING

2 Your turn: Travel in your life

→ △ 142/1

Have you ever read travel texts about a place before you visited it? Were you disappointed afterwards, or did the place meet your expectations? Share your experience.

A travel guide

Station 1 focuses on the kind of travel writing you find in a travel guide (in book form or online). Travel guides are often helpful for general information about a destination.

OCABULARY

3 Before you read

After you've read the text below, be prepared to describe 1–2 things you found particularly interesting about Montana, whose official nickname is the 'Big Sky State'.

S1/31
L3/2

The Rockies: Montana

Believe the hype: Montana really is Big Sky country, a region of snow-capped summits, turbulent rivers, spectacular glacial valleys, heavily wooded forests and sparkling blue lakes under an endless, deep blue sky that seems to stretch for a million miles. The Blackfeet and Shoshone Indians once hunted bison here and today the state is still a land of cowboys, ranches, small cities and nineteenth-century ghost towns. (When the gold ran out, so did the people!) In Montana, so the jokes go, locals keep snow tires on till June. And grizzly bears, elk and bighorn sheep are found in greater numbers in Montana than just about anywhere else on the continent.

The scenery is at its most dramatic on the western side of the state, especially the fantastic Glacier National Park and the surrounding mountain chains, landscapes that featured in 1990s movies *A River Runs Through It* and *The Horse Whisperer*. In contrast, the eastern two-thirds is dusty prairie that attracts far fewer visitors. Each of Montana's small cities has its own proud identity: Enjoyable Missoula is a totally relaxed college town; Butte is a historic copper-mining center; Helena is the elegant state capital; and Bozeman is one of the hippest mountain towns in the USA.

Source: www.roughguides.com

READING

4 Understanding the text

a) *Think back to Ex. 3. Describe the information from the text that you found the most interesting about Montana.*

b) *A closer look: With a partner, go back to the text and list what it tells you about these topics:*

nature | history | cities | sights

c) *Write down questions the text does* ***not*** *answer. What would really interest you about this place? Tell your partner what you'd do to find this information.*

d) *Get into groups of 5–6. Imagine you're in a publisher's meeting. The decision has been made to feature only one photo with the text on p. 103, and not three. Together, decide which photo it should be and then explain your choice to the class. Your notes from b) might help you here.*

READING

5 The characteristics of factual travel writing

Reading skills

If someone is thinking of traveling to a destination, they want some facts from a **travel guide**. But they often want a *feeling* for the place too. So writers of travel guides give their readers atmosphere. Examples from the text on p. 103:
- The facts: The reader learns that there are **rivers** and **forests**.
- But because it's a *travel* guide, the reader also learns that there are **turbulent** rivers and **heavily wooded** forests. Travel writers use **descriptive words** (adverbs, adjectives) like these to achieve a colorful style that is still factual.

But because a factual travel guide is still a factual text (like a news report), the travel writer's opinion and personal experiences are not important. The **focus** is **on the place**, not the writer.

a) *Read the skills box. Then go back to the text on p. 103. List all the collocations in the text that feature an* ***adjective*** *+* ***noun*** *or an* ***adverb and adjective*** *+* ***noun****.*

b) *Which adjectives and adverbs could you use to describe these words from the text? Be creative! (You can use a dictionary too.)*

grizzly bear | lake | river | mountain

WRITING

6 Your turn: Describe a destination you know

a) *Think about the text on p. 103 and what you learned in Ex. 5. Then look at the lines below. Improve them with more / better descriptive words.*

New York is a big city. A lot of people go there. There are skyscrapers, museums and other sights. There are a lot of things to do there. People with different backgrounds live there. There are rich and poor people there. It's interesting.

→ △ 142/2 **b)** *Write 5–6 sentences about a travel destination you know. Make the place sound as attractive for the reader as you can with as many descriptive words as possible.*

A travel blog

Station 2 focuses on personal travel writing, e.g. the kind of writing you find in travel blogs. Matthew Karsten is a US travel blogger who calls himself – and his blog – **The Expert Vagabond**. Read about one of his biggest adventures where he wants to find out if it's possible to safely hitchhike from coast to coast in the US.

SPEAKING

7 Before you read: About hitchhiking

a) *Say what you already know about hitchhiking.*

1. What is it?
2. Why do people do it?

b) *Now read the Across cultures box. Give your opinion on this form of transportation. Explain why or why not you can imagine hitchhiking when you're older.*

Across cultures

Hitchhiking is about getting rides from strangers in their car or truck. Some hitchhikers, especially in rural areas, do this because they have no other way to get around. Others enjoy the adventure of meeting new people. But riding with strangers can be dangerous, which is why hitchhiking is illegal in some US states.

READING

8 Hitchhiking in America: Ride #4

S1/32 L3/3

Susan the Hula Hooper

It was time to get out of Astoria, Oregon and head South back to the town of Seaside. After walking to the edge of town, I picked a busy spot with a large parking lot for potential rides, threw up a new cardboard sign and stuck out my thumb. This time it took 25 minutes before anyone stopped. Not bad! Susan's car was loaded up with a bike on the trunk and a few giant hula hoops in the backseat. Before I could get into the car, she made me promise I wasn't going to murder or rob her. Susan is an auditor from Tacoma, WA and was on her way to Seaside for a short vacation. She's a big hula hoop fan, and actually makes her own out of plastic pipes! We decided to eat lunch together at Norma's Seafood & Steak when we arrived in Seaside. The clam chowder was excellent!

a) *First reaction: Would you have taken a ride with Susan, or waited for the next ride?*

b) *"She made me promise I wasn't going to murder or rob her." Explain why you think Susan says this.*

c) *Go back to the text. Say what you learn more about:* places | people | experiences. *Say why you think Matthew has focused on some things but not on others.*

d) *In Text smart 1 you learned about target groups. Travel writers also have target groups: their readers. Describe who you think Matthew's readers are. Explain why you think so.*

READING

9 The characteristics of personal travel writing

Reading skills

Personal travel writing focuses on a story the writer wants to share:
1. These texts often focus on **experiences** in general. Often, those experiences involve **other people** and what they do and say.
2. Because personal travel writing focuses on the writer's experiences, **facts** about places, history etc. don't play a main role.
3. **Writing styles** can be very different. Some writers depend a lot on humor to get and keep the reader's attention. Others might choose language that makes experiences sound as dramatic as possible. Everyone finds their own style.

a) *Read the skills box. Then go back to Ride #4. Give at least one example of what is mentioned above in points 1–3.*

b) *Describe the main differences between the texts on p. 103 and p. 105.*

READING

10 Hitchhiking in America: Ride #15 → WB 56/2, 57/3

S 1/33
L 3/4

Captain Kitty Litter

In less than 20 minutes a beat-up Chrysler pulled over. I was overly excited to get a ride so quickly, and made the mistake of not properly checking just who it was picking me up. Once inside I knew this would be an interesting ride …
David isn't exactly the cleanest guy around. In fact, I'd describe him as a hoarder of trash. It took him a few minutes to clean all the crap out of the passenger seat for me to sit down. When I did, I soon noticed the kitty litter box full of shit on the floor between my feet. But there was no sign of a kitty. Unless of course the poor creature was somewhere under the mountain of trash in the backseat. (Which wouldn't surprise me.) Over the next 30 minutes I learned that David used to be in the Navy, builds wooden boats that his friends cut up into firewood, has a serious problem with road-rage, and once threw a hitchhiker out of a moving car for not wearing a seat belt – running over his foot in the process. My hand moved a bit closer to the pepper-spray in my pocket. I avoided any controversial subjects and tried not to upset him until he dropped me off outside of Coeur d'Alene, Idaho. David was the kind of guy everyone warned me about.

a) *Answer these questions:*

1. Describe what kind of a person David probably is. Say which lines / words give you the most information about his personality.
2. Would you have accepted a ride from David? Give reasons why / why not.

b) *Which text did you find more interesting: Ride #4 or #15? Explain your opinion.*

WRITING

11 Your turn: Turn yourself into a storyteller

Imagine you and your family were in America and stopped to give Matthew a ride. What would he write about you in his blog? Write an entertaining text for them in a style like Matthew's. (Or, in your own style.)

WRITING

12 Options: Two very different travel destinations

Option A: Write a blog post about a haunted house

a) *Read the travel guide text below about a strange tourist attraction in California.*

After Sarah Winchester's daughter had died (1866), followed by the deaths of her father-in-law (1880) and then her husband (1881), Sarah was sure that she was cursed. Who else in her family will be next? What could she do? The answer came from a man who claimed he could communicate with the spirit world. And it came as a shock for Sarah …

The Winchester family had made a fortune with their famous Winchester rifles. Now, the man told her, the ghosts of all the people who had been killed by those guns had cursed the Winchester family! There was only one way to stop it: Sarah must build a house which was big enough for all the ghosts. And: If Sarah ever stopped building the house, she would die …

So Sarah, scared and with a guilty conscience, began building a mansion in San José, California and didn't stop until the day she died in 1922. There was no plan; the huge house just grew in every direction. Only Sarah understood it; her servants needed a map. Today, visitors see strange staircases that lead to nowhere, windows that open to walls, the endless secret passageways. Perfect places for ghosts to hide? There are many stories of visitors who say they have felt the presence of sad spirits in this big, sad house …

→ △ 142/3
→ S7–9

b) *Creative writing: Imagine you went on a tour of the house and thought it was great – and scary! What could you write about it for a travel blog? Be creative!*

Example: At first I just laughed about ghosts at the Winchester house. What a joke!
Well, after about 20 minutes on the tour, I wasn't laughing anymore …

Option B: Write about a surfer's paradise

→ S7–9

Huntington Beach in southern California is famous for its long pier – and for surfing! Look at the picture. What could you write about it in a travel text? Choose one of the text types below. Also, think of what function your text could have; the word bank on p. 102 can help you.

factual travel text | online rating | blog entry

Write 10–12 sentences in the style that matches the text type you chose.

Find more online: v6z7nj

At home with an American family

Household chores often play a big role at home for American teens. Learn more about it here.

VOCABULARY

1 Warm-up: Collocations for household chores → WB 59/1

a) *Match the verbs and phrases to make collocations about typical household chores.*

do | take | set | vacuum | make | load / empty | clean up | clean

the table | your room | the dishwasher | breakfast | the dishes | the shower | the garbage out | the rug / carpet

b) *Your turn: Describe the chores you have to do at home, how often you do them, and which ones you like / don't like.*

VIEWING

2 Going to a new friend's house

6 → S16

Zach has made a new friend at school: Ravi, from India. The two boys are at Zach's house.

a) *First, just look at stills A–D before you answer these questions:*

1. Describe how you think Ravi is feeling in A. What does his face tell you?
2. Based on what you think about A, look at stills B–D and say what you think is going through Ravi's head here.

b) *Now watch the film to find out if you were right about a). Note other examples in the film that might be strange or different for Ravi.*

c) *Compare notes with a partner: Did you find the same things?*

Useful phrases

- He isn't used to doing … / seeing … / making …
- He thinks it's strange / different to …
- He doesn't understand why …

VIEWING

3 Rules at home

a) *Before you watch the film again, match each word on the right to one of the pictures below.*

allowance | fun | chore | curfew

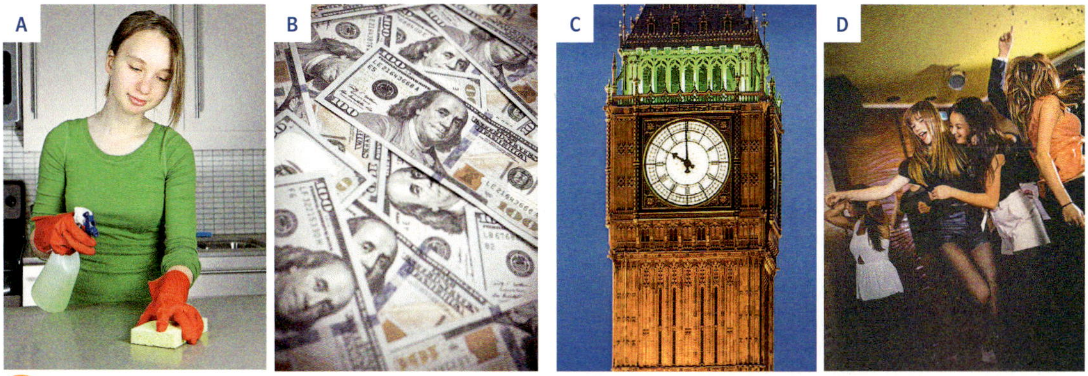

b) *Watch the film. Describe the link between pictures A + B and pictures C + D.*

c) *Give your opinion of Zach's parents. Say if you think they're too strict or not.*

d) *Your turn: Describe the rules that you have to obey at home. Say what happens if you break a rule!*

SPEAKING

4 Role play: Meeting the family

→ S11

You're having a meal with a new American friend at his / her home. Your partner is your friend's father / mother who asks you a lot of questions about these topics:

yourself | your family | your food preferences / issues | chores / rules / allowances

Together, write a short conversation. Then act it out for the class.

SPEAKING

5 < Role play: Showing interest as a guest > → WB 59/2

→ S11

First, draw a simple floor plan of a cool house or apartment. Then take turns to 'show' your partner around your house. Describe the different rooms, how the house is decorated, how you and your family spend time there. Your partner should try to sound interested! The words on the right can help you.

Start like this:

A: So this is the entrance area, and as soon as you walk in, you see …

B: Oh, that's cool. I like houses that have … | Oh, that's interesting over there. Is it …?

Word bank

entrance | staircase | balcony | patio | barbecue / grill area | stairs that go up / down to the … | a door that opens to the …

Tip

When you're invited to somebody's home, it's polite to show interest in their house and family. But it's important not to lie and say you like something when you don't! Try your best to find something you like and focus on that.

Find more online: 9zi457

Unit 4
The Pacific Northwest

A The Space Needle and Mount Rainier are symbols of Seattle, the largest city in the Pacific Northwest (pop. 668,000; 3.6 million in Seattle area). The region consists of Washington and Oregon (in the US) and British Columbia (in Canada).

VOCABULARY

1 The Pacific Northwest: Photos and facts

Seattle population growth between 1900 and 2014

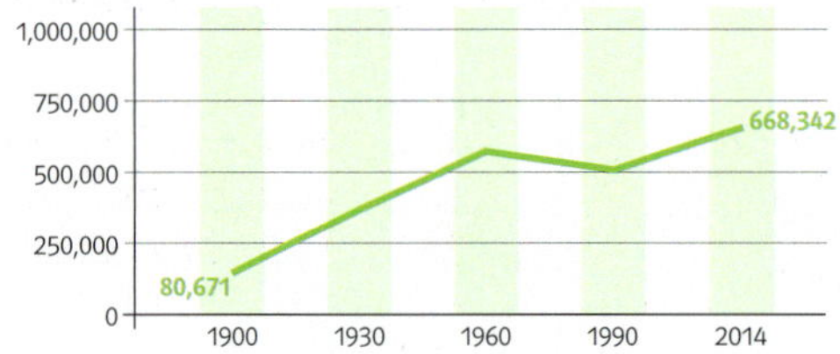

The Seattle area's biggest corporations:
(In numbers of local / total employees)

1. **Boeing** (airplanes): 78,000 / 160,000
2. **Microsoft** (software): 43,000 / 112,000
3. **Amazon** (online retail): 26,000 / 230,000
4. **Costco** (retail): 9,200 / 194,000
5. **Starbucks** (coffee): 3,500 / 182,000

Sources: US Census Bureau (chart); company websites, Seattle Times, Statistic Brain (employee statistics)

→ S5 **a)** *Look at the photos and the captions. Describe what a visitor to the region could do there.*

→ S6 **b)** *Look at the statistics about Seattle. What do they tell us about the population and economy there?*

c) *If Seattle keeps growing so fast, explain how the life you see in the photos could change.*

In Unit 4 you learn
… about life in the Pacific Northwest region of the US. You learn:
- about aspects of city and outdoor life
- about aspects of the Native American experience and influence there
- the language for arguing a point

Seattle is a business boomtown, just like Portland (Oregon) and Vancouver (Canada).

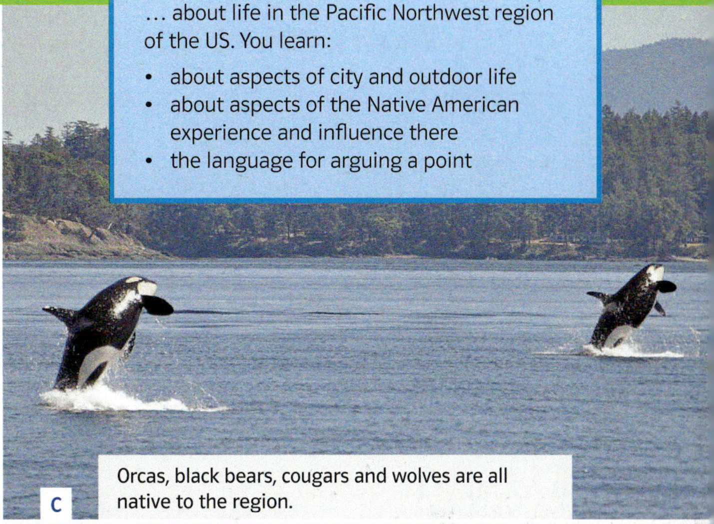
C Orcas, black bears, cougars and wolves are all native to the region.

This beach in Seattle – and many more like it – are never far away in the Northwest.

E Mount Rainier is an active volcano! Mountains and forests are key features of the landscape here.

LISTENING

2 On a Seattle boat tour → WB 60/1–2

L 3/5–7 → S15

a) *First, look at the map of Seattle and the Pacific Northwest at the back of your book. Then listen to a tour guide on a boat tour of the Seattle waterfront, Elliot Bay and Puget Sound.*

1. What makes Seattle special?
2. What makes the Pacific Northwest special?

b) *Listen again and take notes about the topics on the right. Sum up what the guide says about each.*

Seattle | the economy | the outdoors | natural disasters | Native Americans

c) *Your turn: Say which topic interests you the most and explain why.*

READING

3 ‹ Internet research about the Northwest ›

→ S18

In groups of five, each of you should choose ***one*** *of the topics in Ex. 2b) and do some internet research to find out more. Share your results with the class.*

L 3/9

You've got no soul!

The Hilstads live in downtown Seattle. Erik Hilstad's twin sister, Haley, is going to leave Seattle for a weekend in the mountains with their parents and her friend, Ava.

Haley: Oh, Erik! Why don't you come with us? Don't just hang out in the city when you could be outdoors in the fresh mountain air!

Erik: I did that every weekend of my life when we were kids! I don't want to waste my free time in the wilderness anymore. Don't you miss the action of the city?

Haley: Never! We're so lucky to have the outdoors and national parks so close to home. Being close to nature gives me feelings of peace and calm and freedom …

Erik: You aren't *serious*, are you? – Er, you *are*! That's scary.

Haley: No, it's just that you've got no soul! What are *you* going to do all weekend?

Erik: I'm staying with my friend Jake – you haven't met him, have you?

Haley: No, but you talk about him a lot! His uncle is a farmer, isn't he?

Erik: That's right. Jake helps him out at Pike Place Market on Saturdays. He might give me a job there too – I'm going to talk to him today. I hope I get it!

Later, Erik is with Jake at a café. Jake's pretty sister, Kim, is there too.

Erik: Your uncle is cool – I can't wait to start work! It'll be fun, won't it?

Jake: Sure! Come on – meet my friends. All of the guys here work at the market on weekends – and we hang out after work on weekends too. We went on the Great Wheel down at the waterfront the other day, didn't we, Kim?

Kim: Yeah, and now we're planning a hiking trip to Mount Rainier. Come with us, Erik! I'm crazy about the mountains. How about you?

Erik: Er… well … yeah – I like the outdoors. Totally. Yeah, I'm a nature guy. Those mountains give me feelings of, er, peace and calm and freedom …

Kim: Hey, just like me! I *knew* you were my kind of guy!

READING

1 Who is the *real* Erik? → WB 61/3

a) *In what ways are Erik's and Haley's weekend plans different?*

b) *Contrast the opinions Erik expresses to Haley and to Kim. Explain who you think the 'real' Erik is.*

c) *Your turn: Is it always important to 'be true to yourself'? State your opinion and give examples.*

SPEAKING

2 [Revision: Keep the ball bouncing with question tags] → G8 → WB 61/4

a) *Remember, question tags can help to 'keep the ball bouncing' in a conversation:*

Example: His uncle **is** a farmer, **isn't he**? → Haley wants Erik to give an answer.

Find three more examples from p. 112. What do you remember about question tags and how they work? Compare your notes with a partner. Add information if necessary.

b) *Now add the missing question tags to the conversation Erik had with Jake's uncle, Tom.*

Tom: You've never had a Saturday job before, [1] ?
Erik: No, but I'm excited! It's super busy here, [2] ?
Tom: Yeah – you'll be very tired at the end of the day!
Erik: But it's good work experience for me, [3] ?
Tom: Of course. You don't live far from here, [4] ?
Erik: No, 5 minutes away. I'll have to start early, [5] ?
Tom: That's right. But you can be here by 7:30 a.m., [6] ?
Erik: Sure. You won't need me on Sundays, [7] ?
Tom: No – you need some free time, [8] ? So the job is yours if you want it. That's good news, [9] ?

c) *Role play: With your partner, write a short dialogue about different part-time jobs. Use question tags.*

Example:
A: Babysitting **is** an easy job, **isn't it**?
B: I don't know. But a job at a summer camp **would** be more interesting, **wouldn't it**?

LANGUAGE

3 *The, a/an* or no article → G9 → WB 62/5

→ △ 143/1

Erik wants to see Kim again – but without Jake this time!
Read their dialogue. Decide where you need ***the, a/an*** *or* ***no article.***

Erik: Kim, I've got an idea, but don't laugh. At [1] school today, I was thinking: I'm from Seattle but I've never been to [2] top of the Space Needle.
Kim: Are you serious? Then we should go! Let's meet downtown tomorrow. We can go by [3] bus to the Needle. Or we can walk. But it's kind of [4] long way.
Erik: Let's walk. It won't take more than [5] few minutes from my apartment downtown. And we aren't in [6] hurry, are we? We can go to Arnie's for [7] lunch on [8] way. Do you know Arnie's?
Kim: No, I know [9] most of the diners downtown but not Arnie's. Is it good?
Erik: My cousin says it's [10] best in town. He's [11] waiter there. It'll be my treat!
Kim: Really? That's so sweet of you! But then let's go to Emilio's after we've been to the Needle. [12] ice cream he has there is just unbelievable! And of course that will be *my* treat. Have we got ourselves [13] deal?
Erik: We sure have. Sounds great. I love [14] ice cream.

LANGUAGE

4 [Abstract nouns: Excitement and more in Seattle] → G9 → WB 62/6

→ △ 143/2
→ ▲ 143/3

The Seattle tourist board held a competition for teenagers. The idea: With just three photos and a few words, local teens had to show how they feel about their city. Jenna Emory's entry, which you see here, has become part of the tourist board's website …

MY SEATTLE

Fun is great, but excitement is much better! For me, excitement is watching the hydroplane race on Lake Washington each summer during Seafair. 250,000 people on rubber rafts and boats:It's like being in a gigantic swimming pool with 250,000 friends! 😀

Best of all about Seattle? The feelings of peace and calm I get when it's just me, my paddleboard and the water …

It's complete happiness for me to go to the Seahawks games on Sundays with 70,000 other screaming fans. Seahawks fans are the loudest in the NFL – that's a fact! (It's also a major feeling of freedom to get out of the house and away from my homework!)

a) *What kind of a person do you think Jenna is? Give reasons why you think so.*

b) *Find the rule: Make a list of all the* ***nouns*** *in the leaflet. Then say what the difference is between nouns like 'freedom' / 'excitement' and the other nouns in the text.*

c) *Your turn: Make a leaflet like Jenna's about your hometown. Use abstract nouns where possible.*

SPEAKING

5 America and its national parks

Across cultures

In 1832, the artist George Caitlin wrote that he was very worried about the destruction of the American wilderness and the Indian civilization as more and more people moved West. In 1872, the American government created **the world's first national park**: Yellowstone, in Wyoming. Today, there are 59 US national parks which help to protect the natural environment.

Crater Lake National Park in Oregon

a) *Say what has been done to protect the environment where you live.*

b) *Describe your feelings about protecting the environment. How important is it to you?*

MEDIATION

6 Staying safe in Mount Rainier National Park → WB 63/7

→ S13–14

Erik and his friends go up to Mount Rainier National Park one Sunday. When they arrive at the visitor center, there are information leaflets in several languages – but none left in English! A German teenager gives Erik the main information.

a) *Read the skills box. Then look at the marked words in the leaflet. Paraphrase their meaning for your partner.*

b) *Now read the whole leaflet. Find the information you think Erik should know. Then sum it up for your partner in English.*

Mediation skills

- If you don't know a word or a phrase in English, then find another way to say it. This is called **paraphrasing**.
- With mediation, when you sum up the main ideas, always think of your **conversation partner**. What would he / she find useful when you give information?
- In conversation, you can **buy time** with phrases like these: Just a second … | Let me think …

Wilde Tiere sollen wild bleiben!

Biologen haben festgestellt, dass sich das natürliche Verhalten der Tierwelt im Mount Rainier National Park hier in Washington State zunehmend verändert. Da sie ihre Scheu vor Menschen verloren haben, versuchen die Tiere zum Beispiel, den Proviant der Parkbesucher zu stehlen. Das ist für Mensch und Tier gefährlich. Bitte füttern Sie die Tiere nicht, bewahren sie Nahrungsmittel in geschlossenen Behältern auf und nehmen Sie Ihren Müll wieder mit.

Sicherheit geht beim Wandern vor!

Auf dem Mount Rainier kann das Wetter sehr schnell umschlagen. Ersatzkleidung und Regenschutz dürfen daher nicht fehlen – sowie selbstverständlich feste Wanderschuhe. Außerdem sind Bergwanderungen enorm anstrengend. Achten Sie auf regelmäßige Pausen und essen Sie genug. Sie brauchen sehr viel Energie!

Gute Vorbereitung ist alles!

Um auf kleinere Verletzungen, plötzliche Wetterumschwünge oder Verzögerungen vorbereitet zu sein, benötigen Sie auf alle Fälle die richtige Ausrüstung. Folgende absolut unverzichtbare Dinge sollten Sie immer bei sich tragen (Sie können diese im Shop kaufen):

1. Karte des Parkgebiets
2. Kompass
3. Streichhölzer
4. Taschenlampe
5. Kerze
6. Taschenmesser
7. Sonnenbrille und Sonnencreme
8. Regenkleidung
9. Erste-Hilfe-Set

c) *The man behind the desk suddenly calls Erik and the others back. He's just found an information leaflet in English for them! Compare your phrases with the English version at the back of your book on p. 269.*

SPEAKING

7 Nature lovers or city people? → WB 63/8

→ △ 144/4

a) *In pairs, write six questions to find out if other students are nature lovers or city people. Then separate from your partner and ask your questions to six students each.*

b) *Back with your partner, compare your results. The box on the right can help you.*

Useful phrases

I found that all of the people … | most of … | some of … | a few of … | none of …

L 3/13 ◎

Native Americans in the Northwest

The Coast Salish tribes of the Pacific Northwest have a history that goes back thousands of years. Find out more about Northwest Indian culture on these pages.

The Thunderbird and the Orca

Life on the river was good for the Cowichan people and the waters were full of fish, especially salmon. However, there was one time in their history when something very strange happened – the river suddenly went silent! The people knew that there was something very wrong. They panicked as they realized that the salmon had stopped coming. How would the people live? They left their homes and followed their leaders to the river; they sailed downriver to try to find the cause. They needed an answer – and they soon found it. It was a nightmare: At the mouth of the river, they discovered a supernatural killer whale (the Orca) who was eating all the salmon! They paddled their huge war canoes out to the Orca and made loud noises to scare it away – but it just continued eating the salmon right in front of their eyes. The tribe's medicine people knew there was only one hope now: They must call for the powerful support of a supernatural creature known as Tzinquaw (the Thunderbird).

For four days and four nights the people sang spiritual songs to the Thunderbird and they waited. Finally, it appeared. Tzinquaw and the Orca then fought for many hours. It was a terrible battle but, in the end, Tzinquaw won. The salmon run was saved and life was good again. The people went home happily and slept peacefully again that night, dreaming about the powerful Thunderbird!

Adapted from the version of the legend by Joe Jack (Cowichan tribe), British Columbia

READING

8 Understanding the legend

→ S1

a) *Answer these questions about the text:*

1. What problem do the Cowichan people face?
2. What is the reason for this problem?
3. What do the people do to solve the problem?
4. Who is Tzinquaw?

→ △ 144/5

b) *The Thunderbird and the Orca story is an example of a traditional legend. Give reasons why you think this legend has survived for a very long time. These key words might help:*

culture | religion | food | nature

L3/14

This was our river first!

by Laura Chen | August 24, 2014

Port Angeles, WA – Yesterday morning the Lower Elwha Klallam tribe held their traditional First Salmon Ceremony at the mouth of their sacred Elwha River. This year, the tribe chose 15-year old Koi to carry the symbolic salmon. He had caught a large salmon himself directly before the ceremony. As the sun rose, Koi's people sang. You could hear the sound of a drum for miles around as the tribe put the huge salmon onto a wooden raft on the river. Everyone prayed to the gods for enough salmon for the next year. "I feel proud of my people," said Koi, when I saw him later. "They've suffered."

He was talking about the Elwha Dam, which was built in 1914. It was built to produce power for the timber industry – but its dramatic effect was to cut off the salmon run which the tribe needed to survive. 100 years of protest followed. But now, at last, the dam has been removed. "The river is free again!" said Koi. "There's no concrete to hold it back. This was our river first – my people fought the government and we won our lives back!"

Before I left, I asked Koi if he had heard about the Education Project, which sends young Native Americans to school outside their reservations. "Yeah, I've heard about it," he replied. "I'll probably go – I mean, many reservation schools aren't exactly the best, so it's a great chance. But I get nervous when I think about how I would fit into the outside world. By the time I come back, everything will have changed again." Removing the dam was the largest project of its kind in US history and has given the Lower Elwha Klallam tribe a second chance. But the young people still have some difficult decisions to make.

READING

9 Changes in the air → WB 64/9

→ S1 a) *State what information the text gives about the life of the Lower Elwha Klallam tribe. Talk about their past, present and future when you give your answer.*

→ △ 144/6 b) *Describe the kind of problems new students at a new school might have. Say which of these problems you think might affect Koi if he changed schools.*

→ S11 c) *Role play: Act out your ideas from b). Play yourself once and give Koi (your partner) advice. Then swap roles: Now you're Koi; your partner gives you advice.*

WRITING

10 Comparing the legend and the news report

→ △ 144/7 *Compare the story and the news report. What do they tell us about the following points?*

history and the Native American lifestyle | how important salmon are to local tribes

SPEAKING

11 Native Americans in the Northwest: Past and present

Across cultures

The coasts, forests, rivers and lakes of what we now call British Columbia, Washington and Oregon have been home to tribes like the Snohomish, the Stillaguamish, the Cowichan or the Klallam for over 5,000 years. These **Coast Salish tribes** often have their own language; many have their own reservation too.

The Coast Salish are known for their typical **architecture**, **designs** and **artwork** and wood has always played a big role: Longhouses were built to live in and for ceremonies, while colorful masks and totem poles brought the Indians' religion and legends to life.

Point out what you find the most interesting about the Native Americans in the Northwest.

LANGUAGE

12 Transitive and intransitive verbs → WB 64/10

A verb is **transitive** when it takes an **object**:	An **intransitive verb** doesn't take an object:
I **ride my bike** every day.	I **go** to school by bike.

Some verbs are transitive (= incomplete without an object, e.g. *want*, *need*, *thank*, *invite*). Some are intransitive (= don't need an object, e.g. *go*, *come*, *laugh*). Other verbs can be used with or without an object, e.g. *sing (a song)*, *write (e-mails)*, *leave (the house)*:

She **writes long e-mails**.	She **writes** beautifully. (→ No change in meaning)
He **left the box** on the table.	Isn't Tim here? – No, he **left** five minutes ago. (→ Change.)

a) *Make a grid. Sort the verbs on the right into three lists:*

transitive | intransitive | both

sing, discover, win, need, make, appear, dream, continue, fight, sleep, happen, follow

b) *Go back to the texts on pages 116–117. You take one text; your partner takes the other. In your text, find at least two examples of each of the three verb categories from a). Write the examples down in a list and then check each other's work.*

LANGUAGE

13 Transitive and intransitive verbs: Write your own sentences

→ △ 145/8
→ ▲ 145/9

*Write a transitive **and** an intransitive sentence with each of the verbs on the right.*

follow, leave, sing, answer, break, hear

WRITING 14 How to: Argue effectively in writing → WB 65/11–12

→ S7 **a)** *There are plans to attract tourists to Koi's reservation with a new visitor center there. Read what Koi and his friend Suni have posted on their tribe's web forum.*

In my opinion, having a visitor center here is a great idea. One point in favor is that it will bring more tourists to our land and this will mean more jobs for our people. Another advantage is that it will help us to continue our traditional lifestyle because the tourists will want to buy our jewelry and art. A final big benefit would be that we young people would have a chance to meet new people from the outside world. Some people are always against change; but change is also a chance! Overall, this is a great idea! – Koi

My view is that a visitor center would be bad news for our community. The main disadvantage is that our natural environment would be destroyed by all the new buildings and roads. Another point against it is that these roads would bring more noisy cars into our lives. What's more, the cars bring pollution and pollution brings serious health problems. Although there are people who will say more cars means more business, it's a bad deal for our health. So overall, it's an awful idea! – Suni

b) *Now read the skills box. Then go back to the two posts and collect phrases which match the points in the box.*

c) *Your turn: What do you think of the plan for Koi's reservation? Think of three arguments to support your opinion. Then write a post for the web forum. Use phrases from the two posts.*

Writing skills

To argue a point, you need to do these things:

1. **State your opinion** at the start: Are you for or against the question?
2. **Introduce points** which support your opinion, with typical phrases to introduce your points (e.g. *One advantage …; A benefit …*)
3. Show that you know what **the other side** would argue and that you've got the better arguments.
4. **Sum up** your view at the end.

LANGUAGE 15 < Find the rule: The future perfect > → G10 → WB 66/13–14

a) *Look at the sentences in the box on the right. How do you form the **future perfect**?*

→ △ 145/10 **b)** *Go back to the news story about Koi on p. 117. What other changes do you think Koi thinks about? Make sentences about him with the future perfect.*

By the time I come back …

1. the children / become teenagers
2. the old people / die
3. the salmon / disappear again
4. they / build a visitor center
5. my parents / get older
6. my old friends / forget me

c) *Your turn: Make sentences about yourself with the future perfect.*

Tip

By the time I come back, everything **will have changed**.
By the time I get to the party, everyone **might** already **have left**.

In place of **will**, you can also use **won't**, **might** or **mightn't**.

How to argue a point in conversation

Across cultures

Mount Rainier is sacred to the Skagit tribe; its original name is Tahoma. It's the largest mountain in the Northwest (14,417 ft.) and an **active volcano** on the Pacific **Ring of Fire**. The eruption of Mount St. Helens in 1980 destroyed everything nearby. Experts say an eruption of Mount Rainier would be much worse. It's also much closer to the millions of people in the Seattle area than Mount St. Helens.

What natural disasters have you heard about?

The May 1980 eruption

1 Mount Rainier and a family discussion → WB 67/15

L 3/16 → S15

a) *Listen to a family discussion about a point nobody can agree on:*

1. What decision are they trying to reach?
2. What role does Mount Rainier play?

b) *Listen again and collect two sets of arguments:* ***Pro*** *and* ***Con****.*

Mount Rainier: a perfect picture. For now …

2 Formal or informal?

a) *The phrases for writing a pro/con text on p. 119 were quite formal. Which ones were used in the family discussion?*

b) *Which of the more* ***informal*** *phrases in the box here were also used?*

Useful phrases

I agree/disagree with you. | Sure, you've got a point but … | Don't you think you're over-exaggerating? | You always see the glass as half empty! | You can see the positive side too, can't you? | I'm not going to change my mind unless you can really convince me! | Why can't you see the bigger picture? | I can relate to both sides. | Only the facts count: Don't make decisions based on your feelings!

3 Pro or con: Mini-debates in a double circle

→ S11

Sit in a double circle. Students on the outside are going to argue ***for*** *a move to the Mount Rainier village. Students on the inside will argue* ***against*** *it. After two minutes, everyone in the inner circle moves one chair to start a debate with their new partner.*

Examples:

A: Moving so close to Mount Rainier is a bad idea, isn't it? B: I disagree with you! I think …

Moving to America: Time for a family conference!

In Across cultures 1, you learned about contrasts in America. In Unit 1, you heard about some young people whose families were moving to America for their parents' work. Imagine your family is planning to move there for work. There are five city options. **Which city should you move to?** Have a family conference to decide!

Step 1

Form expert groups for one city

Divide into five expert groups. Each group will research one of the five cities above. Later, everyone in your group will go to one of the other groups. These new groups will be your 'family'. Your goal: You'll need to convince the other members of your family that the city you have researched is the best one to move to!

Step 2

Do your research → WB 67/16

Together, research information about the topics on the right.

climate | outdoor activities | dangers | standard of living

Step 3

Prepare arguments for your city → WB 68/17

Prepare arguments to convince your family members. In your expert group, discuss and write down ideas on these points:

1. What positive points will you make about your city?
2. What positive points do you think the members of your family will make about their cities?
3. What negative points will your family members make about your city?

→ How to argue effectively, p. 120 → Vocabulary (pp. 110–111; p. 115, ex. 7; p. 120)

Step 4

Have your family conference → WB 68/18

After you've formed your families, have your conference. Each family has one member who will argue for each city. There are two parents and three teenagers in each group. Who has the most success in convincing the others?

S1/40–45
L3/18–23

The Absolutely True Diary of a Part-Time Indian

SPEAKING

1 Before you read

Look at the cartoons only; ***don't read the text yet****. Say what you think the cartoons tell you about the story. Make predictions.*

Arnold (also known as 'Junior') is a 14-year old Spokane Indian in Washington State who wants to make something of his life. But as he lives on an Indian reservation, he knows it won't be easy: Reservation life is tough. One of his teachers believes in him and persuades Arnold's parents to let him leave the 'rez' and go to school outside. His best friend, Rowdy, hates him for leaving. In this scene, Arnold's dad drives him to his new 'white' school on his first day.

"Just remember this," my father said. "Those white people aren't better than you."

But he was so wrong. And he knew he was wrong. He was the loser Indian father of a loser Indian son living in a world built for winners.

But he loved me so much. He hugged me even closer.

"This is a great thing," he said. "You're so brave. You're a warrior."

It was the best thing he could have said.

"Hey, here's some lunch money," he said and gave me a dollar.

We were poor enough to get a free school lunch, but I didn't want to be the only Indian and the only kid who needed charity.

"Thanks, Dad," I said.

"I love you," he said.

"I love you too."

I felt stronger so I stepped out of the car and walked to the front door. It was locked.

So I stood alone on the sidewalk and watched my father drive away. I hoped he'd drive right home and not stop in a bar and spend whatever money he had left.

I hoped he'd remember to come back and pick me up after school.

I stood alone at the front door for a few very long minutes.

It was still early and I had a black eye from Rowdy's good-bye punch. No, I had a purple, blue, yellow, and black eye. It looked like modern art.

Then the white kids began arriving for school. They surrounded me. Those kids were so white. I could see the blue veins running through their skin like rivers.

Most of the kids were my size or smaller, but there were ten or twelve monster dudes. Giant white guys. They looked like men, not boys. They had to be seniors. Some of them looked like they had to shave two or three times a day.

They stared at me, the Indian boy with the black eye and swollen nose, my going-away gifts from Rowdy. Those white kids couldn't believe their eyes. They stared at me like I was Bigfoot or a UFO. What was I doing at Reardan, whose mascot was an Indian? That made me the only *other* Indian in town.

So what was I doing in racist Reardan, where more than half the students went to college? Nobody in my family had ever gone near a college.

Reardan was the opposite of the rez. It was the opposite of my family. It was the opposite of me.

ADING

2 The story so far

a) *Point out lines from the text above that tell you why Arnold would want to leave his 'rez' for a new school.*

b) *Describe the differences Arnold notices between himself and the others at his new school.*

c) *Now look at the cartoon in detail. Describe how it represents Arnold's feelings.*

d) *Give your opinion on how the following things should / shouldn't play a role when you try to find your place in a new environment:*

clothes | humor | looks | sports | being friendly | being cool

After some time at his new school, Arnold still struggles with feeling different. Many of the kids don't like him at all; some even hate him. But some like him too …

Traveling between Reardan and Wellpinit, between the little white town and the reservation, I always felt like a stranger. I was half Indian in one place and half white in the other. It was like being Indian was my job, but it was only a part-time job. And it didn't pay well at all. The only person who made me feel great all the time was Penelope.

Well, I shouldn't say that. I mean, my mother and father were working hard for me too. They were constantly scraping together enough money to pay for gas, to get me lunch money, to buy me a new pair of jeans and a few new shirts. My parents gave me just enough money so that I could pretend to have more money than I did. I lied about how poor I was.

Everybody in Reardan assumed we Spokanes made lots of money because we had a casino. But that casino, mismanaged and too far away from major highways, was a money-losing business. In order to make money from the casino, you had to work at the casino. And white people everywhere have always believed that the government just gives money to Indians.

And since the kids and parents at Reardan thought I had a lot of money, I did nothing to change their minds. I figured it wouldn't do me any good if they knew I was dirt poor. What would they think of me if they knew I sometimes had to hitchhike to school?

Yeah, so I pretended to have a little money. I pretended to be middle class. I pretended I belonged. Nobody knew the truth.

Of course, you can't lie forever. Lies have short shelf lives. Lies go bad.

READING

3 A closer look at Arnold

a) *"It was like being Indian was my job, but it was only a part-time job. And it didn't pay well at all." (p. 123, lines 7–9) Describe what Arnold means with these key lines.*

b) *Describe Arnold's strategies for pretending not to be poor in the text and cartoon too.*

c) *Point out examples of how Arnold tries to make his struggles sound funny. Explain why you think he does this.*

Arnold becomes friends with Penelope but continues to struggle with feeling different …

In December, I took Penelope to the Winter Formal. The thing is, I only had five dollars, not nearly enough to pay for anything – not for photos, not for food, not for gas, not for a hot dog and soda pop. If it had been any other dance, a regular dance, I would have stayed home with an imaginary illness. But I couldn't skip Winter Formal. And if I didn't take Penelope then she would have gone with somebody else.

Because I didn't have money for gas, and because I couldn't have driven the car if I wanted to, and because I didn't want to double date, I told Penelope I'd meet her at the gym for the dance. She wasn't too happy about that. But the worst thing is that I had to wear one of Dad's old suits. I was worried that people would make fun of me, right? And they probably would have if Penelope hadn't screamed with delight when she first saw me walk into the gym.

"Oh, my, God!" she yelled for everybody to hear. "That suit is so beautiful. It's so retroactive. It's so retroactive that it's radioactive!"

And every dude there suddenly wished he'd worn his father's lame polyester suit.

One day at school, Arnold is really missing his ex-best friend from the rez, Rowdy. Arnold is telling his new friend Gordy about it …

"Rowdy used to be my best friend. He hates me now."

"Why does he hate you?" Gordy asked.

"Because I left the rez," I said.

"But you still live there, don't you? You're just going to school here."

"I know, I know, but some Indians think you have to act white to make your life better. Some Indians think you become white if you try to make your life better, if you become successful."

"If that were true, then wouldn't all white people be successful?"

Man, Gordy was smart. I wished I could take him to the rez and let him educate Rowdy. Of course, Rowdy would probably punch Gordy until he was brain-dead. Or maybe Rowdy, Gordy, and I could become a superhero trio, fighting for truth, justice, and the Native American way. Well, okay, Gordy was white, but anybody can start to act like an Indian if he hangs around us long enough.

"The people at home," I said. "A lot of them call me an apple."

"Do they think you're a fruit or something?" he asked.

"No, no," I said. "They call me an apple because they think I'm red on the outside and white on the inside."

"Ah, so they think you're a traitor."

"Yep."

"Well, life is a constant struggle between being an individual and being a member of the community."

Can you believe there is a kid who talks like that? Like he's already a college professor who's impressed with the sound of his own voice?

"Gordy," I said. "I don't understand what you're trying to say to me."

"Well, in the early days of humans, the community was our only protection against predators, and against starvation. We survived because we trusted one another."

"So?"

"So, back then, weird people threatened the strength of the tribe. If you weren't good for making food, shelter, or babies, then you were tossed out on your own."

"But we're not primitive like that anymore."

"Oh, yes, we are. Weird people still get tossed out."

"You mean weird people like me," I said.

"And me," Gordy said.

"All right, then," I said. "So we have a tribe of two."

I had the sudden urge to hug Gordy, and he had the sudden urge to stop me from hugging him.

"Don't get sentimental," he said.

Yep, even the weird boys are afraid of their emotions.

by Sherman Alexie (2007);
artwork by Ellen Forney

READING

4 Understanding key messages → WB 69/19

The following are key lines from the last excerpt. Choose one of them and explain why it's key for understanding the story.

"They call me an apple because they think I'm red on the outside and white on the inside." (lines 58–60)

"Life is a constant struggle between being an individual and being a member of the community." (lines 63–65)

READING

5 Friends

a) *First, describe what good qualities a typical comic-book superhero usually has.*

b) *In the last excerpt (lines 48–50), Arnold wishes that this could happen:*

"Maybe Rowdy, Gordy, and I could become a superhero trio, fighting for truth, justice, and the Native American way."

Explain why you think Arnold would have this wish.

SPEAKING

6 Your overall reaction to Arnold's story

Give your reaction to the story by completing one of the sentence beginnings below. Exchange your ideas in class.

The story made me …	wish that … | realize that … | decide that … | wonder about … | hope that … | see that … | believe that …

Example:
A: The story made me hope that there's always a chance to …
B: For me, the story made me wonder about how people …

WRITING

7 Creative writing: Important people in Arnold's life → WB 69/20

→ S7–9

In the excerpts above, four characters all played major roles in Arnold's life:

Arnold's father | Rowdy | Penelope | Gordy

These four characters never meet in the book Part-Time Indian. *But imagine they met and started talking about Arnold. What kind of things would they say about a boy like Arnold who is so unique? What would they say to each other?*

1. First, think of **adjectives** to describe each of the characters the way they were presented in the excerpts. This will affect the words you put in their mouths.
2. Based on your idea of these four characters, write some **dialogue** between them. Make sure they show the kinds of feelings that match their **personalities**!

A trip to die for? → S16

VIEWING

1 At the beach in Sandy Hook, New Jersey

7 a) *Wesley is with his neighbor, Rebecca, and another friend, Ben. Watch the film till 02:05. Then answer these questions:*

1. Where is Ben from, and why is he in New Jersey now, on the East Coast?
2. What differences between Ben's home region and the East Coast do they talk about?

b) *Now watch the film till 04:00 and answer these questions:*

1. Describe what Rebecca and the boys do in this part of the film.
2. How do the boys react to the suspicious behavior they see? Give an explanation – and suggest what you think Rebecca and the man are doing.

c) *Now watch the rest of the film and sum up what happens. In what ways did the ending surprise you – or not?*

VIEWING

2 Misunderstandings as a narrative technique → WB 70/21

a) *Read the skills box. Then say how the misunderstanding in this film works.*

b) *Starting at 04:49, Rebecca makes some comments about food: "I could kill for some clam chowder", "Death by Chocolate is really to die for" and a "great way to die". Explain how these everyday expressions make the boys look so worried.*

c) *Your turn: Have you ever experienced a misunderstanding that was funny/embarrassing after you found out it was a misunderstanding? Describe the situation for the class. Then write a short text about it.*

Film skills

A lot of writers and filmmakers like to use **misunderstandings** as part of their plots. This is a popular narrative technique for the following reasons:
- It can be **a test for the viewers**. Can the viewers see that there's a misunderstanding? Or are they tricked into believing something just like the characters in the film?
- The moment in the film when the characters realize there has been a misunderstanding can often be **entertaining** for the viewers.

Legende

Diese Symbole und Erklärungen zeigen dir, wie du mit den Hilfen, Aufgaben und Aktivitäten auf den *Diff pool*-Seiten arbeiten kannst.

△ Hilfe zur Unit-Aufgabe | oder eine leichtere Variante der Unit-Aufgabe | oder eine zusätzliche Aufgabe

▲ eine zusätzliche Herausforderung

Unit 1

△ 1 Welcome to America! → Help with Introduction, p. 13/3

*Read the questions below **before** you listen. They can help you to sum things up in Ex. 3 on p. 13.*

- Why are the European teens in America?
- Why is Josh the right person to talk to them?
- What is he going to talk about?
- Where does Josh live?
- What does he say about American apartment buildings?
- Where does he meet his friends?
- What does he say about city life?
- What is good about life in the suburbs?
- How are suburbs different from cities?
- What can you do in your free time if you live in the suburbs?
- Where will the Europeans go to school?
- What does Josh say about lockers?
- Where else do students meet?
- Do American students have to work hard?
- What does Josh say about other activities at school?
- What do Americans do in their free time?
- What else does Josh think is important?

△ 2 Different categories of gerunds → Help with Station 1, p. 15/3b)

Copy the grid into your exercise books. Complete it with the gerund phrases below.

Gerund after adjective + preposition	Gerund after verb + preposition	Gerund as sentence subject	Gerund as sentence object
I'm scared of changing		Living here isn't bad	

I miss seeing my old friends | Getting there is difficult | I like hanging out with … | We talked about organizing a party | Living here isn't bad ✔ | I miss having a garden | I'm looking forward to starting school | I enjoyed meeting you | Being in a city is cool | I love having a big bedroom | Can you imagine walking up 22 floors? | I'm scared of changing ✔ | I'm looking forward to making friends | I'm good at swimming | How about meeting up? | Stop worrying about losing your old friends | Meeting up isn't easy | I keep forgetting your dad is American | I'm getting used to living on the 22nd floor

△ 3 Do you like talking to your partner? → After Station 1, p. 16/4

Work with a partner to create little dialogues about things you like and don't like. You can use these phrases to start with. Can you think of more?

Do you like skiing? / Do you …? Are you good at playing chess? Do you feel like reading a book? Do you enjoy going for long walks? Are you crazy about texting your friends? Is dancing good for you?	✔	Yes, … is great / fantastic / fun. Yes, I love … / like … / always enjoy …
	✘	No, … takes too much time / makes me sick / is boring / isn't interesting at all. No, I hate … / don't like … at all / find … boring.

Example: Do you feel like going swimming? – No, I hate swimming.

△ 4 Gerunds to talk about likes and dislikes → Instead of Station 1, p. 16/6

Gerunds are often helpful when you want to talk about likes and dislikes. Here, Lena is talking to her new friend, Madison. Finish the sentences below with ***gerund phrases****. Each sentence with a gerund phrase should have the same meaning as the original sentence with the same number.*

Lena
1. I'm a bit shy when I meet new people, but it's OK.
2. Maybe I'll go to the mall; I'm not sure yet.
3. Mom tells me to unpack every day!
4. There's a dress code so I don't wear crazy T-shirts to school anymore.

Madison
5. My brother learned to drive when he was 16.
6. Would you like to meet some more people in the area?
7. I can't wait to plan our Thanksgiving party!
8. I listen to music all the time!

Lena
1. I don't mind meeting …
2. I'm thinking of …
3. Mom keeps …
4. I've stopped …

Madison
5. My brother started …
6. Are you interested in …
7. I'm looking forward to …
8. I love …

△ 5 I like / I hate → Help with Station 1, p. 17/7

What do you like or hate? The words and phrases on the right can help you with sentences. Write your ideas down first before you talk to your partner.

Examples:
- I love chilling out on the sofa, but I hate washing the dishes.
- I'm really interested in …, but I'm scared of …

take tests | chill out with friends | travel around the world | discover new countries | go hiking | see / find dangerous animals | chill out on the sofa | text my friends | play games on my phone | watch TV | clean the kitchen | listen to music | tidy my room / the kitchen

▲ 6 Role play: Matt, his angel and his devil → After Station 2, p. 18/9

In groups of three, write a short role play for Matt, his angel and his devil:

- Matt talks out loud about his dilemma;
- his angel and his devil try to tell him what to do from their different points of view.

The ideas below can help you to write your role play. Then act it out for the class.

hang out with geeks | (not) be an outsider | enjoy having fun | great to do sth for others | Is it really important to …? | love being part of the in-crowd | make the world a better place | What's wrong with being …?

△ 7 Infinitives with question words → Help with Station 2, p. 19/11a)

Compare A and B: Which words are left out in B? What is used instead? What else is different? This can help you to do Ex. 11a) on p. 19.

A		B
Matt asks himself a lot of questions at lunchtime:		He told his parents about it when he came home. He didn't know …
How do I pay for my lunch?	→	… how to pay for his lunch.
Where do I sit?	→	… where to sit.
What can I say to the other students?	→	… what to say to the other students.
Should I talk about the lessons?	→	… whether to talk about the lessons.

△ 8 Do you know how to help a friend? → After Station 2, p. 19/11

*A group of kids from Matt's school is hiking in the hills of Pennsylvania. Suddenly Scott stumbles[1], falls down and doesn't get up again. Everyone is worried and asking questions. Turn their questions into **infinitive sentences**. Use words like these:*

wonder | ask themselves | not know | have no idea | not sure

Example: How can we help him? → They're wondering **how to help** him.

1. Should we feel his pulse[2]?
2. Do we have to check his breathing[3]?
3. Do we have to put up his legs?
4. Should we stay here?
5. Should we cover him with our jackets?
6. Shouldn't we try to find some adults?
7. Who can we call?
8. Where can we find some water for him?

1 **to stumble** ['stʌmbl] stolpern | 2 **pulse** [pʌls] Puls | 3 **breathing** ['bri:ðɪŋ] Atmung

▲ 9 New at our school → After Station 2, p. 19/11

a) *What kinds of things do new students want to know about their new school? Work with a partner to finish the sentences on the left with information on the right.*

1. Students who are new at our school want to know where to …
2. They wonder whether …
3. Some ask themselves how …
4. They would like to know who …
5. They don't know when …

find the cafeteria / the computer room | use the computers | borrow books | say hello to the teachers | ask for the computer passwords | bring books back to the library

b) *Work with a partner to write down questions a new student at your school might have.*

△ 10 I want you to write back! → After Station 2, p. 20/13b)

a) *Lena has told her grandma back in Germany what she is worrying about. First, read the tips and advice that her grandma wrote back.*

> Liebe Lena,
> ich möchte, dass du dich in Amerika zu Hause fühlst. 😀😀😀 Und ich möchte natürlich nicht, dass du traurig bist! 😔😔😔 Das tut mir so leid! Ich hätte gern, dass du Matt schreibst und ihm sagst, wie du dich fühlst. Natürlich würde ich es vorziehen, dass ER dir zuerst schreibt, aber er scheint sehr beschäftigt zu sein. Deshalb kannst du auch nicht erwarten, dass er dir sofort antwortet. Aber wenn du möchtest, dass er sich mit dir trifft, musst DU etwas tun.
> Jetzt hätte ich gern, dass du mir bald antwortest! --Oma 😍😀😍

But Lena isn't so sure about her grandma's advice and wants Madison's opinion. Write what Lena could tell Madison about it.

Start like this: Grandma wants me to feel at home in America, and she doesn't …
She's really sorry for me. She'd like me to …

b) *Lots of people tell Matt what to do too. Write sentences about him:*

Eva and Scott would like Matt to …

spend the lunch break with them | go to the mall with them | not hang out with the geeks

Here's what Matt's parents expect from him:

always do his homework right after school | find new friends quickly | do what they say

And here's what Matt would prefer his friends to do:

everyone like each other | not talk bad about others | all his friends have lunch together

▲ 11 What I'd like others to do → After Station 2, p. 20/13b)

Think of all your teachers (or classmates / parents / friends): What do they do, what don't they do? What do you like about it, what don't you like? Make a list of things you'd like them to do or not to do! Use ***infinitive constructions****. Be creative!*

Examples: I'd like my English teacher to give us less homework. | I'd prefer the Math teacher to stop writing silly numbers on the board. | I expect …

△ 12 Infinitive or gerund? → Help with Station 2, p. 21/15b)

Copy the grid into your exercise books. Then read the text below. Complete the grid with the verbs in yellow and decide: How do you write them when they're used with a ***gerund****? And how do you write them with an* ***infinitive****? Write the German translation of the verbs into your grid.*

Verb	Gerund	Infinitive
remember	sich erinnern, etwas getan zu haben	…
…	…	…

Matt's mom remembers her last trip from England to the US: "I'll never forget losing my passport last year. I had forgotten to put it into my suitcase. I remember holding it in my hand and thinking that I shouldn't put it into my purse[1], and then I tried to open the suitcase – but the zipper[2] got stuck[3]. I tried using soap[4] on the zipper after someone had told me it helps, but it didn't. Then the doorbell rang, and I stopped to answer it. Well, once I stop doing something, I don't always remember to finish it, and that's what happened. I stopped thinking about the passport and put it into my purse. But my purse was stolen on my way to the airport! So I missed the flight *and* lost my passport!"

△ 13 Useful phrases for Lena's video chat → Help with Station 2, p. 21/16

Altkleidersammlung | keine Lust mehr haben, … zu tun | sich fragen wie … sein wird | Obdachlosenunterkunft | Kleider spenden | gut darin sein zu … / das gute Gefühl haben, … | Vorteile | von etwas profitieren | entrümpeln | etwas von jemandem erwarten

△ 14 What *really* happened at the mall → Help with Story, p. 24/4c)

These pictures and phrases can help you to write your own version of the story:

A

B

C

Lena sees group of young people with big signs | no Madison | the crowd pushes; Lena falls, loses her phone | sees her phone | grabs it before somebody steals it

tells officer that phone was stolen | Lena not worried; she knows she'll see the others at 5:00 | officer looks worried; tells her she might not see her phone again

Matt calls Lena's phone, Madison answers | phone was in Madison's bag the whole time | Lena waits at bench at 5:00 | Matt and Madison walk towards her

1 purse [pɜːs] Handtasche | **2 zipper** [ˈzɪpə] Reißverschluss | **3 get stuck** [stʌk] sich verhaken | **4 soap** [səʊp] Seife

Text smart 1

△ 1 How to create an ad → Help with Station, p. 35/2b)

These words and phrases can help you to describe the ad on p. 35:

Useful phrases

- The ad for … is a typical …
- There's a large / small / funny / interesting eye-catcher on the left / right side …
- The eye-catcher shows … / is a photo of …
- It works as an eye-catcher because …
- Several photos show …
- The ad also gives / presents information on …
- The slogan is the part that says "…"
- The slogan focuses on …
- The ad copy tells the reader about …

△ 2 Talking about a target group → Help with Station, p. 36/4a)

Look at the different target groups in the first box below. Which ones would find the Fa$hion Fabulou$ ad attractive? And the Retro 4ever ad?

large families | fashion models | husbands who need a present for their wife's birthday | teachers | students | people with lots of / with little money | fashion addicts | tourists | hipsters | people who need an outfit for a wedding / for a party | skaters

These words might be able to help you to give more information about the target group:

people who want everyday / sporty[1] / cheap / nice / trendy[2] / … clothes | people who want to spend / save money | people who want …

△ 3 Improving an ad → Help with Station, p. 37/5b)

These questions might help you to find ideas for improving the ads on pages 35–36:

Visuals: Is there a link between the eye-catcher and the product? | Does the eye-catcher make the customer curious[3]? | Do the visuals cause positive / negative feelings? | Do the visuals present the product in the best possible way?

Slogan / ad copy: Does the slogan match the product? | Is the slogan catchy? | Does it tell the customer what the product is good for? | Does the ad copy tell the reader clearly where he / she can buy the product? | Does the ad copy clearly speak to a special target group?

Humor: Does the humor of the ad work for everyone? | Does it hurt anybody's feelings? | Are there ways it could be funnier?

Product: Does the ad feature enough information about the product?

Target group: Is it clear who the target group is? | Is there more than one target group? Could the target group be bigger if you changed the ad?

Effectiveness: Would you buy the product? | Do you know anybody who would buy it?

1 **sporty** ['spɔːti] sportlich | 2 **trendy** ['trendi] trendig | 3 **curious** ['kjʊəriəs] neugierig

Unit 2

△ 1 Big city life → Help with Introduction, p. 41/2a)

These words and phrases can help you to talk about life in a big city:

Pros: entertainment: (movie) theaters, concerts, live shows | **activities:** sports clubs, big parks | **education:** schools, museums, special offers for kids | **culture:** music, art, many nationalities[1] and cultures

Cons: people: too many people on the streets, crowded places, full buses and underground trains | **traffic:** too many cars, too much noise, pollution | **crime:** criminal gangs, violence, organized crime

△ 2 Your turn: In New York City → Help with Introduction, p. 41/3

Read the text about one of the photos from the Introduction. Which photo does it match? The text can help you to write your own text about one of the other photos.

I can hear lots of cars and voices – and so many different languages! Everyone seems to be busy. I can feel the magic of a big city with people from lots of different countries. The air smells of strange and spicy[2] food. I'm trying to catch a taxi, but that isn't so easy. Other people are waiting for a taxi too. But I'm not bored: There are so many things to discover and look at, like the colorful shop signs that I can't read and the mix of American and Chinese[3] culture.

△ 3 Tourists in New York → After Station 1, p. 43/2

*Use the phrases below to make sentences with **defining relative clauses**.*

Example: 1. Everyone **who is in New York for the first time** wants to visit the Empire State Building.

are looking for designer clothes | are interested in history | is in New York for the first time ✔ | love paintings and sculptures | want to get a great view of New York | are traveling with children | enjoy outdoor activities | don't have time

1. Everyone wants to visit the Empire State Building.
2. Most tourists spend a day in Central Park.
3. People often come to New York to visit the Museum of Modern Art.
4. Tourists love the Museum of Immigration on Ellis Island.
5. Most visitors travel by taxi.
6. Families always enjoy a visit to the Museum of Natural History.
7. Shoppers love the big department stores[4] like Bloomingdales.
8. Many tourists go up to the top of Rockefeller Center.

1 **nationality** [ˌnæʃnˈæləti] Nationalität | 2 **spicy** [ˈspaɪsi] würzig; scharf | 3 **Chinese** [tʃaɪˈniːz] chinesisch | 4 **department store** [dɪˈpɑːtmənt ˌstɔː] Kaufhaus

4 A stopover[1] in New York
→ After Station 1, p. 43/2

Imagine you have a two-hour stopover in Manhattan. What would you like to see and do? Write a short text. Give reasons for your choice of activities and places.

5 Defining or non-defining?
→ After Station 1, p. 44/6

*Use the phrases to make sentences about Rylee and Lea in New York City. Decide if you need **defining** or **non-defining relative clauses**.*

Example: 1. Lea and Rylee, **who are in New York for the first time**, only have one day to spend in the city.

Diego shows the girls | Diego thinks of | is only a few blocks from Central Park | are in New York for the first time ✓ | catches Diego and the girls at the top of Rockefeller Center | calls himself 'The Naked Cowboy' | Diego and the girls visit | works in a diner

1. Lea and Rylee only have one day to spend in the city.
2. Diego takes the girls on a sightseeing tour of New York.
3. The places are for free.
4. The first place is a famous music school.
5. The man is a popular tourist attraction.
6. At the Alvin Ailey Dance Studio people take dance classes.
7. The big surprise is the view from Rockefeller Center.
8. The security man is Diego's father.

6 Typical German food
→ Help with Station 1, p. 45/9

Match the English phrases on the left with the German expressions on the right. The English words can help you with Ex. 9 on p. 45.

black pudding | liver sausage | grow in the earth | serve with | vegetarian | point to the sky | chopped apples | the main ingredients | a popular dish

Leberwurst | die Hauptzutaten | in den Himmel ragen | ein beliebtes Gericht | Blutwurst | in der Erde wachsen | mit … servieren | vegetarisch | zerkleinerte Äpfel

7 *Since* or *for*?
→ After Station 2, p. 47/12

*Complete the sentences with **since** or **for**.*

1. People have been calling New York 'The Big Apple' ___ a very long time.
2. A large Christmas tree has decorated Rockefeller Center every year ___ Christmas 1933.
3. Carnegie Hall has been one of the world's most famous concert halls ___ it was opened in 1891.
4. New Amsterdam has been called New York ___ Peter Stuyvesant had to give the city to the English in 1664.
5. Yellow taxis have been driving around New York ___ more than a hundred years.
6. New York has been important in foreign trade[2] ___ the opening of the Erie Canal in 1825.

1 **stopover** ['stɒpˌəʊvə] Zwischenstopp | 2 **foreign trade** [ˌfɒrɪn 'treɪd] Außenhandel

△ 8 Present perfect progressive or past perfect progressive? → After Station 2, p. 48/15

*Complete the text with the right verb forms and **since** or **for**.*

Lisa checked the time. She 1 (wait) 2 half an hour now, and still the airport bus wasn't in sight. Others were waiting with her. She noticed a woman who 3 (talk) to someone on her phone 4 20 minutes. "I 5 (live) here 6 May last year, and you haven't been here to see me once!" She'd heard her say. How could anyone not want to visit a friend in New York? Lisa 7 (dream) of coming to New York 8 she was a teenager. One day her boss had told her: "We 9 (look) for someone to take over our office in New York 10 last summer, and it seems that you're the best person for the job!" Lisa, who 11 (think of) moving to New York 12 several months, had accepted at once. "This is the chance I 13 (wait) for 14 I started working for this company," she'd told her husband. But now, after the first week in New York, she missed her husband and her kids. If only the airport bus would come …

▲ 9 Mixed bag: Different tenses → After Station 2, p. 48/15

*As a taxi driver in New York, Emilio meets lots of interesting people. Here's a story he told his son Diego. Use the right tense for the verbs in brackets: **simple past**, **past progressive**, **present perfect**, **past perfect** or **past perfect progressive**.*

I 1 (drive) around for a while when I 2 (pass[1]) the airport bus stop at Grand Central Station. There 3 (be) an accident on Lexington Avenue and traffic 4 (be) very slow. I 5 (notice) a family with a little boy and a teenage girl who 6 (point) at my taxi, so I 7 (stop). The man 8 (tell) me that they 9 (wait) for the airport bus for more than an hour. The family and another woman with a big suitcase 10 (get) into the taxi. They 11 (agree) to share a taxi and pay for it together. When we 12 (arrive) at the airport, the man 13 (say) he'd put it on his credit card[2]. But my credit card machine 14 (not work), so I 15 (ask) them to pay in cash[3]. Well, guess what – the family 16 (spend) all their cash and so they 17 (not be able to) pay. "Don't worry, I'll pay," the other woman 18 (say). "They can give it back to me later." She 19 (give) them her address in New York and 20 (pay): nearly $90! Isn't that cool? I 21 (never meet) such a generous person before.

△ 10 What had been happening before? → Instead of Station 2, p. 48/16

*Complete the sentences with the ideas below. Use the **past perfect progressive**.*

study hard for weeks | walk around Central Park for half an hour | look for rabbits in a muddy field for hours | chill out and talk for two hours | cry all morning | work hard all day | wait for him to call since 10 o'clock

1. I was very tired when I got home after school because I'd been …
2. Dave got the best grade on the test because he …
3. We … when there was a heavy storm and we had to go back.
4. When Kelly arrived at the café, her friends …
5. Our dog was very dirty. He …
6. Lisa thought her friend would never call. She …
7. Mary's eyes were very red. She …

1 **to pass** [pɑːs] vorbeikommen an | 2 **credit card** [ˈkredɪt ˌkɑːd] Kreditkarte | 3 **cash** [kæʃ] Bargeld

△ 11 Stylistic elements in a graphic novel → Help with Story, p. 59/3c)

Which of these stylistic elements can you find in the story? Use the prompts to talk about the effect they have in Asphalt Tribe.

set the scene | introduce the setting | create a distance / a quiet atmosphere

show action in the story | show reactions / feelings of characters

introduce fast action / speed | create suspense | make the reader live through the story

△ 12 Write the story! → Help with Story, p. 60/6

a) *Look at these beginnings of different parts of the story. What scene do they match?*

A: These streets, so busy and hectic during the day, but so dark and scary at night, were our home.

B: I ran away as fast as I could, but when I turned around, I saw that Maybe wasn't following me.

C: After a hard day in the streets we enjoyed our food – even if it was from the dumpster.

b) *Choose one of the opening sentences from a) and use the information and phrases below to continue the story.*

A: sleep under bridges | no family, only gang members | fight to survive | lonely | hard life | depressing | often hungry | invent new names

B: shout at Maybe | run at top speed | stupid rich ladies | no chance to catch us in their designer shoes | hope that handbag full of money

C: relax for a moment | glad to be with friends, not so lonely | suddenly hear police car | scared to death | drop everything and run away into the dark

Text smart 2

△ 1 Reasons → Help with Station 1, p. 72/5

There are different reasons why people would want to stage a hoax or why they believe in conspiracy theories. Maybe some of these statements can help you with Ex. 5 on p. 72:

You could make a lot of money with it!

Governments or companies will do anything to look good or to cover up bad news!

When something is hard to explain, it's easy to say it was a government trick or a cover-up.

A boring person becomes interesting with a good story.

Some people will do anything for attention!

It's fun to trick people, and some people will believe anything!

△ 2 Your turn: Write your own blog response → Help with Station 1, 73/9

These ideas and arguments can help you to write your answer to the blog post on p. 72. Which ones support the blogger's theory? Which ones don't?

- moon landing not important → being better than the Soviet Union important
- good entertainment important → fake or real, only the show counts
- faking it → a good idea; good way to save money for a *real* trip to the moon
- flying to the moon → no benefits; too expensive
- reasons for not going anymore → other problems / challenges in world now; one successful mission enough
- clear facts → astronauts brought back stones, took photos

△ 3 A film rating gone wrong → After Station 2, p. 75/14a)

Look back at the skills box on p. 75. Then read the rating below. Talk to your partner about what's wrong here and how you could improve the text. Then write a new version.

Star Wars Episode 7: How bad can a film get?!
The film tells the story of a group of heroes who fight the dark powers and try to find Luke Skywalker. On some websites people give this movie a rating of 4 or even 5 stars. Are they crazy?! Stupid?! Or both?! Were we watching the same movie?! THIS IS THE WORST STAR WARS FILM EVER! Let's start with the awful actors: Harrison Ford and Carrie Fisher are both too old and ugly to play their parts. I wish they had costumes like Chewbacca's so we wouldn't have to see their faces! Another joke: There are so many badly-done special effects! Han Solo's spaceship, the Millennium Falcon, was used in so many battles for the Rebel Alliance that it just looks like a silly old toy now. And can we talk about Rey, the new female[1] hero? As a girl, let me just say that it wasn't convincing for her to win a fight against Kylo Ren, Han Solo's son! Seriously! A woman who is good at mechanics[2], engineering[3] AND fighting?! Completely unbelievable!!! I wish I could give NO stars, but I have to give at least one, so here it is. ★
POSTED BY SCARY_CHICK ON DEC. 14 AT 10:08 PM

1 female [ˈfiːmeɪl] weiblich | **2 mechanics** [məˈkænɪks] Technik | **3 engineering** [ˌendʒɪˈnɪərɪŋ] Maschinenbau

Unit 3

△ 1 How to become an innovative country → Instead of Introduction, p. 78/1c

Your country needs more innovation – but you only have money for three of these ideas. Which ones would you choose? Discuss it with your partner first. Then share your ideas in class.

- Innovation as a subject at school
- Special classes for very good students
- Advertisements to keep people informed about inventions that are needed
- Talent scouts[1] who look for innovative students at schools
- Innovation competitions for all age groups
- A national agency where everyone with an innovative idea can apply for[2] money
- 'Germany's next top inventor' TV show
- An inventor's magazine to keep people informed about new inventions

▲ 2 What was in the diary? → After Station 1, p. 82/1a)

Write the diary entry in German that Tim's grandma translated for him. Add some more information, then exchange with a partner. Now one of you is Tim, the other his grandma. Translate your partner's text, and read it out to the class.

△ 3 Adjectives and adverbs → After Station 1, p. 83/4

Decide if you need an ***adjective*** *or an* ***adverb****.*

When Ursula Förstner was sent back, she felt **1** (awful): The journey to New York had been so **2** (hard), and now she had to go all the way back to Germany again! Ursula found the journey home **3** (terrible), but she did her best to keep **4** (calm). The ship looked **5** (empty) because most people had been allowed to stay in New York, and it felt **6** (strange) to be alone on board. When she arrived in Hamburg, her uncle was waiting **7** (impatient[3]) for her. He seemed **8** (happy) to see her again and asked her a lot of questions – after all, she had been to New York! Back there, her parents and brother missed her **9** (terrible) while they were trying **10** (hard) to get used to their new life. Everything was so much faster than at home …

1 talent scout ['tæləntˌskaʊt] Talentsucher/-in | **2 to apply for sth** [ə'plaɪ] sich um etw. bewerben | **3 impatient** [ɪm'peɪʃnt] ungeduldig

▲ 4 What would Ursula's parents have said? → After Station 1, p. 83/4

Role play: Back in 1901, nobody had a mobile phone, of course – and there was no way for Ursula to call her parents to say that she was safe! Imagine she'd had a phone: What would she have told her parents about the journey home? What would they have told their daughter? Work with a partner to write their conversation. Then present it to the class.

△ 5 The Italian lady's story → After Station 1, p. 84/6b)

a) *Go back to your grid from Ex. 6b) on p. 84. Add the participles for these verbs:*

shock | frighten | interest | fascinate

b) *Now use the participles from your grid to continue the story:*

Example: "Everything was different from home, and I was **frightened** at first – but then I saw …

△ 6 A great Indian chief → After Station 2, p. 87/11

Use linking words to improve this text about Sitting Bull.

although | and | as | because | but | even though | since | when

Sitting Bull was born a member of the Lakota Sioux tribe in South Dakota. His father named him 'Slow' **1** he was always very careful and slow to take action, **2** after his son's first battle at the age of 14, he gave him the name Sitting Bull. In the middle of the 19th century, a growing number of settlers began to move West. **3** the Americans showed no respect for their land, life became very difficult for the Native Americans. At first Sitting Bull hoped for peace[1] with the white man, **4** then even more people arrived **5** he began to fight them.

In 1874, **6** gold was found in the Black Hills of South Dakota, the United States wanted all the Sioux to move to a reservation. Sitting Bull refused[2] **7** he felt that reservations were like prisons. **8** the US Army began to hunt down[3] the Sioux that lived outside the reservation, Sitting Bull formed a war camp where many Sioux and members of other tribes joined him. On June 26, 1876, Colonel[4] George Custer of the US Army attacked. The Native Americans were able to defeat him **9** Custer hadn't realized the size of Sitting Bull's army. **10** the Battle of Little Bighorn was a great victory[5] for the Native Americans, soon more soldiers arrived in South Dakota.

1 **peace** [pi:s] Frieden | 2 **to refuse** [rɪ'fju:z] ablehnen | 3 **to hunt down sb** ['hʌnt ˌdaʊn] Jagd auf jmdn. machen | 4 **colonel** ['kɜ:nl] Oberst | 5 **victory** ['vɪktri] Sieg

△ 7 Doc Maynard and his Native American friend → After Station 2, p. 88/13

*Remember the rules for **conditional clauses types 2 and 3**. Then combine the two sentences to make conditional clauses.*

Example: 1. If Native Americans **played** a greater role in history books, we'**d know** more about them.

1. Native Americans don't play a great role in history books. So we don't know much about them. ✔
2. Chief Seattle was born to parents from two different tribes. He learned both their dialects when he grew up.
3. As a young man, Seattle had fought against other tribes. He learned how death and war upset a community.
4. In 1850, Doc Maynard left Ohio and moved to Puget Sound in the Pacific Northwest. There he met Chief Seattle.
5. Doc Maynard respected the Native Americans. He wanted to find a good way for Native Americans and the white man to live together.
6. Maynard was an important person in the Pacific Northwest. He was able to name the new city after his Native American friend.
7. Today there is a statue of Chief Seattle at Tilikum Place in Seattle. So people remember him.

▲ 8 More inventions → After Station 2, p. 88/13

Think of two other important inventions that were made in the past and describe them to your classmates. Say how the world would be different today if they hadn't been invented.

Example: If the smartphone hadn't been invented, people would still … Now, with this new invention … It can …

△ 9 Different text types → Help with Story, p. 94/4a)

Work with your partner to compare this text about the Oregon Trail with Lilly's diary entries. How are the two text types different? What are their purposes? Make notes and share your results with the class.

There were many difficulties along the Oregon Trail that the settlers had to deal with.
Here are some of them:

- Even if the settlers were careful, they had accidents and became sick during the trip. Some fell from the slow-moving wagons and were killed by the heavy wheels.
- Some people drowned when they tried to cross the rivers.
- People were scared of attacks by Native Americans.
- As the trip went on, the animals pulling the wagons got tired and weaker. The travelers began to throw out heavy things – furniture, clothing and tools to make things easier for them.
- Travelers needed to make sure they left at the right time of the year. If they left too early, the grass wouldn't be long enough and the animals wouldn't find enough to eat. If they left too late, it would get too cold by the time they got close to Oregon.

Text smart 3

△ 1 Your turn: Travel in your life → Help with Introduction, p. 102/2

Read about Simon's experiences with travel texts. Look for useful expressions he uses; they could help you to talk about your experiences. Also, notice which tenses he uses.

My parents and I were really looking forward to our trip to Spain last year. Before we left, I'd checked the hotel on their website and read some online ratings about it too, so I was sure everything would be OK. Everyone who had visited the hotel seemed to have a nice time there.

We arrived very late at night – but couldn't sleep because it was so loud! The hotel's club was right below our room. The next day, we realized that the pool area was too small for so many people. When I look at my photos, the pool area is much smaller than in the pictures I'd seen before my trip. And the pool smelled awful so I didn't go in. That was bad enough, but the food at the restaurant looked strange, smelled awful and tasted worse! We were really disappointed and my parents complained. The hotel had looked so fantastic, but it was a nightmare! It makes me wonder who wrote all the positive ratings …

△ 2 Writing about a great destination → Help with Station 1, p. 104/6b)

The adjectives and the nouns below might be able to give you ideas for your text:

Adjectives:
comfortable | delicious | amazing | awesome | excellent | fantastic | gigantic | massive | interesting | colorful | great | funny | cool | friendly | extreme

Nouns:
destination | view | scenery | hotel | pool | bed | restaurant | staff[1] | food | sports equipment | instructors | beach | market | downtown

△ 3 A scary house → Help with Options, p. 107/12, Option A

The word bank below can give you some ideas for your text on the Winchester Mystery House. Lots of things can happen in a haunted house!

Word bank

Things that can happen:
hear footsteps[2] behind you | feel a cold wind when all the windows are closed | lights suddenly go out | feel something cold on your skin[3] | see a shadow where nobody is really standing | see a ghost / a person who wasn't there a moment before | hear a strange sound / a voice / a gunshot[4] | see a door close / open by itself

How you feel:
shocked | scared to death | afraid | unable to move | in a state of panic[5]

What you do:
try to run away | not move | shout for help | switch on a flashlight[6] / grab your friend's arm | ask if he/she saw that too | get out as fast as possible | take a photo | call a friend

1 **staff** [stɑːf] Personal | 2 **footstep** ['fʊtstep] Schritt | 3 **skin** [skɪn] Haut | 4 **gunshot** ['gʌnʃɒt] Gewehrschuss | 5 **state of panic** [ˌsteɪt‿əv 'pænɪk] Panikzustand | 6 **flashlight** ***(AE)*** ['flæʃlaɪt] Taschenlampe

Unit 4

△ 1 Whale[1] watching
→ After Station 1, p. 113/3

*Read the following text and decide if you need **the**, **a/an** or **no article**.*

[1] Pacific Ocean is famous for its sea life: [2] whales and [3] seals[2] are just some of [4] animals you can see if you go on [5] whale watching tour by [6] boat. For many people who come to Seattle, [7] whales everyone wants to see the most are the orcas. [8] exciting boat tour like this wouldn't be complete without [9] *really* good photo of [10] orca. So don't forget [11] camera! [12] best thing: Most of [13] tour organizers in the Seattle area promise that you can come again [14] next day for free if no whales were spotted[3] during your tour.

△ 2 The tourist board competition
→ After Station 1, p. 114/4

*It wasn't easy for the Seattle tourist board to decide which text they wanted to use for their leaflet. Read the dialogue and decide if you need a **definite article** or not:*

Kate: What we want for our leaflet is a text about [1] excitement and [2] fun.

Luis: I agree, but I don't think [3] fun that Mark's text talks about is what we're looking for. It's all about [4] kind of excitement you feel on [5] paddleboard on Elliot Bay when those big cruise ships[4] come in. He has no idea of [6] danger he was in when he took that selfie with [7] ship in [8] background!

Kate: Yeah, you're right. Some teenagers have a different idea of [9] danger than adults. – But what about Jenna's text here? She loves [10] nature and [11] water.

Luis: Yeah, this photo of her on her paddleboard is much better than Mark's. It's more peaceful[5], but cool too; not boring. I mean, her picture shows how [12] life in Seattle can offer you [13] peace and [14] fun at the same time.

Kate: OK, but we also need a word about [15] entertainment. Wait – she talks about the Seahawks games! And [16] picture of her with her friends is perfect!

Luis: Well, that really is [17] best entertainment I can think of here in Seattle!

Kate: We've got our winner then. Jenna's text sounds like she's in [18] love with Seattle!

▲ 3 My abstract word cloud
→ After Station 1, p. 114/4

*Choose one of the **abstract nouns** from Ex. 4 on p. 114. Then follow these steps:*

1. Write a short text (5–6 sentences) about your word and what it means to you. Use some other abstract nouns too.
2. Pick the words out of your text that you think are the key words about your abstract noun. Then arrange them in a word cloud like the example on the right for the word 'nature'.

1 whale [weɪl] Wal | **2 seal** [si:l] Seehund | **3 to spot** [spɒt] sichten | **4 cruise ship** ['kru:z ˌʃɪp] Kreuzfahrtschiff | **5 peaceful** ['pi:sfl] friedlich

△ 4 Nature lover or city person? → Help with Station 1, p. 115/7

This list of activities can give you ideas for questions about nature lovers and city people:

love great places to shop | enjoy national parks | like to have lots of movie theaters in the area | hate crowds / enjoy peace and calm | be where the action is | spend time in open spaces with few people | prefer watching TV | spend weekends with computer games | do a lot of outdoor activities | like long walks | like museums | hate bad weather | love being comfortable on the sofa | like tall buildings | want to see wild animals

△ 5 Understanding the legend → Help with Station 2, p. 116/8b)

These phrases can help you to explain why the legend is still important today:

tell stories as a part of their culture | be close to nature | depend on fishing to survive | understand how important salmon is | be thankful for the fish as food | show gratitude | teach next generation to respect nature

△ 6 Leaving the reservation → Help with Station 2, p. 117/9b)

Read this blog post by a Native American named Lisa from the Seattle area.
Some of the things she experienced might be the things Koi is thinking about now:

On my first day at the new school, my head told me, "This is where you should be, this is a great new school. This is your big chance!" But my heart told me, "You're only 12 years old; don't you want to be with your old friends at your old school?" But I listened to my head and went to the new school, and I was really worried that first day:
– Will I be smart enough for all the different subjects?
– What will the rich white kids wear? Will they laugh at my clothes?
– Will I be able to remember the teachers' names, and all the students' names? (My new school was MUCH, MUCH BIGGER than my old one!)
– What will I do if the other students are mean to me and say rude things?

When I look back (I'm 20 now), I can't believe how worried I was. Sure, it wasn't easy. But I always just said to myself: "You never know until you try" and "Just be yourself". And everything was fine! 😀 (Well, almost everything. But nothing is ever perfect, is it?)
--Lisa

△ 7 Comparing the legend and the news report → Help with Station 2, p. 117/10

Which of these characteristics are typical of a legend, which ones are typical of a news report? Use them to talk about the texts on pp. 116–117.

present facts | talk about adventures | mention places, dates and names | talk about heroes | be about mythical[1] figures | give detailed information | talk about real events | use lots of adjectives and adverbs to describe things | use a factual / fictional style

1 **mythical** ['mɪθɪkl] mythisch

△ 8 A walk in the woods → After Station 2, p. 118/13

*Find the **transitive** and **intransitive verbs** in the text. Sort them into your grid from Ex. 12 on p. 118.*

Bill loves long walks through the woods. One day he decided to walk the Appalachian Trail, one of the longest hiking trails in the world – it's about 2,400 miles long! It takes months to hike the whole trail, which leads through a number of eastern states like Pennsylvania, Virginia and Georgia. Along the trail, hikers can sleep in shelters[1] which are open on one side. You have to be careful not to leave food outside the shelters because of the bears. (If you see one, don't try to save your food!) Hikers must have enough food and drink for several days because the trail doesn't take you through villages and cities – only through the woods! (But you can of course stop on the way and leave the trail for a hotel, if you want.) So Bill and a friend left early in March, and the greatest adventure of their lives began. For weeks, they followed the trail through the woods. But finally, when the trail crossed a national road, they realized they had had enough and stopped a car to take them into the next village.

▲ 9 Walking the Pacific Crest Trail → After Station 2, p. 118/13

*The Pacific Crest Trail takes you along the West Coast and through Mount Rainier National Park. Go back to p. 115 and use the information there to write a short text on what could happen to you if you hiked a trail in Mount Rainier National Park. (If you have more information about the area, use that too.) Use **transitive** and **intransitive** verbs.*

△ 10 Things to worry about → After Station 2, p. 119/15

*Before Bill left for the Appalachian Trail, he discussed things with his wife – who didn't like the idea. Use the **future perfect** and the phrases below to write down their discussion. Decide if you need **will / won't / might / mightn't**.*

Example: Bill: When I come back in September, **I'll have slept** in shelters most of the time.
Wife: You **won't have slept** in shelters, I think **you'll have slept** in hotels.

sleep in shelters / sleep in hotels ✔ | cook our own meals every night at the campfire[2] / try to find restaurants as often as possible | see some cougars / see lots of trees | enjoy the spring sun / get caught in bad weather | follow the blazes[3] that mark the trail / lose your way again and again | meet lots of other hikers / be very lonely | admire[4] the wildlife / survive a bear attack | discover how beautiful the mountains are / find out how heavy your bag is

1 **shelter** ['ʃeltə] Hütte; Unterstand | 2 **campfire** ['kæmpfaɪə] Lagerfeuer | 3 **blaze** [bleɪz] Wegmarkierung | 4 **to admire** [əd'maɪə] bewundern

Reading skills

S1 Schnelllesetechniken

Wenn du eine Aufgabe zu einem Text bekommst oder bestimmte Informationen suchst, liest du dir den Text ganz gezielt durch. Die folgenden Techniken können dir helfen, wenn die Zeit begrenzt ist:

Skimming („den Rahm abschöpfen")	Scanning („maschinell durchsuchen")
Wenn du danach gefragt wirst, worum es in einem Text geht, sollst du ihn nicht einfach nacherzählen, sondern nur das Wichtigste *(gist)* zusammenfassen. Dazu kannst du den ganzen Text überfliegen und darauf achten, ob bestimmte Wörter *(key words)* oder Personen häufiger vorkommen. Auch die Überschrift oder Bilder können dir helfen einzuschätzen, was wichtig ist und was nicht. Diese Art des Schnelllesens nennt man *skimming*.	Wenn du nach bestimmten Einzelheiten *(details)* in einem Text gefragt wirst, musst du ihn überfliegen und die Stellen mit den wichtigen Informationen finden. Dazu suchst du gezielt nach passenden Stichwörtern *(key words)*. Sie helfen dir dabei herauszufinden, welche Teile du genauer lesen solltest, um die gesuchten Informationen zu erhalten. Diese Art des Überfliegens nennt man auch *scanning*.

S2 Gliederung als Hilfe

Im geliehenen Buch darfst du das zwar nicht, aber auf Kopien oder in Arbeitsheften solltest du dir angewöhnen, wichtige Stellen in Texten zu markieren und Randnotizen zu machen (z. B. Fragen oder Anmerkungen). Verwende am besten verschiedene Farben:

Markiere z. B. wichtige inhaltliche Punkte grün und Informationen zu den Figuren / Charakteren blau. Diejenigen Wörter, die du nachschlagen musst, solltest du auch hervorheben. Du kannst sie unterstreichen und die richtige Übersetzung am Rand notieren. So fällt dir das erneute Lesen leichter.

Um einen Text besser zu verstehen, kann es dir auch helfen, ihn in mehrere Abschnitte zu gliedern. Orientiere dich dabei z. B. an Absätzen und inhaltlichen Punkten, die du dir markiert hast. Überlege anschließend, was in den einzelnen Teilen jeweils das Wichtigste ist und formuliere passende Überschriften. Dies erleichtert es dir, Texte zusammenzufassen oder *Mediation*-Aufgaben zu lösen.

S3 Umgang mit neuen Wörtern

Viele Wörter in einem Text kannst du verstehen, obwohl du sie noch nicht gelernt hast. Die folgenden Tipps können dir dabei helfen:

Ähnlichkeit mit Wörtern, die du schon kennst

Oft haben verwandte Wörter den gleichen Stamm, aber andere Präfixe oder Suffixe. Wenn du z. B. *usual* schon kennst, wirst du *unusual* sicher verstehen. Und wenn du das Wort *guide* als Nomen kennst, kannst du dir bestimmt denken, was das Verb *to guide* oder die Zusammensetzung *travel guide bedeutet.*

Ähnlichkeit mit Wörtern, die du aus einer anderen Sprache kennst

Viele englische Wörter gibt es genauso oder ähnlich auch im Deutschen, z. B. *computer* oder *hobby*. Manchmal hilft dir auch ein Wort, das du aus einer anderen Sprache kennst, ein englisches Wort zu verstehen, z. B. weil es ähnlich geschrieben wird oder ähnlich klingt.

Verstehen der Wörter im Zusammenhang

Manchmal kannst du dir anhand eines Bildes oder einer Überschrift denken, was ein Wort in einem Text bedeutet. Und wenn du alle Wörter in einem Satz verstehst außer einem, kann dieses oft nur eine bestimmte Bedeutung haben. Was bedeutet z. B. *ridiculous* in folgendem Satz: *That's the silliest thing I've ever heard. It's **ridiculous**!*

Auf den Zusammenhang musst du auch achten, wenn du Wörter im Wörterbuch nachschlägst, denn dort findest du meist mehrere Bedeutungen für ein Wort. Schau dir die folgenden Beispiele an:

*Take the second street on the **right**. That's the **right** way for the station.*
*I haven't got **time** to sit and chat today. We can chat when I come next **time**.*
*This is a very small **room**. There's **room** for only one bed.*

S4 Wichtige Merkmale von literarischen Texten erkennen

Story

Wenn du eine Geschichte genauer liest oder analysierst, solltest du nicht nur über die Handlung *(plot)* selbst nachdenken, sondern auch darüber, wie die Geschichte erzählt wird. Zu den wichtigsten Erzähltechniken *(narrative techniques)* gehören:

Atmosphere / Mood	Bestimmte Wörter und Beschreibungen schaffen in einer Geschichte eine gewisse Stimmung *(atmosphere* oder *mood)*. Stimmung entsteht z. B. dadurch, dass die fünf Sinne *(five senses)* angesprochen werden: Wenn man liest, was die Figuren sehen, hören, riechen, schmecken und fühlen, ist es leichter, sich in sie hineinzuversetzen.
Climax	Der Höhepunkt *(climax)* ist der Hauptwendepunkt in einer Geschichte. Die Spannung ist hier am höchsten. Die Hauptfigur befindet sich oft in einer schwierigen Situation und macht Veränderungen durch, sie wird z. B. stärker oder selbstbewusster. Siehe auch *turning point*.

Flashback	Eine Rückblende *(flashback)* erzählt Ereignisse, die vor einem bestimmten Zeitpunkt in der Geschichte stattgefunden haben. So wird z. B. die Erinnerung einer Figur an etwas Vergangenes beschrieben.
Narrative perspective	Die Wirkung, die eine Geschichte auf den Leser hat, wird stark von der Erzählperspektive *(narrative perspective)* beeinflusst. Wer ist der Erzähler und wie ist seine Einstellung zu den Figuren der Geschichte? Was erzählt er und wann? Die häufigsten Erzählperspektiven sind: **Ich-Erzähler *(first-person narrator)*** Der Ich-Erzähler erzählt aus seiner eigenen Perspektive und oft (aber nicht immer) ist er die Hauptfigur der Geschichte. Der Leser und der Ich-Erzähler erleben die Geschichte sozusagen „gemeinsam". **Er- / Sie-Erzähler *(third-person narrator)*** Dieser Erzähler erzählt die Geschichte „von außen". Die Perspektive ist nicht die der Hauptfigur.
Suspense	Spannung *(suspense)* ist eine wichtige Erzähltechnik, um den Leser in die Geschichte hineinzuziehen. Spannung kann direkt in den ersten Zeilen oder aber langsam im Verlauf der Geschichte aufgebaut werden. Sie wird z. B. durch starke, dramatische Sprache oder durch das Zurückhalten von Informationen erzeugt.
Turning point	Ein Wendepunkt *(turning point)* ist der Teil einer Geschichte, in dem eine Figur eine wichtige Entscheidung treffen muss. Diese Entscheidung beeinflusst den weiteren Verlauf der Geschichte. Sie kann für die Hauptfigur und die anderen Figuren gut oder schlecht sein. Siehe auch *climax*.

Graphic novel

In Comicromanen *(graphic novel)* wird eine Geschichte nicht nur mit Worten, sondern vor allem mit Bildern erzählt. Es ist deshalb wichtig, dass du nicht nur auf die Sprechblasen *(speech bubbles)* und die Bildtexte *(captions)* achtest, sondern auch auf die Gestaltung und Anordnung der einzelnen Bilder *(panels)*.

Poetry

Ein Gedicht ist wie eine Zeichnung oder ein Gemälde, das mit Wörtern „gemalt" wurde, daher ist bei der Interpretation jedes einzelne Wort wichtig. Denke daran: Beim Verständnis von Gedichten geht es nicht darum, die „richtige" Bedeutung zu finden – das gleiche Gedicht kann von verschiedenen Menschen ganz unterschiedlich verstanden werden. Wichtig ist aber, dass du deine Interpretation am Text belegen kannst. Dazu ist es hilfreich, auch formale Merkmale zu untersuchen und mit dem Inhalt in Verbindung zu bringen. Zu den wichtigsten Merkmalen von Gedichten gehören:

Rhyme scheme	Gedichte, die sich reimen, folgen immer einem bestimmten Reimschema *(rhyme scheme)*. Typische Reimschemata sind: **AABB** und **ABAB** sowie **ABCB**. Es gibt aber auch Gedichte, die sich nicht reimen, sogenannte *free verse poems*.
Rhythm / Stress	Ein Gedicht funktioniert nur mit dem richtigen Rhythmus *(rhythm)*. Er bestimmt, welche Stelle in jeder Zeile betont wird. Die Betonung *(stress)* liegt dann immer an der gleichen Stelle. Bei Gedichten, die sich nicht reimen, ist es wichtig, dass du selbst entscheidest, wo die Betonung liegt oder wo eine Pause gemacht werden sollte.
Symbol / Simile / Metaphor	In Gedichten spielen Symbole eine wichtige Rolle. Ein **Symbol** *(symbol)* steht stellvertretend für etwas anderes, z. B. für ein Gefühl, eine Idee oder eine Handlung. So ist das Herz ein Symbol für die Liebe. Bei einem **Vergleich** *(simile)* werden Dinge oder Personen mit etwas anderem verglichen, um auszudrücken, dass sie die gleichen Eigenschaften besitzen. Dabei wird *like* oder *as* verwendet, z. B. *Happy as a rainbow*. Eine **Metapher** *(metaphor)* ist ein verkürzter Vergleich ohne *like* oder *as*, z. B. *I'll be the light to guide you*.

Drama

Theaterstücke sind in Akte *(act)* und Szenen *(scene)* unterteilt. Sie sind dafür gedacht, von Schauspielern auf der Bühne aufgeführt zu werden. Es gibt in der Regel keinen Erzähler, der die Figuren genauer beschreibt. Stattdessen wird die Handlung direkt durch die gesprochene Sprache und durch die Darstellung der Figuren vermittelt. Deshalb ist es bei der Interpretation von Theaterstücken besonders wichtig, neben dem Text auch auf die Sprechweise, Gestik und Mimik zu achten. So kannst du Rückschlüsse auf Charaktereigenschaften, Gedanken und Gefühle der Figuren ziehen.

Characters	Die Figuren *(characters)* stellen oft klassische Typen oder Rollen dar. Auf der einen Seite gibt es einen Helden *(good guy)*, dem ein Bösewicht *(bad guy)* gegenübersteht.
Language	In Theaterstücken wird die Handlung durch gesprochene Sprache vermittelt. Die Figuren sprechen in Dialogen miteinander.
Stage directions	Alles, was nicht durch gesprochene Sprache vermittelt werden kann, wird in Regieanweisungen *(stage directions)* vorgegeben. Diese Anweisungen beschreiben, wie die Schauspieler ihre Rolle spielen und wie sie sprechen sollen. Hier werden auch Angaben zu Requisiten *(props)*, Bühnenbild und Licht gemacht. Wenn man ein Theaterstück liest, können die Regieanweisungen wichtige Hinweise z. B. auf die Stimmung der Szene und die Gefühle der Figuren geben. Sieht man das Theaterstück auf der Bühne, wird die Handlung und Stimmung des Stückes durch Körpersprache, Bewegungen, Bühnenbild, Licht, usw. getragen.

Dealing with visuals

S5 Fotos beschreiben und analysieren

Wenn du ein Foto beschreiben und analysieren sollst, kannst du in folgenden Schritten vorgehen:

1. Beschreibe, was auf dem Foto zu sehen ist. Dafür verwendest du das *simple present*. Konzentriere dich zunächst auf Personen oder Dinge, die im Vordergrund zu sehen sind, aber vergiss nicht, auch Personen oder Dinge im Hintergrund zu beschreiben. Wenn du ausdrücken willst, was auf dem Foto passiert, verwendest du das *present progressive*.
2. Nachdem du das Foto beschrieben hast, kannst du deine Meinung dazu äußern oder du kannst erklären, was es deiner Meinung nach ausdrücken möchte. Für die Analyse des Fotos verwendest du das *simple present*.

Useful phrases

Describing photos:
- At the top / bottom you can see …
- In the foreground / background / middle …
- On the left / right there is / are …
- The people in the photo are talking / having fun / celebrating / fighting / …

Analysing photos:
- I like / don't like the photo because …
- The photo is interesting / boring / exciting / … because …
- The photo shows … / represents …
- The photo tries to show … but I think a photo with … instead of … would work better because …

S6 Statistiken auswerten

Mit Diagrammen lässt sich eine Vielzahl von Informationen auf sehr kleinem Raum zusammenfassen. Häufig findest du die folgenden Diagramme, die jeweils einen anderen Schwerpunkt in der Darstellung haben:

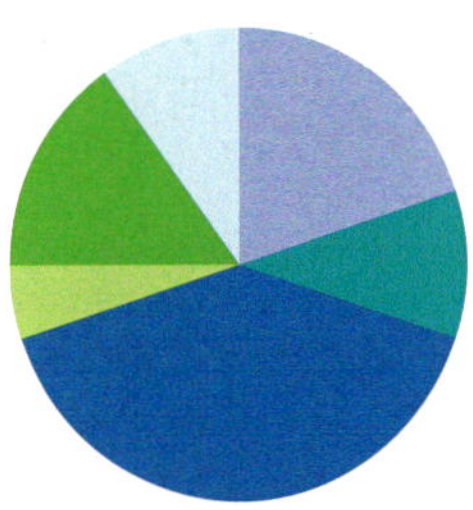

Mit einem Kuchendiagramm *(pie chart)* lassen sich Prozentzahlen darstellen, ausgehend vom gesamten Kreis (= 100 %).

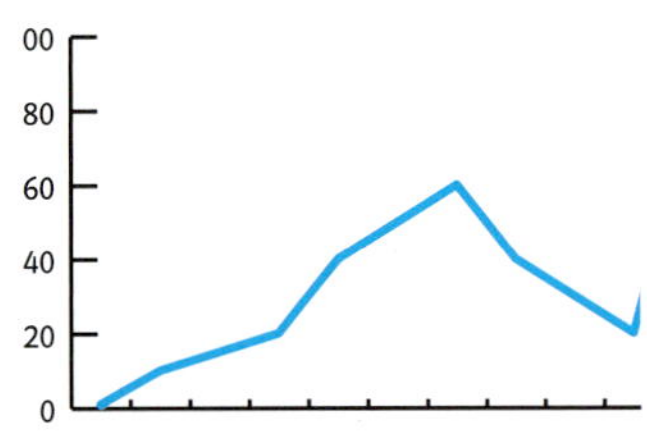

Ein Kurvendiagramm *(line graph)* verwendest du, um eine Entwicklung über einen längeren Zeitraum hinweg darzustellen.

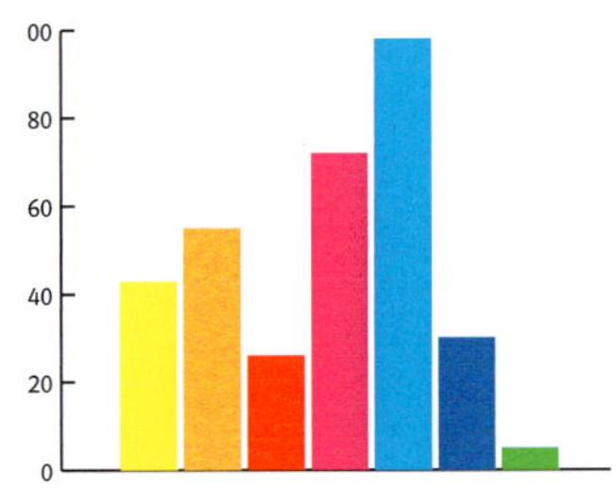

Ein Säulen- oder Balkendiagramm *(bar graph)* nutzt du, um Zahlen direkt miteinander zu vergleichen.

Wenn du deine Auswertung eines Diagramms präsentieren sollst, hilft es dir, schrittweise vorzugehen:

1. Sage zunächst, um welche Art von Diagramm es sich handelt und was es darstellt. Vergiss nicht, die Quelle und das Jahr der Veröffentlichung zu nennen.
2. Beschreibe, was du aus dem Diagramm ablesen kannst.
3. Fasse die wichtigsten Aussagen des Diagramms in 1–2 Sätzen zusammen.

Useful phrases

- The table / bar graph / line graph / pie chart / … was published by … in …
- It's about … / deals with … / …
- The (next) largest group of … | The majority / minority of … | Half of … | Most of … | 30 percent of the people …
- The number of … goes up / grows by … / drops / goes down / doesn't change.
- The numbers / figures show / suggest that …
- We can draw the conclusion that …

Writing skills

S7 Textsorten und ihre Besonderheiten

Du kennst schon einige wichtige Textsorten und ihre Haupteigenschaften:

Print ads	Werbeanzeigen in Zeitungen, Zeitschriften oder auf Plakaten versuchen, den Leser davon zu überzeugen, ein bestimmtes Produkt zu kaufen. Hierzu sprechen sie den Leser direkt an und verwenden emotionale Sprache. Wichtige Elemente sind ein *eye-catcher* (ein Bild und / oder ein Text), ein ansprechender Slogan, weitere Textelemente *(ad copy)*, 1–2 Fotos des Produkts sowie Kontaktinformationen bzw. Angaben, wo das Geschäft oder die Firma zu finden ist.
Blog post	Ein Blog ist eine Art Online-Tagebuch, in dem regelmäßig Beiträge veröffentlicht werden. Es gibt unterschiedliche Arten von Blogs, z. B. Reiseblogs, Nachrichtenblogs oder Musikblogs. Meist sind Blog-Einträge aus der Ich-Perspektive geschrieben und drücken den persönlichen Standpunkt des Bloggers aus.
Dialogue / Film script	Wenn du einen Dialog schreibst, z. B. für eine Filmszene, denke daran, dass du ihn kurz hältst und echte mündliche Sprache verwendest, also z. B. *short forms*, *question tags*, verstärkende Ausdrücke, usw. Achte bei den *stage directions* für ein Film- oder Theaterskript darauf, dass du nur das angibst, was man auch sehen oder darstellen kann. Gedanken kann man nicht sehen, aber du kannst in den *stage directions* Hinweise auf die Gefühle einer Person geben, z. B. durch Anweisungen für Gesichtsausdrücke und Körpersprache.
Diary entry	Ein Tagebucheintrag erzählt und kommentiert vergangene und erwartete Ereignisse aus der ganz persönlichen Sicht einer Person und ist normalerweise nicht für andere Leser bestimmt. Verwende ausdrucksstarke Adjektive und Adverbien, um die Gedanken und Gefühle dieser Person zu beschreiben.

E-mail / Letter / Postcard / Invitation	Achte auf die richtige Anrede für den Adressaten, z. B. *Dear …*, Grußformeln am Schluss, z. B. *Yours / Love / Best wishes*, und beachte die Höflichkeitsregeln. Bei formellen E-Mails oder Briefen verwendet man eher die Langformen, z. B. *I am* statt *I'm*. Denke bei einem Brief an die Angabe der Empfänger- und Absenderadresse und an das Datum.
Flyer	Ein Flyer sollte gut lesbar sein (Schriftart- und größe) und alle wichtigen Informationen enthalten: *Who? What? When? Where? Why?* Formuliere außerdem einen ansprechenden Slogan.
Instructions	Anweisungen sind meist in mehrere, klare Schritte gegliedert. Diese Schritte können von Überschriften eingeleitet werden. Sprachlich werden vor allem Imperative und *phrases* wie *Make sure …*, *You / It must …* oder *Never …* verwendet.
News report	Konzentriere dich bei einem Tatsachenbericht auf die Fakten und spare deine persönliche Meinung aus. Achte außerdem auf eine sachliche Sprache und vermeide emotionale Ausdrücke. Die Schlagzeile *(headline)* sollte direkt auf das Thema des Artikels hinweisen und außerdem das Interesse des Lesers wecken. Beachte, dass in Zeitungsberichten häufig Passivformen verwendet werden.
Prompt cards	Wenn du dich auf eine Präsentation vorbereitest, notiere dir auf Karteikarten nur Stichwörter, die dich an die einzelnen Punkte des Vortrags erinnern. Schreibe z. B. wichtige Namen, Ereignisse, Orte und Daten auf.
Report	Bei einem Bericht ist die Vollständigkeit und Verständlichkeit der sachlichen Informationen das Wichtigste. Er wird im *simple past* geschrieben.
Review / Online rating	Eine Rezension bzw. Kritik hilft dem Leser zu entscheiden, ob es sich lohnt, einen bestimmten Film anzuschauen oder ein bestimmtes Buch zu lesen. Zuerst beschreibst du kurz die wichtigsten Details, dann folgt deine Bewertung, die du mit guten Argumenten belegen solltest.
Story	Wenn du deine eigene Geschichte schreibst, schmücke sie aus und gestalte sie sprachlich abwechslungsreich. Meistens sind Geschichten im *simple past* geschrieben. Wenn du eine Geschichte vervollständigen sollst, muss dein Teil zum vorgegebenen Text passen. Vermeide also inhaltliche Widersprüche. Außerdem sollten sich die Erzählperspektive und die Erzählzeit im Verlauf der Geschichte nicht ändern.
Wiki text	Ein Wiki-Eintrag hat zum Ziel, ähnlich wie ein Lexikonartikel Informationen zu vermitteln. Da jede beliebige Person die Texte schreiben bzw. ergänzen oder abändern kann, ist es wichtig, dass du auch nach anderen zuverlässigen Informationsquellen suchst und dich nicht nur auf die Informationen in dem Wiki verlässt.

S8 Einen eigenen Text schreiben

Es ist wichtig, dass du deine Texte gut planst und zuerst einen Entwurf schreibst, den du dann überarbeitest. So wird es für den Leser einfacher, deinen Gedanken zu folgen und deinen Text flüssig zu lesen.

1. Die Planung deines Textes

Nimm dir für diese Phase ausreichend Zeit. Lies die Aufgabenstellung genau durch und überlege, für wen dein Text bestimmt ist (Adressat) und welche Textsorte verlangt wird (Bericht, Zusammenfassung, Kommentar, usw.). Vor dem Schreiben machst du dir am besten einen Plan: Notiere in Stichwörtern, was in der Einleitung, dem Hauptteil und dem Schluss deines Textes stehen soll. So vergisst du nichts Wichtiges und findest auch leichter eine interessante Einleitung und einen passenden Schluss.

Ein guter Text besteht normalerweise aus den folgenden drei Teilen:

Einleitung *(introduction)*: Hier erfährt der Leser, worum es in deinem Text geht. Du kannst auch eine Fragestellung einführen, die in deinem Text erörtert werden soll.

Hauptteil *(main part)*: Der Hauptteil ist in mehrere Abschnitte gegliedert und beinhaltet die Details (Fakten, Argumente, Beispiele, usw.) zu deinem Thema.

Schluss *(conclusion)*: Deinen Text solltest du mit einem geeigneten Schlussteil beenden. Dies kann eine Zusammenfassung von dem sein, was du im Hauptteil geschrieben hast, oder eine persönliche Äußerung.

2. Der erste Entwurf

Auf der Grundlage deiner Planung kannst du einen ersten Entwurf schreiben. Denke daran, dass du für jede neue Idee einen eigenen Abschnitt beginnst. Tipps für einen guten Schreibstil findest du im folgenden Kapitel (→ S9).

3. Die Überarbeitung

Nachdem du den ersten Entwurf erstellt hast, ist es wichtig, dass du oder einer deiner Mitschüler den Text noch einmal kritisch durchliest. Am hilfreichsten ist es, wenn du den Text mehrmals liest, jedes Mal mit einem anderen Schwerpunkt. Dabei kann dir eine Checkliste helfen (siehe rechts).

Überarbeite anschließend die kritischen Stellen. Wenn du Feedback von einem Mitschüler bekommen hast, sieh es dir genau an und entscheide, was davon du für deinen Text übernehmen möchtest. Wenn du von einem Mitschüler gebeten wirst, seinen Text zu lesen, achte darauf, dass du bei deiner Kritik fair bleibst.

Inhalt:
- Sind alle wesentlichen Punkte enthalten?
- Gibt es keine inhaltlichen Fehler?
- Ist der Text logisch aufgebaut und hat eine klare Struktur?

Rechtschreibung:
- Sind die Wörter richtig geschrieben?
- Stimmt die Zeichensetzung?
- Ist der Text einheitlich im *British* oder *American English* geschrieben?

Grammatik:
- Stimmen die Zeitformen?
- Ist die Formenbildung richtig (z. B. Adjektive, Adverbien, usw.)?

S9 Tipps für einen guten Schreibstil

Je größer dein Wortschatz wird, desto mehr Möglichkeiten eröffnen sich dir beim Schreiben deiner eignene Texte. Lies die folgenden Tipps aufmerksam durch, bevor du mit dem Schreiben beginnst:

Adjektive und Adverbien

Du kannst deine Sätze interessanter gestalten, indem du z. B. Nomen durch Adjektive näher beschreibst. Verben kannst du durch Adverbien oder adverbiale Bestimmungen ergänzen. Vergleiche die folgenden beiden Sätze:

A *I went to the shop.*
B *I went to the big pet shop with my sister last Saturday.*

Achte darauf, dass du Adjektive wie *good*, *bad*, *nice* und *big* nicht zu häufig verwendest. In der Tabelle findest du Beispiele für Adjektive, die du stattdessen verwenden kannst:

good	*amazing, awesome, beautiful, brilliant, exciting, fantastic, fascinating, great, interesting, spectacular, wonderful*
bad	*awful, boring, terrible*
nice	*amazing, beautiful, fascinating, interesting, lovely, pretty, wonderful*
big	*gigantic, great, huge, large, wide*

Konjunktionen *(linking words)*

Ein Text liest sich leichter, wenn die Sätze darin miteinander verknüpft sind. Mit Hilfe von Konjunktionen werden logische Zusammenhänge hergestellt. Vergleiche die beiden folgenden Textausschnitte. Der erste wirkt durch die unverbundenen Hauptsätze abgehackt. Der zweite liest sich durch Satzgefüge aus Haupt- und Nebensätzen und durch Konjunktionen flüssiger. Außerdem geben die vielen Adjektive und Adverbien genauere Informationen und machen den Text interessanter.

A *I went to the shop. I wanted a guinea pig. We looked at all the guinea pigs. I didn't like them. We wanted to leave. A girl came in with a box. She brought back a guinea pig. It was cute! I bought it. I'm happy.*
B *I went to the big pet shop with my sister last Saturday because I wanted to buy a nice guinea pig. We looked at all the guinea pigs, but I didn't like them. Just when I wanted to leave, a girl came in with a box. She brought back a guinea pig which was really cute. So I bought it and I'm very happy now.*

Relativsätze *(defining and non-defining relative clauses)*

Mit Relativsätzen kannst du Sätze verbinden oder zusätzliche Informationen zu einer Person oder Sache einführen:

- *This is the food cart which sells the best hot dogs in New York. (defining relative clause)*
- *The food cart with the city's best hot dogs, which I'd never even heard about until last week, is really worth a visit. (non-defining relative clause)*

Zeitangaben *(time markers)*

Adverbiale Bestimmungen der Zeit können dem Leser helfen, sich in einem Text oder einer Geschichte zeitlich zurechtzufinden. Du kannst *time markers* auf unterschiedliche Weise einsetzen:

- um die Ereignisse zeitlich einzuordnen: *two years ago, last summer, when I came home yesterday, ...*
- um zu zeigen, in welcher Reihenfolge sie passieren: *at first, next, finally, ...*
- um zu verdeutlichen, wie viel Zeit zwischen den Ereignissen vergeht: *for two hours, just five minutes later, ...*
- um auszudrücken, wie schnell oder langsam etwas passiert: *immediately, quickly, it took hours, ...*
- um zu sagen, dass mehrere Ereignisse zeitgleich passieren: *while I was waiting, during lunch, ...*

S10 Eine Zusammenfassung schreiben

Die folgenden Schritte können dir helfen, einen Text schriftlich zusammenzufassen:

1. Lies dir den Ausgangstext einmal komplett durch, damit du weißt, um was es geht. Achte dabei auch auf die Überschrift, denn sie verrät meist schon viel über den Inhalt des Textes.
2. Dann lies den Text noch einmal durch, um weitere Details zu verstehen. Erst wenn du den Text im Detail verstanden hast, kannst du entscheiden, welche Aspekte du in deiner Zusammenfassung *(summary)* erwähnen solltest und welche nicht. Du kannst dir Notizen dazu machen oder wichtige Stellen im Text markieren (wenn er nicht in deinem Englischbuch steht). Beim Verständnis des Textes können dir auch die *wh*-Fragen helfen *(Who? What? Where? When? Why?)*.
3. Entscheide, welche Informationen du in deine Zusammenfassung übernehmen möchtest. Beispiele, Zahlen, direkte Rede, Wertungen oder Interpretationen gehören nicht in eine Zusammenfassung.
4. Schreibe einen ersten Entwurf deiner Zusammenfassung. Beginne mit einer Einleitung, die wichtige Informationen wie z. B. Titel, Autor, Thema und Hauptaussage des Textes beinhaltet. Wenn du einen Zeitungsartikel zusammenfasst, solltest du hier auch die Quelle nennen. Verwende für deine Zusammenfassung das *simple present* und achte darauf, dass du nicht einfach nur den Text abschreibst, sondern deine eigenen Worte findest.

Tip

Denke daran, dass du die Personen in deiner Zusammenfassung ändern musst. Ist der Ausgangstext aus der Perspektive der 1. Person geschrieben („ich", „wir"), musst du für deine Zusammenfassung die 3. Person verwenden („er", „sie").

5. Lies deine Zusammenfassung am Ende noch einmal sorgfältig durch und vergleiche sie mit dem Ausgangstext. Hast du alle wichtigen Aspekte genannt und unwichtige Details weggelassen? Ist dein Text durchgängig im *simple present* geschrieben? Achte auch auf Rechtschreibung und grammatische Stolpersteine.

Speaking skills

S11 Gespräche führen

Es ist nicht immer leicht, sich mit Menschen zu unterhalten, die man noch nicht so lange kennt oder gerade erst kennengelernt hat. Mach dir vor dem Gespräch klar, mit wem du redest. Wenn du dich mit einem gleichaltrigen Jugendlichen unterhältst, kannst du viel informeller sprechen als wenn du mit jemand Älterem sprichst. Überlege auch, ob es kulturelle Unterschiede gibt, und passe deine Sprache entsprechend an.

Die folgenden Schritte können dir helfen, ein Gespräch zu beginnen und aufrecht zu erhalten:

1. Beginne freundlich, z. B. mit etwas, was euch beide verbindet (der Ort, die Situation, usw.).
2. Halte die Unterhaltung am Laufen. Es ist wichtig, deinem Dialogpartner immer das Gefühl zu geben, dass er einbezogen wird. Dazu dienen *feedback phrases*, Nachfragen und *question tags*, wie du anhand des folgenden Beispiels sehen kannst:

   Then we went to the new shoe shop in town, you know. And there were these amazing trainers – I showed you a photo, didn't I? Guess what Linda said when she saw them!

   Wenn du etwas nicht verstehst, frage höflich nach *(What was that you mentioned about …? Sorry, I didn't catch what you just said about …)*. Wenn du etwas nicht sagen kannst, weil dir der nötige Wortschatz fehlt, versuche es zu umschreiben oder bitte deinen Gesprächspartner um Hilfe.
3. Beende das Gespräch so freundlich, wie du es angefangen hast, und verabschiede dich. Vergiss nicht, dich zu bedanken, wenn du um Hilfe gebeten hast.

In vielen Situationen des täglichen Lebens – im Klassenzimmer, mit Freunden, in der Familie – hast du es in Diskussionen mit unterschiedlichen Meinungen zu tun. Umso wichtiger ist es, Kompromisse zu finden. Die *useful phrases* können dir helfen, typische Diskussionssituationen zu meistern.

Tip

Lass dich nicht verunsichern, wenn du beim Sprechen ins Stocken gerätst. In der gesprochenen Sprache ist es normal, dass Pausen, unvollständige Sätze, Wiederholungen oder Füllwörter vorkommen: *Well, I – I really don't know. It's – er, maybe you want to …?*

Useful phrases

Asking for an opinion: How do you feel about …? | What do you think about …?
Making a suggestion: Why don't we …? | I've got an idea. Can we …? | If we did it this way, we could …
Agreeing: Yes, we should do that. | No, I don't mind doing that.
Disagreeing: You've got a point but … | I don't think that's a good idea. It would be better to …
Finding a compromise: Can we meet halfway? | If we did it this way, we could …

S12 Eine Präsentation vorbereiten und halten

Ob in der Schule oder später im Beruf, die Fähigkeit, eine gut vorbereitete und klar strukturierte Präsentation zu halten, spielt eine wichtige Rolle. Die folgenden Schritte können dir bei der Vorbereitung und Durchführung deiner Präsentation helfen:

1. Recherchiere Informationen zu deinem Thema und strukturiere sie, indem du z. B. eine Gliederung anlegst.
2. Überlege dir, mit welchem Material du deine Präsentation unterstützen willst. Gestalte dein Poster / deine Folie / dein Handout.
3. Bereite deine Präsentation vor, indem du nummerierte Karteikarten *(prompt cards)* anlegst, auf denen du dir die wichtigsten Punkte in Stichworten notierst.
4. Übe deine Präsentation zu Hause vor dem Spiegel oder vor einem kleinen Publikum (Eltern, Großeltern, Freunde). Stoppe die Zeit, die du brauchst, damit du bei deiner Präsentation nicht in Zeitnot gerätst.
5. Wenn du deine Präsentation hältst, achte darauf, dass du die Aufmerksamkeit aller Zuhörer hast. Dann erkläre kurz, worüber du sprechen wirst und wie deine Präsentation aufgebaut ist. Sprich langsam und möglichst frei. Verwende deine *prompt cards* nur als Hilfestellung. Beende deine Präsentation mit einer kurzen Zusammenfassung der wichtigsten Punkte. Bedanke dich fürs Zuhören und frage nach, ob deine Zuhörer Fragen haben.

Useful phrases

- My presentation is about … | Today I'll talk about … | First I'd like to talk about … Then …
- Here's a new word. It's … in German.
- On my poster you can see … | The mind map shows … | I've prepared a handout for you.
- That's the end of my presentation. Do you have any questions?
- Thanks for listening.

Mediation skills

S13 Bearbeitung von *Mediation*-Aufgaben

Mediation ist die Übertragung wichtiger Informationen aus einem gesprochenen oder geschriebenen Text in eine andere Sprache, z. B. aus dem Englischen ins Deutsche oder umgekehrt. Das machst du, wenn du einen Text für jemanden zusammenfassen sollst, der die Sprache des Ausgangstextes nicht versteht. Gelegentlich kann es auch sein, dass du dolmetschen musst, also zwischen Gesprächspartnern vermittelst, die nicht dieselbe Sprache sprechen. Ganz wichtig: Es geht bei der *mediation* niemals um eine wörtliche Übersetzung *(translation)*!

Lies dir die *Mediation*-Aufgabe gut durch und beachte besonders folgende Dinge:

Adressat:
Für wen ist die Information bestimmt?
--> Je nachdem, wer die Person ist und wie viel sie schon weiß, sprichst du sie unterschiedlich an.

Zweck:
Wozu benötigt die Person die Information?
--> Du musst nur die Informationen wiedergeben, die für den Adressaten in der jeweiligen Situation wichtig sind. Alles andere kannst du weglassen. Es kann aber auch vorkommen, dass du Dinge zusätzlich erklären musst.

Beispiel: Dein Ausgangstext ist die Infobroschüre eines Museums. Wenn dein Gegenüber dich fragt, ob das Museum heute geöffnet ist, musst du nicht unbedingt alle anderen Öffnungszeiten nennen. Will die Person den Eintrittspreis wissen, kommt es auf ihr Alter an und darauf, ob sie allein oder mit einer Gruppe unterwegs ist.

Einen schriftlichen Ausgangstext kannst du in Ruhe durchlesen und die wichtigsten Informationen auswählen. Dabei helfen dir die Lesetechniken, die unter *Reading skills* beschrieben werden (→ S1). Formuliere die entsprechenden Inhalte so, dass der Adressat sie gut verstehen kann.

Tip

Achte bei einer schriftlichen *mediation* darauf, dass dein Text nicht länger als ca. 35–40 % des Ausgangstextes ist, ähnlich wie bei einer Zusammenfassung (→ **S10**).

Bei einer Dolmetschaufgabe wird eine echte mündliche Gesprächssituation simuliert. Deshalb musst du schneller reagieren, um möglichst viel von dem sinngemäß wiederzugeben, was die Gesprächspartner zueinander sagen. Nicht ganz einfach ist es, wenn du Durchsagen am Flughafen oder am Bahnhof aus dem Englischen ins Deutsche übertragen sollst, da sie oft unbekannte Wörter enthalten und durch die Hintergrundgeräusche schwer zu verstehen sind. Hier kann es dir helfen, dich auf die Namen von Personen oder Orten, Zahlen, Zeitangaben oder auf andere wichtige Schlüsselwörter *(key words)* zu konzentrieren.

S14 Paraphrasieren

Wenn du wichtige Informationen aus einer Sprache in die andere übertragen willst, kann es vorkommen, dass dir ein Wort nicht einfällt, besonders in Gesprächssituationen, wenn alles sehr schnell gehen muss. Bleibe ganz ruhig und versuche, das Wort zu umschreiben *(paraphrasing)*.

Useful phrases

- It's somebody / a person who …
- It's something that you use to …
- It's a place that / where …
- It's the same as … | It's the opposite of …

Wenn du Zeit brauchst, um das richtige Wort oder eine Umschreibung dafür zu finden, kannst du dir mit folgenden *phrases* behelfen: *Just a second …* | *Let me think …*

Listening skills

S15 Hörverstehen üben

Es ist immer sinnvoll, viele authentische englische Texte anzuhören, z. B. Nachrichten in Radio und Fernsehen oder Hörbücher. Dabei ist es nicht schlimm, wenn du nicht jedes Wort verstehst. Dir wird außerdem auffallen, wie unterschiedlich die Aussprache des Englischen je nach Herkunft des Sprechers sein kann. So gibt es neben Unterschieden zwischen britischem und amerikanischem Englisch auch innerhalb Großbritanniens verschiedene Dialekte oder regionale Akzente. Auch dann ist es nicht schlimm, wenn du nicht alles verstehst. Selbst ein Engländer aus London könnte Schwierigkeiten haben, einen Schotten aus Glasgow auf Anhieb zu verstehen.

Manchmal hilft dir beim Hörverstehen auch die Kenntnis von typischen Textsorten und Situationen. Wenn du die Textsorte des Hörtextes kennst, überlege dir, worauf es beim Telefonieren, beim Dolmetschen, bei Präsentationen, Durchsagen, Radio- oder Fernsehsendungen ankommt und welche Themen jeweils zu erwarten sind. Gelegentlich geben dir auch Bilder Hinweise zur entsprechenden Situation: Wenn z. B. bestimmte Personen oder Orte dargestellt sind, kannst du leichter einschätzen, worum es in dem Hörtext geht. Achte beim Hören auf Geräusche sowie Stimme und Tonfall des Sprechers. In echten Gesprächssituationen oder Filmen können dir Gestik und Mimik das Verständnis erleichtern.

Analog zum Lesen (→ S1) helfen dir beim Hörverstehen die folgenden Techniken:

Listening for gist	Listening for detail
Versuche, das Wichtigste *(gist)* in einem Hörtext zu erkennen und zusammenzufassen. Achte dabei besonders auf Wörter und Themen, die mehrmals vorkommen und vermutlich eine wichtige Rolle spielen.	Versuche gezielt, dem Text bestimmte Einzelinformationen *(details)* zu entnehmen. Achte dabei besonders auf Wörter, die du in der Antwort erwartest, und die Informationen dazu.

Viewing skills

S16 Wichtige filmische Mittel

Genre

Es gibt viele unterschiedliche Arten von Filmen, man nennt sie auch Genres. Du erkennst Filme eines Genres normalerweise daran, dass sie ähnliche Hauptmerkmale aufweisen.

Crime

Fantasy

Hier sind einige Beispiele:

Action	In Actionfilmen geht es meist um einen Helden oder eine Heldin im Kampf gegen das Böse. Dabei kommen häufig spektakuläre Stunts, Verfolgungsjagden und Gewaltszenen vor.
Crime	Im Mittelpunkt eines Kriminalfilms steht ein Verbrechen, das meist im Laufe des Films aufgeklärt wird. Dabei gibt es viele spannende Szenen und überraschende Wendungen.
Comedy	Komödien haben eine humorvolle Handlung, die zum Lachen anregt. Häufig werden die Charaktere übertrieben dargestellt und Sprachwitz spielt eine wichtige Rolle.
Fantasy	Fantasyfilme handeln von magischen oder übernatürlichen Kräften. Häufig steht ein Held oder eine Heldin im Mittelpunkt der Handlung.
Historical	Historienfilme spielen in einer bestimmten geschichtlichen Epoche. Häufig basieren sie auf wahren Begebenheiten. Die Kostüme und Requisiten sind meist aufwendig gestaltet.
Romance	In Liebesfilmen steht die Beziehung zwischen zwei Figuren im Mittelpunkt. Das Ende dieser Filme fällt meist positiv aus.
Science Fiction	Science Fiction Filme handeln z. B. von Erfindungen in Wissenschaft und Technik, von Zeitreisen oder Außerirdischen. Sie spielen häufig in der Zukunft und wirken unrealistisch.

Story
Wenn du einen Film anschaust, achte darauf, wo und wann der Film spielt *(setting)*, auf die Besetzung der Rollen *(cast)*, auf den Schauplatz *(location)* und die Handlung *(plot)*.

Audio-visual effects
Ein Film erzählt eine Geschichte mit Worten, aber auch mit Bildern, Geräuschen, Licht, Farben und Musik. Diese audiovisuellen Effekte *(audio-visual effects)* schaffen eine ganz bestimmte Atmosphäre *(atmosphere)* und verstärken damit die Wirkung des Gesehenen. So wird z. B. eine Actionszene meist mit schneller, lauter Musik unterlegt, eine romantische Szene eher mit ruhiger, leiser Musik.

Camera
Die Kameraeinstellung *(shot)* beeinflusst, wie wir Szenen wahrnehmen, ob z. B. Personen oder Objekte als Nahaufnahme *(close-up)*, aus der mittleren Distanz *(medium shot)* oder als Totale *(long shot)* aufgenommen sind.

Long shot

Medium shot

Close-up

Study skills

S17 Vokabeln ordnen und strukturieren

Wörter sind die Bausteine der Sprache. Du musst sie natürlich lernen und jedes für sich verstehen. Zur Beherrschung einer Sprache gehört aber auch zu wissen, welche Kombinationen dieser Bausteine möglich sind. Schreibe deshalb Wörter möglichst immer in typischen Zusammenhängen auf:

- Lerne bei Verben passende Ergänzungen mit *(collocations)*, z. B. *a dry / wet / hot / cool climate* | *to read a book / a magazine / a comic* | *to write a letter / an e-mail / a blog* | *to go swimming / shopping / home / to the cinema.*
- Schreibe dir auf, welche grammatischen Formen auf bestimmte Wörter folgen, z. B. *I would like to swim / to read / to go shopping.* | *I like swimming / reading / going shopping.*
- Notiere dir Beispiele bei Wörtern mit Präpositionen, z. B. *The party is on Friday / at seven.* | *My house is in Dover Street.* | *We're on the road to London.* | *London is on the Thames.*

Deinen Wortschatz kannst du auch erweitern, indem du die Wörter eines Wortfeldes *(word field)* lernst, da thematisch zusammenhängende Vokabeln leichter zu merken sind. Oder du kannst dir Wörter aus derselben Wortfamilie *(word family)* notieren und die Liste mit Hilfe deines Wörterbuchs ergänzen:

Wortfeld:

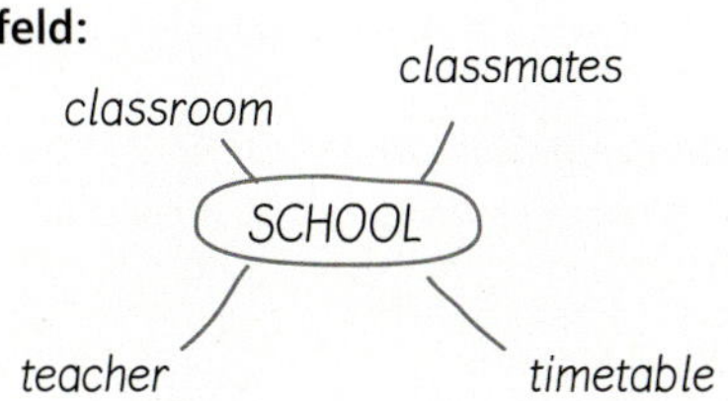

Wortfamilie:

shop – to shop – shopper – shopping
music – musician – musical
immigration – to immigrate – immigrant
colony – to colonize – colonist
information – to inform – informative

Achte beim Lesen unterschiedlicher Textsorten auf hilfreiche Formulierungen *(useful phrases)*. Diese kannst du später in eigenen Texten immer wieder verwenden.

S18 Im Internet recherchieren

Das Internet bietet eine Fülle von Informationen, die in der Regel frei zugänglich sind. Die folgenden Tipps können dir dabei helfen, genau die Informationen zu finden, die du für eine Präsentation oder für die Erstellung eines Textes brauchst:

1. Überlege dir gute Stichwörter, die du in eine Suchmaschine eingeben kannst. Wenn du z. B. eine Übersicht über das amerikanische Schulsystem suchst, kannst du als Stichwort *US school system* eingeben. Je mehr Stichwörter du eingibst, desto genauer sind deine Ergebnisse.
2. Wenn du eine Webseite mit interessanten Informationen gefunden hast, achte darauf, wer die Webseite erstellt hat. Sind die Informationen zuverlässig (Online-Lexikon, seriöse Zeitung, usw.) oder handelt es sich eher um persönliche Meinungen (Forum, Blog, usw.)?
3. Kopiere nicht einfach ganze Artikel aus dem Internet. Mache dir Notizen zu den wichtigsten Informationen und gebe sie anschließend in deinen eigenen Worten wieder.
4. Ordne dein Material und suche gezielt weiter, falls du zusätzliche Informationen brauchst.

Grammar

Liebe Schülerin, lieber Schüler,

in diesem Grammatik-Anhang findest du ausführliche Erklärungen zu allen grammatischen Themen, die in *Green Line 4* behandelt werden. Die Grammatikkapitel (G) helfen dir, die Grammatik zu verstehen, einzelne Punkte nachzuholen oder bestimmte Regeln für Hausaufgaben und die Vorbereitung von Tests und Klassenarbeiten nachzuschlagen.

Regeln sind mit einem blauen Punkt (⊙) gekennzeichnet. Ein Ausrufezeichen (!) bedeutet, dass du hier besonders aufpassen musst. Die englische Zusammenfassung der wichtigsten Regeln findest du in der **English summary**. Mit **Test yourself** überprüfst du, ob du alles verstanden hast. Die Lösungen hierzu findest du auf S. 266–267.

Grammatical terms

English term		Example	*Deutsche Bezeichnung*
(use of) adjectives	G6	The **long** journey on the **huge**, **overcrowded** ship hadn't been **easy**.	*Verwendung von Adjektiven*
defining and non-defining relative clauses	G4	Diego is the boy **who took us around New York**. Diego, **who knows NY like the back of his hand**, showed the girls some great places.	*notwendige und nicht-notwendige Relativsätze*
definite and indefinite article	G9	Erik goes to **school** in Seattle. **The school** he goes to is very modern.	*bestimmter und unbestimmter Artikel*
future perfect	G10	By the time I come back, everything **will have changed**.	*Futur II*
gerund	G1	**Living** in New York is great. I just **love being** here.	*Gerundium*
gerund or infinitive	G3	Stop **shouting**! Let's stop **to have** something to eat.	*Gerundium oder Infinitiv mit* to
infinitive with and without *to*	G2	Would you like **to go** to the movie theater after school? – Sorry, I can't. My parents always make me **come** straight home.	*Infinitiv mit und ohne* to
sentences with linking words	G7	I didn't go to the party **because** we had a Math test the next day. I didn't go to the party **although** most of my friends went.	*Sätze mit Konjunktionen*
past perfect progressive	G5	Emilio was tired because he **had been driving** around New York all day.	*Verlaufsform des Plusquamperfekts*
question tags	G8	This is a cool shop, **isn't it**?	*Bestätigungsfragen*

Unit 1

G1 Living here isn't bad

→ Seiten 14–17

Das Gerundium
The gerund (verb + -ing)

Living in rural Pennsylvania isn't bad. But I really **miss seeing** my friends at home and I'm **scared of changing** too much. What's Pittsburgh like? I'm **thinking of coming** to visit soon. How about **meeting up** there?

Pittsburgh is amazing. I just **love being** here. It's really cool. But I still can't **get used to living** on the 22nd floor! I'm afraid I'm very busy here, so **meeting up** isn't easy right now.

Das **gerund** (verb + -ing) *ist eine Verbform, die es im Deutschen nicht gibt.*
Im Satz kann es verschiedene Funktionen haben. Es wird folgendermaßen verwendet:

1. *als Subjekt* (**Living** here isn't …),
2. *als Objekt nach bestimmten Verben* (I miss **seeing** …),
3. *nach Präpositionen* (I'm scared of **changing** … / I'm thinking of **coming** … / How about **meeting** …).

- *Das* **gerund** *sieht aus wie das* present participle (playing, taking, running) *und wird genauso gebildet. Es gelten auch die gleichen Schreibregeln:*
  try + -ing → trying   liv**e** + -ing → living   get + -ing → ge**tt**ing
- *Im Deutschen wird das* **gerund** *mit dem* ***Infinitiv*** *wiedergegeben:*
  I miss **seeing** my friends.   *Ich vermisse es, meine Freunde **zu sehen**.*
  Living here isn't bad.   *Es ist nicht schlecht hier **zu leben**.*

a) *Das* gerund *als Subjekt des Satzes*

Meeting up isn't easy right now.	*Sich zu treffen ist im Moment nicht einfach.*
Finding new friends can be difficult.	*Neue Freunde zu finden kann schwierig sein.*
Living in America is awesome.	*In Amerika zu leben ist toll.*

- *Als Subjekt des Satzes steht das* **gerund** *am Satzanfang und wird wie ein Nomen gebraucht.*
- *Es kann allein stehen* (**Meeting up**), *zusammen mit einem Nomen verwendet werden* (**Finding new friends**) *und auch eine adverbiale Bestimmung bei sich haben* (**Living in America**).

b) *Das gerund als Objekt des Satzes nach bestimmten Verben*

Matt **enjoys**	**being** in Pittsburgh.	*Matt ist gerne in Pittsburgh.*
Sophie **didn't mind**	**moving** to America.	*Sophie hatte nichts dagegen, nach Amerika umzuziehen.*
Lena **keeps**	**thinking about** her friends in Germany.	*Lena denkt immer wieder an ihre Freunde in Deutschland.*
She **misses**	**hanging out** with them.	*Sie vermisst es, Zeit mit ihnen zu verbringen.*

- *Als Objekt des Satzes steht* ***nach bestimmten Verben*** *das* **gerund** *anstelle eines Infinitivs mit* to, *z. B.* Matt **enjoys being** in Pittsburgh *(nicht:* Matt enjoys to be …*).*
- *Häufig sind es Verben, die allgemeine Vorlieben oder Abneigungen ausdrücken, wie* enjoy, like, dislike, love, hate.
- *Weitere Verben, nach denen ein* ***Verb*** *als* **gerund** *stehen* ***muss****, sind:* keep, miss, imagine *und* suggest.

c) *Das gerund als Objekt nach Präpositionen*

1. ***Adjektiv + Präposition + gerund***

Lena is **scared of**	**changing** too much.	*Lena hat Angst davor, sich zu sehr zu verändern.*
Sophie is **tired of**	**living** in the middle of nowhere.	*Sophie hat es satt, am Ende der Welt zu wohnen.*
Matt isn't **worried about**	**being** bored in Pittsburgh.	*Matt macht sich keine Sorgen, dass er sich in Pittsburgh langweilen könnte.*

- *Weitere Verbindungen von Adjektiv + Präposition, nach denen ein* **gerund** *stehen* ***muss****, sind:* good at, interested in, crazy about.

2. ***Verb + Präposition + gerund***

Lena is **looking forward to**	**seeing** Matt again.	*Lena freut sich darauf, Matt wiederzusehen.*
But Matt doesn't **feel like**	**meeting** up with her.	*Aber Matt hat keine Lust, sich mit ihr zu treffen.*
He is **thinking of**	**inviting** Sophie to a baseball game.	*Er denkt darüber nach, Sophie zu einem Baseballspiel einzuladen.*

- *Weitere Verbindungen von Verb + Präposition, nach denen ein* **gerund** *steht, sind:* talk about, get used to, dream of, forgive somebody for, worry about.

! *Bei* look forward **to** *(sich freuen* ***auf****) und* get used **to** *(sich gewöhnen* ***an****) ist das* **to** *eine Präposition, die zum vorangestellten Verb gehört und auf die das* **gerund** *folgt:*
Sophie can't get used **to sharing** a room with her messy cousin.
She's looking forward **to moving** to Pittsburgh soon.

English summary

The gerund has the same form as the present participle: going, living etc. It can be used …

1. as the subject of the sentence. — **Living** in rural Pennsylvania is OK.
2. as the object of the sentence after certain verbs, e. g. *enjoy, like, hate, imagine, mind.* — Lena doesn't mind **being** there.
3. after prepositions
   a) adjective + preposition + gerund — She isn't worried about **having to** travel for two hours to get there.
   b) verb + preposition + gerund — She's looking forward to **going** to the mall.

Test yourself *Use a gerund to rewrite the sentences.*

Example: What would you like to do today? (be interested in)
→ What would you be interested in doing today?

1. Why don't we visit a museum? (How about)
2. I don't really want to go to a museum today. (feel like)
3. OK, then, what would you like to do? (suggest)
4. Mom tells me every day about the spectacular views from Mt. Washington. (keep)
5. My mom goes there a lot too. (love)
6. She talks about the place all the time. (never stop)

G2 That's the worst thing to do!

→ Seiten 18–20

Der Infinitiv mit und ohne to
The infinitive with and without *to*

Scott and Eva don't **want me to talk** to Henry and Tyler. They say that's the **worst thing to do**. I don't **want to listen** to them. But to be honest I'm **not sure what to do**.

I'm glad I don't have your problems, Matt, but mine aren't much better, you know. I **can** never **meet** friends after school because my parents always **make me come** straight home. They won't **let me do** anything.

Der ***Infinitiv*** *ist die Grundform des Verbs. Im Englischen findet sich der Infinitiv in zwei Formen:* ***mit*** **to** *(to be, to go, to play) und* ***ohne*** **to** *(be, go, play).*
Der ***Infinitiv mit*** **to** *steht nach zahlreichen Verben, Adjektiven und Nomen.*
Der ***Infinitiv ohne*** **to** *wird vor allem nach Hilfsverben* (can, must, should), *aber auch nach anderen Verben wie* let *oder* make *+ Objekt gebraucht.*

a) ***Der Infinitiv mit* to *nach bestimmten Verben***

Would you **like**	to watch the movie on TV this evening?
No, I**'d prefer**	to go to the movie theater.
OK. I'll **try**	to get some tickets.

- *Verben auf die der* ***Infinitiv mit* to** *folgt, können in folgende Gruppen unterteilt werden:*
  1. ***Wünsche und Absichten***, *z.B.* want, would like, hope, decide, expect, offer, plan, promise
  2. ***Vorlieben***, *die sich auf konkrete Situationen beziehen, z.B.* choose, prefer
  3. ***Versuche*** oder ***Bemühungen***, *z.B.* try, learn, manage.

b) ***Der Infinitiv mit* to *nach Verb + Fragewort oder nach* whether**

Direkte Frage	*Indirekte Frage*	*mit* can, should, must, have to *mit Infinitiv* + to
Where do I have to go?	Matt doesn't **know**	where he has to go. **where** to go.
Who can I ask?	He **isn't sure**	who he can ask. **who** to ask.
Should I sit with Henry and Tyler?	He **wonders**	**if** he should sit with Henry and Tyler. **whether** to sit with Henry and Tyler.

- *Nach* **know, be sure, decide, wonder** + ***Fragewort*** (what, when, where, which, whether) *steht der* ***Infinitiv mit* to** *oft anstelle einer indirekten Frage (mit* can, should, must, have to*).*

! *Bei Entscheidungsfragen wird bei der Infinitivkonstruktion* if *(ob) durch* **whether** *ersetzt.*

c) ***Der Infinitiv mit* to nach Superlativen**

Hauptsatz + Relativsatz	*Hauptsatz + Infinitiv mit* to
You are the first person who has said that.	You are **the first** (person) to say that.
I was the only one who ordered meat.	I was **the only one** to order meat.
That's the worst thing that you can do.	That's **the worst thing** to do.

- *Nach* **the first, the last, the only one** *und nach* ***Superlativen*** (the worst thing, the most important thing) *ersetzt der* ***Infinitiv mit* to** *einen Relativsatz.*

d) **Der *Infinitiv mit* to nach Verb + Objekt**

Verb	*Objekt*	*Infinitiv mit* to
Henry and Tyler **want**	**people**	to think about sweatshops and child labor.
They **would like**	**them**	to join their protest at the mall.
Scott and Eva **expect**	**Matt**	to ignore them.

- *Auf die folgenden Verben kann die Verbindung von* ***Objekt + Infinitiv mit** to *folgen:*
  ask *(bitten)*, expect, prefer, tell, warn, want *und* would like.

❗ *Nach* want *(wollen, dass) und* would like *(möchten, dass) darfst du keinen Nebensatz mit* that *anschließen. Vergleiche:*

Matt: Scott and Eva want **me** **to drop** Henry and Tyler.
Scott und Eva wollen, **dass ich** Henry und Tyler fallen lasse.

e) ***Der Infinitiv ohne** to **nach*** **let** ***und*** **make** ***+ Objekt***

Verb	*Objekt*	*Infinitiv ohne* to
Sophie's parents won't **let**	**her**	**meet** her friends after school.
They **make**	**her**	**come** straight home.
Do your parents **let**	**you**	**do** what you want?
Or do they **make**	**you**	**come** home early too?

- *Nach* make *+ Objekt (veranlassen, zwingen) und* let *+ Objekt (zulassen, erlauben) wird der* ***Infinitiv ohne** to *gebraucht.*

English summary

The infinitive with *to* is used …

1. after certain verbs, e.g. *want, expect, decide, would like/would prefer* — Sophie's parents always **want to know** where she is. They**'d like to take** control of her life.
2. after certain verbs + questions words — Sophie **isn't sure what to do**.
3. after superlatives *(the first/last/only one/the best thing)* — She's **the only one to have** parents who are so strict.
4. after *want, would like, expect, ask, tell* + object — She **would like them to relax** more.

The infinitive without *to* is used …

1. after modal verbs *(can, should, must, have to)* — They **should trust** her.
2. after *let/make* + object — They should **let her go out** with her friends.

Test yourself *Complete the second sentence so that the meaning is similar to the first. Use infinitive constructions.*

1. I'll be home before 6 p.m., I promise. — I promise …
2. I didn't know what I could say. — I didn't know what …
3. My parents say that I shouldn't watch too much TV. — My parents don't want …
4. I was surprised when he invited me to his party. — I didn't expect …
5. They always say that she can do what she wants. — They always let …
6. Our football coach says we have to train every day. — Our football coach makes …
7. The best thing that we can do is say nothing at all. — The best thing …

G3 Gerund or infinitive: It depends on the meaning

→ Seite 21

Das gerund *oder der Infinitiv mit* to: *Bedeutungsunterschiede*

Nach einigen wenigen Verben (forget, go on, mean, remember, stop, try) *wird je nach Bedeutung entweder ein* **gerund** *oder ein* ***Infinitiv mit*** **to** *verwendet.*

a) *Nach* go on, mean, stop und try *hängt die* **Bedeutung des Verbs** *davon ab, ob ihm ein* **gerund** *oder ein* ***Infinitiv mit*** **to** *folgt.*

to go on doing sth *etwas fortsetzen / weitermachen*	to go on to do sth *etwas anschließend machen*
They **went on talking**. Sie redeten weiter.	Then they **went on to talk about** child labor. Anschließend sprachen sie über Kinderarbeit.

to mean doing sth *bedeuten*	to mean to do sth *wollen, beabsichtigen*
That **means walking**. Das bedeutet, dass wir laufen müssen.	I **meant to send** you a text, but I forgot. Ich wollte dir eine SMS schicken, aber …

to stop doing sth *aufhören, etwas zu tun*	to stop to do something *anhalten, um etwas Neues zu tun*
Stop shouting! Hör auf, zu schreien!	Let's **stop to have** a drink. Lasst uns anhalten, um etwas zu trinken.

to try doing sth *eine Methode ausprobieren*	to try to do sth *eine konkrete Handlung ausprobieren*
If you can't sleep, **try counting** sheep. … probier's mal mit Schäfchen zählen.	I **tried to sleep** in the car, but it wasn't possible. Ich habe versucht, im Auto zu schlafen, aber …

b) *Nach* remember *und* forget *steht das* **gerund** *für eine Handlung, die* ***bereits stattgefunden*** *hat und an die man sich erinnert. Der* ***Infinitiv mit*** **to** *weist hingegen auf eine Handlung hin, die* ***beabsichtigt ist*** *und* ***noch bevorsteht***.

to remember doing sth *sich erinnern an*	to remember to do sth *daran denken, etwas zu tun*
Sophie can't **remember visiting** London. She was too young. *Sophie kann sich nicht daran erinnern, dass sie London besucht hat. …*	Please **remember to learn** the irregular verbs for the test. *Denkt bitte daran, die unregelmäßigen Verben für den Test zu lernen.*

to forget doing sth *vergessen, wie man etwas getan hat*	to forget to do sth *vergessen, etwas zu tun*
Lena will never **forget having to say goodbye** to her friends in Hamburg. *Lena wird nie vergessen, wie sie sich von ihren Freunden … verabschieden musste.*	Please don't **forget to tidy** your room before your friends arrive. *Vergiss nicht, dein Zimmer aufzuräumen, bevor deine Freunde kommen.*

! *Nach* to begin, to start *und* to like *(im Sinne von „genießen") kann sowohl das* **gerund** *als auch der* ***Infinitiv mit*** **to** *stehen. Die Bedeutung ist in beiden Fällen gleich!*

It started to rain.	It started raining.
I like to go to the movie theater.	I like going to the movie theater.

English summary

Some English verbs such as *forget, go on, mean, remember, stop* and *try* can be followed by a gerund or by an infinitive with *to*, but with a change in meaning.

We **stopped to buy** some eggs from the farm.
We've **stopped buying** them from the supermarket.

Test yourself *After Lena received Matt's e-mail, this is what she wrote in her diary. Put the verb into the right form: gerund or infinitive with* to.

Dear Diary,
Bad news! I got a mail from Matt today and it seems he can't stop (think) about Sophie. I'm sure Matt didn't mean (hurt) me, but … When I told Madison, she said I should try (forget) him. But how? M. thinks I should try (do) yoga! She says she can remember (feel) upset about something once, and it really helped her. But I'm not sure. I'm not really sure about anything at the moment: Should I go on (write) him? Should I tell him how I feel? I don't know. The only thing I know right now is that it's really late and I mustn't forget (set) my alarm clock! Madison's mom is driving us to the mall outside Pittsburgh tomorrow. We want (get) there early and it's two hours in the car, so that means (leave) at 8 a.m.! Oh well, at least we can stop (have) breakfast somewhere on the way.

Unit 2

G4 The boy who ... / Diego, who ...

→ Seiten 42–44

Notwendige und nicht-notwendige Relativsätze
Defining and non-defining relative clauses

Diego is the boy **who took us around New York**. He showed us sights in New York **(which) you would never find in a guidebook**.	Diego, **who knows New York like the back of his hand**, showed the two girls some great places. All the sights were amazing, but Rockefeller Center, **which they visited last**, was just awesome.

Relativsätze sind Nebensätze, die ihr **Bezugswort** *im Hauptsatz a) näher bestimmen (***the boy** who took us around New York*) oder b) zusätzlich beschreiben (***Diego**, who knows New York like the back of his hand, ...*).*
Im Englischen nennt man diese zwei Arten von Relativsätzen **defining** *und* **non-defining relative clauses.**

a) Defining relative clauses

Two girls who / that are spending the day in New York visit a diner.
A boy (who / that) they meet there takes them on a tour of the city.
Some of the **sights (which / that) he shows them** are amazing.

- **Defining relative clauses** *bestimmen ihr vorangestelltes* **Bezugswort** *im Hauptsatz näher. Sie legen fest, wer oder was gemeint ist. Ohne den Relativsatz wäre in den obigen Beispielen nicht klar, von welchen beiden Mädchen, von welchem Jungen oder von welchen Sehenswürdigkeiten genau die Rede ist.*
- *Relativsätze, die ihr Bezugswort näher bestimmen, stehen* **ohne Komma**. *Beim Sprechen macht man keine Pause.*

- **Defining relative clauses** *werden durch Relativpronomen wie* **who** *oder* **that** *(bei Personen) und* **which** *oder* **that** *(bei Sachen) eingeleitet, wenn sie das Subjekt im Relativsatz sind.* *Sind die Relativpronomen* who, which, that *das Objekt im Relativsatz, können sie weggelassen werden (*a boy (**who / that**) they meet …; some of the sights (**that**) he shows …*). Diese Relativsätze nennt man* **contact clauses**.

b) **Non-defining relative clauses**

Rylee and Lea, **who are spending the day in New York**, visit a diner.
Diego, **who they meet there**, takes them on a tour of the city.
At **Rockefeller Center**, **which they visit last**, they have a scary experience.

- *Bei* **non-defining relative clauses** *ist das vorangestellte* ***Bezugswort bereits definiert****.* *Auch ohne den Relativsatz bleibt klar, wer oder was gemeint ist:* Rylee and Lea, Diego *und das* Rockefeller Center. *Die Relativsätze bestimmen daher ihr Bezugswort* ***nicht*** *näher.* *Sie enthalten lediglich eine zusätzliche oder ergänzende Information, die ebenso gut in Klammern stehen oder entfallen könnte, ohne dass die Aussage im Hauptsatz verändert wird.*
- *Relativsätze, die Zusatzinformationen enthalten, werden vom Hauptsatz immer* ***durch Kommas abgetrennt****. Beim Sprechen wird eine Pause gemacht.*
- *Im Gegensatz zu* defining relative clauses *beginnen* **non-defining relative clauses** ***immer mit einem Relativpronomen****: Für Personen verwendet man* **who**. *Für Dinge verwendet man* **which**. *Das Relativpronomen* **that** *ist in einem* **non-defining relative clause** ***nicht möglich****.*

English summary

There are two types of relative clauses: **defining** and **non-defining**.

1. Defining relative clauses tell you which person or thing the speaker is talking about. **No comma** is used between the noun and the relative clause.
   Lea is a German girl **who / that** comes from Berlin.
2. Non-defining relative clauses are used after nouns that are definite already. They give extra information about a person or thing. You always need a **comma** to separate the main clause from the relative clause.
   Lea, **who** is German, is Rylee's cousin from Berlin.
3. Non-defining relative clauses always begin with a relative pronoun. You use ***who*** for people and ***which*** for things. You **never** use ***that***.
   They walked to the Alvin Ailey Dance Studio, **which** is close to Central Park.

Test yourself *Copy these sentences into your exercise book. Underline the noun(s) to which the relative clauses refer (*das Bezugswort*) and add commas where needed.*

1. Last year we visited New York which is the largest city in the USA.
2. We stayed with some friends who live there.
3. They showed us some amazing sights which we would never have found on our own.
4. But they also took us to famous sights like Rockefeller Center which was awesome too.
5. In Times Square we saw the Naked Cowboy who is really only *almost* naked.
6. He is a street performer who has become one of New York's biggest tourist attractions.

G5 How long had they been doing that?

→ Seiten 46–48

Die Verlaufsform des Plusquamperfekts
The past perfect progressive

When Emilio arrived home, he felt tired. He **had been working** hard all day.

Das **past perfect** *wird verwendet, um Vorzeitigkeit vor einem bestimmten Zeitpunkt in der Vergangenheit auszudrücken.*
Mit dem **past perfect simple** (I had done) *betonst du* ***das Ergebnis*** *einer abgeschlossenen Handlung, z. B.* Emilio felt tired. He **had had** a hard day.
Mit dem **past perfect progressive** (I had been doing) *betonst du den* ***Verlauf*** *oder die* ***Dauer*** *dieser Handlung, z. B.* Emilio felt tired. He **had been working** hard all day.

- *Das* **past perfect progressive** *bildest du aus* **had been** + **present participle** (verb + -ing)

Aussage:	He **had been listening**.
Verneinung:	He **hadn't been listening**.
Ergänzungsfrage:	How long **had** he **been listening**?
Entscheidungsfrage mit Kurzantwort:	**Had** he **been listening**? Yes, he **had**. / No, he **hadn't**.

- *Das* **past perfect progressive** *benutzt du für Handlungen, die vor einem Zeitpunkt in der Vergangenheit angefangen haben und bis zu diesem Zeitpunkt andauerten. Hierbei wird die Dauer der Handlung häufig durch eine Zeitangabe betont, z.B.* for ten years, since 2015, all day / week / year, all the time *usw.*

Past perfect progressive + *Zeitangabe*	*Vergangenheit*
Emilio **had been waiting** **for 20 minutes** *... wartete schon seit ...*	before his first passenger arrived.
His second passenger **hadn't been sitting** in his taxi **for long** *... hatte noch nicht lange im Taxi gesessen ...*	when he started to ask lots of questions.

- *Der Gebrauch des* **past perfect progressive** *ist mit der Verwendung des* **present perfect progressive** *vergleichbar. Die beschriebenen Handlungen dauern jedoch nicht bis in die Gegenwart an, sondern nur bis zu einem Zeitpunkt in der Vergangenheit.*

Present (now) ←←←←	Present perfect progressive
Emilio **is** tired	because he **has been driving** around New York all day.
Past (yesterday) ←←←	**Past perfect progressive**
Emilio **was** tired	because he **had been driving** around New York all day.

! *Beachte, dass du das* **past perfect progressive** *wie alle Verlaufsformen* ***nur bei Tätigkeitsverben*** *verwenden kannst (z.B.* wait, work, live*). Bei Verben, die keine Tätigkeit, sondern einen Zustand bezeichnen (z.B.* be, know, belong*) benutzt du das* **past perfect simple**, *z.B.* Emilio had only been at the taxi stand for a few minutes when his next passenger got in.

English summary

You use the past perfect progressive to stress how long an activity continued before another event in the past happened. It is often used with an expression of time, e.g. *since, for, all day* etc.

Last week Diego found a new assistant for his diner. He **had been looking for** help since the summer.

Test yourself *Use the past perfect simple or the past perfect progressive to complete the text.*

After Julia and Andrea from Germany (walk) around Manhattan all morning, they were very hungry. So they decided to go to Diego's Diner, which they (read) about in the guidebook they (buy) the day before. When they got there at 12:30, the diner was already very busy. Some of the people (wait) to get their lunch for quite some time. The girls (learn) English since the age of ten, so they had no language problems. But when they tried to order, nobody seemed to notice them. Finally, after they (try) to get a waiter's attention for about 15 minutes, a friendly Hispanic American came to their table and took their order.

Unit 3

G6 The long, hard voyage to America

→ Seiten 82–85

Die Verwendung von Adjektiven
The use of adjectives

Johan was **thrilled**. At last they had arrived. The **long** journey from Europe on the **huge**, **overcrowded** ship hadn't been **easy**. Many people had become **sick** on the way, and two had even died. Ursula, who had found it **difficult** to sleep on board, now found it **difficult** to keep her eyes open. She felt very **tired**, and her **red** eyes made her look **terrible**. But she was **happy**. After three **long** weeks, they had finally reached their destination. Now the **next exciting new** chapter in their lives could begin.

Adjektive beschreiben Personen oder Dinge näher. Mit der Verwendung von Adjektiven kannst du Texte interessanter und lebhafter gestalten.

- *Wie im Deutschen steht ein Adjektiv* ***vor*** *dem* ***Nomen****, auf das es sich bezieht* (long journey; huge, overcrowded ship), *oder* ***nach*** *einer Form des Verbs* **be** (Johan was thrilled; the journey hadn't been easy).
- *Außer* **be** *gibt es weitere Verben, nach denen nicht ein Adverb, sondern ein Adjektiv steht:*

Verben der Sinneswahrnehmung: **feel, look, sound, taste, smell**	Ursula **felt tired** and she **looked terrible**.
Zustandsverben wie: **seem, remain, stay, keep**	But she **seemed happy**.
Verben, die dem deutschen Wort „werden" entsprechen: **become, grow, get**	Many people on the ship **became sick**.
Verben wie **find, make, keep, see, like + noun / pronoun**	Ursula **found it difficult** to keep her eyes open.

❗ *Beschreiben Verben der Sinneswahrnehmung einen Zustand, so folgt ihnen ein Adjektiv, z. B.* He looked nervous. *(= Er sah nervös aus.). Beschreiben sie eine Tätigkeit, so muss ihnen ein Adverb folgen, z. B.* He looked at me nervously. *(= Er sah mich nervös an.).*

- *Auch Partizipien werden als Adjektive verwendet. Das* present participle *(*exciting, disappointing*) hat aktive Bedeutung und wird verwendet, um etwas oder jemanden zu beschreiben.*

- *Das* past participle (thrilled, excited) *hat als Adjektiv passive Bedeutung und wird verwendet, um ein Ergebnis auszudrücken.*

English summary

You use adjectives to give more information about a noun or a pronoun. They tell you what people or things are like.

Adjectives are used before nouns.	It was difficult to sleep on the **huge**, **overcrowded** ship.
They are also used after verbs like ***be, feel, look, remain, become*** etc. These verbs don't describe an activity, but tell you what someone or something is like or how they feel.	Ursula felt **terrible** and her red eyes made her look **awful**.

Test yourself *Many years later, Johan tells his grandchildren about his journey to America. Complete the text with these adjectives:*

good – bad – frightening – difficult – poor – live – happy – lots – great – sick – seasick – hard – rich – exciting – huge – awful – strange – terrible – fresh – broken

In 1901, we left Germany and sailed over to America on a 1 ship. For the 2 first- and second-class passengers the journey was 3 : they had 4 food, 5 music, 6 air and 7 of space to move about. But for the hundreds of 8 third-class passengers like us, the journey was 9 : Below deck, the food was 10 , the drinking water tasted 11 , the beds were 12 , the toilets were 13 , and there was no entertainment at all to keep us 14 . Some of the passengers were 15 , others were 16 with fever. The air was so 17 that we often found it 18 to breathe. For us, the journey wasn't 19 . It was very, very 20 .

G7 The Pony Express

→ Seiten 86–88

Sätze mit Konjunktionen
Sentences with linking words

In 1860, **when** communication between the Midwest and the West of the US was still very slow, three men – William H. Russell, William B. Waddell and Alexander Majors – came up with a great idea for a fast new mail delivery service, **and** founded the Pony Express. This new service by horseback now made it possible to carry mail from Missouri to California within about ten days. **Although** the Pony Express ended after less than two years, the legend of its brave, young riders and their race across the dangerous mountains and deserts of the great Wild West still lives on today.

Linking words *sind Konjunktionen (Bindewörter), die Sätze miteinander verknüpfen. Texte lassen sich dadurch interessanter gestalten und leichter lesen.*

a) ***Hauptsatz + Hauptsatz***
Konjunktionen wie and, but *oder* so *(deshalb) verbinden zwei Hauptsätze miteinander.*

Hauptsatz (main clause)		*Hauptsatz* (main clause)
The Pony Express started in April 1860,	**and**	it operated until October 1861.
It was a great service,	**but**	the electric telegraph was even better.
With this new technology, messages were sent across the continent instantly,	**so**	the Pony Express service was no longer needed.

b) ***Hauptsatz + Nebensatz***
Konjunktionen wie when, although, because *usw. verknüpfen einen Hauptsatz mit einem Nebensatz und leiten damit den Nebensatz ein. Sie lassen sich ordnen nach:*

Zeit: when, while, after, before, as *(als)*, until, as soon as, by the time	Bill was looking for a job with horses **when** he saw an interesting advertisement in the newspaper.
Einräumung: although, even though, while	The Pony Express offered Bill a job **even though** he was only 14 years old. **While** most riders were 16 or 17 years old, some were as young as 14.
Zweck: so, so that *(damit)*	All riders had to be skinny **so that** the horses could travel faster.
Grund: because, since, as *(da)*	The Pony Express was a great improvement **because** delivery only took ten days.

- *Der Nebensatz kann dem Hauptsatz auch vorangestellt werden und wird dann durch ein Komma vom Hauptsatz getrennt:*
  While Bill was reading the newspaper, he saw an interesting advertisement.

English summary

Linking words are words that you can use to create longer sentences and make your text flow better.

Although the Pony Express was well-organized, it only lasted 18 months.

Test yourself *Use each of these linking words once to complete the sentences:*

while | because | and | but | so | as | although

1. In 1700, about 250,000 colonists lived in North America, ___ by 1775 this number had grown to around 2.5 million.
2. ___ the population continued to grow, the land in the East became very crowded.
3. More space was needed, ___ people began to look West.
4. In 1803, President Jefferson bought large parts of North America from the French ___ offered it to new settlers for little money.
5. ___ many people moved West around this time to farm the new land, others left the East ___ they didn't like the new industries or the cities that were developing there.
6. ___ the journey West was hard and full of dangers, many people saw it as a chance to build better lives for themselves.

Unit 4

G8 You aren't serious, are you?

→ Seiten 112–113

Bestätigungsfragen
Question tags

Bestätigungsfragen sind kurze Fragen am Ende eines Aussagesatzes. Sie kommen in der gesprochenen Sprache vor und entsprechen dem deutschen „nicht wahr?", „oder?" und „stimmt's?". Sie dienen vorwiegend dazu, das Gespräch in Gang zu halten („Keep the ball bouncing"*). Die Antwort, die erwartet wird, ist meist nur eine Bestätigung der Aussage.*

- Question tags *bestehen aus einem Hilfsverb + Personalpronomen. Bei der Bildung der Bestätigungsfrage wiederholst du das Hilfsverb des Aussagesatzes* (is, have, will, can …). *Das Subjekt des Aussagesatzes wird zum Personalpronomen. Ist der Aussagesatz bejaht, wird die Bestätigungsfrage verneint und umgekehrt.*

Aussagesatz (Hilfsverb – bejaht)	Question tag	*Aussagesatz (Hilfsverb – verneint)*	Question tag
Erik is looking for a job,	**isn't he**?	**Tom and Anna aren't** angry,	**are they**?
We can talk about this later,	**can't we**?	**You won't** be late,	**will you**?
Haley has got a twin brother,	**hasn't she**?	**Jake hasn't** met Haley yet,	**has he**?

! *Apostroph + s kann für* is *oder* has *stehen. Vergleiche*:
Erik**'s** talking to Jake, **isn't** he?
Erik**'s** got a twin sister, **hasn't** he?

- *Enthält der Aussagesatz **kein** Hilfsverb, verwendest du **do / does** oder **did**:*
  You **know** what to do, **don't** you?
  Your mom **went** shopping, **didn't** she?

! have / has / had *gilt nur in zusammengesetzten Verbformen* (have got, have done, had seen) *als Hilfsverb.*
They**'ve got** a dog, haven't they? You **have had** breakfast, **haven't** you?
Steht have / has / had *im Aussagesatz als einzige Verbform, gilt es als Vollverb.*
They **have** a dog, **don't** they? You **had** breakfast this morning, **didn't** you?

English summary

Question tags are short questions that are often put at the end of a sentence in spoken English. Negative tags are used after positive sentences, and positive tags after negative sentences.

Question tags begin with the auxiliary verb and are followed by the pronoun form of the sentence subject.

The weather **is** great today, **isn't** it?
You **haven't** seen Erik, **have** you?

If the sentence has no auxiliary verb, *do / does* or *did* is used.

You **like** going to the movies, don't you?

Test yourself *Haley and her friend Ava are shopping for clothes in downtown Seattle. Complete their conversation with question tags.*

Ava: This is a cool store, 1 ?
Haley: Yes, they've got some nice clothes here, but they aren't cheap, 2 ?
Ava: No, but good quality costs money, 3 ? Hey, these shorts look great, 4 ? And they'll go really well with my new top, 5 ? Oh, 40 dollars. You couldn't lend me some money, 6 ?
Haley: You aren't serious, 7 ? Listen, I've got a better idea. Let's go back to the store next door. They had some cool clothes there too, 8 ? And they were a lot cheaper.

G9 For me, excitement is ...

→ Seiten 112–114

Der bestimmte und der unbestimmte Artikel
The definite and the indefinite article

Für den Gebrauch und das Weglassen des bestimmten Artikels **the** *und des unbestimmten Artikels* **a / an** *gibt es im Englischen feste Regeln. Diese unterscheiden sich in einigen Fällen von der Verwendung des bestimmten und unbestimmten Artikels im Deutschen.*

a) ***Der bestimmte Artikel* the**

- ***Mit** dem bestimmten Artikel stehen:*

Familiennamen im Plural	**the** Hilstads
Gebirge, Flüsse, Meere	**the** Cascade Mountains, **the** Alps, **the** Rhine, **the** Pacific Ocean
Ländernamen im Plural	**the** US, **the** UK, **the** Netherlands
Adjektive im Superlativ	**the** most famous / **the** most popular / **the** best (sights)
Musikinstrumente	I don't play **the piano** but I play **the guitar**.

- ***Ohne** den bestimmten Artikel stehen:*

Personennamen im Singular	Haley, Erik, poor Kim
Eigennamen von Bergen und Seen	Mount Rainier, Lake Washington
Namen von Straßen, Städten und Ländernamen im Singular	Fifth Avenue, Oxford Street, Seattle, London, England, Germany, Poland
„die meisten" (ohne Einschränkung)	**Most** people like chocolate. *(= fast alle Leute)*
„die meisten" (mit Einschränkung)	**Most of the** people I know like chocolate. *(= fast alle Leute, die ich kenne)*

- ***Mit und ohne** den bestimmten Artikel stehen:*

  - *Konkrete Begriffe (Dinge, die du sehen und berühren kannst)*
  - *Abstrakte Begriffe (Dinge wie* life, history, friendship, love …*)*
  - *Mahlzeiten (*breakfast, lunch, dinner*) und stoffliche Bezeichnungen (*milk, water, air*)*
  - *Institutionen (*school, church, prison, hospital*)*
  - *Verkehrsmittel*

Wenn die genannten Begriffe im allgemeinen Sinne verwendet werden, stehen sie ohne den bestimmten Artikel:	***Wenn die genannten Begriffe durch eine Ergänzung (oft einen Relativsatz oder* of*-phrase) näher bestimmt werden, stehen sie mit dem bestimmten Artikel:***
I know **people** all over the world.	But I don't know **the people** who live next door.
Life is hard.	I'm reading a book about **the life of** a part-time Indian.
Let's have **lunch** at Arnie's.	**The lunch** I had there last week was really good.
Water isn't a problem in Seattle.	**The water** in Seattle is very clean.
Erik goes to **school** in Seattle.	**The school** he goes to is very modern.
We usually go into town by **bus**.	**The bus** to Seattle leaves in five minutes.

b) *Der unbestimmte Artikel* a / an

- *Der unbestimmte Artikel steht* ***vor****:*

Berufsbezeichnungen	Jack is **a** vet.	Jack ist Tierarzt.
Maßeinheiten (= pro / je)	Two euros **a pound.**	Zwei Euro **das Pfund**.
Zeiteinheiten (= pro / je)	three times **a** day / year	dreimal **am** Tag / **im** Jahr
100 und 1000	**a** hundred, **a** thousand	hundert / tausend

- *sowie* ***nach:***

half	half **an** hour / half **a** kilo	**eine halbe** Stunde / **ein halbes** Kilo
quite	**quite a / kind of a** long way	**ein ziemlich** langer Weg
such	**such a** nice day	**so ein** schöner Tag

- *und in* phrases *wie: in* ***a*** *hurry (in Eile); for* ***a*** *long time (lange Zeit);* have **a** headache *(Kopfschmerzen haben).*

English summary

You use the definite article (*the*) before:

1. nouns that refer to specific people or things. — The sun is shining.
2. names of rivers, seas, mountain chains, plural names of countries and musical instruments. — the Mississippi, the Thames, the Rockies, the US, the guitar

You do **not** use the definite article before:

1. an abstract noun — What does happiness mean to you?
2. names of mountains, lakes, towns, roads, countries and *most* when it means *almost all*. — Mt. Rainier, Lake Ontario, Park road / Most people like ice cream.

You use the indefinite article (*a / an*) before:

1. jobs, units of measurement, time, 100, 1000 — Mr. Summer is a pilot.
2. after *half, quite, such* — I've been waiting for half an hour.
3. and in certain expressions — I'm in a hurry.

Test yourself *Complete what this young Seattleite has to say about his hometown and his dreams. Put in the definite or indefinite article. If no article is needed, write (–).*

I live in Seattle, which is **1** largest city in **2** Northwest of **3** US. For me, it's **4** best place to live in **5** whole world. I just love **6** excitement of the city, especially in **7** summer months. There's always so much to do, from water sports on **8** Lake Washington to whale watching on Puget Sound or camping on **9** Mount Rainier in **10** Cascade Mountains. In Seattle, **11** life is never boring. But I'm not only interested in **12** outdoors, I'm really into **13** music too. I play **14** guitar and I practice at least two hours **15** day. My parents would like me to study to become **16** doctor when I finish **17** school. But that's not my dream. My dream is to become **18** famous pop star. Who knows? Maybe one day I'll be able to turn my dream into **19** reality.

G10 ‹ By the time I come back, everything will have changed ›

→ Seite 119

Das Futur II
The future perfect

Tomorrow I'm moving to my new school. It's going to be a crazy day for me – really exciting but really sad too. By this time tomorrow afternoon I**'ll have said** my goodbyes to all my family and friends and I**'ll have left** the reservation. But I **won't have left** forever – or will I?

Mit dem **future perfect** *drückst du aus, dass eine Handlung oder ein Vorgang zu einem bestimmten Zeitpunkt in der Zukunft abgeschlossen sein wird. Dieser Zeitpunkt wird häufig durch eine Zeitangabe wie* **by the time, by Friday, this time tomorrow** *usw. festgelegt.*

- *Das* **future perfect** *bildest du aus* will / won't have + past participle *(3. Verbform)*

Aussage:	By tomorrow afternoon Koi **will have left** the reservation.
Verneinung:	Of course, he **won't have said** goodbye forever.
Entscheidungsfrage mit Kurzantwort:	But **will** his friends **have forgotten** about him by the time he gets back? – Yes, they **will**. / No, they **won't**.

- *Anstatt* will *verwendest du* might*, um eine Vermutung, und* should*, um eine Erwartung auszudrücken:*
  This time next year Koi might / should have finished school.

English summary

You use the future perfect for an action which will have been completed at a given point of time in the future.

Call me after 2 p.m. I'll have had lunch by then.

Test yourself *Look at Tom's plans for this week. What will he / won't he have done* **by Wednesday***?*

Monday	Tuesday	Wednesday	Thursday	Friday
give presentation on Native American culture	take books back to library	French test / vocab	finish Geography project	speak to Mr. Day about basketball practice

Vocabulary

Im ***Vocabulary*** findest du alle wichtigen englischen Wörter und Redewendungen aus *Green Line* 4. Sie stehen in der Reihenfolge, in der sie im Buch vorkommen. Diese Wörter solltest du lernen und anwenden können. Andere nützliche Wörter (*Vocabulary for instructions and activities*), die du **nicht** auswendig lernen musst, findest du auf S. 264–265.
Auf das *Vocabulary* folgt das ***Dictionary (English – German)***. Falls du ein Wort vergessen hast, kannst du in dieser alphabetischen Wortliste nachsehen.

Englische Begriffe wie *e-mail*, *cool* oder *cornflakes*, die du auch im Deutschen verwendest, stehen nicht im *Vocabulary*. Du kannst ihre Aussprache und Übersetzung aber im *Dictionary* nachschlagen. Das gleiche gilt für Wörter, die auf Englisch und Deutsch fast gleich geschrieben und ausgesprochen werden, wie z. B. *park* oder *partner*.

In den drei Teilen von ***Text smart*** musst du nicht alle neuen Vokabeln auswendig lernen. Die Wörter und Ausdrücke, die im *Vocabulary* aufgelistet sind, sind die wichtigsten und sie solltest du lernen und anwenden können. Alle anderen neuen Wörter aus *Text smart* kannst du ebenfalls im *Dictionary* ab S. 220 nachschlagen.

Abkürzungen und Zeichen

pl	Mehrzahl (Plural)	!	Achtung!
sg	Einzahl (Singular)	↔	ist das Gegenteil von
AE	amerikanisch-englisches Wort	→	ist verwandt mit
coll/ugs	umgangssprachlich	=	entspricht
liter	literarisch	≠	entspricht nicht
5	In dieser Übung kommen die Wörter vor.	*Fr./Lat.*	verwandte Wörter in anderen Fremdsprachen

Englische Laute

Konsonanten

[b]	**b**ed	[p]	**p**icture
[d]	**d**ay	[r]	**r**ed
[ð]	**th**e	[s]	**s**ix
[f]	**f**amily	[ʃ]	**sh**e
[g]	**g**o	[t]	**t**en
[ŋ]	morni**ng**	[tʃ]	**ch**air
[h]	**h**ouse	[v]	**v**ideo
[j]	**y**ou	[w]	**w**e, **o**ne
[k]	**c**an, mil**k**	[z]	ea**s**y
[l]	**l**etter	[ʒ]	revi**s**ion
[m]	**m**an	[dʒ]	pa**ge**
[n]	**n**o	[θ]	**th**ank you

Vokale

[ɑː]	c**ar**	[i]	happ**y**
[æ]	**a**pple	[iː]	t**ea**cher
[e]	p**e**n	[ɒ]	d**o**g
[ə]	**a**gain	[ɔː]	b**a**ll
[ɜː]	g**ir**l	[ʊ]	b**oo**k
[ʌ]	b**u**t	[u]	Jan**u**ary
[ɪ]	**i**t	[uː]	t**oo**, tw**o**

Doppellaute

[aɪ]	**I**, m**y**
[aʊ]	n**ow**, m**ou**se
[eɪ]	n**a**me, th**ey**
[eə]	th**ere**, p**air**
[ɪə]	h**ere**, id**ea**
[əʊ]	hell**o**
[ɔɪ]	b**oy**
[ʊə]	s**ure**

[ː] der vorangehende Laut ist lang, z. B. *you* [juː]
[‿] der Bindebogen zeigt, dass zwei Wörter in der Aussprache verbunden werden
[ˈ] die folgende Silbe trägt den Hauptakzent
[ˌ] die folgende Silbe trägt den Nebenakzent

Der Aussprachestandard in *Green Line* ist *British English*. Auch Wörter, die den Zusatz *AE* haben, werden entsprechend lautschriftlich dargestellt. Bei den Tonträgern und Filmsequenzen wird die jeweils passende Aussprache verwendet.

Across cultures 1 The USA: Country of contrasts

contrast ['kɒntrɑ:st]	Kontrast; Unterschied; Gegensatz	! Notice the stress on the first syllable. *Fr.* contraste *(m)*
the US (= the United States) [ðə ˌju:'es]	die USA (= die Vereinigten Staaten)	*The US* is a country of contrasts.
urban ['ɜ:bn]	städtisch; Stadt-	Towns and cities are *urban* areas. *Lat.* urbs *(f)*
endless ['endləs]	endlos	School lessons sometimes seem *endless*. *endless* → end
sparse [spɑ:s]	dünn; spärlich	I only have *sparse* information on this topic.
populated ['pɒpjəleɪtɪd]	bevölkert; besiedelt	
rural ['rʊərl]	ländlich	*rural* ↔ urban *Fr.* rural/-e
single ['sɪŋgl]	einzeln; einzig; alleinstehend	a *single* room = ein Einzelzimmer not a *single* person = kein einziger Mensch I'm *single.* = Ich bin alleinstehend.
tractor ['træktə]	Traktor	
desert ['dezət]	Wüste	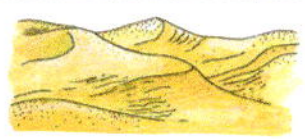
(the) Southwest [ˌsaʊθ'west]	(der) Südwesten; im Südwesten; südwestlich	*southwest* → northwest
temperature ['temprətʃə]	Temperatur	What's the *temperature* today? *Fr.* température *(f)*
degree Fahrenheit (°F) ['færnhaɪt]	Grad Fahrenheit	110 *°F* is about 43°C.
cactus ['kæktəs]	Kaktus	
cool [ku:l]	kühl	The weather can be cold, *cool*, warm or hot.
zone [zəʊn]	Zone	There are different climate *zones* in the US.
immigrant ['ɪmɪgrənt]	Immigrant/-in; Einwanderer/-in	! He's an *immigrant* **from** Asia. He's an *immigrant* **to** the US. *Fr.* immigrant *(m)*; *Lat.* immigrare
European [ˌjʊərə'pi:ən]	Europäer/-in; europäisch; aus Europa	*European* → Europe
cultural ['kʌltʃrl]	kulturell	There are *cultural* differences between people who come from different countries.
redwood (tree) ['redwʊd ˌtri:]	Mammutbaum	= a huge tree that grows in California
foot [fʊt], **feet** [fi:t] *(pl)*	Fuß *(Längenmaß: 30,48 cm)*	I'm 1.82 m tall, that's about 6 *feet*.

	skyscraper ['skaɪskreɪpə]	Wolkenkratzer	The Empire State Building is the most famous *skyscraper* in New York.
	state [steɪt]	Staat; Bundesstaat; Land	The US has 50 *states*.
	to **fly** [flaɪ], **flew** [flu:], **flown** [fləʊn]	hissen	Flags *are flown* on a lot of public buildings and on homes in the US.
	a (day/week/year) [ə 'deɪ/wi:k/jɪə]	pro (Tag/Woche/Jahr)	An apple *a day* keeps the doctor away. = Einen Apfel pro Tag und man bleibt gesund.
	population [ˌpɒpjə'leɪʃn]	Bevölkerung; Population	*population* → populated *Fr.* population *(f)*
	billionaire ['bɪliəneə]	Milliardär/-in	
1	**scenery** ['si:nri]	Landschaft	= what you see around you when you're somewhere with a view, e.g. out in the country
	simply ['sɪmpli]	einfach nur	Americans usually call their country *simply* 'America'.
	dense [dens]	dicht	*dense* ↔ sparse
	in the country [ˌɪn ðə 'kʌntri]	auf dem Land	
	mountainous ['maʊntɪnəs]	bergig	
	flat [flæt]	flach; platt	Countryside with no hills is *flat*.
	gigantic [dʒaɪ'gæntɪk]	gigantisch; riesig	Those mountains are *gigantic*!
	wealthy ['welθi]	wohlhabend; reich	*wealthy* ↔ poor
	wasteful ['weɪstfl]	verschwenderisch	Don't be *wasteful* with water!
	luxury ['lʌkʃri]	Luxus	Wealthy people often spend their money on all kinds of *luxury*.
	to **represent** [ˌreprɪ'zent]	repräsentieren; darstellen; stehen für	*to represent* = to stand for *Fr.* représenter
	to **symbolize** *(AE)* ['sɪmbəlaɪz]	symbolisieren	*to symbolise* → symbol *Fr.* symboliser
2	**harsh** [hɑ:ʃ]	rau; hart	Don't be so *harsh* with him. He already feels bad enough.
	extreme [ɪk'stri:m]	extrem; radikal	
	standard of living [ˌstændəd‿əv 'lɪvɪŋ]	Lebensstandard	In Germany, we enjoy a high *standard of living*.
4	to **become friends** [bɪˌkʌm‿'frendz]	sich anfreunden; Freundschaft schließen	Tristan and Callum *became friends* some years ago.
	vacation *(AE)* [və'keɪʃn]	Ferien; Urlaub	Summer *vacation* at American schools is at least two, sometimes three months.
	dude *(coll)* [du:d]	Mann; Alter *(ugs.)*	Hey, *dude*! What's up?
	awesome ['ɔ:səm]	super; spitze	*awesome* = great
	US [ˌju:'es]	US-amerikanisch	Most *US* teens don't know what it's like to have school uniforms.
	to **have no clue** [ˌhæv nəʊ 'klu:]	keine Ahnung haben	What's the time? – I *have no clue*.

route planner ['ru:t ˌplænə]	Routenplaner	
Brit [brɪt]	Brite/Britin *(ugs.)*	
colonist ['kɒlənɪst]	Siedler/-in; Kolonist/-in	*colonist* → colony *(n)*
corn [kɔ:n]	Korn; Mais; Getreide	
wheat [wi:t]	Weizen	In the Midwest you can see endless corn and *wheat* fields.
to **ride** [raɪd], **rode** [rəʊd], **ridden** ['rɪdn]	fahren; reiten	You can *ride* a bike or a horse.
epic ['epɪk]	episch; *hier:* geil	The party was *epic*!
massive ['mæsɪv]	riesig; massiv; *hier:* super	*massive* = awesome
complete [kəm'pli:t]	vollständig; komplett; völlig	Is your picture of America *complete*?

Unit 1 Kids in America

kid [kɪd]	Jugendliche/-r; Kind	Hey *kids*, let's go swimming! *kid* = child

Introduction

1	**impression** [ɪm'preʃn]	Impression; Eindruck	What is your *impression* of the US?
3	**orientation** [ˌɔ:riən'teɪʃn]	Orientierung; Orientierungs-	At the *orientation* weekend teenagers get information about teen life in the US.
	to **give a talk** [ˌgɪv‿ə 'tɔ:k]	einen Vortrag halten	I'm nervous. I have to *give a talk* at school.
	suburb ['sʌbɜ:b]	Vorort	Wimbledon is a *suburb* of London.
	suburban [sə'bɜ:bn]	Vorstadt-	*Suburban* houses often have lots of space. *suburban* → suburb
	front yard *(AE)* [ˌfrʌnt 'jɑ:d]	Vorgarten	*front yard* ↔ backyard
	shopping mall ['ʃɒpɪŋ ˌmɔ:l]	Einkaufszentrum	
	middle school *(AE)* ['mɪdl ˌsku:l]	Mittelschule *(weiterführende Schule in den USA, Mittelstufe)*	Children at *middle school* in the US are usually 13 to 14 years old.
	high school *(AE)* ['haɪ ˌsku:l]	High School *(weiterführende Schule in den USA, Oberstufe)*	= a school in the US for students between the ages of 15 and 18
	hallway ['hɔ:lweɪ]	Flur; Diele; Korridor	
	hall pass ['hɔ:l pɑ:s]	*Erlaubnis, sich während des Unterrichts auf dem Flur aufzuhalten*	During lessons students are not allowed to be in the hallway without a *hall pass*.
	dress code ['dres ˌkəʊd]	Kleiderordnung; Bekleidungsvorschriften	The school has a *dress code*, so she can't wear such a short skirt.
	restroom *(AE)* ['restrʊm]	Toilette	

Urban vs. rural

urban centers
city life
crowded, densely populated,
not enough space
short distances
skyscrapers, tall buildings, downtown
suburb, suburban

rural areas
country life, in the country
farms, corn/wheat fields, mountains
long distances, endless roads
sparsely populated,
open spaces/lots of space

Write five sentences with these words or phrases.

Station 1: Living here isn't bad

movie *(AE)* [ˈmuːvi]	Film	In *movies*, teen life is often shown as all fun and games.
walk-in closet [ˌwɔːkɪn ˈklɒzɪt]	begehbarer Kleiderschrank	American houses often have *walk-in closets*.
to **be around** [ˌbiː əˈraʊnd]	da sein; zusammen sein mit	There *aren't* many restaurants *around*, just a few.
not until [ˌnɒt‿ənˈtɪl]	nicht vor; erst um/im	My birthday *isn't until* six weeks!
store *(AE)* [stɔː]	Laden; Geschäft	There's a cool new *store* at the mall. Let's check it out!
drive [draɪv]	Fahrt; Anfahrt; Autofahrt	*drive* → to drive
along for the ride [əˌlɒŋ fə ðə ˈraɪd]	mit dabei	My brother doesn't always want me *along for the ride*.
ride [raɪd]	Fahrt; Ritt	*ride* → to ride
curfew [ˈkɜːfjuː]	Sperrstunde; Ausgangssperre	In Germany, the *curfew* for teenagers between sixteen and eighteen is 10 p.m. They have to be home by 10 o'clock.
to **meet up** [ˌmiːt‿ˈʌp]	sich treffen	
downtown *(AE)* [ˌdaʊnˈtaʊn]	im Stadtzentrum	Don't you think malls are boring? Shopping *downtown* is cooler!
to **get used to sth** [ˌget ˈjuːzd tə]	sich an etw. gewöhnen	I don't like to get up early in the morning, but I *got used to* it.
floor [flɔː]	Stockwerk	! What you call the first *floor* in Germany is the second *floor* in the US.
elevator *(AE)* [ˈelɪveɪtə]	Aufzug; Lift	
luckily [ˈlʌkɪli]	glücklicherweise	*Luckily*, he found his money and could pay for his lunch.
movie theater *(AE)* [ˈmuːvi ˌθɪətə]	Kino	Let's go to the movies. – OK, which *movie theater*?
soccer *(AE)* [ˈsɒkə]	Fußball	*Soccer* is becoming very popular in the US.
I'm afraid ... [ˌaɪm‿əˈfreɪd]	Leider ...	*I'm afraid* I'm very busy right now.

	to **keep in touch** [ˌkiːp‿ɪn ˈtʌtʃ]	in Kontakt bleiben	Let's *keep in touch*.
	to **keep** [kiːp], **kept** [kept], **kept** [kept]	*hier:* weiter tun; immer wieder tun	*Keep* smiling, and everything will be fine! = Everything feels better when you smile.
	no wonder [ˌnəʊ ˈwʌndə]	kein Wunder	Your dad is American; *no wonder* your English is so good.
2	**Pilgrim** [ˈpɪlgrɪm]	Pilger/-in	In 1620 the *Pilgrims* left England for America.
	to **practice a religion** [ˌpræktɪs‿ə rɪˈlɪdʒn]	eine Religion ausüben	
	survivor [səˈvaɪvə]	Überlebende/-r	*survivor* → to survive
	Native American [ˌneɪtɪv‿əˈmerɪkən]	Ureinwohner/-in Amerikas; Indianer/-in; indianisch	
	harvest [ˈhɑːvɪst]	Ernte	
	to **give thanks** [ˌgɪv ˈθæŋks]	danken	At Thanksgiving people *give thanks* for the good things in their lives.
	Indian [ˈɪndiən]	Indianer/-in; indianisch	! The terms *‚Indian'* and ‚Native American' are both fine for describing the original population of what is now the US.
	menu [ˈmenjuː]	Speisekarte	
	dish [dɪʃ]	Gericht; Speise	What's your favorite *dish*?
3	**instead of** [ɪnˈsted‿əv]	statt; anstatt; an Stelle von	This year we're going to go on vacation in the winter *instead of* the summer.
4	**social media** [ˌsəʊʃl ˈmiːdiə]	soziale Netzwerke	Why aren't you on *social media* like everybody else? – Why do I have to do what everybody else does?
	to **mind** [maɪnd]	etwas dagegen haben; einem etwas ausmachen	Do you *mind* if I open the window? – No, I don't *mind*.
	in the middle of nowhere [ɪn ðə ˌmɪdl‿əv ˈnəʊweə]	mitten im Nirgendwo	
5	to **find one's way around** [ˌfaɪnd wʌnz ˌweɪ‿əˈraʊnd]	sich zurechtfinden	I know New York very well. I know how to *find my way around* in New York.
	to **be tired of** [bi ˈtaɪəd‿əv]	es müde sein (zu); es leid sein (zu); es satt haben (zu)	I'm really *tired of* cleaning up your room all the time. = I really don't want to clean up your room anymore.
6	**likes** *(pl)* [laɪks]	Vorlieben	
	dislikes *(pl)* [dɪsˈlaɪks]	Abneigungen	What are your likes and *dislikes*? = What do you like and what don't you like?
	to **unpack** [ʌnˈpæk]	auspacken	
7	to **dislike** [dɪsˈlaɪk]	nicht mögen	*to dislike* ↔ to like
	to **dream** [driːm], **dreamt** [dremt], **dreamt** [dremt]	träumen	I *dream* of having my own restaurant one day. = I really want my own restaurant one day. ! *to dream, dreamt/dreamed, dreamt/dreamed*
	to **be crazy about** [bi ˈkreɪzi‿əbaʊt]	verrückt sein nach; abfahren auf	He's *crazy about* posting new selfies. = He loves it when he can post new selfies.

	insecure [ˌɪnsɪˈkjʊə]	unsicher	Meeting new people makes me feel *insecure*.
8	**foreground** [ˈfɔːgraʊnd]	Vordergrund	*foreground* ↔ background

Likes and dislikes

There are different ways to express likes and dislikes. Sometimes you can use the same verb, sometimes there are totally different ways to express things.

I'm **interested in** meeting new friends.	I'm **interested in** new friends. / It's great to meet new friends.
Living here isn't bad / is cool.	**Life** here isn't bad/is cool.
I **like/love** having a big bedroom.	I **like/love** my big bedroom.
I **hate/dislike** sharing my room.	A bedroom on my own **would be great**.
I **miss** seeing my old friends.	I **miss** my old friends.
I'm **scared of** changing too much.	I'm **scared of** too many changes.
I **enjoyed** meeting you.	It was **great** to meet you.
How about meeting up?	**Let's** meet up.
I haven't **got used to** living on the 22nd floor.	I haven't **got used to** our apartment on the 22nd floor.
I **look forward to** starting school.	I **look forward to** my first day at school.
I'm **good at** swimming.	I'm a **good** swimmer.
Don't **worry about** losing your old friends.	Don't **worry about** your old friends; you won't lose them.
I **keep** forgetting your dad is American.	I **always forget about** the fact that your dad is American.
I **didn't mind** moving to America.	A new life in America **was no problem** for me.
I **don't feel like** going anywhere.	I don't **want to** go anywhere.
He's **tired of** answering her questions.	He **doesn't like** it when he has to answer her questions.
I **dream of** going to Australia.	I **dream of** a trip to Australia.
She's **crazy about** going shopping.	She **loves** shopping. / She **loves** it when she can go to cool stores.

Can you think of other ways to say these two sentences?

1. She talked about organizing a party.
2. Stop worrying.

Station 2: That's the worst thing to do!

committee [kəˈmɪti]	Komitee; Ausschuss	*Fr.* comité *(m)*
8th-grader *(AE)* [ˈeɪtθˌgreɪdə]	Achtklässler/-in	An *8th-grader* is a student in the 8th year of school.
period *(AE)* [ˈpɪəriəd]	Stunde; Unterrichtsstunde	At our school, first *period* starts at 8:00 a.m.
geek [giːk]	Außenseiter/-in	Just because a person isn't super popular doesn't mean he/she is a *geek*.
What a … [ˈwɒt‿ə]	Was für ein/-e …	*What a* dilemma!
shopper [ˈʃɒpə]	Käufer/-in	*shopper* → shopping → shop
child labor *(AE)* [ˌtʃaɪld ˈleɪbə]	Kinderarbeit	
sweatshop [ˈswetʃɒp]	Ausbeuterbetrieb	

to **demonstrate** ['demənstreɪt]	demonstrieren	
right [raɪt]	Recht	Child labor goes against the *rights* of children.
11 **whether** ['weðə]	ob	*whether* = if *(in indirect speech)*

Phrases with superlatives

Why don't you come with us? You're **the only one** to stay at home.	Warum kommst du nicht mit? Du bist die Einzige, die zu Hause bleibt.
If you don't want to walk, it's **the cheapest thing** to take the bus.	Wenn du nicht zu Fuß gehen willst, ist es am günstigsten, den Bus zu nehmen.
On the weekends my dad is always **the first** to get up. My sister is **the last** to have breakfast.	Am Wochenende steht mein Vater immer als Erster auf. Meine Schwester frühstückt als Letzte.
My friends are great. They're **the funniest people** to go out with.	Meine Freunde sind toll! Mit ihnen ist es am lustigsten auszugehen.
Don't stay home alone. It's **the worst thing** to do when you're sad.	Bleib nicht allein zu Hause. Das ist das Schlimmste, was du tun kannst, wenn du traurig bist.
Should I stay or should I go? What's **the best thing** to do?	Soll ich bleiben oder gehen? Was ist am besten?

Write three more sentences with superlative phrases.

Phrases with question words

Matt didn't know **what** to think.	Er wusste nicht, **was** er davon halten sollte.
He was wondering **who** to sit with in the cafeteria.	Er fragte sich, zu **wem** er sich in der Cafeteria setzen sollte/konnte.
He wanted to know **where** to go.	Er wollte wissen, **wohin** er gehen sollte.
He wasn't sure **how much** money to bring.	Er war sich nicht sicher, **wie viel** Geld er mitbringen sollte/musste.
He didn't know **when** to use his locker.	Er wusste nicht, **wann** er seinen Spind benutzen sollte/durfte.
He didn't know **whether** to use his own laptop.	Er wusste nicht, **ob** er seinen eigenen Laptop benutzen sollte/konnte.

Write three more sentences with question words.

13 to **prefer** [prɪ'fɜː]	vorziehen	= to like more/better *Fr.* préférer
14 to **control** [kən'trəʊl]	kontrollieren; steuern	My parents *control* everything I do.
might [maɪt]	könnte/-n (vielleicht)	Maybe he'll play well in the match. He *might* even win it!
15 to **argue** ['ɑːgjuː]	argumentieren; streiten	In a discussion, you use arguments to *argue* for or against something.
16 to **clean out** [ˌkliːn‿'aʊt]	ausräumen; entrümpeln	
clothing drive ['kləʊðɪŋ ˌdraɪv]	Kleidersammlung	Let's clean out our attic for the *clothing drive*.

	homeless shelter ['həʊmləs ˌʃeltə]	Obdachlosenunterkunft	= a place where homeless people can sleep
	homeless ['həʊmləs]	obdachlos	
	to **wish** [wɪʃ]	(sich) wünschen	*to wish* → wish
	to **donate** [də'neɪt]	spenden; stiften	= to give money, food, etc. to sb
	benefit ['benɪfɪt]	Vorteil; Nutzen; Unterstützung	What's the *benefit* of a clothing drive?
	pound [paʊnd]	Pfund *(Maßeinheit)*	In the US, people weigh things in *pounds*, not in kilos.
	item ['aɪtəm]	Gegenstand; Objekt	We'll get a few cents for every *item* we donate.
	drop-off ['drɒpɒf]	Abgabe	The *drop-off* point for clothes is in the cafeteria.

Story: Nightmare at the mall!

	nightmare ['naɪtmeə]	Alptraum	= a scary dream
1	**believable** [bɪ'li:vəbl]	glaubwürdig	The novel has *believable* characters. *believable* → to believe
	exaggerated [ɪg'zædʒreɪtɪd]	übertrieben	*Fr.* exagéré/-e
	unrealistic [ˌʌnrɪə'lɪstɪk]	unrealistisch	Your plan won't work because it's *unrealistic*.
	coincidence [kəʊ'ɪnsɪdns]	Zufall	There are too many unrealistic *coincidences* in this movie!
	to **open** ['əʊpn]	eröffnen	He's going to *open* a new sports store.
	to **sign** [saɪn]	unterschreiben; unterzeichnen	Please *sign* the letter. *Fr.* signer; *Lat.* signare
	amazed [ə'meɪzd]	erstaunt; verblüfft	
	scared [skeəd]	verängstigt; ängstlich	This film is scary. I feel *scared*.
	right [raɪt]	direkt	I'm looking for my pen. – It's *right* next to your exercise book.
	cheer [tʃɪə]	Jubel; Hurraruf	
	dizzy ['dɪzi]	schwindelig	Some people feel *dizzy* if they look down from a skyscraper.
	down [daʊn]	nieder	*Down* with child labor!
	to **escape (from)** [ɪ'skeɪp frəm]	fliehen; entfliehen; flüchten; entkommen	= to run away from sth or sb
	protester ['prəʊtestə]	Protestierende/-r; Demonstrant/-in	! Be careful with the pronunciaton.
	to **touch** [tʌtʃ]	berühren; antippen	Don't *touch* the dog, it bites.
	troublemaker ['trʌblmeɪkə]	Unruhestifter/-in	*troublemaker* → trouble
	to **leave sb alone** [ˌli:v‿ə'ləʊn]	jmdn. in Ruhe lassen	*Leave me alone!*
	obvious ['ɒbviəs]	offensichtlich	= easy to see or understand *obvious* = clear
	twice [twaɪs]	zweimal	= two times

2	**mess** [mes]	Unordnung; Durcheinander; Schweinerei	There's a *mess* in my room. I'll have to tidy it up.
	to **mix** [mɪks]	zusammenpassen	These colors don't *mix*.

Action USA! Go on, text her!

	Go on! [ˌɡəʊ‿ˈɒn]	Los!	*Go on*, don't wait too long!
1	**attractive** [əˈtræktɪv]	attraktiv	! Be careful with the word stress.
	boyfriend [ˈbɔɪfrend]	Freund *(in einer Paarbeziehung)*	Is he just a friend, or your *boyfriend*?
	attitude [ˈætɪtjuːd]	Haltung; Einstellung	Your *attitude* to/towards life is the way you feel about it. *Fr.* attitude *(f)*
2	to **overdo** [əʊvəˈduː], **overdid** [əʊvəˈdɪd], **overdone** [əʊvəˈdʌn]	übertreiben; zu weit gehen	Don't you think that's *overdoing* it? I mean, it's a great party outfit, but for school?
3	**date** [deɪt]	Verabredung; Date	Have you got a *date* for the dance yet?

Skills: How to write in the appropriate style

1	**content** [ˈkɒntent]	Inhalt	= the information or ideas e.g. in a book, film, photo, etc.
	toothpaste [ˈtuːθpeɪst]	Zahnpasta	
3	**ironic** [ˌaɪˈrɒnɪk]	ironisch	I love writers with an *ironic* sense of humor.
	informative [ɪnˈfɔːmətɪv]	informativ	Brochures are usually *informative*.
	natural [ˈnætʃrl]	natürlich; Natur-	! Be careful with the pronunciation. *natural* → nature
	individual [ˌɪndɪˈvɪdʒuəl]	Einzelperson; Einzelne/-r; Individuum	Each person is an *individual* with his/her own personality.
	pose [pəʊz]	Pose; Haltung	
	season [ˈsiːzn]	Saison; Jahreszeit	Summer is the warmest *season*.
	championship [ˈtʃæmpiənʃɪp]	Meisterschaft	She was the youngest player ever to win the national *championship*.

Unit task: An American-style yearbook

double [ˈdʌbl]	Doppel-; zweimal	The pictures don't fit on one page, I'll need a *double* page for them.
concert [ˈkɒnsət]	Konzert	

Important differences

	AE		BE	
Different spelling	cent**er**		cent**re**	
	Dr.		Dr	
	Mr./Mrs./Ms.		Mr/Mrs/Ms	
	neighb**o**r(hood)		neighb**ou**r(hood)	
	to symboli**z**e		to symboli**s**e	
Different words	apartment	mom	flat	mum
	downtown	movie	city centre	film
	elevator	movie theater	lift	cinema
	front yard	period	garden	lesson
	high school	restroom	grammar school	bathroom, toilets
	middle school	soccer	comprehensive school	football
	8th-grader, 8th-grade student	store	Year 8 student	shop
		vacation		holiday

Text smart 1 Advertisements

ad(vertisement) [əd'vɜːtɪsmənt]	Anzeige; Werbespot	
product ['prɒdʌkt]	Produkt; Erzeugnis	! Be careful with the pronunciation. *product* → to produce
just about anywhere [ˌdʒʌst‿əˌbaʊt 'eniweə]	praktisch überall	You can see advertisements for products *just about anywhere* you look.
advertiser ['ædvətaɪzə]	Werbefachmann/-frau	
to **win** sb **over** [ˌwɪn‿'əʊvə]	jmdn. für sich gewinnen; jmdn. überzeugen	Advertisers try to *win* customers *over*.

Introduction

1 **brand** [brænd]	Marke	= a particular product or line of products made by one company and sold under a special name
immediately [ɪ'miːdiətli]	sofort; gleich	I don't want to wait any longer. Let's go *immediately*.
to **give away** [ˌɡɪv‿ə'weɪ]	verteilen; verschenken	
sample ['sɑːmpl]	Probe; Muster	My favorite chocolate company is giving away free *samples* today.
chocolate bar ['tʃɒklət ˌbɑː]	Schokoriegel	

to **fall for** ['fɔ:l fə]	hereinfallen auf	You didn't *fall for* that trick, did you?
hair [heə]	Haar; Haare	! Ihre Haare **sind** lang. = Her *hair* **is** long.
to **advertise** ['ædvətaɪz]	Werbung machen; werben; anpreisen; inserieren	Have you heard about that new phone? They *advertise* it a lot on TV.
receptive [rɪ'septɪv]	empfänglich	*receptive* → to receive
temptation [temp'teɪʃn]	Versuchung	*temptation* → to tempt
sceptical ['skeptɪkl]	skeptisch	= when you have your doubts about sth
advertising *(no pl)* ['ædvətaɪzɪŋ]	Werbung; Reklame	*advertising* → to advertise → advertisement → advertiser

You, one, they

In English there are different words for the German word 'man'. Sometimes you can also translate it with a passive sentence.

You can see advertisements for products just about anywhere **you** look.	**Man** sieht Werbung praktisch überall, wohin **man** schaut.
On the radio, **they** mentioned a big sale at a clothes store.	Im Radio erwähnte **man** einen großen Ausverkauf in einem Kleiderladen./Im Radio **wurde** ein großer Ausverkauf in einem Kleiderladen erwähnt.
One can never know what will happen.	**Man** kann nie wissen, was passieren wird.

'You' and 'they' are very common, but 'one' is for a more formal kind of English, e.g. for business, in formal writing and sometimes in literature too.

Station: Did you see that new ad?

	to **spice up** [ˌspaɪs_ˈʌp]	aufpeppen	*Spice up* your style with some color!
	highly ['haɪli]	höchst-	*highly* = very, extremely
	brand-new [ˌbrænd'nju:]	brandneu	
	available [ə'veɪləbl]	erhältlich; verfügbar	If sth is *available*, you can get it or buy it.
	glamorous ['glæmrəs]	glamourös	She looks so *glamorous*, like a movie star!
	lovely ['lʌvli]	schön; hübsch	Thank you, that's a *lovely* present.
	nerd [nɜ:d]	Nerd *(Person, die intelligent, aber sozial unbeholfen ist)*	
2	**target** ['tɑ:gɪt]	Ziel; Ziel-	Who is the *target* group of this advertisement?
	eye-catcher ['aɪkætʃə]	Blickfang; Hingucker	Her dress is an *eye-catcher*.
	visual ['vɪʒuəl]	Bild	Ads depend a lot on *visuals*.
	ad copy ['æd ˌkɒpi]	Werbetext	We've got the visuals for the new ad, but we still need the *ad copy* for it.
	image ['ɪmɪdʒ]	Bild; Abbildung	*Fr.* image *(f)*
	billboard ['bɪlbɔ:d]	Plakatwand	= large outdoor sign for advertisements
4	**approach** [ə'prəʊtʃ]	Herangehensweise; Vorgehensweise; Ansatz; Annäherung	We get the same results but we have different *approaches*. *Fr.* approche *(f)*

	truckload ['trʌkləʊd]	Lastwagenladung	The shop gets *truckloads* of new clothes every day so the customers always find something new.
	arrival [ə'raɪvl]	Ankommende/-r; Neuzugang	*arrival* → to arrive
	to **settle for less** [ˌsetl fə 'les]	sich mit weniger zufrieden geben	I want the best, so why should I *settle for less*?
	effective [ɪ'fektɪv]	effektiv; wirkungsvoll	Featuring famous people in ads can be very *effective*.
	to **attract** [ə'trækt]	anziehen	What target group are they trying to *attract*?
	fabulous ['fæbjələs]	sagenhaft; fantastisch	*Fr.* fabuleux/fabuleuse
5	**effectiveness** [ɪ'fektɪvnəs]	Effektivität; Wirksamkeit	*effectiveness* → effective

Options

6	**trash** *(AE)* [træʃ]	Abfall; Müll	There's so much *trash* on TV!
	ugly ['ʌgli]	hässlich	*ugly* ↔ beautiful

Across cultures 2 School life – dos and don'ts

1	**corridor** ['kɒrɪdɔː]	Gang; Flur; Korridor	
	gym(nasium) [dʒɪm; dʒɪm'neɪziəm]	Turnhalle	= the room in a school where PE lessons often take place
	lab(oratory) [læb; lə'bɒrətri]	Labor	
	cell phone *(AE)* ['selfəʊn]	Mobiltelefon; Handy	If you can't reach him at home, try him on his *cell phone*.
	to **skip** [skɪp]	auslassen; schwänzen	The girls decided to *skip* class after lunch. Bad idea! That always means trouble.
	to **cheat** [tʃiːt]	mogeln; betrügen	She *cheated* on the test, so she had to repeat it. She's *cheating* on her boyfriend. = She's going out with sb else, but her boyfriend doesn't know.
	to **get caught** [ˌget 'kɔːt]	erwischt werden; ertappt werden	She *got caught* by the teacher while she was cheating on a test.
	principal *(AE)* ['prɪnsɪpl]	Schulleiter/-in	= the boss of a school in the US
	to **be suspended** [bi sə'spendɪd]	suspendiert werden; zeitweilig vom Unterricht ausgeschlossen werden	One of my classmates *was suspended* for two weeks for skipping class so often.
	detention [dɪ'tenʃn]	Nachsitzen; Haft; Verhaftung	The whole class got *detention* today.
2	**lunchtime** ['lʌnʃtaɪm]	Mittagszeit; Mittagspause	At *lunchtime* the students eat in the cafeteria.
	to **complete** [kəm'pliːt]	fertigstellen; vervollständigen; vollenden	After ten years the director finally *completed* his epic, 3-hour film.

	consequence ['kɒnsɪkwəns]	Konsequenz; Folge	
	otherwise ['ʌðəwaɪz]	sonst	I have to do my homework now. *Otherwise* I won't be able to go to the mall later.
3	to **stand in line** *(AE)* [ˌstænd‿ɪn 'laɪn]	anstehen; Schlange stehen; (sich) anstellen	In the US, you'll be unpopular very quickly if you don't *stand in line*. 
	to **switch off** [ˌswɪtʃ‿'ɒf]	ausschalten	*to switch off* = to turn off
5	to **be about to do sth** [bi‿ə'baʊt tə]	im Begriff sein, etw. zu tun	Can you help me with my presentation? – I'*m about to go* shopping; I'll help you later.
	to **get into trouble** [ˌget‿ɪntə 'trʌbl]	in Schwierigkeiten geraten	
	so (that) [ˌsəʊ 'ðæt]	damit; so dass	Some students fake hall passes *so that* they can skip classes.
	cheat sheet ['tʃi:t ʃi:t]	Spickzettel	I've never used a *cheat sheet* in my life!
	You'd better ... *(= You had better)* ['ju:d ˌbetə]	Du solltest lieber ...	It's late. *I'd better* go home.
	If I were you ... [ˌɪf aɪ wɜ: 'ju:]	Wenn ich du wäre ...	*If I were you*, I wouldn't say a word to my parents.
	No risk, no fun! [nəʊ ˌrɪsk nəʊ 'fʌn]	Wer nicht wagt, der nicht gewinnt.	You never take any risks. *No risk, no fun!*
	mad [mæd]	wütend	He's *mad* at me. = He's angry with me.
	I can't see the point of ... [aɪ ˌkɑ:nt si: ðə 'pɔɪnt‿əv]	Ich sehe keinen Sinn darin ...	*I can't see the point of* talking to the teacher. He won't change his mind.
	waste [weɪst]	Verschwendung	It's a *waste* of time telling him what to do. He'll never change!

Unit 2 City of dreams: New York

Introduction

	intersection [ˌɪntə'sekʃn]	Kreuzung	= where two or more roads meet
	district ['dɪstrɪkt]	Distrikt; Bezirk	! Be careful with the word stress.
	lung [lʌŋ]	Lunge	*Lungs* need fresh air.
1	**a pocketful of** [ə 'pɒkɪtfl‿əv]	Unmengen von/an	*a pocketful of* = a lot of
	gonna (= going to) *(coll)* ['gɒnə]	wird/werden	! *Gonna* is often used in conversations and in songs.
	to **make it** ['meɪk‿ɪt]	es schaffen	If I can *make it* here, I can *make it* anywhere.
	by any means [baɪ‿enɪ 'mi:nz]	mit allen Mitteln	I'm going to make it in show business *by any means*, I don't care how!
	to **inspire** [ɪn'spaɪə]	inspirieren; anregen	= to give the idea for sth (e.g. a poem or a song)

melting pot ['meltɪŋ ˌpɒt]	Schmelztiegel	= a place where people from different origins come together to live and form a new culture
jungle ['dʒʌŋgl]	Dschungel	A lot of people call New York a 'concrete *jungle*'.

Station 1: Saving the best for last

to **save the best for last** [ˌseɪv ðə ˌbest fə 'lɑːst]	sich das Beste bis zum Schluss aufheben	
to **take the day off** [ˌteɪk ðə ˌdeɪ‿'ɒf]	sich den Tag freinehmen	Diego isn't working. He's *taken the day off*.
diner *(AE)* ['daɪnə]	einfaches Restaurant mit Theke und Tischen	I have breakfast in the *diner* around the corner every morning before I go to work.
conference ['kɒnfrns]	Konferenz; Tagung	*Fr.* conférence *(f)*
guidebook ['gaɪdbʊk]	Reiseführer	In a *guidebook* you can find all the important sights of a city.
to **gasp** [gɑːsp]	tief Luft holen; keuchen	"Oh no! That's terrible!" she *gasped*.
classical ['klæsɪkl]	klassisch	
bank [bæŋk]	Bank	! *bank* (Geldinstitut) ≠ *bench* (Bank zum Sitzen).
sculpture ['skʌlptʃə]	Skulptur	! Be careful with the pronunciation.
since [sɪns]	da	! '*Since*' has two meanings: – *since* I was little = seit … – *since* it's too late = da …
naked ['neɪkɪd]	nackt	! Be careful with the pronunciation: two syllables!
for free [fə 'friː]	umsonst; kostenlos	
on a shoestring [ˌɒn‿ə 'ʃuːstrɪŋ]	für/mit wenig Geld	Living *on a shoestring* isn't easy in an expensive city like New York.
to **time** [taɪm]	den richtigen Zeitpunkt wählen	If we *time* it right, we'll be at the Empire State Building before it closes.
block [blɒk]	Block; Häuserblock	= an area of land (in a town) with streets on all sides
enthusiasm [ɪn'θjuːziæzm]	Enthusiasmus; Begeisterung	He talks about his city with so much *enthusiasm*!
just in time [ˌdʒʌst‿ɪn 'taɪm]	gerade rechtzeitig	I got to the airport *just in time*. People were already getting on the plane.
sunset ['sʌnset]	Sonnenuntergang	
to **sneak** [sniːk], **snuck** [snʌk], **snuck** [snʌk]	schleichen; schmuggeln	He *snuck* into his bedroom quietly; his parents never knew he'd been gone.
service ['sɜːvɪs]	Service; Dienstleistung; Dienst	*Fr.* service *(m)*; *Lat.* servitium *(nt)*
Leave that to me. [ˌliːv ðæt tə 'miː]	Überlass das mir.	Oh no, what are we going to do? – *Leave that to me*. I always know what to do.
bright [braɪt]	hell; leuchtend; strahlend	In the summer, the sun is very *bright*.
2 **tour company** ['tʊə ˌkʌmpəni]	Reiseanbieter	I like *tour companies* that offer unusual tours.

3	to **be located** [bi ləʊ'keɪtɪd]	gelegen sein; liegen	Where *is* the museum *located*? = Where exactly is the museum? *to be located in* → location *(n)*
4	**subway** *(AE)* ['sʌbweɪ]	U-Bahn	
	to **groan** [grəʊn]	stöhnen	= a sound that shows you're hurt, unhappy or disappointed
6	**statue** ['stætʃu:]	Statue; Standbild	Oh look, that's not a *statue*; it's a man!
	liberty ['lɪbəti]	Freiheit	*Fr.* liberté *(f)*
	artist ['ɑ:tɪst]	Künstler/-in	*artist* → art
	tablet ['tæblət]	Tafel	The Statue of Liberty is holding a torch and a *tablet*.
	spike [spaɪk]	Spitze; Stachel	The Statue of Liberty's crown has seven *spikes*.
	to **base on** ['beɪs‿ɒn]	stützen auf	The character in the story is *based on* a real person.
	goddess ['gɒdes]	Göttin	What's the name of the Roman *goddess* of liberty?
	to **be known as** [bi 'nəʊn‿əz]	bekannt sein als	
	enlightenment [ɪn'laɪtnmənt]	Aufklärung; Erleuchtung	The Statue of Liberty's torch stands for *enlightenment*.
8	**ethnic** ['eθnɪk]	ethnisch; Volks-; *hier:* exotisch	What's your *ethnic* background? – I'm half German and half Spanish.
	from the outside [ˌfrəm ði‿aʊt'saɪd]	von außen	*From the outside*, the restaurant doesn't look very nice.
	delicious [dɪ'lɪʃəs]	köstlich	Mmm, this cake is *delicious*.
	fried [fraɪd]	gebraten *(in der Pfanne)*	*Fried* food is delicious – but you mustn't eat too much of it.
	pastry ['peɪstri]	Teig; Teigtasche	
	filling ['fɪlɪŋ]	Füllung	This pastry has a vegetarian *filling*.
	Jewish ['dʒu:ɪʃ]	jüdisch	A bagel with lox is typical *Jewish* food.
	truck *(AE)* [trʌk]	*hier:* Wagen	Are there any food *trucks* in the area?
	cart [kɑ:t]	Karren	an ice-cream *cart* 
	New Yorker [ˌnju: 'jɔ:kə]	New Yorker/-in	= a person who is from New York City
	to **combine** [kəm'baɪn]	kombinieren; verbinden	Can you *combine* red and pink?
	flavor *(AE)* ['fleɪvə]	Geschmack; Aroma	Two ice creams, please. – What *flavor*? – One chocolate and one banana.
	specialty *(AE)* ['speʃlti]	Spezialität; Besonderheit	
	combination [ˌkɒmbɪ'neɪʃn]	Kombination; Verbindung	*combination* → to combine
10	**hometown** ['həʊmtaʊn]	Heimatstadt	*hometown* → home
	spot [spɒt]	Fleck; Ort	We found a quiet *spot* in the park and sat down on the grass.

Station 2: Life is a trip

to **lift** [lɪft]	heben; hochheben; anheben	You can really hurt yourself if you try to *lift* something that's too heavy.
trunk *(AE)* [trʌŋk]	Kofferraum	
to **be done with** [bi 'dʌn wɪð]	fertig sein mit	I'*m done with* you, I don't want to see you again!
break [breɪk]	Durchbruch	He'd been hoping for his big *break* for five years.
rejection [rɪ'dʒektʃn]	Ablehnung; Absage	He got one *rejection* after the other.
to **come true** [ˌkʌm 'truː]	wahr werden; in Erfüllung gehen	Wouldn't it be wonderful if our dreams always *came true*?
good luck [ˌgʊd 'lʌk]	(viel) Glück	Emilio wished the man *good luck*.
sidewalk *(AE)* ['saɪdwɔːk]	Gehweg; Gehsteig	
businessman ['bɪznɪsmæn]	Geschäftsmann	The passenger looked like a successful *businessman*.
not necessarily [ˌnɒt nesə'serəli]	nicht notwendigerweise; nicht unbedingt	Seeing New York on a shoestring is impossible! – That's *not necessarily* true. Central Park, for example, is free.
however [haʊ'evə]	jedoch	The man had lots of money. *However*, he wasn't happy with his life.
bill *(AE)* [bɪl]	Geldschein; Rechnung	The suitcase was full of 100$ *bills*. We'd like to pay. Can you bring us the *bill*, please?
change [tʃeɪndʒ]	Münzgeld; Wechselgeld	That'll be $8.50, please. – Here's $10.00. Keep the *change*.
to **get in** [ˌget‿'ɪn]	einsteigen	Agree on the price before you *get in* a taxi.
yet [jet]	doch; und trotzdem; und dennoch	*Yet* is used to add sth that seems surprising after what has been said.
to **complain** [kəm'pleɪn]	sich beschweren; sich beklagen	My soup was cold, so I *complained*.
to **shop** [ʃɒp]	einkaufen; shoppen	New York City is a great place to *shop*.
needless to say [ˌniːdləs tə 'seɪ]	natürlich; selbstverständlich	When we got home, our teenage kids were having a huge, loud party. *Needless to say*, we weren't happy!
tip [tɪp]	Trinkgeld	In the US, before you leave a café or restaurant, it's normal to leave a *tip* of at least 15%, often 20%.
16 **grade** *(AE)* [greɪd]	Note	! The best *grade* in American schools is A+; the worst is F (there's no E). Some schools use a number system: 4.00 is the best; 0.00 the worst.
18 **busker** ['bʌskə]	Straßenmusikant/-in	= sb who plays music or sings for money in city streets or stations
to **perform** [pə'fɔːm]	aufführen; auftreten	If you *perform* a play, you act it in front of people who come to watch it.
freeway *(AE)* ['friːweɪ]	Autobahn	
to **transport** [træn'spɔːt]	transportieren; befördern	= to take from one place to another *Fr.* transporter

	lorry ['lɒri]	Lastwagen	
19	to **fail to do sth** ['feɪl tə]	versäumen, etw. zu tun; es nicht schaffen, etw. zu tun	A lot of actors *fail to* find success.
	rags to riches [ˌrægz təˈrɪtʃɪz]	vom Tellerwäscher zum Millionär	There are lots of Hollywood movies with a *rags to riches* storyline.
	to **make a living (from)** [ˌmeɪk‿ə 'lɪvɪŋ frəm]	seinen Lebensunterhalt bestreiten (mit)	She *makes a living* from piano lessons.
	either ... or ... ['aɪðə/'iːðə ... ɔː]	entweder ... oder ...	You have to decide now: You can have *either* this one *or* that one, but not both.

Story: Asphalt Tribe

3	**panel** ['pænl]	Bild *(eines Comics)*	
	lead-in ['liːdɪn]	Einführung; Einleitung	
	shape [ʃeɪp]	Form	
	sequence ['siːkwəns]	Abfolge; Reihenfolge	The *sequence* of comic panels is very important.
	consecutive [kən'sekjʊtɪv]	aufeinanderfolgend; fortlaufend	The panels here are arranged *consecutively.*
	to **overlap** [ˌəʊvə'læp]	(sich) überlappen	The pictures in the book *overlap*, which I think looks cool.
	to **lay** [leɪ], **laid** [leɪd], **laid** [leɪd]	legen	
	to **make use of** [meɪk 'juːz‿əv]	benutzen; verwenden	What tricks do they *make use of*?
	long shot ['lɒŋ ʃɒt]	Totale *(Kameraeinstellung)*	Let's use a *long shot* for this scene so we can see everything that's going on.
	medium shot ['miːdiəm ʃɒt]	Halbtotale *(Kameraeinstellung)*	
	medium ['miːdiəm]	mittel; mittelgroß	What size do you wear: small, *medium* or large?
	effect [ɪ'fekt]	Effekt; Wirkung	You should always think of the *effects* of your actions before you do something. *Fr.* effet *(m)*
	stylistic [staɪ'lɪstɪk]	Stil-; stilistisch	*stylistic* → style
	speed [spiːd]	Geschwindigkeit	This movie has a lot of *speed.*

Action USA! New Yorkers don't do things like that!

1	to **cringe** [krɪndʒ]	schaudern; sich ducken	If you *cringe* about sth, you feel very embarrassed by it. Usually, it's what sb else has done.
2	**unexpected** [ˌʌnɪk'spektɪd]	unerwartet	*unexpected* → to expect

Skills: How to conduct a podcast interview

	to **conduct** [kən'dʌkt]	durchführen; ausführen	*to conduct* an interview

1	**path** [pɑ:θ]	Pfad; Weg	Rita's *path* to success was long and hard.
2	**follow-up** [ˈfɒləʊʌp]	Fortsetzung; Folge-	*follow-up* → to follow → the following
	talk [tɔ:k]	Gespräch; Unterhaltung	*talk* → to talk

Important differences

	AE		BE	
Different spelling	flavor, labor		flavour, labour	
	specialty		speciality	
	to realize		to realise	
	to practice		to practise	
	traveling		travelling	
Different words	bill	sidewalk	note	pavement
	cell phone	subway	mobile phone	underground
	freeway	trash	motorway	rubbish
	grade	truck	class	lorry
	intersection	trunk	crossroad	boot
	period	yard	lesson	garden
	principal		head teacher	

Text smart 2 Internet texts

Introduction

	reliable [rɪˈlaɪəbl]	verlässlich; zuverlässig; vertrauenswürdig	He's very *reliable*. He always does what he says he'll do.
1	**inconvenient** [ˌɪnkənˈvi:niənt]	unbequem; lästig	Hi, can I ask you something? – Er, it's a bit *inconvenient* right now. Later?
	up-to-date [ˌʌptəˈdeɪt]	modern; zeitgemäß; aktuell	
	tutorial [tju:ˈtɔ:riəl]	Tutorium; Tutorial	I often watch *tutorials* about cooking on the Internet.
3	**moon landing** [ˈmu:n ˌlændɪŋ]	Mondlandung	
	science [saɪəns]	Wissenschaft; Naturwissenschaft	*science* → scientist ***Fr.*** science *(f)*; ***Lat.*** scientia *(f)*
	astronaut [ˈæstrənɔ:t]	Astronaut/-in	

human ['hju:mən]	Mensch	Neil Armstrong was the first *human* on the moon.
to **be considered (to be) sth** [bi kən'sɪdəd tə]	als etw. gelten	Germany *is considered to* be one of the richest countries in the world.

Station 1: An online wiki text

wiki (text) ['wɪkɪ ˌtekst]	Wikitext	
mission ['mɪʃn]	Mission; Auftrag	Our *mission* as a team is to win the championship.
to **touch down** [tʌtʃ 'daʊn]	landen	In 1969 Apollo 11 *touched down* on the moon.
surface ['sɜ:fɪs]	Oberfläche	***Fr.*** surface *(f)*
to **announce** [ə'naʊns]	ankündigen; durchsagen	*to announce* → announcement ***Fr.*** annoncer; ***Lat.*** ad + nuntiare
to **step** [step]	treten; steigen	*to step* → step
president ['prezɪdnt]	Präsident/-in	! Watch the word stress.
priority [praɪ'ɒrəti]	Priorität; Vorrang	The moon landing was one of President John F. Kennedy's top *priorities*.
to **challenge** ['tʃælɪndʒ]	herausfordern	*to challenge* → challenge
engineer [ˌendʒɪ'nɪə]	Ingenieur/-in; Techniker/-in	
political [pə'lɪtɪkl]	politisch	Do you like watching TV programs about *political* problems?
5 **hoax** [həʊks]	Täuschung; Trick	Some people say that the moon landing was a *hoax*.
conspiracy [kən'spɪrəsi]	Verschwörung	Is there a *conspiracy* against the Queen? ***Fr.*** conspiration *(f)*; ***Lat.*** conspiratio *(f)*
theory ['θɪəri]	Theorie	
to **stage** [steɪdʒ]	inszenieren; aufführen	How difficult would it be to *stage* something like the moon landing?
the public [ðə 'pʌblɪk]	die Öffentlichkeit	Stars sometimes want to hide from *the public*. ***Fr.*** public *(m)*; ***Lat.*** publicum *(nt)*
to **involve** [ɪn'vɒlv]	involvieren; einbeziehen; beteiligen	If you *involve* sb in sth, you include them, e.g. in a situation or activity.
cover-up ['kʌvərʌp]	Vertuschung	*cover-up* → to cover
government ['gʌvnmənt]	Regierung	= a group of people whose job it is to run a country and deal with its problems
6 **complicated** ['kɒmplɪkeɪtɪd]	kompliziert	The rules of this game are too *complicated*!
impossible [ɪm'pɒsəbl]	unmöglich	*impossible* ↔ possible ***Fr.*** impossible
to **make sense** [ˌmeɪk 'sens]	Sinn ergeben; einleuchten	If sth *makes sense*, you can understand it.
at the time [ˌət ðə 'taɪm]	damals	
to **run** [rʌn]	betreiben; leiten; führen	My parents *run* a restaurant.
tech [tek]	Technologie; Technik	The US is famous for its *tech* companies, e.g. in Silicon Valley or Seattle.
7 **respect** [rɪ'spekt]	Respekt	Honest bloggers will enjoy their readers' *respect*.
entertaining [ˌentə'teɪnɪŋ]	unterhaltsam	*entertaining* ↔ boring

8	**function** ['fʌŋkʃn]	Funktion	Every text has a *function*.
	to **trick** [trɪk]	austricksen; täuschen	*to trick* → trick
	to **estimate** ['estɪmeɪt]	schätzen	I *estimate* her stay in hospital to take a week.
	to **question** ['kwestʃən]	fragen; hinterfragen	Our trainer always *questions* our motivation.
	critical ['krɪtɪkl]	kritisch	*critical* → self-critical

Station 2: Online ratings

10	to **rate** [reɪt]	bewerten; einstufen	*to rate* → rating
11	**space** [speɪs]	Weltraum; Weltall	There's endless space in *space*.
	space program ['speɪs ˌprəʊgræm]	Raumfahrtprogramm	There's a Mars *space program*, but will there ever really be a human on Mars?
12	**breathtaking** ['breθˌteɪkɪŋ]	atemberaubend	The visuals in the movie were *breathtaking*.
	well-written [ˌwel'rɪtn]	gut geschrieben	I think the story is *well-written*.
	disappointing [ˌdɪsə'pɔɪntɪŋ]	enttäuschend	How was the movie? – It was very *disappointing*. A waste of time!
14	**special effect** [ˌspeʃl‿ɪ'fekt]	Spezialeffekt	In action movies the *special effects* are often as important as the story.
	well-developed [ˌweldɪ'veləpt]	gut entwickelt; ausgereift	You know a character is *well-developed* when he/she seems believable, like sb you know.
	undeveloped [ˌʌndɪ'veləpt]	unentwickelt; unausgereift	*undeveloped* ↔ well-developed

How words can start or end

You can use prefixes and suffixes to make new words from the same word family.

adjectives

in-	direct, convenient, secure	help, hope, thank, use	**-ful**
im-	possible	help, end, use	**-less**
ir-	regular	health, luck, cloud	**-y**
un-	expected, developed, realistic		
dis-	honest		

verbs

dis-	appear, agree, obey
re-	build, read, tell, write
un-	wrap, pack
mis-	behave, understand

! Be careful with the pronunciation:
In English, you don't put the stress on the prefix.
<u>ho</u>nest – dis<u>ho</u>nest

nouns

re-	action, discovery	interview, report, sing	**-er**
ex-	change	champion, friend, relation	**-ship**
in-	dependence	surf, swim(m)	**-ing**
		invent, narrat(e), surviv(e)	**-or**
		demonstrat(e), organiz(e)	**-ion/-ation**
		settle, improve	**-ment**

Write sentences with one word from each group.

badly-written [ˌbædli'rɪtn]	schlecht geschrieben	*badly-written* ↔ well-written
weak [wi:k]	schwach	*weak* ↔ strong

Across cultures 3 What you say and how you say it

register ['redʒɪstə]	Sprachebene; Register	It's important to change your *register* to match the situation you're in. That means you should always use the right language for the right situation.
2 **Canadian** [kə'neɪdiən]	kanadisch; Kanadier/-in	= sb or sth from Canada
to **pronounce** [prə'naʊns]	aussprechen	! Be careful with the spelling: to pron**ou**nce [aʊ] – pron**u**nciation [ʌ]
schedule *(AE)* ['ʃedju:l; 'skedʒu:l]	Stundenplan; Fahrplan; Terminkalender	
though [ðəʊ]	doch; jedoch; obwohl	I tried my best, but I just couldn't win the race. I don't mind *though*. Winning isn't everything.
water fountain ['wɔ:tə ˌfaʊntɪn]	Wasserspender	
4 **informal** [ɪn'fɔ:ml]	informell; zwanglos	*informal* ↔ formal
nope *(infml)* [nəʊp]	nee; nö	= a very informal word for 'no'
It sucks. *(slang)* [ɪt 'sʌks]	Das ist zum Kotzen.	! Only use this phrase when you talk to your friends.
ain't (= isn't/aren't) [eɪnt]	ist nicht; sind nicht	! It isn't good English to use *ain't*, but one hears it quite often. It's typical to use it in ‚double negative' sentences which are incorrect grammar: „I'm not doing anything for her!" → „I *ain't* doing nothing for her!"
totally ['təʊtli]	völlig; total	*totally* = completely
whatever [wɒt'evə]	was/wie auch immer; egal (was/welche)	
no more [ˌnəʊ 'mɔ:]	nicht mehr	*no more* = not anymore
(I) didn't mean to ... [aɪ ˌdɪdnt 'mi:n tə]	Ich wollte nicht ...	Sorry! *I didn't mean to* be rude.
auntie ['ɑ:nti]	Tantchen	
not ... either [nɒt ... 'aɪðə; nɒt ... 'i:ðə]	auch nicht	He doesn't like her. She does*n't* like him *either*.
to **mind sth** [maɪnd]	auf etw. aufpassen	*Mind* your language: Don't be rude.

Unit 3 A nation invents itself

	nation ['neɪʃn]	Nation	*nation* → national *Fr.* nation *(f)*

Introduction

1	**innovation** [ˌɪnə'veɪʃn]	Innovation; Neuerung	*Fr.* innovation *(f)*
	transportation *(AE)* [ˌtrænspɔː'teɪʃn]	Transport	*transportation* → to transport
	innovative [ɪ'nəʊvətɪv; 'ɪnəvətɪv]	innovativ; kreativ	*innovative* → innovation
3	**after** ['ɑːftə]	nachdem	! Look at the difference: *after* the show *after* the show finished
	to **colonize** *(AE)* ['kɒlənaɪz]	kolonisieren	*to colonize* → colony
	permanent ['pɜːmnənt]	permanent; dauerhaft	*permanent* ↔ for a short time *Fr.* permanent; ***Lat.*** permanere
	settlement ['setlmənt]	Siedlung	
	by the time [ˌbaɪ ðə 'taɪm]	bis *(zu dem Zeitpunkt)*	*By the time* of the Revolutionary War in the 1770s, there were 13 British colonies.
	eastern ['iːstn]	östlich; Ost-	
	to **declare** [dɪ'kleə]	erklären	In 1776 the 13 British colonies *declared* independence from Britain.
	to **treat** [triːt]	behandeln	If you don't *treat* your dog right, you'll have trouble with it.
	army ['ɑːmi]	Armee	*Fr.* armée *(f)*
	general ['dʒenrl]	General	
	settler ['setlə]	Siedler/-in	*settler* → settlement
	to **suffer (from)** ['sʌfə frəm]	leiden (unter)	The Native Americans were treated badly and had to *suffer*. *Fr.* souffrir; ***Lat.*** sufferre
	peak [piːk]	Haupt-; Spitzen-	The *peak* immigration period was from 1880 to 1930.
	a total of [ə 'təʊtl‿əv]	insgesamt	For my vacation I paid *a total of* 500 dollars.
	to **pass** [pɑːs]	durchgehen; vorbeigehen (an); passieren	The train has just *passed* a bridge.
	united [juː'naɪtɪd]	vereint; vereinigt	the *United* States of America, the *United* Kingdom
	stranger ['streɪndʒə]	Fremde/-r	I don't know that man – he's a *stranger*.
	especially [ɪ'speʃli]	besonders; vor allem	*especially* → special
	to **descend from** [dɪ'send frəm]	abstammen von; herstammen von	Most Americans are *descended from* immigrants.
4	**belongings** *(pl)* [bɪ'lɒŋɪŋz]	Habseligkeiten; Hab und Gut	= the things (often everything) that a person owns *belongings* → to belong to

	covered wagon [ˌkʌvəd ˈwægən]	Planwagen	

Station 1: This story sounds great!

	bat [bæt]	Schläger *(Tischtennis; Baseball)*	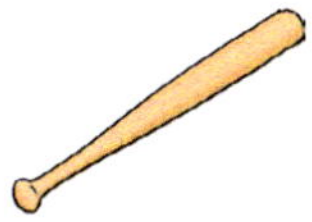
	last name *(AE)* [ˈlɑːst neɪm]	Nachname; Familienname	
	to **pass** [pɑːs]	bestehen	When you*'ve passed* your driving test, you're allowed to drive a car alone.
	medical [ˈmedɪkl]	medizinisch; ärztlich; Medizin-	*medical* → medicine
	examination [ɪgˌzæmɪˈneɪʃn]	Untersuchung; Prüfung	
	to **disappear** [ˌdɪsəˈpɪə]	verschwinden	My bike *has disappeared*, perhaps it was stolen.
1	**great-great-grandfather** [ˌgreɪtgreɪtˈgrænˌfɑːðə]	Ururgroßvater	The father of my father's or mother's grandfather is my *great-great-grandfather.*
2	**terrible** [ˈterəbl]	schrecklich; schlimm; furchtbar	*terrible* = awful *Fr.* terrible
	to **catch an infection** [ɪnˈfekʃn]	sich eine Infektion holen; sich einen Infekt holen	A spider bit me and now I've *caught an infection.*
3	**calm** [kɑːm]	ruhig; friedlich	*calm* ↔ nervous

Adverbs

Adverbs do not only refer to ***verbs*** *(example: She* ***talks loudly****.),* ***adjectives*** *(example: He's* ***extremely cool****.) or other* ***adverbs*** *(example: My dad drives* ***really carefully****.). Adverbs can also refer to a* ***whole sentence****. Most of them are at the beginning of a sentence. Here are some that you've already used.*

Luckily, they didn't get hurt in the accident.	Glücklicherweise wurden sie beim Unfall nicht verletzt.
Honestly, I don't care that her new boyfriend is so good-looking. He's an idiot.	Es ist mir ehrlich gesagt egal, dass ihr neuer Freund so gut aussieht. Er ist ein Idiot.
Actually, we aren't even friends, so I don't know why everyone thinks we're best friends.	Eigentlich sind wir nicht einmal Freunde, also weiß ich nicht, warum alle meinen, wir seien beste Freunde.
Perhaps we shouldn't skip class.	Wir sollten den Unterricht vielleicht nicht schwänzen.
Obviously, he doesn't know where to go.	Offensichtlich weiß er nicht, wohin er gehen soll.
Of course you're invited to my party.	Natürlich bist du zu meiner Party eingeladen.
I'm not going to watch the game; I don't like football **anyway**.	Ich schaue mir das Spiel nicht an; ich mag Fußball sowieso nicht.
America is a rich country. Many people, **however**, have a low standard of living.	Amerika ist ein reiches Land. Dennoch haben viele Menschen einen niedrigen Lebensstandard.

4	**drinking water** ['drɪŋkɪŋ ˌwɔ:tə]	Trinkwasser	
5	**in fact** [ɪn 'fækt]	tatsächlich; eigentlich; genau genommen	*in fact* → fact
	to **manage (to do sth)** ['mænɪdʒ tə]	schaffen (etw. zu tun)	Thanks, I don't need any help. I can *manage* on my own.
	reservation [ˌrezə'veɪʃn]	Reservat	= land that belongs to the Native Americans
	to **recognize** *(AE)* ['rekəgnaɪz]	erkennen; anerkennen	I didn't *recognize* him, he was wearing a costume.
	in addition to [ɪn‿ə'dɪʃn tə]	neben; daneben; darüber hinaus	A lot of Germans speak English *in addition to* German.
6	to **comfort** ['kʌmfət]	trösten; ermutigen	She *comforted* the crying child.
	frightened ['fraɪtnd]	verängstigt	*frightened* = scared
	relieved [rɪ'li:vd]	erleichtert	I was *relieved* when I knew my friends weren't hurt in the accident.
	exhausting [ɪg'zɔ:stɪŋ]	anstrengend	Running a marathon is *exhausting*.
	had gotten off *(AE)* [hæd ˌgɒtn‿'ɒf]	waren ausgestiegen	In American English people say *'gotten'* instead of 'got'.
	papers *(pl)* ['peɪpəz]	Unterlagen; Papiere	He signed the *papers* and then got the keys to his new apartment.
7	to **start all over again** [ˌstɑ:t‿ɔ:l‿'əʊvər‿əˌgen]	ganz von vorn beginnen	*Starting all over again* may be frightening. to start from the very beginning
8	**statistics** *(pl)* [stə'tɪstɪks]	Statistik	*Statistics* show facts in the form of figures.
	table ['teɪbl]	Tabelle	*table* → timetable
	bar graph ['bɑ: grɑ:f]	Säulendiagramm; Balkendiagramm	
	line graph ['laɪn grɑ:f]	Kurvendiagramm	
	pie chart ['paɪ ˌtʃɑ:t]	Kuchendiagramm; Tortendiagramm	For a lot of presentations you need to feature graphs and charts, e.g. *pie charts*.
	to **publish** ['pʌblɪʃ]	veröffentlichen; publizieren; verlegen	= to prepare and print (a book, newspaper, magazine, etc.)
	majority [mə'dʒɒrəti]	Mehrheit; Mehrzahl	The *majority* of Americans live in cities. ! *Majority* is used with a plural verb form. *Fr.* majorité *(f)*
	minority [maɪ'nɒrəti]	Minderheit	= less than half of the people or things in a group *minority* ↔ majority *Fr.* minorité *(f)*
	percent, percent *(pl)* [pə'sent]	Prozent	60 *percent* of 10 students = 6 students
	to **grow by** ['grəʊ baɪ]	steigen um	The world population *has grown by* 12 percent over the last ten years.
	to **suggest** [sə'dʒest]	andeuten; nahelegen	*to suggest* → suggestion
	conclusion [kən'klu:ʒn]	Schluss; Schlussfolgerung	What *conclusion* do you draw from these facts? *conclusion* ↔ introduction

Station 2: Necessity is the mother of invention

necessity [nəˈsesəti]	Notwendigkeit	Food is a basic *necessity*. *Fr.* nécessité *(f)*
communications network [kəˌmju:nɪˈkeɪʃnz ˌnetwɜ:k]	Kommunikationsnetz; Nachrichtennetz	
face-to-face [ˌfeɪs tə ˈfeɪs]	von Angesicht zu Angesicht; Auge in Auge	Let's meet and talk to each other *face-to-face*.
to **migrate** [maɪˈgreɪt]	wandern; umherziehen	Large numbers of people *migrated* from the East to the West in the 19th century.
pioneer [ˌpaɪəˈnɪə]	Pionier/-in	
western [ˈwestən]	westlich; West-	Many states in the *western* US have a dry climate.
mass migration [ˌmæs maɪˈgreɪʃn]	Massenwanderung	*mass migration* → to migrate
to **expand** [ɪkˈspænd]	(sich) ausdehnen; erweitern	The company wanted to *expand* and so they looked for more workers.
wanted [ˈwɒntɪd]	gesucht	
skinny [ˈskɪni]	dünn; mager	It isn't healthy to be too *skinny*.
fellow [ˈfeləʊ]	Bursche; Kerl	= an old word for 'guy' or 'man'
rider [ˈraɪdə]	Reiter/-in; Fahrer/-in	*rider* → to ride 
to **risk** [rɪsk]	riskieren	
mail [meɪl]	Post	*mail* → e-mail
to **employ** [ɪmˈplɔɪ]	einstellen; anstellen; beschäftigen	If you *employ* people, you pay them to work for you. *Fr.* employer
as [æz; əz]	da; weil	*As* I'm never allowed to go out, I have no friends.
even though [ˌi:vn ˈðəʊ]	auch wenn; obwohl	I love my brother *even though* he isn't always nice to me.
to **replace (by/with)** [rɪˈpleɪs]	ersetzen (durch)	Our old fridge was *replaced by* a new one. *Fr.* remplacer
to **develop** [dɪˈveləp]	(sich) entwickeln	*to develop* → well-developed *Fr.* développer
to **connect (to)** [kəˈnekt tə]	verbinden (mit); vermitteln; anschließen	You can *connect* two words to make other words: 'school' and 'bag' make 'schoolbag'.
instantly [ˈɪnstəntli]	sofort	
10 **long-lasting** [ˈlɒŋlɑ:stɪŋ]	lang anhaltend	The Pony Express wasn't a *long-lasting* success.
11 **in order to** [ɪn‿ˈɔ:də tə]	um … zu; mit der Absicht	You often have to be creative *in order to* reach a goal.
to **start off** [ˌstɑ:t‿ˈɒf]	anfangen; beginnen; starten	Modern communication *started off* in the US.
motor car [ˈməʊtə ˌkɑ:]	Automobil	= a more historical way to say 'car'
12 **motion picture** [ˌməʊʃn ˈpɪktʃə]	Film; Spielfilm	= a more formal way to say 'film' or 'movie'

importance [ɪm'pɔ:tns]	Bedeutung; Wichtigkeit	*importance* → important *Fr.* importance *(f)*
15 **colonial** [kə'ləʊniəl]	kolonial; Kolonial-	*colonial* → colony → colonist → to colonize
spirit ['spɪrɪt]	Geist; Stimmung	In the true *spirit* of sport, taking part is more important than winning.
to **shape** [ʃeɪp]	formen	Having friends from different countries *has shaped* my personality.
barbecue ['bɑ:bɪkju:]	Grill(party)	
stripe [straɪp]	Streifen	The US flag is called 'the Stars and *Stripes*'. 

American history

17th century
to colonize – colony – colonist – colonial
to settle – settlement – settler
Native American – tribe – tribal

20th century
to descend from – great-great-grandparents
to migrate – migration – immigration – immigrant
to pass the immigration center / a medical examination

18th and 19th century
Revolutionary War = War of Independence
to declare independence
to expand
reservation
pioneer

Skills: How to write a report

1 **grandmother** ['græn,mʌðə]	Großmutter	*grandmother* → mother → grandfather
insurance [ɪn'ʃʊərns]	Versicherung	My dad works at an *insurance* company.

Unit task: Oral historian for a day

oral ['ɔ:rl]	mündlich	An *oral* exam is a test in which you have to show how good your speaking skills are.
historian [hɪ'stɔ:riən]	Historiker/-in	*historian* → history → historical

Story: A journey into the unknown

the unknown [ði ˌʌn'nəʊn]	das Unbekannte	*the unknown* → to know
Ma [mɑ:]	Mama	= a historical word for 'Mom'
to **come up to** [ˌkʌm‿'ʌp tə]	zukommen auf	Ma *came up to* me and gave me a diary.

to **keep a diary** [ˌkiːp‿ə ˈdaɪəri]	ein Tagebuch führen	I *keep a diary* because I like to write down my feelings about the things I experience.
apart [əˈpɑːt]	auseinander; getrennt	
Pa [pɑː]	Papa	= a historical word for 'Dad'
trail [treɪl]	Weg; Pfad	
preparation [ˌprepr'eɪʃn]	Vorbereitung	*preparation* → to prepare
to **head (for)** [ˈhed fə]	zusteuern auf	If you *head for* a place, you move towards it.
to **farm** [fɑːm]	Landwirtschaft betreiben	*to farm* → farm → farmer
by *(+ gerund)* [baɪ]	indem	You can't catch fish just *by* putting your hand in the river.
to **wave** [weɪv]	winken; schwenken	The star *is waving* to her fans.
to **pack** [pæk]	packen; einpacken	= to put your things in a bag before you go away
grass [grɑːs]	Gras	
furniture *(singular noun with plural meaning)* [ˈfɜːnɪtʃə]	Möbel	! The *furniture* is new. = Die Möbel sind neu.
to **abandon** [əˈbændən]	aufgeben; zurücklassen	*Fr.* abandonner
proper [ˈprɒpə]	richtig; ordentlich; angemessen	For many in Britain, a *proper* English breakfast includes bacon and eggs, sausages, baked beans and tomatoes, with tea or coffee.
to **own** [əʊn]	besitzen	This is our own house. We *own* it.
to **wonder** [ˈwʌndə]	sich Gedanken machen; sich fragen	I often *wonder* why …
up to [ˈʌp tə]	bis zu	How many people are there in the stadium? – *Up to* 30,000 people.
chest [tʃest]	Brust; Brustkorb	
to **join in** [ˌdʒɔɪn‿ˈɪn]	teilnehmen; mitmachen	After the big storm, the neighbors needed our help with their yard. So we all *joined in* and cleaned everything up.
bottom [ˈbɒtəm]	Boden; unterer Teil; Grund	*bottom* ↔ top
flour [flaʊə]	Mehl	
to **reach (for)** [ˈriːtʃ fə]	greifen (nach)	She *reached for* the last piece of cake, but her brother was faster.
spicy [ˈspaɪsi]	würzig; pikant	Indian food is usually very *spicy*.
Russian [ˈrʌʃn]	Russe/Russin; russisch; Russisch	
in spite of [ɪn ˈspaɪt‿əv]	trotz	*In spite of* the rain we went for a walk.
recent [ˈriːsnt]	kürzlich; neueste/-r/-s; letzte/-r/-s	*Recent* events are things that happened only a short time ago. *Fr.* récent; *Lat.* recens
alive [əˈlaɪv]	lebend; am Leben; lebendig	*alive* ↔ dead
to **get well** [ˌget ˈwel]	gesund werden	I hope you'll *get well* soon.
none [nʌn]	keine/-r/-s	*None* of us wants to go to the museum.
5 **herd** [hɜːd]	Herde; Rudel	Sheep live in *herds*.

bison ['baɪsn], **bison** ['baɪsn] *(pl)*	Bison; Büffel	
to **be stuck** [bi 'stʌk]	festsitzen; feststecken; hängen bleiben	If you*'re stuck* in a place, you can't get out.

Action USA!

2	**honor** *(AE)* ['ɒnə]	Ehre	! Be careful with the pronunciation.
	equal ['i:kwəl]	gleich; gleichwertig	Do you think all Americans are *equal*?
	no matter [nəʊ 'mætə]	egal; ganz gleich	*No matter* what the problem is, just call if you need my help!

Text smart 3 Travel texts

Introduction

1	**incredible** [ɪn'kredəbl]	unglaublich	The movie I saw was *incredibly* bad. ***Fr.*** incroyable; ***Lat.*** incredibilis
	to **scare sb to death** [ˌskeə tə 'deθ]	jmdn. zu Tode erschrecken	The tarantula *scared her to death*.
	to **fear** [fɪə]	(sich) fürchten	
	heat *(no pl)* [hi:t]	Hitze; Wärme	Death Valley is feared for its *heat*.
	to **be aware of sth** [bi‿ə'weər‿əv]	sich etw. bewusst sein	I*'m aware* of the dangers of driving alone in the desert.
	rough [rʌf]	rau; grob; uneben; holprig	The roads are *rough* in Death Valley.
	reception [rɪ'sepʃn]	Empfang	In the desert there's often no cell phone *reception*. *receptive* → to receive
	to **educate** ['edʒʊkeɪt]	erziehen; bilden	*to educate* → education
2	to **meet sb's expectations** [ˌmi:t sʌmbədiz‿ekspek'teɪʃnz]	jmds. Erwartungen erfüllen	The concert wasn't as good as I thought it would be. It really didn't *meet my expectations*.

Station 1: A travel guide

	general ['dʒenrl]	allgemein	Do you want details or just *general* information?
3	**snow-capped** ['snəʊkæpt]	schneebedeckt	
	summit ['sʌmɪt]	Gipfel; Berggipfel	The view from the *summit* is awesome!
	turbulent ['tɜ:bjələnt]	turbulent; aufgewühlt	It was really *turbulent* in the streets downtown with all the protesters.

glacial ['gleɪsiəl; 'gleɪʃl]	eisig; Gletscher-	The landscapes were formed in *glacial* times.
valley ['væli]	Tal	*valley* ↔ mountain *Fr.* vallée *(f)*
wooded ['wʊdɪd]	bewaldet	*Wooded* areas are nice and cool on a hot summer day. *wooded* → wood
sparkling ['spɑ:klɪŋ]	glitzernd; funkelnd	
to **hunt** [hʌnt]	jagen	Indian tribes once *hunted* bison.
snow tire *(AE)* ['snəʊ ˌtaɪə]	Winterreifen	In winter cars need *snow tires*.
grizzly bear ['grɪzli ˌbeə]	Grizzlybär	Park visitors should hope they don't come face to face with a *grizzly bear*.
elk [elk]	Elch	
bighorn sheep [ˌbɪghɔ:n 'ʃi:p]	Dickhornschaf	
chain [tʃeɪn]	Kette	The Rockies are North America's most famous mountain *chain*. *Fr.* chaîne *(f)*
dusty ['dʌsti]	staubig	If you don't clean your room often enough, everything starts to get *dusty*.
enjoyable [ɪn'dʒɔɪəbl]	angenehm; unterhaltsam	*enjoyable* → to enjoy
copper-mining ['kɒpəˌmaɪnɪŋ]	Kupferbergbau	*Copper-mining* has a long history in Montana.

Station 2: A travel blog

	to **hitchhike** ['hɪtʃhaɪk]	trampen; per Anhalter fahren	He tried to *hitchhike* from coast to coast.
7	**hitchhiking** ['hɪtʃˌhaɪkɪŋ]	Trampen	
	to **get a ride** [ˌget‿ə 'raɪd]	eine Mitfahrgelegenheit bekommen	
	truck *(AE)* [trʌk]	Truck; Lastwagen	My friend got a ride home in a *truck*.
	hitchhiker ['hɪtʃˌhaɪkə]	Tramper/-in	
8	**edge of town** [ˌedʒ‿əv 'taʊn]	Stadtrand	My family lives on the *edge of town*. It's too boring there for me!
	parking lot ['pɑ:kɪŋ ˌlɒt]	Parkplatz	
	cardboard ['kɑ:dbɔ:d]	Pappe; Karton	He made a *cardboard* sign for hitchhiking.
	to **stick out** [ˌstɪk‿'aʊt], **stuck out** [ˌstʌk‿'aʊt], **stuck out** [ˌstʌk‿'aʊt]	hinausstrecken	Hitchhikers *stick out* their thumbs when they want a ride.
	backseat ['bæksi:t]	Rücksitz	= the seat behind the driver in a car
	to **murder** ['mɜ:də]	ermorden; umbringen	*to murder* = to kill *to murder* → murder
	to **rob** [rɒb]	ausrauben; rauben; berauben	*to rob* → robber
10	**kitty litter** ['kɪti ˌlɪtə]	Katzenstreu	The *kitty litter* box for our cat is in the bathroom.
	passenger seat ['pæsndʒə ˌsi:t]	Beifahrersitz	= the seat next to the driver in a car

	unless [ən'les]	es sei denn, (dass) ...; wenn nicht	
	creature ['kri:tʃə]	Kreatur; Lebewesen; Geschöpf	There are some strange *creatures* in that movie.
	seat belt ['si:t belt]	Sicherheitsgurt	In my car, everybody wears a *seat belt*.
	to **run over** [ˌrʌn‿'əʊvə]	überfahren	My friend *ran over* my foot with his car. Great friend!
	to **drop sb off** [ˌdrɒp‿'ɒf]	jmdn. absetzen; jmdn. aussteigen lassen	*to drop sb off* ↔ to pick sb up
11	**storyteller** ['stɔ:riˌtelə]	Geschichtenerzähler/-in	*storyteller* → to tell

Across cultures 4 At home with an American family

	household ['haʊshəʊld]	Haushalt	
	chore [tʃɔ:]	(lästige) Pflicht; Bürde	Tidying up and cleaning the kitchen are some of the *chores* in a household.
1	to **set the table** [ˌset ðə 'teɪbl]	den Tisch decken	*Set the table*, please. Breakfast is ready.
	to **vacuum** ['vækju:m]	staubsaugen	
	to **load** [ləʊd]	einräumen; laden	*Load* the dishwasher please.
	to **empty** ['emti]	leeren; ausräumen	*to empty* ↔ to load *to empty* → empty
	to **clean up** [ˌkli:n‿'ʌp]	aufräumen; sauber machen	
	dishwasher ['dɪʃˌwɒʃə]	Spülmaschine	
	to **do the dishes** [ˌdu: ðə 'dɪʃɪz]	den Abwasch machen	
	dishes *(pl)* ['dɪʃɪz]	Geschirr	
	garbage *(AE)* ['gɑ:bɪdʒ]	Müll; Abfall	It's necessary to separate our *garbage*.
	rug [rʌg]	Vorleger; Teppich	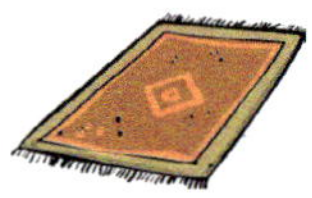
3	**allowance** *(AE)* [ə'laʊəns]	Taschengeld	*allowance* → to allow
	to **obey** [ə'beɪ]	gehorchen	If you *obey* orders, you do what you've been told to do. *Fr.* obéir
4	**preference** ['prefrns]	Vorliebe	*preference* → to prefer *Fr.* préférence *(f)*
	issue ['ɪʃu:; 'ɪsju:]	Abneigung; Problem	Have you got any food *issues*? – Yes, I don't eat meat or anything with milk in it.

Unit 4 The Pacific Northwest

Introduction

	to **consist of** [kən'sɪst‿əv]	bestehen aus	The US *consists of* 50 states.
	boomtown ['bu:mtaʊn]	schnell wachsende Stadt	Seattle is a business *boomtown*.
	orca ['ɔ:kə]	Schwertwal	
	cougar ['ku:gə]	Puma; Berglöwe	= a kind of big wild cat
	wolf [wʊlf], **wolves** [wʊlvz] *(pl)*	Wolf	
	native ['neɪtɪv]	einheimisch; eingeboren	What kind of plants and flowers are *native* to your region?
	volcano [vɒl'keɪnəʊ], **volcanoes** [vɒl'keɪnəʊz] *(pl)*	Vulkan	
1	**economy** [ɪ'kɒnəmi]	Ökonomie; Wirtschaft	Germany's *economy* is usually healthy. *Fr.* économie *(f)*
	growth [grəʊθ]	Wachstum	*growth* → to grow
	corporation [ˌkɔ:pr'eɪʃn]	Konzern; Unternehmen	Microsoft and SAP are huge *corporations*.
	total ['təʊtl]	gesamt; Gesamt-	Do you know the *total* number of students in your school?
	employee [ɪm'plɔɪi:]	Angestellte/-r; Mitarbeiter/-in; Arbeitnehmer/-in	= sb who works for a company or business and is employed *employee* → to employ
	airplane ['eəpleɪn]	Flugzeug	Boeing and Airbus produce *airplanes*.
	retail ['ri:teɪl]	Einzelhandel	Amazon makes money in online *retail*.
2	**waterfront** ['wɔ:təfrʌnt]	Hafenviertel; Ufer	Seattle's *waterfront* offers boat tours.
	the outdoors [ði ˌaʊt'dɔ:z]	die Natur	I love *the outdoors*. = I love sepnding time in nature.

Station 1: You've got no soul!

	You've got no soul! [ju:v ˌgɒt nəʊ 'səʊl]	*hier:* Du hast kein Feingefühl!	
	soul [səʊl]	Seele	Humans consist of body, mind and *soul*.
	wilderness ['wɪldənəs]	Wildnis	! Be careful with the pronunciation: wild [aɪ] – wilderness [ɪ]
	national park [ˌnæʃnl 'pɑ:k]	Nationalpark; Naturpark	There are 59 *national parks* in the US. *Fr.* parc national *(m)*
	peace [pi:s]	Frieden	to make/keep *peace*, to be at *peace*
	calm [kɑ:m]	Ruhe	Nature gives me feelings of peace, *calm* and freedom.
	great wheel [ˌgreɪt 'wi:l]	Riesenrad	*Great wheels* are often called 'Ferris wheels' too.
1	to **be true to oneself** [bi 'tru: tu wʌnˌself]	sich selbst treu bleiben	You should always *be true to yourself*. = You shouldn't pretend to be someone you aren't.
2	**part-time** [ˌpɑ:t'taɪm]	Teilzeit-; Halbtags-	My new job is a *part-time* job. I only work half-days.

3	**kind of** [ˈkaɪnd‿əv]	ziemlich	It's *kind of* a long way from New York to Los Angeles. – *Kind of*? That's a huge distance!
	to **be in a hurry** [ˌbi‿ɪn‿ə ˈhʌri]	es eilig haben; in Eile sein	If you're always *in a hurry*, you feel there isn't enough time to do everything you want/need to do.
	waiter [ˈweɪtə]	Kellner/-in; Bedienung	= the person who brings you your food in a restaurant
	It's my treat. [ɪts ˈmaɪ ˌtriːt]	Das geht auf meine Rechnung.	Order whatever you want! *It's my treat* today.
	unbelievable [ˌʌnbɪˈliːvəbl]	unglaublich; unglaubwürdig	Some novels have *unbelievable* characters.
	deal [diːl]	Abmachung; Übereinkunft	It's a *deal*. = Abgemacht.

Nouns and articles

Countable (*zählbar*), singular nouns, e.g. 'cat', must have an article:
Yesterday there was **a cat** in our garden.

But there are also nouns that don't need an article:

1. **Plural nouns** that refer to things or people in general don't need an article:
   My dog likes **cats**, but they don't like him! **BUT:** Have you fed the cats yet?

2. **Uncountable (*unzählbar*) nouns** that refer to things in general don't need an article:
   I love **ice cream**.
   I need **information**.
   Tennis is great. **BUT:** The tennis played by Novak Djokovic is awesome.

3. **Common (*allgemein*) nouns with a general meaning** don't need an article, especially when they are used with a preposition:
   - at school/college/university/home **BUT:** The school I went to as a child …
   - after work
   - in bed
   - in prison/hospital/church
   - before breakfast/lunch/dinner
   - in spring/summer/fall/winter **BUT:** The summer of 1969 …
   - after Christmas/Easter/New Year
   - by bike/train/car
   - on foot

4. **Proper nouns (*Eigennamen*)** don't need an article:
   - in Central Park/Hollywood
   - on Broadway
   - in America/Germany

Write a sentence for every category (1–4).

4	to **hold a competition** [ˌhəʊld‿ə ˌkɒmpəˈtɪʃn]	einen Wettbewerb durchführen	The tourist board *held a competition* for teens. *Fr.* compétition *(f)*
	entry [ˈentri]	Beitrag; Einsendung	What's your *entry* for the writing competition?
	hydroplane [ˈhaɪdrəpleɪn]	Gleitboot	Seattle is famous for its *'hydro'* races.
	rubber raft [ˌrʌbə ˈrɑːft]	Schlauchboot	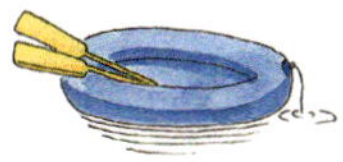
	happiness [ˈhæpɪnəs]	Glück; Zufriedenheit; Fröhlichkeit	*happiness* → happy
	major [ˈmeɪdʒə]	wichtig; bedeutend; Haupt-	This book has been made into a *major* film. *Lat.* maior *(adj)*
	paddleboard [ˈpædlbɔːd]	Paddling Board *(eine Art Surfbrett, auf dem man aufrecht stehend paddelt)*	The *paddleboard* trend started in the US.
5	to **protect sb/sth (from)** [prəˈtekt frəm]	jmdn./etw. (be)schützen (vor)	National parks *protect* the natural environment.
6	to **buy time** [ˌbaɪ ˈtaɪm]	Zeit gewinnen	In a conversation, you sometimes need to *buy time* while you think of what to say next.
	Just a second … [ˌdʒʌst‿ə ˈseknd]	Einen Augenblick …	
	second [ˈseknd]	Sekunde	
7	**nature lover** [ˈneɪtʃə ˌlʌvə]	Naturfreund/-in	Are you a *nature lover* or a city person? *Lat.* natura *(f)*

All of, most of, some of, …

All of my friends love ice cream.	**Alle** meine Freunde lieben Eis.
Most of them love chocolate ice cream.	**Die meisten** von ihnen lieben Schokoladeneis.
Some of them don't like banana ice cream.	**Einige** mögen kein Bananeneis.
A few of them only buy freshly made ice cream.	**Wenige** kaufen nur frisch gemachtes Eis.
None of my friends has ever made ice cream themselves.	**Keiner** meiner Freunde hat Eis jemals selbst gemacht.

Station 2: Native Americans in the Northwest

people [ˈpiːpl]	Volk	The Cowichan *people* are one of the Coast Salish tribes.
salmon [ˈsæmən], **salmon** [ˈsæmən] *(pl)*	Lachs	*Salmon* are interesting fish: During their lives, they live in rivers and oceans.
to **go** *(+ adj)* [gəʊ]	werden	A lot of people *go white* when they get scared.
leader [ˈliːdə]	Führer/-in; Anführer/-in	= the person or team that is in front of the others
downriver [ˌdaʊnˈrɪvə]	flussabwärts; stromabwärts	
cause [kɔːz]	Grund; Ursache	*cause* → to cause → because
mouth [maʊθ]	Mündung	Where's the *mouth* of the Mississippi River?

	whale [weɪl]	Wal	An orca is a kind of *whale*.
	to **paddle** ['pædl]	paddeln	*to paddle* → paddle board
	canoe [kə'nu:]	Kanu	
	medicine people ['medsn ˌpi:pl]	Medizinmänner	
	support *(no pl)* [sə'pɔ:t]	Unterstützung; Hilfe	*support* → to support
	spiritual ['spɪrɪtjuəl]	spirituell; geistig	*Fr.* spirituel/-le
	to **appear** [ə'pɪə]	auftauchen; erscheinen	= to be there suddenly *to appear* ↔ to disappear
	salmon run ['sæmən ˌrʌn]	Lachswanderung	
	peaceful ['pi:sfl]	friedlich	*peaceful* → peace
9	**ceremony** ['serɪməni]	Zeremonie	
	sacred ['seɪkrɪd]	heilig	The Elwha River is *sacred* to the Lower Elwha Klallam tribe.
	symbolic [sɪm'bɒlɪk]	symbolisch	*symbolic* → symbol
	to **rise** [raɪz], **rose** [rəʊz], **risen** ['rɪzn]	aufgehen *(Sonne)*	As the sun *rose*, the ceremony started. *to rise* = to go up
	drum [drʌm]	Trommel	
	raft [rɑ:ft]	Floß	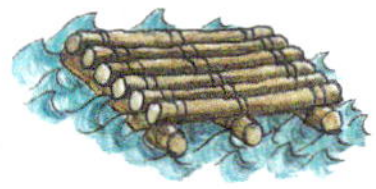
	the gods *(liter)* [ðə 'gɒdz]	die Götter *(literarisch)*	*The gods* must be angry with me at the moment because everything went wrong today!
	dam [dæm]	Damm; Staumauer	A *dam* is built to make water form a lake.
	power [paʊə]	Strom; Elektrizität; Energie	Electricity is a form of *power*.
	timber ['tɪmbə]	Holz; Bauholz	= wood that is used for building houses and furniture
	to **remove** [rɪ'mu:v]	entfernen; abreißen	= to take away (sth that you don't want) *to remove* → to move
	outside world ['aʊtsaɪd ˌwɜ:ld]	Außenwelt	*here:* the world outside the reservation
	Everything will have changed. [ˌevriθɪŋ wɪl hæv 'tʃeɪndʒd]	Alles wird sich geändert haben.	
11	**architecture** ['ɑ:kɪtektʃə]	Architektur	If you study *architecture*, you learn how to plan and design buildings.
	artwork ['ɑ:twɜ:k]	Illustrationen; Bebilderung	Every Indian tribe has its typical *artwork*.
	longhouse ['lɒŋhaʊs]	Langhaus	= a typical house of the Coast Salish tribes

	totem pole ['təʊtəm ˌpəʊl]	Totempfahl	
14	**in favor (of)** *(AE)* [ɪn 'feɪvər‿əv]	(da)für; zugunsten (von)	If you vote for sth, you are *in favor of* it.
	advantage [əd'vɑ:ntɪdʒ]	Vorteil	In basketball, it's an *advantage* to be tall. *Fr.* avantage *(m)*
	overall [ˌəʊvr'ɔ:l]	insgesamt	*Overall*, I think it's a great idea, but I have one small issue with it.
	view [vju:]	Ansicht; Einstellung; Standpunkt	*view* = point of view
	community [kə'mju:nəti]	Gemeinde; Gemeinschaft	Are you active in your *community*? – Yes, I help with food drives and clothing drives.
	disadvantage [ˌdɪsəd'vɑ:ntɪdʒ]	Nachteil	*disadvantage* ↔ advantage
	to **destroy** [dɪ'strɔɪ]	zerstören	Too many new buildings and roads *destroy* the natural environment. *Fr.* détruire
	what's more [ˌwɒts 'mɔ:]	außerdem; überdies	Cars are noisy. *What's more*, they cause pollution.
	deal [di:l]	Handel; Geschäft	It's a bad *deal* for our health.

Skills: How to argue a point in conversation

	to **argue** ['ɑ:gju:]	erörtern	Let's *argue* this point more widely.
	eruption [ɪ'rʌpʃn]	Ausbruch *(Vulkan)*	In 1980 there was an *eruption* of Mount St. Helens.
	nearby [ˌnɪə'baɪ]	in der Nähe	= not far away
2	to **over-exaggerate** [ˌəʊvərɪg'zædʒreɪt]	völlig übertreiben	If you *over-exaggerate* sth, you make it sound much better or worse than it really is. *Fr.* exagérer
	to **see the bigger picture** [ˌsi: ðə ˌbɪgə 'pɪktʃə]	über den Tellerrand hinausschauen	Why can't you *see the bigger picture*? You only see yourself.
	based on ['beɪst‿ɒn]	basierend auf; beruhend auf	Don't make decisions *based on* your feelings.
3	**debate** [dɪ'beɪt]	Debatte	= a formal discussion about the pros and cons of sth
	move [mu:v]	Umzug	That was our third *move* in five years. Can't we stay here for a while?

Story: The Absolutely True Diary of a Part-Time Indian

junior ['dʒu:niə]	Junior; der/die Jüngere	Arnold's family calls him *'Junior'*.
loser ['lu:zə]	Verlierer/-in; Loser/-in	*loser* → to lose
black eye [blæk‿'aɪ]	blaues Auge	

	punch [pʌnʃ]	Faustschlag; Boxhieb	Arnold had a black eye from his friend's *punch*.
	to **surround** [səˈraʊnd]	umgeben; umringen	At school the white kids *surrounded* Arnold.
	skin [skɪn]	Haut; Fell	When I'm in the sun for too long, my *skin* goes red.
	gift [gɪft]	Geschenk; Gabe	*gift* = present; talent
	racist [ˈreɪsɪst]	rassistisch; Rassist/-in	Did you just make a joke about Native Americans? That's *racist* and it isn't funny.
	college [ˈkɒlɪdʒ]	Universität *(in den USA)*	! Notice the difference: He goes to *college*. – Where exactly? – He goes to the University of Washington.
2	to **struggle** [ˈstrʌgl]	kämpfen; Mühe haben; ringen	Arnold *struggles* with feeling different.
	gas(oline) *(AE)* [ˈgæsliːn]	Benzin	I hope we have enough *gas*. I don't want to be trapped in Death Valley!
	highway *(AE)* [ˈhaɪweɪ]	Landstraße; Bundesautobahn *(amerik.)*; Highway	In the US, *highways* are main roads, but not the fastest. Freeways are the fastest roads.
	It wouldn't do me any good. [ˌɪt wʊdnt ˌduː miː eni ˈgʊd]	Es würde mir nichts nützen.	I thought telling the truth *wouldn't do me any good*. So I lied, but that was worse.
	to **go bad** [ˌgəʊ ˈbæd]	schiefgehen; schlecht werden; verderben	Let's eat that salmon before it *goes bad*. It was expensive.
3	**strategy** [ˈstrætədʒi]	Strategie	! Watch the spelling and the pronunciation. *Fr.* stratégie *(f)*
	struggle [ˈstrʌgl]	Anstrengung; Kampf	When you try very hard to do sth difficult, it's a *struggle*. *struggle* → to struggle
	soda pop *(AE)* [ˈsəʊdə ˌpɒp]	Limo	We aren't allowed to drink *soda pop* at home. Bad for your teeth!
	imaginary [ɪˈmædʒɪnri]	erfunden; eingebildet	= not real, only in the mind *imaginary* → to imagine
	illness [ˈɪlnəs]	Krankheit	*illness* → ill
	suit [suːt]	Anzug; Kostüm	! Watch the pronunciation.
	to **make fun of** [ˌmeɪk ˈfʌn‿əv]	sich lustig machen über	If you *make fun of* sb, you make jokes about them.
	lame [leɪm]	lahm; langweilig	*lame* = boring
	to **punch** [pʌnʃ]	mit der Faust schlagen; boxen	*to punch* → punch
	brain-dead [ˈbreɪnˌded]	hirntot	
	superhero [ˈsuːpəˌhɪərəʊ]	Superheld	Superman is a famous *superhero*.
	justice [ˈdʒʌstɪs]	Gerechtigkeit	Superheroes fight for truth and *justice*.
	traitor [ˈtreɪtə]	Verräter/-in	
	constant [ˈkɒnstənt]	ständig; konstant; stetig; gleichmäßig	He texts me *constantly* and won't stop.
	to **toss out** [ˌtɒs‿ˈaʊt]	ausstoßen; hinauswerfen	I'm sure it isn't a nice feeling when you're *tossed out* of a community just because you're different.
7	**unique** [juːˈniːk]	einzigartig	= being the only one of its kind *Fr.* unique

Action USA! A trip to die for?

	It's to die for! [ˌɪts tə ˈdaɪ fɔː]	Dafür könnte ich sterben!; Das ist unwiderstehlich!	Mmm, those bagels *are to die for*!
1	**suspicious** [səˈspɪʃəs]	verdächtig	His behavior looks *suspicious* to me.
2	**misunderstanding** [ˌmɪsʌndəˈstændɪŋ]	Missverständnis	

Important differences

	AE	BE
Different spelling	to coloni**ze**, to recogni**ze** in fav**or** of, hum**or** jewe**lr**y	to coloni**se**, to recogni**se** in fav**our** of, hum**our** jewe**ller**y
Different words	allowance gas highway last name line schedule transportation	pocket money petrol motorway surname queue timetable transport

Dictionary

In dieser alphabetischen Wortliste findest du das gesamte Vokabular von *Green Line* 1, 2, 3 und 4.
Namen stehen in einer extra Liste am Ende des *Dictionary*.
Einträge, die aus mehreren Wörtern bestehen, kannst du meist unter verschiedenen Stichwörtern nachschlagen. So ist z.B. *after all* unter *after* und unter *all* eingetragen.
Die Fundstellen stehen immer hinter dem jeweiligen Wort und zeigen dir an, wo es zum ersten Mal vorkommt, z. B.:
advantage [əd'vɑ:ntɪdʒ] Vorteil **IV U4**, 119 kommt zum ersten Mal vor in Band 4, Unit 4, Seite 119
advertising *(no pl)* ['ædvətaɪzɪŋ] Werbung; Reklame **IV TS1**, 34 kommt zum ersten Mal vor in Band 4, Text smart 1, Seite 34
U = Unit, AC = Across cultures, TS = Text smart
Die mit * gekennzeichneten Verben sind unregelmäßig.
Die mit ° gekennzeichneten Vokabeln sind rezeptiv.
Die mit ⟨ ⟩ gekennzeichneten Vokabeln sind fakultativ.

A

a [ə] ein/-e **I**
- **a** bit [ə 'bɪt] ein bisschen; ein wenig **II**
- **a** couple of [ə 'kʌpl‿əv] ein paar **I**
- **a** few [ə 'fju:] ein paar; wenige; einige **I**
- **a** little [ə 'lɪtl] ein wenig; etwas **I**
- **a** lot [ə 'lɒt] viel **I**
- **a** lot of [ə 'lɒt‿əv] viel/-e; eine Menge **I**
- **a** total of [ə 'təʊtl‿əv] insgesamt **IV U3**, 81
- **a** (day/week/year) [ə 'deɪ/wi:k/jɪə] pro (Tag/Woche/Jahr) **IV AC1**, 9
- **a** lot to learn [ə ˌlɒt tə 'lɜ:n] viel zu lernen **I**

a.m. [ˌeɪ'em] vormittags *(Uhrzeit)* **I**
to **abandon** [ə'bændən] aufgeben; zurücklassen **IV U3**, 92
*to be **able** to (do sth) [bi‿'eɪbl tə] fähig sein zu; können; dürfen **II**
aboard [ə'bɔ:d] an Bord **I**
about [ə'baʊt] ungefähr; circa; etwa **I**
about [ə'baʊt] über; von **I**
- *to be **about** to do sth [bi‿ə'baʊt tə] im Begriff sein, etw. zu tun **IV AC2**, 39
- out and **about** [ˌaʊt‿ən‿ə'baʊt] unterwegs **II**
- What **about** …? ['wɒt‿əbaʊt] Wie wär's mit …?; Was ist mit …? **I**
- What is … **about**? [ˌwɒt‿ɪz …‿ə'baʊt] Worum geht es in/im …? **I**

above [ə'bʌv] oben **II**
abroad [ə'brɔ:d] im Ausland; ins Ausland **III**
absolutely [ˌæbsə'lu:tli] absolut; völlig **II**
abstract ['æbstrækt] abstrakt °**IV U4**, 114
accent ['æksnt] Akzent **II**
to **accept** [ək'sept] akzeptieren; hinnehmen; annehmen **III**
accident ['æksɪdnt] Unfall **II**
according to [ə'kɔ:dɪŋ tə] laut; gemäß °**IV U3**, 88
account settings [ə'kaʊnt ˌsetɪŋz] Profileinstellungen **III**
to **achieve** [ə'tʃi:v] erreichen; erlangen °**IV TS3**, 104
across [ə'krɒs] auf der anderen Seite von; über; hinüber; herüber; quer durch **I**
- **Across** cultures [əˌkrɒs 'kʌltʃəz] Interkulturelles **I**

to **act** [ækt] spielen *(Theater)* **I**; sich verhalten; handeln °**IV AC2**, 38
- to **act** like ['ækt laɪk] tun als ob **II**
- to **act** out [ækt 'aʊt] nachspielen **II**
- **acting** a scene [ˌæktɪŋ‿ə 'si:n] eine Theaterszene spielen **I**

acting ['æktɪŋ] Schauspielen **II**
action ['ækʃn] Handlung; Action; Aktion **I**
active ['æktɪv] aktiv **III**
activity [æk'tɪvəti] Aktivität **I**
actor ['æktə] Schauspieler **II**
actual ['æktʃuəl] tatsächlich; wirklich; eigentlich °**IV U2**, 62
actually ['æktʃuəli] tatsächlich; wirklich; eigentlich ⟨**IV TS3**, 105⟩
ad [əd'vɜ:tɪsmənt] Anzeige; Werbespot **IV TS1**, 34
- **ad** copy ['æd ˌkɒpi] Werbetext **IV TS1**, 35

AD (= Anno Domini) [ˌeɪ'di:] nach Christus **III**
adapted [ə'dæptɪd] adaptiert; angepasst °**IV U4**, 116
to **add** [æd] hinzufügen; ergänzen **I**
addict ['ædɪkt] Süchtige/-r; Abhängige/-r **III**
in **addition** to [ɪn‿ə'dɪʃn tə] neben; daneben; darüber hinaus **IV U3**, 84
additional [ə'dɪʃnl] zusätzlich **II**
address [ə'dres] Adresse **I**
to **address** [ə'dres] ansprechen; sich wenden an °**IV U3**, 94
adjective ['ædʒɪktɪv] Adjektiv; Eigenschaftswort **II**
adult ['ædʌlt] Erwachsene/-r **II**
advantage [əd'vɑ:ntɪdʒ] Vorteil **IV U4**, 119
adventure [əd'ventʃə] Abenteuer **II**
adverb ['ædvɜ:b] Adverb **II**
adverbial clause [ədˌvɜ:biəl 'klɔ:z] Adverbialsatz °**IV U3**, 87
advert ['ædvɜ:t] Anzeige; Werbespot **III**
to **advertise** ['ædvətaɪz] Werbung machen; werben; anpreisen; inserieren **IV TS1**, 34
advertisement [əd'vɜ:tɪsmənt] Anzeige; Werbespot **IV TS1**, 34
advertiser ['ædvətaɪzə] Werbefachmann/-frau **IV TS1**, 34
advertising *(no pl)* ['ædvətaɪzɪŋ] Werbung; Reklame **IV TS1**, 34
advice [əd'vaɪs] Rat; Ratschlag **II**
to **affect** [ə'fekt] beeinflussen; beeinträchtigen; betreffen °**IV U4**, 117
to **afford** [ə'fɔ:d] sich leisten **III**
*to be **afraid** (of) [bi‿ə'freɪd‿əv] (sich) fürchten; Angst haben (vor) **III**
I'm **afraid** … [ˌaɪm‿ə'freɪd] Leider … **IV U1**, 14
after ['ɑ:ftə] nach *(zeitlich)* **I**
- **after** all [ˌɑ:ftər‿'ɔ:l] doch; schließlich; immerhin **I**
- **after** that [ˌɑ:ftə 'ðæt] danach **I**

after ['ɑ:ftə] nachdem **IV U3**, 80
afternoon [ˌɑ:ftə'nu:n] Nachmittag **I**
- this **afternoon** [ðɪs 'ɑ:ftənu:n] heute Nachmittag **II**

afterwards ['ɑ:ftəwədz] danach; hinterher °**IV TS1**, 37
again [ə'gen] wieder; noch einmal; noch mal **I**
- over and over **again** [ˌəʊvər‿ən‿ˌəʊvər‿ə'gen] immer wieder **III**

against [ə'genst] gegen **II**
- **against** all odds [əˌgenst‿ɔ:l‿'ɒdz] entgegen allen Erwartungen **III**

age [eɪdʒ] Alter **III**
- Bronze **Age** ['brɒnz eɪdʒ] Bronzezeit *(ca. 2200–800 v. Chr.)* **II**
- golden **age** [ˌgəʊldn 'eɪdʒ] goldenes Zeitalter **III**

travel **agency** ['trævlˌeɪdʒnsi] Reisebüro **III**
travel **agent's** ['trævlˌeɪdʒnts] Reisebüro **II**
aggressive [ə'gresɪv] aggressiv **II**
ago [ə'gəʊ] vor *(zeitlich)* **II**
agony aunt ['ægəniˌɑ:nt] Kummerkastentante **II**
to **agree** (on) [ə'gri:] sich einigen (auf) **II**
to **agree** (with) [ə'gri:] einer Meinung sein (mit); zustimmen **II**
ain't (= isn't/aren't) [eɪnt] ist nicht; sind nicht **IV AC3**, 77

air [eə] Luft **III**
air-conditioning [ˌeəkən'dɪʃnɪŋ] Klimaanlage **III**
air-force base ['eəfɔ:s ˌbeɪs] Luftwaffenstützpunkt ⟨**IV TS2**, 72⟩
airplane ['eəpleɪn] Flugzeug **IV U4**, 110
airport ['eəpɔ:t] Flughafen **II**
aisle [aɪl] Mittelgang ⟨**IV U4**, 123⟩
aka [ˌeɪkeɪ'eɪ] alias °**IV U2**, 49
alarm clock [ə'lɑ:m ˌklɒk] Wecker **II**
alien ['eɪliən] Außerirdische/-r; außerirdisches Wesen **I**
alive [ə'laɪv] lebend; am Leben; lebendig **IV U3**, 93
all [ɔ:l] alle/-s; ganz **I**
after **all** [ˌɑ:ftər‿'ɔ:l] doch; schließlich; immerhin **I**
all alone [ˌɔ:l‿ə'ləʊn] ganz allein ⟨**IV TS2**, 74⟩
all day [ˌɔ:l 'deɪ] den ganzen Tag **II**
all night [ˌɔ:l 'naɪt] die ganze Nacht **I**
all over [ˌɔ:l‿'əʊvə] überall (in) **I**
all right [ˌɔ:l 'raɪt] in Ordnung; alles klar ⟨**IV U4**, 125⟩
all the time [ˌɔ:l ðə 'taɪm] die ganze Zeit **II**
at **all** [ət‿'ɔ:l] überhaupt **I**
all of them ['ɔ:l‿əv ˌðem] alle **I**
all of us ['ɔ:l‿əv ˌʌs] wir alle **II**
to start **all** over again [ˌstɑ:t‿ɔ:l‿'əʊvər‿əˌgen] ganz von vorn beginnen **IV U3**, 85
to pledge **allegiance** [ˌpledʒ‿ə'li:dʒns] Treueschwur leisten ⟨**IV U1**, 19⟩
allergic to [ə'lɜ:dʒɪk tə] allergisch gegen ⟨**IV U4**, 124⟩
bowling **alley** ['bəʊlɪŋ‿ˌæli] Bowlingbahn **I**
*to be **allowed** to (do sth) [bi‿ə'laʊd tə] dürfen **II**
allowance *(AE)* [ə'laʊəns] Taschengeld **IV AC4**, 109
all-purpose ['ɔ:lˌpɜ:pəs] für alle Lebenslagen ⟨**IV U4**, 124⟩
almost ['ɔ:lməʊst] fast; beinahe **II**
alone [ə'ləʊn] allein; ohne fremde Hilfe **I**
all **alone** [ˌɔ:l‿ə'ləʊn] ganz allein ⟨**IV TS2**, 74⟩
*to leave sb **alone** [ˌli:v‿ə'ləʊn] jmdn. in Ruhe lassen **IV U1**, 23
along [ə'lɒŋ] entlang **I**
to clap **along** [ˌklæp‿ə'lɒŋ] mitklatschen ⟨**IV U3**, 93⟩
*to sing **along** [ˌsɪŋ‿ə'lɒŋ] mitsingen **III**
along for the ride [əˌlɒŋ fə ðə 'raɪd] mit dabei **IV U1**, 14
alphabet ['ælfəbet] Alphabet **I**
alphabetical [ˌælfə'betɪkl] alphabetisch **II**
already [ɔ:l'redi] schon; bereits **I**
also ['ɔ:lsəʊ] auch **II**
although [ɔ:l'ðəʊ] obwohl **III**
always ['ɔ:lweɪz] immer; ständig **I**
amazed [ə'meɪzd] erstaunt; verblüfft **IV U1**, 22
amazing [ə'meɪzɪŋ] unglaublich; toll; erstaunlich **II**
ambulance ['æmbjələns] Krankenwagen **III**
American [ə'merɪkən] Amerikanisch; amerikanisch; aus Amerika; Amerikaner/-in **II**
Native **American** [ˌneɪtɪv‿ə'merɪkən] Ureinwohner/-in Amerikas; Indianer/-in; indianisch **IV U1**, 15
among [ə'mʌŋ] unter; inmitten **III**
amount (of) [ə'maʊnt] Menge °**IV TS2**, 75
an [ən] ein/-e **I**
to **analyze** *(AE)* ['ænlaɪz] analysieren °**IV U1**, 13
ancient ['eɪnʃnt] alt; altertümlich; antik ⟨**IV TS2**, 72⟩
and [ænd; ənd] und **I**
angel ['eɪndʒl] Engel **III**
anger *(no pl)* ['æŋgə] Zorn; Wut **III**
angry ['æŋgri] wütend; zornig; verärgert; böse **I**
*to make sb **angry** [meɪk 'æŋgri] jmdn. wütend machen; jmdn. verärgern **III**
animal ['ænɪməl] Tier **I**
animal shelter ['ænɪml ˌʃeltə] Tierheim **III**
ankle ['æŋkl] Fußgelenk; Fußknöchel **II**
to twist your **ankle** [ˌtwɪst jɔ:r‿'æŋkl] sich den Knöchel verrenken **II**
to **announce** [ə'naʊns] ankündigen; durchsagen **IV TS2**, 71
announcement [ə'naʊnsmənt] Ankündigung; Durchsage **II**
anonymous [ən'ɒnɪməs] anonym **II**
another [ə'nʌðə] ein/-e andere/-r/-s; noch ein/-e; ein/-e andere/-r/-s **I**
one **another** [ˌwʌn‿ə'nʌðə] einander; gegenseitig ⟨**IV U4**, 125⟩
answer ['ɑ:nsə] Antwort **I**
short **answer** [ˌʃɔ:t‿'ɑ:nsə] Kurzantwort **I**
to **answer** ['ɑ:nsə] antworten; beantworten **I**
to **answer** the phone [ˌɑ:nsə ðə 'fəʊn] einen Anruf entgegennehmen **I**
answering machine ['ɑ:nsrɪŋ məˌʃi:n] Anrufbeantworter **I**
anthem ['ænθəm] Hymne **III**
any ['eni] irgendein/-e/-er; irgendwelche **I**
not **any** more [ˌnɒt‿eni 'mɔ:] nicht mehr **I**
not … **any** [nɒt … eni] kein/-e/-en **I**
not **anymore** *(AE)* [ˌnɒt‿eni'mɔ:] nicht mehr **IV AC1**, 9
anyone else [ˌeniwʌn 'els] jemand anderes **II**
Anything else? [ˌeniθɪŋ‿'els] Sonst noch etwas? **I**
not … **anything** [ˌnɒt 'eniθɪŋ] nichts **I**
anyway ['eniweɪ] trotzdem; jedenfalls; sowieso **II**
anywhere ['eniweə] irgendwo; überall (egal, wo) **II**
just about **anywhere** [ˌdʒʌst‿əˌbaʊt 'eniweə] praktisch überall **IV TS1**, 34
apart [ə'pɑ:t] auseinander; getrennt **IV U3**, 92
apart from [ə'pɑ:t frəm] abgesehen von; außer **III**
apartment *(AE)* [ə'pɑ:tmənt] Apartment; Wohnung **IV U1**, 13
to **apologise** [ə'pɒlədʒaɪz] sich entschuldigen **III**
app [æp] App **II**
to **appear** [ə'pɪə] auftauchen; erscheinen **IV U4**, 116
apple ['æpl] Apfel **I**
approach [ə'prəʊtʃ] Herangehensweise; Vorgehensweise; Ansatz; Annäherung **IV TS1**, 36
appropriate [ə'prəʊpriət] angemessen **III**
April ['eɪprəl] April **I**
Arab ['ærəb] arabisch **III**
architect ['ɑ:kɪtekt] Architekt/-in **II**
architecture ['ɑ:kɪtektʃə] Architektur **IV U4**, 118
area ['eəriə] Areal; Gebiet; Fläche **II**
run **area** ['rʌn ˌeəriə] Gehege; Auslauf **III**
to **argue** ['ɑ:gju:] argumentieren; streiten **IV U1**, 21; erörtern **IV U4**, 120
argument ['ɑ:gjəmənt] Auseinandersetzung; Streit; Argument **III**
argumentative [ˌɑ:gjə'mentətɪv] erörternd °**IV U4**, 119
arm [ɑ:m] Arm **II**
army ['ɑ:mi] Armee **IV U3**, 80
around [ə'raʊnd] um … herum; umher **I**
*to be **around** [ˌbi: ə'raʊnd] da sein; zusammen sein mit **IV U1**, 14
*to find one's way **around** [ˌfaɪnd wʌnz ˌweɪ‿ə'raʊnd] sich zurechtfinden **IV U1**, 16
*to hang **around** [ˌhæŋ‿ə'raʊnd] herumhängen (bei) ⟨**IV U4**, 125⟩
to show sb **around** (a place) [ˌʃəʊ‿ə'raʊnd] jmdn. (an einem Ort) herumführen ⟨**IV AC4**, 109⟩
to turn **around** [tɜ:n‿(ə)'raʊnd] (sich) umdrehen; wenden **II**
to **arrange** [ə'reɪndʒ] arrangieren; anordnen **III**
to **arrest** [ə'rest] festnehmen; verhaften **II**
arrival [ə'raɪvl] Ankunft **III**; Ankommende/-r; Neuzugang **IV TS1**, 36
arrivals hall [ə'raɪvlz ˌhɔ:l] Ankunftshalle **III**
to **arrive** [ə'raɪv] ankommen **II**
arrow ['ærəʊ] Pfeil **III**
arrowhead ['ærəʊhed] Pfeilspitze ⟨**IV U3**, 93⟩
Art [ɑ:t] Kunstunterricht **I**
art [ɑ:t] Kunst **II**
article ['ɑ:tɪkl] Artikel; Bericht *(in einer Zeitschrift, Zeitung)* **II**
reference **article** ['refrns ˌɑ:tɪkl] Referenzartikel **III**
artist ['ɑ:tɪst] Künstler/-in **IV U2**, 44
artwork ['ɑ:twɜ:k] Illustrationen; Bebilderung **IV U4**, 118
as [æz; əz] als **II**
as if [əz‿'ɪf] als ob **III**

as [æz] während; indem **I**; wie **II**
as soon **as** [əz 'su:n‿əz] sobald **II**
as … **as** [əz … əz] so … wie **I**
… **as** well **as** … [əz 'wel‿əz] sowie; und (auch) °**IV U3**, 91
as [æz; əz] da; weil **IV U3**, 86
to **ask** [ɑ:sk] fragen; bitten **I**
Ask about … ['ɑ:sk‿əˌbaʊt] Frage/Fragt nach … **I**
to **ask** for ['ɑ:sk fə] fragen nach; bitten um **I**
*to be **asleep** [ˌbi ə'sli:p] schlafen **II**
*to fall **asleep** [ˌfɔ:l‿ə'sli:p] einschlafen **I**
aspect ['æspekt] Aspekt; Gesichtspunkt °**IV U1**, 12
asphalt ['æsfælt] Asphalt ⟨**IV U2**, 50⟩
assembly [ə'sembli] Versammlung; Morgenappell **II**
assistant [ə'sɪstnt] Assistent/-in; Verkäufer/-in **II**
to **assume** [ə'sju:m] annehmen ⟨**IV U4**, 123⟩
astronaut ['æstrənɔ:t] Astronaut/-in **IV TS2**, 70
at [æt; ət] in; auf; bei; an; um *(bei Uhrzeitangaben)* **I**
at 7:30 [ət ˌsevn‿'θɜ:ti] um halb acht **I**
at all [ət‿'ɔ:l] überhaupt **I**
at first [ət 'fɜ:st] zuerst; zunächst **II**
at home [ət 'həʊm] zu Hause **I**
at last [ət 'lɑ:st] endlich; schließlich **I**
at least [ət 'li:st] mindestens; wenigstens **II**
at the back of [ət ðə 'bæk‿əv] hinten; am Ende; im hinteren Teil **II**
at the moment [ət ðə 'məʊmənt] im Moment; gerade **I**
at the same time [ət ðə ˌseɪm 'taɪm] zur selben Zeit; gleichzeitig **I**
at the time [ˌət ðə 'taɪm] damals **IV TS2**, 72
at the weekend [ət ðə ˌwi:k'end] am Wochenende **I**
athletics *(no pl)* [æθ'letɪks] Leichtathletik **III**
atlas ['ætləs] Atlas **II**
atmosphere ['ætməsfɪə] Atmosphäre; Stimmung **II**
to **attack** [ə'tæk] angreifen **III**
flight **attendant** ['flaɪt‿əˌtendnt] Flugbegleiter/-in **III**
attention [ə'tenʃn] Aufmerksamkeit; Beachtung **II**
*to pay **attention** to sb/sth [ˌpeɪ‿ə'tenʃn tʊ] jmdn./etw. beachten **III**
attic ['ætɪk] Dachboden **II**
attitude ['ætɪtju:d] Haltung; Einstellung **IV U1**, 25
to **attract** [ə'trækt] anziehen **IV TS1**, 36
attraction [ə'trækʃn] Attraktion; Sehenswürdigkeit **II**
attractive [ə'træktɪv] attraktiv **IV U1**, 25
audience ['ɔ:diəns] Publikum **II**
audio ['ɔ:diəʊ] Audio-; Hör- **I**
audio tour ['ɔ:diəʊ ˌtʊə] Audioführung **II**
audio-visual effect [ˌɔ:diəʊvɪʒuəl ɪ'fekt] audiovisueller Effekt **II**
audition [ɔ:'dɪʃn] Vorsprechen; Vorsingen; Vortanzen **III**
auditor ['ɔ:dɪtə] Wirtschaftsprüfer/-in ⟨**IV TS3**, 105⟩
August ['ɔ:gəst] August **I**
aunt [ɑ:nt] Tante **I**
agony **aunt** ['ægəni‿ɑ:nt] Kummerkastentante **II**
auntie ['ɑ:nti] Tantchen **IV AC3**, 77
Australian [ɒs'treɪliən] australisch; Australier/-in **III**
author ['ɔ:θə] Autor/-in **III**
available [ə'veɪləbl] erhältlich; verfügbar **IV TS1**, 35
to **avoid** [ə'vɔɪd] vermeiden; meiden; aus dem Weg gehen **III**
to stay **awake** [ˌsteɪ‿ə'weɪk] wach bleiben ⟨**IV U2**, 60⟩
award [ə'wɔ:d] Auszeichnung; Preis **II**
to be **aware** of sth [bi‿ə'weər‿əv] sich etw. bewusst sein **IV TS3**, 102
away [ə'weɪ] weg **I**
*to give **away** [ˌgɪv‿ə'weɪ] verteilen; verschenken **IV TS1**, 34; verraten; preisgeben °**IV U2**, 63
right **away** [ˌraɪt‿ə'weɪ] sofort; gleich **I**
*to run **away** [ˌrʌn‿ə'weɪ] wegrennen **I**
straight **away** [ˌstreɪt‿ə'weɪ] sofort; gleich **III**
*to throw **away** [ˌθrəʊ‿ə'weɪ] wegwerfen **I**
awesome ['ɔ:səm] super; spitze **IV AC1**, 11
awful ['ɔ:fl] schrecklich; furchtbar **I**
axe [æks] Axt **III**

B

baby ['beɪbi] Baby; Säugling **I**
babysitting ['beɪbɪsɪtɪŋ] Babysitting **IV U4**, 113
back [bæk] Rückseite; Rücken **II**
at the **back** of [ət ðə 'bæk‿əv] hinten; am Ende; im hinteren Teil **II**
back to **back** [ˌbæk tʊ 'bæk] Rücken an Rücken **I**
back [bæk] zurück **I**
back then [bæk 'ðen] damals **III**
*to go right **back** to [ˌgəʊ raɪt 'bæk tə] zurückgehen auf **II**
to turn **back** [tɜ:n 'bæk] umkehren; zurückgehen **II**
backache ['bækeɪk] Rückenschmerzen; Rückenweh **II**
backcountry *(no pl)* ['bækkʌntri] Hinterland ⟨**IV TS3**, 102⟩
background ['bækgraʊnd] Hintergrund **I**
backing ['bækɪŋ] Hintergrund-; Background- **III**
backing dancer ['bækɪŋ ˌdɑ:nsə] Backgroundtänzer/-in **III**
backpack ['bækpæk] Rucksack **III**
backseat ['bæksi:t] Rücksitz **IV TS3**, 105
backyard [ˌbæk'jɑ:d] Garten; Hinterhof **III**
bacon ['beɪkn] Schinkenspeck; Speck **I**
bad [bæd] schlecht; böse; schlimm *(ugs.)* **I**
*to go **bad** [ˌgəʊ 'bæd] schiefgehen; schlecht werden; verderben **IV U4**, 124
Too **bad**! [ˌtu: 'bæd] Zu dumm!; Schade! **I**
badly-written [ˌbædli'rɪtn] schlecht geschrieben **IV TS2**, 75
badminton ['bædmɪntən] Badminton **I**
bag [bæg] Tasche; Tüte **I**
tea **bag** ['ti: bæg] Teebeutel **III**
bagel ['beɪgl] Bagel *(weiches, ringförmiges Brötchen)* ⟨**IV U2**, 45⟩
bagpipes *(pl)* ['bægpaɪps] Dudelsack **III**
bake sale ['beɪk seɪl] Kuchenverkauf ⟨**IV U4**, 124⟩
baked beans *(pl)* [ˌbeɪkt 'bi:nz] weiße Bohnen in Tomatensoße **I**
balcony ['bælkəni] Balkon ⟨**IV AC4**, 109⟩
ball [bɔ:l] Ball **I**
*to keep the **ball** bouncing [ˌki:p ðə bɔ:l 'baʊntsɪŋ] *hier:* das Gespräch am Laufen halten **III**
to **ban** [bæn] bannen; verbieten; sperren **III**
banana [bə'nɑ:nə] Banane **I**
band [bænd] Band; Musikgruppe **III**
Bang! [bæŋ] Peng! **II**
bank [bæŋk] Ufer **II**; Bank **IV U2**, 42
word **bank** ['wɜ:d ˌbæŋk] Wortsammlung **III**
bar [bɑ:] Bar **IV U4**, 122
bar graph ['bɑ: grɑ:f] Säulendiagramm; Balkendiagramm **IV U3**, 85
chocolate **bar** ['tʃɒklət ˌbɑ:] Schokoriegel **IV TS1**, 34
snack **bar** ['snæk ˌbɑ:] Café; Imbissstube **I**
barbecue ['bɑ:bɪkju:] Grillparty **IV U3**, 89
barbed wire [ˌbɑ:bd 'waɪə] Stacheldraht ⟨**IV U2**, 60⟩
bare [beə] nackt; bloß **III**
bargain ['bɑ:gɪn] Schnäppchen **I**
to **bark** [bɑ:k] bellen **I**
air-force **base** ['eəfɔ:s ˌbeɪs] Luftwaffenstützpunkt ⟨**IV TS2**, 72⟩
to **base** on ['beɪs‿ɒn] stützen auf **IV U2**, 44
baseball ['beɪsbɔ:l] Baseball **IV U1**, 16
based on ['beɪst‿ɒn] basierend auf; beruhend auf **IV U4**, 120
basic ['beɪsɪk] grundlegend; Grund- **II**
basics *(pl)* ['beɪsɪks] Grundlagen **III**
basketball ['bɑ:skɪtbɔ:l] Basketball **I**
bat [bæt] Schläger *(Tischtennis; Baseball)* **IV U3**, 82
bath [bɑ:θ] Bad; Badewanne **I**
baths *(pl)* [bɑ:θs] Badehaus; Therme **III**
bathroom ['bɑ:θrʊm] Bad; Badezimmer **I**
battery ['bætri] Batterie; Akku **II**
battle ['bætl] Schlacht; Kampf **III**
BC (= before Christ) [ˌbi:'si:] vor Christus **III**
*to **be** [bi:] sein **I**

*to **be** able to (do sth) [bi‿'eɪbl tə] fähig sein zu; können; dürfen **II**
*to **be** about [bi:‿ə'baʊt] sich handeln um **I**
*to **be** about to do sth [bi‿ə'baʊt tə] im Begriff sein, etw. zu tun **IV AC2**, 39
*to **be** afraid (of) [bi‿ə'freɪd‿əv] (sich) fürchten; Angst haben (vor) **III**
*to **be** allowed to (do sth) [bi‿ə'laʊd tə] dürfen **II**
*to **be** around [ˌbi: ə'raʊnd] da sein; zusammen sein mit **IV U1**, 14
*to **be** asleep [ˌbi ə'sli:p] schlafen **II**
to **be** aware of sth [bi‿ə'weər‿əv] sich etw. bewusst sein **IV TS3**, 102
*to **be** born [bi 'bɔ:n] geboren werden **III**
*to **be** buried six feet under [bi 'berid sɪks fi:t ˌʌndə] begraben sein; beerdigt sein ⟨**IV U3**, 89⟩
*to **be** called [bi 'kɔ:ld] heißen; genannt werden **III**
*to **be** called to do sth [bi 'kɔ:ld tə du:] auserwählt sein, etw. zu tun **III**
*to **be** connected [bi kə'nektɪd] zusammenhängen; in Zusammenhang stehen **II**
*to **be** considered (to be) sth [bi kən'sɪdəd tə] als etw. gelten **IV TS2**, 70
*to **be** crazy about [bi 'kreɪzi‿əbaʊt] verrückt sein nach; abfahren auf **IV U1**, 17
*to **be** done with [bi 'dʌn wɪð] fertig sein mit **IV U2**, 46
*to **be** fed up (with) [bi fed‿'ʌp wɪð] sauer sein (auf); die Nase voll haben (von) **III**
*to **be** gone [bi: 'gɒn] verschwunden sein; weg sein **II**
*to **be** good at [bi: 'gʊd‿ət] gut sein in **I**
*to **be** grounded [bi 'graʊndɪd] Hausarrest haben **III**
*to **be** hard on sb [bi 'hɑ:d‿ɒn] streng mit jmdm. sein **III**
*to **be** homesick [bi 'həʊmsɪk] Heimweh haben **III**
*to **be** in [bi‿'ɪn] dabei sein; mitmachen **II**
*to **be** in a hurry [ˌbi‿ɪn‿ə 'hʌri] es eilig haben; in Eile sein **IV U4**, 113
*to **be** in charge (of) [bi‿ɪn 'tʃɑ:dʒ‿əv] die Verantwortung tragen (für); zuständig sein (für) **III**
*to **be** in sb's shoes [ˌbi: ɪn sʌmbɒdɪz 'ʃu:z] an jmds. Stelle sein; in jmds. Haut stecken **III**
*to **be** in the way [bi:‿ɪn ðə 'weɪ] im Weg sein/stehen **I**
*to **be** interested in [bi‿'ɪntrəstɪd‿ɪn] interessiert sein an; sich interessieren für **II**
*to **be** into [bi:‿'ɪntə] mögen; stehen auf **I**
*to **be** jealous (of) [bi: 'dʒeləs] eifersüchtig sein (auf); neidisch sein (auf) **I**
*to **be** known as [bi 'nəʊn‿əz] bekannt sein als **IV U2**, 44
*to **be** late [bi: 'leɪt] zu spät dran sein; zu spät kommen **I**

*to **be** like [bi 'laɪk] sein **III**
*to **be** located [bi ləʊ'keɪtɪd] gelegen sein; liegen **IV U2**, 43
*to **be** lucky [bi‿'lʌki] Glück haben **II**
*to **be** made of [bi 'meɪd‿əv] bestehen aus **III**
*to **be** on [bi‿'ɒn] an sein; laufen **II**
*to **be** on fire [ˌbi:‿ɒn 'faɪə] brennen **III**
*to **be** right [bi 'raɪt] recht haben **I**
*to **be** sb's size [ˌbi sʌmbɒdiz 'saɪz] so groß sein wie jmd. ⟨**IV U4**, 122⟩
*to **be** scared (of) [bi: 'skeəd‿əv] Angst haben (vor) **I**
*to **be** set (in) [bi 'set ɪn] spielen (in); seinen Schauplatz haben (in) **III**
*to **be** sick [bi 'sɪk] sich übergeben **III**
*to **be** sorry [bi: 'sɒri] leid tun **I**
*to **be** stressed out [bi ˌstrest‿'aʊt] völlig gestresst sein **III**
*to **be** stuck [bi 'stʌk] festsitzen; feststecken; hängen bleiben **IV U3**, 94
*to **be** surprised [bi sə'praɪzd] überrascht sein **II**
*to **be** suspended [bi sə'spendɪd] suspendiert werden; zeitweilig vom Unterricht ausgeschlossen werden **IV AC2**, 38
*to **be** tired of [bi 'taɪəd‿əv] es müde sein (zu); es leid sein (zu); es satt haben (zu) **IV U1**, 16
*to **be** trapped [bi 'træpt] eingeschlossen sein; in der Falle sitzen **III**
*to **be** true to oneself [bi 'tru: tu wʌnˌself] sich selbst treu bleiben **IV U4**, 112
*to **be** unlucky [bi:‿ʌn'lʌki] Pech haben **I**
*to **be** up to [bi‿'ʌp tə] vorhaben **II**
*to **be** used to [bi 'ju:s‿tə] gewöhnt sein an; gewohnt sein **III**
*to **be** walled in [ˌbi wɔ:ld‿'ɪn] von Wänden eingeschlossen sein ⟨**IV U2**, 60⟩
*to **be** worried [bi 'wʌrid] beunruhigt sein; besorgt sein **II**
*to **be** worth [bi: 'wɜ:θ] wert sein **I**
*to **be** wrong [bi: 'rɒŋ] unrecht haben; sich irren **I**
Be careful! [bi: 'keəfl] Vorsicht!; Pass/Passt auf! **I**
Be polite. [bi: pə'laɪt] Sei/Seid höflich. **I**
Here you **are**. [ˌhɪə ju‿'ɑ:] Bitte schön. **I**
I'**m** from … [ˌaɪm frɒm] Ich bin aus … **I**
Is this how you (do) …? [ɪz 'ðɪs haʊ jʊ ˌdu:] Machst du so …? **I**
beach [bi:tʃ] Strand **II**
bead [bi:d] Perle ⟨**IV U3**, 93⟩
baked **beans** *(pl)* [ˌbeɪkt 'bi:nz] weiße Bohnen in Tomatensoße **I**
bear [beə] Bär **II**
grizzly **bear** ['grɪzli ˌbeə] Grizzlybär **IV TS3**, 103
*to **beat** [bi:t] schlagen; besiegen **II**
beat-up ['bi:tʌp] ramponiert ⟨**IV TS3**, 106⟩
beautiful ['bju:tɪfl] schön; hübsch; wunderbar **II**

because [bɪ'kɒz] weil; da **I**
because of [bɪ'kɒz‿əv] wegen **II**
*to **become** [bɪ'kʌm] werden **II**
*to **become** extinct [bɪˌkʌm‿ɪk'stɪŋkt] aussterben **III**
*to **become** friends [bɪˌkʌm‿'frendz] sich anfreunden; Freundschaft schließen **IV AC1**, 11
bed [bed] Bett **I**
*to go to **bed** [ˌgəʊ tə 'bed] ins Bett gehen **I**
bedroom ['bedrʊm] Schlafzimmer **I**
bee [bi:] Biene **II**
Beefeater ['bi:fˌi:tə] königlicher Leibgardist **II**
before [bɪ'fɔ:] schon einmal; vorher; zuvor **II**
before [bɪ'fɔ:] vor *(zeitlich)*; bevor **I**
*to **begin** [bɪ'gɪn] beginnen; anfangen **II**
beginning [bɪ'gɪnɪŋ] Anfang; Beginn **II**
to **behave** [bɪ'heɪv] sich benehmen; sich verhalten **III**
behavior *(no pl) (AE)* [bɪ'heɪvjə] Verhalten; Benehmen; Betragen **IV AC2**, 39
behaviour *(no pl)* [bɪ'heɪvjə] Verhalten; Benehmen; Betragen **III**
behind [bɪ'haɪnd] hinter **I**
*to leave **behind** [ˌli:v bɪ'haɪnd] zurücklassen **III**
believable [bɪ'li:vəbl] glaubwürdig **IV U1**, 22
to **believe** [bɪ'li:v] glauben **I**
He couldn't **believe** his eyes. [hi ˌkʊdnt bɪˌli:v hɪz‿'aɪz] Er traute seinen Augen nicht. **II**
bell [bel] Glocke **II**
saved by the **bell** [ˌseɪvd baɪ ðə 'bel] noch mal Glück gehabt **III**
belongings *(pl)* [bɪ'lɒŋɪŋz] Habseligkeiten; Hab und Gut **IV U3**, 81
to **belong** [bɪ'lɒŋ] dazugehören ⟨**IV U4**, 124⟩
where I **belong** [ˌweər‿aɪ bɪ'lɒŋ] wo ich hingehöre **III**
to **belong** (to) [bɪ'lɒŋ (tə)] gehören (zu) **II**
below [bɪ'ləʊ] unterhalb; unten **I**
belt [belt] Gürtel **III**
seat **belt** ['si:t belt] Sicherheitsgurt **IV TS3**, 106
bench [benʃ] Bank; Sitzbank **III**
benefit ['benɪfɪt] Vorteil; Nutzen; Unterstützung **IV U1**, 21
besides [bɪ'saɪdz] neben **II**
(the) **best** [best] (der/die/das) Beste **II**
to save the **best** for last [ˌseɪv ðə ˌbest fə 'lɑ:st] sich das Beste bis zum Schluss aufheben **IV U2**, 42
best [best] beste/-r/-s; am besten **I**
Best wishes [ˌbest 'wɪʃɪz] Viele Grüße; Herzliche Grüße **II**
the **best** … ever ['best … ˌevə] der/die/das beste … überhaupt **III**
I **bet** [aɪ 'bet] ich wette **II**
better ['betə] besser; lieber **I**

You'd **better** ... *(= You had better)* ['ju:d ˌbetə] Du solltest lieber ... **IV AC2**, 39
between [bɪ'twi:n] zwischen **I**
in **between** [ˌɪn bɪ'twi:n] dazwischen **III**
bicycle motocross [ˌbaɪsɪkl 'məʊtəʊkrɒs] Fahrradmotocross **II**
big [bɪg] groß **I**
big deal [bɪg 'di:l] große Sache **III**
bighorn sheep [ˌbɪghɔ:n 'ʃi:p] Dickhornschaf **IV TS3**, 103
bike [baɪk] Fahrrad **I**
mountain **biking** ['maʊntɪn ˌbaɪkɪŋ] Mountainbikefahren **II**
bilingual [baɪ'lɪŋgwl] zweisprachig **II**
bill *(AE)* [bɪl] Geldschein; Rechnung **IV U2**, 46
billboard ['bɪlbɔ:d] Plakatwand **IV TS1**, 35
billion ['bɪliən] Milliarde **III**
billionaire ['bɪliəneə] Milliardär/-in **IV AC1**, 9
biographical [ˌbaɪəʊ'græfɪkl] biografisch **III**
bird [bɜ:d] Vogel **II**
birdwatching ['bɜ:dˌwɒtʃɪŋ] Vogelbeobachtung **II**
date of **birth** [ˌdeɪt‿əv 'bɜ:θ] Geburtsdatum **III**
birthday ['bɜ:θdeɪ] Geburtstag **I**
Happy **Birthday**! [ˌhæpi 'bɜ:θdeɪ] Alles Gute zum Geburtstag!; Herzlichen Glückwunsch zum Geburtstag! **I**
biscuit ['bɪskɪt] Keks **I**
bison ['baɪsn], **bison** ['baɪsn] *(pl)* Bison; Büffel **IV U3**, 94
a **bit** [ə 'bɪt] ein bisschen; ein wenig **II**
bit by **bit** [ˌbɪt baɪ 'bɪt] Stück für Stück **III**
to **bitch** *(coll)* [bɪtʃ] meckern; sich aufregen über ⟨**IV U2**, 57⟩
*to **bite** [baɪt] beißen **II**
black [blæk] schwarz **I**
black eye [blæk‿'aɪ] blaues Auge **IV U4**, 122
*to go **black** [ˌgəʊ 'blæk] schwarz werden **II**
block [blɒk] Block; Häuserblock **IV U2**, 42
building **block** ['bɪldɪŋ blɒk] Baustein **II**
to **block** [blɒk] blockieren; abblocken **II**
blog [blɒg] Blog; Internettagebuch **III**
blogger ['blɒgə] Blogger/-in **IV TS3**, 105
bloke *(fam)* [bləʊk] Typ *(ugs.)* **III**
blond [blɒnd] blond **III**
blood [blʌd] Blut **III**
blow [bləʊ] Hieb; Schlag; Windstoß ⟨**IV U3**, 89⟩
*to **blow** out [ˌbləʊ‿'aʊt] ausblasen; auspusten **I**
blue [blu:] blau **I**
blurred [blɜ:d] verschwommen; verwischt **III**
BMX [ˌbi:em'eks] BMX **II**
board [bɔ:d] Brett; Tafel **III**
tourist **board** ['tʊərɪst bɔ:d] Touristeninformation **II**
boarding ['bɔ:dɪŋ] Boarding **III**
boarding card ['bɔ:dɪŋ ˌkɑ:d] Bordkarte **III**
boat [bəʊt] Boot **I**
boating lake ['bəʊtɪŋ ˌleɪk] See zum Rudern **I**
body ['bɒdi] Körper **III**
human **body** [ˌhju:mən 'bɒdi] menschlicher Körper **II**
bodyguard ['bɒdigɑ:d] Bodyguard **IV U1**, 22
bold [bəʊld] fett gedruckt **III**
bone-crushing ['bəʊnˌkrʌʃɪŋ] knochenbrecherisch; vernichtend ⟨**IV U4**, 123⟩
bonfire ['bɒnfaɪə] Lagerfeuer; Freudenfeuer **I**
book [bʊk] Buch **I**
exercise **book** ['eksəsaɪz ˌbʊk] Übungsheft **I**
to **book** [bʊk] buchen; reservieren **II**
to **boom** [bu:m] dröhnen **II**
boomtown ['bu:mtaʊn] schnell wachsende Stadt **IV U4**, 111
boot [bu:t] Stiefel; Kofferraum **III**
bored [bɔ:d] gelangweilt **I**
boring ['bɔ:rɪŋ] langweilig **I**
*to be **born** [bi 'bɔ:n] geboren werden **III**
to **borrow** ['bɒrəʊ] (sich) ausleihen **II**
boss [bɒs] Boss; Chef **III**
bossy ['bɒsi] herrisch; rechthaberisch **III**
both [bəʊθ] beide **II**
to **bother** ['bɒðə] stören; belästigen **III**
bottle ['bɒtl] Flasche **I**
bottom ['bɒtəm] Boden; unterer Teil; Grund **IV U3**, 93
to **bounce** [baʊnts] springen; hüpfen **III**
*to keep the ball **bouncing** [ˌki:p ðə bɔ:l 'baʊntsɪŋ] *hier:* das Gespräch am Laufen halten **III**
bowl [bəʊl] Schale; Schälchen; Schüssel **I**
to play **bowls** [ˌpleɪ 'bəʊlz] Bowling spielen **III**
bowling alley ['bəʊlɪŋ‿ˌæli] Bowlingbahn **I**
box [bɒks] Box; Kasten; Schachtel; Kiste **I**
phone **box** ['fəʊn ˌbɒks] Telefonzelle **III**
boxing ['bɒksɪŋ] Boxen **II**
round of **boxing** [ˌraʊnd‿əv 'bɒksɪŋ] Boxrunde **II**
boy [bɔɪ] Junge **I**
cabin **boy** ['kæbɪn ˌbɔɪ] Schiffsjunge **I**
boyfriend ['bɔɪfrend] Freund *(in einer Paarbeziehung)* **IV U1**, 25
bracelet ['breɪslət] Armband **I**
bracket ['brækɪt] Klammer **II**
brain(s) [breɪn(z)] Gehirn; Verstand **IV U4**, 125
brain-dead ['breɪnˌded] hirntot **IV U4**, 125
to **brainstorm** ['breɪnstɔ:m] Ideen sammeln °**IV U1**, 27
brand [brænd] Marke **IV TS1**, 34
brand-new [ˌbrænd'nju:] brandneu **IV TS1**, 35
brave [breɪv] mutig; tapfer **I**
bread [bred] Brot **I**
bread roll ['bred rəʊl] Brötchen **III**
break [breɪk] Pause **II**; Durchbruch **IV U2**, 46
half-term **break** [ˌhɑ:ftɜ:m 'breɪk] Halbjahresferien **I**
lunch **break** ['lʌnʃbreɪk] Mittagspause **I**
*to **break** [breɪk] brechen; zerbrechen **I**
broken ['brəʊkn] gebrochen; kaputt **I**
breakfast ['brekfəst] Frühstück **I**
*to have **breakfast** [ˌhæv 'brekfəst] frühstücken **I**
breath [breθ] Atem; Atemzug **III**
*to take a **breath** [ˌteɪk‿ə 'breθ] Luft holen; Atem holen **III**
Take a deep **breath**. [ˌteɪk‿ə ˌdi:p 'breθ] Atme(t) tief ein. **II**
to **breathe** [bri:ð] atmen **II**
breathtaking ['breθˌteɪkɪŋ] atemberaubend **IV TS2**, 74
bridge [brɪdʒ] Brücke **II**
bright [braɪt] hell; leuchtend; strahlend **IV U2**, 42
*to **bring** [brɪŋ] bringen; mitbringen **I**
on the **brink** of [ˌɒn ðə 'brɪŋk‿əv] am Rande von; kurz vor **III**
Brit [brɪt] Brite/Britin *(ugs.)* **IV AC1**, 11
British ['brɪtɪʃ] britisch; Brite/Britin **I**
brochure ['brəʊʃə] Broschüre; Prospekt **I**
broken ['brəʊkn] gebrochen; kaputt **I**
Bronze Age ['brɒnz eɪdʒ] Bronzezeit *(ca. 2200–800 v. Chr.)* **II**
brother ['brʌðə] Bruder **I**
brown [braʊn] braun **I**
bucket ['bʌkɪt] Eimer **II**
*to **build** [bɪld] bauen **II**; aufbauen **III**
building ['bɪldɪŋ] Gebäude **I**
building block ['bɪldɪŋ blɒk] Baustein **II**
cyber **bully** [ˌsaɪbə 'bʊli] *jemand, der andere in sozialen Netzwerken belästigt oder mobbed* **II**
*to give the **bumps** [ˌgɪv ðə 'bʌmps] hochleben lassen **I**
a **bunch** of junk [ə‿ˌbʌnʃ‿əv 'dʒʌŋk] ein Haufen Müll ⟨**IV U2**, 54⟩
burger ['bɜ:gə] Hamburger **I**
*to be **buried** six feet under [bi 'berid sɪks fi:t ˌʌndə] begraben sein; beerdigt sein ⟨**IV U3**, 89⟩
*to **burn** [bɜ:n] brennen; verbrennen **III**
*to **burn** down [ˌbɜ:n 'daʊn] abbrennen; niederbrennen **III**
bus [bʌs] Bus **I**
bus station ['bʌs ˌsteɪʃn] Busbahnhof **I**
bush [bʊʃ] Busch *(Buschlandschaft)*; Wildnis **III**
business ['bɪznɪs] Geschäft; Business **III**
businessman ['bɪznɪsmæn] Geschäftsmann **IV U2**, 46
busker ['bʌskə] Straßenmusikant/-in **IV U2**, 49
busy ['bɪzi] belebt; beschäftigt **I**
but [bʌt] aber **I**
butter ['bʌtə] Butter **III**
button ['bʌtn] Knopf **III**
*to **buy** [baɪ] kaufen **I**

*to **buy** time [ˌbaɪ ˈtaɪm] Zeit gewinnen **IV U4**, 115
buyer [ˈbaɪə] Käufer/-in **I**
by [baɪ] bei; neben; an **II**; von **III**
by the river [baɪ ðə ˈrɪvə] am Fluss **II**
by the time [ˌbaɪ ðə ˈtaɪm] bis *(zu dem Zeitpunkt)* **IV U3**, 80
one **by** one [ˌwʌn baɪ ˈwʌn] eine/-r/-s nach dem/der anderen ⟨**IV U3**, 93⟩
by any means [baɪ‿enɪ ˈmiːnz] mit allen Mitteln **IV U2**, 40
by *(+ gerund)* [baɪ] indem **IV U3**, 92
by *(bike)* [baɪ] mit *(dem Fahrrad)* **I**
Bye! [baɪ] Tschüss! **II**

C

cabin boy [ˈkæbɪn ˌbɔɪ] Schiffsjunge **I**
cache [kæʃ] Cache **II**
cactus [ˈkæktəs] Kaktus **IV AC1**, 8
café [ˈkæfeɪ] Café **I**
cafeteria [ˌkæfəˈtɪəriə] Cafeteria **I**
cake [keɪk] Kuchen; Torte **I**
calendar [ˈkæləndə] Kalender **III**
(phone) call [ˈfəʊn ˌkɔːl] Anruf; Telefonanruf **I**
to call [kɔːl] nennen; anrufen; rufen **I**
*to be **called** [bi ˈkɔːld] heißen; genannt werden **III**
*to be **called** to do sth [bi ˈkɔːld tə duː] auserwählt sein, etw. zu tun **III**
caller [ˈkɔːlə] Anrufer/-in **I**
call-in [ˈkɔːlɪn] *Sendung, bei der sich das Publikum telefonisch beteiligen kann* **III**
calm [kɑːm] Ruhe **IV U4**, 112
to calm down [ˌkɑːm ˈdaʊn] sich beruhigen **II**
calm [kɑːm] ruhig; friedlich **IV U3**, 83
camel racing [ˈkæml ˌreɪsɪŋ] Kamelrennen **II**
camera [ˈkæmrə] Fotoapparat; Kamera **II**
caught on **camera** [ˌkɔːt‿ɒn ˈkæmrə] ertappt; mit der Kamera festgehalten **II**
summer **camp** [ˈsʌmə kæmp] Sommerferienlager **II**
to camp [kæmp] campen; zelten **II**
to campaign (for) [kæmˈpeɪn fɔː] demonstrieren (für); aufmerksam machen (auf); sich engagieren (für) **III**
camping [ˈkæmpɪŋ] Camping; Zelten **II**
can [kæn] Dose; Büchse **I**
tin **can** [ˈtɪn kæn] Blechdose **III**
can [kæn; kən] können; dürfen **I**
can't [kɑːnt] kann nicht; können nicht **I**
Canadian [kəˈneɪdiən] kanadisch; Kanadier/-in **IV AC3**, 76
cancer [ˈkænsə] Krebs *(Krankheit)* ⟨**IV U4**, 123⟩
candle [ˈkændl] Kerze **I**
candlelight *(no pl)* [ˈkændlaɪt] Kerzenlicht **II**
cannot [ˈkænɒt] kann nicht; können nicht **II**
canoe [kəˈnuː] Kanu **IV U4**, 116
canvas [ˈkænvəs] Segeltuch ⟨**IV U4**, 123⟩
capital [ˈkæpɪtl] Hauptstadt **II**
capital letter [ˌkæpɪtl ˈletə] Großbuchstabe **I**
capitalistic [ˌkæpɪtlˈɪstɪk] kapitalistisch ⟨**IV U2**, 57⟩
captain [ˈkæptɪn] Kapitän/-in; Mannschaftsführer/-in **I**
caption [ˈkæpʃn] Bildunterschrift; Untertitel **III**
to capture [ˈkæptʃə] ergreifen; einfangen **III**
car [kɑː] Auto **I**
motor **car** [ˈməʊtə ˌkɑː] Automobil **IV U3**, 87
card [kɑːd] Karte; Spielkarte **I**
boarding **card** [ˈbɔːdɪŋ ˌkɑːd] Bordkarte **III**
prompt **card** [ˈprɒmpt kɑːd] Stichwortkarte; Rollenkarte **II**
cardboard [ˈkɑːdbɔːd] Pappe; Karton **IV TS3**, 105
*to take **care** of sb/sth [ˌteɪk‿ˈkeər‿əv] sich um jmdn./etw. kümmern; für jmdn. sorgen **III**
to care (about) [ˈkeər‿əˌbaʊt] wichtig nehmen; sich kümmern (um); sich interessieren (für) **II**
career [kəˈrɪə] Beruf; Laufbahn; Karriere **III**
careful [ˈkeəfl] vorsichtig; sorgfältig **II**
Be **careful**! [biː ˈkeəfl] Vorsicht!; Pass/Passt auf! **I**
carnival [ˈkɑːnɪvl] Karneval **II**
carpet [ˈkɑːpɪt] Teppich **II**
carrot [ˈkærət] Karotte; Möhre **I**
to carry [ˈkæri] tragen **II**
cart [kɑːt] Karren **IV U2**, 45
cartoon [kɑːˈtuːn] Cartoon; Zeichentrickfilm **III**
cash *(no pl)* [kæʃ] Bargeld ⟨**IV U2**, 54⟩
casino [kəˈsiːnəʊ] Kasino; Spielkasino ⟨**IV U4**, 123⟩
plaster **cast** [ˈplɑːstə kɑːst] Gipsverband **III**
casting [ˈkɑːstɪŋ] Casting; Rollenbesetzung **III**
castle [ˈkɑːsl] Schloss; Burg **II**
cat [kæt] Katze **I**
*to catch [kætʃ] fangen **II**; mitbekommen *(ugs.)*; mitkriegen *(ugs.)* **III**; erwischen ⟨**IV U2**, 53⟩
*to **catch** an infection [ɪnˈfekʃn] sich eine Infektion holen; sich einen Infekt holen **IV U3**, 83
*to **catch** up with sb [ˌkætʃ‿ˈʌp wɪð] jmdn. einholen ⟨**IV U3**, 93⟩
catchy [ˈkætʃi] eingängig; einprägsam **III**
category [ˈkætəgri] Kategorie; Klasse **II**
caught on camera [ˌkɔːt‿ɒn ˈkæmrə] ertappt; mit der Kamera festgehalten **II**
*to get **caught** [ˌget ˈkɔːt] erwischt werden; ertappt werden **IV AC2**, 38
cause [kɔːz] Grund; Ursache **IV U4**, 116
to cause [kɔːz] verursachen **II**
cave [keɪv] Höhle **II**
to cave in [keɪv‿ˈɪn] einstürzen; zusammenbrechen ⟨**IV U3**, 89⟩
to celebrate [ˈseləbreɪt] feiern **I**
celebration [ˌseləˈbreɪʃn] Feier ⟨**IV U2**, 60⟩
celebrity [səˈlebrəti] Prominente/-r; berühmte Person **III**
cell [sel] Zelle ⟨**IV U2**, 60⟩
cell phone *(AE)* [ˈselfəʊn] Mobiltelefon; Handy **IV AC2**, 38
Celt [kelt] Kelte/Keltin **III**
Celtic [ˈkeltɪk; ˈseltɪk] keltisch **II**
cent [sent] Cent *(Währung)* **I**
center *(AE)* [ˈsentə] Zentrum; Center **IV AC1**, 8
central [ˈsentrl] zentral; Zentral- **II**
centre [ˈsentə] Zentrum; Center **I**
community **centre** [kəˈmjuːnəti ˌsentə] Gemeindezentrum **I**
leisure **centre** [ˈleʒə ˌsentə] Freizeitzentrum **I**
tourist information **centre** [ˌtʊərɪst ɪnfəˈmeɪʃn ˌsentə] Touristeninformation **I**
century [ˈsenʃri] Jahrhundert **II**
cereal *(no pl)* [ˈsɪəriəl] Frühstückszerealie; Getreideprodukt *(z. B. Cornflakes oder Müsli)* **I**
ceremony [ˈserɪməni] Zeremonie **IV U4**, 117
certain [ˈsɜːtn] bestimmt; sicher; gewiss °**IV U3**, 94
chain [tʃeɪn] Kette **IV TS3**, 103
chair [tʃeə] Stuhl; Sessel **I**
challenge [ˈtʃælɪndʒ] Herausforderung **II**
to challenge [ˈtʃælɪndʒ] herausfordern **IV TS2**, 71
champion [ˈtʃæmpiən] Gewinner/-in; Sieger/-in; Champion **III**
championship [ˈtʃæmpiənʃɪp] Meisterschaft **IV U1**, 26
chance [tʃɑːns] Chance; Gelegenheit; Möglichkeit **II**
change [tʃeɪndʒ] Änderung; Veränderung; Wechsel **II**; Münzgeld; Wechselgeld **IV U2**, 46
to change [tʃeɪndʒ] wechseln; (sich) ändern **II**
to **change** (onto) [tʃeɪndʒ (ˈɒntʊ)] umsteigen (in) **II**
to **change** one's mind [ˌtʃeɪndʒ wʌnz ˈmaɪnd] seine Meinung ändern **III**
Everything will have **changed**. [ˌevriθɪŋ wɪl hæv ˈtʃeɪndʒd] Alles wird sich geändert haben. **IV U4**, 117
chant [tʃɑːnt] Sprechgesang **II**
chaos [ˈkeɪɒs] Chaos; Durcheinander **III**
chapter [ˈtʃæptə] Kapitel **III**
character [ˈkærəktə] Charakter; Figur **I**
characteristic [ˌkærəktəˈrɪstɪk] typisches Merkmal °**IV TS2**, 73
*to be in **charge** (of) [bi‿ɪn ˈtʃɑːdʒ‿əv] die Verantwortung tragen (für); zuständig sein (für) **III**
charity [ˈtʃærɪti] Wohltätigkeitsverein; wohltätige Zwecke; Wohlfahrt **I**

charity shop ['tʃærɪti ʃɒp] Second-Hand-Laden **I**
lucky **charm** [ˌlʌki 'tʃɑ:m] Glücksbringer; Talisman **I**
chart [tʃɑ:t] Diagramm **IV U3**, 85; Tabelle °**IV U4**, 110
pie **chart** ['paɪ ˌtʃɑ:t] Kuchendiagramm; Tortendiagramm **IV U3**, 85
to **chase** [tʃeɪs] jagen; nachjagen **I**
chat [ˌtʃæt] Chat **III**
chat room ['tʃæt rʊm] Chatroom **II**
video **chat** ['vɪdiəʊ ˌtʃæt] Videochat **II**
to **chat** [tʃæt] plaudern; chatten *(sich online unterhalten)* **I**
chatroom ['tʃætrʊm] Chatroom *(Internet-forum, wo man sich online unterhalten kann)* **III**
cheap [tʃi:p] billig; preiswert **I**
to **cheat** [tʃi:t] mogeln; betrügen **IV AC2**, 38
cheat sheet ['tʃi:t ʃi:t] Spickzettel **IV AC2**, 39
to **check** [tʃek] überprüfen; prüfen; kontrollieren **I**
to **check** out *(coll)* [ˌtʃek‿'aʊt] prüfen; abchecken; auschecken **III**
Check-in ['tʃekɪn] Einchecken **I**
checklist ['tʃeklɪst] Checkliste **II**
Check-out ['tʃekaʊt] Auschecken **I**
checkpoint ['tʃekpɔɪnt] Kontrollpunkt **III**
cheer [tʃɪə] Jubel; Hurraruf **IV U1**, 22
to **cheer** [tʃɪə] anfeuern; jubeln; zujubeln **II**
to **cheer** sb up [ˌtʃɪər‿'ʌp] jmdn. aufheitern **III**
Cheers! [tʃɪəz] Danke! **III**
cheese [tʃi:z] Käse **I**
chess [tʃes] Schach **II**
chest [tʃest] Brust; Brustkorb **IV U3**, 93
chewing gum ['tʃu:ɪŋ ˌgʌm] Kaugummi **III**
chick *(slang)* [tʃɪk] Puppe *(Jargon)*; Mieze *(Jargon)* ⟨**IV U2**, 54⟩
chicken ['tʃɪkɪn] Huhn; Hähnchen **I**
chicken tikka masala [ˌtʃɪkɪn ˌtɪkə mə'sɑ:lə] *indisches Hühnchengericht* **I**
child [tʃaɪld], **children** ['tʃɪldrən] *(pl)* Kind **I**
child labor *(AE)* [ˌtʃaɪld 'leɪbə] Kinderarbeit **IV U1**, 18
only **child** ['əʊnli ˌtʃaɪld] Einzelkind **I**
to **chill** out [tʃɪl‿'aʊt] chillen **III**
chimney ['tʃɪmni] Kamin; Schornstein **II**
chips *(pl)* [tʃɪps] Pommes frites **I**
chocolate ['tʃɒklət] Schokolade **I**
chocolate bar ['tʃɒklət ˌbɑ:] Schokoriegel **IV TS1**, 34
choice [tʃɔɪs] Wahl; Auswahl **II**
°to **choose** [tʃu:z] auswählen; wählen **II**
chore [tʃɔ:] (lästige) Pflicht; Bürde **IV AC4**, 108
chorus ['kɔ:rəs] Refrain **III**
in **chorus** [ɪn 'kɔ:rəs] im Chor **III**
clam **chowder** [ˌklæm 'tʃaʊdə] Muschelsuppe ⟨**IV TS3**, 105⟩; °**IV U4**, 127
Christmas ['krɪsməs] Weihnachten **I**
church [tʃɜ:tʃ] Kirche **I**
cinema ['sɪnəmə] Kino **I**
circle ['sɜ:kl] Kreis; Ring **I**
°to go round in **circles** [gəʊ ˌraʊnd ɪn 'sɜ:klz] sich im Kreis drehen **III**
city ['sɪti] Stadt; Großstadt **I**
civilization [ˌsɪvlaɪ'zeɪʃn] Kultur; Zivilisation ⟨**IV U4**, 114⟩
to **claim** [kleɪm] behaupten °**IV TS2**, 72
clam chowder [ˌklæm 'tʃaʊdə] Muschelsuppe ⟨**IV TS3**, 105⟩; °**IV U4**, 127
to **clap** [klæp] klatschen **I**
to **clap** along [ˌklæp‿ə'lɒŋ] mitklatschen ⟨**IV U3**, 93⟩
Clap your hands. [ˌklæp jɔ: 'hændz] Klatsch/Klatscht in die Hände. **I**
clarification [ˌklærɪfɪ'keɪʃn] Klärung; Klarstellung **III**
class [klɑ:s] Klasse; Schulklasse **I**; *hier:* Unterricht **II**
class display ['klɑ:s dɪˌspleɪ] Ausstellung in der Klasse **I**
class poster ['klɑ:s ˌpəʊstə] Klassenposter **I**
middle **class** [ˌmɪdl 'klɑ:s] Mittelschicht ⟨**IV U4**, 124⟩
classical ['klæsɪkl] klassisch **IV U2**, 42
classmate ['klɑ:smeɪt] Klassenkamerad/-in; Mitschüler/-in **I**
classroom ['klɑ:srʊm] Klassenzimmer **I**
adverbial **clause** [əd,vɜ:biəl 'klɔ:z] Adverbialsatz °**IV U3**, 87
conditional **clause** [kənˌdɪʃnl 'klɔ:z] Bedingungssatz ⟨**IV U3**, 88⟩
contact **clause** ['kɒntækt ˌklɔ:z] *Relativsatz ohne Relativpronomen* **II**
defining relative **clause** [dɪˌfaɪnɪŋ 'relətɪv ˌklɔ:z] notwendiger Relativsatz **II**
if-**clause** ['ɪfˌklɔ:z] if-Satz **II**
main **clause** ['meɪn ˌklɔ:z] Hauptsatz **II**
non-defining relative **clause** [ˌnɒndɪfaɪnɪŋ 'relətɪv ˌklɔ:z] nicht notwendiger Relativsatz °**IV U2**, 43
clay pipe ['kleɪ paɪp] Tonpfeife **II**
to **clean** [kli:n] säubern; reinigen **I**
to **clean** out [ˌkli:n‿'aʊt] ausräumen; entrümpeln **IV U1**, 21
to **clean** up [ˌkli:n‿'ʌp] aufräumen; sauber machen **IV AC4**, 108
clean [kli:n] sauber **III**
to **clear** out [ˌklɪər‿'aʊt] ausräumen; entrümpeln **I**
clear [klɪə] klar; deutlich **I**
clever ['klevə] schlau; klug **II**
click [klɪk] Klicken; Klick **II**
to **click** on ['klɪk‿ɒn] anklicken **II**
cliff [klɪf] Klippe; Kliff **III**
climate ['klaɪmət] Klima **III**
climax ['klaɪmæks] Höhepunkt **III**
to **climb** [klaɪm] klettern; besteigen; steigen **I**
climbing ['klaɪmɪŋ] Klettern **II**
clique [kli:k] Clique **IV U1**, 18
clock [klɒk] Uhr **I**
alarm **clock** [ə'lɑ:m ˌklɒk] Wecker **II**
o'**clock** [ə'klɒk] Uhr *(Zeitangabe bei vollen Stunden)* **I**
to **clone** [kləʊn] klonen **III**
close [kləʊs] schmaler Durchgang **III**
to **close** [kləʊz] schließen; zumachen **I**
to **close** oneself away from [ˌkləʊz ə'weɪ frəm] sich abschotten von **III**
close [kləʊs] eng; knapp **I**; nahe **II**
Look **closely** … [ˌlʊk 'kləʊsli] Schau(t) genau … **II**
That was **close**! [ˌðæt wəz 'kləʊs] Das war knapp! **I**
closed [kləʊzd] geschlossen; zu **III**
closet ['klɒzɪt] Schrank; Wandschrank **IV U1**, 14
walk-in **closet** [ˌwɔ:kɪn 'klɒzɪt] begehbarer Kleiderschrank **IV U1**, 14
close-up ['kləʊsʌp] Nahaufnahme **II**
clothes *(pl)* [kləʊðz] Kleider; Kleidung **I**
clothing ['kləʊðɪŋ] Kleidung **IV U1**, 21
clothing drive ['kləʊðɪŋ ˌdraɪv] Kleidersammlung **IV U1**, 21
cloud [klaʊd] Wolke **II**
word **cloud** ['wɜ:d ˌklaʊd] Wörterwolke **II**
cloudy ['klaʊdi] bedeckt; bewölkt **II**
clown [klaʊn] Clown **II**
club [klʌb] Klub; Verein; AG **I**
Cooking **Club** ['kʊkɪŋ ˌklʌb] Koch-AG **I**
clue [klu:] Hinweis; Spur **II**
°to have no **clue** [ˌhæv nəʊ 'klu:] keine Ahnung haben **IV AC1**, 11
coach [kəʊtʃ] Trainer/-in **I**; Reisebus **II**
coast [kəʊst] Küste **III**
coastal path [ˌkəʊstl 'pɑ:θ] Küstenweg **II**
coastline ['kəʊstlaɪn] Küste; Küstenverlauf **II**
coconut ['kəʊkənʌt] Kokosnuss **II**
code [kəʊd] Code; Verschlüsselung **IV U3**, 86
dress **code** ['dres ˌkəʊd] Kleiderordnung; Bekleidungsvorschriften **IV U1**, 13
coffee ['kɒfi] Kaffee **I**
coin [kɔɪn] Münze **I**
coincidence [kəʊ'ɪnsɪdns] Zufall **IV U1**, 22
coke ['kəʊk] Cola **I**
cold [kəʊld] Erkältung **II**; Kälte ⟨**IV U2**, 60⟩
cold [kəʊld] kalt **II**
collage [kɒl'ɑ:ʒ] Collage °**IV U3**, 78
to **collect** [kə'lekt] sammeln **I**
collection [kə'lekʃn] Kollektion; Sammlung **II**
college ['kɒlɪdʒ] Universität *(in den USA)* **IV U4**, 123
collocation [ˌkɒlə'keɪʃn] Wortverbindung **II**
colonial [kə'ləʊniəl] kolonial; Kolonial- **IV U3**, 89
colonist ['kɒlənɪst] Siedler/-in; Kolonist/-in **IV AC1**, 11
to **colonize** *(AE)* ['kɒlənaɪz] kolonisieren **IV U3**, 80
colony ['kɒləni] Kolonie **II**

colorful *(AE)* ['kʌləfl] farbenfroh; bunt **IV TS3**, 104
colour ['kʌlə] Farbe **I**
What **colour** is …? [ˌwɒt 'kʌlər‿ɪz] Welche Farbe hat …? **I**
colourful ['kʌləfl] farbenfroh; bunt **I**
column ['kɒləm] Spalte **III**
combination [ˌkɒmbɪ'neɪʃn] Kombination; Verbindung **IV U2**, 45
to **combine** [kəm'baɪn] kombinieren; verbinden **IV U2**, 45
*to **come** [kʌm] kommen **I**
*to **come** down [ˌkʌm 'daʊn] herunterkommen **I**
*to **come** in [ˌkʌm‿'ɪn] hereinkommen **II**
*to **come** to one's mind [ˌkʌm tə wʌnz 'maɪnd] jmdm. in den Sinn kommen; jmdm. einfallen °**IV U3**, 78
*to **come** true [ˌkʌm 'tru:] wahr werden; in Erfüllung gehen **IV U2**, 46
*to **come** up [ˌkʌm‿'ʌp] vorkommen **III**
*to **come** up to [ˌkʌm‿'ʌp tə] zukommen auf **IV U3**, 92
Come off it! [ˌkʌm‿'ɒf‿ɪt] Komm wieder runter! ⟨**IV U2**, 56⟩
Come on! [ˌkʌm‿'ɒn] Komm schon!; Komm jetzt! **I**
comedian [kə'mi:diən] Komiker/-in; Comedian **II**
comedy ['kɒmədi] Komödie **III**
comedy show ['kɒmədi ˌʃəʊ] Comedy Show **II**
to **comfort** ['kʌmfət] trösten; ermutigen **IV U3**, 84
comfortable ['kʌmftəbl] komfortabel; bequem **II**
comic ['kɒmɪk] Comicheft **II**
comma ['kɒmə] Komma °**IV U2**, 43
command [kə'mɑ:nd] Befehl **III**
command module [kə'mɑ:nd ˌmɒdju:l] Kommandokapsel ⟨**IV TS2**, 71⟩
commander [kə'mɑ:ndə] Kommandant/-in ⟨**IV TS2**, 71⟩
comment ['kɒment] Kommentar **II**
to **comment** (on) ['kɒment‿(ɒn)] kommentieren **II**
committee [kə'mɪti] Komitee; Ausschuss **IV U1**, 18
*to have in **common** [ˌhæv‿ɪn 'kɒmən] gemeinsam haben **III**
to **communicate** [kə'mju:nɪkeɪt] kommunizieren; sich verständigen **II**
communication [kəˌmju:nɪ'keɪʃn] Kommunikation **II**
communications network [kəˌmju:nɪ'keɪʃnz ˌnetwɜ:k] Kommunikationsnetz; Nachrichtennetz **IV U3**, 86
community [kə'mju:nəti] Gemeinde; Gemeinschaft **IV U4**, 119
community centre [kə'mju:nəti ˌsentə] Gemeindezentrum **I**

company ['kʌmpəni] Gesellschaft; Firma; Unternehmen **III**
tour **company** ['tʊə ˌkʌmpəni] Reiseanbieter **IV U2**, 43
comparative [kəm'pærətɪv] Komparativ **II**
to **compare** (with/to) [kəm'peə] vergleichen (mit) **I**
comparison [kəm'pærɪsn] Vergleich **II**
to **compete** (with) [kəm'pi:t] konkurrieren (mit); sich messen (mit); in Wettbewerb treten (mit) **III**
competition [ˌkɒmpə'tɪʃn] Wettbewerb; Turnier **II**
*to hold a **competition** [ˌhəʊld‿ə ˌkɒmpə'tɪʃn] einen Wettbewerb durchführen **IV U4**, 114
competitive [kəm'petɪtɪv] leistungsorientiert; konkurrierend **III**
to **complain** [kəm'pleɪn] sich beschweren; sich beklagen **IV U2**, 46
to **complete** [kəm'pli:t] fertigstellen; vervollständigen; vollenden **IV AC2**, 38
complete [kəm'pli:t] vollständig; komplett; völlig **IV AC1**, 11
completely [kəm'pli:tli] völlig **II**
complicated ['kɒmplɪkeɪtɪd] kompliziert **IV TS2**, 72
compound word ['kɒmpaʊnd wɜ:d] Kompositum *(zusammengesetztes Wort)* **II**
compromise ['kɒmprəmaɪz] Kompromiss **II**
to **compromise** ['kɒmprəmaɪz] Kompromisse eingehen **III**
computer [ˌkəm'pju:tə] Computer **I**
computing power [ˌkəm'pju:tɪŋ ˌpaʊə] Rechenleistung ⟨**IV TS2**, 72⟩
con [kɒn] Argument dagegen **II**
to **concentrate** ['kɒnsntreɪt] (sich) konzentrieren **III**
concept ['kɒnsept] Vorstellung; Idee; Konzept °**IV U3**, 95
concert ['kɒnsət] Konzert **IV U1**, 27
conclusion [kən'klu:ʒn] Schluss; Schlussfolgerung **IV U3**, 85
concrete ['kɒŋkri:t] Beton **III**
concrete ['kɒŋkri:t] konkret °**IV U4**, 114
condition [kən'dɪʃn] Kondition; Bedingung **II**
conditional clause [kənˌdɪʃnl 'klɔ:z] Bedingungssatz ⟨**IV U3**, 88⟩
conditional sentence [kənˌdɪʃnl 'sentəns] Bedingungssatz **II**
to **conduct** [kən'dʌkt] durchführen; ausführen **IV U2**, 62
conference ['kɒnfrns] Konferenz; Tagung **IV U2**, 42
confident ['kɒnfɪdnt] selbstsicher; selbstbewusst **II**
confused [kən'fju:zd] verwirrt; wirr; konfus **III**
to **connect** (to) [kə'nekt tə] verbinden (mit); vermitteln; anschließen **IV U3**, 86
*to be **connected** [bi kə'nektɪd] zusammenhängen; in Zusammenhang stehen **II**

connection [kə'nekʃn] Verbindung **II**
conscience ['kɒnʃns] Gewissen **III**
guilty **conscience** [ˌgɪlti 'kɒnʃns] Schuldbewusstsein; schlechtes Gewissen ⟨**IV TS3**, 107⟩
consecutive [kən'sekjʊtɪv] aufeinanderfolgend; fortlaufend **IV U2**, 59
consequence ['kɒnsɪkwəns] Konsequenz; Folge **IV AC2**, 38
*to be **considered** (to be) sth [bi kən'sɪdəd tə] als etw. gelten **IV TS2**, 70
to **consist** of [kən'sɪst‿əv] bestehen aus **IV U4**, 110
conspiracy [kən'spɪrəsi] Verschwörung **IV TS2**, 72
constant ['kɒnstənt] ständig; konstant; stetig; gleichmäßig **IV U4**, 125
construction [kən'strʌkʃn] Konstruktion °**IV U1**, 13
contact ['kɒntækt] Kontakt **II**
contact clause ['kɒntækt ˌklɔ:z] *Relativsatz ohne Relativpronomen* **II**
to **contain** [kən'teɪn] enthalten **III**
content ['kɒntent] Inhalt **IV U1**, 26
contest ['kɒntest] Wettkampf; Wettbewerb **I**
continent ['kɒntɪnənt] Kontinent; Erdteil **IV U2**, 44
to **continue** [kən'tɪnju:] fortfahren; andauern; weitermachen; weitergehen **III**
contrast ['kɒntrɑ:st] Kontrast; Unterschied; Gegensatz **IV AC1**, 8
to **contrast** [kən'trɑ:st] kontrastieren; gegenüberstellen °**IV U4**, 112
control [kən'trəʊl] Kontrolle **III**
mission **control** [ˌmɪʃn kən'trəʊl] Bodenkontrollzentrum ⟨**IV TS2**, 71⟩
to **control** [kən'trəʊl] kontrollieren; steuern **IV U1**, 20
controversial [ˌkɒntrə'vɜ:ʃl] umstritten; kontrovers ⟨**IV TS3**, 106⟩
conversation [ˌkɒnvə'seɪʃn] Konversation; Gespräch; Unterhaltung **I**
to hog a **conversation** [ˌhɒg‿ə kɒnvə'seɪʃn] ein Gespräch für sich in Beschlag nehmen; ein Gespräch dominieren **III**
to **convert** [kən'vɜ:t] umwandeln; verwandeln; umsetzen in ⟨**IV U2**, 60⟩
to **convince** [kən'vɪns] überzeugen **II**
convinced [kən'vɪnst] überzeugt **III**
convincing [kən'vɪnsɪŋ] überzeugend **III**
to **cook** [kʊk] kochen **II**
cooker ['kʊkə] Herd **I**
cooking ['kʊkɪŋ] Kochen **I**
Cooking Club ['kʊkɪŋ ˌklʌb] Koch-AG **I**
*to leave it to **cool** [ˌli:v‿ɪt tə 'ku:l] kalt stellen **I**
cool [ku:l] cool; super **I**; kühl **IV AC1**, 8
cop *(coll)* [kɒp] Polizist/-in *(ugs.)* ⟨**IV U2**, 58⟩
copper ['kɒpə] Kupfer **IV TS3**, 103
copper-mining ['kɒpəˌmaɪnɪŋ] Kupferbergbau **IV TS3**, 103
ad **copy** ['æd ˌkɒpi] Werbetext **IV TS1**, 35

to **copy** ['kɒpi] abschreiben; kopieren **I**
corn [kɔ:n] Korn; Mais; Getreide **IV AC1**, 11
cornbread ['kɔ:nbred] Maisbrot ⟨**IV U3**, 93⟩
corner ['kɔ:nə] Ecke **II**
Cornish ['kɔ:nɪʃ] in Cornwall **II**
corporation [ˌkɔ:pr'eɪʃn] Konzern; Unternehmen **IV U4**, 110
Correct … [kə'rekt] Korrigiere/Korrigiert … **I**
correct [kə'rekt] richtig; korrekt **I**
corridor ['kɒrɪdɔ:] Gang; Flur; Korridor **IV AC2**, 38
*to **cost** [kɒst] kosten **I**
costume ['kɒstju:m] Kostüm **I**
cougar ['ku:gə] Puma; Berglöwe **IV U4**, 111
cough [kɒf] Husten **II**
to **cough** [kɒf] husten ⟨**IV U4**, 124⟩
could [kʊd] könnte/-n **II**; konnte/-n **III**
to **count** (on) ['kaʊnt_ɒn] zählen (auf) **I**
country ['kʌntri], **countries** ['kʌntriz] *(pl)* Land **I**
in the **country** [ˌɪn ðə 'kʌntri] auf dem Land **IV AC1**, 10
countryside ['kʌntrisaɪd] Land **II**
couple ['kʌpl] Paar **II**
a **couple** of [ə 'kʌpl_əv] ein paar **I**
course [kɔ:s] Kurs **II**
of **course** [əv 'kɔ:s] natürlich; selbstverständlich **I**
court [kɔ:t] Spielfeld **II**
cousin ['kʌzn] Cousin/Cousine **I**
cover ['kʌvə] Cover; Titelblatt **III**
cover version ['kʌvə ˌvɜ:ʃn] Coverversion **III**
to **cover** ['kʌvə] abdecken; bedecken; zudecken **III**
covered wagon [ˌkʌvəd 'wægən] Planwagen **IV U3**, 81
cover-up ['kʌvərʌp] Vertuschung **IV TS2**, 72
cow [kaʊ] Kuh **II**
cowboy ['kaʊbɔɪ] Cowboy; Rinderhirte **IV U2**, 42
crack [kræk] Knacken; Krachen **III**
cracking ['krækɪŋ] knackend; brechend **III**
cramp [kræmp] Krampf **II**
cranberry ['krænbri] Cranberry ⟨**IV U1**, 15⟩
crane [kreɪn] Kran **III**
crap *(vulg)* [kræp] Scheiß ⟨**IV TS3**, 106⟩
to **crash** [kræʃ] abstürzen **II**; zusammenstoßen **III**
crazy ['kreɪzi] verrückt **I**
*to be **crazy** about [bi 'kreɪzi_əbaʊt] verrückt sein nach; abfahren auf **IV U1**, 17
*to go **crazy** [ˌgəʊ 'kreɪzi] ausflippen; durchdrehen; verrückt werden **II**
cream [kri:m] Creme; Sahne **I**
ice **cream** [ˌaɪs 'kri:m] Eis; Eiscreme **I**
to **create** [kri'eɪt] schaffen; erschaffen; erfinden **I**
creative [kri'eɪtɪv] kreativ **I**
creature ['kri:tʃə] Kreatur; Lebewesen; Geschöpf **IV TS3**, 106
credit ['kredɪt] Guthaben **II**

cricket ['krɪkɪt] Cricket **II**
crime [kraɪm] Verbrechen; Kriminalität **II**
criminal ['krɪmɪnəl] Kriminelle/-r; Verbrecher/-in **II**
to **cringe** [krɪndʒ] schaudern; sich ducken **IV U2**, 61
crisp [krɪsp] Kartoffelchip **I**
criterion [kraɪ'tɪəriən], **criteria** [kraɪ'tɪəriə] *(pl)* Kriterium; Argument **III**
critical ['krɪtɪkl] kritisch **IV TS2**, 73
croissant ['krwæsɑ̃ŋ] Croissant ⟨**IV U2**, 45⟩
cronut ['krəʊnʌt] Cronut ⟨**IV U2**, 45⟩
crop [krɒp] Ernte ⟨**IV U3**, 92⟩
to **crop** (a photo) [krɒp] (ein Foto) zurechtschneiden **III**
cross [krɒs] Kreuz **II**
to **cross** [krɒs] überqueren; kreuzen **II**
*to keep your fingers **crossed** [ki:p jɔ: ˌfɪŋgəz 'krɒst] die Daumen drücken **I**
crowd [kraʊd] Menschenmenge **II**
crowded ['kraʊdɪd] überfüllt **III**
crown [kraʊn] Krone **III**
crown jewels [ˌkraʊn 'dʒu:əlz] Kronjuwelen **II**
cruel ['kru:əl] grausam **II**
crushed [krʌʃt] eingequetscht; eingeklemmt **III**
to **cry** [kraɪ] schreien; rufen **II**; weinen **III**
CU *(= See you)* ['si: ju] Bis dann!; Bis … **I**
cultural ['kʌltʃrl] kulturell **IV AC1**, 8
culture ['kʌltʃə] Kultur **I**
Across **cultures** [əˌkrɒs 'kʌltʃəz] Interkulturelles **I**
cup [kʌp] Tasse **III**
cupboard ['kʌbəd] Küchenschrank; Schrank **I**
curfew ['kɜ:fju:] Sperrstunde; Ausgangssperre **IV U1**, 14
currency ['kʌrnsi] Währung **III**
curry ['kʌri] Curry *(Gewürz oder Gericht)* **I**
to **curse** [kɜ:s] fluchen; verfluchen; verdammen ⟨**IV TS3**, 107⟩
custard ['kʌstəd] Vanillesoße; Vanillepudding **I**
custom ['kʌstəm] Gewohnheit; Brauch; Sitte **III**
customer ['kʌstəmə] Kunde/Kundin **II**
customs *(sg)* ['kʌstəmz] Zoll **III**
*to **cut** (off) [kʌt (ɒf)] schneiden; abschneiden **II**
*to **cut** up [kʌt_'ʌp] zerschneiden °**IV U2**, 61
cute [kju:t] niedlich; süß **I**
cyber bully [ˌsaɪbə 'bʊli] *jemand, der andere in sozialen Netzwerken belästigt oder mobbed* **II**
to **cycle** ['saɪkl] Fahrrad fahren **IV U1**, 16
cycling ['saɪklɪŋ] Radfahren **I**

D

dad [dæd] Papa **I**
dam [dæm] Damm; Staumauer **IV U4**, 117
dance [dɑ:ns] Tanz; Tanzveranstaltung **III**

to **dance** [dɑ:ns] tanzen **I**
to **dance** to ['dɑ:ns tə] tanzen zu **III**
dancer ['dɑ:nsə] Tänzer/-in **II**
backing **dancer** ['bækɪŋ ˌdɑ:nsə] Backgroundtänzer/-in **III**
danger ['deɪndʒə] Gefahr **III**
dangerous ['deɪndʒrəs] gefährlich **I**
the **dark** [ðə 'dɑ:k] Dunkelheit **II**
dark [dɑ:k] dunkel **II**
darkness ['dɑ:knəs] Dunkelheit **II**
date [deɪt] Datum **I**; Verabredung; Date **IV U1**, 25
date of birth [ˌdeɪt_əv 'bɜ:θ] Geburtsdatum **III**
to double **date** [ˌdʌbl 'deɪt] mit einem anderen Paar ausgehen; zu viert ausgehen ⟨**IV U4**, 124⟩
daughter ['dɔ:tə] Tochter **III**
day [deɪ] Tag **I**
all **day** [ˌɔ:l 'deɪ] den ganzen Tag **II**
one **day** [wʌn 'deɪ] eines Tages **II**
*to take the **day** off [ˌteɪk ðə ˌdeɪ_'ɒf] sich den Tag freinehmen **IV U2**, 42
the other **day** [ðiˌʌðə 'deɪ] neulich **III**
these **days** [ˌði:z 'deɪz] zurzeit **III**
a (**day**/week/year) [ə 'deɪ/wi:k/jɪə] pro (Tag/Woche/Jahr) **IV AC1**, 9
a **day** out in … [ə ˌdeɪ_'aʊt ɪn] ein Tag in … **II**
the next **day** [ðə ˌnekst 'deɪ] am nächsten Tag **II**
dead [ded] tot **II**
deal [di:l] Abmachung; Übereinkunft **IV U4**, 113; Handel; Geschäft **IV U4**, 119
big **deal** [bɪg 'di:l] große Sache **III**
*to **deal** (with) [di:l] sich befassen mit; umgehen mit **II**
Oh **dear**! [ˌəʊ 'dɪə] Oje! **II**
Dear … [dɪə] Lieber …; Liebe … *(Anrede in Briefen)* **I**
Dear Sir or Madam [dɪə ˌsɜ:r_ɔ: 'mædəm] Sehr geehrte Dame, sehr geehrter Herr **II**
death [deθ] Tod **III**
to scare sb to **death** [ˌskeə tə 'deθ] jmdn. zu Tode erschrecken **IV TS3**, 102
debate [dɪ'beɪt] Debatte **IV U4**, 120
December [dɪ'sembə] Dezember **I**
to **decide** [dɪ'saɪd] (sich) entscheiden **I**
decision [dɪ'sɪʒn] Entscheidung **II**
*to make a **decision** [ˌmeɪk_ə dɪ'sɪʒn] eine Entscheidung treffen **II**
deck [dek] Deck **I**
to **declare** [dɪ'kleə] erklären **IV U3**, 80
to **decorate** ['dekəreɪt] dekorieren; verzieren; schmücken **I**; streichen; tapezieren; dekorieren ⟨**IV AC4**, 109⟩
decorations *(pl)* [ˌdekə'reɪʃnz] Dekoration; Schmuck **I**
deep [di:p] tief **II**
to **defeat** [dɪ'fi:t] besiegen **III**
defining relative clause [dɪˌfaɪnɪŋ 'relətɪv ˌklɔ:z] notwendiger Relativsatz **II**

definitely ['defɪnətli] bestimmt; definitiv; eindeutig **III**
definition [ˌdefɪ'nɪʃn] Definition **II**
degree Fahrenheit (°F) ['færnhaɪt] Grad Fahrenheit **IV AC1**, 8
delay [dɪ'leɪ] Verzögerung; Verspätung **III**
to **delete** [dɪ'li:t] löschen **III**
deli ['deli] Feinkostgeschäft ⟨**IV U2**, 55⟩
delicate ['delɪkət] empfindlich ⟨**IV U2**, 56⟩
delicious [dɪ'lɪʃəs] köstlich **IV U2**, 45
delight [dɪ'laɪt] Vergnügen; Entzücken ⟨**IV U4**, 124⟩
to **demonstrate** ['demənstreɪt] demonstrieren **IV U1**, 18
dense [dens] dicht **IV AC1**, 10
to **depart** [dɪ'pɑ:t] abfahren **II**
departure [dɪ'pɑ:tʃə] Abflug; Abreise **III**
departure lounge [dɪ'pɑ:tʃə ˌlaʊndʒ] Abflughalle **III**
to **depend** (on) [dɪ'pend‿(ɒn)] abhängen von **II**
depressing [dɪ'presɪŋ] deprimierend; bedrückend **III**
to **descend** from [dɪ'send frəm] abstammen von; herstammen von **IV U3**, 80
to **describe** [dɪ'skraɪb] beschreiben **I**
description [dɪ'skrɪpʃn] Beschreibung **II**
descriptive [dɪ'skrɪptɪv] beschreibend °**IV TS3**, 104
desert ['dezət] Wüste **IV AC1**, 8
to **deserve** [dɪ'zɜ:v] verdienen **II**
design [dɪ'zaɪn] Design; Gestaltung; Entwurf **II**
to **design** [dɪ'zaɪn] entwerfen; gestalten **II**
designer [dɪ'zaɪnə] Designer/-in **III**
web **designer** ['web dɪˌzaɪnə] Webdesigner **III**
desk [desk] Schalter **III**
destination [ˌdestɪ'neɪʃn] Ziel; Reiseziel **III**
to **destroy** [dɪ'strɔɪ] zerstören **IV U4**, 119
destruction [dɪ'strʌkʃn] Zerstörung ⟨**IV U4**, 114⟩
detail ['di:teɪl] Detail; Einzelheit **II**
detective [dɪ'tektɪv] Detektiv/-in; Detektivgeschichte; Kriminalroman; Kriminalfilm; Krimi **III**
private **detective** [ˌpraɪvət dɪ'tektɪv] Privatdetektiv/-in **II**
detention [dɪ'tenʃn] Nachsitzen; Haft; Verhaftung **IV AC2**, 38
to **develop** [dɪ'veləp] (sich) entwickeln **IV U3**, 86
devil ['devl] Teufel **III**
diabetes [ˌdaɪə'bi:ti:z] Diabetes; Zuckerkrankheit ⟨**IV U4**, 123⟩
diagram ['daɪəgræm] Diagramm **I**
dialect ['daɪəlekt] Dialekt **II**
dialogue ['daɪəlɒg] Dialog; Gespräch **I**
diary ['daɪəri] Tagebuch **II**
diary entry ['daɪəri entri] Tagebucheintrag **II**
*to keep a **diary** [ˌki:p‿ə 'daɪəri] ein Tagebuch führen **IV U3**, 92
dice [daɪs] Würfel **II**
Roll two **dice**. [ˌrəʊl ˌtu: 'daɪs] Würfle/Würfelt mit zwei Würfeln. **I**
throw the **dice** twice [ˌθrəʊ ðə daɪs 'twaɪs] würfle zweimal **II**
dictionary ['dɪkʃnri] Wörterbuch **I**
to **die** [daɪ] sterben **III**
It's to **die** for! [ˌɪts tə 'daɪ fɔ:] Dafür könnte ich sterben!; Das ist unwiderstehlich! **IV U4**, 127
difference ['dɪfrəns] Unterschied **I**
different ['dɪfrnt] anders; unterschiedlich; verschieden **I**
difficult ['dɪfɪklt] schwierig **II**
difficulty ['dɪfɪklti] Schwierigkeit °**IV U3**, 94
*to **dig** [dɪg] graben **II**
dilemma [daɪ'lemə] Dilemma; Zwickmühle **III**
diner *(AE)* ['daɪnə] einfaches Restaurant mit Theke und Tischen **IV U2**, 42
dinner ['dɪnə] Abendessen **I**
dinosaur ['daɪnəsɔ:] Dinosaurier **II**
direct [dɪ'rekt] direkt **III**
direct speech [dɪˌrekt 'spi:tʃ] direkte Rede **III**
direction [dɪ'rekʃn] Richtung **I**
stage **direction** ['steɪdʒ dɪˌrekʃn] Regieanweisung **III**
director [dɪ'rektə] Regisseur/-in **III**
dirt [dɜ:t] Schmutz; Dreck **III**
dirty ['dɜ:ti] dreckig; schmutzig **II**
disadvantage [ˌdɪsəd'vɑ:ntɪdʒ] Nachteil **IV U4**, 119
to **disagree** [ˌdɪsə'gri:] anderer Meinung sein; nicht einverstanden sein **III**
to **disappear** [ˌdɪsə'pɪə] verschwinden **IV U3**, 82
disappointed [ˌdɪsə'pɔɪntɪd] enttäuscht **I**
disappointing [ˌdɪsə'pɔɪntɪŋ] enttäuschend **IV TS2**, 74
disaster [dɪ'zɑ:stə] Desaster; Katastrophe; Unglück **II**
to **discover** [dɪ'skʌvə] entdecken **II**
discovery [dɪ'skʌvri] Entdeckung **III**
to **discuss** [dɪ'skʌs] diskutieren **I**
discussion [dɪ'skʌʃn] Diskussion **II**
dish [dɪʃ] Gericht; Speise **IV U1**, 15
dishes *(pl)* ['dɪʃɪz] Geschirr **IV AC4**, 108
*to do the **dishes** [ˌdu: ðə 'dɪʃɪz] den Abwasch machen **IV AC4**, 108
dishonest [dɪ'sɒnɪst] unehrlich **III**
dishwasher ['dɪʃˌwɒʃə] Spülmaschine **IV AC4**, 108
to **dislike** [dɪs'laɪk] nicht mögen **IV U1**, 17
dislikes *(pl)* [dɪs'laɪks] Abneigungen **IV U1**, 16
to **disobey** [ˌdɪsə'beɪ] nicht gehorchen; ungehorsam sein **III**
display [dɪ'spleɪ] Ausstellung **II**
class **display** ['klɑ:s dɪˌspleɪ] Ausstellung in der Klasse **I**
distance ['dɪstns] Distanz; Entfernung **II**
district ['dɪstrɪkt] Distrikt; Bezirk **IV U2**, 40
to **divide** (up) [dɪ'vaɪd] aufteilen **III**
dizzy ['dɪzi] schwindelig **IV U1**, 22
DJ [ˌdi:'dʒeɪ] DJ; Discjockey **III**
*to **do** [du:] machen; tun **I**
*to be **done** with [bi 'dʌn wɪð] fertig sein mit **IV U2**, 46
*to **do** about ['du:‿əˌbaʊt] unternehmen wegen **II**
*to **do** our hair [ˌdu:‿aʊə 'heə] uns frisieren; unsere Haare machen **I**
*to **do** the dishes [ˌdu: ðə 'dɪʃɪz] den Abwasch machen **IV AC4**, 108
*to **do** the shopping [ˌdu: ðə 'ʃɒpɪŋ] Einkäufe machen; Besorgungen machen **III**
*to **do** well [ˌdu: 'wel] gute Leistungen erbringen **III**
Don't worry! [ˌdəʊnt 'wʌri] Keine Sorge! **I**
dos and **don'ts** [ˌdu:z‿ənd 'dəʊnts] Gebote und Verbote; was man tun und was man nicht tun sollte **III**
It wouldn't **do** me any good. [ˌɪt wʊdnt ˌdu: mi: eni 'gʊd] Es würde mir nichts nützen. **IV U4**, 124
We **did** it! [ˌwi: 'dɪd‿ɪt] Wir haben es geschafft! **II**
You can **do** it! [ˌju: kən 'du: ɪt] Du schaffst es! **III**
doctor ['dɒktə] Arzt/Ärztin **II**
to **document** ['dɒkjəment] dokumentieren; festhalten ⟨**IV TS2**, 71⟩
dog [dɒg] Hund **I**
hot **dog** ['hɒt ˌdɒg] Hot Dog *(Würstchen im Brötchen)* ⟨**IV U2**, 45⟩
to walk the **dog** [ˌwɔ:k ðə 'dɒg] den Hund ausführen; mit dem Hund spazieren gehen **I**
I'm **dog-tired**. [ˌaɪm ˌdɒg'taɪəd] Ich bin hundemüde. **I**
dollar ['dɒlə] Dollar *(Währung)* **III**
dolphin ['dɒlfɪn] Delfin **III**
dominoes ['dɒmɪnəʊz] Domino **III**
to **donate** [də'neɪt] spenden; stiften **IV U1**, 21
door [dɔ:] Tür **I**
front **door** [ˌfrʌnt 'dɔ:] Haustür **II**
next **door** [ˌnekst 'dɔ:] (von) nebenan **III**
doorbell ['dɔ:bel] Türklingel **III**
double ['dʌbl] Doppel-; zweimal **IV U1**, 27
to **double** date [ˌdʌbl 'deɪt] mit einem anderen Paar ausgehen; zu viert ausgehen ⟨**IV U4**, 124⟩
doubt [daʊt] Zweifel **III**
doughnut ['dəʊnʌt] Donut *(frittierter Teigkringel)* ⟨**IV U2**, 45⟩
down [daʊn] nach unten; herunter; hinunter **II**; nieder **IV U1**, 22
*to come **down** [ˌkʌm 'daʊn] herunterkommen **I**
*to go **down** [ˌgəʊ 'daʊn] hinuntergehen; nach unten gehen; entlanggehen **I**

to note **down** [ˌnəʊt ˈdaʊn] notieren; aufschreiben **II**
to pull **down** [ˌpʊl‿ˈdaʊn] abreißen **III**
*to sit **down** [ˌsɪt ˈdaʊn] sich hinsetzen; sich setzen **I**
to slow **down** [ˌsləʊ ˈdaʊn] langsamer werden; bremsen 〈**IV U2**, 60〉
to touch **down** [tʌtʃ ˈdaʊn] landen **IV TS2**, 71
*to write **down** [ˌraɪt ˈdaʊn] aufschreiben **I**
to **download** [ˌdaʊnˈləʊd] herunterladen *(aus dem Internet)* **II**
downriver [ˌdaʊnˈrɪvə] flussabwärts; stromabwärts **IV U4**, 116
downstairs [ˌdaʊnˈsteəz] nach unten; im Untergeschoss; unten **II**
downtown *(AE)* [ˌdaʊnˈtaʊn] im Stadtzentrum **IV U1**, 14
draft [drɑːft] Entwurf; Konzept **I**
drama [ˈdrɑːmə] Theater; Drama **II**
dramatic [drəˈmætɪk] dramatisch **II**
*to **draw** [drɔː] zeichnen **I**; ziehen **II**
*to **draw** the reader into the story/action [ˌdrɔː ðə ˌriːdə ɪntə ðə ˈstɔːri/ˈækʃn] den Leser/die Leserin in die Geschichte/Handlung hineinziehen **III**
drawing [ˈdrɔːɪŋ] Zeichnung **I**
dreadlocks *(pl)* [ˈdredlɒks] Rastalocken 〈**IV U2**, 60〉
dream [driːm] Traum **II**
*to **dream** [driːm] träumen **IV U1**, 17
dress [dres] Kleid **III**
dress code [ˈdres ˌkəʊd] Kleiderordnung; Bekleidungsvorschriften **IV U1**, 13
fancy **dress** [ˈfænsi dres] Verkleidung; Kostüm **II**
to **drift** [drɪft] schweben; treiben 〈**IV U3**, 89〉
drink [drɪŋk] Getränk **I**
*to **drink** [drɪŋk] trinken **I**
drinking water [ˈdrɪŋkɪŋ ˌwɔːtə] Trinkwasser **IV U3**, 83
drive [draɪv] Fahrt; Anfahrt; Autofahrt **IV U1**, 14
clothing **drive** [ˈkləʊðɪŋ ˌdraɪv] Kleidersammlung **IV U1**, 21
*to **drive** [draɪv] fahren **III**
*to **drive** off [draɪv‿ˈɒf] wegfahren **III**
driver [ˈdraɪvə] Fahrer/-in **II**
drizzle [ˈdrɪzl] Nieselregen **III**
to **drop** [drɒp] fallen (lassen) **II**
to **drop** out (of) [ˌdrɒp ˈaʊt‿əv] abbrechen **III**
to **drop** sb off [ˌdrɒp‿ˈɒf] jmdn. absetzen; jmdn. aussteigen lassen **IV TS3**, 106
drop-off [ˈdrɒpɒf] Abgabe **IV U1**, 21
to **drown** [draʊn] ertrinken; ertränken **III**
drum [drʌm] Trommel **IV U4**, 117
drums *(pl)* [drʌmz] Schlagzeug **III**
dry [draɪ] trocken **III**
dude *(coll)* [duːd] Mann; Alter *(ugs.)* **IV AC1**, 11
dumpster [ˈdʌmpstə] Müllcontainer 〈**IV U2**, 55〉
during *(+ noun)* [ˈdjʊərɪŋ] während *(+ Nomen)* **II**
dusty [ˈdʌsti] staubig **IV TS3**, 103
duty-free [ˌdjuːtiˈfriː] zollfrei **III**
DVD [ˌdiːviːˈdiː] DVD **I**

E

e.g. *(= for example)* [ˌiːˈdʒiː] z.B. *(= zum Beispiel)* **I**
each [iːtʃ] jede/-r/-s **I**
each other [ˌiːtʃ‿ˈʌðə] einander; sich; sich gegenseitig **I**
each [iːtʃ] pro Person; pro Stück **I**
ear [ɪə] Ohr **III**
early [ˈɜːli] früh **I**
this **early** [ˈðɪs ˌɜːli] so früh **III**
to **earn** [ɜːn] verdienen **I**
earth [ɜːθ] Erdboden; Erde; die Erde **II**
What on **earth** …? [ˌwɒt‿ɒn‿ˈɜːθ] Was um alles in der Welt …? **II**
east [iːst] Osten; Ost- **I**
Easter [ˈiːstə] Ostern **I**
eastern [ˈiːstn] östlich; Ost- **IV U3**, 80
easy [ˈiːzi] einfach; leicht **I**
easy-going [ˌiːziˈgəʊɪŋ] locker; unkompliziert **III**
*to **eat** [iːt] essen; fressen **I**
Eco [ˈiːkəʊ] Öko- **II**
economy [ɪˈkɒnəmi] Ökonomie; Wirtschaft **IV U4**, 110
edge of town [ˌedʒ‿əv ˈtaʊn] Stadtrand **IV TS3**, 105
to **edit** out [ˌedɪt‿ˈaʊt] herausschneiden **III**
to **educate** [ˈedʒʊkeɪt] erziehen; bilden **IV TS3**, 102
education *(no pl)* [ˌedʒʊˈkeɪʃn] Erziehung; Bildung **III**
effect [ɪˈfekt] Effekt; Wirkung **IV U2**, 59
audio-visual **effect** [ˌɔːdiəʊvɪʒuəl ɪˈfekt] audiovisueller Effekt **II**
special **effect** [ˌspeʃl‿ɪˈfekt] Spezialeffekt **IV TS2**, 75
effective [ɪˈfektɪv] effektiv; wirkungsvoll **IV TS1**, 36
effectiveness [ɪˈfektɪvnəs] Effektivität; Wirksamkeit **IV TS1**, 37
egg [eg] Ei **I**
Egyptian [ɪˈdʒɪpʃn] Ägypter/-in; ägyptisch **III**
eight [eɪt] acht **I**
either … or … [ˈaɪðə/ˈiːðə … ɔː] entweder … oder … **IV U2**, 49
not … **either** [nɒt … ˈaɪðə; nɒt … ˈiːðə] auch nicht **IV AC3**, 77
elderly [ˈeldəli] älter **III**
electric [ɪˈlektrɪk] elektrisch **III**
electrician [ˌelɪkˈtrɪʃn] Elektriker/-in **II**
electricity [ˌelɪkˈtrɪsəti] Elektrizität; Strom **II**
electrics [ɪˈlektrɪks] Elektrik **II**
electronic [ˌelekˈtrɒnɪk] elektronisch **II**
elegant [ˈelɪgnt] elegant **IV TS3**, 103
element [ˈelɪmənt] Element **II**
elephant [ˈelɪfənt] Elefant **III**
elevator *(AE)* [ˈelɪveɪtə] Aufzug; Lift **IV U1**, 14
eleven [ɪˈlevn] elf **I**
elk [elk] Elch **IV TS3**, 103
else [els] andere/-r/-s; sonst noch **III**
nobody **else** [ˈnəʊbədi els] niemand anderes **II**
what **else** [ˌwɒt‿ˈels] was sonst; was noch **I**
e-mail [ˈiːmeɪl] E-Mail **I**
to **e-mail** [ˈiːmeɪl] mailen; per E-Mail schicken **II**
embarrassed [ɪmˈbærəst] verlegen **II**
embarrassing [ɪmˈbærəsɪŋ] peinlich **II**
emotion [ɪˈməʊʃn] Gefühl; Emotion 〈**IV TS2**, 74〉
emotional [ɪˈməʊʃnl] emotional; Gefühls- **III**
emperor [ˈemprə] Kaiser **III**
empire [ˈempaɪə] Reich; Kaiserreich **III**
to **employ** [ɪmˈplɔɪ] einstellen; anstellen; beschäftigen **IV U3**, 86
employee [ɪmˈplɔɪiː] Angestellte/-r; Mitarbeiter/-in; Arbeitnehmer/-in **IV U4**, 110
to **empty** [ˈemti] leeren; ausräumen **IV AC4**, 108
empty [ˈemti] leer **III**
encyclopaedia [ɪnˌsaɪkləˈpiːdiə] Enzyklopädie; Lexikon °**IV TS2**, 71
end [end] Ende; Schluss **I**
in the **end** [ˌɪn ði‿ˈend] schließlich; zum Schluss **II**
to **end** [end] enden; beenden **II**
to **end** up [ˌend‿ˈʌp] enden; landen **II**
ending [ˈendɪŋ] Ende; Schluss *(einer Geschichte)* **I**
happy **ending** [ˌhæpi ˈendɪŋ] Happy End **III**
endless [ˈendləs] endlos **IV AC1**, 8
enemy [ˈenəmi] Feind/-in **III**
energy [ˈenədʒi] Energie; Kraft **III**
search **engine** [ˈsɜːtʃ‿endʒɪn] Suchmaschine °**IV U1**, 12
steam **engine** [ˈstiːm‿endʒɪn] Dampfmaschine **III**
engineer [ˌendʒɪˈnɪə] Ingenieur/-in; Techniker/-in **IV TS2**, 71
engineering [ˌendʒɪˈnɪərɪŋ] Technik; Maschinenbau 〈**IV TS2**, 72〉
English [ˈɪŋglɪʃ] englisch; Englisch; aus England; Engländer/-in **I**
English-speaking [ˈɪŋglɪʃˌspiːkɪŋ] englischsprachig **I**
I'm **English**. [aɪm‿ˈɪŋglɪʃ] Ich bin Engländer/-in. **I**
to **enjoy** [ɪnˈdʒɔɪ] genießen; sich freuen an **II**
to **enjoy** oneself [ɪnˈdʒɔɪ] Spaß haben; sich amüsieren **III**
enjoyable [ɪnˈdʒɔɪəbl] angenehm; unterhaltsam **IV TS3**, 103

enlightenment [ɪn'laɪtnmənt] Aufklärung; Erleuchtung **IV U2**, 44
enough [ɪ'nʌf] genug; genügend **I**
to **enter** ['entə] hineingehen; betreten; eintreten; *hier:* mitmachen **II**
to **entertain** [ˌentə'teɪn] unterhalten **III**
entertainer [ˌentə'teɪnə] Entertainer/-in; Unterhaltungskünstler/-in **IV U2**, 42
entertaining [ˌentə'teɪnɪŋ] unterhaltsam **IV TS2**, 73
entertainment *(no pl)* [ˌentə'teɪnmənt] Unterhaltung **III**
enthusiasm [ɪn'θju:ziæzm] Enthusiasmus; Begeisterung **IV U2**, 42
entrance ['entrəns] Eingang; Eintritt **III**
entry ['entri] Eintrag **III**; Beitrag; Einsendung **IV U4**, 114
diary **entry** ['daɪəri entri] Tagebucheintrag **II**
environment [ɪn'vaɪrnmənt] Umwelt; Umgebung **II**
epic ['epɪk] episch; *hier:* geil **IV AC1**, 11
equal ['i:kwəl] gleich; gleichwertig **IV U3**, 95
equipment [ɪ'kwɪpmənt] Ausstattung; Ausrüstung **II**
er [ɜ:] äh **I**
era ['ɪərə] Ära; Zeitalter **III**
ergonomic [ˌɜ:gə'nɒmɪk] ergonomisch ⟨**IV U4**, 123⟩
eruption [ɪ'rʌpʃn] Ausbruch *(Vulkan)* **IV U4**, 120
escalator ['eskəleɪtə] Rolltreppe **I**
escape [ɪ'skeɪp] Flucht **III**
to **escape** (from) [ɪ'skeɪp frəm] fliehen; entfliehen; flüchten; entkommen **IV U1**, 22
especially [ɪ'speʃli] besonders; vor allem **IV U3**, 80
to **estimate** ['estɪmeɪt] schätzen **IV TS2**, 73
etc. *(= et cetera)* [ɪt'setrə] usw. *(= und so weiter)* **II**
ethnic ['eθnɪk] ethnisch; Volks-; *hier:* exotisch **IV U2**, 45
euro ['jʊərəʊ] Euro *(Währung)* **I**
European [ˌjʊərə'pi:ən] Europäer/-in; europäisch; aus Europa **IV AC1**, 8
even ['i:vn] sogar; selbst **I**
even though [ˌi:vn 'ðəʊ] auch wenn; obwohl **IV U3**, 86
evening ['i:vnɪŋ] Abend **I**
in the **evenings** [ɪn ði‿'i:vnɪŋz] abends **I**
event [ɪ'vent] Ereignis; Veranstaltung **I**
ever ['evə] jemals **II**
the best … **ever** ['best … ˌevə] der/die/das beste … überhaupt **III**
every ['evri] jede/-r/-s **I**
everybody ['evribɒdi] jeder; alle **II**
everyday ['evrideɪ] alltäglich **III**
everyone ['evriwʌn] jeder; alle **I**
everything ['evriθɪŋ] alles **I**
Everything will have changed. [ˌevriθɪŋ wɪl hæv 'tʃeɪndʒd] Alles wird sich geändert haben. **IV U4**, 117
everywhere ['evriweə] überall **I**
ex- [eks] ehemalige/-r/-s ⟨**IV U4**, 125⟩
exactly [ɪg'zæktli] genau **II**
to **exaggerate** [ɪg'zædʒəreɪt] übertreiben **III**
exaggerated [ɪg'zædʒəreɪtɪd] übertrieben **IV U1**, 22
exam [ɪg'zæm] Examen; Prüfung **II**
examination [ɪgˌzæmɪ'neɪʃn] Untersuchung; Prüfung **IV U3**, 82
example [ɪg'zɑ:mpl] Beispiel **I**
for **example** [fər‿ɪg'zɑ:mpl] zum Beispiel **II**
excellent ['ekslnt] exzellent; hervorragend ⟨**IV TS2**, 74⟩
except [ɪk'sept] außer; bis auf **III**
excerpt ['eksɜ:pt] Auszug °**IV U2**, 59
exchange [ɪks'tʃeɪndʒ] Austausch; Austausch- **III**
exchange student [ɪks'tʃeɪndʒ ˌstju:dnt] Austauschschüler/-in **III**
student **exchange** ['stju:dnt ɪksˌtʃeɪndʒ] Schüleraustausch **III**
to **exchange** [ɪks'tʃeɪndʒ] austauschen **II**
excited [ɪk'saɪtɪd] aufgeregt; begeistert **I**
excitement *(no pl)* [ɪk'saɪtmənt] Aufregung **III**
exciting [ɪk'saɪtɪŋ] spannend; aufregend **I**
excuse [ɪk'skju:s] Entschuldigung; Ausrede ⟨**IV U4**, 124⟩
Excuse me … [ɪk'skju:z mi] Entschuldigung!; Entschuldigen Sie! **I**
exercise ['eksəsaɪz] Übung; Aufgabe **I**
exercise book ['eksəsaɪz ˌbʊk] Übungsheft **I**
exhausting [ɪg'zɔ:stɪŋ] anstrengend **IV U3**, 84
to **expand** [ɪk'spænd] (sich) ausdehnen; erweitern **IV U3**, 86
to **expect** [ɪk'spekt] erwarten **III**
expectation [ˌekspek'teɪʃn] Erwartung **IV TS3**, 102
*to meet sb's **expectations** [ˌmi:t sʌmbədiz‿ekspek'teɪʃnz] jmds. Erwartungen erfüllen **IV TS3**, 102
expensive [ɪk'spensɪv] teuer **I**
experience [ɪk'spɪəriəns] Erfahrung **II**
to **experience** [ɪk'spɪəriəns] erfahren; erleben **III**
expert ['ekspɜ:t] Experte/Expertin **II**
to **explain** [ɪk'spleɪn] erklären **I**
explanation [ˌeksplə'neɪʃn] Erklärung; Erläuterung °**IV U4**, 127
exploration [ˌeksplə'reɪʃn] Erforschung; Erkundung ⟨**IV TS2**, 74⟩
to **explore** [ɪk'splɔ:] auf Entdeckungsreise gehen; sich umschauen; erkunden; erforschen **I**
to **express** [ɪk'spres] ausdrücken **II**
expression [ɪk'spreʃn] Ausdruck; Wendung; Äußerung **II**
facial **expression** [ˌfeɪʃl ɪk'spreʃn] Gesichtsausdruck **III**
*to become **extinct** [bɪˌkʌm‿ɪk'stɪŋkt] aussterben **III**
extinction *(no pl)* [ɪks'tɪŋkʃn] Aussterben **III**
extra ['ekstrə] extra; zusätzlich **I**
extreme [ɪk'stri:m] extrem; radikal **IV AC1**, 10
extremely [ɪk'stri:mli] äußerst; sehr ⟨**IV TS3**, 102⟩
eye [aɪ] Auge **II**
black **eye** [blæk‿'aɪ] blaues Auge **IV U4**, 122
to roll one's **eyes** [ˌrəʊl wʌnz‿'aɪz] die Augen verdrehen **III**
He couldn't believe his **eyes**. [hi ˌkʊdnt bɪˌli:v hɪz‿'aɪz] Er traute seinen Augen nicht. **II**
eyebrow ['aɪbraʊ] Augenbraue ⟨**IV U2**, 60⟩
eye-catcher ['aɪkætʃə] Blickfang; Hingucker **IV TS1**, 35
eyewitness ['aɪwɪtnəs] Augenzeuge/Augenzeugin **II**

F

fabulous ['fæbjələs] sagenhaft; fantastisch **IV TS1**, 36
face [feɪs] Gesicht **I**
face to **face** [ˌfeɪs tə 'feɪs] von Angesicht zu Angesicht; Auge in Auge **IV U3**, 86
Put … **face** down. [pʊt ˌfeɪs 'daʊn] Lege/Legt … umgedreht hin. **I**
to **face** [feɪs] gegenüber stehen; konfrontiert werden mit **III**
Let's **face** it. [lets 'feɪs‿ɪt] Machen wir uns doch nichts vor. **III**
face-to-face [ˌfeɪstə'feɪs] *hier:* persönlich; von Angesicht zu Angesicht **II**
facial **expression** [ˌfeɪʃl ɪk'spreʃn] Gesichtsausdruck **III**
fact [fækt] Fakt; Tatsache **II**
in **fact** [ɪn 'fækt] tatsächlich; eigentlich; genau genommen **IV U3**, 84
factory ['fæktri] Fabrik; Werk **III**
factual ['fæktʃʊəl] sachlich **III**
factual text [ˌfæktʃʊəl 'tekst] Sachtext **III**
degree **Fahrenheit** (°F) ['færnhaɪt] Grad Fahrenheit **IV AC1**, 8
to **fail** to do sth ['feɪl tə] versäumen, etw. zu tun; es nicht schaffen, etw. zu tun **IV U2**, 49
fair [feə] gerecht; fair **I**
fair play [feə 'pleɪ] Fairplay **III**
to **fake** [feɪk] vortäuschen; fälschen **II**
fake [feɪk] falsch; gefälscht **III**
*to **fall** [fɔ:l] fallen; hinfallen **I**
*to **fall** asleep [ˌfɔ:l‿ə'sli:p] einschlafen **I**
*to **fall** down [ˌfɔ:l‿'daʊn] stürzen; hinunterfallen **III**
*to **fall** for ['fɔ:l fə] hereinfallen auf **IV TS1**, 34
*to **fall** off [ˌfɔ:l‿'ɒf] herunterfallen; hinunterfallen **II**
*to **fall** over [ˌfɔ:l‿'əʊvə] hinfallen; umkippen **I**

*to get **familiar** [ˌget fəˈmɪliə] sich vertraut machen °**IVTS3**, 102
family [ˈfæmli] Familie **I**
family tree [ˈfæmli ˌtriː] Stammbaum **I**
host **family** [ˈhəʊst ˌfæmli] Gastfamilie **III**
famous [ˈfeɪməs] berühmt **I**
fan [fæn] Fan; Anhänger/-in **II**
fancy dress [ˈfænsi dres] Verkleidung; Kostüm **II**
fantastic [fænˈtæstɪk] fantastisch; großartig **II**
fantasy [ˈfæntəsi] Fantasie; Traum- **I**; Fantasy **III**
fanzine [fænˈziːn] Fanzeitschrift **II**
FAQ [ˌefeɪˈkjuː] Liste mit häufig gestellten Fragen **III**
far [fɑː] weit **II**
so **far** [ˌsəʊ ˈfɑː] bis jetzt **II**
in the **far** west [ɪn ðə fɑː ˈwest] im äußersten Westen **II**
fare [feə] Fahrpreis **II**
farm [fɑːm] Farm; Bauernhof **I**
to **farm** [fɑːm] Landwirtschaft betreiben **IV U3**, 92
farmer [ˈfɑːmə] Farmer/-in; Landwirt/-in **II**
fascinating [ˈfæsɪneɪtɪŋ] faszinierend **III**
fashion [ˈfæʃn] Mode **II**
fast [fɑːst] schnell **I**
father [ˈfɑːðə] Vater **I**
father-in-law [ˌfɑːðərɪnˈlɔː] Schwiegervater ⟨**IVTS3**, 107⟩
in **favor** (of) *(AE)* [ɪn ˈfeɪvər‿əv] dafür; zugunsten (von) **IV U4**, 119
favourite [ˈfeɪvrɪt] Favorit/-in; Günstling **III**
favourite [ˈfeɪvrɪt] Lieblings- **I**
My **favourite** … [maɪ ˈfeɪvrɪt] Mein/e Lieblings … **I**
What's your **favourite** …? [ˈwɒts jə ˌfeɪvrɪt] Was ist dein/-e Lieblings…? **I**
fear [fɪə] Angst; Furcht; Befürchtung **II**
to **fear** [fɪə] (sich) fürchten **IVTS3**, 102
fearful [ˈfɪəfl] ängstlich **III**
feast [fiːst] Festmahl ⟨**IV U2**, 55⟩
feather [ˈfeðə] Feder **III**
feature [ˈfiːtʃə] Eigenschaft; Merkmal **III**
to **feature** [ˈfiːtʃə] zeigen; aufweisen **III**; eine Hauptrolle spielen ⟨**IVTS3**, 103⟩
February [ˈfebruri] Februar **I**
*to be **fed** up (with) [bi fed‿ˈʌp wɪð] sauer sein (auf); die Nase voll haben (von) **III**
fee [fiː] Gebühr **II**
school **fees** *(pl)* [ˈskuːl fiːz] Schulgeld; Schulgebühren **III**
*to **feed** [fiːd] füttern; ernähren **II**
feedback [ˈfiːdbæk] Feedback; Rückmeldung **II**
*to **feel** [fiːl] fühlen; sich fühlen **I**
*to **feel** left out [ˌfiːl leftˈaʊt] sich ausgeschlossen fühlen **II**
*to **feel** sick [ˌfiːl ˈsɪk] Übelkeit verspüren; sich schlecht fühlen **II**
*to **feel** sorry for [ˌfiːl ˈsɒri fɔː] Mitleid haben mit; bedauern **III**
feeling [ˈfiːlɪŋ] Gefühl **II**
fellow [ˈfeləʊ] Bursche; Kerl **IV U3**, 86
ferry [ˈferi] Fähre **III**
festival [ˈfestɪvl] Festival; Fest **I**
to **fetch** [fetʃ] holen; abholen **III**
fever [ˈfiːvə] Fieber **II**
swamp **fever** *(no pl)* [ˈswɒmp ˌfiːvə] Sumpffieber ⟨**IV U3**, 92⟩
few [fjuː] wenige **II**
a **few** [ə ˈfjuː] ein paar; wenige; einige **I**
fiction *(no pl)* [ˈfɪkʃn] Erzählliteratur; Erfindung; Prosa; Fiktion **III**
science **fiction** [ˌsaɪəns ˈfɪkʃn] Science-Fiction *(Zukunftsdichtung)* **II**
fictional [ˈfɪkʃnl] fiktional; fiktiv; erdichtet **III**
field [fiːld] Feld; Spielfeld; Wiese; Weide; Acker **II**
field trip [ˈfiːld trɪp] Schulausflug; Exkursion ⟨**IV U4**, 124⟩
fifteen [ˌfɪfˈtiːn] fünfzehn **I**
fight [faɪt] Kampf; Streit **II**
*to **fight** [faɪt] kämpfen; (sich) streiten **II**
figure [ˈfɪɡə] Figur; Gestalt **II**; Ziffer; Zahl **III**
wax **figure** [ˈwæks ˌfɪɡə] Wachsfigur **II**
to **figure** [ˈfɪɡə] sich vorstellen; glauben; schätzen ⟨**IV U4**, 124⟩
to **fill** [fɪl] (sich) füllen **III**
to **fill** in [ˌfɪlˈɪn] ausfüllen **II**
filling [ˈfɪlɪŋ] Füllung **IV U2**, 45
film [fɪlm] Film **I**
to **film** [fɪlm] filmen; drehen **II**
filmmaker [ˈfɪlmˌmeɪkə] Filmemacher/-in **II**
final [ˈfaɪnl] endgültig **II**; letzte/-r/-s **III**
finally [ˈfaɪnli] schließlich; endlich; zum Schluss; letztlich **II**
*to **find** [faɪnd] finden; herausfinden **I**
*to **find** one's way around [ˌfaɪnd wʌnz ˌweɪ‿əˈraʊnd] sich zurechtfinden **IV U1**, 16
*to **find** out [ˌfaɪnd‿ˈaʊt] herausfinden **I**
fine [faɪn] gut; in Ordnung; schön **I**
I'm **fine**. [ˌaɪm ˈfaɪn] Mir geht's gut. **I**
finger [ˈfɪŋɡə] Finger **I**
*to keep your **fingers** crossed [ˌkiːp jɔː ˌfɪŋɡəz ˈkrɒst] die Daumen drücken **I**
finish line [ˈfɪnɪʃ ˌlaɪn] Ziellinie **II**
to **finish** [ˈfɪnɪʃ] beenden; enden; fertigstellen; aufhören **I**
finished [ˈfɪnɪʃt] fertig **II**
fire [faɪə] Feuer **III**
*to be on **fire** [ˌbiː‿ɒn ˈfaɪə] brennen **III**
firewood [ˈfaɪəwʊd] Brennholz ⟨**IVTS3**, 106⟩
fireworks *(pl)* [ˈfaɪəwɜːks] Feuerwerk **I**
firm [fɜːm] fest ⟨**IV U3**, 93⟩
first [fɜːst] zuerst; als Erstes; erste/-r/-s **I**
at **first** [ət ˈfɜːst] zuerst; zunächst **II**
first language [ˌfɜːst ˈlæŋɡwɪdʒ] Muttersprache **II**
first person narrator [ˌfɜːst ˌpɜːsn nəˈreɪtə] Ich-Erzähler/-in **III**
fish [fɪʃ], **fish** [fɪʃ] *(pl)* Fisch **I**
fishing [ˈfɪʃɪŋ] Angeln; Fischen; Fischerei **II**
to **fit** [fɪt] passen **II**
*to get **fit** [ˌget ˈfɪt] in Form kommen; fit werden **I**
five [faɪv] fünf **I**
to **fix** [fɪks] reparieren; befestigen **II**
flag [flæɡ] Flagge; Fahne **III**
flair [fleə] Flair; Atmosphäre **II**
flame [fleɪm] Flamme **III**
flash [flæʃ] Blitz; Lichtblitz **III**
flashback [ˈflæʃbæk] Rückblende; Flashback **III**
flat [flæt] Wohnung **I**
flat [flæt] flach; platt **IV AC1**, 10
flavor *(AE)* [ˈfleɪvə] Geschmack; Aroma **IV U2**, 45
flea market [ˈfliː ˌmɑːkɪt] Flohmarkt **I**
flight [flaɪt] Flug **III**
flight attendant [ˈflaɪt‿əˌtendnt] Flugbegleiter/-in **III**
to **float** [fləʊt] gleiten; treiben ⟨**IV U3**, 93⟩
floor [flɔː] Fußboden **I**; Stockwerk **IV U1**, 14
floor plan [ˈflɔː plæn] Grundriss ⟨**IV AC4**, 109⟩
flour [flaʊə] Mehl **IV U3**, 93
to **flow** out [fləʊ‿ˈaʊt] hinausfließen **II**
flower [ˈflaʊə] Blume **II**
*to **fly** [flaɪ] fliegen **III**; hissen **IV AC1**, 9
flyer [ˈflaɪə] Flyer **I**
focus [ˈfəʊkəs] Blickpunkt; Schwerpunkt; Fokus **III**
out of **focus** [ˌaʊt‿əv ˈfəʊkəs] unscharf **III**
to **focus** (on) [ˈfəʊkəs‿ɒn] sich konzentrieren (auf) **II**
folder [ˈfəʊldə] Ordner; Mappe **I**
folks *(infml) (pl)* [fəʊks] Leute ⟨**IV U3**, 92⟩
to **follow** [ˈfɒləʊ] folgen; hinterhergehen; befolgen **II**
the **following** [ðə ˈfɒləʊɪŋ] folgende/-r/-s **II**
follow-up [ˈfɒləʊʌp] Fortsetzung; Folge- **IV U2**, 62
food [fuːd] Essen; Lebensmittel **I**; Futter **III**
foot [fʊt], **feet** [fiːt] *(pl)* Fuß **I**; Fuß *(Längenmaß: 30,48 cm)* **IV AC1**, 9
*to keep one's **feet** or hands still [ˌkiːp wʌnzː ˈfiːt‿ɔː ˈhændz stɪl] die Beine und Hände ruhig halten **III**
on **foot** [ɒn ˈfʊt] zu Fuß **II**
football [ˈfʊtbɔːl] Fußball **I**
for [fɔː; fə] wegen **II**
for example [fər‿ɪɡˈzɑːmpl] zum Beispiel **II**
for free [fə ˈfriː] umsonst; kostenlos **IV U2**, 42
for *(+ Zeitraum)* [fɔː; fə] seit **III**
for … [fɔː; fə] … lang **II**
force [fɔːs] Kraft; Macht **III**
weather **forecast** [ˈweðə ˌfɔːkɑːst] Wettervorhersage **II**
foreground [ˈfɔːɡraʊnd] Vordergrund **IV U1**, 17
foreign [ˈfɒrɪn] ausländisch; fremd **III**

foreign language [ˌfɒrɪn ˈlæŋgwɪdʒ] Fremdsprache **II**
forest [ˈfɒrɪst] Wald **II**
forever [fəˈrevə] für immer; ewig **II**
*to **forget** [fəˈget] vergessen **I**
*to **forgive** [fəˈgɪv] vergeben; verzeihen **II**
fork [fɔːk] Gabel **III**
form [fɔːm] Form **I**; Formular **II**
negative **form** [ˈnegətɪv ˌfɔːm] verneinte Form **I**
past **form** [ˈpɑːst fɔːm] Vergangenheitsform **II**
possessive **form** [pəˌsesɪv ˈfɔːm] Possessivform **I**
short **form** [ˈʃɔːt fɔːm] Kurzform **I**
to **form** [fɔːm] formen; bilden **II**
formal [ˈfɔːml] formal; formell; förmlich **II**
fortune [ˈfɔːtʃuːn] Vermögen; Reichtum ⟨**IV TS3**, 107⟩
forum [ˈfɔːrəm] Forum **II**
forward [ˈfɔːwəd] vorwärts **III**
to look **forward** to [ˌlʊk ˈfɔːwəd tə] sich freuen auf **II**
to **found** [faʊnd] gründen **III**
foundation [faʊnˈdeɪʃn] Stiftung; Gründung °**IV U3**, 85
water **fountain** [ˈwɔːtə ˌfaʊntɪn] Wasserspender **IV AC3**, 76
four [fɔː] vier **I**
four-walled [ˈfɔːwɔːld] mit vier Wänden ⟨**IV U2**, 60⟩
fox [fɒks] Fuchs **II**
freeze **frame** [ˈfriːz ˌfreɪm] Standbild **III**
free [friː] frei; kostenlos **I**
free time [ˌfriː ˈtaɪm] Freizeit **I**
for **free** [fə ˈfriː] umsonst; kostenlos **IV U2**, 42
freedom *(no pl)* [ˈfriːdəm] Freiheit; Unabhängigkeit **III**
freeway *(AE)* [ˈfriːweɪ] Autobahn **IV U2**, 49
freeze frame [ˈfriːz ˌfreɪm] Standbild **III**
French [frenʃ] französisch; Französisch **II**
frequently asked [ˌfriːkwəntli‿ˈɑːskt] häufig gefragt **I**
fresh [freʃ] frisch **I**
Friday [ˈfraɪdeɪ] Freitag **I**
fridge [frɪdʒ] Kühlschrank **I**
fried [fraɪd] gebraten *(in der Pfanne)* **IV U2**, 45
friend [frend] Freund/-in **I**
*to become **friends** [bɪˌkʌm‿ˈfrendz] sich anfreunden; Freundschaft schließen **IV AC1**, 11
*to make **friends** [ˌmeɪk ˈfrendz] Freundschaft schließen **II**
That's what **friends** are for. [ˌðæts wɒt ˈfrendz‿ɑː ˌfɔː] Dafür sind Freunde da. **I**
friendly [ˈfrendli] freundlich; nett **II**
friendship [ˈfrendʃɪp] Freundschaft **II**
frightened [ˈfraɪtnd] verängstigt **IV U3**, 84
frightening [ˈfraɪtnɪŋ] furchterregend **IV U3**, 85
fringe [frɪndʒ] Rand-; Alternativ- **III**
from [frɒm; frəm] aus; von **I**
from the outside [ˌfrəm ði‿aʊtˈsaɪd] von außen **IV U2**, 45
from … to [frəm … tə] von … bis **I**
Where … **from**? [ˌweə … ˈfrɒm] Woher …? **I**
from around the world [frɒm əˌraʊnd ðə ˈwɜːld] aus aller Welt **II**
front [frʌnt] Vorderseite; Front-; Vorder- **II**
front door [ˌfrʌnt ˈdɔː] Haustür **II**
front yard *(AE)* [ˌfrʌnt ˈjɑːd] Vorgarten **IV U1**, 13
in **front** of [ɪn ˈfrʌnt‿əv] vor **I**
fruit [fruːt] Frucht; Obst **I**
full (of) [fʊl‿əv] voll (von) **I**
to talk with your mouth **full** [ˌtɔːk wɪð jɔː ˈmaʊθ fʊl] mit vollem Mund sprechen **III**
fun [fʌn] Freude; Spaß **I**
*to have **fun** [ˌhæv ˈfʌn] Spaß haben; sich amüsieren **I**
*to make **fun** of [ˌmeɪk ˈfʌn‿əv] sich lustig machen über **IV U4**, 124
It's **fun**. [ɪts ˈfʌn] Es macht Spaß. **I**
No risk, no **fun**! [nəʊ ˌrɪsk nəʊ ˈfʌn] Wer nicht wagt, der nicht gewinnt. **IV AC2**, 39
fun [fʌn] lustig; witzig; fröhlich **I**
function [ˈfʌŋkʃn] Funktion **IV TS2**, 73
funny [ˈfʌni] lustig; witzig **I**; merkwürdig; komisch **III**
furniture *(singular noun with plural meaning)* [ˈfɜːnɪtʃə] Möbel **IV U3**, 92
further [ˈfɜːðə] weiter (weg) **III**
future [ˈfjuːtʃə] Zukunft **II**
future perfect [ˌfjuːtʃə ˈpɜːfɪkt] vollendetes Futur; Futur II ⟨**IV U4**, 119⟩
future [ˈfjuːtʃə] zukünftig **III**

G

gadget [ˈgædʒɪt] Gerät; technische Spielerei **III**
Gaelic [ˈgeɪlɪk] gälisch; Gälisch **II**
gallery walk [ˈgælri ˌwɔːk] Museumsrundgang; Vernissage **I**
game [geɪm] Spiel **I**
guessing **game** [ˈgesɪŋ ˌgeɪm] Ratespiel **II**
gap [gæp] Lücke; Spalt; Abstand **I**
garage [ˈgærɑːʒ] Garage **I**
garbage *(AE)* [ˈgɑːbɪdʒ] Müll; Abfall **IV AC4**, 108
garden [ˈgɑːdn] Garten **I**
garlic [ˈgɑːlɪk] Knoblauch **III**
gas(oline) *(AE)* [ˈgæsliːn] Benzin **IV U4**, 123
to **gasp** [gɑːsp] tief Luft holen; keuchen **IV U2**, 42
gate [geɪt] Gate; Flugsteig; Ausgang **III**
geek [giːk] Außenseiter/-in **IV U1**, 18
general [ˈdʒenrl] General **IV U3**, 80
general [ˈdʒenrl] allgemein **IV TS3**, 103
in **general** [ɪn ˈdʒenrl] im allgemeinen °**IV TS3**, 106
generation [ˌdʒenəˈreɪʃn] Generation **III**
generous [ˈdʒenrəs] großzügig **III**
genius [ˈdʒiːniəs] Genie **II**
genre [ˈʒɑ̃ːnrə] Gattung **III**
gentleman [ˈdʒentlmən], **gentlemen** [ˈdʒentlmen] *(pl)* Gentleman; feiner Herr **III**
geocaching [ˈdʒiːəʊkæʃɪŋ] Geocaching **II**
geography [dʒiˈɒgrəfi] Geografie; Erdkunde **II**
German [ˈdʒɜːmən] deutsch; Deutsch; aus Deutschland; Deutsche/-r **I**
gerund [ˈdʒernd] Gerundium °**IV U1**, 13
gesture [ˈdʒestʃə] Geste; Gebärde **III**
*to **get** [get] holen; bringen; bekommen; besorgen; kaufen **I**; werden **II**
*to **get** a ride [ˌget‿ə ˈraɪd] eine Mitfahrgelegenheit bekommen **IV TS3**, 105
*to **get** around [ˌget‿əˈraʊnd] *hier:* sich fortbewegen **II**
*to **get** away with [ˌget‿əˈweɪ wɪð] davonkommen mit **II**
*to **get** caught [ˌget ˈkɔːt] erwischt werden; ertappt werden **IV AC2**, 38
*to **get** familiar [ˌget fəˈmɪliə] sich vertraut machen °**IV TS3**, 102
*to **get** fit [ˌget ˈfɪt] in Form kommen; fit werden **I**
*to **get** in [ˌget‿ˈɪn] einsteigen **IV U2**, 46
*to **get** in the way [ˌget‿ɪn ðə ˈweɪ] stören; im Weg stehen **II**
*to **get** into [ˌget‿ˈɪntə] einsteigen; hineingelangen **I**
*to **get** into trouble [ˌget‿ɪntə ˈtrʌbl] in Schwierigkeiten geraten **IV AC2**, 39
*to **get** lost [ˌget ˈlɒst] verloren gehen; sich verirren **II**
*to **get** off (a bus/train) [ˌget‿ˈɒf] aussteigen (aus einem Bus/Zug) **II**
*to **get** on (the bus) [ˌget‿ˈɒn] einsteigen (in den Bus) **II**
*to **get** on people's nerves [ˌget‿ɒn sʌmbɒdiz ˈnɜːvz] jemandem auf die Nerven gehen **I**
*to **get** organised [get ˈɔːgənaɪzd] sich organisieren **II**
*to **get** out of [get ˌaʊt‿əv] aussteigen; herauskommen aus **II**
*to **get** right [get ˈraɪt] richtig beantworten **II**
*to **get** started [ˌget ˈstɑːtɪd] anfangen **II**
*to **get** sth out of one's head [get ˌaʊt‿əv wʌnz ˈhed] etw. aus dem Kopf bekommen **III**
*to **get** there [ˈget ðeə] hinkommen **I**
*to **get** to [ˈget tə] kommen zu; kommen nach; erreichen **I**
*to **get** to know [ˌget tə ˈnəʊ] kennenlernen **II**
*to **get** up [ˌget‿ˈʌp] aufstehen *(aus dem Bett)* **I**

*to **get** used to sth [ˌget ˈjuːzd tə] sich an etw. gewöhnen **IV U1**, 14
*to **get** well [ˌget ˈwel] gesund werden **IV U3**, 93
had **gotten** off *(AE)* [hæd ˌgɒtn‿ˈɒf] waren ausgestiegen **IV U3**, 84
Time to **get** up! [ˌtaɪm tə ˌget‿ˈʌp] Es ist Zeit aufzustehen! **I**
ghost [gəʊst] Geist **II**
giant [dʒaɪənt] Riesen-; riesig ⟨**IV TS2**, 71⟩
gift [gɪft] Geschenk; Gabe **IV U4**, 123
gig [gɪg] Auftritt; Gig **III**
gigantic [dʒaɪˈgæntɪk] gigantisch; riesig **IV AC1**, 10
girl [gɜːl] Mädchen **I**
girlfriend [ˈgɜːlfrend] Freundin *(in einer Paarbeziehung)* **II**
gist [dʒɪst] das Wesentliche **II**
*to **give** [gɪv] geben; schenken **I**
*to **give** a talk [ˌgɪv‿ə ˈtɔːk] einen Vortrag halten **IV U1**, 13
*to **give** away [ˌgɪv‿əˈweɪ] verteilen; verschenken **IV TS1**, 34; verraten; preisgeben °**IV U2**, 63
*to **give** reasons [ˌgɪv ˈriːznz] Gründe nennen/angeben ⟨**IV U2**, 60⟩
*to **give** sb a piggyback [gɪv‿ə ˈpɪgibæk] jmdn. Huckepack nehmen **III**
*to **give** sb funny looks [ˌgɪv fʌni ˈlʊks] jmdn. schief anschauen **III**
*to **give** thanks [ˌgɪv ˈθæŋks] danken **IV U1**, 15
*to **give** the bumps [ˌgɪv ðə ˈbʌmps] hochleben lassen **I**
*to **give** up [ˌgɪv‿ˈʌp] aufgeben **III**
glacial [ˈgleɪsiəl; ˈgleɪʃl] eisig; Gletscher- **IV TS3**, 103
glad [glæd] froh **III**; fein ⟨**IV U4**, 123⟩
glamorous [ˈglæmrəs] glamourös **IV TS1**, 35
to **glance** at [ˈglɑːns‿ət] einen Blick werfen auf; blicken auf ⟨**IV U2**, 60⟩
glass [glɑːs] Glas **I**
glasses *(pl)* [ˈglɑːsɪz] Brille **II**
to **glint** [glɪnt] glitzern ⟨**IV U2**, 60⟩
glossary [ˈglɒsri] Glossar; Stichwortverzeichnis **III**
glove [glʌv] Handschuh **I**
*to **go** [gəʊ] gehen; fahren **I**
*to **go** *(+ adj)* [gəʊ] werden **IV U4**, 116
*to **go** bad [ˌgəʊ ˈbæd] schiefgehen; schlecht werden; verderben **IV U4**, 124
*to **go** black [ˌgəʊ ˈblæk] schwarz werden **II**
*to **go** crazy [ˌgəʊ ˈkreɪzi] ausflippen; durchdrehen; verrückt werden **II**
*to **go** down [ˌgəʊ ˈdaʊn] hinuntergehen; nach unten gehen; entlanggehen **I**
*to **go** for a walk [ˌgəʊ fər‿ə ˈwɔːk] spazieren gehen **II**
*to **go** on [ˌgəʊ‿ˈɒn] weitergehen; weitermachen; weiterführen; fortfahren **I**
*to **go** out [ˌgəʊ‿ˈaʊt] ausgehen; hinausgehen **II**
*to **go** over to [ˌgəʊ ˈəʊvə tə] hinübergehen zu; zu jmdm. nach Hause gehen **II**
*to **go** right back to [ˌgəʊ raɪt ˈbæk tə] zurückgehen auf **II**
*to **go** round in circles [gəʊ ˌraʊnd ɪn ˈsɜːklz] sich im Kreis drehen **III**
*to **go** shopping [ˌgəʊ ˈʃɒpɪŋ] einkaufen gehen **I**
*to **go** swimming [ˌgəʊ ˈswɪmɪŋ] Schwimmen gehen **I**
*to **go** to bed [ˌgəʊ tə ˈbed] ins Bett gehen **I**
*to **go** together [ˌgəʊ təˈgeðə] zueinander passen; zueinander gehören **I**
*to **go** with [ˈgəʊ wɪð] passen zu; gehören zu **I**
*to **go** wrong [ˌgəʊ ˈrɒŋ] schiefgehen **I**
*to let **go** (of) [ˌlet ˈgəʊ (əv)] loslassen **II**
Go on! [ˌgəʊ‿ˈɒn] Los! **IV U1**, 25
It's **gone**. [ɪts ˈgɒn] Es ist weg. **II**
What's **going** on? [wɒts ˌgəʊɪŋ‿ˈɒn] Was ist los?; Was geht ab? **III**
goal [gəʊl] Tor; Ziel **I**
God [gɒd] Gott ⟨**IV U1**, 19⟩
the **gods** *(liter)* [ðə ˈgɒdz] die Götter *(literarisch)* **IV U4**, 117
goddess [ˈgɒdes] Göttin **IV U2**, 44
gold [gəʊld] Gold **III**
golden age [ˌgəʊldn ˈeɪdʒ] goldenes Zeitalter **III**
golf [gɒlf] Golf **II**
*to be **gone** [biː ˈgɒn] verschwunden sein; weg sein **II**
gonna (= going to) *(coll)* [ˈgɒnə] wird/werden **IV U2**, 40
good [gʊd] gut **I**
*to be **good** at [biː ˈgʊd‿ət] gut sein in **I**
good luck [ˌgʊd ˈlʌk] viel Glück **IV U2**, 46
Good morning. [ˌgʊd ˈmɔːnɪŋ] Guten Morgen. **I**
It wouldn't do me any **good**. [ˌɪt wʊdnt ˌduː miː eni ˈgʊd] Es würde mir nichts nützen. **IV U4**, 124
goodbye [gʊdˈbaɪ] auf Wiedersehen **I**
gorge scrambling [ˈgɔːdʒ ˌskræmblɪŋ] Schluchtenklettern **II**
gotta (= got to) *(coll)* [ˈgɒtə] muss/müssen ⟨**IV U3**, 89⟩
government [ˈgʌvnmənt] Regierung **IV TS2**, 72
to **grab** [græb] greifen; ergreifen; schnappen **II**
grade *(AE)* [greɪd] Note **IV U2**, 48
8th-**grader** *(AE)* [ˈeɪtθˌgreɪdə] Achtklässler/-in **IV U1**, 18
grammar [ˈgræmə] Grammatik **II**
grammar school [ˈgræmə ˌskuːl] Gymnasium **II**
grandad [ˈgrændæd] Opa **I**
great-great-**grandfather** [ˌgreɪtgreɪtˈgrænˌfɑːðə] Urgroßvater **IV U3**, 82
grandma [ˈgrænmɑː] Oma **I**
grandmother [ˈgrænˌmʌðə] Großmutter **IV U3**, 90
grandparents *(pl)* [ˈgrænˌpeərənts] Großeltern **I**
granny [ˈgræni] Oma **I**
graph [grɑːf] Diagramm; Schaubild **IV U3**, 85
bar **graph** [ˈbɑː grɑːf] Säulendiagramm; Balkendiagramm **IV U3**, 85
line **graph** [ˈlaɪn grɑːf] Kurvendiagramm **IV U3**, 85
graphic novel [ˌgræfɪk ˈnɒvl] Bildergeschichte; Comic **III**
grass [grɑːs] Gras **IV U3**, 92
gratitude [ˈgrætɪtjuːd] Dankbarkeit **III**
great [greɪt] großartig; toll; super **I**
great wheel [ˌgreɪt ˈwiːl] Riesenrad **IV U4**, 112
It's **great** for … [ɪts ˈgreɪt fə] Es ist super zum/für … **I**
great-great-grandfather [ˌgreɪtgreɪtˈgrænˌfɑːðə] Urgroßvater **IV U3**, 82
green [griːn] grün **I**
Greenwich Mean Time *(= GMT)* [ˌgrenɪdʒ ˈmiːn ˌtaɪm] westeuropäische Zeit **I**
greeting [ˈgriːtɪŋ] Gruß **I**
grey [greɪ] grau **I**
grid [grɪd] Gitter; Tabelle; Raster **I**
grill [grɪl] Grill ⟨**IV AC4**, 109⟩
grizzly bear [ˈgrɪzli ˌbeə] Grizzlybär **IV TS3**, 103
groan [grəʊn] Stöhnen **III**
to **groan** [grəʊn] stöhnen **IV U2**, 44
ground [graʊnd] Boden; Erdboden **III**
*to be **grounded** [bi ˈgraʊndɪd] Hausarrest haben **III**
group [gruːp] Gruppe; Klasse **I**
tutor **group** [ˈtjuːtə ˌgruːp] Klasse *(in einer englischen Schule)* **I**
to **group** (around) [gruːp (əˈraʊnd)] gruppieren (um) **III**
*to **grow** [grəʊ] wachsen **II**; anbauen; züchten **III**
*to **grow** by [ˈgrəʊ baɪ] steigen um **IV U3**, 85
*to **grow** up [ˌgrəʊ‿ˈʌp] aufwachsen; erwachsen werden **III**
growth [grəʊθ] Wachstum **IV U4**, 110
guard [gɑːd] Wache; Wächter/-in **II**
to **guess** [ges] raten; erraten; vermuten **I**; annehmen **III**
guessing game [ˈgesɪŋ ˌgeɪm] Ratespiel **II**
guest [gest] Gast **III**
guide [gaɪd] Führer/-in; Reiseführer **II**
to **guide** [gaɪd] führen; leiten **III**
guidebook [ˈgaɪdbʊk] Reiseführer **IV U2**, 42
guilty [ˈgɪlti] schuldig **III**

guilty conscience [ˌgɪlti ˈkɒnʃns] Schuldbewusstsein; schlechtes Gewissen ⟨**IVTS3**, 107⟩
guinea pig [ˈgɪni: ˌpɪg] Meerschweinchen **I**
guitar [gɪˈtɑ:] Gitarre **III**
chewing **gum** [ˈtʃu:ɪŋ ˌgʌm] Kaugummi **III**
gun [gʌn] Schusswaffe ⟨**IVTS3**, 107⟩
guy [gaɪ] Typ; Kerl; *(Pl.)* Leute **II**
gym(nasium) [dʒɪm; dʒɪmˈneɪziəm] Turnhalle **IV AC2**, 38

H

haggis [ˈhægɪs] Haggis *(schottisches Gericht aus in einem Schafsmagen gekochten Schafsinnereien und Haferschrot)* **III**
hair [heə] Haar; Haare **IVTS1**, 34
*to do our **hair** [ˌdu:ˌaʊə ˈheə] uns frisieren; unsere Haare machen **I**
hairbrush [ˈheəbrʌʃ] Haarbürste **III**
half [hɑ:f], **halves** [hɑ:vz] *(pl)* (of) die Hälfte **I**
half [hɑ:f] halb **I**
half an hour [ˌhɑ:fˌənˌˈaʊər] eine halbe Stunde **III**
half past [ˌhɑ:f ˈpɑ:st] halb *(bei Uhrzeitangaben)* **I**
half-sister [ˈhɑ:fˌsɪstə] Halbschwester **I**
half-term break [ˌhɑ:ftɜ:m ˈbreɪk] Halbjahresferien **I**
*to meet **halfway** [ˌmi:t hɑ:fˈweɪ] sich auf halbem Weg treffen **III**
hall [hɔ:l] Halle; Saal; Flur; Diele; Korridor **II**
arrivals **hall** [əˈraɪvlz ˌhɔ:l] Ankunftshalle **III**
hall pass [ˈhɔ:l pɑ:s] *Erlaubnis, sich während des Unterrichts auf dem Flur aufzuhalten* **IV U1**, 13
hallway [ˈhɔ:lweɪ] Flur; Diele; Korridor **IV U1**, 13
ham [hæm] Schinken **III**
hammer [ˈhæmə] Hammer **II**
hand [hænd] Hand **I**
Clap your **hands**. [ˌklæp jɔ: ˈhændz] Klatsch/Klatscht in die Hände. **I**
On the one **hand** ..., (but) on the other **hand** ... [ɒn ðəˌˈwʌn ˌhænd ... (bʌt) ɒn ðiˌˈʌðə ˌhænd ...] Einerseits ..., (aber) andererseits ... **II**
handful [ˈhænfʊl] Handvoll ⟨**IV U3**, 93⟩
*to **hang** around [ˌhæŋˌəˈraʊnd] herumhängen (bei) ⟨**IV U4**, 125⟩
*to **hang** on [ˌhæŋˌˈɒn] (einen Augenblick) warten **III**
*to **hang** out (with) *(infml)* [ˌhæŋˌˈaʊt wɪð] sich herumtreiben (mit); rumhängen (mit); sich treffen (mit) **III**
*to **hang** up [ˌhæŋˌˈʌp] aufhängen **II**
to **happen** [ˈhæpn] geschehen; passieren **I**
happiness [ˈhæpɪnəs] Glück; Zufriedenheit; Fröhlichkeit **IV U4**, 114
happy [ˈhæpi] glücklich; froh; fröhlich **I**
happy ending [ˌhæpi ˈendɪŋ] Happy End **III**
Happy Birthday! [ˌhæpi ˈbɜ:θdeɪ] Alles Gute zum Geburtstag!; Herzlichen Glückwunsch zum Geburtstag! **I**
harbour [ˈhɑ:bə] Hafen **II**
hard [hɑ:d] hart; schwer; schwierig; *hier:* stark **II**
*to be **hard** on sb [bi ˈhɑ:dˌɒn] streng mit jmdm. sein **III**
hardly [ˈhɑ:dli] kaum **III**
harsh [hɑ:ʃ] rau; hart **IV AC1**, 10
harvest [ˈhɑ:vɪst] Ernte **IV U1**, 15
hat [hæt] Hut **I**
to **hate** [heɪt] hassen; nicht mögen **II**
haunted house [ˌhɔ:ntɪd ˈhaʊs] Geisterhaus ⟨**IVTS3**, 107⟩
*to **have** [hæv] haben **I**
*to **have** *(a sweet)* [hæv] *(ein Bonbon)* nehmen; *(ein Bonbon)* essen **I**
*to **have** a look (at) [ˌhævˌə ˈlʊk] anschauen **II**
*to **have** a point [ˌhævˌə ˈpɔɪnt] nicht ganz Unrecht haben **III**
*to **have** a short shelf life [ˌhævˌə ˌʃɔ:t ˈʃelf laɪf] eine kurze Haltbarkeit haben ⟨**IV U4**, 124⟩
*to **have** breakfast [ˌhæv ˈbrekfəst] frühstücken **I**
*to **have** fun [ˌhæv ˈfʌn] Spaß haben; sich amüsieren **I**
*to **have** got [hæv ˈgɒt] besitzen; haben **I**
*to **have** in common [ˌhævˌɪn ˈkɒmən] gemeinsam haben **III**
*to **have** no clue [ˌhæv nəʊ ˈklu:] keine Ahnung haben **IV AC1**, 11
*to **have** to [ˈhæv tə] müssen **II**
he [hi:] er **I**
head [hed] Kopf **I**
*to get sth out of one's **head** [get ˌaʊtˌəv wʌnz ˈhed] etw. aus dem Kopf bekommen **III**
head of state [ˌhedˌəv ˈsteɪt] Staatsoberhaupt **II**
With a very big **head**! [ˌwɪð ə ˌveri bɪg ˈhed] Und ein Angeber! **II**
to **head** (for) [ˈhed fə] zusteuern auf **IV U3**, 92
headache *(no pl)* [ˈhedeɪk] Kopfschmerzen; Kopfweh **II**
heading [ˈhedɪŋ] Überschrift; Titel **I**
headline [ˈhedlaɪn] Schlagzeile **III**
headphones *(pl)* [ˈhedfəʊnz] Kopfhörer **II**
health [helθ] Gesundheit **II**
healthy [ˈhelθi] gesund **I**
*to **hear** [hɪə] hören **I**
I **hear** ... [aɪ ˈhɪə] Ich habe gehört, dass ... **I**
heart [hɑ:t] Herz; *hier:* Zentrum **II**
*to learn ... by **heart** [ˌlɜ:n baɪ ˈhɑ:t] auswendig lernen **I**
heat *(no pl)* [hi:t] Hitze; Wärme **IVTS3**, 102
heating [ˈhi:tɪŋ] Heizung **III**
underfloor **heating** *(no pl)* [ˌʌndəflɔ: ˈhi:tɪŋ] Fußbodenheizung **III**
heavy [ˈhevi] schwer; stark **III**
hectic [ˈhektɪk] hektisch ⟨**IV U2**, 51⟩
hedgehog [ˈhedʒhɒg] Igel **III**
height [haɪt] Höhe ⟨**IVTS2**, 72⟩
hell [hel] Hölle ⟨**IVTS3**, 102⟩
Hello. [helˈəʊ] Hallo. **I**
*to say **hello** (to) [ˌseɪ helˈəʊ tə] grüßen; Grüße ausrichten (an) **I**
help [help] Hilfe **I**
to **help** [help] helfen **I**
to **help** out [ˌhelpˌˈaʊt] aushelfen **III**
helpful [ˈhelpfl] hilfsbereit; hilfreich **I**
helpless [ˈhelpləs] hilflos **I**
her [hɜ:] ihr/-e; sie **I**
herb [hɜ:b] Kraut **III**
herd [hɜ:d] Herde; Rudel **IV U3**, 94
here [hɪə] hier **I**
right **here** [ˌraɪt ˈhɪə] genau hier **II**
Here you are. [ˌhɪə juˌˈɑ:] Bitte schön. **I**
hero [ˈhɪərəʊ], **heroes** [ˈhɪərəʊz] *(pl)* Held **II**
heroine [ˈherəʊɪn] Heldin **II**
to **hesitate** [ˈhezɪteɪt] zögern **III**
Hey! [heɪ] Hi.; He!; Hallo. **I**
Hi. [haɪ] Hi.; Hallo. **I**
hibernation [ˌhaɪbəˈneɪʃn] Winterschlaf **III**
*to **hide** [haɪd] (sich) verstecken **II**
high [haɪ] hoch; groß **II**
high school *(AE)* [ˈhaɪ ˌsku:l] High School *(weiterführende Schule in den USA, Oberstufe)* **IV U1**, 13
high tide [ˈhaɪ ˌtaɪd] Flut **II**
the **high** street [ðə ˈhaɪ ˌstri:t] die Haupteinkaufsstraße **III**
highlight [ˈhaɪlaɪt] Highlight; Höhepunkt **II**
highly [ˈhaɪli] höchst- **IVTS1**, 35
highway *(AE)* [ˈhaɪweɪ] Landstraße; Bundesautobahn *(amerik.)*; Highway **IV U4**, 123
hiking [ˈhaɪkɪŋ] Wandern **II**
hill [hɪl] Berg; Hügel **II**
him [hɪm] ihn; ihm **I**
himself [hɪmˈself] er/sich (selbst); selber **II**
hint [hɪnt] Hinweis; Andeutung; Tipp **III**
hip [hɪp] hip; total in **IVTS3**, 103
his [hɪz] sein/-e **I**
historian [hɪˈstɔ:riən] Historiker/-in **IV U3**, 91
historic [hɪˈstɒrɪk] historisch **III**
historical [hɪˈstɒrɪkl] historisch; geschichtlich **I**
history [ˈhɪstri] Geschichte **II**
living **history** show [ˌlɪvɪŋ ˈhɪstəri ˌʃəʊ] *Show, in der historischer Alltag nachgespielt wird* **II**
*to **hit** [hɪt] schlagen; treffen **I**
to **hitchhike** [ˈhɪtʃhaɪk] trampen; per Anhalter fahren **IVTS3**, 105
hitchhiker [ˈhɪtʃˌhaɪkə] Tramper/-in **IVTS3**, 105
hitchhiking [ˈhɪtʃˌhaɪkɪŋ] Trampen **IVTS3**, 105

hoarder of trash [ˌhɔːdər‿əv ˈtræʃ] Messy ⟨**IV TS3**, 106⟩
hoax [həʊks] Täuschung; Trick **IV TS2**, 72
hobby [ˈhɒbi], **hobbies** [ˈhɒbiz] *(pl)* Hobby **I**
hockey [hɒki] Hockey **II**
to **hog** a conversation [ˌhɒg‿ə kɒnvəˈseɪʃn] ein Gespräch für sich in Beschlag nehmen; ein Gespräch dominieren **III**
*to **hold** [həʊld] halten; festhalten **I**
*to **hold** a competition [ˌhəʊld‿ə ˌkɒmpəˈtɪʃn] einen Wettbewerb durchführen **IV U4**, 114
*to **hold** onto [ˌhəʊld‿ˈɒntə] (sich) festhalten an **III**
*to **hold** open [ˌhəʊld‿ˈəʊpn] aufhalten **III**
hole [həʊl] Loch **II**
holiday [ˈhɒlədeɪ] Urlaub; Feiertag **I**
holidays *(pl)* [ˈhɒlədeɪz] Ferien **I**
home [həʊm] Zuhause; Heim **I**
at **home** [ət ˈhəʊm] zu Hause **I**
home [həʊm] nach Hause **I**
homeless [ˈhəʊmləs] obdachlos **IV U1**, 21
homeless shelter [ˈhəʊmləs ˌʃeltə] Obdachlosenunterkunft **IV U1**, 21
homepage [ˈhəʊmpeɪdʒ] Homepage **I**
*to be **homesick** [bi ˈhəʊmsɪk] Heimweh haben **III**
hometown [ˈhəʊmtaʊn] Heimatstadt **IV U2**, 45
homework [ˈhəʊmwɜːk] Hausaufgabe(n) **I**
honest [ˈɒnɪst] ehrlich **III**
honey [ˈhʌni] Honig **III**
honor *(AE)* [ˈɒnə] Ehre **IV U3**, 95
to **hook** [hʊk] *hier:* fesseln **III**
hula **hoop** [ˈhuːlə ˌhuːp] Hulahoop-Reifen ⟨**IV TS3**, 105⟩
hula **hooper** [ˈhuːlə ˌhuːpə] Hulahooper/-in ⟨**IV TS3**, 105⟩
hope [həʊp] Hoffnung **II**
to **hope** [həʊp] hoffen **I**
hopeful [ˈhəʊpfl] hoffnungsvoll **I**
horn [hɔːn] Horn **III**
horrified [ˈhɒrɪfaɪd] entsetzt **I**
horror [ˈhɒrə] Horrorgeschichte; Horrorfilm; Horror **III**
horse [hɔːs] Pferd **I**
hospital [ˈhɒspɪtl] Hospital; Krankenhaus **II**
host family [ˈhəʊst ˌfæmli] Gastfamilie **III**
hostel [ˈhɒstl] Herberge **III**
hostile [ˈhɒstaɪl] feindlich; ablehnend ⟨**IV TS2**, 74⟩
hot [hɒt] heiß **III**
hot dog [ˈhɒt ˌdɒg] Hot Dog *(Würstchen im Brötchen)* ⟨**IV U2**, 45⟩
hotel [həʊˈtel] Hotel **II**
hour [aʊə] Stunde **II**
half an **hour** [ˌhɑːf‿ən‿ˈaʊər] eine halbe Stunde **III**
house [haʊs] Haus **I**
haunted **house** [ˌhɔːntɪd ˈhaʊs] Geisterhaus ⟨**IV TS3**, 107⟩
to move (**house**) [muːv (haʊs)] umziehen **II**
household [ˈhaʊshəʊld] Haushalt **IV AC4**, 108
how [haʊ] wie **I**
How many …? [ˌhaʊ ˈmeni] Wie viele …? **I**
How are you? [ˌhaʊ‿ˈɑː jə] Wie geht es dir/euch/Ihnen?; Wie geht es euch?; Wie geht es Ihnen? **I**
How much (is/are) …? [ˌhaʊ ˈmʌtʃ‿ɪz/ɑː] Wie viel (kostet/kosten) …? **I**
How old are you? [haʊ‿ˈəʊld‿ə ˌjuː] Wie alt bist du?; Wie alt sind Sie? **I**
How to … [ˈhaʊ tə] Wie man … **I**
Is this **how** you (do) …? [ɪz ˈðɪs haʊ jʊ ˌduː] Machst du so …? **I**
that's **how** [ðæts ˈhaʊ] so **II**
however [haʊˈevə] jedoch **IV U2**, 46
to **hug** [hʌg] umarmen **I**
huge [hjuːdʒ] riesig; riesengroß; gewaltig **II**
hula hoop [ˈhuːlə ˌhuːp] Hulahoop-Reifen ⟨**IV TS3**, 105⟩
hula hooper [ˈhuːlə ˌhuːpə] Hulahooper/-in ⟨**IV TS3**, 105⟩
to **hum** [hʌm] summen **II**
human [ˈhjuːmən] Mensch **IV TS2**, 70
human body [ˌhjuːmən ˈbɒdi] menschlicher Körper **II**
Humanities *(pl)* [hjuːˈmænətiz] Sozialwissenschaften **II**
humor *(no pl) (AE)* [ˈhjuːmə] Humor; Stimmung **IV U4**, 123
humour *(no pl)* [ˈhjuːmə] Humor; Stimmung **III**
sense of **humour** *(no pl)* [ˌsens‿əv ˈhjuːmə] Sinn für Humor **III**
hundreds of [ˈhʌndrədz‿əv] Hunderte (von) **III**
hungry [ˈhʌŋgri] hungrig **I**
to **hunt** [hʌnt] jagen **IV TS3**, 103
*to be in a **hurry** [ˌbi‿ɪn‿ə ˈhʌri] es eilig haben; in Eile sein **IV U4**, 113
to **hurry** [ˈhʌri] eilen; sich beeilen **I**
*to **hurt** [hɜːt] verletzen; weh tun **II**
hurt [hɜːt] verletzt **II**
husband [ˈhʌzbənd] Ehemann **II**
hydroplane [ˈhaɪdrəpleɪn] Gleitboot **IV U4**, 114
hype [haɪp] Hype; Wirbel ⟨**IV TS3**, 103⟩

I

I [aɪ] ich **I**
I don't know! [ˌaɪ ˌdəʊnt ˈnəʊ] Ich weiß (es) nicht! **I**
I don't like … [aɪ ˈdəʊnt laɪk] Ich mag … nicht.; Ich mache … nicht gern. **I**
I hear … [aɪ ˈhɪə] Ich habe gehört, dass … **I**
I like … [aɪ ˈlaɪk] Mir gefällt …; Ich mag … **I**
I love you. [aɪ ˈlʌv ju] Ich liebe dich.; Ich mag dich. **I**
I love … [aɪ ˈlʌv] Ich liebe …; Ich mag … total gern. **I**
I'd like to … *(= I would like to)* [aɪd ˈlaɪk tə] Ich möchte …; Ich würde gern … **I**
I'd rather [aɪd ˈrɑːðə] ich würde lieber **III**
I'm (not) scared of … [ˌaɪm (nɒt) ˈskeəd‿əv] Ich habe (keine) Angst vor … **I**
I'm afraid … [ˌaɪm‿əˈfreɪd] Leider … **IV U1**, 14
I'm dog-tired. [ˌaɪm ˌdɒgˈtaɪəd] Ich bin hundemüde. **I**
I'm English. [aɪm‿ˈɪŋglɪʃ] Ich bin Engländer/-in. **I**
I'm fine. [ˌaɪm ˈfaɪn] Mir geht's gut. **I**
I'm from … [ˌaɪm frɒm] Ich bin aus … **I**
I'm sorry! [ˌaɪm ˈsɒri] Tut mir leid! **I**
ice [aɪs] Eis **I**
ice cream [ˌaɪs ˈkriːm] Eis; Eiscreme **I**
ice rink [ˈaɪs ˌrɪŋk] Eisbahn; Schlittschuhbahn **I**
icebreaker [ˈaɪsˌbreɪkə] Eisbrecher *(Sätze, um mit jmdm. ins Gespräch zu kommen)* **III**
idea [aɪˈdɪə] Idee; Einfall **I**
no **idea** [ˌnəʊ‿aɪˈdɪə] keine Ahnung **II**
to **identify** with [aɪˈdentɪfaɪ wɪð] sich identifizieren mit **III**
identity [aɪˈdentəti] Identität **II**
idiot [ˈɪdiət] Idiot/-in **II**
if [ɪf] wenn; falls; ob **I**
as **if** [əz‿ˈɪf] als ob **III**
if-clause [ˈɪfˌklɔːz] if-Satz **II**
If I were you … [ˌɪf aɪ wɜː ˈjuː] Wenn ich du wäre … **IV AC2**, 39
to **ignite** [ɪgˈnaɪt] anzünden; entfachen ⟨**IV U3**, 89⟩
to **ignore** [ɪgˈnɔː] ignorieren; außer Acht lassen **III**
ill [ɪl] krank **III**
illegal [ɪˈliːgl] illegal; unrechtmäßig; rechtswidrig **III**
illness [ˈɪlnəs] Krankheit **IV U4**, 124
to **illustrate** [ˈɪləstreɪt] veranschaulichen; darstellen; illustrieren °**IV U3**, 78
image [ˈɪmɪdʒ] Bild; Abbildung **IV TS1**, 35
imaginary [ɪˈmædʒɪnri] erfunden; eingebildet **IV U4**, 124
imagination [ɪˌmædʒɪˈneɪʃn] Fantasie; Vorstellungskraft **III**
imaginative [ɪˈmædʒɪnətɪv] einfallsreich; fantasievoll **III**
to **imagine** [ɪˈmædʒɪn] sich (etwas) vorstellen **I**
immediately [ɪˈmiːdiətli] sofort; gleich **IV TS1**, 34
immigrant [ˈɪmɪgrənt] Immigrant/-in; Einwanderer/-in **IV AC1**, 8
immigration [ˌɪmɪˈgreɪʃn] Immigration; Einwanderung; Einreise **III**
immigration office [ˌɪmɪˈgreɪʃn ˌɒfɪs] Einwanderungsbehörde **III**

imperative [ɪm'perətɪv] Imperativ; Befehlsform **III**
impolite [ˌɪmp'laɪt] unhöflich **III**
importance [ɪm'pɔ:tns] Bedeutung; Wichtigkeit **IV U3**, 88
important [ɪm'pɔ:tnt] wichtig **I**
impossible [ɪm'pɒsəbl] unmöglich **IV TS2**, 72
impressed [ɪm'prest] beeindruckt **II**
impression [ɪm'preʃn] Impression; Eindruck **IV U1**, 12
to improve [ɪm'pru:v] sich verbessern; verbessern **I**
improvement [ɪm'pru:vmənt] Verbesserung °**IV TS1**, 37
in [ɪn] in; im; rein; herein **I**
in addition to [ɪn‿ə'dɪʃn tə] neben; daneben; darüber hinaus **IV U3**, 84
in between [ˌɪn bɪ'twi:n] dazwischen **III**
in chorus [ɪn 'kɔ:rəs] im Chor **III**
in fact [ɪn 'fækt] tatsächlich; eigentlich; genau genommen **IV U3**, 84
in favor (of) *(AE)* [ɪn 'feɪvər‿əv] dafür; zugunsten (von) **IV U4**, 119
in front of [ɪn 'frʌnt‿əv] vor **I**
in general [ɪn 'dʒenrl] im allgemeinen °**IV TS3**, 106
in need [ɪn 'ni:d] bedürftig; in Not **II**
in order to [ɪn‿'ɔ:də tə] um ... zu; mit der Absicht **IV U3**, 87
in secret [ɪn 'si:krət] heimlich **II**
in spite of [ɪn 'spaɪt‿əv] trotz **IV U3**, 93
in the country [ˌɪn ðə 'kʌntri] auf dem Land **IV AC1**, 10
in the end [ˌɪn ði‿'end] schließlich; zum Schluss **II**
in the evenings [ɪn ði‿'i:vnɪŋz] abends **I**
in the mornings [ˌɪn ðə 'mɔ:nɪŋz] morgens; vormittags **I**
in the photo(s) [ˌɪn ðə 'fəʊtəʊ(z)] auf dem Foto/den Fotos **I**
in the street [ˌɪn ðə 'stri:t] in der Straße; auf der Straße **I**
in the process [ˌɪn ðə 'prəʊsəs] in dem Zusammenhang ⟨**IV TS3**, 106⟩
to include [ɪn'klu:d] einschließen; beinhalten **II**; aufnehmen; einbeziehen **III**
incomplete [ˌɪnkəm'pli:t] unvollständig °**IV U4**, 118
inconvenient [ˌɪnkən'vi:niənt] unbequem; lästig **IV TS2**, 70
incredible [ɪn'kredəbl] unglaublich **IV TS3**, 102
in-crowd ['ɪnkraʊd] Szene; die Angesagten; die Beliebten **III**
independence *(no pl)* [ˌɪndɪ'pendəns] Unabhängigkeit **III**
independent [ˌɪndɪ'pendənt] unabhängig **III**
Indian ['ɪndiən] Inder/-in; indisch **I**; Indianer/-in; indianisch **IV U1**, 15
indirect ['ɪndɪrekt] indirekt **III**
indirect speech [ˌɪndɪrekt 'spi:tʃ] indirekte Rede **III**

individual [ˌɪndɪ'vɪdʒuəl] Einzelperson; Einzelne/-r; Individuum **IV U1**, 26
individual [ˌɪndɪ'vɪdʒuəl] individuell; einzeln **II**
indivisible [ˌɪndɪ'vɪzəbl] unteilbar ⟨**IV U1**, 19⟩
industry ['ɪndəstri] Industrie; Branche; Gewerbe **III**
infection [ɪn'fekʃn] Infektion; Infekt; Ansteckung **IV U3**, 83
*to catch an **infection** [ɪn'fekʃn] sich eine Infektion holen; sich einen Infekt holen **IV U3**, 83
infinitive [ɪn'fɪnətɪv] Infinitiv **I**
influence ['ɪnfluəns] Einfluss °**IV U4**, 111
to influence ['ɪnfluəns] beeinflussen **II**
to inform [ɪn'fɔ:m] informieren °**IV U3**, 94
informal [ɪn'fɔ:ml] informell; zwanglos **IV AC3**, 77
information *(no pl)* [ˌɪnfə'meɪʃn] Information; Informationen **I**
informative [ɪn'fɔ:mətɪv] informativ **IV U1**, 26
ingredient [ɪn'gri:diənt] Zutat **II**
injury ['ɪndʒəri] Verletzung **II**
inline skating ['ɪnlaɪn ˌskeɪtɪŋ] Inlineskatefahren **I**
inner ['ɪnə] innere/-r/-s; Innen- °**IV U4**, 120
innovation [ˌɪnə'veɪʃn] Innovation; Neuerung **IV U3**, 78
innovative [ɪ'nəʊvətɪv; 'ɪnəvətɪv] innovativ; kreativ **IV U3**, 78
insecure [ˌɪnsɪ'kjʊə] unsicher **IV U1**, 17
on the inside [ˌɒn ði‿'ɪnsaɪd] innen °**IV U4**, 120
inside [ˌɪn'saɪd] innen; im Innern; hinein; nach drinnen; in; drin **I**
to inspire [ɪn'spaɪə] inspirieren; anregen **IV U2**, 40
instantly ['ɪnstəntli] sofort **IV U3**, 86
instead [ɪn'sted] stattdessen **III**
instead of [ɪn'sted‿əv] statt; anstatt; an Stelle von **IV U1**, 15
instruction [ɪn'strʌkʃn] Instruktion; Anweisung **I**
instructor [ɪn'strʌktə] Lehrer/-in; Betreuer/-in **II**
instrument ['ɪnstrəmənt] Instrument **IV U3**, 93
insurance [ɪn'ʃʊərns] Versicherung **IV U3**, 90
interest ['ɪntrəst] Interesse **II**
to interest ['ɪntrəst] (sich) interessieren **II**
*to be interested in [bi‿'ɪntrəstɪd‿ɪn] interessiert sein an; sich interessieren für **II**
interesting ['ɪntrəstɪŋ] interessant **I**
international [ˌɪntə'næʃnl] international **I**
internet ['ɪntənet] Internet **I**
intersection [ˌɪntə'sekʃn] Kreuzung **IV U2**, 40
interview ['ɪntəvju:] Interview; Befragung **I**
to interview ['ɪntəvju:] interviewen; befragen **I**
interviewee [ˌɪntəvju'i:] Befragte/-r; Interviewte/-r °**IV U2**, 63

interviewer ['ɪntəvju:ə] Interviewer/-in; Befrager/-in °**IV U2**, 62
into ['ɪntə] in; in ... hinein **I**
*to be **into** [bi:‿'ɪntə] mögen; stehen auf **I**
intransitive [ɪn'trænsətɪv] intransitiv °**IV U4**, 116
to introduce [ˌɪntrə'dju:s] einführen; einleiten **III**
Introduce ... [ˌɪntrə'dju:s] Stelle/Stellt ... vor. **I**
introduction [ˌɪntrə'dʌkʃn] Einführung; Einleitung; Vorstellung **II**
to invade [ɪn'veɪd] einmarschieren (in); eindringen (in); überfallen **III**
to invent [ɪn'vent] erfinden **III**
invention [ɪn'venʃn] Erfindung **III**
inventor [ɪn'ventə] Erfinder/-in **III**
invisible [ɪn'vɪzəbl] unsichtbar **III**
invitation [ˌɪnvɪ'teɪʃn] Einladung **I**
to invite [ɪn'vaɪt] einladen **I**
to involve [ɪn'vɒlv] involvieren; einbeziehen; beteiligen **IV TS2**, 72
inward ['ɪnwəd] ankommend **II**
Irish ['aɪrɪʃ] irisch; Irisch **II**
ironic [ˌaɪ'rɒnɪk] ironisch **IV U1**, 26
irregular [ɪ'regjələ] unregelmäßig **I**
island ['aɪlənd] Insel **II**
issue ['ɪʃu:; 'ɪsju:] Abneigung; Problem **IV AC4**, 109
it [ɪt] es **I**
*to make **it** ['meɪk‿ɪt] es schaffen **IV U2**, 40
It wouldn't do me any good. [ˌɪt wʊdnt ˌdu: mi: eni 'gʊd] Es würde mir nichts nützen. **IV U4**, 124
It's fun. [ɪts 'fʌn] Es macht Spaß. **I**
It's great for ... [ɪts 'greɪt fə] Es ist super zum/für ... **I**
It's to die for! [ˌɪts tə 'daɪ fɔ:] Dafür könnte ich sterben!; Das ist unwiderstehlich! **IV U4**, 127
It's your turn. [ˌɪts 'jɔ: tɜ:n] Du bist dran. **I**
It's, like, so wild to ... [ˌɪts laɪk səʊ 'waɪld tə] Es ist echt klasse ... ⟨**IV AC3**, 77⟩
It's .../They're ... [ɪts/ðeə] Es kostet .../ Sie kosten ... **I**
IT *(= Information Technology)* [ˌaɪ'ti:] Informatik; Informationstechnik **III**
Italian [ɪ'tæliən] italienisch; Italienisch; aus Italien °**IV U3**, 84
item ['aɪtəm] Gegenstand; Objekt **IV U1**, 21
its [ɪts] sein/-e; ihr/-e **I**
ivory *(no pl)* ['aɪvri] Elfenbein **III**

J

jacket ['dʒækɪt] Jacke **III**
jam [dʒæm] Marmelade; Konfitüre **III**
January ['dʒænjuri] Januar **I**
*to be jealous (of) [bi: 'dʒeləs] eifersüchtig sein (auf); neidisch sein (auf) **I**
jeans *(pl)* [dʒi:nz] Jeans ⟨**IV U3**, 88⟩

jelly ['dʒeli] Tortenguss; Götterspeise; Wackelpudding; Gelee **I**
jewel ['dʒu:əl] Juwel; Edelstein **III**
crown **jewels** [ˌkraʊn 'dʒu:əlz] Kronjuwelen **II**
jewellery ['dʒu:əlri] Schmuck **I**
jewelry *(AE)* ['dʒu:əlri] Schmuck **IV U4**, 119
Jewish ['dʒu:ɪʃ] jüdisch **IV U2**, 45
job [dʒɒb] Arbeit; Aufgabe; Job **I**
mouth **jogging** ['maʊθ ˌdʒɒgɪŋ] Training für den Mund **I**
to **join** [dʒɔɪn] beitreten; sich anschließen; verbinden **II**
to **join** in [ˌdʒɔɪn‿'ɪn] teilnehmen; mitmachen **IV U3**, 93
joke [dʒəʊk] Witz **I**
to **joke** [dʒəʊk] scherzen **II**
journey ['dʒɜ:ni] Reise; Fahrt **II**
to **judge** [dʒʌdʒ] beurteilen; bewerten **III**
juggling ['dʒʌglɪŋ] Jonglieren **II**
juice [dʒu:s] Saft **I**
July [dʒʊ'laɪ] Juli **I**
to **jump** [dʒʌmp] springen **I**
to **jump** back [ˌdʒʌmp‿'bæk] zurückspringen; *hier:* zurückschrecken **II**
to **jump** the queue [ˌdʒʌmp ðə 'kju:] sich vordrängeln **I**
June [dʒu:n] Juni **I**
jungle ['dʒʌŋgl] Dschungel **IV U2**, 40
junior ['dʒu:niə] Junior; der/die Jüngere **IV U4**, 122
a bunch of **junk** [ə‿ˌbʌnʃ‿əv 'dʒʌŋk] ein Haufen Müll ⟨**IV U2**, 54⟩
piece of **junk** [ˌpi:s‿əv 'dʒʌŋk] Stück Schrott **III**
just [dʒʌst] gerade; nur; einfach **I**
Just a second … [ˌdʒʌst‿ə 'seknd] Einen Augenblick … **IV U4**, 115
just about anywhere [ˌdʒʌst‿əˌbaʊt 'eniweə] praktisch überall **IV TS1**, 34
just in time [ˌdʒʌst‿ɪn 'taɪm] gerade rechtzeitig **IV U2**, 42
justice ['dʒʌstɪs] Gerechtigkeit **IV U4**, 125
juvenile ['dʒu:vnaɪl] Jugend- ⟨**IV U2**, 58⟩

K

*to **keep** [ki:p] behalten; aufbewahren; halten **I**; weiter tun; immer wieder tun **IV U1**, 14
*to **keep** a diary [ˌki:p‿ə 'daɪəri] ein Tagebuch führen **IV U3**, 92
*to **keep** away from [ˌki:p‿ə'weɪ frəm] (sich) fernhalten von **II**
*to **keep** going [ˌki:p 'gəʊɪŋ] aufrechterhalten **II**
*to **keep** in mind [ˌki:p‿ɪn 'maɪnd] beachten; im Gedächtnis behalten °**IV U2**, 49
*to **keep** in touch [ˌki:p‿ɪn 'tʌtʃ] in Kontakt bleiben **IV U1**, 14
*to **keep** one's feet or hands still [ˌki:p wʌnz: 'fi:t‿ɔ: 'hændz stɪl] die Beine und Hände ruhig halten **III**
*to **keep** out (of) [ˌki:p‿'aʊt əv] draußen bleiben; draußen halten **III**
*to **keep** the ball bouncing [ˌki:p ðə bɔ:l 'baʊntsɪŋ] *hier:* das Gespräch am Laufen halten **III**
*to **keep** up (with) [ˌki:p‿'ʌp (wɪð)] mithalten (mit); Schritt halten (mit) **II**
*to **keep** your fingers crossed [ˌki:p jɔ: ˌfɪŋgəz 'krɒst] die Daumen drücken **I**
key [ki:] Schlüssel **II**
key ring ['ki: ˌrɪŋ] Schlüsselbund; Schlüsselanhänger **III**
key word ['ki: wɜ:d] Stichwort; Schlüsselbegriff **I**
khakis ['kɑ:kiz] Khakihose ⟨**IV U4**, 123⟩
to **kick** [kɪk] schießen; treten **II**
kid [kɪd] Jugendliche/-r; Kind **IV U1**, 12
to **kill** [kɪl] töten; umbringen **III**
killer ['kɪlə] Killer/-in **IV U4**, 116
kilometre (km) ['kɪləˌmi:tə; kɪ'lɒmɪtə] Kilometer **III**
kilt [kɪlt] Kilt; Schottenrock **III**
kind [kaɪnd] Art; Sorte **I**
kind of ['kaɪnd‿əv] ziemlich **IV U4**, 113
king [kɪŋ] König **I**
kitchen ['kɪtʃɪn] Küche **I**
kitty ['kɪti] Miezekatze ⟨**IV TS3**, 106⟩
kitty litter ['kɪti ˌlɪtə] Katzenstreu **IV TS3**, 106
knife [naɪf], **knives** [naɪvz] *(pl)* Messer **III**
knight [naɪt] Ritter **II**
knob [nɒb] Griff **II**
*to **know** [nəʊ] kennen; wissen **I**
*to be **known** as [bi 'nəʊn‿əz] bekannt sein als **IV U2**, 44
*to get to **know** [ˌget tə 'nəʊ] kennenlernen **II**
I don't **know**! [ˌaɪ ˌdəʊnt 'nəʊ] Ich weiß (es) nicht! **I**
You **know** how to … [ju: 'nəʊ ˌhaʊ tə] Du weißt, wie man …; Ihr wisst, wie man … **I**
koala [kəʊ'ɑ:lə] Koala **III**
Korean [kə'ri:ən] koreanisch; Koreanisch; Koreaner/-in **II**
South **Korean** [ˌsaʊθ kə'ri:ən] Südkoreaner/-in; südkoreanisch; Südkoreanisch **II**

L

lab(oratory) [læb; lə'bɒrətri] Labor **IV AC2**, 38
child **labor** *(AE)* [ˌtʃaɪld 'leɪbə] Kinderarbeit **IV U1**, 18
laboratory [læb; lə'bɒrətri] Labor **IV AC2**, 38
ladder ['lædə] Leiter **II**
lady ['leɪdi] Lady; Dame **III**
lady-in-waiting [ˌleɪdiɪn'weɪtɪŋ] Hofdame **III**
laid-back [ˌleɪd'bæk] entspannt; locker **III**
lake [leɪk] See **I**
boating **lake** ['bəʊtɪŋ ˌleɪk] See zum Rudern **I**
lamb [læm] Lamm; Lämmchen **I**
lame [leɪm] lahm; langweilig **IV U4**, 124
land [lænd] Land **I**
to **land** [lænd] landen **II**
landing ['lændɪŋ] Landung **III**
moon **landing** ['mu:n ˌlændɪŋ] Mondlandung **IV TS2**, 70
landscape ['lændskeɪp] Landschaft **II**
language ['læŋgwɪdʒ] Sprache **I**
first **language** [ˌfɜ:st 'læŋgwɪdʒ] Muttersprache **II**
foreign **language** [ˌfɒrɪn 'læŋgwɪdʒ] Fremdsprache **II**
official **language** [əˌfɪʃl 'læŋgwɪdʒ] Amtssprache **II**
laptop ['læptɒp] Laptop **II**
large [lɑ:dʒ] groß; riesig **II**
lassi ['lʌsi] Lassi **I**
last [lɑ:st] letzte/-r/-s **I**
at **last** [ət 'lɑ:st] endlich; schließlich **I**
last name *(AE)* ['lɑ:st neɪm] Nachname; Familienname **IV U3**, 82
to save the best for **last** [ˌseɪv ðə ˌbest fə 'lɑ:st] sich das Beste bis zum Schluss aufheben **IV U2**, 42
late [leɪt] spät; zu spät **I**
*to be **late** [bi: 'leɪt] zu spät dran sein; zu spät kommen **I**
later ['leɪtə] später **I**
latest ['leɪtɪst] neueste/-r/-s **III**
to **laugh** [lɑ:f] lachen **I**
lavish ['lævɪʃ] üppig; verschwenderisch **III**
*to **lay** [leɪ] legen **IV U2**, 59
layer (of) ['leɪər‿əv] Schicht (aus); Lage (aus) **III**
layout ['leɪaʊt] Layout; Anordnung **III**
lazy ['leɪzi] faul **III**
*to **lead** [li:d] führen; anführen **III**
*to **lead** off [li:d‿'ɒf] wegführen **III**
lead [li:d] Haupt- **III**
lead part [ˌli:d 'pɑ:t] Hauptrolle **III**
leader ['li:də] Führer/-in; Anführer/-in **IV U4**, 116
lead-in ['li:dɪn] Einführung; Einleitung **IV U2**, 59
leaflet ['li:flət] Broschüre; Informationsblatt; Prospekt **III**
leap [li:p] Sprung; Satz ⟨**IV TS2**, 71⟩
*to **learn** [lɜ:n] lernen **I**
*to **learn** a lesson from [ˌlɜ:n‿ə 'lesn frəm] lernen aus ⟨**IV U2**, 56⟩
*to **learn** about ['lɜ:n‿əˌbaʊt] erfahren über **III**
*to **learn** … by heart [ˌlɜ:n baɪ 'hɑ:t] auswendig lernen **I**
a lot to **learn** [ə ˌlɒt tə 'lɜ:n] viel zu lernen **I**
at **least** [ət 'li:st] mindestens; wenigstens **II**

*to **leave** [liːv] verlassen; lassen; abfahren; losgehen **II**
*to **leave** a message [ˌliːv‿ə 'mesɪdʒ] eine Nachricht hinterlassen **I**
*to **leave** behind [ˌliːv‿bɪ'haɪnd] zurücklassen **III**
*to **leave** it to cool [ˌliːv‿ɪt tə 'kuːl] kalt stellen **I**
*to **leave** out [ˌliːv‿'aʊt] auslassen; weglassen °**IV U1**, 24
*to **leave** sb alone [ˌliːv‿ə'ləʊn] jmdn. in Ruhe lassen **IV U1**, 23
*to **leave** space [liːv 'speɪs] Platz lassen **I**
Leave that to me. [ˌliːv ðæt tə 'miː] Überlass das mir. **IV U2**, 42
left [left] linke/-r/-s; links **I**
on the **left** [ɒn ðə 'left] auf der linken Seite; links **I**
left [left] übrig **I**
left-hand ['lefthænd] linke/-r/-s °**IV U1**, 15
leg [leg] Bein **II**
legend ['ledʒənd] Legende; Sage **II**
leisure ['leʒə] Freizeit; Freizeit- **I**
leisure centre ['leʒə ˌsentə] Freizeitzentrum **I**
lemon ['lemən] Zitrone **II**
lemonade [ˌlemə'neɪd] Limonade **I**
*to **lend** ['lend tə] leihen; verleihen **III**
less [les] weniger **III**
to settle for **less** [ˌsetl fə 'les] sich mit weniger zufrieden geben **IV TS1**, 36
lesson ['lesn] Unterrichtsstunde; Schulstunde; Unterricht **I**
*to learn a **lesson** from [ˌlɜːn‿ə 'lesn frəm] lernen aus ⟨**IV U2**, 56⟩
*to **let** [let] lassen **I**
*to **let** go (of) [ˌlet 'gəʊ (əv)] loslassen **II**
Let's face it. [lets 'feɪs‿ɪt] Machen wir uns doch nichts vor. **III**
letter ['letə] Buchstabe **I**; Brief **II**
capital **letter** [ˌkæpɪtl 'letə] Großbuchstabe **I**
liberty ['lɪbəti] Freiheit **IV U2**, 44
library ['laɪbri] Bibliothek; Bücherei **III**
lie [laɪ] Lüge **III**
white **lie** [ˌwaɪt 'laɪ] Notlüge **III**
to **lie** [laɪ] lügen **II**
*to **lie** [laɪ] liegen **II**
life [laɪf], **lives** [laɪvz] *(pl)* Leben **II**
*to have a short shelf **life** [ˌhæv‿ə ˌʃɔːt 'ʃelf laɪf] eine kurze Haltbarkeit haben ⟨**IV U4**, 124⟩
lifeboat ['laɪfbəʊt] Rettungsboot **I**
lifebuoy ['laɪfbɔɪ] Rettungsring **I**
lifestyle ['laɪfstaɪl] Lebensstil; Lifestyle **III**
to **lift** [lɪft] heben; hochheben; anheben **IV U2**, 46
light [laɪt] Licht; Lampe **II**
light [laɪt] leicht **III**
to **lighten** ['laɪtn] aufhellen **III**
lightning *(no pl)* ['laɪtnɪŋ] Blitz **II**
to **like** [laɪk] mögen; gern haben **I**
would **like** [wʊd 'laɪk] würde/-st/-n/-t gern; hätte/-st/-n/-t gern **I**
I don't **like** … [aɪ 'dəʊnt laɪk] Ich mag … nicht.; Ich mache … nicht gern. **I**
I **like** singing and dancing. [ˌaɪ laɪk ˌsɪŋɪŋ‿ənd 'dɑːnsɪŋ] Ich singe und tanze gern. **I**
I **like** … [aɪ 'laɪk] Mir gefällt …; Ich mag … **I**
I'd **like** to … *(= I would like to)* [aɪd 'laɪk tə] Ich möchte …; Ich würde gern … **I**
Would you **like** …? [ˌwʊd jʊ 'laɪk] Möchtest du …?; Möchten Sie …?; Möchtet ihr …? **II**
like [laɪk] wie; als ob **I**
*to be **like** [bi 'laɪk] sein **III**
like that [laɪk 'ðæt] so **I**
like this [laɪk 'ðɪs] so **I**
What was it **like**? [ˌwɒt wɒz‿ɪt 'laɪk] Wie war es? **III**
likes *(pl)* [laɪks] Vorlieben **IV U1**, 16
limit ['lɪmɪt] Limit; Grenze **III**
line [laɪn] Zeile; Linie **I**
finish **line** ['fɪnɪʃ ˌlaɪn] Ziellinie **II**
line graph ['laɪn grɑːf] Kurvendiagramm **IV U3**, 85
opening **line** ['əʊpnɪŋ‿ˌlaɪn] der erste Satz **III**
*to stand in **line** *(AE)* [ˌstænd‿ɪn 'laɪn] anstehen; Schlange stehen; (sich) anstellen **IV AC2**, 39
time **line** ['taɪm ˌlaɪn] Zeitstrahl **I**
lines *(pl)* [laɪnz] Text **III**
to **line** up [laɪn‿'ʌp] (sich) aufstellen **III**
link [lɪŋk] Link; Verbindung **II**
to **link** [lɪŋk] verbinden **II**
linking word ['lɪŋkɪŋ ˌwɜːd] Bindewort **I**
lion [laɪən] Löwe **II**
list [lɪst] Liste **I**
to **listen** (to) ['lɪsn] zuhören; anhören **I**
Listen again. [ˌlɪsn‿ə'gen] Hör/Hört noch einmal zu. **I**
to **listen** for ['lɪsn fə] horchen auf **I**
listener ['lɪsənə] Zuhörer/-in **II**
listening ['lɪsnɪŋ] Hören **I**
litre (l) ['liːtə] Liter **III**
kitty **litter** ['kɪti ˌlɪtə] Katzenstreu **IV TS3**, 106
to **litter** ['lɪtə] verschmutzen; verunreinigen; Müll herumliegen lassen **III**
little ['lɪtl] klein **I**
a **little** [ə 'lɪtl] ein wenig; etwas **I**
little ['lɪtl] wenig °**IV U2**, 61
to **live** [lɪv] wohnen; leben **I**
standard of **living** [ˌstændəd‿əv 'lɪvɪŋ] Lebensstandard **IV AC1**, 10
live [laɪv] live **III**
lively ['laɪvli] lebendig **II**
*to make a **living** (from) [ˌmeɪk‿ə 'lɪvɪŋ frəm] seinen Lebensunterhalt bestreiten (mit) **IV U2**, 49
living history show [ˌlɪvɪŋ 'hɪstəri ˌʃəʊ] *Show, in der historischer Alltag nachgespielt wird* **II**
living room ['lɪvɪŋ rʊm] Wohnzimmer **I**
to **load** [ləʊd] einräumen; laden **IV AC4**, 108
to **load** up [ləʊd‿'ʌp] beladen ⟨**IV TS3**, 105⟩
local ['ləʊkl] Ortsansässige/-r; Einheimische/-r ⟨**IV TS3**, 103⟩
local ['ləʊkl] örtlich; lokal **II**
*to be **located** [bi ləʊ'keɪtɪd] gelegen sein; liegen **IV U2**, 43
location [ləʊ'keɪʃn] Handlungsort; Lage; Standort **II**
loch [lɒx; lɒk] See *(in Schottland)* **III**
locked [lɒkt] abgeschlossen **II**
locker ['lɒkə] Schließfach; Spind **I**
loft [lɒft] Dachboden **I**
logbook ['lɒgbʊk] Logbuch °**IV TS2**, 72
logic ['lɒdʒɪk] Logik **III**
LOL (= laughing out loud) [lɒl] LOL **II**
Londoner ['lʌndənə] Londoner/-in **I**
lonely ['ləʊnli] einsam **I**
long [lɒŋ] lang **I**
long shot ['lɒŋ ʃɒt] Totale *(Kameraeinstellung)* **IV U2**, 59
(not) any **longer** [nɒt‿ˌeni 'lɒŋgə] (nicht) mehr; (nicht) länger **II**
longhouse ['lɒŋhaʊs] Langhaus **IV U4**, 118
long-lasting ['lɒŋlɑːstɪŋ] lang anhaltend **IV U3**, 87
look [lʊk] Blick **I**
*to give sb funny **looks** [ˌgɪv fʌni 'lʊks] jmdn. schief anschauen **III**
*to have a **look** (at) [ˌhæv‿ə 'lʊk] anschauen **II**
*to take a **look** at [ˌteɪk‿ə 'lʊk‿æt] einen Blick werfen auf **II**
to **look** [lʊk] schauen; sehen; aussehen **I**
Look! [lʊk] Schau/Schaut mal! **I**
to **look** after [ˌlʊk‿'ɑːftə] aufpassen auf; hüten; sich kümmern um **I**
to **look** at ['lʊk‿ət] anschauen; ansehen **I**
to **look** for ['lʊk fɔː] suchen nach **I**
to **look** forward to [ˌlʊk 'fɔːwəd tə] sich freuen auf **II**
to **look** out [ˌlʊk‿'aʊt] aufpassen **II**
to **look** up [ˌlʊk‿'ʌp] nachschlagen; nachschauen **I**
Look closely … [ˌlʊk 'kləʊsli] Schau(t) genau … **II**
looks *(pl)* [lʊks] Aussehen **III**
lord [lɔːd] Lord; Herr **III**
lorry ['lɒri] Lastwagen **IV U2**, 49
*to **lose** [luːz] verlieren **II**
loser ['luːzə] Verlierer/-in; Loser/-in **IV U4**, 122
lost [lɒst] verloren ⟨**IV TS2**, 74⟩
*to get **lost** [ˌget 'lɒst] verloren gehen; sich verirren **II**
a **lot** [ə 'lɒt] viel **I**
a **lot** of [ə 'lɒt‿əv] viel/-e; eine Menge **I**
lots (of) ['lɒts‿əv] viel/-e; jede Menge **I**
parking **lot** ['pɑːkɪŋ ˌlɒt] Parkplatz **IV TS3**, 105
loud [laʊd] laut **I**

*to read out **loud** [ˌriːd‿aʊt ˈlaʊd] laut vorlesen **III**
*to sing out **loud** [ˌsɪŋ‿aʊt ˈlaʊd] laut vorsingen **III**
departure **lounge** [dɪˈpɑːtʃə ˌlaʊndʒ] Abflughalle **III**
love [lʌv] Liebe **II**
Love … [lʌv] Liebe Grüße *(am Briefende)*; Herzliche Grüße *(am Briefende)* **I**
to **love** [lʌv] lieben; gern mögen **I**
would **love** [wʊd ˈlʌv] würde/-st/-n/-t sehr gern; hätte/-st/-n/-t sehr gern **I**
I **love** you. [aɪ ˈlʌv ju] Ich liebe dich.; Ich mag dich. **I**
I **love** … [aɪ ˈlʌv] Ich liebe …; Ich mag … total gern. **I**
lovebirds *(pl)* [ˈlʌvˌbɜːdz] Turteltauben **II**
lovely [ˈlʌvli] schön; hübsch **IV TS1**, 35
lover [ˈlʌvə] Freund/-in; Liebhaber/-in **IV U4**, 115
nature **lover** [ˈneɪtʃə ˌlʌvə] Naturfreund/-in **IV U4**, 115
low [ləʊ] niedrig **II**
low tide [ˈləʊ ˌtaɪd] Ebbe **II**
lox [lɑːks] Räucherlachs ⟨**IV U2**, 45⟩
good **luck** [ˌgʊd ˈlʌk] viel Glück **IV U2**, 46
What **luck**! [wɒt ˈlʌk] Was für ein Glück! **III**
luckily [ˈlʌkɪli] glücklicherweise **IV U1**, 14
lucky … [ˈlʌki] … der/die Glückliche **I**
*to be **lucky** [bi‿ˈlʌki] Glück haben **II**
lucky charm [ˌlʌki ˈtʃɑːm] Glücksbringer; Talisman **I**
luggage *(no pl)* [ˈlʌgɪdʒ] Gepäck **III**
lunch [lʌnʃ] Mittagessen **I**
lunch break [ˈlʌnʃbreɪk] Mittagspause **I**
lunchtime [ˈlʌnʃtaɪm] Mittagszeit; Mittagspause **IV AC2**, 38
lung [lʌŋ] Lunge **IV U2**, 41
the **lungs** *(pl)* [ðə ˈlʌŋz] die Lunge **III**
luxury [ˈlʌkʃri] Luxus **IV AC1**, 10
(song) **lyrics** *(pl)* [sɒŋ ˈlɪrɪks] Liedtext **III**

M

Ma [mɑː] Mama **IV U3**, 92
machine [məˈʃiːn] Automat; Maschine; Apparat; Gerät **I**
answering **machine** [ˈɑːnsrɪŋ məˌʃiːn] Anrufbeantworter **I**
vending **machine** [ˈvendɪŋ məˌʃiːn] Automat **III**
washing **machine** [ˈwɒʃɪŋ məˌʃiːn] Waschmaschine **II**
mad [mæd] verrückt **II**; wütend **IV AC2**, 39
Dear Sir or **Madam** [dɪə ˌsɜːr‿ɔː ˈmædəm] Sehr geehrte Dame, sehr geehrter Herr **II**
made up from [ˌmeɪd‿ˈʌp frəm] zusammengesetzt aus °**IV TS2**, 72
magazine [ˌmægəˈziːn] Zeitschrift **I**
maggot [ˈmægət] Made ⟨**IV U2**, 56⟩
magic [ˈmædʒɪk] Magie; Zauberei **III**
magical [ˈmædʒɪkəl] magisch; Zauber- **II**
mail [meɪl] Post **IV U3**, 86
to **mail** [ˈiːmeɪl] mailen; per E-Mail schicken **II**
main [meɪn] Haupt- **I**
main clause [ˈmeɪn ˌklɔːz] Hauptsatz **II**
major [ˈmeɪdʒə] wichtig; bedeutend; Haupt- **IV U4**, 114
majority [məˈdʒɒrəti] Mehrheit; Mehrzahl **IV U3**, 85
*to **make** [meɪk] machen; tun; bilden; *hier:* ergeben **I**
*to be **made** of [bi ˈmeɪd‿əv] bestehen aus **III**
*to **make** a decision [ˌmeɪk‿ə dɪˈsɪʒn] eine Entscheidung treffen **II**
*to **make** a living (from) [ˌmeɪk‿ə ˈlɪvɪŋ frəm] seinen Lebensunterhalt bestreiten (mit) **IV U2**, 49
*to **make** a wish [ˌmeɪk‿ə ˈwɪʃ] sich etwas wünschen **I**
*to **make** friends [ˌmeɪk ˈfrendz] Freundschaft schließen **II**
*to **make** fun of [ˌmeɪk ˈfʌn‿əv] sich lustig machen über **IV U4**, 124
*to **make** it [ˈmeɪk‿ɪt] es schaffen **IV U2**, 40
*to **make** money [ˌmeɪk ˈmʌni] Geld verdienen **I**
*to **make** notes [ˌmeɪk ˈnəʊts] Notizen machen **I**
*to **make** sb angry [meɪk ˈæŋgri] jmdn. wütend machen; jmdn. verärgern **III**
*to **make** sb do sth [meɪk] jmdn. dazu bringen, etw. zu tun **II**
*to **make** sense [ˌmeɪk ˈsens] Sinn ergeben; einleuchten **IV TS2**, 72
*to **make** sure [ˌmeɪk ˈʃɔː] sich versichern **I**
*to **make** trouble [ˌmeɪk ˈtrʌbl] Ärger machen; in Schwierigkeiten bringen **I**
*to **make** use of [meɪk ˈjuːz‿əv] benutzen; verwenden **IV U2**, 59
shopping **mall** [ˈʃɒpɪŋ ˌmɔːl] Einkaufszentrum **IV U1**, 13
man [mæn], **men** [men] *(pl)* Mann **I**
to **manage** (to do sth) [ˈmænɪdʒ tə] schaffen (etw. zu tun) **IV U3**, 84
manga [ˈmæŋgə] Manga *(japanischer Comic)* **II**
mango [ˈmæŋgəʊ] Mango **I**
manicure [ˈmænɪkjʊə] Maniküre ⟨**IV U2**, 56⟩
mankind [mænˈkaɪnd] Menschheit ⟨**IV TS2**, 71⟩
manners *(pl)* [ˈmænəz] Manieren; Benehmen **III**
mansion [ˈmænʃn] Herrenhaus; Villa ⟨**IV TS3**, 107⟩
software **manual** [ˈsɒftweə ˌmænjuəl] Softwarehandbuch **III**
many [ˈmeni] viele **I**
How **many** …? [ˌhaʊ ˈmeni] Wie viele …? **I**
map [mæp] Stadtplan; Landkarte **I**
mind **map** [ˈmaɪnd mæp] Wörternetz *(eine Art Schaubild)* **I**
marathon [ˈmærəθn] Marathon **II**
March [mɑːtʃ] März **I**
to **march** [mɑːtʃ] marschieren **III**
mark [mɑːk] Note **III**
to **mark** [mɑːk] markieren; kennzeichnen **II**
marked [mɑːkt] markiert °**IV AC3**, 76
market [ˈmɑːkɪt] Markt **I**
flea **market** [ˈfliː ˌmɑːkɪt] Flohmarkt **I**
marmalade [ˈmɑːməleɪd] Marmelade aus Zitrusfrüchten **III**
to **marry** [ˈmæri] heiraten **III**
mascot [ˈmæskət] Maskottchen ⟨**IV U4**, 123⟩
mashed potatoes *(pl)* [ˌmæʃt pəˈteɪtəʊz] Kartoffelpüree **III**
mask [mɑːsk] Maske **III**
mass [mæs] Masse; Massen- **IV U3**, 86
mass migration [ˌmæs maɪˈgreɪʃn] Massenwanderung **IV U3**, 86
massive [ˈmæsɪv] riesig; massiv; *hier:* super **IV AC1**, 11
raven **master** [ˈreɪvn ˌmɑːstə] Herr der Raben **II**
match [mætʃ] Spiel; Match **II**
to **match** [mætʃ] zuordnen; passen zu; entsprechen **I**
mate [meɪt] Schiffsoffizier; Maat **I**
material [məˈtɪəriəl] Material **II**
Maths [mæθs] Mathematik; Mathe **II**
no **matter** [nəʊ ˈmætə] egal; ganz gleich **IV U3**, 95
What's the **matter**? [ˌwɒts ðə ˈmætə] Was ist los?; Was hast du? **II**
It doesn't **matter**. [ɪt ˌdʌznt ˈmætə] Es ist egal. **III**
May [meɪ] Mai **I**
may [meɪ] (vielleicht) können; dürfen **II**
maybe [ˈmeɪbi] vielleicht **I**
mayo [ˈmeɪəʊ] Mayonnaise ⟨**IV U2**, 57⟩
me [miː] ich; mich; mir **I**
meal [miːl] Mahlzeit; Essen **II**
ready **meal** [ˌredi ˈmiːl] Fertiggericht **I**
*to **mean** [miːn] bedeuten; meinen **II**
(I) didn't **mean** to … [aɪ ˌdɪdnt ˈmiːn tə] Ich wollte nicht … **IV AC3**, 77
mean [miːn] gemein **III**
meaning [ˈmiːnɪŋ] Bedeutung; Sinn **II**
by any **means** [baɪ‿enɪ ˈmiːnz] mit allen Mitteln **IV U2**, 40
meat *(no pl)* [miːt] Fleisch **III**
mechanic [məˈkænɪk] Mechaniker/-in; Kfz-Mechaniker/-in **II**
media [ˈmiːdiə] Medien **II**
social **media** [ˌsəʊʃl ˈmiːdiə] soziale Netzwerke **IV U1**, 16
mediation [ˌmiːdiˈeɪʃn] Sprachmittlung **I**
medical [ˈmedɪkl] medizinisch; ärztlich; Medizin- **IV U3**, 82
medicine *(no pl)* [ˈmedsn] Medizin; Medikamente **III**
medicine people [ˈmedsn ˌpiːpl] Medizinmänner **IV U4**, 116
medieval [ˌmediˈiːvl] mittelalterlich **II**

medium ['mi:diəm] mittel; mittelgroß **IV U2**, 59
medium shot ['mi:diəm ʃɒt] Halbtotale *(Kameraeinstellung)* **IV U2**, 59
*to **meet** [mi:t] treffen; sich treffen **I**
*to **meet** halfway [ˌmi:t hɑ:f'weɪ] sich auf halbem Weg treffen **III**
*to **meet** sb's expectations [ˌmi:t sʌmbədiz‿ekspek'teɪʃnz] jmds. Erwartungen erfüllen **IV TS3**, 102
*to **meet** up [ˌmi:t‿'ʌp] sich treffen **IV U1**, 14
meeting ['mi:tɪŋ] Meeting; Treffen; Besprechung ⟨**IV TS3**, 104⟩
melody ['melədi] Melodie **III**
melting pot ['meltɪŋ ˌpɒt] Schmelztiegel **IV U2**, 40
member ['membə] Mitglied **II**
memory ['memri] Erinnerung; Gedächtnis **II**
menacing ['menɪsɪŋ] drohend ⟨**IV U2**, 60⟩
to **mention** ['menʃn] erwähnen **II**
menu ['menju:] Speisekarte **IV U1**, 15
merchant ['mɜ:tʃənt] Kaufmann; Händler **II**
mess [mes] Unordnung; Durcheinander; Schweinerei **IV U1**, 24
to **mess** sth **up** [ˌmes‿'ʌp] etw. durcheinanderbringen; etw. vergeigen **III**
message ['mesɪdʒ] Botschaft; Nachricht **I**
*to leave a **message** [ˌli:v‿ə 'mesɪdʒ] eine Nachricht hinterlassen **I**
*to take a **message** [ˌteɪk‿ə 'mesɪdʒ] eine Nachricht entgegennehmen; jmdm. etw. ausrichten **I**
text (**message**) ['tekst ˌmesɪdʒ] SMS; Kurznachricht **I**
messy ['mesi] unordentlich **III**
metre ['mi:tə] Meter **II**
middle ['mɪdl] Mitte **I**
middle class [ˌmɪdl 'klɑ:s] Mittelschicht ⟨**IV U4**, 124⟩
middle school *(AE)* ['mɪdl ˌsku:l] Mittelschule *(weiterführende Schule in den USA, Mittelstufe)* **IV U1**, 13
in the **middle** of nowhere [ɪn ðə ˌmɪdl‿əv 'nəʊweə] mitten im Nirgendwo **IV U1**, 16
midnight ['mɪdnaɪt] Mitternacht **III**
might [maɪt] könnte/-n (vielleicht) **IV U1**, 20
It **might** as well be … [ˌɪt maɪt əs 'wel bi: …] Es könnte/-n auch … sein. **III**
to **migrate** [maɪ'greɪt] wandern; umherziehen **IV U3**, 86
migration [maɪ'greɪʃn] Migration; Wanderung **IV U3**, 86
mass **migration** [ˌmæs maɪ'greɪʃn] Massenwanderung **IV U3**, 86
mile [maɪl] Meile *(Längenmaß)* **II**
milk [mɪlk] Milch **I**
to **milk** [mɪlk] melken **II**
million ['mɪljən] Million **II**
I've done this a **million** times before. [ˌaɪv dʌn ðɪs ə ˌmɪljən taɪmz bɪ'fɔ:] Ich habe das schon eine Million Mal gemacht. **II**
millionaire [ˌmɪljə'neə] Millionär/-in **III**
mind [maɪnd] Geist; Verstand; Kopf **III**
to change one's **mind** [ˌtʃeɪndʒ wʌnz 'maɪnd] seine Meinung ändern **III**
*to come to one's **mind** [ˌkʌm tə wʌnz 'maɪnd] jmdm. in den Sinn kommen; jmdm. einfallen °**IV U3**, 78
*to keep in **mind** [ˌki:p‿ɪn 'maɪnd] beachten; im Gedächtnis behalten °**IV U2**, 49
mind map ['maɪnd mæp] Wörternetz *(eine Art Schaubild)* **I**
*to rise up in one's **mind** [raɪz‿ʌp ɪn wʌnz 'maɪnd] jmdm. in den Sinn kommen **III**
to **mind** [maɪnd] etwas dagegen haben; einem etwas ausmachen **IV U1**, 16
to **mind** sth [maɪnd] auf etw. aufpassen **IV AC3**, 77
I don't **mind** … [ˌaɪ dəʊnt 'maɪnd] Ich habe nichts dagegen (zu) …; Mir macht es nichts aus (zu) … **III**
mine [maɪn] Mine **II**
mine [maɪn] mein/-er/-e/-es **II**
mini [mɪni] Mini- **II**
mining ['maɪnɪŋ] Bergbau **II**
minority [maɪ'nɒrəti] Minderheit **IV U3**, 85
minute ['mɪnɪt] Minute **I**
mirror ['mɪrə] Spiegel **III**
mismanaged [ˌmɪs'mænɪdʒd] schlecht geführt ⟨**IV U4**, 123⟩
Miss [mɪs] Fräulein *(Anrede)* **III**
to **miss** [mɪs] verpassen; versäumen; vermissen **II**
missing ['mɪsɪŋ] fehlend; verschwunden **II**
What is **missing**? [ˌwɒt‿ɪz 'mɪsɪŋ] Was fehlt? **I**
mission ['mɪʃn] Mission; Auftrag **IV TS2**, 71
mission control [ˌmɪʃn kən'trəʊl] Bodenkontrollzentrum ⟨**IV TS2**, 71⟩
mist [mɪst] Nebel; Dunst ⟨**IV U2**, 60⟩
mistake [mɪ'steɪk] Fehler **I**
misunderstanding [ˌmɪsʌndə'stændɪŋ] Missverständnis **IV U4**, 127
misunderstood [ˌmɪsʌndə'stʊd] missverstanden **III**
mix [mɪks] Mix **III**
to **mix** [mɪks] zusammenpassen **IV U1**, 24
to **mix** (up) [mɪks‿'ʌp] mischen; vermischen **III**
mobile ['məʊbaɪl] Handy; Mobiltelefon **II**
modal ['məʊdl] Modalverb **II**
model ['mɒdl] Modell; Tonmodell; Model **I**
role **model** ['rəʊl ˌmɒdl] Vorbild ⟨**IV U4**, 123⟩
modelling ['mɒdəlɪŋ] Modeln **III**
modern ['mɒdn] modern **II**
module ['mɒdju:l] Modul; Element ⟨**IV TS2**, 71⟩
command **module** [kə'mɑ:nd ˌmɒdju:l] Kommandokapsel ⟨**IV TS2**, 71⟩
mom *(AE)* [mɒm] Mama **IV AC1**, 11
moment ['məʊmənt] Moment; Augenblick **II**
at the **moment** [ət ðə 'məʊmənt] im Moment; gerade **I**
monarch ['mɒnək] Monarch/-in **III**
Monday ['mʌndeɪ] Montag **I**
on **Mondays** [ɒn 'mʌndeɪz] montags **I**
money ['mʌni] Geld **I**
*to make **money** [ˌmeɪk 'mʌni] Geld verdienen **I**
pocket **money** ['pɒkɪt ˌmʌni] Taschengeld **I**
to raise **money** [ˌreɪz 'mʌni] Geld sammeln **II**
monster ['mɒnstə] Monster; Ungeheuer **I**
montage [mɒn'tɑ:ʒ] Montage °**IV U2**, 61
month [mʌnθ] Monat **II**
monument ['mɒnjəmənt] Monument; Denkmal **II**
mood [mu:d] Stimmung; Laune **II**
moon [mu:n] Mond **IV TS2**, 70
moon landing ['mu:n ˌlændɪŋ] Mondlandung **IV TS2**, 70
moonlight ['mu:nlaɪt] Mondlicht **III**
more [mɔ:] mehr; weitere **I**
no **more** [ˌnəʊ 'mɔ:] nicht mehr **IV AC3**, 77
not any **more** [ˌnɒt‿eni 'mɔ:] nicht mehr **I**
more … than ['mɔ: ðən] mehr … als **I**
morning ['mɔ:nɪŋ] Morgen; Vormittag **I**
in the **mornings** [ˌɪn ðə 'mɔ:nɪŋz] morgens; vormittags **I**
Good **morning**. [ˌgʊd 'mɔ:nɪŋ] Guten Morgen. **I**
(the) **most** [ðə 'məʊst] der/die/das meiste; die meisten **I**
mother ['mʌðə] Mutter **I**
motion picture [ˌməʊʃn 'pɪktʃə] Film; Spielfilm **IV U3**, 88
to **motivate** ['məʊtɪveɪt] motivieren **I**
motivation [ˌməʊtɪ'veɪʃn] Motivation; Beweggründe **III**
motive ['məʊtɪv] Motiv; Beweggrund **III**
bicycle **motocross** [ˌbaɪsɪkl 'məʊtəʊkrɒs] Fahrradmotocross **II**
motor car ['məʊtə ˌkɑ:] Automobil **IV U3**, 87
mountain ['maʊntɪn] Berg **II**
mountain biking ['maʊntɪn ˌbaɪkɪŋ] Mountainbikefahren **II**
mountainous ['maʊntɪnəs] bergig **IV AC1**, 10
mouse [maʊs], **mice** [maɪs] *(pl)* Maus/Mäuse **I**
mouth [maʊθ] Mund **I**; Mündung **IV U4**, 116
mouth jogging ['maʊθ ˌdʒɒgɪŋ] Training für den Mund **I**
to talk with your **mouth** full [ˌtɔ:k wɪð jɔ: 'maʊθ fʊl] mit vollem Mund sprechen **III**
move [mu:v] Bewegung **I**; Umzug **IV U4**, 120
on the **move** [ˌɒn‿ðə 'mu:v] unterwegs **III**
to **move** [mu:v] (sich) bewegen **I**
to **move** (house) [mu:v (haʊs)] umziehen **II**
to **move** in/into [ˌmu:v‿'ɪn/'ɪntə] einziehen in **II**
movie *(AE)* ['mu:vi] Film **IV U1**, 14

movie theater *(AE)* ['mu:vi ˌθɪətə] Kino **IV U1**, 14
Mr ['mɪstə] Herr *(Anrede)* **I**
Mrs ['mɪsɪz] Frau *(Anrede)* **I**
much [mʌtʃ] viel **I**
that **much** [ðæt 'mʌtʃ] so viel **III**
mud [mʌd] Schlamm **II**
muddy ['mʌdi] schlammig **II**
mudlark ['mʌdlɑ:k] *jemand, der im Schlamm nach Sachen sucht, die er dann verkaufen kann* **II**
muesli ['mju:zli] Müsli **III**
mug [mʌg] Becher **III**
multi-ethnic [ˌmʌlti'eθnɪk] Vielvölker-; international **II**
mum [mʌm] Mama **I**
mummy ['mʌmi] Mama; Mami; Mutti **III**
murder ['mɜ:də] Mord **III**
to **murder** ['mɜ:də] ermorden; umbringen **IV TS3**, 105
museum [mju:'zi:əm] Museum **I**
music ['mju:zɪk] Musik **I**
musical ['mju:zɪkl] musikalisch; Musik- **III**
musician [mju:'zɪʃn] Musiker/-in **II**
must [mʌst] müssen **I**
mustn't ['mʌsnt] nicht dürfen **I**
to **mutter** ['mʌtə] murmeln **III**
my [maɪ] mein/-e **I**
My favourite … [maɪ 'feɪvrɪt] Mein/e Lieblings … **I**
My name is … [maɪ 'neɪm‿ɪz] Ich heiße … **I**
myself [maɪ'self] ich/mir/mich (selbst); selber **II**
mysterious [mɪ'stɪəriəs] mysteriös; geheimnisvoll **II**
mystery ['mɪstri] Mysterium; Rätsel; Geheimnis **III**
mythical [mɪθɪkl] sagenhaft; sagenumwoben **III**

N

naked ['neɪkɪd] nackt **IV U2**, 42
name [neɪm] Name **I**
last **name** *(AE)* ['lɑ:st neɪm] Nachname; Familienname **IV U3**, 82
name day ['neɪm ˌdeɪ] Namenstag **I**
My **name** is … [maɪ 'neɪm‿ɪz] Ich heiße … **I**
What's your **name**? [ˌwɒts jə 'neɪm] Wie heißt du?; Wie heißen Sie? **I**
to **name** [neɪm] nennen; benennen **I**
narrative perspective [ˌnærətɪv pə'spektɪv] Erzählperspektive **III**
narrative technique [ˌnærətɪv tek'ni:k] Erzähltechnik °**IV U4**, 127
narrator [nə'reɪtə] Erzähler/-in **III**
first person **narrator** [ˌfɜ:st ˌpɜ:sn nə'reɪtə] Ich-Erzähler/-in **III**
third person **narrator** [ˌθɜ:d ˌpɜ:sn nə'reɪtə] Er/Sie-Erzähler/-in **III**
narrow ['nærəʊ] eng; schmal **III**
NASA *(= National Aeronautics and Space Administration)* ['næsə] NASA **IV TS2**, 70
nasty ['nɑ:sti] garstig; gemein **II**
nation ['neɪʃn] Nation **IV U3**, 78
national ['næʃnl] national; landesweit **I**
national park [ˌnæʃnl 'pɑ:k] Nationalpark; Naturpark **IV U4**, 112
native ['neɪtɪv] einheimisch; eingeboren **IV U4**, 111
Native American [ˌneɪtɪv‿ə'merɪkən] Ureinwohner/-in Amerikas; Indianer/-in; indianisch **IV U1**, 15
natural ['nætʃrl] natürlich; Natur- **IV U1**, 26
nature ['neɪtʃə] Natur **II**
nature lover ['neɪtʃə ˌlʌvə] Naturfreund/-in **IV U4**, 115
near [nɪə] nahe; in der Nähe von **I**
nearby [ˌnɪə'baɪ] in der Nähe **IV U4**, 120
nearly ['nɪəli] fast; annähernd **II**
not **necessarily** [ˌnɒt nesə'serəli] nicht notwendigerweise; nicht unbedingt **IV U2**, 46
necessary ['nesəsri] nötig; notwendig; erforderlich °**IV TS2**, 75
necessity [nə'sesəti] Notwendigkeit **IV U3**, 86
neck [nek] Hals; Nacken; Genick ⟨**IV U2**, 60⟩
necklace ['nekləs] Halskette **III**
in **need** [ɪn 'ni:d] bedürftig; in Not **II**
There's no **need** to … [ˌðeəz nəʊ 'ni:d tə] Es gibt keinen Grund zu … **III**
with special **needs** [wɪð ˌspeʃl 'ni:dz] behindert **II**
to **need** (to) [ni:d] brauchen; benötigen **I**
to **need** (to do) [ni:d] (tun) müssen **I**
needn't ['ni:dnt] nicht brauchen; nicht müssen **I**
needless to say [ˌni:dləs tə 'seɪ] natürlich; selbstverständlich **IV U2**, 46
negative ['negətɪv] negativ; verneint **II**
negative form ['negətɪv ˌfɔ:m] verneinte Form **I**
neighborhood *(AE)* ['neɪbəhʊd] Nachbarschaft **IV U1**, 13
neighbour ['neɪbə] Nachbar/-in **I**
neighbourhood ['neɪbəhʊd] Nachbarschaft **III**
nephew ['nefju:] Neffe **III**
nerd [nɜ:d] Nerd *(Person, die intelligent, aber sozial unbeholfen ist)* **IV TS1**, 35
*to get on people's **nerves** [ˌget‿ɒn sʌmbɒdiz 'nɜ:vz] jemandem auf die Nerven gehen **I**
nervous ['nɜ:vəs] nervös; aufgeregt **II**
net [net] Netz **II**
netball ['netbɔ:l] Korbball **I**
network ['netwɜ:k] Netzwerk **IV U3**, 86
communications **network** [kəˌmju:nɪ'keɪʃnz ˌnetwɜ:k] Kommunikationsnetz; Nachrichtennetz **IV U3**, 86
social **network** [ˌsəʊʃl 'netwɜ:k] soziales Netzwerk **II**
never ['nevə] nie; niemals **I**
new [nju:] neu **I**
New Year's Eve [ˌnju:‿jɪəz‿'i:v] Silvester ⟨**IV U2**, 60⟩
New Yorker [ˌnju: 'jɔ:kə] New Yorker/-in **IV U2**, 45
newly-arrived [ˌnju:li‿ə'raɪvd] frisch angekommen °**IV U3**, 95
news *(sg)* [nju:z] Nachrichten; Neuigkeiten **II**
news report ['nju:z rɪˌpɔ:t] Tatsachenbericht; Nachrichtenbeitrag; Meldung **III**
newspaper ['nju:sˌpeɪpə] Zeitung **III**
next [nekst] nächste/-r/-s; der/die Nächste(n) **I**
next door [ˌnekst 'dɔ:] (von) nebenan **III**
next to ['nekst tə] neben **I**
the **next** day [ðə ˌnekst 'deɪ] am nächsten Tag **II**
next [nekst] als Nächstes **I**
nice [naɪs] nett; schön; lieb **I**
nickname ['nɪkneɪm] Spitzname °**IV TS3**, 103
night [naɪt] Nacht **I**
all **night** [ˌɔ:l 'naɪt] die ganze Nacht **I**
night walk ['naɪt wɔ:k] Nachtwanderung **II**
nightmare ['naɪtmeə] Alptraum **IV U1**, 22
nine [naɪn] neun **I**
2nite *(= tonight)* [tə'naɪt] heute Abend **I**
no [nəʊ] kein/-e **I**
no matter [nəʊ 'mætə] egal; ganz gleich **IV U3**, 95
no more [ˌnəʊ 'mɔ:] nicht mehr **IV AC3**, 77
no one ['nəʊ wʌn] niemand ⟨**IV U3**, 89⟩
no way [ˌnəʊ 'weɪ] auf keinen Fall; keineswegs ⟨**IV U1**, 24⟩; keine Möglichkeit; kein Weg ⟨**IV TS2**, 72⟩
no idea [ˌnəʊ‿aɪ'dɪə] keine Ahnung **II**
no wonder [ˌnəʊ 'wʌndə] kein Wunder **IV U1**, 14
no [nəʊ] nein **I**
nobody ['nəʊbədi] niemand **II**
nobody else ['nəʊbədi els] niemand anderes **II**
noise [nɔɪz] Lärm; Geräusch **II**
noisy ['nɔɪzi] laut **III**
non- [nɒn] nicht- **II**
non-defining relative clause [ˌnɒndɪfaɪnɪŋ 'relətɪv ˌklɔ:z] nicht notwendiger Relativsatz °**IV U2**, 43
none [nʌn] keine/-r/-s **IV U3**, 93
nope *(infml)* [nəʊp] nee; nö **IV AC3**, 77
normal ['nɔ:ml] normal **II**
normally ['nɔ:mli] normalerweise **III**
Norman ['nɔ:mən] Normanne/Normannin; normannisch **III**
north [nɔ:θ] Norden; Nord- **II**
north [nɔ:θ] nördlich; im Norden **III**
nose [nəʊz] Nase **II**
to wrinkle one's **nose** [ˌrɪŋkl wʌnz 'nəʊz] die Nase rümpfen ⟨**IV U2**, 60⟩
not [nɒt] nicht **I**
not any more [ˌnɒt‿eni 'mɔ:] nicht mehr **I**

not anymore *(AE)* [ˌnɒt‿eniˈmɔː] nicht mehr **IV AC1**, 9
not necessarily [ˌnɒt nesəˈserəli] nicht notwendigerweise; nicht unbedingt **IV U2**, 46
not until [ˌnɒt‿ənˈtɪl] nicht vor; erst um/im **IV U1**, 14
not … any [nɒt … eni] kein/-e/-en **I**
not … anything [ˌnɒt ˈeniθɪŋ] nichts **I**
not … either [nɒt … ˈaɪðə; nɒt … ˈiːðə] auch nicht **IV AC3**, 77
not … yet [nɒt ˈjet] noch nicht **II**
note [nəʊt] Notiz; Anmerkung **I**
*to make **notes** [ˌmeɪk ˈnəʊts] Notizen machen **I**
*to take **notes** [ˌteɪk ˈnəʊts] sich Notizen machen **I**
to **note** down [ˌnəʊt ˈdaʊn] notieren; aufschreiben **II**
nothing [ˈnʌθɪŋ] nichts **I**
to **notice** [ˈnəʊtɪs] bemerken; wahrnehmen **II**
noticeboard [ˈnəʊtɪsbɔːd] schwarzes Brett **II**
noun [naʊn] Nomen; Hauptwort **I**
novel [ˈnɒvl] Roman **III**
graphic **novel** [ˌgræfɪk ˈnɒvl] Bildergeschichte; Comic **III**
November [nəˈvembə] November **I**
now [naʊ] jetzt; nun **I**
right **now** [ˌraɪt ˈnaʊ] jetzt gleich; sofort; gerade **II**
nowhere [ˈnəʊweə] nirgendwo; nirgendwohin **II**
in the middle of **nowhere** [ɪn ðə ˌmɪdl‿əv ˈnəʊweə] mitten im Nirgendwo **IV U1**, 16
number [ˈnʌmbə] Zahl; Nummer **I**
nurse [nɜːs] Krankenschwester; Krankenpfleger **III**
nut [nʌt] Nuss **I**

O

o'clock [əˈklɒk] Uhr *(Zeitangabe bei vollen Stunden)* **I**
oak [əʊk] Eiche **III**
to **obey** [əˈbeɪ] gehorchen **IV AC4**, 109
object [ˈɒbdʒɪkt] Objekt **II**; Gegenstand **III**
object pronoun [ˌɒbdʒɪkt ˈprəʊnaʊn] Objektpronomen **III**
obvious [ˈɒbviəs] offensichtlich **IV U1**, 23
October [ɒkˈtəʊbə] Oktober **I**
against all **odds** [əˌgenst‿ɔːl ˈɒdz] entgegen allen Erwartungen **III**
odd [ɒd] seltsam; komisch **III**
of [ɒv; əv] von **I**
of course [əv ˈkɔːs] natürlich; selbstverständlich **I**
of one's own [ˌəv wʌnz‿ˈəʊn] eigen **III**
to drop sb **off** [ˌdrɒp‿ˈɒf] jmdn. absetzen; jmdn. aussteigen lassen **IV TS3**, 106
*to take **off** [ˌteɪk‿ˈɒf] abnehmen; herunternehmen; ausziehen **I**
*to take the day **off** [ˌteɪk ðə ˌdeɪ‿ˈɒf] sich den Tag freinehmen **IV U2**, 42
to turn **off** [ˌtɜːn‿ˈɒf] abschalten; ausschalten **II**
special **offer** [ˌspeʃl‿ˈɒfə] Sonderangebot **I**
to **offer** [ˈɒfə] anbieten **II**
office [ˈɒfɪs] Büro **I**
immigration **office** [ˌɪmɪˈgreɪʃn ˌɒfɪs] Einwanderungsbehörde **III**
ticket **office** [ˈtɪkɪt ˌɒfɪs] Kartenschalter **III**
police **officer** [pəˈliːs‿ɒfɪsə] Polizeibeamter; Polizist/-in **II**
official [əˈfɪʃl] Schiedsrichter/-in **II**; Beamte/-r **III**
official [əˈfɪʃl] offiziell **III**
official language [əˌfɪʃl ˈlæŋgwɪdʒ] Amtssprache **II**
offline [ˈɒflaɪn] offline **II**
often [ˈɒfn] oft; häufig **I**
oh [əʊ] null *(bei Telefonnummern und Uhrzeitangaben)* **I**
Oh! [əʊ] O! **I**
Oh dear! [ˌəʊ ˈdɪə] Oje! **II**
ointment [ˈɔɪntmənt] Salbe **II**
OK [əʊˈkeɪ] o.k.; in Ordnung **I**
okay [əˈkeɪ] okay **III**
old [əʊld] alt **I**
How **old** are you? [haʊ‿ˈəʊld‿ə ˌjuː] Wie alt bist du?; Wie alt sind Sie? **I**
old school [ˈəʊldskuːl] von der alten Schule ⟨**IV U4**, 124⟩
11-year-**old** [ɪˌlevnˈjɪərəʊld] 11-Jährige/-r **II**
OMG! (Oh my god!) [ˌəʊ maɪ ˈgɒd] OMG! (Oh mein Gott!) **IV U1**, 26
on [ɒn] auf; an; am; in; im **I**
*to be **on** [bi‿ˈɒn] an sein; laufen **II**
on Mondays [ɒn ˈmʌndeɪz] montags **I**
on my own [ˌɒn maɪ‿ˈəʊn] allein; für mich **II**
on the brink of [ˌɒn ðə ˈbrɪŋk‿əv] am Rande von; kurz vor **III**
on the inside [ˌɒn ði‿ˈɪnsaɪd] innen °**IV U4**, 120
on the left [ɒn ðə ˈleft] auf der linken Seite; links **I**
on the outside [ˌɒn ði‿ˈaʊtsaɪd] außen °**IV U4**, 120
on the right [ɒn ðə ˈraɪt] auf der rechten Seite; rechts **I**
on time [ɒn ˈtaɪm] pünktlich **II**
on top [ɒn ˈtɒp] oben; obendrauf **I**
Come **on**! [ˌkʌm‿ˈɒn] Komm schon!; Komm jetzt! **I**
on a shoestring [ˌɒn‿ə ˈʃuːstrɪŋ] für/mit wenig Geld **IV U2**, 42
on the move [ˌɒn‿ðə ˈmuːv] unterwegs **III**
once [wʌns] einmal; einst **I**
one [wʌn] eins **I**
no **one** [ˈnəʊ wʌn] niemand ⟨**IV U3**, 89⟩
one another [ˌwʌn‿əˈnʌðə] einander; gegenseitig ⟨**IV U4**, 125⟩
one by **one** [ˌwʌn baɪ ˈwʌn] eine/-r/-s nach dem/der anderen ⟨**IV U3**, 93⟩
one day [wʌn ˈdeɪ] eines Tages **II**
one-way ticket [ˈwʌnweɪ ˌtɪkɪt] einfache Fahrkarte **II**
one [wʌn], **ones** [wʌnz] *(pl)* eine/-r/-s **II**
online [ɒnˈlaɪn] online **II**
only [ˈəʊnli] einzige/-r/-s **II**
only [ˈəʊnli] erst; bloß; nur **I**
only child [ˈəʊnli ˌtʃaɪld] Einzelkind **I**
onto [ˈɒntə] auf … hinauf ⟨**IV TS2**, 71⟩
Oops! [uːps] Hoppla!; Huch! **I**
to **open** [ˈəʊpn] öffnen; aufmachen **I**; *hier:* beginnen **III**; eröffnen **IV U1**, 22
to **open** to [ˈəʊpn tə] führen zu/in ⟨**IV AC4**, 109⟩
open [ˈəʊpn] offen; geöffnet; aufgeschlagen **I**
*to hold **open** [ˌhəʊld‿ˈəʊpn] aufhalten **III**
opening [ˈəʊpnɪŋ] Öffnung; Beginn **III**
opening line [ˈəʊpnɪŋ‿ˌlaɪn] der erste Satz **III**
opinion [əˈpɪnjən] Meinung **II**
opposite [ˈɒpəzɪt] Gegenteil ⟨**IV U4**, 123⟩
opposite [ˈɒpəzɪt] gegenüber; auf der anderen Seite von **I**
optimistic [ˌɒptɪˈmɪstɪk] optimistisch **III**
option [ˈɒpʃn] Möglichkeit; Wahl; Option **III**
or [ɔː] oder **I**
either … **or** … [ˈaɪðə/ˈiːðə … ɔː] entweder … oder … **IV U2**, 49
oral [ˈɔːrl] mündlich **IV U3**, 91
orange [ˈɒrɪndʒ] Orange **I**
orange [ˈɒrɪndʒ] orange **I**
orbit [ˈɔːbɪt] Umlaufbahn; Orbit ⟨**IV TS2**, 71⟩
orca [ˈɔːkə] Schwertwal **IV U4**, 111
order [ˈɔːdə] Reihenfolge; Ordnung **I**; Befehl **III**
in **order** to [ɪn‿ˈɔːdə tə] um … zu; mit der Absicht **IV U3**, 87
out of **order** [ˌaʊt‿əv ˈɔːdə] kaputt; außer Betrieb **III**
word **order** [ˈwɜːd‿ˌɔːdə] Wortstellung; Satzstellung **I**
to **order** [ˈɔːdə] bestellen **III**
organisation [ˌɔːgnaɪˈzeɪʃn] Organisation **II**
to **organise** [ˈɔːgənaɪz] organisieren **I**
*to get **organised** [get ˈɔːgənaɪzd] sich organisieren **II**
to **organize** *(AE)* [ˈɔːgənaɪz] organisieren **IV U3**, 92
orientation [ˌɔːriənˈteɪʃn] Orientierung; Orientierungs- **IV U1**, 13
origin [ˈɒrɪdʒɪn] Ursprung; Herkunft; Abstammung **III**
original [əˈrɪdʒnl] Original **III**
original [əˈrɪdʒnl] original; ursprünglich **III**
originally [əˈrɪdʒnli] ursprünglich **II**
other [ˈʌðə] anders; andere/-r/-s; weitere **I**
each **other** [ˌiːtʃ‿ˈʌðə] einander; sich; sich gegenseitig **I**
the **others** [ði‿ˈʌðəz] die anderen **I**

otherwise ['ʌðəwaɪz] sonst **IV AC2**, 38
Ouch! [aʊtʃ] Aua! **II**
our [aʊə; ɑ:] unser/-e **I**
out [aʊt] außerhalb; heraus; hinaus; nach draußen **I**
to clean **out** [ˌkli:n‿'aʊt] ausräumen; entrümpeln **IV U1**, 21
to clear **out** [ˌklɪər‿'aʊt] ausräumen; entrümpeln **I**
to drop **out** (of) [ˌdrɒp 'aʊt‿əv] abbrechen **III**
*to hang **out** (with) *(infml)* [ˌhæŋ‿'aʊt wɪð] sich herumtreiben (mit); rumhängen (mit); sich treffen (mit) **III**
*to leave **out** [ˌli:v‿'aʊt] auslassen; weglassen °**IV U1**, 24
out and about [ˌaʊt‿ən‿ə'baʊt] unterwegs **II**
out of ['aʊt‿əv] aus … heraus **III**
out of focus [ˌaʊt‿əv 'fəʊkəs] unscharf **III**
out of order [ˌaʊt‿əv 'ɔ:də] kaputt; außer Betrieb **III**
*to run **out** [ˌrʌn‿'aʊt] ausgehen ⟨**IV TS3**, 103⟩
to toss **out** [ˌtɒs‿'aʊt] ausstoßen; hinauswerfen **IV U4**, 125
a day **out** in … [ə ˌdeɪ‿'aʊt ɪn] ein Tag in … **II**
out of tune [ˌaʊt‿əv 'tju:n] verstimmt ⟨**IV U3**, 92⟩
outdoor [ˌaʊt'dɔ:] Freiluft-; Outdoor- **II**
the **outdoors** [ði ˌaʊt'dɔ:z] die Natur **IV U4**, 111
outfit ['aʊtfɪt] Outfit; Kleidung **II**
outgoing [aʊt'gəʊɪŋ] kontaktfreudig **III**
outlaw ['aʊtlɔ:] Geächtete/-r; Gesetzlose/-r **II**
outline ['aʊtlaɪn] Skizze; Umriss **II**
out-of-character [ˌaʊtəv'kærəktə] ungewöhnlich °**IV U1**, 24
from the **outside** [ˌfrəm ðiˌaʊt'saɪd] von außen **IV U2**, 45
on the **outside** [ˌɒn ði‿'aʊtsaɪd] außen °**IV U4**, 120
outside [aʊt'saɪd] nach draußen; draußen; außerhalb **I**
outside world ['aʊtsaɪd ˌwɜ:ld] Außenwelt **IV U4**, 117
outward ['aʊtwəd] abfahrend **II**
over ['əʊvə] hinüber; über **I**; vorüber; vorbei **II**
*to go **over** to [ˌgəʊ 'əʊvə tə] hinübergehen zu; zu jmdm. nach Hause gehen **II**
over and **over** again [ˌəʊvər‿ən‿ˌəʊvər‿ə'gen] immer wieder **III**
*to run **over** [ˌrʌn‿'əʊvə] überfahren **IV TS3**, 106
*to win sb **over** [ˌwɪn‿'əʊvə] jmdn. für sich gewinnen; jmdn. überzeugen **IV TS1**, 34
overall [ˌəʊvr'ɔ:l] allgemein; Gesamt- °**IV U4**, 126
overall [ˌəʊvr'ɔ:l] insgesamt **IV U4**, 119
*to **overdo** [əʊvə'du:] übertreiben; zu weit gehen **IV U1**, 25
to **over-exaggerate** [ˌəʊvərɪg'zædʒreɪt] völlig übertreiben **IV U4**, 120
to **overlap** [ˌəʊvə'læp] (sich) überlappen **IV U2**, 59
overloaded [ˌəʊvə'ləʊdɪd] überladen **III**
overly ['əʊvəli] allzu; übermäßig ⟨**IV TS3**, 106⟩
overnight [ˌəʊvə'naɪt] über Nacht **III**
to **overreact** [ˌəʊvəri'ækt] überreagieren **II**
to **own** [əʊn] besitzen **IV U3**, 92
own [əʊn] eigene/-r/-s **I**
of one's **own** [ˌəv wʌnz‿'əʊn] eigen **III**
on my **own** [ˌɒn maɪ‿'əʊn] allein; für mich **II**

P

p.m. [ˌpi:'em] nachmittags *(Uhrzeit)*; abends *(Uhrzeit)* **I**
Pa [pɑ:] Papa **IV U3**, 92
to **pack** [pæk] packen; einpacken **IV U3**, 92
packet ['pækɪt] Päckchen; Paket; Packung **I**
to **paddle** ['pædl] paddeln **IV U4**, 116
paddleboard ['pædlbɔ:d] Paddling Board *(eine Art Surfbrett, auf dem man aufrecht stehend paddelt)* **IV U4**, 114
page [peɪdʒ] Seite **I**
pain [peɪn] Schmerz **II**
to **paint** [peɪnt] anmalen; malen **I**
painting ['peɪntɪŋ] Malerei; Gemälde **II**
pair [peə] Paar **I**
pair work ['peə wɜ:k] Partnerarbeit **II**
to **pair** [peə] Paare bilden **III**
palm tree ['pɑ:m ˌtri:] Palme **II**
pamphlet ['pæmflɪt] kleine Broschüre; Faltblatt ⟨**IV U3**, 92⟩
panel ['pænl] Bild *(eines Comics)* **IV U2**, 59
to **panic** ['pænɪk] panisch werden **II**
paper ['peɪpə] Papier **I**
piece of **paper** [ˌpi:s‿əv 'peɪpə] Stück Papier **I**
papers *(pl)* ['peɪpəz] Unterlagen; Papiere **IV U3**, 84
paradise ['pærədaɪs] Paradies **II**
paragraph ['pærəgrɑ:f] Paragraf; Absatz °**IV TS2**, 73
to **paraphrase** ['pærəfreɪz] paraphrasieren; umschreiben °**IV U4**, 115
parcel ['pɑ:sl] Paket; Päckchen **I**
parents *(pl)* ['peərənts] Eltern **I**
park [pɑ:k] Park **I**
national **park** [ˌnæʃnl 'pɑ:k] Nationalpark; Naturpark **IV U4**, 112
parking lot ['pɑ:kɪŋ ˌlɒt] Parkplatz **IV TS3**, 105
part [pɑ:t] Teil; Stadtteil **I**; Rolle **III**
lead **part** [ˌli:d 'pɑ:t] Hauptrolle **III**
*to take **part** (in) [ˌteɪk 'pɑ:t (ɪn)] teilnehmen (an) **II**
partially sighted [ˌpɑ:ʃəli 'saɪtɪd] sehbehindert **II**
to **participate** [pɑ:'tɪsɪpeɪt] teilnehmen **II**
participle [pɑ:'tɪsɪpl] Partizip °**IV U3**, 84
past **participle** [ˌpɑ:st pɑ:'tɪsɪpl] Partizip **II**
present **participle** [ˌpreznt pɑ:'tɪsɪpl] Partizip Präsens °**IV U3**, 84
particular [pə'tɪkjələ] bestimmte/-r/-s **III**
particularly [pə'tɪkjələli] besonders °**IV TS3**, 103
partner ['pɑ:tnə] Partner/-in **I**
part-time [ˌpɑ:t'taɪm] Teilzeit-; Halbtags- **IV U4**, 113
party ['pɑ:ti] Party; Feier **I**; Partei **III**; Gruppe; Reisegruppe ⟨**IV U3**, 92⟩
hall **pass** ['hɔ:l pɑ:s] *Erlaubnis, sich während des Unterrichts auf dem Flur aufzuhalten* **IV U1**, 13
to **pass** [pɑ:s] zupassen; zuspielen **II**; durchgehen; vorbeigehen (an); passieren **IV U3**, 81; bestehen **IV U3**, 82
to **pass** (on) [ˌpɑ:s‿'ɒn] weitergeben **I**
passageway ['pæsɪdʒweɪ] Korridor; Gang ⟨**IV TS3**, 107⟩
passenger ['pæsndʒə] Passagier/-in; Fahrgast **III**
passenger seat ['pæsndʒə ˌsi:t] Beifahrersitz **IV TS3**, 106
passive ['pæsɪv] Passiv **III**
passive ['pæsɪv] passiv **III**
passport ['pɑ:spɔ:t] Pass; Reisepass **III**
past [pɑ:st] Vergangenheit **II**
past form ['pɑ:st fɔ:m] Vergangenheitsform **II**
past participle [ˌpɑ:st pɑ:'tɪsɪpl] Partizip **II**
past perfect [ˌpɑ:st 'pɜ:fɪkt] Plusquamperfekt **III**
past perfect progressive [ˌpɑ:st ˌpɜ:fɪkt prə'gresɪv] Verlaufsform des Plusquamperfekts °**IV U2**, 47
past progressive [ˌpɑ:st prə'gresɪv] Verlaufsform der Vergangenheit **II**
simple **past** [ˌsɪmpl 'pɑ:st] Vergangenheitsform **II**
past [pɑ:st] nach *(bei Uhrzeitangaben)*; vorbei (an); vorüber (an) **I**
half **past** [ˌhɑ:f 'pɑ:st] halb *(bei Uhrzeitangaben)* **I**
quarter **past**/to ['kwɔ:tə pɑ:st/tə] Viertel nach/vor **I**
pasta ['pæstə] Pasta; Nudeln **I**
pastry ['peɪstri] Teig; Teigtasche **IV U2**, 45
patchwork ['pætʃwɜ:k] Flicken-; Patchwork- ⟨**IV U2**, 60⟩
path [pɑ:θ] Pfad; Weg **IV U2**, 62
coastal **path** [ˌkəʊstl 'pɑ:θ] Küstenweg **II**
patio ['pætiəʊ] Terrasse; Innenhof ⟨**IV AC4**, 109⟩
pattern ['pætn] Muster **II**
pause [pɔ:z] Pause **III**
pawn shop ['pɔ:n ʃɒp] Pfandhaus; Pfandleihe **III**
*to **pay (for)** [peɪ] bezahlen **I**

*to **pay** attention to sb/sth [ˌpeɪ‿ə'tenʃn tʊ] jmdn./etw. beachten **III**
PC *(= Personal Computer)* [pi:'si:] PC **II**
PE *(= Physical Education)* [ˌpi:'i:; ˌfɪzɪkl‿edʒʊ'keɪʃn] Sportunterricht **II**
peace [pi:s] Frieden **IV U4**, 112
peaceful ['pi:sfl] friedlich **IV U4**, 116
peach [pi:tʃ] Pfirsich **III**
peak [pi:k] Haupt-; Spitzen- **IV U3**, 81
peer pressure ['pɪə ˌpreʃe] Gruppenzwang **III**
to **peer-edit** ['pɪər‿ˌedɪt] gegenseitig kontrollieren **II**
pen [pen] Füller **I**
pencil ['pensl] Bleistift; Buntstift **I**
pencil-case ['pensl ˌkeɪs] Federmäppchen; Mäppchen **I**
penicillin [ˌpenɪ'sɪlɪn] Penicillin **III**
penny ['peni], **pence** [pens] *(pl)* Penny; Pence *(brit. Währungseinheit)* **I**
penthouse ['penthaʊs] Penthouse; Wohnung mit Dachterrasse **IV U2**, 49
people ['pi:pl] Volk **IV U4**, 116
people *(pl)* ['pi:pl] Leute; Menschen **I**
medicine **people** ['medsn ˌpi:pl] Medizinmänner **IV U4**, 116
pepper-spray ['pepəspreɪ] Pfefferspray ⟨**IV TS3**, 106⟩
per [pɜ:; pə] pro **II**
percent, **percent** *(pl)* [pə'sent] Prozent **IV U3**, 85
future **perfect** [ˌfju:tʃə 'pɜ:fɪkt] vollendetes Futur; Futur II ⟨**IV U4**, 119⟩
past **perfect** [ˌpɑ:st 'pɜ:fɪkt] Plusquamperfekt **III**
past **perfect** progressive [ˌpɑ:st ˌpɜ:fɪkt prə'gresɪv] Verlaufsform des Plusquamperfekts °**IV U2**, 47
present **perfect** [ˌpreznt 'pɜ:fɪkt] das Perfekt **II**
present **perfect** progressive [ˌpreznt ˌpɜ:fɪkt prə'gresɪv] Verlaufsform des Perfekts **III**
perfect ['pɜ:fɪkt] perfekt; vollkommen **I**
to **perform** [pə'fɔ:m] aufführen; auftreten **IV U2**, 49
performance [pə'fɔ:məns] Aufführung; Vorstellung **III**
perhaps [pə'hæps] vielleicht **III**
period ['pɪəriəd] Periode; Zeitspanne **III**
period *(AE)* ['pɪəriəd] Stunde; Unterrichtsstunde **IV U1**, 18
permanent ['pɜ:mənənt] permanent; dauerhaft **IV U3**, 80
person ['pɜ:sn], **people** ['pi:pl] *(pl)* Person; Mensch **I**
first **person** narrator [ˌfɜ:st ˌpɜ:sn nə'reɪtə] Ich-Erzähler/-in **III**
third **person** narrator [ˌθɜ:d ˌpɜ:sn nə'reɪtə] Er/Sie-Erzähler/-in **III**
personal ['pɜ:snl] persönlich **I**
personality [ˌpɜ:sn'æləti] Persönlichkeit **III**

perspective [pə'spektɪv] Perspektive; Blickwinkel **II**
narrative **perspective** [ˌnærətɪv pə'spektɪv] Erzählperspektive **III**
to **persuade** [pə'sweɪd] überreden **II**
persuasive [pə'sweɪsɪv] überzeugend **III**
pet [pet] Haustier **I**
phone [fəʊn] Telefon; Handy **I**
to answer the **phone** [ˌɑ:nsə ðə 'fəʊn] einen Anruf entgegennehmen **I**
cell **phone** *(AE)* ['selfəʊn] Mobiltelefon; Handy **IV AC2**, 38
phone box ['fəʊn ˌbɒks] Telefonzelle **III**
phone call ['fəʊn ˌkɔ:l] Anruf; Telefonanruf **I**
rotary **phone** ['rəʊtri fəʊn] Telefon mit Wählscheibe **III**
to **phone** [fəʊn] anrufen; telefonieren **III**
photo ['fəʊtəʊ] Foto; Fotografie **I**
in the **photo**(s) [ˌɪn ðə 'fəʊtəʊ(z)] auf dem Foto/den Fotos **I**
photo shoot ['fəʊtəʊ ˌʃu:t] Fotoshooting; Fotoaufnahmen **III**
photo story ['fəʊtəʊ ˌstɔ:ri] Fotostory; Bildgeschichte **I**
*to take **photos** [ˌteɪk 'fəʊtəʊz] fotografieren; Fotos machen **I**
to **photobomb** ['fəʊtəʊbɒm] ins Foto laufen **III**
photographer [fə'tɒgrəfə] Fotograf/-in **III**
phrase [freɪz] Redewendung; Ausdruck; Satz **I**
Useful **phrases** [ˌju:sfl 'freɪsɪz] nützliche Ausdrücke **I**
piano [pi'ænəʊ] Klavier; Piano **IV U2**, 47
to **pick** [pɪk] auswählen; aussuchen **II**
to **pick** up [ˌpɪk‿'ʌp] aufheben; mitnehmen; abholen **III**
pick-up ['pɪkʌp] Pick-up; Wiederaufnehmen **I**
picnic ['pɪknɪk] Picknick **I**
picture ['pɪktʃə] Bild; Foto **I**
motion **picture** [ˌməʊʃn 'pɪktʃə] Film; Spielfilm **IV U3**, 88
*to see the bigger **picture** [ˌsi: ðə ˌbɪgə 'pɪktʃə] über den Tellerrand hinausschauen **IV U4**, 120
pie [paɪ] Kuchen; Pastete **I**
pie chart ['paɪ ˌtʃɑ:t] Kuchendiagramm; Tortendiagramm **IV U3**, 85
pumpkin **pie** [ˌpʌmpkɪn 'paɪ] Kürbiskuchen ⟨**IV U1**, 15⟩
piece [pi:s] Stück **I**
piece of junk [ˌpi:s‿əv 'dʒʌŋk] Stück Schrott **III**
piece of paper [ˌpi:s‿əv 'peɪpə] Stück Papier **I**
pier [pɪə] Pier; Hafendamm **I**
piercing ['pɪəsɪŋ] Piercing ⟨**IV U2**, 60⟩
pig [pɪg] Schwein **I**
guinea **pig** ['gɪni: ˌpɪg] Meerschweinchen **I**

*to give sb a **piggyback** [gɪv‿ə 'pɪgibæk] jmdn. Huckepack nehmen **III**
Pilgrim ['pɪlgrɪm] Pilger/-in **IV U1**, 15
pill [pɪl] Pille; Tablette **II**
pilot ['paɪlət] Pilot/-in **II**
pineapple ['paɪnæpl] Ananas **III**
pink [pɪŋk] pink; rosa **I**
pioneer [ˌpaɪə'nɪə] Pionier/-in **IV U3**, 86
pipe [paɪp] Rohr; Rohrleitung; Pfeife **II**
clay **pipe** ['kleɪ paɪp] Tonpfeife **II**
pitch [pɪtʃ] Spielfeld; Platz **II**
pizza ['pi:tsə] Pizza **I**
place [pleɪs] Ort; Stelle; Platz **I**
starting **place** ['stɑ:tɪŋ pleɪs] Startpunkt **II**
*to take **place** [ˌteɪk 'pleɪs] stattfinden **I**
to **place** [pleɪs] legen **II**
placemat ['pleɪsmæt] Placemat; Platzdeckchen **I**
plan [plæn] Plan; Entwurf **I**
floor **plan** ['flɔ: plæn] Grundriss ⟨**IV AC4**, 109⟩
to **plan** [plæn] planen **I**
plane [pleɪn] Flugzeug **III**
planet ['plænɪt] Planet **II**
planner ['plænə] Handbuch; Kalender **I**
route **planner** ['ru:t ˌplænə] Routenplaner **IV AC1**, 11
plant [plɑ:nt] Pflanze **II**
to **plant** [plɑ:nt] pflanzen; anpflanzen **II**
plaster cast ['plɑ:stə kɑ:st] Gipsverband **III**
plastic ['plæstɪk] Plastik; Kunststoff; Plastik- ⟨**IV U3**, 89⟩
plate [pleɪt] Teller **III**
platform ['plætfɔ:m] Plattform; Bahnsteig **II**
play [pleɪ] Theaterstück **III**
fair **play** [feə 'pleɪ] Fairplay **III**
play on words [ˌpleɪ‿ɒn 'wɜ:dz] Wortspiel **III**
role **play** ['rəʊl ˌpleɪ] Rollenspiel **I**
to **play** [pleɪ] spielen **I**
to **play** a trick (on) [ˌpleɪ‿ə 'trɪk‿ɒn] einen Streich spielen **I**
to **play** bowls [ˌpleɪ 'bəʊlz] Bowling spielen **III**
player ['pleɪə] Spieler/-in; Mitspieler/-in **II**
Please. [pli:z] Bitte. **I**
to **pledge** allegiance [ˌpledʒ‿ə'li:dʒns] Treueschwur leisten ⟨**IV U1**, 19⟩
plot [plɒt] Handlung **III**
plumber ['plʌmə] Installateur/-in; Klempner/-in **II**
plumbing ['plʌmɪŋ] Sanitärarbeit **II**
plural ['plʊərəl] Plural; Mehrzahl **I**
poaching *(no pl)* ['pəʊtʃɪŋ] Wilderei **III**
pocket ['pɒkɪt] Tasche; Hosentasche **III**
pocket money ['pɒkɪt ˌmʌni] Taschengeld **I**
a **pocketful** of [ə 'pɒkɪtfl‿əv] Unmengen von/an **IV U2**, 40
podcast ['pɒdkɑ:st] Podcast **IV U2**, 62
poem ['pəʊɪm] Gedicht **I**
point [pɔɪnt] Punkt; Zeitpunkt **II**

*to have a **point** [ˌhæv‿ə ˈpɔɪnt] nicht ganz Unrecht haben **III**
point of view [ˌpɔɪnt‿əv ˈvjuː] Standpunkt; Ansicht; Perspektive **II**
to the **point** [tə ðə ˈpɔɪnt] prägnant; treffend **III**
turning **point** [ˈtɜːnɪŋ ˌpɔɪnt] Wendepunkt **III**
I can't see the **point** of … [aɪ ˌkɑːnt siː ðə ˈpɔɪnt‿əv] Ich sehe keinen Sinn darin … **IV AC2**, 39
to **point** at sb/sth [ˈpɔɪnt æt] mit dem Finger auf jmdn./etw. zeigen **III**
to **point** out sth [ˌpɔɪnt‿ˈaʊt] hinweisen auf etw. °**IV AC1**, 11
Point to … [ˈpɔɪnt tə] Zeige/Zeigt auf … **I**
totem **pole** [ˈtəʊtəm ˌpəʊl] Totempfahl **IV U4**, 118
police [pəˈliːs] Polizei **II**
police officer [pəˈliːs‿ɒfɪsə] Polizeibeamter; Polizist/-in **II**
polite [pəˈlaɪt] höflich **I**
Be **polite**. [biː pəˈlaɪt] Sei/Seid höflich. **I**
political [pəˈlɪtɪkl] politisch **IV TS2**, 71
pollution [pəˈluːʃn] Verschmutzung **II**
polyester [ˌpɒliˈestə] Polyester ⟨**IV U4**, 124⟩
pond [pɒnd] Teich **II**
pony [ˈpəʊni] Pony **I**
pony trekking [ˈpəʊni ˌtrekɪŋ] Ponyreiten im Gelände **II**
swimming **pool** [ˈswɪmɪŋ ˌpuːl] Swimmingpool; Schwimmbecken **III**
the **poor** [ðə pʊə] die Armen **II**
poor [pɔː; pʊə] arm **III**
soda **pop** *(AE)* [ˈsəʊdə ˌpɒp] Limo **IV U4**, 124
popular [ˈpɒpjələ] beliebt; populär **I**
populated [ˈpɒpjəleɪtɪd] bevölkert; besiedelt **IV AC1**, 8
population [ˌpɒpjəˈleɪʃn] Bevölkerung; Population **IV AC1**, 9
pose [pəʊz] Pose; Haltung **IV U1**, 26
positive [ˈpɒzətɪv] positiv **II**
possessive form [pəˌsesɪv ˈfɔːm] Possessivform **I**
possibility [ˌpɒsəˈbɪləti] Möglichkeit **II**
possible [ˈpɒsəbl] möglich **I**
post [pəʊst] Post *(Eintrag im Internet)* **I**
to **post** [pəʊst] online stellen; posten **II**
postcard [ˈpəʊstkɑːd] Postkarte **II**
poster [ˈpəʊstə] Poster **I**
class **poster** [ˈklɑːs ˌpəʊstə] Klassenposter **I**
postman [ˈpəʊstmən] Briefträger **II**
melting **pot** [ˈmeltɪŋ ˌpɒt] Schmelztiegel **IV U2**, 40
potato [pəˈteɪtəʊ], **potatoes** [pəˈteɪtəʊz] *(pl)* Kartoffel **III**
mashed **potatoes** *(pl)* [ˌmæʃt pəˈteɪtəʊz] Kartoffelpüree **III**
sweet **potatoes** *(pl)* [ˈswiːt pəˌteɪtəʊz] Süßkartoffeln ⟨**IV U1**, 15⟩
potential [pəˈtenʃl] potenziell; möglich ⟨**IV TS3**, 105⟩
pound [paʊnd] Pfund *(Maßeinheit)* **IV U1**, 21
pound (£) [paʊnd] Pfund *(brit. Währungseinheit)* **I**
to **pour** [pɔː] einschenken; eingießen; schütten **I**
power [paʊə] Kraft; Macht; Stärke **II**
computing **power** [ˌkəmˈpjuːtɪŋ ˌpaʊə] Rechenleistung ⟨**IV TS2**, 72⟩
Word **power** [ˈwɜːd ˌpaʊə] die Kraft der Wörter *(Wortschatzübung)* **I**
those in **power** [ˌðəʊz ɪn ˈpaʊə] die Regierenden; die Herrschenden **III**
power [paʊə] Strom; Elektrizität; Energie **IV U4**, 117
power cut [ˈpaʊə ˌkʌt] Stromausfall **II**
powerful [ˈpaʊəfl] stark; mächtig **II**
practical [ˈpræktɪkl] praktisch **II**
practice [ˈpræktɪs] Training; Übung **III**
to **practice** *(AE)* [ˈpræktɪs] üben; ausüben; praktizieren; trainieren **IV U1**, 15
to **practice** a religion [ˌpræktɪs‿ə rɪˈlɪdʒn] eine Religion ausüben **IV U1**, 15
to **practise** [ˈpræktɪs] üben; trainieren **I**
practising [ˈpræktɪsɪŋ] Üben **I**
prairie [ˈpreəri] Prärie **IV U3**, 92
to **pray** [preɪ] beten **III**
predator [ˈpredətə] Raubtier ⟨**IV U4**, 125⟩
prediction [prɪˈdɪkʃn] Vorhersage; Voraussage **II**
to **prefer** [prɪˈfɜː] vorziehen **IV U1**, 20
preference [ˈprefrns] Vorliebe **IV AC4**, 109
prehistoric [ˌpriːhɪˈstɒrɪk] vorgeschichtlich **II**
preparation [ˌprepr'eɪʃn] Vorbereitung **IV U3**, 92
to **prepare** [prɪˈpeə] vorbereiten; zubereiten **I**
preposition [ˌprepəˈzɪʃn] Präposition **I**
pre-reading [ˌpriːˈriːdɪŋ] vor dem Lesen **I**
prescription [prɪˈskrɪpʃn] Rezept *(für Arzneimittel)* **II**
presence [ˈprezns] Anwesenheit ⟨**IV TS3**, 107⟩
present [ˈpreznt] Geschenk **I**
present [ˈpreznt] Gegenwart; Präsens **II**
present participle [ˌpreznt pɑːˈtɪsɪpl] Partizip Präsens °**IV U3**, 84
present perfect [ˌpreznt ˈpɜːfɪkt] das Perfekt **II**
present perfect progressive [ˌpreznt ˌpɜːfɪkt prəˈgresɪv] Verlaufsform des Perfekts **III**
present progressive [ˌpreznt prəˈgresɪv] Verlaufsform des Präsens/der Gegenwart **I**
simple **present** [ˌsɪmpl ˈpreznt] Gegenwart; Präsens **I**
to **present** [prɪˈzent] präsentieren; vorstellen **I**
present [ˈpreznt] heutig; Gegenwarts- **III**
presentation [ˌpreznˈteɪʃn] Präsentation; Vortrag **I**
presenter [prɪˈzentə] Moderator/-in **I**
president [ˈprezɪdnt] Präsident/-in **IV TS2**, 71
to **press** [pres] drücken; pressen **II**
peer **pressure** [ˈpɪə ˌpreʃə] Gruppenzwang **III**
to **pretend** [prɪˈtend] vortäuschen; tun als ob **III**
pretty [ˈprɪti] hübsch **III**
pretty [ˈprɪti] ziemlich; ganz schön ⟨**IV TS2**, 74⟩
price [praɪs] Preis **I**
primary school [ˈpraɪmri ˌskuːl] Grundschule **I**
primitive [ˈprɪmɪtɪv] primitiv ⟨**IV U4**, 125⟩
principal *(AE)* [ˈprɪnsɪpl] Schulleiter/-in **IV AC2**, 38
print [prɪnt] gedruckt; Druck- **II**
priority [praɪˈɒrəti] Priorität; Vorrang **IV TS2**, 71
prison [ˈprɪzn] Gefängnis **II**
prisoner [ˈprɪznə] Gefangene/-r ⟨**IV U2**, 60⟩
private detective [ˌpraɪvət dɪˈtektɪv] Privatdetektiv/-in **II**
prize [praɪz] Preis; Gewinn **I**
pro [prəʊ] Argument dafür **II**
probable [ˈprɒbəbli] wahrscheinlich ⟨**IV TS3**, 102⟩
probably [ˈprɒbəbli] möglicherweise; wahrscheinlich **II**
problem [ˈprɒbləm] Problem; Schwierigkeit **I**
in the **process** [ˌɪn ðə ˈprəʊsəs] in dem Zusammenhang ⟨**IV TS3**, 106⟩
to **produce** [prəˈdjuːs] herstellen; produzieren **III**
product [ˈprɒdʌkt] Produkt; Erzeugnis **IV TS1**, 34
production [prəˈdʌkʃn] Produktion; Inszenierung **III**
professor [prəˈfesə] Professor/-in ⟨**IV U4**, 125⟩
profile [ˈprəʊfaɪl] Profil; Porträt **I**
program *(AE)* [ˈprəʊgræm] Programm; Sendung **IV TS2**, 74
space **program** [ˈspeɪs ˌprəʊgræm] Raumfahrtprogramm **IV TS2**, 74
programme [ˈprəʊgræm] Programm; Sendung **II**
progress [ˈprəʊgres] Fortschritt **II**
past perfect **progressive** [ˌpɑːst ˌpɜːfɪkt prəˈgresɪv] Verlaufsform des Plusquamperfekts °**IV U2**, 47
past **progressive** [ˌpɑːst prəˈgresɪv] Verlaufsform der Vergangenheit **II**
present perfect **progressive** [ˌpreznt ˌpɜːfɪkt prəˈgresɪv] Verlaufsform des Perfekts **III**
present **progressive** [ˌpreznt prəˈgresɪv] Verlaufsform des Präsens/der Gegenwart **I**
project [ˈprɒdʒekt] Projekt **I**
to **promise** [ˈprɒmɪs] versprechen **II**
prompt [prɒmpt] Stichwort **III**

prompt card [ˈprɒmpt kɑːd] Stichwortkarte; Rollenkarte **II**
pronoun [ˈprəʊnaʊn] Pronomen; Fürwort °**IV U1**, 20
object **pronoun** [ˌɒbdʒɪkt ˈprəʊnaʊn] Objektpronomen **III**
reflexive **pronoun** [rɪˌfleksɪv ˈprəʊnaʊn] Reflexivpronomen **III**
relative **pronoun** [ˌrelətɪv ˈprəʊnaʊn] Relativpronomen **II**
to **pronounce** [prəˈnaʊns] aussprechen **IV AC3**, 76
pronunciation [prəˌnʌnsiˈeɪʃn] Aussprache **I**
prop [prɒp] Requisite **II**
proper [ˈprɒpə] richtig; ordentlich; angemessen **IV U3**, 92
protagonist [prəʊˈtægnɪst] Protagonist/-in; Hauptfigur **III**
to **protect** sb/sth (from) [prəˈtekt frəm] jmdn./etw. beschützen (vor) **IV U4**, 114
protection [prəˈtekʃn] Schutz ⟨**IV U4**, 125⟩
protest [ˈprəʊtest] Protest **III**
protester [ˈprəʊtestə] Protestierende/-r; Demonstrant/-in **IV U1**, 22
proud (of) [ˈpraʊd‿əv] stolz (auf) **II**
the **public** [ðə ˈpʌblɪk] die Öffentlichkeit **IV TS2**, 72
public [ˈpʌblɪk] öffentlich **II**
public transport *(no pl)* [ˌpʌblɪk ˈtrænspɔːt] öffentliche Verkehrsmittel **II**
publication [ˌpʌblɪˈkeɪʃn] Veröffentlichung °**IV U3**, 85
to **publish** [ˈpʌblɪʃ] veröffentlichen; publizieren; verlegen **IV U3**, 85
publisher [ˈpʌblɪʃə] Verleger/-in; Verlagshaus ⟨**IV TS3**, 104⟩
pudding [ˈpʊdɪŋ] Pudding; Nachtisch **I**
to **pull** [pʊl] ziehen **I**
to **pull** down [ˌpʊl‿ˈdaʊn] abreißen **III**
to **pull** over [ˌpʊl‿ˈəʊvə] (heranfahren und) anhalten ⟨**IV TS3**, 106⟩
pumpkin pie [ˌpʌmpkɪn ˈpaɪ] Kürbiskuchen ⟨**IV U1**, 15⟩
punch [pʌnʃ] Faustschlag; Boxhieb **IV U4**, 122
to **punch** [pʌnʃ] mit der Faust schlagen; boxen **IV U4**, 125
to **purchase** *(fml)* [ˈpɜːtʃəs] kaufen; erwerben ⟨**IV U4**, 123⟩
purple [ˈpɜːpl] violett; lila **I**
purpose [ˈpɜːpəs] Ziel; Absicht; Zweck **III**
to **push** [pʊʃ] stoßen; schieben; schubsen **II**
to **push** oneself [ˈpʊʃ wʌnˌself] sich alles abverlangen; sich Mühe geben **III**
pushy [ˈpʊʃi] aufdringlich; penetrant; aggressiv **III**
*to **put** [pʊt] setzen; stellen; legen **I**
Put in … [pʊt‿ˈɪn] Setze/Setzt ein … **I**
Put it in … [ˌpʊt‿ɪt‿ˈɪn] Lege/Legt es in …; Stelle/Stellt es in … **I**
*to **put** on [ˌpʊt‿ˈɒn] anziehen **III**
*to **put** through [ˌpʊt‿ˈθruː] verbinden **I**
*to **put** up [ˌpʊt‿ˈʌp] aufstellen; errichten; aufhängen **II**
Put … face down. [pʊt ˌfeɪs ˈdaʊn] Lege/Legt … umgedreht hin. **I**
puzzle [ˈpʌzl] Rätsel; Puzzle **I**
pyjamas *(pl)* [pɪˈdʒɑːməz] Schlafanzug; Pyjama **II**

Q

quality [ˈkwɒləti] Qualität **I**
quarter past/to [ˈkwɔːtə pɑːst/tə] Viertel nach/vor **I**
queen [kwiːn] Königin **II**
question [ˈkwestʃən] Frage **I**
question tag [ˈkwestʃən ˌtæg] Frageanhängsel; Bestätigungsfrage **II**
to **question** [ˈkwestʃən] fragen; hinterfragen **IV TS2**, 73
questionnaire [ˌkwestʃəˈneə] Fragebogen **III**
queue [kjuː] Schlange; Warteschlange **I**
to jump the **queue** [ˌdʒʌmp ðə ˈkjuː] sich vordrängeln **I**
quick [kwɪk] schnell **I**
quickly [ˈkwɪkli] schnell **II**
quiet [kwaɪət] still; ruhig; leise **I**
quill [kwɪl] Federkiel **III**
quite [kwaɪt] ziemlich; ganz; völlig **III**
quiz [kwɪz] Quiz; Rätsel **I**
quotation [kwəˈteɪʃn] Zitat; Belegstelle °**IV U2**, 49
quote [kwəʊt] Zitat **II**

R

rabbit [ˈræbɪt] Kaninchen **I**
race [reɪs] Wettlauf; Rennen **II**
camel **racing** [ˈkæml ˌreɪsɪŋ] Kamelrennen **II**
racist [ˈreɪsɪst] rassistisch; Rassist/-in **IV U4**, 123
racquet [ˈrækɪt] Schläger **II**
radio [ˈreɪdiəʊ] Radio **II**
radioactive [ˌreɪdiəʊˈæktɪv] radioaktiv ⟨**IV U4**, 124⟩
raffle [ˈræfl] Tombola **I**
raft [rɑːft] Floß **IV U4**, 117
rubber **raft** [ˌrʌbə ˈrɑːft] Schlauchboot **IV U4**, 114
rags to riches [ˌrægz tə‿ˈrɪtʃɪz] vom Tellerwäscher zum Millionär **IV U2**, 49
rain [reɪn] Regen **III**
to **rain** [reɪn] regnen **II**
rainbow [ˈreɪnbəʊ] Regenbogen **III**
raincoat [ˈreɪnkəʊt] Regenmantel **III**
to **raise** money [ˌreɪz ˈmʌni] Geld sammeln **II**
ranch [rɑːntʃ; ræntʃ] Ranch **IV TS3**, 103
rap [ræp] Rap **I**
to **rap** [ræp] rappen **I**
rat [ræt] Ratte **I**
to **rate** [reɪt] bewerten; einstufen **IV TS2**, 74
I'd **rather** [aɪd ˈrɑːðə] ich würde lieber **III**
rating [ˈreɪtɪŋ] Kritik **III**
raven [ˈreɪvn] Rabe **II**
raven master [ˈreɪvn ˌmɑːstə] Herr der Raben **II**
RE *(= Religious Education)* [ˌɑːrˈiː; rɪˌlɪdʒəs‿edʒʊˈkeɪʃn] Religion *(Schulfach)* **II**
to **reach** [riːtʃ] erreichen; dran kommen **II**
to **reach** (for) [ˈriːtʃ fə] greifen (nach) **IV U3**, 93
to **react** [riˈækt] reagieren **III**
reaction [riˈækʃn] Reaktion **II**
*to **read** [riːd] lesen **I**
*to **read** out loud [ˌriːd‿aʊt ˈlaʊd] laut vorlesen **III**
reader [ˈriːdə] Leser/-in **I**
*to draw the **reader** into the story/action [ˌdrɔː ðə ˌriːdə ɪntə ðə ˈstɔːri/ˈækʃn] den Leser/die Leserin in die Geschichte/Handlung hineinziehen **III**
reading [ˈriːdɪŋ] Lesen **I**
ready [ˈredi] fertig; bereit **II**
ready meal [ˌredi ˈmiːl] Fertiggericht **I**
real [rɪəl] echt; richtig; wirklich **II**
to **realise** [ˈrɪəlaɪz] erkennen; realisieren **III**
realistic [ˌrɪəˈlɪstɪk] realistisch **II**
reality [riˈæləti] Realität; Wirklichkeit ⟨**IV U4**, 123⟩
to **realize** *(AE)* [ˈrɪəlaɪz] erkennen; realisieren **IV U1**, 22
really [ˈrɪəli] wirklich **I**
reason [ˈriːzn] Grund **II**
*to give **reasons** [ˌgɪv ˈriːznz] Gründe nennen/angeben ⟨**IV U2**, 60⟩
*to **rebuild** [ˌriːˈbɪld] wieder aufbauen **III**
to **receive** [rɪˈsiːv] empfangen; erhalten; bekommen **II**
recent [ˈriːsnt] kürzlich; neueste/-r/-s; letzte/-r/-s **IV U3**, 93
recently [ˈriːsntli] kürzlich; neulich °**IV TS2**, 75
reception [rɪˈsepʃn] Empfang **IV TS3**, 102
receptive [rɪˈseptɪv] empfänglich **IV TS1**, 34
recipe [ˈresɪpi] Rezept **III**
to **recite** [rɪˈsaɪt] vortragen; rezitieren **III**
to **reckon** [ˈrekn] vermuten; meinen ⟨**IV U3**, 93⟩
to **recognize** *(AE)* [ˈrekəgnaɪz] erkennen; anerkennen **IV U3**, 84
to **record** [rɪˈkɔːd] aufnehmen; aufzeichnen **II**
recorder [rɪˈkɔːdə] Flöte **III**
recording [rɪˈkɔːdɪŋ] Aufnahme; Aufzeichnung **I**
recording studio [rɪˈkɔːdɪŋ ˌstjuːdiəʊ] Aufnahmestudio; Tonstudio **I**
recycling [ˌriːˈsaɪklɪŋ] Recycling; Wiederaufbereitung **II**
red [red] rot **I**
redwood (tree) [ˈredwʊd ˌtriː] Mammutbaum **IV AC1**, 9
to **reef** the sails [ˌriːf ðə ˈseɪlz] die Segel einholen **I**

to **refer** to [rɪ'fɜː tə] sich beziehen auf °**IV TS2**, 73
reference article ['refrns ˌɑːtɪkl] Referenzartikel **III**
referendum [ˌrefr'endəm] Referendum; Volksentscheid **III**
reflexive [rɪ'fleksɪv] reflexiv; Reflexiv- **III**
reflexive pronoun [rɪˌfleksɪv 'prəʊnaʊn] Reflexivpronomen **III**
refugee [ˌrefjʊ'dʒiː] Flüchtling **III**
region ['riːdʒn] Region; Gegend **II**
register ['redʒɪstə] Sprachebene; Register **IV AC3**, 76
registration [ˌredʒɪs'treɪʃn] Anwesenheitskontrolle **II**
regular ['regjələ] regelmäßig; gleichmäßig **I**; normal; üblich ⟨**IV U4**, 124⟩
regulator ['regjəleɪtə] Regulator/-in; Aufsicht führende Person °**IV TS2**, 71
to **rehearse** [rɪ'hɜːs] proben **III**
reign [reɪn] Herrschaft; Regierungszeit **III**
to **reign** [reɪn] herrschen; regieren **III**
rejection [rɪ'dʒekʃn] Ablehnung; Absage **IV U2**, 46
to **relate** to [rɪ'leɪt tə] Zugang finden zu **III**
relationship [rɪ'leɪʃnʃɪp] Beziehung **II**
defining **relative** clause [dɪˌfaɪnɪŋ 'relətɪv ˌklɔːz] notwendiger Relativsatz **II**
non-defining **relative** clause [ˌnɒndɪfaɪnɪŋ 'relətɪv ˌklɔːz] nicht notwendiger Relativsatz °**IV U2**, 43
relative pronoun [ˌrelətɪv 'prəʊnaʊn] Relativpronomen **II**
to **relax** [rɪ'læks] sich entspannen; sich ausruhen; sich beruhigen **II**
relaxed [rɪ'lækst] entspannt; locker; gelassen ⟨**IV TS3**, 103⟩
reliable [rɪ'laɪəbl] verlässlich; zuverlässig; vertrauenswürdig **IV TS2**, 70
relieved [rɪ'liːvd] erleichtert **IV U3**, 84
religion [rɪ'lɪdʒn] Religion **IV U1**, 15
to practice a **religion** [ˌpræktɪs‿ə rɪ'lɪdʒn] eine Religion ausüben **IV U1**, 15
religious [rɪ'lɪdʒəs] religiös; gläubig **I**
to **rely** (on) [rɪ'laɪ‿ɒn] sich verlassen (auf); vertrauen (auf) **III**
to **remember** [rɪ'membə] sich erinnern (an); sich merken; denken an **I**
Remember? [rɪ'membə] Erinnerst du dich?; Erinnert ihr euch? **I**
to **remind** (sb of sth/sb) [rɪ'maɪnd əv] (jmdn. an etw./jmdn.) erinnern **III**
to **remove** [rɪ'muːv] entfernen; abreißen **IV U4**, 117
to **rent** (out) [ˌrent‿'aʊt] mieten **III**
to **repeat** [rɪ'piːt] wiederholen **II**
repetition [ˌrepɪ'tɪʃn] Wiederholung **III**
to **replace** (by/with) [rɪ'pleɪs] ersetzen (durch) **IV U3**, 86
reply [rɪ'plaɪ] Antwort; Erwiderung; Entgegnung **I**

to **reply** [rɪ'plaɪ] antworten; erwidern; entgegnen **I**
report [rɪ'pɔːt] Bericht; Meldung **II**
news **report** ['njuːz rɪˌpɔːt] Tatsachenbericht; Nachrichtenbeitrag; Meldung **III**
travel **report** [ˌtrævl rɪ'pɔːt] Reisebericht **II**
to **report** [rɪ'pɔːt] berichten; wiedergeben **III**
reporter [rɪ'pɔːtə] Reporter/-in **II**
to **represent** [ˌreprɪ'zent] repräsentieren; darstellen; stehen für **IV AC1**, 10
republic [rɪ'pʌblɪk] Republik ⟨**IV U1**, 19⟩
request [rɪ'kwest] Bitte **III**
*to **reread** ['riːriːd] noch einmal lesen **III**
rescue ['reskjuː] Rettung **II**
to **rescue** ['reskjuː] retten **III**
research *(no pl)* [rɪ'sɜːtʃ] Recherche; Forschung; Untersuchung **III**
to **research** [rɪ'sɜːtʃ] recherchieren; erforschen; untersuchen °**IV U4**, 121
reservation [ˌrezə'veɪʃn] Reservat **IV U3**, 84
respect [rɪ'spekt] Respekt **IV TS2**, 73
response [rɪ'spɒns] Antwort; Erwiderung; Rückmeldung °**IV TS2**, 73
responsible [rɪs'pɒnsəbl] verantwortlich; verantwortungsvoll **III**
the **rest** [rest] der Rest **I**
restaurant ['restrɒnt] Restaurant; Gaststätte **I**
restroom *(AE)* ['restrʊm] Toilette **IV U1**, 13
result [rɪ'zʌlt] Ergebnis; Resultat **II**
retail ['riːteɪl] Einzelhandel **IV U4**, 110
*to **retell** [ˌriː'tel] nacherzählen; nochmals erzählen **I**
retroactive [ˌretrəʊ'æktɪv] rückwirkend; retro ⟨**IV U4**, 124⟩
return ticket [rɪ'tɜːn ˌtɪkɪt] Hin- und Rückfahrkarte **II**
to **return** [rɪ'tɜːn] zurückkehren; zurückfahren **II**
revision [rɪ'vɪʒn] Wiederholung **II**
*to **rewrite** [ˌriː'raɪt] umschreiben; neu schreiben **III**
rhino ['raɪnəʊ] Rhinozeros; Nashorn **III**
rhyme [raɪm] Reim **I**
rhyme scheme ['raɪm skiːm] Reimschema **III**
to **rhyme** [raɪm] (sich) reimen **III**
rhyming ['raɪmɪŋ] sich reimend **III**
rhythm ['rɪðm] Rhythmus **I**
the **rich** [ðə rɪtʃ] die Reichen **II**
rich [rɪtʃ] reich **III**
rags to **riches** [ˌrægz tə‿'rɪtʃɪz] vom Tellerwäscher zum Millionär **IV U2**, 49
ride [raɪd] Fahrt; Ritt **IV U1**, 14
*to get a **ride** [ˌget‿ə 'raɪd] eine Mitfahrgelegenheit bekommen **IV TS3**, 105
along for the **ride** [əˌlɒŋ fə ðə 'raɪd] mit dabei **IV U1**, 14
*to **ride** [raɪd] fahren; reiten **IV AC1**, 11
rider ['raɪdə] Reiter/-in; Fahrer/-in **IV U3**, 86
rifle ['raɪfl] Gewehr ⟨**IV TS3**, 107⟩

rigging ['rɪgɪŋ] Takelage **I**
right [raɪt] Recht **IV U1**, 18
right [raɪt] richtig; korrekt; rechts; rechte/-r/-s **I**
all **right** [ˌɔːl 'raɪt] in Ordnung; alles klar ⟨**IV U4**, 125⟩
*to be **right** [bi 'raɪt] recht haben **I**
*to get **right** [get 'raɪt] richtig beantworten **II**
on the **right** [ɒn ðə 'raɪt] auf der rechten Seite; rechts **I**
right [raɪt] direkt **IV U1**, 22
right away [ˌraɪt‿ə'weɪ] sofort; gleich **I**
right here [ˌraɪt 'hɪə] genau hier **II**
right now [ˌraɪt 'naʊ] jetzt gleich; sofort; gerade **II**
ring [rɪŋ] Ring **III**
key **ring** ['kiː ˌrɪŋ] Schlüsselbund; Schlüsselanhänger **III**
*to **ring** [rɪŋ] klingeln; läuten **I**; anrufen **III**
ice **rink** ['aɪs ˌrɪŋk] Eisbahn; Schlittschuhbahn **I**
*to **rise** [raɪz] steigen; sich erheben **III**
*to **rise** [raɪz] aufgehen *(Sonne)* **IV U4**, 117
*to **rise** up in one's mind [raɪz‿ʌp ɪn wʌnz 'maɪnd] jmdm. in den Sinn kommen **III**
No **risk**, no fun! [nəʊ ˌrɪsk nəʊ 'fʌn] Wer nicht wagt, der nicht gewinnt. **IV AC2**, 39
*to take a **risk** [ˌteɪk‿ə 'rɪsk] ein Risiko eingehen **III**
to **risk** [rɪsk] riskieren **IV U3**, 86
river ['rɪvə] Fluss **I**
by the **river** [baɪ ðə 'rɪvə] am Fluss **II**
road [rəʊd] Straße **II**
road trip ['rəʊd ˌtrɪp] Tour; Trip ⟨**IV TS3**, 102⟩
road-rage ['rəʊdreɪdʒ] Aggression beim Autofahren ⟨**IV TS3**, 106⟩
to **roar** [rɔː] dröhnen; brüllen; rauschen **III**
roaring ['rɔːrɪŋ] dröhnend; tosend; donnernd **III**
roast turkey [rəʊst 'tɜːki] Putenbraten ⟨**IV U1**, 15⟩
to **rob** [rɒb] ausrauben; rauben; berauben **IV TS3**, 105
robber ['rɒbə] Räuber/-in **II**
robot ['rəʊbɒt] Roboter; Automat ⟨**IV U2**, 60⟩
rock [rɒk] Fels; Stein ⟨**IV TS2**, 71⟩
rock [rɒk] Rock *(Musik)* **III**
rock 'n' roll [ˌrɒk‿ən 'rəʊl] Rock 'n' Roll **II**
to **rock** [rɒk] schaukeln **III**
rocky ['rɒki] felsig; steinig **II**
role [rəʊl] Rolle **I**
role model ['rəʊl ˌmɒdl] Vorbild ⟨**IV U4**, 123⟩
role play ['rəʊl ˌpleɪ] Rollenspiel **I**
to swap **roles** [ˌswɒp 'rəʊlz] Rollen tauschen **I**
bread **roll** ['bred rəʊl] Brötchen **III**
rock 'n' **roll** [ˌrɒk‿ən 'rəʊl] Rock 'n' Roll **II**
to **roll** off [rəʊl] hinunterrollen; herunterrollen **II**

to **roll** one's eyes [ˌrəʊl wʌnz‿'aɪz] die Augen verdrehen **III**
Roll two dice. [ˌrəʊl ˌtu: 'daɪs] Würfle/ Würfelt mit zwei Würfeln. **I**
Roman ['rəʊmən] Römer/-in; römisch **II**
romance [rə'mæns] Liebesgeschichte; Liebesfilm **III**
Romanian [rʊ'meɪniən] Rumäne/Rumänin; rumänisch; Rumänisch **II**
roof [ru:f] Dach **II**
room [ru:m; rʊm] Zimmer; Raum **I**
chat **room** ['tʃæt rʊm] Chatroom **II**
living **room** ['lɪvɪŋ rʊm] Wohnzimmer **I**
side **room** ['saɪd ˌrʊm] Nebenraum **III**
roommate ['ru:mmeɪt] Zimmergenosse/ Zimmergenossin **I**
rope [rəʊp] Seil **III**
rotary phone ['rəʊtri fəʊn] Telefon mit Wählscheibe **III**
rough [rʌf] rau; grob; uneben; holprig **IV TS3**, 102
round [raʊnd] Runde **II**
round of boxing [ˌraʊnd‿əv 'bɒksɪŋ] Boxrunde **II**
the **Round** Table [ðə ˌraʊnd 'teɪbl] die Tafelrunde **II**
round [raʊnd] um … herum **II**
*to go **round** in circles [gəʊ ˌraʊnd ɪn 'sɜ:klz] sich im Kreis drehen **III**
to turn **round** [ˌtɜ:n‿(ə)'raʊnd] (sich) umdrehen; wenden **II**
route [ru:t] Strecke; Route **II**
route planner ['ru:t ˌplænə] Routenplaner **IV AC1**, 11
routine [ru:'ti:n] Routine **III**
royal ['rɔɪəl] königlich **I**
rubber ['rʌbə] Radiergummi **I**
rubber raft [ˌrʌbə 'rɑ:ft] Schlauchboot **IV U4**, 114
rubbish ['rʌbɪʃ] Müll; Gerümpel **I**
rude [ru:d] unhöflich; unverschämt **I**
rug [rʌg] Vorleger; Teppich **IV AC4**, 108
rugby ['rʌgbi] Rugby **II**
to **ruin** ['ru:ɪn] ruinieren; zerstören **II**
rule [ru:l] Regel **I**
What's the **rule** for …? [ˌwɒts ðə 'ru:l fə] Was ist die Regel für …? **I**
to **rule** [ru:l] herrschen; regieren **II**
ruler ['ru:lə] Lineal **I**
run [rʌn] Rennen; Lauf **II**
run area ['rʌn ˌeəriə] Gehege; Auslauf **III**
salmon **run** ['sæmən ˌrʌn] Lachswanderung **IV U4**, 116
*to **run** [rʌn] rennen; laufen **I**; betreiben; leiten; führen **IV TS2**, 72
*to **run** away [ˌrʌn‿ə'weɪ] wegrennen **I**
*to **run** out [ˌrʌn‿'aʊt] ausgehen ⟨**IV TS3**, 103⟩
*to **run** over [ˌrʌn‿'əʊvə] überfahren **IV TS3**, 106
runner ['rʌnə] Läufer/-in **II**
running ['rʌnɪŋ] Laufen; Rennen **II**
rural ['rʊərl] ländlich **IV AC1**, 8
Russian ['rʌʃn] Russe/Russin; russisch; Russisch **IV U3**, 93

S

sacred ['seɪkrɪd] heilig **IV U4**, 117
sad [sæd] traurig **I**
safe [seɪf] sicher; ungefährlich **II**
to reef the **sails** [ˌri:f ðə 'seɪlz] die Segel einholen **I**
to **sail** [seɪl] segeln; umsegeln **III**
sailboat ['seɪlbəʊt] Segelboot **II**
sailor ['seɪlə] Seemann; Matrose **I**
salad ['sæləd] Salat **I**
sale [seɪl] Verkauf **II**
bake **sale** ['beɪk seɪl] Kuchenverkauf ⟨**IV U4**, 124⟩
salmon ['sæmən], **salmon** ['sæmən] *(pl)* Lachs **IV U4**, 116
salmon run ['sæmən ˌrʌn] Lachswanderung **IV U4**, 116
the **same** [ðə 'seɪm] der-/die-/dasselbe; der/ die/das gleiche **I**
the **same** way as [ˌðə seɪm 'weɪ æz] genauso wie **II**
samosa [sə'məʊsə] *mit Kartoffeln oder Hackfleisch gefüllte indische Teigtasche* ⟨**IV U2**, 45⟩
sample ['sɑ:mpl] Probe; Muster **IV TS1**, 34
sandal ['sændl] Sandale **III**
sandwich ['sænwɪdʒ] Sandwich; belegtes Brot **I**
sandy ['sændi] sandig; Sand- **II**
Saturday ['sætədeɪ] Samstag **I**
sauce [sɔ:s] Soße **III**
sausage ['sɒsɪdʒ] Wurst; Bratwurst **III**
to **save** [seɪv] retten; bergen **I**; sparen **III**
to **save** the best for last [ˌseɪv ðə ˌbest fə 'lɑ:st] sich das Beste bis zum Schluss aufheben **IV U2**, 42
saved by the bell [ˌseɪvd baɪ ðə 'bel] noch mal Glück gehabt **III**
sax ['sæks] Saxofon **I**
saxophone ['sæksəfəʊn] Saxofon **I**
*to **say** [seɪ] sagen; aufsagen; sprechen **I**
needless to **say** [ˌni:dləs tə 'seɪ] natürlich; selbstverständlich **IV U2**, 46
*to **say** hello (to) [ˌseɪ hel'əʊ tə] grüßen; Grüße ausrichten (an) **I**
saying ['seɪɪŋ] Redensart; Sprichwort **III**
to **scan** [skæn] scannen; nach Details durchsuchen **II**
to **scare** sb [skeə] jmdm. Angst machen; jmdn. erschrecken **IV TS3**, 102
to **scare** sb to death [ˌskeə tə 'deθ] jmdn. zu Tode erschrecken **IV TS3**, 102
scared [skeəd] verängstigt; ängstlich **IV U1**, 22
*to be **scared** (of) [bi: 'skeəd‿əv] Angst haben (vor) **I**
scary ['skeəri] unheimlich; gruselig; beängstigend **II**
scene [si:n] Szene **I**; Schauplatz **II**
acting a **scene** [ˌæktɪŋ‿ə 'si:n] eine Theaterszene spielen **I**
scenery ['si:nri] Landschaft **IV AC1**, 10
sceptical ['skeptɪkl] skeptisch **IV TS1**, 34
schedule *(AE)* ['ʃedju:l; 'skedʒu:l] Stundenplan; Fahrplan; Terminkalender **IV AC3**, 76
rhyme **scheme** ['raɪm ski:m] Reimschema **III**
schnitzel ['ʃnɪtsl] Schnitzel ⟨**IV U2**, 45⟩
school [sku:l] Schule **I**
grammar **school** ['græmə ˌsku:l] Gymnasium **II**
high **school** *(AE)* ['haɪ ˌsku:l] High School *(weiterführende Schule in den USA, Oberstufe)* **IV U1**, 13
middle **school** *(AE)* ['mɪdl ˌsku:l] Mittelschule *(weiterführende Schule in den USA, Mittelstufe)* **IV U1**, 13
primary **school** ['praɪmri ˌsku:l] Grundschule **I**
school fees *(pl)* ['sku:l fi:z] Schulgeld; Schulgebühren **III**
old **school** ['əʊldsku:l] von der alten Schule ⟨**IV U4**, 124⟩
schoolbag ['sku:lbæg] Schultasche **I**
schoolwork ['sku:lwɜ:k] Schularbeiten **III**
Science [saɪəns] Naturwissenschaften **II**
science [saɪəns] Wissenschaft; Naturwissenschaft **IV TS2**, 70
science fiction [ˌsaɪəns 'fɪkʃn] Science-Fiction *(Zukunftsdichtung)* **II**
scientist ['saɪəntɪst] Wissenschaftler/-in **III**
score [skɔ:] Punktestand; Spielstand **II**
Scot [skɒt] Schotte/Schottin **III**
Scottish ['skɒtɪʃ] schottisch **II**
gorge **scrambling** ['gɔ:dʒ ˌskræmblɪŋ] Schluchtenklettern **II**
to **scrape** [skreɪp] kratzen; schürfen ⟨**IV U4**, 123⟩
scream [skri:m] Schrei ⟨**IV U3**, 89⟩
to **scream** [skri:m] schreien; kreischen **II**
script [skrɪpt] Drehbuch; Skript **III**
sculpture ['skʌlptʃə] Skulptur **IV U2**, 42
sea [si:] Meer **I**
seafood ['si:fu:d] Meeresfrüchte ⟨**IV TS3**, 105⟩
seal [si:l] Siegel °**IV U3**, 80
search [sɜ:tʃ] Suche; Such- **II**
search engine ['sɜ:tʃ‿endʒɪn] Suchmaschine °**IV U1**, 12
to **search** for ['sɜ:tʃ fə] suchen (nach) **III**
seasick ['si:sɪk] seekrank **III**
season ['si:zn] Saison; Jahreszeit **IV U1**, 26
seat [si:t] Sitz; Sitzplatz **III**
passenger **seat** ['pæsndʒə ˌsi:t] Beifahrersitz **IV TS3**, 106
seat belt ['si:t belt] Sicherheitsgurt **IV TS3**, 106
second ['seknd] Sekunde **IV U4**, 115

Just a **second** … [ˌdʒʌst‿ə 'seknd] Einen Augenblick … **IV U4**, 115
second ['seknd] zweite/-r/-s **I**
secret ['siːkrət] Geheimnis **II**
in **secret** [ɪn 'siːkrət] heimlich **II**
secret ['siːkrət] geheim **III**
section ['sekʃn] Abschnitt; Paragraf **II**
security [sɪ'kjʊərəti] Sicherheit; Schutz; Wachdienst; Wach-; Sicherheits- **III**
*to **see** [siː] sehen **I**
*to **see** the bigger picture [ˌsiː ðə ˌbɪgə 'pɪktʃə] über den Tellerrand hinausschauen **IV U4**, 120
See you! ['siː jə] Bis dann!; Bis … **I**
I can't **see** the point of … [aɪ ˌkɑːnt siː ðə 'pɔɪnt‿əv] Ich sehe keinen Sinn darin … **IV AC2**, 39
Wait and **see**! [ˌweɪt‿ənd 'siː] Warte ab! **I**
to **seem** [siːm] scheinen **III**
self [self], **selves** [selvz] *(pl)* das Selbst **III**
self-critical ['selfˌkrɪtɪkl] selbstkritisch **II**
self-evaluation [ˌselfɪˌvælju'eɪʃn] Selbsteinschätzung **I**
selfie ['selfi] Selfie **II**
*to **sell** [sel] verkaufen **I**
seller ['selə] Verkäufer/-in *(auf einem Flohmarkt)* **I**
*to **send** [send] schicken; senden **I**
*to **send** off [send‿'ɒf] abschicken **II**
senior ['siːniə] Schüler/-in im letzten Schuljahr ⟨**IV U4**, 122⟩
sense [sens] Sinn **III**
*to make **sense** [ˌmeɪk 'sens] Sinn ergeben; einleuchten **IV TS2**, 72
sense of humour *(no pl)* [ˌsens‿əv 'hjuːmə] Sinn für Humor **III**
sensible ['sensɪbl] vernünftig **III**
sentence ['sentəns] Satz **I**
conditional **sentence** [kənˌdɪʃnl 'sentəns] Bedingungssatz **II**
sentimental [ˌsentɪ'mentl] sentimental ⟨**IV U4**, 125⟩
to **separate** ['sepreɪt] (sich) trennen °**IV U2**, 43
separate ['seprət] separat; getrennt; verschieden **II**
September [sep'tembə] September **I**
sequence ['siːkwəns] Sequenz; Szene **III**; Abfolge; Reihenfolge **IV U2**, 59
series ['sɪəriːz], **series** ['sɪəriːz] *(pl)* Serie **III**
serious ['sɪəriəs] ernsthaft; ernst **I**
servant ['sɜːvnt] Diener/-in; Bedienstete/-r ⟨**IV TS3**, 107⟩
service ['sɜːvɪs] Service; Dienstleistung; Dienst **IV U2**, 42
set [set] Umgebung; Rahmen **II**; Aufnahmeort; Drehort **III**
a **set** of [ə 'set‿əv] eine Liste von **III**
*to be **set** (in) [bi 'set ɪn] spielen (in); seinen Schauplatz haben (in) **III**
*to **set** off [ˌset‿'ɒf] *hier:* ein Feuerwerk zünden **III**
*to **set** the table [ˌset ðə 'teɪbl] den Tisch decken **IV AC4**, 108
*to **set** up [ˌset‿'ʌp] einrichten; aufbauen **I**
setting ['setɪŋ] Schauplatz; Rahmen **II**
account **settings** [ə'kaʊnt ˌsetɪŋz] Profileinstellungen **III**
to **settle for less** [ˌsetl fə 'les] sich mit weniger zufrieden geben **IV TS1**, 36
settlement ['setlmənt] Siedlung **IV U3**, 80
settler ['setlə] Siedler/-in **IV U3**, 81
seven ['sevn] sieben **I**
several ['sevrl] einige; mehrere; verschiedene **II**
shadow ['ʃædəʊ] Schatten **III**
*to **shake** [ʃeɪk] schütteln ⟨**IV U2**, 60⟩
shallow ['ʃæləʊ] seicht; flach ⟨**IV U3**, 92⟩
shampoo [ʃæm'puː] Shampoo **IV TS1**, 34
shape [ʃeɪp] Form **IV U2**, 59
to **shape** [ʃeɪp] formen **IV U3**, 89
to **share** [ʃeə] teilen **II**
shark [ʃɑːk] Hai **III**
sharp [ʃɑːp] scharf; schneidend **III**
to **shave** [ʃeɪv] (sich) rasieren ⟨**IV U4**, 122⟩
she [ʃiː] sie **I**
sheep [ʃiːp], **sheep** [ʃiːp] *(pl)* Schaf **II**
bighorn **sheep** [ˌbɪghɔːn 'ʃiːp] Dickhornschaf **IV TS3**, 103
cheat **sheet** ['tʃiːt ʃiːt] Spickzettel **IV AC2**, 39
shelter ['ʃeltə] Obdach; Schutz; Schutzhütte ⟨**IV U4**, 125⟩
animal **shelter** ['ænɪml ˌʃeltə] Tierheim **III**
homeless **shelter** ['həʊmləs ˌʃeltə] Obdachlosenunterkunft **IV U1**, 21
*to **shine** [ʃaɪn] scheinen; glänzen **II**
shinty ['ʃɪnti] Shinty *(eine Art Hockey)* **III**
ship [ʃɪp] Schiff **I**
shipbuilding ['ʃɪpbɪldɪŋ] Schiffsbau **III**
shirt [ʃɜːt] Hemd; Shirt ⟨**IV U4**, 123⟩
shit *(vulg)* [ʃɪt] Scheiße; Scheißdreck ⟨**IV U2**, 54⟩
shock [ʃɒk] Schock **II**
shocked [ʃɒkt] schockiert; geschockt **III**
shoe [ʃuː] Schuh **I**
*to be in sb's **shoes** [ˌbiː ɪn sʌmbɒdɪz 'ʃuːz] an jmds. Stelle sein; in jmds. Haut stecken **III**
tennis **shoes** ['tenɪs ˌʃuːz] Tennisschuhe ⟨**IV U4**, 123⟩
in Jay's **shoes** [ɪn dʒeɪz 'ʃuːz] an Jays Stelle **III**
on a **shoestring** [ˌɒn‿ə 'ʃuːstrɪŋ] für/mit wenig Geld **IV U2**, 42
photo **shoot** ['fəʊtəʊ ˌʃuːt] Fotoshooting; Fotoaufnahmen **III**
*to **shoot** [ʃuːt‿(ət)] schießen (auf) **III**
shop [ʃɒp] Geschäft; Laden **I**
charity **shop** ['tʃærɪti ʃɒp] Second-Hand-Laden **I**
pawn **shop** ['pɔːn ʃɒp] Pfandhaus; Pfandleihe **III**
to **shop** [ʃɒp] einkaufen; shoppen **IV U2**, 46
shopper ['ʃɒpə] Käufer/-in **IV U1**, 18
shopping ['ʃɒpɪŋ] Einkaufen; Einkäufe **I**
*to do the **shopping** [ˌduː ðə 'ʃɒpɪŋ] Einkäufe machen; Besorgungen machen **III**
*to go **shopping** [ˌgəʊ 'ʃɒpɪŋ] einkaufen gehen **I**
shopping mall ['ʃɒpɪŋ ˌmɔːl] Einkaufszentrum **IV U1**, 13
shore [ʃɔː] Ufer; Küste **II**
short [ʃɔːt] kurz **I**
*to have a **short** shelf life [ˌhæv‿ə ˌʃɔːt 'ʃelf laɪf] eine kurze Haltbarkeit haben ⟨**IV U4**, 124⟩
short answer [ˌʃɔːt‿'ɑːnsə] Kurzantwort **I**
short form ['ʃɔːt fɔːm] Kurzform **I**
shorts *(pl)* [ʃɔːts] Shorts; kurze Hose **II**
shot [ʃɒt] Einstellung; Kameraeinstellung **II**; Aufnahme **III**
long **shot** ['lɒŋ ʃɒt] Totale *(Kameraeinstellung)* **IV U2**, 59
medium **shot** ['miːdiəm ˌʃɒt] Halbtotale *(Kameraeinstellung)* **IV U2**, 59
should [ʃʊd] sollte; solltest; sollten; solltet **II**
shouldn't ['ʃʊdnt] sollte(n) nicht **II**
shoulder ['ʃəʊldə] Schulter **II**
to **shout** [ʃaʊt] schreien; rufen **I**
show [ʃəʊ] Show; Schau; Aufführung **II**
comedy **show** ['kɒmədi ˌʃəʊ] Comedy Show **II**
living history **show** [ˌlɪvɪŋ 'hɪstəri ˌʃəʊ] *Show, in der historischer Alltag nachgespielt wird* **II**
talent **show** ['tælənt ˌʃəʊ] Talentwettbewerb **I**
to **show** [ʃəʊ] zeigen **I**
to **show** off [ʃəʊ‿'ɒf] angeben **II**
to **show** sb around (a place) [ˌʃəʊ‿ə'raʊnd] jmdn. (an einem Ort) herumführen ⟨**IV AC4**, 109⟩
shower ['ʃaʊə] Dusche **I**
show-off ['ʃəʊ‿ɒf] Angeber/-in **III**
to **shuffle** ['ʃʌfl] mischen **II**
shutter ['ʃʌtə] Fensterladen **III**
shy [ʃaɪ] schüchtern **II**
sick [sɪk] krank; unwohl **II**
*to be **sick** [bi 'sɪk] sich übergeben **III**
*to feel **sick** [ˌfiːl 'sɪk] Übelkeit verspüren; sich schlecht fühlen **II**
side [saɪd] Seite **II**
side room ['saɪd ˌrʊm] Nebenraum **III**
sidewalk *(AE)* ['saɪdwɔːk] Gehweg; Gehsteig **IV U2**, 46
sight [saɪt] Sehenswürdigkeit; Anblick **II**; *hier:* Blick **III**
sighting ['saɪtɪŋ] Sichten °**IV TS2**, 75
sightseeing ['saɪtsiːɪŋ] Sightseeing-; Besichtigungs- **II**
sign [saɪn] Zeichen; Schild **II**
to **sign** [saɪn] unterschreiben; unterzeichnen **IV U1**, 22
signal ['sɪgnl] Signal; Empfang **III**
signal word ['sɪgnəl ˌwɜːd] Signalwort **I**

silence *(no pl)* ['saɪləns] Stille; Schweigen; Ruhe **III**
silent ['saɪlənt] still; ruhig; schweigsam; stumm **III**
silly ['sɪli] Dummkopf **II**
silly ['sɪli] dumm; doof; albern **I**
silver ['sɪlvə] Silber **II**
similar ['sɪmɪlə] ähnlich **II**
similarity [ˌsɪmɪ'lærəti] Ähnlichkeit; Gemeinsamkeit °**IV TS1**, 37
simple ['sɪmpl] einfach; simpel **III**
simple past [ˌsɪmpl 'pɑ:st] Vergangenheitsform **II**
simple present [ˌsɪmpl 'preznt] Gegenwart; Präsens **I**
simply ['sɪmpli] einfach nur **IV AC1**, 10
since [sɪns] da **IV U2**, 42
since *(+ Zeitpunkt)* [sɪns] seit; seitdem **III**
*to **sing** [sɪŋ] singen **I**
*to **sing** along [ˌsɪŋ‿ə'lɒŋ] mitsingen **III**
*to **sing** out loud [ˌsɪŋ‿aʊt 'laʊd] laut vorsingen **III**
singer ['sɪŋə] Sänger/-in **II**
single ['sɪŋgl] einzeln; einzig; alleinstehend **IV AC1**, 8
single ticket ['sɪŋgl ˌtɪkɪt] einfache Fahrkarte **II**
*to **sink** [sɪŋk] untergehen; sinken **III**
Dear **Sir** or Madam [dɪə ˌsɜ:r‿ɔ: 'mædəm] Sehr geehrte Dame, sehr geehrter Herr **II**
sister ['sɪstə] Schwester **I**
half-**sister** ['hɑ:fˌsɪstə] Halbschwester **I**
*to **sit** [sɪt] sitzen **I**
Sit! [sɪt] Sitz! *(Befehl für Hunde)*; Platz! *(Befehl für Hunde)* **I**
*to **sit** down [ˌsɪt 'daʊn] sich hinsetzen; sich setzen **I**
*to **sit** face to face [ˌsɪt feɪs tə ˌfeɪs] sich gegenüber sitzen **I**
site [saɪt] Webseite **II**
situation [ˌsɪtju'eɪʃn] Situation **I**
six [sɪks] sechs **I**
size [saɪz] Größe; Kleidergröße **I**
*to be sb's **size** [ˌbi sʌmbɒdiz 'saɪz] so groß sein wie jmd. ⟨**IV U4**, 122⟩
to **skate** [skeɪt] Inlineskates fahren; Schlittschuh laufen **I**
skateboard ['skeɪtbɔ:d] Skateboard **II**
skateboarding ['skeɪtbɔ:dɪŋ] Skateboardfahren **I**
skates *(pl)* [skeɪts] Inlineskates; Rollschuhe; Schlittschuhe **I**
(inline) **skating** ['ɪnlaɪn ˌskeɪtɪŋ] Inlineskatefahren **I**
skill [skɪl] Fertigkeit; Geschick **I**
to **skim** [skɪm] überfliegen **II**
skin [skɪn] Haut; Fell **IV U4**, 122
skinny ['skɪni] dünn; mager **IV U3**, 86
to **skip** [skɪp] auslassen; schwänzen **IV AC2**, 38
skirt [skɜ:t] Rock **II**
sky [skaɪ] Himmel **III**
skyscraper ['skaɪskreɪpə] Wolkenkratzer **IV AC1**, 9
slave [sleɪv] Sklave/Sklavin **III**
sleep [sli:p] Schlaf **III**
*to **sleep** [sli:p] schlafen **I**
sleepover ['sli:pˌəʊvə] Übernachtung **I**
to **slice** [slaɪs] in Scheiben schneiden **I**
slide [slaɪd] Rutschbahn **I**
water **slide** ['wɔ:tə ˌslaɪd] Wasserrutsche **I**
*to **slide** [slaɪd] gleiten lassen ⟨**IV U2**, 60⟩
to **slip** into [slɪp‿'ɪntə] schlüpfen in °**IV TS1**, 37
slogan ['sləʊgən] Slogan; Werbespruch **II**
time **slot** ['taɪm slɒt] Zeitfenster **II**
to **slow** down [ˌsləʊ 'daʊn] langsamer werden; bremsen ⟨**IV U2**, 60⟩
slow [sləʊ] langsam **I**
to step into a story **slowly** [step‿ˌɪntʊ ə ˌstɔ:ri 'sləʊli] eine Geschichte langsam entwickeln **III**
small [smɔ:l] klein **I**
small talk ['smɔ:l ˌtɔ:k] Smalltalk **III**
smart [smɑ:t] schlau; klug; intelligent **III**
smartcard ['smɑ:tkɑ:d] Chipkarte **II**
smartphone ['smɑ:tfəʊn] Smartphone **II**
to **smash** [smæʃ] zerschlagen; zerschmettern **III**
*to **smell** [smel] riechen; duften **III**
smile [smaɪl] Lächeln **I**
to **smile** [smaɪl] lächeln **I**
smoke [sməʊk] Rauch **III**
smoky ['sməʊki] verraucht **III**
smuggler ['smʌglə] Schmuggler/-in **III**
snack [snæk] Snack; Imbiss **I**
snack bar ['snæk ˌbɑ:] Café; Imbissstube **I**
word **snake** ['wɜ:d ˌsneɪk] Wortschlange **I**
*to **sneak** [sni:k] schleichen; schmuggeln **IV U2**, 42
*to **sneak** around [ˌsni:k‿ə'raʊnd] herumschleichen **II**
to **snore** [snɔ:] schnarchen **I**
snow [snəʊ] Schnee **III**
snow tire *(AE)* ['snəʊ ˌtaɪə] Winterreifen **IV TS3**, 103
snow-capped ['snəʊkæpt] schneebedeckt **IV TS3**, 103
so [səʊ] so; also **I**
so far [ˌsəʊ 'fɑ:] bis jetzt **II**
so is ['səʊ ɪz] ebenso wie **III**
so (that) [ˌsəʊ 'ðæt] damit; so dass **IV AC2**, 39
to **soak** up [səʊk‿'ʌp] aufsaugen **III**
soccer *(AE)* ['sɒkə] Fußball **IV U1**, 14
social ['səʊʃl] sozial; gesellschaftlich **IV U1**, 16
social media [ˌsəʊʃl 'mi:diə] soziale Netzwerke **IV U1**, 16
social network [ˌsəʊʃl 'netwɜ:k] soziales Netzwerk **II**
society [sə'saɪəti] Verein; Gesellschaft **II**
soda pop *(AE)* ['səʊdə ˌpɒp] Limo **IV U4**, 124
sofa ['səʊfə] Sofa; Couch **I**
software ['sɒftweə] Software *(Computerprogramme)* **IV U4**, 110
software manual ['sɒftweə ˌmænjuəl] Softwarehandbuch **III**
soldier ['səʊldʒə] Soldat/-in **III**
solution [sə'lu:ʃn] Lösung **II**
to **solve** [sɒlv] lösen **II**
Somali [sə'mɑ:li] Somali **III**
some [sʌm; səm] einige; ein paar; etwas **I**
somebody ['sʌmbədi] jemand **I**
someone ['sʌmwʌn] jemand **II**
something ['sʌmθɪŋ] etwas **I**
sometimes ['sʌmtaɪmz] manchmal **I**
somewhere ['sʌmweə] irgendwo **II**
son [sʌn] Sohn **III**
song [sɒŋ] Song; Lied **I**
theme **song** ['θi:m sɒŋ] Titelmelodie °**IV U2**, 61
soon [su:n] bald **II**
as **soon** as [əz 'su:n‿əz] sobald **II**
Sorry! ['sɒri] Entschuldigung!; Tut mir leid! **I**
*to be **sorry** [bi: 'sɒri] leid tun **I**
*to feel **sorry** for [ˌfi:l 'sɒri fɔ:] Mitleid haben mit; bedauern **III**
I'm **sorry**! [ˌaɪm 'sɒri] Tut mir leid! **I**
to **sort** [sɔ:t] sortieren °**IV U3**, 88
to **sort** into [sɔ:t 'ɪntʊ] einsortieren; sortieren nach **III**
soul [səʊl] Seele **IV U4**, 112
You've got no **soul**! [ju:v ˌgɒt nəʊ 'səʊl] *hier:* Du hast kein Feingefühl! **IV U4**, 112
sound [saʊnd] Ton; Geräusch; Klang **I**
to **sound** [saʊnd] klingen **I**
soup [su:p] Suppe **III**
source [sɔ:s] Quelle **II**
south [saʊθ] Süden; Süd- **II**
South Korean [ˌsaʊθ kə'ri:ən] Südkoreaner/-in; südkoreanisch; Südkoreanisch **II**
the **Southeast** [ðə ˌsaʊθ'i:st] der Südosten ⟨**IV U3**, 84⟩
southern ['sʌðən] südlich; Süd- ⟨**IV TS3**, 107⟩
(the) **Southwest** [ˌsaʊθ'west] (der) Südwesten; im Südwesten; südwestlich **IV AC1**, 8
souvenir [ˌsu:vn'ɪə] Souvenir; Andenken **II**
space [speɪs] Raum; Fläche; Platz; Ort **II**
*to leave **space** [li:v 'speɪs] Platz lassen **I**
space [speɪs] Weltraum; Weltall **IV TS2**, 74
space program ['speɪs ˌprəʊgræm] Raumfahrtprogramm **IV TS2**, 74
spaceship ['speɪsʃɪp] Raumschiff **II**
Spanish ['spænɪʃ] spanisch; Spanisch; die Spanier **III**
spark [spɑ:k] Funke ⟨**IV U3**, 89⟩
sparkling ['spɑ:klɪŋ] glitzernd; funkelnd **IV TS3**, 103
sparse [spɑ:s] dünn; spärlich **IV AC1**, 8
*to **speak** [spi:k] sprechen **I**
speaker ['spi:kə] Redner/-in; Sprecher/-in **I**
speaking ['spi:kɪŋ] Sprechen **I**
spear [spɪə] Speer **II**
special ['speʃl] besonders; speziell **I**

special effect [ˌspeʃl‿ɪˈfekt] Spezialeffekt **IV TS2**, 75
special offer [ˌspeʃl‿ˈɒfə] Sonderangebot **I**
with **special** needs [wɪð ˌspeʃl ˈniːdz] behindert **II**
specialty *(AE)* [ˈspeʃlti] Spezialität; Besonderheit **IV U2**, 45
specific [spəˈsɪfɪk] spezifisch; speziell **III**
spectacular [spekˈtækjələ] spektakulär **III**
speech [spiːtʃ] Rede **III**
direct **speech** [dɪˌrekt ˈspiːtʃ] direkte Rede **III**
indirect **speech** [ˌɪndɪrekt ˈspiːtʃ] indirekte Rede **III**
speech bubble [ˈspiːtʃ ˌbʌbl] Sprechblase **I**
speed [spiːd] Geschwindigkeit **IV U2**, 59
*to **spell** [spel] buchstabieren **I**
spelling [ˈspelɪŋ] Rechtschreibung **I**
*to **spend** [spend] ausgeben *(Geld)* **I**; verbringen *(Zeit)* **II**
to **spice** up [ˌspaɪs‿ˈʌp] aufpeppen **IV TS1**, 35
spicy [ˈspaɪsi] würzig; pikant **IV U3**, 93
spider [ˈspaɪdə] Spinne **III**
spike [spaɪk] Spitze; Stachel **IV U2**, 44
*to **spill** [spɪl] verschütten; auslaufen **III**
spirit [ˈspɪrɪt] Geist; Stimmung **IV U3**, 89
spirit world [ˈspɪrɪt ˌwɜːld] Geisterreich ⟨**IV TS3**, 107⟩
spiritual [ˈspɪrɪtjuəl] spirituell; geistig **IV U4**, 116
in **spite** of [ɪn ˈspaɪt‿əv] trotz **IV U3**, 93
spoken [ˈspəʊkn] gesprochen **II**
sponge [spʌndʒ] Rühr-; Biskuit- **I**
spontaneous [spɒnˈteɪniəs] spontan **II**
spoon [spuːn] Löffel **III**
sport [spɔːt] Sport; Sportart **I**
spot [spɒt] Fleck; Ort **IV U2**, 45
spray [spreɪ] Spray ⟨**IV U2**, 56⟩
spring [sprɪŋ] Frühling **III**
squirrel [ˈskwɪrəl] Eichhörnchen **I**
stadium [ˈsteɪdiəm] Stadion **II**
stage [steɪdʒ] Bühne **III**
stage direction [ˈsteɪdʒ dɪˌrekʃn] Regieanweisung **III**
to **stage** [steɪdʒ] aufführen **III**; inszenieren **IV TS2**, 72
staircase [ˈsteəkeɪs] Treppenhaus; Treppenaufgang ⟨**IV TS3**, 107⟩
stairs *(pl)* [steəz] Treppe **III**
*to **stand** [stænd] stehen **I**
*to **stand** in line *(AE)* [ˌstænd‿ɪn ˈlaɪn] anstehen; Schlange stehen; (sich) anstellen **IV AC2**, 39
*to **stand** in the way of sb/sth [ˌstænd ɪn ðə ˈweɪ‿əv] jmdm./etw. im Weg stehen **III**
*to **stand** up [ˌstænd‿ˈʌp] aufstehen *(von einer Sitzgelegenheit)* **I**
standard of living [ˌstændəd‿əv ˈlɪvɪŋ] Lebensstandard **IV AC1**, 10
star [stɑː] Star; Stern **I**
to **stare** [steə] starren; anstarren **I**
start [stɑːt] Anfang; Start **III**
to **start** [stɑːt] anfangen; beginnen; starten **I**; *hier:* gründen **III**
*to get **started** [ˌget ˈstɑːtɪd] anfangen **II**
to **start** all over again [ˌstɑːt‿ɔːl‿ˈəʊvər‿əˌgen] ganz von vorn beginnen **IV U3**, 85
to **start** off [ˌstɑːt‿ˈɒf] anfangen; beginnen; starten **IV U3**, 87
starting place [ˈstɑːtɪŋ pleɪs] Startpunkt **II**
starvation *(no pl)* [stɑːˈveɪʃn] Hungertod; Verhungern ⟨**IV U4**, 125⟩
state [steɪt] Staat; Bundesstaat; Land **IV AC1**, 9
head of **state** [ˌhed‿əv ˈsteɪt] Staatsoberhaupt **II**
to **state** [steɪt] darlegen; darstellen °**IV U4**, 112
statement [ˈsteɪtmənt] Aussage; Behauptung; Erklärung **II**
station [ˈsteɪʃn] Haltestelle; Bahnhof; Station **I**; Sender **II**
bus **station** [ˈbʌs ˌsteɪʃn] Busbahnhof **I**
statistics *(pl)* [stəˈtɪstɪks] Statistik **IV U3**, 85
statue [ˈstætʃuː] Statue; Standbild **IV U2**, 44
to **stay** [steɪ] bleiben **I**; übernachten **II**
to **stay** awake [ˌsteɪ‿əˈweɪk] wach bleiben ⟨**IV U2**, 60⟩
to **stay** away from [ˌsteɪ‿əˈweɪ frəm] fernbleiben von; meiden **II**
to **stay** in touch (with) [ˌsteɪ ɪn ˈtʌtʃ wɪð] in Kontakt bleiben (mit) **II**
to **stay** with [ˈsteɪ wɪð] wohnen bei **II**
Stay the way you are. [ˌsteɪ ðə weɪ ju ˈɑː] Bleib wie du bist. **III**
steady [ˈstedi] kontinuierlich; unaufhörlich **III**
steak [steɪk] Steak **I**
*to **steal** [stiːl] stehlen **II**
steam [stiːm] Dampf **III**
steam engine [ˈstiːm‿endʒɪn] Dampfmaschine **III**
step [step] Stufe; Schritt **I**
step-by-**step** [ˌstepbaɪˈstep] Schritt-für-Schritt- **II**
to **step** [step] treten; steigen **IV TS2**, 71
to **step** into a story slowly [step‿ˌɪntʊ ə ˌstɔːri ˈsləʊli] eine Geschichte langsam entwickeln **III**
stepmum [ˈstepmʌm] Stiefmutter **I**
*to **stick** [stɪk] stecken ⟨**IV U2**, 58⟩
*to **stick** out [ˌstɪk‿ˈaʊt] hinausstrecken **IV TS3**, 105
still [stɪl] Standbild **II**
still [stɪl] still **I**
*to keep one's feet or hands **still** [ˌkiːp wʌnz‿ˈfiːt‿ɔː ˈhændz stɪl] die Beine und Hände ruhig halten **III**
still [stɪl] noch; immer noch **I**; dennoch **II**
*to **sting** [stɪŋ] stechen **III**
stomach [ˈstʌmək] Magen; Bauch **II**
stomachache [ˈstʌməkeɪk] Bauchschmerzen; Bauchweh **II**
stone [stəʊn] Stein; Stein- **III**
stop [stɒp] Haltestelle; Halt **II**
to **stop** [stɒp] aufhören (mit); anhalten; stoppen **I**
Stop and think [ˌstɒp‿ənd ˈθɪŋk] Warte/Wartet und denk/denkt nach. **I**
Stop it! [ˈstɒp‿ɪt] Mach/Macht das aus!; Hör/Hört auf! **I**
store *(AE)* [stɔː] Laden; Geschäft **IV U1**, 14
storm [stɔːm] Sturm **I**
story [ˈstɔːri], **stories** [ˈstɔːriz] *(pl)* Story; Geschichte; Erzählung **I**
photo **story** [ˈfəʊtəʊ ˌstɔːri] Fotostory; Bildgeschichte **I**
to step into a **story** slowly [step‿ˌɪntʊ ə ˌstɔːri ˈsləʊli] eine Geschichte langsam entwickeln **III**
storyline [ˈstɔːrilaɪn] Handlung °**IV U1**, 24
storyteller [ˈstɔːriˌtelə] Geschichtenerzähler/-in **IV TS3**, 106
straight [streɪt] gerade; direkt; geradewegs **III**
straight away [ˌstreɪt‿əˈweɪ] sofort; gleich **III**
straight on [streɪt‿ˈɒn] geradeaus **I**
strange [streɪndʒ] fremd; seltsam; merkwürdig **I**
stranger [ˈstreɪndʒə] Fremde/-r **IV U3**, 80
strategy [ˈstrætədʒi] Strategie **IV U4**, 124
street [striːt] Straße *(in der Stadt)* **I**
in the **street** [ˌɪn ðə ˈstriːt] in der Straße; auf der Straße **I**
the high **street** [ðə ˈhaɪ ˌstriːt] die Haupteinkaufsstraße **III**
streetlight [ˈstriːtlaɪt] Straßenlampe ⟨**IV U2**, 60⟩
strength [streŋθ] Stärke; Kraft ⟨**IV U4**, 125⟩
stress [stres] Betonung **III**
to **stress** [stres] betonen; hervorheben **III**
*to be **stressed** out [bi ˌstrest‿ˈaʊt] völlig gestresst sein **III**
to **stretch** [stretʃ] strecken; dehnen ⟨**IV TS3**, 103⟩
strict [strɪkt] streng; strikt **III**
stringy [ˈstrɪŋi] strähnig ⟨**IV U2**, 60⟩
stripe [straɪp] Streifen **IV U3**, 89
strong [strɒŋ] stark **II**
structure [ˈstrʌktʃə] Struktur; Aufbau; Gliederung **III**
to **structure** [ˈstrʌktʃə] strukturieren; gliedern °**IV TS2**, 75
struggle [ˈstrʌgl] Anstrengung; Kampf **IV U4**, 124
to **struggle** [ˈstrʌgl] kämpfen; Mühe haben; ringen **IV U4**, 123
*to be **stuck** [bi ˈstʌk] festsitzen; feststecken; hängen bleiben **IV U3**, 94
stuck in the middle of … [ˌstʌk ɪn ðə ˈmɪdl‿əv] mitten in … stecken; feststecken in … **III**
student [ˈstjuːdnt] Schüler/-in; Student/-in **I**
exchange **student** [ɪksˈtʃeɪndʒ ˌstjuːdnt] Austauschschüler/-in **III**

student exchange ['stju:dnt ɪksˌtʃeɪndʒ] Schüleraustausch **III**
studies *(pl)* ['stʌdiz] Studium; Lernen; Arbeit für die Schule **II**
studio ['stju:diəʊ] Studio; Atelier **IV U2**, 42
recording **studio** [rɪ'kɔ:dɪŋ ˌstju:diəʊ] Aufnahmestudio; Tonstudio **I**
to **study** ['stʌdi] studieren; lernen **III**
stuff [stʌf] Zeug **I**
stupid ['stju:pɪd] dumm; blöd **II**
style [staɪl] Stil **III**
stylistic [staɪ'lɪstɪk] Stil-; stilistisch **IV U2**, 59
subject ['sʌbdʒɪkt] Schulfach; Subjekt; Satzgegenstand **II**; Thema **III**
substitute ['sʌbstɪtju:t] Ersatz; Ersatz- **II**
suburb ['sʌbɜ:b] Vorort **IV U1**, 13
suburban [sə'bɜ:bn] Vorstadt- **IV U1**, 13
subway *(AE)* ['sʌbweɪ] U-Bahn **IV U2**, 44
to **succeed** (in) [sək'si:d‿ɪn] Erfolg haben (in/bei/mit) **III**
success [sək'ses] Erfolg **III**
successful [sək'sesfl] erfolgreich **III**
such [sʌtʃ] solch; solche/-r/-s **II**
It **sucks**. *(slang)* [ɪt 'sʌks] Das ist zum Kotzen. **IV AC3**, 77
sudden ['sʌdn] plötzlich ⟨**IV U4**, 125⟩
suddenly ['sʌdnli] plötzlich; auf einmal **I**
to **suffer** (from) ['sʌfə frəm] leiden (unter) **IV U3**, 81
sugar ['ʃʊgə] Zucker **III**
to **suggest** [sə'dʒest] vorschlagen **III**; andeuten; nahelegen **IV U3**, 85
suggestion [sə'dʒestʃn] Vorschlag; Anregung **I**
suit [su:t] Anzug; Kostüm **IV U4**, 124
suitcase ['su:tkeɪs] Koffer **III**
to **sum** up [ˌsʌm‿'ʌp] zusammenfassen **II**
to **summarise** ['sʌmraɪz] zusammenfassen **III**
to **summarize** *(AE)* ['sʌmraɪz] zusammenfassen **IV U3**, 85
summary ['sʌmri] Zusammenfassung **III**
summer ['sʌmə] Sommer **II**
summer camp ['sʌmə kæmp] Sommerferienlager **II**
summit ['sʌmɪt] Gipfel; Berggipfel **IV TS3**, 103
sun [sʌn] Sonne **II**
Sunday ['sʌndeɪ] Sonntag **I**
sunflower ['sʌnflaʊə] Sonnenblume **III**
sunset ['sʌnset] Sonnenuntergang **IV U2**, 42
super ['su:pə] super **IV U1**, 14
superhero ['su:pəˌhɪərəʊ] Superheld **IV U4**, 125
superlative [su:'pɜ:lətɪv] Superlativ **II**
supermarket ['su:pəˌmɑ:kɪt] Supermarkt **I**
supernatural ['su:pəˌnætʃrl] übernatürlich **III**
superpower ['su:pəˌpaʊə] Supermacht **II**
supper ['sʌpə] spätes Abendessen ⟨**IV U2**, 56⟩
supply [sə'plaɪ] Vorrat; Versorgung ⟨**IV U3**, 93⟩
to **supply** [sə'plaɪ] versorgen **II**
support *(no pl)* [sə'pɔ:t] Unterstützung; Hilfe **IV U4**, 116
to **support** [sə'pɔ:t] unterstützen **III**
sure [ʃʊə; ʃɔ:] sicher **I**
*to make **sure** [ˌmeɪk 'ʃɔ:] sich versichern **I**
I'm (not) **sure** … [ˌaɪm nɒt 'ʃʊə] Ich bin mir (nicht) sicher … **III**
surface ['sɜ:fɪs] Oberfläche **IV TS2**, 71
surfer ['sɜ:fə] Surfer/-in; Wellenreiter/-in ⟨**IV TS3**, 107⟩
surfing ['sɜ:fɪŋ] Surfen **II**
surgery ['sɜ:dʒəri] Arztpraxis; Praxis; Praxisräume **I**
surprise [sə'praɪz] Überraschung **I**
to **surprise** [sə'praɪz] überraschen **II**
*to be **surprised** [bi sə'praɪzd] überrascht sein **II**
surprising [sə'praɪzɪŋ] überraschend **II**
to **surround** [sə'raʊnd] umgeben; umringen **IV U4**, 122
surrounding [sə'raʊndɪŋ] umgebend ⟨**IV TS3**, 103⟩
survey ['sɜ:veɪ] Umfrage; Studie **I**
to **survive** [sə'vaɪv] überleben **III**
survivor [sə'vaɪvə] Überlebende/-r **IV U1**, 15
*to be **suspended** [bi sə'spendɪd] suspendiert werden; zeitweilig vom Unterricht ausgeschlossen werden **IV AC2**, 38
suspense [sə'spens] Spannung **II**
suspicious [sə'spɪʃəs] misstrauisch; argwöhnisch **III**; verdächtig **IV U4**, 127
swamp fever *(no pl)* ['swɒmp ˌfi:və] Sumpffieber ⟨**IV U3**, 92⟩
to **swap** [swɒp] tauschen °**IV TS1**, 37
to **swap** roles [ˌswɒp 'rəʊlz] Rollen tauschen **I**
sweatshop ['swetʃɒp] Ausbeuterbetrieb **IV U1**, 18
sweet [swi:t] süß **I**
sweet potatoes *(pl)* ['swi:t pəˌteɪtəʊz] Süßkartoffeln ⟨**IV U1**, 15⟩
sweets *(pl)* [swi:ts] Süßigkeiten; Bonbons **I**
*to **swim** [swɪm] schwimmen **I**
swimming ['swɪmɪŋ] Schwimmen **I**
*to go **swimming** [ˌgəʊ 'swɪmɪŋ] Schwimmen gehen **I**
swimming pool ['swɪmɪŋ ˌpu:l] Swimmingpool; Schwimmbecken **III**
switch [swɪtʃ] Schalter **III**
to **switch** off [ˌswɪtʃ‿'ɒf] ausschalten **IV AC2**, 39
swollen ['swəʊlən] geschwollen ⟨**IV U4**, 123⟩
syllable ['sɪləbl] Silbe **III**
symbol ['sɪmbl] Symbol **II**
symbolic [sɪm'bɒlɪk] symbolisch **IV U4**, 117
to **symbolize** *(AE)* ['sɪmbəlaɪz] symbolisieren **IV AC1**, 10
system ['sɪstəm] System **IV U3**, 87

T

table ['teɪbl] Tisch **I**; Tabelle **IV U3**, 85
*to set the **table** [ˌset ðə 'teɪbl] den Tisch decken **IV AC4**, 108
the Round **Table** [ðə ˌraʊnd 'teɪbl] die Tafelrunde **II**
tablet ['tæblət] Tablet **II**; Tafel **IV U2**, 44
taco ['tækəʊ] Taco *(mexikanische gefüllte Teigtasche)* ⟨**IV U2**, 45⟩
taekwondo [ˌtækwʌn'du:] Taekwondo **II**
question **tag** ['kwestʃən ˌtæg] Frageanhängsel; Bestätigungsfrage **II**
tail [teɪl] Schwanz; Schweif **I**
*to **take** [teɪk] nehmen; mitnehmen; wegnehmen; bringen; mitbringen **I**; dauern; (Zeit) brauchen **II**
*to **take** a breath [ˌteɪk‿ə 'breθ] Luft holen; Atem holen **III**
*to **take** a look at [ˌteɪk‿ə 'lʊk‿æt] einen Blick werfen auf **II**
*to **take** a message [ˌteɪk‿ə 'mesɪdʒ] eine Nachricht entgegennehmen; jmdm. etw. ausrichten **I**
*to **take** a risk [ˌteɪk‿ə 'rɪsk] ein Risiko eingehen **III**
*to **take** a test [ˌteɪk‿ə 'test] einen Test machen **II**
*to **take** a vote [ˌteɪk‿ə 'vəʊt] abstimmen **I**
*to **take** care of sb/sth [ˌteɪk‿'keər‿əv] sich um jmdn./etw. kümmern; für jmdn. sorgen **III**
*to **take** notes [ˌteɪk 'nəʊts] sich Notizen machen **I**
*to **take** off [ˌteɪk‿'ɒf] abnehmen; herunternehmen; ausziehen **I**
*to **take** part (in) [ˌteɪk 'pɑ:t (ɪn)] teilnehmen (an) **II**
*to **take** photos [ˌteɪk 'fəʊtəʊz] fotografieren; Fotos machen **I**
*to **take** place [ˌteɪk 'pleɪs] stattfinden **I**
*to **take** the day off [ˌteɪk ðə ˌdeɪ‿'ɒf] sich den Tag freinehmen **IV U2**, 42
Take a deep breath. [ˌteɪk‿ə ˌdi:p 'breθ] Atme(t) tief ein. **II**
Take turns. [ˌteɪk 'tɜ:nz] Wechselt euch ab. **I**
take-off ['teɪk‿ɒf] Start; Abheben **III**
talent ['tælənt] Talent **I**
talent show ['tælənt ˌʃəʊ] Talentwettbewerb **I**
talk [tɔ:k] Vortrag; Rede **IV U1**, 13; Gespräch; Unterhaltung **IV U2**, 62
*to give a **talk** [ˌgɪv‿ə 'tɔ:k] einen Vortrag halten **IV U1**, 13
small **talk** ['smɔ:l ˌtɔ:k] Smalltalk **III**
to **talk** [tɔ:k] sprechen; reden **I**
to **talk** about … ['tɔ:k‿əbaʊt] sprechen über; erzählen von **I**
to **talk** to ['tɔ:k tə] reden mit **I**
to **talk** with your mouth full [ˌtɔ:k wɪð jɔ: 'maʊθ fʊl] mit vollem Mund sprechen **III**
talker ['tɔ:kə] Sprecher/-in **III**
talking ['tɔ:kɪŋ] Sprechen **I**
tall [tɔ:l] groß; hoch **II**
to **tap** [tæp] antippen **II**
tarantula [tə'ræntjələ] Tarantel *(Spinnenart)* ⟨**IV TS3**, 102⟩

target ['tɑ:gɪt] Ziel; Ziel- **IV TS1**, 35
tartan ['tɑ:tn] Schottenkaro *(bestimmtes Muster eines Clans)*; karierter Schottenstoff **III**
task [tɑ:sk] Aufgabe; Auftrag **I**
to taste [teɪst] schmecken; probieren **III**
tattoo [tæt'u:] Tattoe; Tätowierung **III**
to tattoo [tæt'u:] tätowieren ⟨**IV U2**, 60⟩
taxi ['tæksi] Taxi **II**
tea [ti:] Tee **I**
tea bag ['ti: bæg] Teebeutel **III**
*to teach [ti:tʃ] unterrichten; lehren; beibringen **II**
*to **teach** somebody a lesson [ˌti:tʃ‿ə 'lesn] jmdm. eine Lehre/Lektion erteilen **II**
teacher ['ti:tʃə] Lehrer/-in **I**
team [ti:m] Team; Gruppe **II**
tear [tɪə] Träne ⟨**IV U2**, 54⟩
to tease sb [ti:z] jmdn. aufziehen; jmdn. hänseln; jmdn. ärgern **III**
tech [tek] Technologie; Technik **IV TS2**, 72
technique [tek'ni:k] Methode; Technik °**IV U2**, 61
narrative **technique** [ˌnærətɪv tek'ni:k] Erzähltechnik °**IV U4**, 127
Technology [tek'nɒlədʒi] Technik; Computerunterricht **II**
technology [tek'nɒlədʒi] Technologie **II**
teen [ti:n] Jugend- **II**; Teenager; Jugendliche/-r **III**
teenage ['ti:neɪdʒ] jugendlich; Jugend- **III**
teenager ['ti:nˌeɪdʒə] Teenager; Jugendliche/-r **I**
telegraph ['telɪgrɑ:f] Telegraf **IV U3**, 86
telephone ['telɪfəʊn] Telefon **I**
*to tell [tel] erzählen; sagen; mitteilen **I**
Tell me about ... ['tel mi:‿əˌbaʊt] Erzähle mir von ... **I**
temperature ['temprətʃə] Temperatur **IV AC1**, 8
to tempt [tempt] in Versuchung führen; reizen **III**
temptation [temp'teɪʃn] Versuchung **IV TS1**, 34
tempted ['temptɪd] in Versuchung gebracht **III**
tempting ['temptɪŋ] verführerisch **III**
ten [ten] zehn **I**
ten times [ten 'taɪmz] zehnmal **I**
tennis ['tenɪs] Tennis **I**
tennis shoes ['tenɪs ˌʃu:z] Tennisschuhe ⟨**IV U4**, 123⟩
tense [tens] Zeit; Zeitform *(grammatisch)* **II**
term [tɜ:m] Begriff **III**
terrible ['terəbl] schrecklich; schlimm; furchtbar **IV U3**, 83
test [test] Test; Klassenarbeit; Prüfung **I**
*to take a **test** [ˌteɪk‿ə 'test] einen Test machen **II**
to test [test] testen; prüfen **II**
text [tekst] Text **I**
factual **text** [ˌfæktʃʊəl 'tekst] Sachtext **III**
text (message) ['tekst ˌmesɪdʒ] SMS; Kurznachricht **I**
wiki **(text)** ['wɪkɪ ˌtekst] Wikitext **IV TS2**, 71
to text [tekst] eine SMS schicken **II**
than [ðæn] als *(bei Vergleichen)* **II**
more ... **than** ['mɔ: ðən] mehr ... als **I**
*to give thanks [ˌgɪv 'θæŋks] danken **IV U1**, 15
to thank [θæŋk] danken **II**
Thank you. ['θæŋk ju] Danke. **I**
thankful ['θæŋkfl] dankbar **I**
Thanks. [θæŋks] Danke. **I**
that [ðæt] so *(Betonung)* **III**
that much [ðæt 'mʌtʃ] so viel **III**
that [ðæt; ðət] dass **I**
so **(that)** [ˌsəʊ 'ðæt] damit; so dass **IV AC2**, 39
that [ðæt] das; jenes **I**
after **that** [ˌɑ:ftə 'ðæt] danach **I**
like **that** [laɪk 'ðæt] so **I**
That was close! [ˌðæt wəz 'kləʊs] Das war knapp! **I**
that's how [ðæts 'haʊ] so **II**
That's what friends are for. [ˌðæts wɒt 'frendz‿ɑ: ˌfɔ:] Dafür sind Freunde da. **I**
that's why [ðæts 'waɪ] deshalb **II**
That's ... [ðæts] Das macht ... **I**
that [ðæt] der; dem; den; die; das *(Relativpronomen)* **II**
the [ðə; ði] der; die *(auch Pl.)*; das **I**
the others [ði‿'ʌðəz] die anderen **I**
the same [ðə 'seɪm] der-/die-/dasselbe; der/die/das gleiche **I**
the ... **the** [ðə ... ðə] je ... desto **II**
theater *(AE)* ['θɪətə] Theater **IV U2**, 40
movie **theater** *(AE)* ['mu:vi ˌθɪətə] Kino **IV U1**, 14
theatre ['θɪətə] Theater **I**
their [ðeə] ihr/-e *(Pl.)* **I**
them [ðem] sie *(Pl.)*; ihnen **I**
theme [θi:m] Thema; Motto **I**
theme song ['θi:m sɒŋ] Titelmelodie °**IV U2**, 61
then [ðen] dann; danach **I**
back **then** [bæk 'ðen] damals **III**
theorist ['θɪərist] Theoretiker/-in ⟨**IV TS2**, 72⟩
theory ['θɪəri] Theorie **IV TS2**, 72
there [ðeə] da; dort; dahin; dorthin **I**
there is/are [ðər‿'ɪz/'ɑ:] da ist/sind; es gibt **I**
There's no need to ... [ˌðeəz nəʊ 'ni:d tə] Es gibt keinen Grund zu ... **III**
these [ði:z] diese (hier) **I**
these days [ˌði:z 'deɪz] zurzeit **III**
they [ðeɪ] sie *(Pl.)* **I**
It's .../**They**'re ... [ɪts/ðeə] Es kostet .../ Sie kosten ... **I**
thick [θɪk] dick *(nicht für Personen)* **III**
thief [θi:f], thieves [θi:vz] *(pl)* Dieb/-in ⟨**IV U2**, 52⟩
thin [θɪn] dünn ⟨**IV U3**, 89⟩
thing [θɪŋ] Ding; Sache **I**
*to think [θɪŋk] denken; nachdenken; glauben **I**
Stop and **think** [ˌstɒp‿ənd 'θɪŋk] Warte/ Wartet und denk/denkt nach. **I**
*to **think** of ['θɪŋk‿əv] halten von; denken über **I**; (sich) ausdenken; sich etwas einfallen lassen **II**
Think of ... ['θɪŋk‿əv] Denke/Denkt an ... **I**
*to **think** up [θɪŋk‿'ʌp] (sich) ausdenken; sich einfallen lassen °**IV TS1**, 36
third [θɜ:d] Drittel ⟨**IV TS3**, 103⟩
third [θɜ:d] dritte/-r/-s **I**
third person narrator [ˌθɜ:d ˌpɜ:sn nə'reɪtə] Er/Sie-Erzähler/-in **III**
thirsty ['θɜ:sti] durstig **III**
thirteen [ˌθɜ:'ti:n] dreizehn **I**
this [ðɪs] dies; diese/-r/-s **I**
this afternoon [ðɪs 'ɑ:ftənu:n] heute Nachmittag **II**
this early ['ðɪs ˌɜ:li] so früh **III**
This is ... ['ðɪs‿ɪz] Das (hier) ist ... **I**
thistle ['θɪsl] Distel **III**
those [ðəʊz] diese dort; jene **I**
those in power [ˌðəʊz ɪn 'paʊə] die Regierenden; die Herrschenden **III**
though [ðəʊ] doch; jedoch; obwohl **IV AC3**, 76
even **though** [ˌi:vn 'ðəʊ] auch wenn; obwohl **IV U3**, 86
thought [θɔ:t] Gedanke **II**
thousands of ['θaʊzndz‿əv] tausende (von) **I**
to threaten ['θretn] drohen; bedrohen ⟨**IV U4**, 125⟩
three [θri:] drei **I**
thrilled [θrɪld] aufgeregt; außer sich vor Freude **IV U3**, 85
thrilling ['θrɪlɪŋ] aufregend **IV U3**, 85
through [θru:] durch **I**
*to throw (at) [θrəʊ] werfen (nach) **I**
*to **throw** away [ˌθrəʊ‿ə'weɪ] wegwerfen **I**
*to **throw** up [ˌθrəʊ‿'ʌp] schnell aufs Papier werfen ⟨**IV TS3**, 105⟩
throw the dice twice [ˌθrəʊ ðə daɪs 'twaɪs] würfle zweimal **II**
thumb [θʌm] Daumen **II**
thunder *(no pl)* ['θʌndə] Donner **II**
Thursday ['θɜ:zdeɪ] Donnerstag **I**
to tick [tɪk] abhaken **II**
ticket ['tɪkɪt] Los; Ticket; Eintrittskarte **I**; Fahrschein **II**
one-way **ticket** ['wʌnweɪ ˌtɪkɪt] einfache Fahrkarte **II**
return **ticket** [rɪ'tɜ:n ˌtɪkɪt] Hin- und Rückfahrkarte **II**
single **ticket** ['sɪŋgl ˌtɪkɪt] einfache Fahrkarte **II**
ticket office ['tɪkɪt ˌɒfɪs] Kartenschalter **III**
high tide ['haɪ ˌtaɪd] Flut **II**
low **tide** ['ləʊ ˌtaɪd] Ebbe **II**

to **tidy** *(a room)* ['taɪdi] aufräumen; in Ordnung bringen **I**
to **tie** (to) ['taɪ tə] binden (an); fesseln (an) **III**
tight [taɪt] eng ⟨**IV U2**, 60⟩
till [tɪl] bis **I**
timber ['tɪmbə] Holz; Bauholz **IV U4**, 117
time [taɪm] Zeit **I**; Mal **II**
all the **time** [ˌɔ:l ðə 'taɪm] die ganze Zeit **II**
at the same **time** [ət ðə ˌseɪm 'taɪm] zur selben Zeit; gleichzeitig **I**
at the **time** [ˌət ðə 'taɪm] damals **IV TS2**, 72
*to buy **time** [ˌbaɪ 'taɪm] Zeit gewinnen **IV U4**, 115
by the **time** [ˌbaɪ ðə 'taɪm] bis *(zu dem Zeitpunkt)* **IV U3**, 80
free **time** [ˌfri: 'taɪm] Freizeit **I**
on **time** [ɒn 'taɪm] pünktlich **II**
ten **times** [ten 'taɪmz] zehnmal **I**
time line ['taɪm ˌlaɪn] Zeitstrahl **I**
time slot ['taɪm slɒt] Zeitfenster **II**
I can't wait till next **time**. [aɪ kɑ:nt ˌweɪt tɪl nekst 'taɪm] Ich kann es bis zum nächsten Mal kaum erwarten. **II**
just in **time** [ˌdʒʌst‿ɪn 'taɪm] gerade rechtzeitig **IV U2**, 42
Time to get up! [ˌtaɪm tə ˌget‿'ʌp] Es ist Zeit aufzustehen! **I**
What **time**? [ˌwɒt 'taɪm] Um wie viel Uhr? **I**
What's the **time**? [ˌwɒts ðə 'taɪm] Wie spät ist es?; Wie viel Uhr ist es? **I**
to **time** [taɪm] den richtigen Zeitpunkt wählen **IV U2**, 42
timetable ['taɪmˌteɪbl] Stundenplan; Fahrplan **I**
tin [tɪn] Zinn **II**
tin can ['tɪn kæn] Blechdose **III**
tinned [tɪnd] Dosen-; aus der Dose **I**
tiny ['taɪni] klein; winzig **III**
tip [tɪp] Tipp; Ratschlag **I**; Trinkgeld **IV U2**, 46
to **tiptoe** ['tɪptəʊ] auf Zehenspitzen gehen **II**
tire *(AE)* [taɪə] Reifen **IV TS3**, 103
snow **tire** *(AE)* ['snəʊ ˌtaɪə] Winterreifen **IV TS3**, 103
tired [taɪəd] müde **I**
*to be **tired** of [bi 'taɪəd‿əv] es müde sein (zu); es leid sein (zu); es satt haben (zu) **IV U1**, 16
title ['taɪtl] Titel; Überschrift **II**
to [tʊ; tə] zu; nach; auf; in; vor *(bei Uhrzeitangaben)* **I**
from … **to** [frəm … tə] von … bis **I**
quarter past/**to** ['kwɔ:tə pɑ:st/tə] Viertel nach/vor **I**
to the point [tə ðə 'pɔɪnt] prägnant; treffend **III**
toast [təʊst] Toast **I**
tobacco *(no pl)* [tə'bækəʊ] Tabak **III**
today [tə'deɪ] heute **I**
together [tə'geðə] zusammen; miteinander; gemeinsam **I**
toilet ['tɔɪlət] Toilette **I**
tolerant ['tɒlrnt] tolerant **III**
tomato [tə'mɑ:təʊ], **tomatoes** [tə'mɑ:təʊz] *(pl)* Tomate **I**
tomorrow [tə'mɒrəʊ] morgen **I**
tone [təʊn] Ton; Signalton °**IV U1**, 26
tonight [tə'naɪt] heute Abend; heute Nacht **III**
too [tu:] auch; zu **I**
Too bad! [ˌtu: 'bæd] Zu dumm!; Schade! **I**
You **too**? [ju: 'tu:] Du auch? **I**
tool [tu:l] Werkzeug; Gerät **II**
toothpaste ['tu:θpeɪst] Zahnpasta **IV U1**, 26
top [tɒp] Spitze; oberer Teil; oberes Ende **I**
on **top** [ɒn 'tɒp] oben; obendrauf **I**
to **top** up [tɒp‿'ʌp] aufladen **II**
topic ['tɒpɪk] Thema **II**
torch [tɔ:tʃ] Fackel; Taschenlampe **II**
to **toss** out [ˌtɒs‿'aʊt] ausstoßen; hinauswerfen **IV U4**, 125
total ['təʊtl] gesamt; Gesamt- **IV U4**, 110
a **total** of [ə 'təʊtl‿əv] insgesamt **IV U3**, 81
totally ['təʊtli] völlig; total **IV AC3**, 77
totem pole ['təʊtəm ˌpəʊl] Totempfahl **IV U4**, 118
*to keep in **touch** [ˌki:p‿ɪn 'tʌtʃ] in Kontakt bleiben **IV U1**, 14
to stay in **touch** (with) [ˌsteɪ ɪn 'tʌtʃ wɪð] in Kontakt bleiben (mit) **II**
to **touch** [tʌtʃ] berühren; antippen **IV U1**, 22
to **touch** down [tʌtʃ 'daʊn] landen **IV TS2**, 71
tough [tʌf] hart; rau; zäh ⟨**IV U4**, 122⟩
tour [tʊə] Tour; Fahrt; Rundgang **II**
audio **tour** ['ɔ:diəʊ ˌtʊə] Audioführung **II**
tour company ['tʊə ˌkʌmpəni] Reiseanbieter **IV U2**, 43
tourism ['tʊərɪzm] Tourismus **II**
tourist ['tʊərɪst] Tourist/-in **I**
tourist board ['tʊərɪst bɔ:d] Touristeninformation **II**
tourist information centre [ˌtʊərɪst ɪnfə'meɪʃn ˌsentə] Touristeninformation **I**
towards [tə'wɔ:dz] in Richtung; auf … zu; darauf zu **II**
tower [taʊə] Turm **III**
town [taʊn] Stadt **I**
edge of **town** [ˌedʒ‿əv 'taʊn] Stadtrand **IV TS3**, 105
toy [tɔɪ] Spielzeug **I**
to **trace** [treɪs] verfolgen; nachspüren **I**
tractor ['træktə] Traktor **IV AC1**, 8
to **trade** [treɪd] austauschen **II**
tradition [trə'dɪʃn] Tradition **I**
traditional [trə'dɪʃnl] traditionell **III**
traffic ['træfɪk] Verkehr **III**
trail [treɪl] Weg; Pfad **IV U3**, 92
walking **trail** ['wɔ:kɪŋ treɪl] Wanderweg **II**
train [treɪn] Zug **I**
to **train** [treɪn] trainieren **II**
trainer ['treɪnə] Turnschuh **III**
training ['treɪnɪŋ] Training **II**
traitor ['treɪtə] Verräter/-in **IV U4**, 125
transitive ['trænsətɪv] transitiv *(ein Objekt nach sich ziehend)* °**IV U4**, 116
to **translate** [trænz'leɪt] übersetzen **I**
translation [trænz'leɪʃn] Übersetzung **I**
transport ['trænspɔ:t] Verkehrsmittel; Transport **II**
public **transport** *(no pl)* [ˌpʌblɪk 'trænspɔ:t] öffentliche Verkehrsmittel **II**
to **transport** [træn'spɔ:t] transportieren; befördern **IV U2**, 49
transportation *(AE)* [ˌtrænspɔ:'teɪʃn] Transport **IV U3**, 78
*to be **trapped** [bi 'træpt] eingeschlossen sein; in der Falle sitzen **III**
trash *(AE)* [træʃ] Abfall; Müll **IV TS1**, 37
hoarder of **trash** [ˌhɔ:dər‿əv 'træʃ] Messy ⟨**IV TS3**, 106⟩
travel ['trævl] (das) Reisen; Reise **II**
travel agency ['trævl‿ˌeɪdʒnsi] Reisebüro **III**
travel agent's ['trævl‿ˌeɪdʒnts] Reisebüro **II**
travel report [ˌtrævl rɪ'pɔ:t] Reisebericht **II**
to **travel** ['trævl] fahren; reisen **II**
traveler *(AE)* ['trævlə] Reisende/-r **IV TS3**, 102
traveller ['trævlə] Reisende/-r **III**
travelling *(no pl)* ['trævlɪŋ] (das) Reisen **III**
treasure ['treʒə] Schatz **II**
treat [tri:t] *hier:* Leckerli; Belohnung **III**
It's my **treat**. [ɪts 'maɪ ˌtri:t] Das geht auf meine Rechnung. **IV U4**, 113
to **treat** [tri:t] behandeln **IV U3**, 80
tree [tri:] Baum **I**
family **tree** ['fæmli ˌtri:] Stammbaum **I**
palm **tree** ['pɑ:m ˌtri:] Palme **II**
redwood **tree** ['redwʊd ˌtri:] Mammutbaum **IV AC1**, 9
pony **trekking** ['pəʊni ˌtrekɪŋ] Ponyreiten im Gelände **II**
trial [traɪəl] Qualifikation **II**
tribal ['traɪbl] Stammes- ⟨**IV U3**, 84⟩
tribe [traɪb] Stamm; Volksstamm **III**
trick [trɪk] Trick; Streich **I**
to play a **trick** (on) [ˌpleɪ‿ə 'trɪk‿ɒn] einen Streich spielen **I**
to **trick** [trɪk] austricksen; täuschen **IV TS2**, 73
trifle ['traɪfl] Trifle *(englischer Nachtisch)* **I**
trio ['triəʊ] Trio ⟨**IV U4**, 125⟩
trip [trɪp] Trip; Reise; Ausflug; Fahrt **II**
field **trip** ['fi:ld trɪp] Schulausflug; Exkursion ⟨**IV U4**, 124⟩
road **trip** ['rəʊd ˌtrɪp] Tour; Trip ⟨**IV TS3**, 102⟩
triumph ['traɪəmf] Triumph ⟨**IV TS2**, 71⟩
trouble ['trʌbl] Ärger; Probleme; Schwierigkeiten **II**
*to get into **trouble** [ˌget‿ɪntə 'trʌbl] in Schwierigkeiten geraten **IV AC2**, 39
*to make **trouble** [ˌmeɪk 'trʌbl] Ärger machen; in Schwierigkeiten bringen **I**
troublemaker ['trʌblmeɪkə] Unruhestifter/-in **IV U1**, 23
trousers *(pl)* ['traʊzəz] Hose **II**

trowel ['traʊəl] kleiner Spaten **II**
truck *(AE)* [trʌk] *hier:* Wagen **IV U2**, 45; Truck; Lastwagen **IV TS3**, 105
truckload ['trʌkləʊd] Lastwagenladung **IV TS1**, 36
true [tru:] wahr **II**
*to be **true** to oneself [bi 'tru: tu wʌnˌself] sich selbst treu bleiben **IV U4**, 112
*to come **true** [ˌkʌm 'tru:] wahr werden; in Erfüllung gehen **IV U2**, 46
trunk *(AE)* [trʌŋk] Kofferraum **IV U2**, 46
to **trust** [trʌst] vertrauen **III**
truth [tru:θ] Wahrheit **III**
to **try** [traɪ] versuchen; probieren **I**
to **try** on [ˌtraɪ‿'ɒn] anprobieren **II**
to **try** out [ˌtraɪ‿'aʊt] ausprobieren **III**
T-shirt ['ti:ʃɜ:t] T-Shirt **I**
the **Tube** [ðə 'tju:b] die Londoner U-Bahn **II**
Tudor ['tju:də] Tudor- **III**
Tuesday ['tju:zdeɪ] Dienstag **I**
tune [tju:n] Melodie **III**
out of **tune** [ˌaʊt‿əv 'tju:n] verstimmt ⟨**IV U3**, 92⟩
tunnel ['tʌnl] Tunnel **I**
turbulent ['tɜ:bjələnt] turbulent; aufgewühlt **IV TS3**, 103
roast **turkey** [rəʊst 'tɜ:ki] Putenbraten ⟨**IV U1**, 15⟩
It's your **turn**. [ˌɪts 'jɔ: tɜ:n] Du bist dran. **I**
Take **turns**. [ˌteɪk 'tɜ:nz] Wechselt euch ab. **I**
Your **turn**. ['jɔ: tɜ:n] Du bist dran. **I**
to **turn** [tɜ:n] einbiegen; abbiegen **I**; drehen; (sich) umdrehen **III**
to **turn** (a)round [ˌtɜ:n‿(ə)'raʊnd] (sich) umdrehen; wenden **II**
to **turn** back [tɜ:n 'bæk] umkehren; zurückgehen **II**
to **turn** into [ˌtɜ:n‿'ɪntə] ändern in; umwandeln in **III**
to **turn** off [ˌtɜ:n‿'ɒf] abschalten; ausschalten **II**
to **turn** to ['tɜ:n tə] sich wenden an; sich zuwenden **II**
turning point ['tɜ:nɪŋ ˌpɔɪnt] Wendepunkt **III**
It **turned** out that … [ɪt ˌtɜ:nd‿'aʊt ðæt] Es stellte sich heraus, dass … **III**
tusk [tʌsk] Stoßzahn **III**
tutor ['tju:tə] Klassenlehrer/-in **I**
tutor group ['tju:tə ˌgru:p] Klasse *(in einer englischen Schule)* **I**
tutorial [tju:'tɔ:riəl] Tutorium; Tutorial **IV TS2**, 70
TV (= television) [ˌti:'vi: ('telɪvɪʒn)] Fernsehen; Fernseher **I**
to watch **TV** [ˌwɒtʃ ti:'vi:] fernsehen **I**
tweet [twi:t] Nachricht auf Twitter °**IV U3**, 94
twelve [twelv] zwölf **I**
twice [twaɪs] zweimal **IV U1**, 23
twin [twɪn] Zwilling; Zwillings- **II**
to **twist** your ankle [ˌtwɪst jɔ:r‿'æŋkl] sich den Knöchel verrenken **II**
two [tu:] zwei **I**
the **two** of them [ðə 'tu:‿əv ðəm] beide **II**
two of which ['tu:‿əv wɪtʃ] zwei von ihnen **II**
type [taɪp] Typ; Art; Sorte **III**
typical ['tɪpɪkl] typisch **I**
typically ['tɪpɪkli] typisch **III**
tyre [taɪə] Reifen **IV TS3**, 103

U

u *(= you)* [ju:; jə] du; Sie; ihr **I**
UFO [ˌju:ef'əʊ] UFO **II**
ugly ['ʌgli] hässlich **IV TS1**, 37
umbrella [ʌm'brelə] Regenschirm ⟨**IV U2**, 60⟩
unable [ʌn'eɪbl] unfähig; nicht in der Lage ⟨**IV TS2**, 74⟩
unbelievable [ˌʌnbɪ'li:vəbl] unglaublich; unglaubwürdig **IV U4**, 113
uncle ['ʌŋkl] Onkel **I**
under ['ʌndə] unter **I**
underfloor heating *(no pl)* [ˌʌndəflɔ: 'hi:tɪŋ] Fußbodenheizung **III**
underground ['ʌndəgraʊnd] U-Bahn **II**
to **underline** [ˌʌndə'laɪn] unterstreichen **III**
*to **understand** [ˌʌndə'stænd] verstehen **I**
understanding [ˌʌndə'stændɪŋ] Verständnis **II**
undeveloped [ˌʌndɪ'veləpt] unentwickelt; unausgereift **IV TS2**, 75
unexpected [ˌʌnɪk'spektɪd] unerwartet **IV U2**, 61
unfair [ʌn'feə] unfair **II**
unfamiliar [ˌʌnfə'mɪliə] nicht vertraut; unbekannt **III**
unfriendly [ʌn'frendli] unfreundlich **II**
uniform ['ju:nɪfɔ:m] Uniform **I**
unique [ju:'ni:k] einzigartig **IV U4**, 126
unit ['ju:nɪt] Lektion; Kapitel; Einheit **I**
united [ju:'naɪtɪd] vereint; vereinigt **IV U3**, 80
the **unknown** [ði ˌʌn'nəʊn] das Unbekannte **IV U3**, 92
unless [ən'les] es sei denn, (dass) …; wenn nicht **IV TS3**, 106
*to be **unlucky** [bi:ˌʌn'lʌki] Pech haben **I**
unofficial [ˌʌnə'fɪʃl] inoffiziell **III**
to **unpack** [ʌn'pæk] auspacken **IV U1**, 16
unreal [ˌʌn'rɪəl] irreal **III**
unrealistic [ˌʌnrɪə'lɪstɪk] unrealistisch **IV U1**, 22
unsure [ʌn'ʃʊə] unsicher **III**
until [ʌn'tɪl] bis; erst wenn **II**
not **until** [ˌnɒt‿ən'tɪl] nicht vor; erst um/im **IV U1**, 14
to **unwrap** [ʌn'ræp] auswickeln; auspacken **I**
up [ʌp] hinauf; (nach) oben **II**
*to cut **up** [kʌt‿'ʌp] zerschneiden °**IV U2**, 61
to end **up** [ˌend‿'ʌp] enden; landen **II**
*to get **up** [ˌget‿'ʌp] aufstehen *(aus dem Bett)* **I**
*to give **up** [ˌgɪv‿'ʌp] aufgeben **III**
to look **up** [ˌlʊk‿'ʌp] nachschlagen; nachschauen **I**
*to throw **up** [ˌθrəʊ‿'ʌp] schnell aufs Papier werfen ⟨**IV TS3**, 105⟩
up to ['ʌp tə] bis zu **IV U3**, 93
What's **up**? [ˌwɒts‿'ʌp] Was ist los? **III**
*to **upset** [ʌp'set] aus der Fassung bringen **III**
upset [ʌp'set] aufgebracht; bestürzt **II**
upstairs [ʌp'steəz] nach oben; im Obergeschoss; oben **II**
up-to-date [ˌʌptə'deɪt] modern; zeitgemäß; aktuell **IV TS2**, 70
urban ['ɜ:bn] städtisch; Stadt- **IV AC1**, 8
urge [ɜ:dʒ] Drang ⟨**IV U4**, 125⟩
us [ʌs] uns **I**
US [ˌju:'es] US-amerikanisch **IV AC1**, 11
use [ju:s] Verwendung; Gebrauch; Nutzen °**IV U2**, 47
*to make **use** of [meɪk 'ju:z‿əv] benutzen; verwenden **IV U2**, 59
to **use** [ju:z] benutzen; verwenden; gebrauchen **I**
*to be **used** to [bi 'ju:s‿tə] gewöhnt sein an; gewohnt sein **III**
*to get **used** to sth [ˌget 'ju:zd tə] sich an etw. gewöhnen **IV U1**, 14
used to *(+ infinitive)* ['ju:st tə] pflegte(n) zu; tat(en) früher ⟨**IV TS3**, 106⟩
useful ['ju:sfl] nützlich; hilfreich **I**
Useful phrases [ˌju:sfl 'freɪsɪz] nützliche Ausdrücke **I**
useless ['ju:sləs] nutzlos **III**
usual ['ju:ʒl] üblich **III**
usually ['ju:ʒli] normalerweise; gewöhnlich; meistens **I**

V

vacation *(AE)* [və'keɪʃn] Ferien; Urlaub **IV AC1**, 11
to **vacuum** ['vækju:m] staubsaugen **IV AC4**, 108
vagabond ['vægəbɒnd] Vagabund ⟨**IV TS3**, 105⟩
valley ['væli] Tal **IV TS3**, 103
van [væn] Lieferwagen; Transporter; Kleinbus ⟨**IV U2**, 58⟩
vanishing ['vænɪʃɪŋ] verschwindend ⟨**IV U4**, 123⟩
vegetable ['vedʒtəbl] Gemüse **III**
vegetarian [ˌvedʒɪ'teəriən] Vegetarier/-in **III**
vegetarian [ˌvedʒɪ'teəriən] vegetarisch **III**
vein [veɪn] Vene ⟨**IV U4**, 122⟩
vending machine ['vendɪŋ məˌʃi:n] Automat **III**
verb [vɜ:b] Verb **I**
verse [vɜ:s] Vers; Strophe **III**
version ['vɜ:ʃn] Version **III**
cover **version** ['kʌvə ˌvɜ:ʃn] Coverversion **III**

versus (vs.) ['vɜːsəs] gegen **III**
very ['veri] sehr **I**
very much [ˌveri 'mʌtʃ] sehr **I**
vet [vet] Tierarzt/Tierärztin **I**
Victorian [vɪk'tɔːriən] viktorianisch; Viktorianer/-in **III**
video ['vɪdiəʊ] Video **II**
video chat ['vɪdiəʊ ˌtʃæt] Videochat **II**
view [vjuː] Aussicht; Sicht; Ausblick; Blick **II**; Ansicht; Einstellung; Standpunkt **IV U4**, 119
point of **view** [ˌpɔɪnt‿əv 'vjuː] Standpunkt; Ansicht; Perspektive **II**
viewer ['vjuːə] Zuschauer/-in **II**
viewing ['vjuːɪŋ] Hör-/Sehverstehen **I**
village ['vɪlɪdʒ] Dorf **I**
villain ['vɪlən] Bösewicht **II**
violence *(no pl)* ['vaɪəlns] Gewalt **III**
violent ['vaɪəlnt] gewaltsam; gewalttätig; brutal **III**
visa ['viːzə], **visas** ['viːzəz] *(pl)* Visum, Visa *(Pl.)*; Einreisebewilligung **III**
visit ['vɪzɪt] Besuch **I**
to **visit** ['vɪzɪt] besichtigen; besuchen **I**
visitor ['vɪzɪtə] Besucher/-in **I**
visual ['vɪʒuəl] Bild **IV TS1**, 35
vitamin ['vɪtəmɪn] Vitamin **III**
vocabulary [və'kæbjəlri] Vokabular; Wortschatz **I**
voice [vɔɪs] Stimme **I**
volcano [vɒl'keɪnəʊ], **volcanoes** [vɒl'keɪnəʊz] *(pl)* Vulkan **IV U4**, 111
volleyball ['vɒlibɔːl] Volleyball **I**
*to take a **vote** [ˌteɪk‿ə 'vəʊt] abstimmen **I**
to **vote** [vəʊt] abstimmen; wählen **I**
voyage ['vɔɪɪdʒ] Reise; Fahrt ⟨**IV TS2**, 74⟩

W

wagon ['wægən] Wagen; Waggon; Planwagen; Karren **IV U3**, 81
covered **wagon** [ˌkʌvəd 'wægən] Planwagen **IV U3**, 81
to **wait** (for) [weɪt] warten (auf) **I**
I can't **wait** till next time. [aɪ kɑːnt ˌweɪt tɪl nekst 'taɪm] Ich kann es bis zum nächsten Mal kaum erwarten. **II**
Wait and see! [ˌweɪt‿ənd 'siː] Warte ab! **I**
waiter ['weɪtə] Kellner/-in; Bedienung **IV U4**, 113
*to **wake** up [weɪk‿'ʌp] aufwachen; aufwecken **III**
gallery **walk** ['gæləri ˌwɔːk] Museumsrundgang; Vernissage **I**
*to go for a **walk** [ˌgəʊ fər‿ə 'wɔːk] spazieren gehen **II**
night **walk** ['naɪt wɔːk] Nachtwanderung **II**
to **walk** [wɔːk] gehen; laufen **I**
to **walk** the dog [ˌwɔːk ðə 'dɒg] den Hund ausführen; mit dem Hund spazieren gehen **I**
walk-in closet [ˌwɔːkɪn 'klɒzɪt] begehbarer Kleiderschrank **IV U1**, 14
walking ['wɔːkɪŋ] Wandern **II**
walking trail ['wɔːkɪŋ treɪl] Wanderweg **II**
wall [wɔːl] Wand; Mauer **I**; Online-Pinnwand **III**
*to be **walled** in [ˌbi wɔːld‿'ɪn] von Wänden eingeschlossen sein ⟨**IV U2**, 60⟩
to **want** (to) ['wɒnt tə] wollen; mögen **I**
wanted ['wɒntɪd] gesucht **IV U3**, 86
war [wɔː] Krieg **III**
wardrobe ['wɔːdrəʊb] Kleiderschrank **I**
to **warm** up [ˌwɔːm‿'ʌp] aufwärmen; sich aufwärmen **I**
warm [wɔːm] warm **III**
warm-up ['wɔːm‿ʌp] Aufwärmübung **I**
to **warn** [wɔːn] warnen **III**
warrior ['wɒriə] Krieger **II**
to **wash** [wɒʃ] waschen; sich waschen **I**
to **wash** up [ˌwɒʃ‿'ʌp] angespült werden **II**
washing machine ['wɒʃɪŋ məˌʃiːn] Waschmaschine **II**
waste [weɪst] Verschwendung **IV AC2**, 39
to **waste** [weɪst] verschwenden **II**
wasteful ['weɪstfl] verschwenderisch **IV AC1**, 10
watch [wɒtʃ] Armbanduhr ⟨**IV U4**, 123⟩
wrist **watch** ['rɪst wɒtʃ] Armbanduhr ⟨**IV U4**, 123⟩
to **watch** [wɒtʃ] beobachten; (sich) ansehen; zuschauen **I**
to **watch** TV [ˌwɒtʃ tiː'viː] fernsehen **I**
water ['wɔːtə] Wasser **I**
drinking **water** ['drɪŋkɪŋ ˌwɔːtə] Trinkwasser **IV U3**, 83
water fountain ['wɔːtə ˌfaʊntɪn] Wasserspender **IV AC3**, 76
water slide ['wɔːtə ˌslaɪd] Wasserrutsche **I**
waterfront ['wɔːtəfrʌnt] Hafenviertel; Ufer **IV U4**, 111
wave [weɪv] Welle **I**
to **wave** [weɪv] winken; schwenken **IV U3**, 92
wax [wæks] Wachs **II**
wax figure ['wæks ˌfɪgə] Wachsfigur **II**
way [weɪ] Weg; Art und Weise **I**
*to be in the **way** [biː‿ɪn ðə 'weɪ] im Weg sein/stehen **I**
*to find one's **way** around [ˌfaɪnd wʌnz ˌweɪ‿ə'raʊnd] sich zurechtfinden **IV U1**, 16
*to get in the **way** [ˌget‿ɪn ðə 'weɪ] stören; im Weg stehen **II**
no **way** [ˌnəʊ 'weɪ] auf keinen Fall; keineswegs ⟨**IV U1**, 24⟩; keine Möglichkeit; kein Weg ⟨**IV TS2**, 72⟩
in other **ways** [ɪn‿'ʌðə weɪz] auf andere Weise **II**
the same **way** as [ˌðə seɪm 'weɪ æz] genauso wie **II**
we [wiː; wi] wir **I**
We're from … ['wɪə frəm] Wir sind aus … **I**
weak [wiːk] schwach **IV TS2**, 75
wealthy ['welθi] wohlhabend; reich **IV AC1**, 10
weapon ['wepən] Waffe **III**
*to **wear** [weə] anhaben; tragen *(Kleidung)* **I**
weather ['weðə] Wetter **I**
weather forecast ['weðə ˌfɔːkɑːst] Wettervorhersage **II**
web [web] Netz; Spinnennetz **III**
web designer ['web dɪˌzaɪnə] Webdesigner **III**
website ['websaɪt] Website; Internetauftritt **I**
wedding ['wedɪŋ] Hochzeit **I**
Wednesday ['wenzdeɪ] Mittwoch **I**
week [wiːk] Woche **I**
weekday ['wiːkdeɪ] Wochentag **II**
weekend [ˌwiːk'end] Wochenende **I**
at the **weekend** [ət ðə ˌwiːk'end] am Wochenende **I**
to **weigh** [weɪ] wiegen **III**
weight [weɪt] Gewicht **III**
weird [wɪəd] merkwürdig; seltsam; sonderbar **II**
Welcome! ['welkəm] Willkommen! **II**
to **welcome** ['welkəm] willkommen heißen **II**
You're **welcome**. [ˌjɔː 'welkəm] Bitte schön.; Nichts zu danken.; Gern geschehen. **I**
*to do **well** [ˌduː 'wel] gute Leistungen erbringen **III**
*to get **well** [ˌget 'wel] gesund werden **IV U3**, 93
well-developed [ˌweldɪ'veləpt] gut entwickelt; ausgereift **IV TS2**, 75
well-written [ˌwel'rɪtn] gut geschrieben **IV TS2**, 74
… as **well** as … [əz 'wel‿əz] sowie; und (auch) °**IV U3**, 91
well [wel] tja; nun **I**
Welsh [welʃ] walisisch; Walisisch; Waliser/-in **II**
west [west] Westen; West- **I**
in the far **west** [ɪn ðə fɑː 'west] im äußersten Westen **II**
western ['westən] westlich; West- **IV U3**, 86
wet [wet] nass **II**
whale [weɪl] Wal **IV U4**, 116
what [wɒt] was; welche/-r/-s; was für ein **I**
What a … ['wɒt‿ə] Was für ein/-e … **IV U1**, 18
What about … ? ['wɒt‿əbaʊt] Wie wär's mit …?; Was ist mit …? **I**
What are …? ['wɒt‿ɑː] Welche … sind es? **I**
What colour is …? [ˌwɒt 'kʌlər‿ɪz] Welche Farbe hat …? **I**
what else [ˌwɒt‿'els] was sonst; was noch **I**
What is missing? [ˌwɒt‿ɪz 'mɪsɪŋ] Was fehlt? **I**
What is … about? [ˌwɒt‿ɪz …‿ə'baʊt] Worum geht es in/im …? **I**
what it's like [ˌwɒt‿ɪts 'laɪk] wie das ist **II**

What luck! [wɒt 'lʌk] Was für ein Glück! **III**
What on earth ...? [ˌwɒt: ɒn‿'ɜ:θ] Was um alles in der Welt ...? **II**
What time? [ˌwɒt 'taɪm] Um wie viel Uhr? **I**
what to ... ['wɒt tə] was man ... **I**
What was it like? [ˌwɒt wɒz‿ɪt 'laɪk] Wie war es? **III**
what's more [ˌwɒts 'mɔ:] außerdem; überdies **IV U4**, 119
What's that? [wɒts 'ðæt] Was ist das? **I**
What's the rule for ...? [ˌwɒts ðə 'ru:l fə] Was ist die Regel für ...? **I**
What's up? [ˌwɒts‿'ʌp] Was ist los? **III**
What's your favourite ...? ['wɒts jə ˌfeɪvrɪt] Was ist dein/-e Lieblings...? **I**
What's your name? [ˌwɒts jə 'neɪm] Wie heißt du?; Wie heißen Sie? **I**
What's going on? [wɒts ˌgəʊɪŋ‿'ɒn] Was ist los?; Was geht ab? **III**
What's the matter? [ˌwɒts ðə 'mætə] Was ist los?; Was hast du? **II**
What's the time? [ˌwɒts ðə 'taɪm] Wie spät ist es?; Wie viel Uhr ist es? **I**
... **what** to do. ['wɒt tə du:] ... was ich tun soll. **II**

whatever [wɒt'evə] wie auch immer; egal (was/welche) **IV AC3**, 77
wheat [wi:t] Weizen **IV AC1**, 11
wheel [wi:l] Rad; Steuerrad; Steuer **I**
great **wheel** [ˌgreɪt 'wi:l] Riesenrad **IV U4**, 112
4-**wheel**-drive [ˌfɔ:wi:l'draɪv] Auto mit Vierradantrieb ⟨**IV TS3**, 102⟩
wheelchair ['wi:ltʃeə] Rollstuhl **II**
when [wen] wenn; wann; als **I**
whenever [wen'evə] wann immer; jedes Mal, wenn; so oft **II**
where [weə] wo; wohin **I**
Where ... from? [ˌweə ... 'frɒm] Woher ...? **I**
where I belong [ˌweər‿aɪ bɪ'lɒŋ] wo ich hingehöre **III**
... **where** to go. [ˌweə tə 'gəʊ] ... wohin ich gehen kann. **II**
I go **wherever** the wind takes me. [aɪ ˌgəʊ weəˌrevə ðə wɪnd 'teɪks mi:] Ich lasse mich treiben. **III**
whether ['weðə] ob **IV U1**, 19
which [wɪtʃ] welche/-r/-s **I**
which [wɪtʃ] der; die; das; dem; den *(Relativpronomen)* **II**
a **while** [ə 'waɪl] eine Weile **II**
while [waɪl] während **I**
to **whip** [wɪp] schlagen **I**
whisky ['wɪski] Whisky **III**
to **whisper** ['wɪspə] flüstern **I**
white [waɪt] weiß **I**
white lie [ˌwaɪt 'laɪ] Notlüge **III**
who [hu:] wer; wem; wen **I**
Who ... for? [ˌhu: 'fɔ:] Für wen ...? **I**
Who is it? [ˌhu:‿'ɪz‿ɪt] Wer ist es? **I**
Who's in? [hu:z‿'ɪn] Wer macht mit?; Wer ist dabei? **II**
who [hu:] der; dem; den; die *(Relativpronomen)* **II**
whole [həʊl] ganz **I**
whom [hu:m] wem; wen **III**
whoosh [wʊʃ] wusch **I**
whose [hu:z] wessen °**IV U1**, 14
whose [hu:z] dessen; deren *(Relativpronomen)* **II**
why [waɪ] warum **I**
that's **why** [ðæts 'waɪ] deshalb **II**
wide [waɪd] breit; weit; ausgedehnt **II**
wife [waɪf], **wives** [waɪvz] *(pl)* Ehefrau **II**
wifi ['waɪfaɪ] WLAN **III**
wiki (text) ['wɪkɪ ˌtekst] Wikitext **IV TS2**, 71
wild [waɪld] wild **II**
It's, like, so **wild** to ... [ˌɪts laɪk səʊ 'waɪld tə] Es ist echt klasse ... ⟨**IV AC3**, 77⟩
wilderness ['wɪldənəs] Wildnis **IV U4**, 112
wildlife ['waɪldlaɪf] Tierwelt *(in freier Wildbahn)* **II**
*to **win** [wɪn] gewinnen; siegen **I**
*to **win** sb over [ˌwɪn‿'əʊvə] jmdn. für sich gewinnen; jmdn. überzeugen **IV TS1**, 34
wind [wɪnd] Wind **II**
I go wherever the **wind** takes me. [aɪ ˌgəʊ weəˌrevə ðə wɪnd 'teɪks mi:] Ich lasse mich treiben. **III**
window ['wɪndəʊ] Fenster **I**
windsurfing ['wɪndsɜ:fɪŋ] Windsurfen **II**
wine [waɪn] Wein **I**
winner ['wɪnə] Gewinner/-in; Sieger/-in **I**
winter ['wɪntə] Winter **III**
Winter Formal [ˌwɪntə 'fɔ:ml] Winterfest ⟨**IV U4**, 124⟩
barbed **wire** [ˌbɑ:bd 'waɪə] Stacheldraht ⟨**IV U2**, 60⟩
wish [wɪʃ] Wunsch **I**
*to make a **wish** [ˌmeɪk‿ə 'wɪʃ] sich etwas wünschen **I**
Best **wishes** [ˌbest 'wɪʃɪz] Viele Grüße; Herzliche Grüße **II**
to **wish** [wɪʃ] (sich) wünschen **IV U1**, 21
with [wɪð] mit; bei **I**
within [wɪ'ðɪn] innerhalb °**IV AC3**, 76
without [wɪ'ðaʊt] ohne **I**
witness ['wɪtnəs] Zeuge/Zeugin **II**
wizard ['wɪzəd] Zauberer **II**
wobbly ['wɒbli] wackelig **II**
wolf [wʊlf], **wolves** [wʊlvz] *(pl)* Wolf **IV U4**, 111
woman ['wʊmən], **women** ['wɪmɪn] *(pl)* Frau **I**
no **wonder** [ˌnəʊ 'wʌndə] kein Wunder **IV U1**, 14
to **wonder** ['wʌndə] sich Gedanken machen; sich fragen **IV U3**, 92
wonderful ['wʌndəfl] wunderbar **II**
wood [wʊd] Wald; Wäldchen **III**
wood [wʊd] Holz **III**
wooded ['wʊdɪd] bewaldet **IV TS3**, 103
wooden ['wʊdn] hölzern; aus Holz **III**
Woof! [wʊf] Wau! **I**
word [wɜ:d] Wort **I**
compound **word** ['kɒmpaʊnd wɜ:d] Kompositum *(zusammengesetztes Wort)* **II**
key **word** ['ki: wɜ:d] Stichwort; Schlüsselbegriff **I**
linking **word** ['lɪŋkɪŋ ˌwɜ:d] Bindewort **I**
play on **words** [ˌpleɪ‿ɒn 'wɜ:dz] Wortspiel **III**
signal **word** ['sɪgnəl ˌwɜ:d] Signalwort **I**
word bank ['wɜ:d ˌbæŋk] Wortsammlung **III**
word cloud ['wɜ:d ˌklaʊd] Wörterwolke **II**
word order ['wɜ:d‿ˌɔ:də] Wortstellung; Satzstellung **I**
Word power ['wɜ:d ˌpaʊə] die Kraft der Wörter *(Wortschatzübung)* **I**
word snake ['wɜ:d ˌsneɪk] Wortschlange **I**
word-building ['wɜ:dˌbɪldɪŋ] Wortbildung **II**
work [wɜ:k] Arbeit **I**
pair **work** ['peə wɜ:k] Partnerarbeit **II**
to **work** [wɜ:k] arbeiten **I**; funktionieren **II**
to **work** out [ˌwɜ:k‿'aʊt] herausfinden; ausarbeiten **II**; funktionieren; klappen **III**
workbook ['wɜ:kbʊk] Arbeitsheft; Übungsheft **III**
workshop ['wɜ:kʃɒp] Workshop **I**
world [wɜ:ld] Erde; Welt **I**
outside **world** ['aʊtsaɪd ˌwɜ:ld] Außenwelt **IV U4**, 117
spirit **world** ['spɪrɪt ˌwɜ:ld] Geisterreich ⟨**IV TS3**, 107⟩
from around the **world** [frɒm əˌraʊnd ðə 'wɜ:ld] aus aller Welt **II**
worm [wɜ:m] Wurm **I**
worried ['wʌrid] beunruhigt; besorgt **III**
*to be **worried** [bi 'wʌrid] beunruhigt sein; besorgt sein **II**
to **worry** ['wʌri] sich Sorgen machen **II**
Don't **worry**! [ˌdəʊnt 'wʌri] Keine Sorge! **I**
the **worst** [ðə 'wɜ:st] der/die/das schlimmste; der/die/das schlechteste **II**
*to be **worth** [bi: 'wɜ:θ] wert sein **I**
would [wʊd] würde/-st/-n/-t **III**
would like [wʊd 'laɪk] würde/-st/-n/-t gern; hätte/-st/-n/-t gern **I**
would love [wʊd 'lʌv] würde/-st/-n/-t sehr gern; hätte/-st-/-n/-t sehr gern **I**
Would you like ...? [ˌwʊd jʊ 'laɪk] Möchtest du ...?; Möchten Sie ...?; Möchtet ihr ...? **II**
wounded ['wu:ndɪd] verwundet; verletzt **III**
Wow! [waʊ] Wow! **I**
to **wrap** [ræp] einwickeln; einpacken **I**
wrapping ['ræpɪŋ] Verpackung; Hülle **I**
to **wrinkle** one's nose [ˌrɪŋkl wʌnz 'nəʊz] die Nase rümpfen ⟨**IV U2**, 60⟩
wrist [rɪst] Handgelenk **II**
wrist watch ['rɪst wɒtʃ] Armbanduhr ⟨**IV U4**, 123⟩

*to **write** [raɪt] schreiben **I**
*to **write** down [ˌraɪt 'daʊn] aufschreiben **I**
writer ['raɪtə] Autor/-in; Verfasser/-in **III**
writing ['raɪtɪŋ] Schreiben **I**
wrong [rɒŋ] falsch **I**
*to be **wrong** [bi: 'rɒŋ] unrecht haben; sich irren **I**
*to go **wrong** [ˌgəʊ 'rɒŋ] schiefgehen **I**

X

XOXO [ˌhʌgz‿ən 'kɪsɪz] Umarmungen und Küsse *(am Ende von E-Mails und SMS)* **I**

Y

yard [jɑ:d] Garten; Hof **IV U1**, 13
front **yard** *(AE)* [ˌfrʌnt 'jɑ:d] Vorgarten **IV U1**, 13
yeah *(infml)* [jeə] ja **I**
year [jɪə] Jahr; Schuljahr **I**
New **Year's** Eve [ˌnju:‿jɪəz‿'i:v] Silvester ⟨**IV U2**, 60⟩
11-**year**-old [ɪˌlevn'jɪərəʊld] 11-Jährige/-r **II**
18-**year**-old [ˌeɪti:n 'jɪər‿əʊld] 18-jährig **II**
yearbook ['jɪəbʊk] Jahrbuch **II**
to **yell** [jel] brüllen; laut schreien ⟨**IV U4**, 124⟩
yellow ['jeləʊ] gelb **I**
yep *(infml)* [jep] ja ⟨**IV U4**, 125⟩
yes [jes] ja **I**
yesterday ['jestədeɪ] gestern **II**
yet [jet] schon; noch **II**
not … **yet** [nɒt 'jet] noch nicht **II**
yet [jet] doch; und trotzdem; und dennoch **IV U2**, 46
yoghurt ['jɒgət] Joghurt **I**
you [ju:; jə] du; ihr; Sie **I**
You know how to … [ju: 'nəʊ ˌhaʊ tə] Du weißt, wie man …; Ihr wisst, wie man … **I**
You too? [ju: 'tu:] Du auch? **I**
You'd better … *(= You had better)* ['ju:d ˌbetə] Du solltest lieber … **IV AC2**, 39
You're welcome. [jɔ: 'welkəm] Bitte schön.; Nichts zu danken.; Gern geschehen. **I**
young [jʌŋ] jung **I**
your [jɔ:; jə] dein/-e; euer/eure; Ihr/-e **I**
What's **your** name? [ˌwɒts jə 'neɪm] Wie heißt du?; Wie heißen Sie? **I**
Your turn. ['jɔ: tɜ:n] Du bist dran. **I**
yours [jɔ:z] dein/-er/-e/-es; eure/-r/-s; Ihr/-e **II**
Yours … [jɔ:z] Viele Grüße … *(am Ende von Briefen und Mails)* **II**
yourself [jɔ:'self] du/dir/dich/Sie/sich (selbst); selber **I**
yourselves [jɔ:'selvz] ihr/euch/Sie/sich (selbst); selber **II**
youth [ju:θ] Jugend **III**
yummy ['jʌmi] lecker ⟨**IV U4**, 124⟩

Z

zero ['zɪərəʊ] null **I**
zone [zəʊn] Zone **IV AC1**, 8
zoo [zu:] Zoo; Tierpark **II**
to **zoom** in (on) [ˌzu:m‿'ɪn ɒn] heranzoomen (auf) **III**

Boys' names

Arnie ['ɑ:ni] **IV U4**, 113
Arnold ['ɑ:nld] **IV U4**, 122
Austin ['ɒstɪn] **IV U1**, 26
Ben [ben] **I**
Bob [bɒb] **I**
Brad [bræd] **III**
Brodie ['brəʊdi] **IV AC3**, 77
Callum ['kæləm] **IV AC1**, 11
Carlos ['kɑ:lɒs] **IV U3**, 79
Clayton ['kleɪtn] **IV U3**, 92
Daniel ['dænjəl] **IV U2**, 62
Dave [deɪv] **I**
David ['deɪvɪd] **I**
Desmond ['dezmənd] **I**
Diego [di'eɪgəʊ] **IV U2**, 42
Eddie ['edi] **III**
Emilio [ɪ'mɪliəʊ] **IV U2**, 46
Erik ['erɪk] **IV U4**, 112
Ethan ['i:θn] **III**
Finn [fɪn] **III**
Frank [fræŋk] **II**
Gordy ['gɔ:di] **IV U4**, 125
Harrison ['hærɪsn] **IV U2**, 49
Henry ['henri] **I**
Jack [dʒæk] **I**
Jake [dʒeɪk] **IV U3**, 92
James [dʒeɪmz] **II**
Jamie ['dʒeɪmi] **I**
Jay [dʒeɪ] **I**
Jim [dʒɪm] **III**
John [dʒɒn] **II**
Josh [dʒɒʃ] **IV U1**, 13
Koi [kɔɪ] **IV U4**, 117
Lawrence ['lɔ:rəns] **IV U2**, 61
Lee [li:] **IV U3**, 82
Luke [lu:k] **I**
Mario ['mæriəʊ] **III**
Mark [mɑ:k] **IV TS2**, 74
Marley ['mɑ:li] **II**
Marlon ['mɑ:lən] **IV TS2**, 70
Matt [mæt] **III**
Matthew ['mæθju:] **IV TS3**, 105
Max [mæks] **III**
Mick [mɪk] **II**
Mike [maɪk] **II**
Moses ['məʊzɪz] **IV U3**, 92
Nathan ['neɪθn] **II**
Nick [nɪk] **II**
Peter ['pi:tə] **II**
Ravi ['rɑ:vi] **IV AC4**, 108
Rick [rɪk] **III**
Rob [rɒb] **III**
Rowdy ['raʊdi] ⟨**IV U4**, 122⟩
Scott [skɒt] **IV U1**, 18
Sean [ʃɔ:n] **III**
Shahid [ʃɑ:'hi:d] **I**
Sherman ['ʃɜ:mən] ⟨**IV U4**, 125⟩
Simon ['saɪmən] **III**
Steve [sti:v] **I**
Stuart ['stu:ət] **III**
Suni ['su:ni] **IV U4**, 119
Thomas ['tɒməs] **III**
Tim [tɪm] **IV TS2**, 70
Todd [tɒd] ⟨**IV U2**, 60⟩
Tony ['təʊni] **I**
Tristan ['trɪstən] **IV AC1**, 11
Tyler ['taɪlə] **I**
Wesley ['wezli] **IV U1**, 25
Will [wɪl] **II**
Zach [zæk] **IV AC4**, 108

Girls' names

Abbie ['æbi] **IV U3**, 92
Alice ['ælɪs] **II**
Alicia [ə'lɪsiə; ə'lɪʃə] **I**
Amber ['æmbə] **I**
Anna ['ænə] **I**
Anne [æn] **I**
Annie ['æni] **III**
Anya ['ænjə] **III**
Ashley ['æʃli] **IV U2**, 43
Ava ['ɑ:və] **IV U4**, 112
Carol ['kærəl] **I**
Ceri ['keri] **II**
Christine [krɪ'sti:n] **IV U2**, 61
Claire ['kleə] **I**
Eileen [aɪ'li:n] **IV U3**, 79
Ellen ['elən] ⟨**IV U4**, 125⟩
Emily ['emɪli] **I**
Eva ['i:və] **IV U1**, 18
Frances ['frɑ:nsɪs] **I**
Gwen [gwen] **II**
Haley ['heɪli] **III**
Harriet ['hæriət] **IV U3**, 92
Helen ['helɪn] **II**
Holly ['hɒli] **I**
Irina [ɪ'ri:nə] **I**
Ivy ['aɪvi] **III**
Janie ['dʒeɪni] **IV U1**, 26
Jean [dʒi:n] **III**
Jenna ['dʒenə] **IV U4**, 114
Jenny ['dʒeni] **III**
Jessica ['dʒesɪkə] **IV U1**, 25
Judith ['dʒu:dɪθ] **II**
Julie ['dʒu:li] **I**
June [dʒu:n] **IV AC3**, 77
Kate [keɪt] **II**
Kelly ['keli] **IV U2**, 48
Kim [kɪm] **IV U4**, 112
Kirsty ['kɜ:sti] **III**
Laura ['lɔ:rə] **I**
Lauren ['lɔ:rən] **II**
Leanne [li'æn] **IV U1**, 25
Lilly ['lɪli] **IV U3**, 92
Lou [lu:] **I**
Lucy ['lu:si] **I**
Madison ['mædɪsn] **IV U1**, 14
Margaret ['mɑ:grət] **III**
Mary ['meəri] **II**
Megan ['megən] **II**
Meredith ['merədɪθ] **IV U2**, 47
Myra ['maɪrə] **IV U3**, 92
Nancy ['nænsi] **IV U2**, 44
Norma ['nɔ:mə] ⟨**IV TS3**, 105⟩
Olivia [ɒl'ɪviə] **I**
Penelope [pə'neləpi] **IV U4**, 123
Pia ['pi:ə] **I**
Polly ['pɒli] **II**
Rebecca [rɪ'bekə] **IV U4**, 127
Rita ['ri:tə] **IV U2**, 62
Rose [rəʊz] **I**
Ruby ['ru:bi] **II**
Rylee ['raɪli] **IV U2**, 42
Sally ['sæli] **I**
Sarah ['seərə] **IV U2**, 61
Sophie ['səʊfi] **IV U1**, 14
Susan ['su:zn] **IV TS3**, 105
Tamara [tə'mɑ:rə] **II**
Tina ['ti:nə] **III**
Violet ['vaɪələt] **III**
Vivien ['vɪvjən] **II**

Surnames

Alexie [ə'leksi] ⟨**IV U4**, 125⟩
Ashton ['æʃtən] **II**
Azad [ə'zɑ:d] **I**
Berners-Lee [ˌbɜ:nəz'li:] **IV U3**, 87
Blanchard ['blænʃəd] **IV U2**, 49
Chen [tʃen] **IV U4**, 117
Elliot ['eliət] **I**
Emory ['emri] **IV U4**, 114
Ford [fɔ:d] **IV U1**, 26
Forester ['fɒrɪstə] **IV U3**, 82
Forney ['fɔ:ni] ⟨**IV U4**, 125⟩
Francis ['frɑ:nsɪs] **III**
Fraser ['freɪzə] **I**
Green [gri:n] **I**
Henry ['henri] **IV U3**, 86
Hilstad ['hɪlstæd] **IV U4**, 112
Jameson ['dʒeɪmsn] **IV U3**, 92
Jones [dʒəʊnz] **III**
Karp [kɑ:p] **III**
King [kɪŋ] **III**
Mahmoud **III**
Miller ['mɪlə] **III**
Moreno [mə'ri:nəʊ] **IV U2**, 62
Morse [mɔ:s] **IV U3**, 86
Nicholls ['nɪkəlz] **II**
Parker ['pɑ:kə] **II**
Preston ['prestən] **I**
Richardson ['rɪtʃədsn] **I**
Strasser ['stræsə] ⟨**IV U2**, 60⟩
Swindon ['swɪndən] **I**
Thompson ['tɒmsən] **II**
Vail [veɪl] **IV U3**, 86
Walker ['wɔ:kə] **I**
Watney ['wɒtni] **IV TS2**, 74
Winchester ['wɪntʃɪstə] ⟨**IV TS3**, 107⟩
Woodruff ['wʊdrʌf] **III**
Wright [raɪt] **II**

Place names

Aberdeen [ˌæbə'di:n] *Stadt in Schottland* **III**
Astoria [ə'stɔ:riə] *Stadt in den USA* ⟨**IV TS3**, 105⟩
Baltimore ['bɔ:ltɪmɔ:] *Stadt in den USA* **IV U3**, 86
Bankside ['bæŋksaɪd] *Stadtteil von London* **III**
Bedloe Island [ˌbedləʊ‿'aɪlənd] **IV U2**, 44
Birchview ['bɜ:tʃvju:] *Stadt in den USA* **IV U1**, 14
Birmingham ['bɜ:mɪŋəm] **III**
Black Lake [ˌblæk 'leɪk] *Stadt in den USA* **IV U3**, 92
Boston ['bɒstn] *Stadt in den USA* **IV AC1**, 11
Bozeman ['bəʊzmən] *Stadt in den USA* ⟨**IV TS3**, 103⟩
Bradford ['brædfəd] **II**
Bristol ['brɪstl] **III**
Broadway ['brɔ:dweɪ] *Straße in NYC* **IV AC1**, 11
Brooklyn ['brʊklɪn] *Stadtteil von New York* **IV TS1**, 35
Butte [bju:t] *Stadt in den USA* ⟨**IV TS3**, 103⟩
Caerphilly [keə'fɪli] *walisische Stadt* **II**
Cambridge ['keɪmbrɪdʒ] *Stadt in den USA* **IV U1**, 14
Camden Market ['kæmdən ˌmɑ:kɪt] **II**
Chicago [ʃɪ'kɑ:gəʊ] *Stadt in den USA* **IV AC1**, 9
Coeur d'Alene [ˌkɔ:r də'leɪn] *Stadt in den USA* ⟨**IV TS3**, 106⟩
College Way [ˌkɒlɪdʒ 'weɪ] **I**
Cologne [kə'ləʊn] Köln **I**
Covent Garden [ˌkɒvnt 'gɑ:dn] **II**
Cracow ['krækɒv; 'krɑ:kaʊ] Krakau **I**
Dover ['dəʊvə] *englische Küstenstadt am Ärmelkanal* **III**
Dubai [du:'baɪ] **III**
Edinburgh ['edɪnbrə] **II**
Ellis Island [ˌelɪs‿'aɪlənd] *Insel vor New York City* **IV AC1**, 8
Glasgow ['glɑ:zgəʊ] *Stadt in Schottland* **III**
Heathrow [ˌhi:θ'rəʊ] *Flughafen in London* **III**
Helena ['helɪnə] *Stadt in den USA* ⟨**IV TS3**, 103⟩
Hollywood ['hɒliwʊd] **II**
Houston ['hju:stn] *Stadt in den USA* **IV TS2**, 71
Huntington Beach [ˌhʌntɪŋtən 'bi:tʃ] *Stadt in den USA* ⟨**IV TS3**, 107⟩
Hyde Park [ˌhaɪd 'pɑ:k] **II**
Isle of Man [ˌaɪl‿əv 'mæn] **II**
Jamestown ['dʒeɪmztaʊn] *Stadt in den USA* **IV U3**, 80
Lakeview ['leɪkvju:] *Stadt in den USA* **IV U1**, 21
Liberty Island [ˌlɪbəti‿'aɪlənd] **IV U2**, 44
Liverpool ['lɪvəpu:l] **III**
London ['lʌndən] **I**
Lower Manhattan [ˌləʊə mæn'hætn] **IV U2**, 44
Manhattan [mæn'hætn] *Stadtteil von New York* **IV TS1**, 35
Miami [maɪ'æmi] *Stadt in den USA* **IV U4**, 121
Midtown Manhattan [ˌmɪdtaʊn mæn'hætn] **IV U2**, 41
Missoula [mɪ'zu:lə] *Stadt in den USA* ⟨**IV TS3**, 103⟩
Nashville ['næʃvɪl] *Stadt in den USA* **IV U4**, 121
New York [ˌnju: 'jɔ:k] **III**
Nottingham ['nɒtɪŋəm] **II**
Oxford Street ['ɒksfəd ˌstri:t] **II**
Paddington ['pædɪŋtən] **II**
Philadelphia [ˌfɪlə'delfiə] *Stadt in den USA* **IV TS1**, 35
Phoenix ['fi:nɪks] *Stadt in den USA* **IV U4**, 121
Pittsburgh ['pɪtsbɜ:g] *Stadt in den USA* **IV U1**, 14
Pittsfield ['pɪtsfi:ld] *Stadt in den USA* **IV U3**, 92
Port Angeles [pɔ:t‿'ændʒɪləs] *Stadt in den USA* **IV U4**, 117
Portland ['pɔ:tlənd] *Stadt in den USA* **IV U4**, 111
Reardan ['rɪədən] *Stadt in den USA* ⟨**IV U4**, 123⟩
Roswell ['rɒzwel] *Stadt in den USA* **IV TS2**, 75
San Diego [ˌsæn di'eɪgəʊ] *Stadt in den USA* **IV AC1**, 11
San José [ˌsæn həʊ'zeɪ] *Stadt in den USA* ⟨**IV TS3**, 107⟩
Sandy Hook [ˌsændi 'hʊk] *Stadt in den USA* **IV U4**, 127
Seaside ['si:saɪd] *Stadt in den USA* ⟨**IV TS3**, 105⟩
Seattle [si'ætl] **III**
Stratford-upon-Avon [ˌstrætfədəpɒn'eɪvn] *Geburtsort Shakespeares* **III**
Tacoma [tə'kəʊmə] *Stadt in den USA* ⟨**IV TS3**, 105⟩
Vancouver [væn'ku:və] *Stadt in Kanada* **IV U4**, 111
Washington, D.C. [ˌwɒʃɪŋtən ˌdi:'si:] *Hauptstadt der USA* **IV TS1**, 35
Wellpinit ['welpɪnɪt] *Stadt in den USA* ⟨**IV U4**, 123⟩
Wimbledon ['wɪmbldən] **I**

Geographical names

Africa ['æfrɪkə] Afrika **III**
Alabama [ˌælə'bæmə] *US-amerik. Bundesstaat* **IV U2**, 42
America [ə'merɪkə] Amerika **II**
Arizona [ˌærɪ'zəʊnə] *US-amerik. Bundesstaat* **IV AC1**, 8
Asia ['eɪʒə] Asien **IV AC1**, 8
Atlantic Ocean [ətˌlæntɪk 'əʊʃn] Atlantischer Ozean **II**
Australia [ɒs'treɪliə] Australien **II**
Austria ['ɔ:strɪə] Österreich **II**
Bangladesh [ˌbæŋglə'deʃ] Bangladesch **III**
Ben Nevis [ˌben 'nevɪs] *Berg in Schottland* **III**
Britain ['brɪtn] Großbritannien **I**
British Columbia [ˌbrɪtɪʃ kə'lʌmbiə] *kanadische Provinz* **IV U4**, 110
British Empire [ˌbrɪtɪʃ‿'empaɪə] britisches Königreich **II**
British Isles [ˌbrɪtɪʃ‿'aɪlz] Britische Inseln **II**
California [ˌkælɪ'fɔ:niə] Kalifornien *(US-amerik. Bundesstaat)* **IV AC1**, 9
Canada ['kænədə] Kanada **I**
China ['tʃaɪnə] China **I**
Cornwall ['kɔ:nwɔ:l] **II**
Crater Lake National Park [ˌkreɪtə leɪk ˌnæʃnl 'pɑ:k] **IV U4**, 114
Cuba ['kju:bə] Kuba **IV U2**, 62
Death Valley [ˌdeθ 'væli] **IV TS3**, 102
Egypt ['i:dʒɪpt] Ägypten **III**
Elliot Bay [ˌeliət 'beɪ] **IV U4**, 111
Elwha River [ˌelwə 'rɪvə] (leer) **IV U4**, 117
England ['ɪŋglənd] England **I**
Europe ['jʊərəp] Europa **IV U3**, 81
European Union (EU) [ˌjʊərəpiən 'ju:njən (i:ju:)] Europäische Union **II**
France [frɑ:ns] Frankreich **II**
Germany ['dʒɜ:məni] Deutschland **I**
Glacier National Park [ˌglæsiə ˌnæʃnl 'pɑ:k] **IV TS3**, 103
Great Britain (GB) [ˌgreɪt 'brɪtn] Großbritannien **II**
Idaho ['aɪdəhəʊ] *US-amerik. Bundesstaat* ⟨**IV TS3**, 106⟩
India ['ɪndiə] Indien **II**
Ireland ['aɪələnd] Irland **IV U3**, 85
Italy ['ɪtəli] Italien **II**
Kent [kent] *Grafschaft im Südosten Englands* **II**
Kenya ['kenjə] Kenia **III**
Lake Washington [ˌleɪk 'wɒʃɪŋtən] **IV U4**, 114
Latin America [ˌlætɪn ə'merɪkə] Lateinamerika **IV AC1**, 8
Loch Ness [ˌlɒx 'nes; ˌlɒk 'nes] *See in Schottland* **III**
Maryland ['meərilænd] *US-amerik. Bundesstaat* **IV U3**, 86
Mexico ['meksɪkəʊ] Mexiko **IV U3**, 81
(the) **Midwest** [ˌmɪd'west] (der) Mittlere Westen **IV AC1**, 11
Milwaukee [mɪl'wɔ:ki] *US-amerik. Bundesstaat* **IV U3**, 83
Missouri [mɪ'zʊəri] *US-amerik. Bundesstaat* **IV U3**, 86
Montana [mɒn'tænə] *US-amerik. Bundesstaat* **IV TS3**, 103
Mount Rainier [ˌmaʊnt reɪ'niə] *Berg in den USA* **IV AC1**, 8
Mount St. Helens [ˌmaʊnt snt 'helənz] *Vulkan in den USA* **IV U4**, 120
New Jersey [ˌnju: 'dʒɜ:zi] *US-amerik. Bundesstaat* **IV U4**, 127

New Mexico [ˌnjuː ˈmeksɪkəʊ] *US-amerik. Bundesstaat* **IV TS2**, 75
Normandy [ˈnɔːməndi] die Normandie **II**
North Sea [ˌnɔːθ ˈsiː] Nordsee **II**
Northern Ireland [ˌnɔːðn‿ˈaɪələnd] Nordirland **II**
Oregon [ˈɒrɪgən] *US-amerik. Bundesstaat* **IV U3**, 92
the Pacific Northwest [ðə pəˌsɪfɪk nɔːθˈwest] Pazifischer Nordwesten **IV AC1**, 8
Pacific Ring of Fire [pəˌsɪfɪk ˌrɪŋ‿əv ˈfaɪə] Pazifischer Feuerring *(Vulkangürtel im Pazifischen Ozean)* **IV U4**, 120
Pakistan [ˌpɑːkɪˈstɑːn] **I**
Pennsylvania [ˌpensɪlˈveɪniə] *US-amerik. Bundesstaat* **IV U1**, 14
Poland [ˈpəʊlənd] Polen **I**
Puget Sound [ˌpjuːdʒət ˈsaʊnd] *Bucht vor Seattle* **IV U4**, 111
Republic of Ireland [rɪˌpʌblɪk‿əv‿ˈaɪələnd] Republik Irland **II**
the Rockies (= the Rocky Mountains) [ðə ˈrɒkiz] *Gebirge in the USA* **IV AC1**, 11
Russia [ˈrʌʃə] Russland **IV AC1**, 9
Scandinavia [ˌskændɪˈneɪviə] Skandinavien **III**
Scotland [ˈskɒtlənd] Schottland **II**
Sherwood Forest [ˌʃɜːwʊd ˈfɒrɪst] **II**
the Shetland Islands [ðə ˈʃetlənd ˌaɪləndz] die Shetlandinseln **III**
Snowdonia National Park [snəʊˌdəʊniə ˌnæʃnl ˈpɑːk] **II**
Somalia [səˈmɑːliə] Somalia **III**
South Africa [ˌsaʊθ‿ˈæfrɪkə] Südafrika **II**
Soviet Union [ˌsəʊviət ˈjuːnjən] Sowjetunion **IV TS2**, 71
Spain [speɪn] Spanien **II**
Sweden [ˈswiːdn] Schweden **IV AC1**, 9
Thames [temz] **I**
United Kingdom (UK) [juːˈkeɪ] Vereinigtes Königreich von Großbritannien und Nordirland **I**
the US (= the United States) [ðə juːˈes] die USA (= die Vereinigten Staaten) **IV AC1**, 8
USA (United States of America) [juːesˈeɪ (juːˌnaɪtɪd ˌsteɪts‿əv‿əˈmerɪkə)] USA (Vereinigte Staaten von Amerika) **II**
Virginia [vəˈdʒɪnjə] *US-amerik. Bundesstaat* **IV U3**, 80
Wales [weɪlz] **II**
Washington State [ˌwɒʃɪŋtən ˈsteɪt] *US-amerik. Bundesstaat* **IV AC1**, 8
Wisconsin [wɪˈskɒnsɪn] *US-amerik. Bundesstaat* **IV U2**, 46
Wyoming [waɪˈəʊmɪŋ] *US-amerik. Bundesstaat* **IV U4**, 114
Yellowstone National Park [ˌjeləʊstəʊn ˌnæʃnl ˈpɑːk] **IV U4**, 114

Other names

A River Runs Through it [ə ˌrɪvə ˌrʌnz ˈθruː‿ɪt] Aus der Mitte entspringt ein Fluss *(Filmtitel)* ⟨**IV TS3**, 103⟩
Air Jordan [ˌeə ˈdʒɔːdn] ⟨**IV U4**, 123⟩
Amazon [ˈæməzn] **IV U4**, 110
Apollo 11 [əˌpɒləʊ ɪˈlevn] *Raumfähre* **IV TS2**, 71
Area 51 [ˌeəriə ˌfɪftiˈwʌn] **IV TS2**, 72
Astor Place Cube [ˌæstə pleɪs ˈkjuːb] *Kunstwerk* **IV U2**, 42
Auguste Bartholdi [ɔːˌgʊst bɑːˈtəʊldi] *frz. Bildhauer* **IV U2**, 44
Auld Lang Syne [ˌɔːld læŋ ˈsaɪn] *schottisches Volkslied* **III**
Austro-Hungarian Empire [ˌɔːstrəʊhʌŋˌgeəriən ˈempaɪə] Österreichisch-Ungarische Monarchie **IV U3**, 85
Best Young Tech Entrepreneur [ˌbest jʌŋ ˌtek ɒntrəprəˈnɜː] **III**
Big Ben [ˌbɪg ˈben] **II**
Bigfoot [ˈbɪgfʊt] *Wesen einer Legende* ⟨**IV U4**, 123⟩
Blackfeet [ˈblækfiːt] *Indianerstamm* ⟨**IV TS3**, 103⟩
Boeing [ˈbəʊɪŋ] *Flugzeughersteller* **IV U4**, 110
British Airways [ˌbrɪtɪʃ‿ˈeəweɪz] *Fluggesellschaft* **III**
British Museum [ˌbrɪtɪʃ mjuːˈziːəm] **II**
Buckingham Palace [ˌbʌkɪŋəm ˈpælɪs] **II**
Capricorn One [ˌkæprɪkɔːn ˈwʌn] *Filmtitel* **IV TS2**, 74
Census Bureau [ˈsensəs ˌbjʊərəʊ] *US-amerik. Bundesbehörde für Volkszählung* **IV U3**, 85
Central Park [ˌsentrl ˈpɑːk] *Park in New York* **IV U2**, 41
Changing of the Guards [ˌtʃeɪndʒɪŋ əv ðə ˈgɑːdz] *Wachwechsel vor dem Buckingham Palace* **II**
Cherokee [ˈtʃerəkiː] *Nordamerik. Indianerstamm* **IV U3**, 84
Chinatown [ˈtʃaɪnətaʊn] **IV U2**, 41
Chrysler [ˈkraɪslə] *Automarke* ⟨**IV TS3**, 106⟩
Chrysler Building [ˈkraɪslə ˌbɪldɪŋ] *Wolkenkratzer in New York* **IV U2**, 41
Church of England [ˌtʃɜːtʃ‿əv ˈɪŋglənd] **III**
Coast Salish [ˌkəʊst ˈseɪlɪʃ] *Indianerstamm* **IV U4**, 116
Cold War [ˌkəʊld ˈwɔː] Kalter Krieg **IV TS2**, 71
Columbia [kəˈlʌmbiə] *Raumkapsel* **IV TS2**, 71
Costco [ˈkɒstkəʊ] *US-amerik. Großhandelskette* **IV U4**, 110
Cowichan [ˈkaʊɪtʃən] *Indianerstamm* **IV U4**, 116
Devil's Inn [ˌdevlz‿ˈɪn] ⟨**IV TS3**, 102⟩
Docklands Light Railway *(DLR)* [ˌdɒklændz ˌlaɪt ˈreɪlweɪ] *Regionalbahn im Osten Londons* **I**
Eagle [ˈiːgl] *Raumkapsel* **IV TS2**, 71
Edinburgh Fringe Festival [ˌedɪnbrə ˈfrɪndʒ ˌfestɪvl] **III**

Empire State Building [ˌempaɪə ˈsteɪt ˌbɪldɪŋ] *Wolkenkratzer in NYC* **IV AC1**, 9
Empire State of Mind [ˌempaɪə ˌsteɪt‿əv ˈmaɪnd] *Liedtitel* **IV U2**, 40
Fashion Fabulous [ˌfæʃn ˈfæbjələs] **IV TS1**, 36
the Globe Theatre [ðə ˌgləʊb ˈθɪətə] **III**
God Save the Queen [ˈgɒd seɪv ðə ˌkwiːn] Gott schütze die Königin *(britische Nationalhymne)* **III**
Halloween [ˌhæləʊˈiːn] *Tag vor Allerheiligen* **I**
Hogmanay [ˈhɒgməneɪ] *traditionelles schottisches Neujahrsfest* **III**
the Houses of Parliament [ðə ˌhaʊzɪz‿əv ˈpɑːləmənt] *britisches Parlamentsgebäude* **II**
Independence Day [ˌɪndɪˈpendəns ˌdeɪ] amerikanischer Unabhängigkeitstag **IV AC1**, 11
Industrial Revolution [ɪnˌdʌstriəl revlˈuːʃn] die industrielle Revolution **III**
Juillard School [ˈdʒuːljəd ˌskuːl] *Hochschule für Tanz* **IV U2**, 42
Kmart [ˈkeɪmɑːt] ⟨**IV U4**, 123⟩
London Eye [ˌlʌndən‿ˈaɪ] **II**
Lower Elwha Klallam [ˌləʊə ˌelwə ˈklæləm] *Indianerstamm* **IV U4**, 117
Madame Tussauds [ˌmædəm tʊˈsɔːdz] **II**
Mars [mɑːz] **IV TS2**, 74
Meridian Line [məˌrɪdiən ˈlaɪn] Nullmeridian **I**
Metropolitan Museum of Art [metrəˌpɒlɪtn mjuːˌziːəm‿əv‿ˈɑːt] *Museum in New York* **IV U2**, 42
Microsoft [ˈmaɪkrəsɒft] **IV U4**, 110
Millennium Footbridge [mɪˌleniəm ˈfʊtbrɪdʒ] **II**
Natural History Museum [ˌnætʃrl ˈhɪstri mjuːˌziːəm] **II**
Navajo [ˈnævəhəʊ] *Nordamerik. Indianerstamm* **IV U3**, 84
Navy [ˈneɪvi] Marine **III**
OG [əʊˈdʒiː] **IV U2**, 49
The Oregon Trail [ði‿ˌɒrɪgən ˈtreɪl] **IV U3**, 92
Oyster card [ˈɔɪstə ˌkɑːd] **II**
Park Avenue [ˌpɑːk‿ˈævənjuː] *Straße in New York* **IV U2**, 46
Pike Place Market [ˌpaɪk pleɪs ˈmɑːkɪt] **IV U4**, 112
Pledge of Allegiance [ˌpledʒ‿əv‿əˈliːdʒns] *Treueeid auf die amerikanische Flagge* **IV U1**, 18
Pony Express [ˌpəʊni ɪkˈspres] *Postzustellung zu Pferde* **IV U3**, 86
Ralph Lauren [ˌrælf ˈlɔːrən] ⟨**IV U4**, 123⟩
Retro 4ever [ˌretrəʊ fəˈrevə] **IV TS1**, 35
Revolutionary War [revlˌuːʃnri ˈwɔː] Amerikanischer Unabhängigkeitskrieg **IV U3**, 80
Rockefeller Center [ˌrɒkəfelə ˈsentə] *Gebäude in New York* **IV U2**, 42
Roman Empire [ˌrəʊmən ˈempaɪə] Römisches Reich **III**
Royal Observatory [ˌrɔɪəl‿əbˈzɜːvətri] **I**

Famous names

In the classroom

Tip

Die Wörter und Ausdrücke auf diesen Seiten musst du nicht auswendig lernen. Aber in vielen Situationen im Klassenzimmer wirst du sie nützlich finden!

Vocabulary for instructions and activities

(Die mit * gekennzeichneten Begriffe werden im Fachlehrplan von mindestens einem Bundesland als Operatoren definiert. Die Verwendung der geforderten Operatoren in Green Line beginnt in Band 1 und wird Band für Band ausgebaut.)

Act (out) one of the scenes. / Act (out) the dialogues.	Spiele eine der Szenen. / Spiele die Dialoge.
Add more words / ideas.	Füge weitere Wörter / Ideen hinzu.
Ask your partner questions.	Stelle deinem Partner / deiner Partnerin Fragen.
Answer your partner's questions.	Beantworte die Fragen deines Partners / deiner Partnerin.
Check your partner's text.	Überprüfe den Text deines Partners / deiner Partnerin.
Choose a character / one of the situations / options.	Wähle eine Figur / eine der Situationen / Optionen aus.
Collect ideas.	Sammle Ideen.
***Compare** English and German.	Vergleiche das Englische und das Deutsche.
Complete the answers.	Vervollständige die Antworten.
Copy the grid / the mind map.	Schreibe die Tabelle / das Wörternetz ab.
Correct the wrong sentences.	Korrigiere die falschen Sätze.
***Describe** what you see / how it makes you feel.	Beschreibe, was du siehst / wie du dich dabei fühlst.
Decide who writes which part.	Entscheidet, wer welchen Teil schreibt.
***Discuss** different ideas.	Diskutiert verschiedene Ideen.
Divide your class up into two groups.	Teilt eure Klasse in zwei Gruppen auf.
Draw a picture.	Zeichne ein Bild.
Exchange your flyers / questions.	Tauscht eure Flyer / Fragen untereinander aus.
***Explain** your answer. / Explain why.	Erkläre deine Antwort. / Erkläre warum.
Fill in your grid / the form.	Fülle deine Tabelle / das Formular aus.
Find the rule / the right word order.	Finde die Regel / die richtige Wortstellung.
Finish your brochure.	Stelle deine Broschüre fertig.
Form expert groups.	Bildet Expertengruppen.
Get organised.	Organisiert euch.
Give reasons / examples.	Nenne Gründe / Beispiele.
Give feedback.	Gib ein Feedback.
Go back to your home group.	Gehe zurück zu deiner ersten Gruppe.

Guess the new words.	Errate die neuen Wörter.
Imagine you're one of the people in the story.	Stelle dir vor, du bist eine der Personen in der Geschichte.
Improve your text / part of the report.	Verbessere deinen Text / deinen Teil des Berichts.
Learn your text by heart.	Lerne deinen Text auswendig.
Listen to the sentences / the dialogue.	Höre dir die Sätze / den Dialog an.
Look at the picture / the examples.	Schau dir das Bild / die Beispiele an.
***Look up** the words.	Schlage die Wörter nach.
Make a poster / a grid / a mind map / notes.	Fertige ein Poster / eine Tabelle / ein Wörternetz / Notizen an.
***Match** the sentence parts.	Ordne die Satzteile einander zu.
Note down what is missing.	Notiere, was fehlt.
Plan the scenes.	Plane die Szenen.
Practise your scenes / the dialogues.	Übe deine Szenen / die Dialoge.
***Present** the information from your text.	Präsentiere die Informationen aus deinem Text.
Put in the correct forms.	Setze die richtigen Formen ein.
Put the verbs in the right / correct form.	Bringe die Verben in die richtige Form.
Read your text aloud. / Read your text out loud.	Lies deinen Text laut vor.
Record your final report / dialogue.	Nehmt euren fertigen Bericht / Dialog auf.
Repeat the sentences / the dialogues.	Wiederhole die Sätze / die Dialoge.
***Report** what the people say.	Berichte, was die Leute sagen.
Say the words / the sounds.	Sage die Wörter / die Laute.
Scan the text for details.	Suche den Text nach Details ab.
Share the information with your partner.	Teile die Informationen mit deinem Partner / deiner Partnerin.
Skim the text for the gist.	Überfliege den Text und finde die wichtigsten Aussagen.
***Sum up / Summarise** what happens in the story.	Fasse zusammen, was in der Geschichte passiert.
Swap roles.	Tauscht die Rollen.
Take notes.	Mache dir Notizen.
Take turns.	Wechselt euch ab.
***Talk** with / to your partner (about …).	Sprich mit deinem Partner / deiner Partnerin (über …).
***Tell** your partner about your experiences.	Erzähle deinem Partner / deiner Partnerin von deinen Erfahrungen.
Think about different problems.	Denke über verschiedene Probleme nach.
Think of ideas for …	Überlege dir Ideen für …
***Translate** the words / sentences.	Übersetze die Wörter / Sätze.
Underline the words that change.	Unterstreiche die Wörter, die sich ändern.
Use the ideas / the vocabulary.	Verwende die Ideen / die Vokabeln.
Watch the film.	Sieh dir den Film an.
Work with a partner or in a group.	Arbeite mit einem Partner / einer Partnerin oder in einer Gruppe.
***Write** dialogues / a short text / a reply / a summary.	Schreibe Dialoge / einen kurzen Text / eine Antwort / eine Zusammenfassung.
Write about your friends.	Schreibe über deine Freunde.
Write down your ideas / key words.	Schreibe deine Ideen / Schlüsselwörter auf.

Find more online: a6q5h3

Irregular verbs

■ ■ ■ Grundform, *simple past* und *past participle* sind identisch
■ ● ● Grundform unterscheidet sich vom *simple past* und *past participle*
■ ● ■ Grundform und *past participle* sind identisch, nur das *simple past* hat eine andere Form
■ ● ▲ Grundform, *simple past* und *past participle* haben alle eine andere Form

■ Grundform	■ simple past	■ past participle	Deutsch
cost [kɒst]	cost [kɒst]	cost [kɒst]	kosten
cut [kʌt]	cut [kʌt]	cut [kʌt]	schneiden
hit [hɪt]	hit [hɪt]	hit [hɪt]	schlagen, treffen
hurt [hɜ:t]	hurt [hɜ:t]	hurt [hɜ:t]	verletzen, sich weh tun
let [let]	let [let]	let [let]	lassen
put [pʊt]	put [pʊt]	put [pʊt]	legen, setzen, stellen

■ Grundform	● simple past	● past participle	Deutsch
bring [brɪŋ]	brought [brɔ:t]	brought [brɔ:t]	(mit)bringen
build [bɪld]	built [bɪlt]	built [bɪlt]	bauen
burn [bɜ:n]	burnt [bɜ:nt]	burnt [bɜ:nt]	(ver)brennen
buy [baɪ]	bought [bɔ:t]	bought [bɔ:t]	kaufen
catch [kætʃ]	caught [kɔ:t]	caught [kɔ:t]	fangen; mitbekommen
dream [dri:m]	dreamed [dri:md] / dreamt [dremt]	dreamed [dri:md] / dreamt [dremt]	träumen
feel [fi:l]	felt [felt]	felt [felt]	fühlen
find [faɪnd]	found [faʊnd]	found [faʊnd]	finden
get [get]	got [gɒt]	got [gɒt]	bekommen; werden
hang [hæŋ]	hung [hʌŋ]	hung [hʌŋ]	hängen
have [hæv]	had [hæd]	had [hæd]	haben
hear [hɪə]	heard [hɜ:d]	heard [hɜ:d]	hören
hold [həʊld]	held [held]	held [held]	halten
keep [ki:p]	kept [kept]	kept [kept]	(auf)bewahren, behalten
lead [li:d]	led [led]	led [led]	(an)führen
learn [lɜ:n]	learned [lɜ:nd] / learnt [lɜ:nt]	learned [lɜ:nd] / learnt [lɜ:nt]	lernen
leave [li:v]	left [left]	left [left]	(ver)lassen
lend [lend]	lent [lent]	lent [lent]	(ver)leihen
make [meɪk]	made [meɪd]	made [meɪd]	machen, tun
meet [mi:t]	met [met]	met [met]	treffen
pay [peɪ]	paid [peɪd]	paid [peɪd]	(be)zahlen
read [ri:d]	read [red]	read [red]	lesen
say [seɪ]	said [sed]	said [sed]	sagen
sell [sel]	sold [səʊld]	sold [səʊld]	verkaufen
send [send]	sent [sent]	sent [sent]	senden, verschicken
shoot [ʃu:t]	shot [ʃɒt]	shot [ʃɒt]	schießen (auf)
sit [sɪt]	sat [sæt]	sat [sæt]	sitzen
sleep [sli:p]	slept [slept]	slept [slept]	schlafen
smell [smel]	smelt [smelt]	smelt [smelt]	riechen, duften

spell [spel]	spelt [spelt]	spelt [spelt]	buchstabieren
spend [spend]	spent [spent]	spent [spent]	ausgeben, verbringen
spill [spɪl]	spilt [spɪlt]	spilt [spɪlt]	verschütten, auslaufen
stand (up) [stænd]	stood (up) [stʊd]	stood (up) [stʊd]	(auf)stehen
sting [stɪŋ]	stung [stʌŋ]	stung [stʌŋ]	stechen
teach [ti:tʃ]	taught [tɔ:t]	taught [tɔ:t]	lehren, unterrichten
tell [tel]	told [təʊld]	told [təʊld]	erzählen
think [θɪŋk]	thought [θɔ:t]	thought [θɔ:t]	(nach)denken, glauben
understand [ˌʌndəˈstænd]	understood [ˌʌndəˈstʊd]	understood [ˌʌndəˈstʊd]	verstehen
win [wɪn]	won [wʌn]	won [wʌn]	gewinnen, siegen

■ Grundform	● simple past	■ past participle	Deutsch
become [bɪˈkʌm]	became [bɪˈkeɪm]	become [bɪˈkʌm]	werden
come [kʌm]	came [keɪm]	come [kʌm]	kommen
run [rʌn]	ran [ræn]	run [rʌn]	laufen, rennen

■ Grundform	● simple past	▲ past participle	Deutsch
be [bi:]	was / were [wɒz / wɜ:]	been [bi:n]	sein
blow (out) [bləʊ]	blew [blu:]	blown [bləʊn]	(aus)blasen, (aus)pusten
break [breɪk]	broke [brəʊk]	broken [ˈbrəʊkn]	(zer)brechen, kaputt machen
choose [tʃu:z]	chose [tʃəʊz]	chosen [tʃəʊzn]	(aus)wählen
do [du:]	did [dɪd]	done [dʌn]	machen, tun
draw [drɔ:]	drew [dru:]	drawn [drɔ:n]	zeichnen
drink [drɪŋk]	drank [dræŋk]	drunk [drʌŋk]	trinken
drive [draɪv]	drove [drəʊv]	driven [ˈdrɪvn]	fahren
eat [i:t]	ate [et]	eaten [i:tn]	essen
fall [fɔ:l]	fell [fel]	fallen [ˈfɔ:lən]	fallen
fly [flaɪ]	flew [flu:]	flown [fləʊn]	fliegen
forget [fəˈget]	forgot [fəˈgɒt]	forgotten [fəˈgɒtn]	vergessen
give [gɪv]	gave [geɪv]	given[ˈgɪvn]	geben
go [gəʊ]	went [went]	gone [gɒn]	gehen, fahren
grow [grəʊ]	grew [gru:]	grown [grəʊn]	wachsen; anbauen
know [nəʊ]	knew [nju:]	known [nəʊn]	kennen, wissen
ring [rɪŋ]	rang [ræŋ]	rung [rʌŋ]	klingeln; anrufen
rise [raɪz]	rose [rəʊz]	risen [ˈrɪzn]	steigen, sich erheben
see [si:]	saw [sɔ:]	seen [si:n]	sehen
show [ʃəʊ]	showed [ʃəʊd]	shown [ʃəʊn]	zeigen
sing [sɪŋ]	sang [sæŋ]	sung [sʌŋ]	singen
sink [sɪŋk]	sank [sæŋk]	sunk [sʌŋk]	sinken, untergehen
speak [spi:k]	spoke [spəʊk]	spoken [ˈspəʊkn]	sprechen
swim [swɪm]	swam [swæm]	swum [swʌm]	schwimmen
take [teɪk]	took [tʊk]	taken [ˈteɪkn]	nehmen
throw [θrəʊ]	threw [θru:]	thrown [θrəʊn]	werfen
wake up [ˌweɪk‿ˈʌp]	woke up [ˌwəʊk‿ˈʌp]	woken up [ˌwəʊkn‿ˈʌp]	aufwachen; aufwecken
wear [weə]	wore [wɔ:]	worn [wɔ:n]	anhaben, tragen
write [raɪt]	wrote [rəʊt]	written [ˈrɪtn]	schreiben

Grammar solutions

Unit 1

G1 Living here isn't bad

1. How about visiting a museum?
2. I don't really feel like going to a museum today.
3. OK, then, what would you suggest doing?
4. Mom keeps telling me about the spectacular views from Mt. Washington.
5. My mom loves going there too.
6. She never stops talking about the place.

G2 That's the worst thing to do!

1. I promise to be home before 6 p.m.
2. I didn't know what to say.
3. My parents don't want me to watch too much TV.
4. I didn't expect him to invite me to his party.
5. They always let her do what she wants.
6. Our football coach makes us train every day.
7. The best thing to do is say nothing at all.

G3 Gerund or infinitive: It depends on the meaning

Dear Diary,
Bad news! I got a mail from Matt today and it seems he can't stop **thinking** about Sophie. I'm sure Matt didn't mean **to hurt** me, but ... When I told Madison, she said I should try **to forget** him. But how? M. thinks I should try **doing** yoga! She says she can remember **feeling** upset about something once, and it really helped her. But I'm not sure. I'm not really sure about anything at the moment: Should I go on **writing** to him? Should I tell him how I feel? I don't know. The only thing I know right now is that it's really late and I mustn't forget **to set** my alarm clock. Madison's mom is driving us to the mall outside Pittsburgh tomorrow. We want **to get** there early and it's two hours in the car, so that means **leaving** at 8 a.m.! Oh well, at least we can stop **to have** breakfast somewhere on the way.

Unit 2

G4 The boy who ... / Diego, who ...

1. Last year we visited **New York**, which is the largest city in the USA.
2. We stayed with **some friends** who live there.
3. They showed us **some amazing sights** which we would never have found on our own.
4. But they also took us to famous sights like **Rockefeller Center**, which was awesome too.
5. In Times Square we saw **the Naked Cowboy**, who is really only *almost* naked.
6. He is a **street performer** who has become one of New York's biggest tourist attractions.

G5 How long had they been doing that?

After Julia and Andrea from Germany **had been walking** around Manhattan all morning, they were very hungry. So they decided to go to Diego's Diner, which they **had read** about in the guidebook they **had bought** the day before. When they got there at 12:30, the diner was already very busy. Some of the people **had been waiting** to get their lunch for quite some time. The girls **had been learning** English since the age of ten, so they had no language problems. But when they tried to order, nobody seemed to notice them. Finally, after they **had been trying** to get a waiter's attention for about 15 minutes, a friendly Hispanic American came to their table and took their order.

Unit 3

G6 The long, hard voyage to America

In 1901 we left Germany and sailed over to America on a **huge** ship. For the rich first- and second-class passengers the journey was **great**: they had **good** food, **live** music, **fresh** air and **lots** of space to move about. But for the hundreds of **poor** third-class passengers like us, the journey was **terrible**: Below deck, the food was **bad**, the drinking water tasted **strange**, the beds were **hard**, the toilets were **broken**, and there was no entertainment at all to keep us **happy**. Some of the passengers were **seasick**, others were **sick** with fever. The air was so **awful** that we often found it **difficult** to breathe. For us, the journey wasn't **exciting**. It was very, very **frightening**.

G7 The Pony Express

1. In 1700, about 250,000 colonists lived in North America, **but** by 1775 this number had grown to around 2.5 million.
2. **As** the population continued to grow, the land in the East became very crowded.
3. More space was needed, **so** people began to look West.
4. In 1803, President Jefferson bought large parts of North America from the French **and** offered it to new settlers for little money.
5. **While** many people moved West around this time to farm the new land, others left the East **because** they did not like the new industries or the cities that were developing there.
6. **Although** the journey West was hard and full of dangers, many people saw it as a chance to build better lives for themselves.

Unit 4

G8 You aren't serious, are you?

Ava: This is a cool store, isn't it?
Haley: Yes, they've got some nice clothes here, but they aren't cheap, are they?

Ava: No, but good quality costs money, doesn't it? Hey, these shorts look great, don't they? And they'll go really well with my new top, won't they? Oh, 40 dollars. You couldn't lend me some money, could you?

Haley: You aren't serious, are you? Listen, I've got a better idea. Let's go back to the store next door. They had some cool clothes there too, didn't they? And they were a lot cheaper.

G9 For me, excitement is ...

I live in Seattle, which is **the** largest city in **the** Northwest of **the** US. For me, it's **the** best place to live in **the** whole world. I just love **the** excitement of the city, especially in **the** summer months. There's always so much to do, from water sports on (-) Lake Washington to whale watching on Puget Sound or camping on (-) Mount Rainier in **the** Cascade Mountains. In Seattle, (-) life is never boring. But I'm not only interested in **the** outdoors, I'm really into (-) music too. I play **the** guitar and I practice at least two hours **a** day. My parents would like me to study to become **a** doctor when I finish (-) school. But that's not my dream. My dream is to become **a** famous pop star. Who knows? Maybe one day I'll be able to turn my dream into (-) reality.

G10 By the time I come back, everything will have changed

1. Tom will have given his presentation on Native American culture.
2. He'll have taken his books back to the library.
3. He'll have learned the vocabulary for the French test.
4. He won't have finished his Geography project.
5. He won't have spoken to Mr. Day about basketball practice.

Unit solutions

Unit 4, Mediation: English version of leaflet → page 115, ex. 6

Keep wildlife wild!

Biologists at Mount Rainier National Park here in Washington State have noticed a change in the natural behavior of the park's wildlife. The animals have lost their natural fear of humans, and one result of this, for example, is that the animals try to steal food from the park visitors. This is unsafe for both the wildlife and the visitors. Please don't feed the animals, keep all food in closed containers and take all your garbage away with you.

Safety first for hikers!

The weather can change very suddenly on Mount Rainier. Make sure you have extra clothes and rain gear with you – and you will, of course, need strong walking boots. Also, please remember that mountain hiking is very tiring. Make sure you rest regularly and eat often enough. You'll need lots of energy!

Good preparation is the key!

To be prepared for minor injuries, sudden weather changes or delays, you must always carry the following essentials with you (you can buy them in our shop):

1. a map of the park
2. a compass
3. matches
4. a flashlight
5. a candle
6. a pocket knife
7. sunglasses and sunscreen
8. rain gear
9. a first aid kit

The US school system

For most kids in the US, school starts at the age of 3–4 with pre-school (or nursery school), which can be compared to German *Kindergarten*. Different to Germany, kindergarten in the US comes after pre-school.

School systems differ around the US, but everywhere high school ends with the **high school diploma** after 12th grade. Then students can decide if they want to find a job or continue their education at college or university. A dual vocational training[1] like in Germany doesn't exist in the US.

State-run schools in the US are called **public schools**. The others are **private schools** mostly operated by religious institutions and organizations.

School takes up a lot of time

In America kids are at school all day. How early the day starts depends on how they get to school – with a school bus, by public or private transportation. Either the kids bring a bag lunch from home or eat a hot lunch in the school cafeteria. But even when classes are over in the afternoon, a lot of kids still don't go home because there are all kinds of activities going on. If you don't have sports practice for a school team, you might have a drama or chess club meeting. That means that many students don't get home until the evening.

Even on the weekend students spend a lot of time at school. Going to school sports events is a big social activity that involves a lot of different students, especially at the high school level. The school band plays at the game, the cheerleaders cheer, the dance team performs at half-time and the school newspaper photographer takes pictures.

High schools typically have formal dances several times a year. The most popular are the homecoming[2] dance after a football game and the prom[3] at the end of the school year.

Other school activities have more to do with the community. The students might organize a food or clothing drive to help poor families.

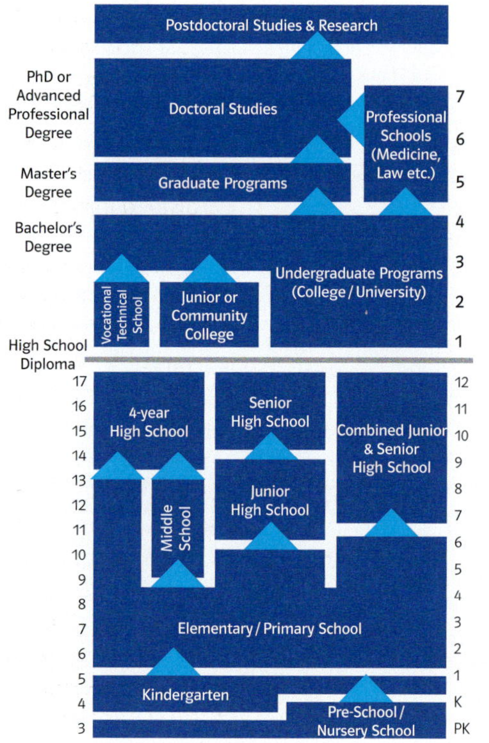

Source: DeutscheInDenUSA.com

Surprising facts

- About 2 million students are home-schooled in America.
- Going to a private school can cost $50,000 a year.
- The largest high school in America has over 8,000 students.

Or they spend their weekend helping to build a playground in the neighborhood. Most of the students really do want to help, but they also know that participating in these activities will look good on their college applications[4]. Getting into a good college or university can be very competitive and kids start thinking about it at the beginning of high school already!

1 **dual vocational training** [djuːəl vəʊˌkeɪʃnl ˈtreɪnɪŋ] duale Berufsausbildung | 2 **homecoming** [ˈhəʊmˌkʌmɪŋ] Ehemaligentreffen | 3 **prom** [prɒm] *Ball am Ende des Schuljahres* | 4 **application** [ˌæplɪˈkeɪʃn] Bewerbung

New York, New York

New York City, which was originally founded as a trading post in 1624, is the largest city in America with an estimated population of 8.6 million people (Berlin has about 3.5 million). In area, New York City is about half the size of Saarland.

The city is divided into five sections called **boroughs**[1]. The borough with the third-largest population is the smallest – **Manhattan**. This is home to the city's famous skyscrapers and three of the world's ten most-visited tourist attractions (Times Square, Central Park and the Grand Central Terminal). About 60 million tourists visit the city each year.

The least-populated borough and probably the most different compared to Manhattan is **Staten Island**. Most of the island is a residential[2] area. It is connected to Brooklyn by a bridge and the free Staten Island Ferry.

The **Bronx** is home to the world's largest metro zoo and the New York Yankees professional baseball team. However, it's probably most well-known as the birthplace of rap and hip-hop culture. More than half of the population is Hispanic.

Queens is the largest borough in area and is considered the most ethnically diverse[3] urban area in the world. Almost 50 % of the residents are foreign-born and 50 % of New York City's Asian population lives here. Queens annually hosts the US Open tennis tournament at Flushing Meadows. Two of the world's busiest airports, John F. Kennedy and LaGuardia, are also located here.

The most populous borough is **Brooklyn**. There is wide cultural, social and ethnic diversity. The rapidly growing Chinese-American population has established[4] several Chinatowns. Brooklyn is also home to a strong independent art scene but also to many high-tech start-ups.

Surprising facts

- New York was originally called New Amsterdam.
- The name 'Manhattan' goes back to the Native American tribe that lived in the area, called the Mannahatta.
- Almost half of the city's residents over the age of five speak a language other than English.

New York's importance in the world

New York City is often called the cultural and financial center of the world. The city is home to the world's two largest stock exchanges[5], where global trading goes on continuously. The United Nations has been located in New York since soon after its creation in 1945. The world's perhaps most famous theater district is simply known by the street that hosts it – Broadway. This is the place to go for plays and musicals. Besides performing arts like the symphony and ballet, there are also important art museums in New York, like the Museum of Modern Art, or MoMA for short. New York City has a huge advertising industry too. It used to be concentrated on Madison Avenue, but has now spread out across the city.

1 **borough** ['bʌrə] Stadtteil | 2 **residential** [rezɪ'denʃl] Wohn- | 3 **diverse** [daɪ'vɜ:s] vielfältig | 4 **to establish** [ɪ'stæblɪʃ] gründen | 5 **stock exchange** ['stɒk ɪksˌtʃeɪndʒ] Börse

Native Americans and their cultures

About 5.2 million people in the US are recorded as Native American; that's 1.7% of the total population. Native Americans traditionally lived in different tribes and they still identify with those tribes today.

Only about 20% of Native Americans live on the more than 300 reservations in the US. A reservation is an area of land that is managed by and belongs to a tribe alone. The largest reservation, which is about half the size of Germany, belongs to the Navajo nation. Today many reservations are allowed to have casinos, which have become a tourist attraction and a major source of income[1] for the tribes.

Referring to the first Americans only as 'the Indians' or 'the Native Americans' would be the same as calling all the very different peoples of Europe only 'the Europeans'. The tribes of the prairies, deserts and coasts had very different lifestyles, culture, traditions and art. Some tribes lived in one place and were farmers, like the Choctaw from the Southeast, and other tribes were nomadic[2]. The Lakota, for example, were hunters[3] and followed the buffalo herds. They lived in teepees, which could be packed up quickly and easily transported. Tribes of the Pacific Northwest such as the Chinook were known for their woodcarving, including totem poles[4]. The Anasazi, a desert tribe, were known for their black and white pottery[5].

Native Americans have their own languages – almost 300 of them! The most widely spoken one is Cherokee, which became a written language in the 1820s.

Surprising facts

- Words like 'Mississippi', 'Michigan', 'barbecue' and 'husky' originally come from Native American languages.
- These languages were used during World War II to send coded messages.
- The Cherokee language has 17 verb tenses, 10 persons, and 75% of the words are verbs.

The lives of Native Americans in the US were largely influenced by the arrival of European settlers. Here are some important dates of their common history:

1783	end of war between British and Americans; Native American territories are 'given' to America
1830–1850	**Trail of Tears:** forced relocations[6] of Native American tribes; many died on the way
1876	**Battle of the Little Bighorn:** one of the Native Americans' biggest victories[7] in the wars against America's expansion
1890	**Wounded Knee Massacre:** final clash between US troops and the Sioux; about 150 Native Americans were killed
1924	Native Americans were given US citizenship[8]
1968	Native Americans were granted all civil rights[9]
2009	**Historic apology** by US government to all Native Peoples

1 **source of income** [ˌsɔːs‿əv ˈɪnkʌm] Einnahmequelle | 2 **nomadic** [nəʊˈmædɪk] nicht sesshaft | 3 **hunter** [ˈhʌntə] Jäger/-in | 4 **totem pole** [ˈtəʊtəm ˌpəʊl] Totempfahl | 5 **pottery** [ˈpɒtri] Töpferei | 6 **relocation** [ˌriːləʊˈkeɪʃn] Umsiedlung | 7 **victory** [ˈvɪktri] Sieg | 8 **citizenship** [ˈsɪtɪznʃɪp] Staatsbürgerschaft | 9 **civil rights** [ˌsɪvl ˈraɪts] Bürgerrechte

National parks in the US

In 1872, President Ulysses S. Grant signed the law[1] that would eventually lead to the creation of 59 national parks in the US. The first national park was Yellowstone in Wyoming, Montana and Idaho. The area is geologically very active – rivers, waterfalls, canyons, geysers, bubbling mudpots, hot springs and volcanic activity. The park was named after the yellow-colored rock in its canyons. If you include national monuments, historical sites, seashores etc., there are more than 400 sites today and since 1916 the National Park Service has been in charge of preserving[2] them.

The largest park isn't visited very often due to its location. Wrangell-St. Elias National Park and Preserve in Alaska is 53,000 km^2 in size – that's bigger than Switzerland. The park with the most visitors is the Great Smoky Mountains in North Carolina and Tennessee with more than 10 million a year. People go there to hike since the park has 850 miles of trails. The Grand Canyon comes in 2nd place for the number of visitors and Yosemite in California is 3rd. California has the most national parks (nine), including Sequoia (giant trees) and Joshua Tree (a desert park full of huge cacti). Alaska is close behind with eight parks and then Utah with five. The newest national park, Pinnacles (2013), is also in California and is full of spectacular canyons and cliffs.

The role of the National Park Service (NPS)

The logo of the NPS symbolizes its role in preserving the country's natural beauty. However, preservation isn't the only purpose of a national park. Another main goal is the education of the millions of visitors who enjoy the parks every year. When tourists first started visiting Yellowstone, they threw objects into the pools, springs and geysers just for the fun of it. One such pool, which used to be a beautiful bright blue, was forced to erupt[4] in 1950 and out came socks, bath towels, handkerchiefs and coins. Back then it was also common practice to feed animals in the parks, including bears! Today this is forbidden for the safety of the people and the animals. In general, the park rangers do a lot to educate. There are campfire ranger talks, guided nature walks, museums and junior ranger programs for kids and teens which aim at getting them actively involved in the park.

Surprising facts

- The US invented the concept of national parks, but they are also the second-most polluting[3] country, after China.
- The Grand Canyon is almost exactly the same size as the country of Slovakia.
- Sequoia National Park is home to the largest living single-stem tree in the world. The tree is about 275 ft. (84 m) tall.

1 **law** [lɔ:] Gesetz | 2 **to preserve** [prɪ'zɜ:v] erhalten; schützen | 3 **to pollute** [pə'lu:t] verschmutzen | 4 **to erupt** [ɪ'rʌpt] ausbrechen; explodieren

Time line of US history

12,000 BC

The people we now call **Native Americans** came from Siberia to Alaska. But the first humans to arrive in America probably came from Southeast Asia by boat long before that.

1000 AD

The **Vikings** were the first Europeans to arrive in what is now the northeast corner of Canada. Little is known about their settlements there, which weren't permanent and which remained basically unknown in Europe.

1492

Christopher Columbus of Italy wasn't the first European to discover the 'New World' when his Spanish ships reached some islands in the Caribbean in 1492. But his four voyages for Spain – and the countless others by other explorers which followed – led to permanent European colonization of North and South America. The colonial race between the European powers was on.

1607

England was becoming a growing European power and wanted a piece of the colonial pie too. The first permanent English settlement established for the English crown was in **Jamestown**, Virginia.

1621

Some settlers came for different reasons, not for trade. Starting in 1621, the **Pilgrims**, for example, came to the New World to practice their religion freely – something they weren't allowed to do back in England. The Pilgrims colonized what is now Massachusetts in New England.

1675–1676

There had always been **conflicts between European settlers and Indians**, but most of the time there was peace during the early years. King Philip's War in 1675–76 (Philip was an Indian chief) was the first serious war and started two centuries of bloody warfare between whites and Native Americans.

1776

The 'Founding Fathers'gather to sign the famous Declaration of Independence

When the 13 British colonies in America declared their **independence from Britain** and then won it in the Revolutionary War, it was the beginning of a new country: The United States of America. The famous **Declaration of Independence** was a milestone in democratic thinking. From the start, America was built on the ideas of personal freedom and political involvement by the people for the people.

1803

After President Jefferson had bought huge parts of North America from the French in 1803 (the Louisiana Purchase), he sent the **explorers Lewis and Clark** out West to see what the country had bought.

Endless land-scapes of mountains and prairies: typical of the West, then and now

he first battle
1 the US Civil
Var was fought
t Fort Sumter,
outh Carolina

1861–1865

The South was a slave-holding, agricultural society; the North was more industrialized. Because of these differences, the southern states wanted to be separate, and a terrible **Civil War** followed. The victory of the North saved the unity of the US and freed the slaves.

Railroad workers had to face the challenge of endless miles of difficult and often mountainous terrain

1869

The first transcontinental railroad – the Pacific Railroad – opened in 1869. It was regarded as the greatest technological achievement of the 19th century. With more and more railroads linking the massive country, the US was able to grow together – and the economy could grow too.

1914–1918
1941–1945

World War I and **World War II** both ended with victories for America and its allies. By the time WWI was over, the US had become one of the leading world powers. By the time WWII was over, America had become one of two superpowers; the Soviet Union was the other.

1929–1938

The US, together with the rest of the world, entered a period of economic depression, often called the **Great Depression**. With a radical shift in economic policy, President Franklin D. Roosevelt and his **New Deal** helped to overcome the crisis.

Following WWII

Throughout the 20th century, **American influence** on all aspects of international life became more and more important, from business to politics to culture – especially after World War II. Great inventors, writers, artists and Hollywood actors turned the 20th century into the 'American century'.

Hollywood, especially in the 1940s and 1950s, would have been unthinkable without its glamorous movie stars

1950s–1960s

Rosa Parks and Martin Luther King Jr., among others, protested against the unfair treatment of African-Americans in the **civil rights movement** of the 1950s and 1960s. Eventually, protests grew so strong that the policy of segregation finally came to an end. But this didn't yet mean the end of race problems in the US.

2001

The **9/11 terrorist attacks** in New York and Washington, D.C., were a huge shock for Americans. But fighting terrorism with military means turned out to be very problematic, as the Americanled wars in Afghanistan and Iraq following 9/11 showed.

2009–2017

YES, WE CAN!

Barack Obama became the first **African-American president** in US history. This was a huge milestone in race relations for the entire country.

Barack Obama taking the oath of office, Jan. 2009

THE PACIFIC NORTHWEST

NEW YORK
THE BRONX
W 155th St.
W 145th St.
Harlem River Dr.
HARLEM
W 125th St.
7th Avenue
Lenox Avenue
Broadway
Henry Hudson Pkwy.
MANHATTAN
Park Avenue
2nd Avenue
1st Avenue
Amsterdam Ave.
Central Park
E 106th St.
Hudson River
UPPER WEST SIDE
5th Avenue
E 96th St.
W 81st St.
UPPER EAST SIDE
The Metropolitan Museum of Art
E 84th St.
The Juilliard School
Lincoln Center
Broadway
E 79th St.
Park Avenue
3rd Avenue
2nd Avenue
1st Avenue
E 66th St.
10th Avenue
9th Avenue
Central Park S.
Lincoln Tunnel
Alvin Ailey American Dance Theater
Avenue of the Americas
Museum of Modern Art
QUEENS
12th Avenue
W 42nd St.
Rockefeller Center
Queensboro Bridge
Times Square
W 34th St.
5th Avenue
Chrysler Building
The High Line
E 42nd St.
MIDTOWN
United Nations
Empire State Building
Queens Midtown Tunnel
NEW JERSEY
9th Avenue
8th Avenue
7th Avenue
Broadway
W 14th St.
E 23rd St.
West Side Highway
Bleecker St.
Greenwich Village
E 14th St.
Hudson St.
Holland Tunnel
Soho
Broadway
Astor Place
Avenue D
LOWER WEST SIDE
Broome St.
Little Italy
E Houston St.
Canal St.
LOWER EAST SIDE
East River
Chinatown
Bowery
Williamsburg Bridge
One World Trade Center
9/11 Memorial
FDR Drive
Brooklyn Bridge
Manhattan Bridge
Ellis Island
Liberty Island
Statue of Liberty
Brooklyn Battery Tunnel
BROOKLYN
MANHATTAN
THE BRONX
NEW JERSEY
QUEENS
BROOKLYN
STATEN ISLAND

Bildquellen:
U1.1 Getty Images RF (E+/wundervisuals), München; **U1.2** shutterstock (Stuart Monk), New York, NY; **2.1** Corbis, Düsseldorf; **3.1** Getty Images (DEA/A. DAGLI ORTI/De Agostini), München; **4.1** Alamy Images (Sean Pavone), Abingdon, Oxon; **6.1** laif (Lars Schneider/Aurora), Köln; **8.1** Corbis (Matt Mawson), Düsseldorf; **8.2** Corbis (Bill Stormont), Düsseldorf; **8.3** shutterstock (Pi-Lens), New York, NY; **8.4** Corbis (Nick Roush), Düsseldorf; **8.5** shutterstock (Everett Historical), New York, NY; **9.1** Corbis (Louie Psihoyos), Düsseldorf; **9.2** Corbis (Gavin Hellier/JAI), Düsseldorf; **9.3** Corbis (Hill Street Studios/Blend Images), Düsseldorf; **9.4** Corbis (Lynn Christiansen), Düsseldorf; **9.5** Corbis (David Butow), Düsseldorf; **10.1** shutterstock (granata1111), New York, NY; **11.1** Corbis (Robert Niedring), Düsseldorf; **11.2** Corbis (Hero Images), Düsseldorf; **12.1** Corbis (Kevin Dodge/ Masterfile), Düsseldorf; **12.2** shutterstock (LizCoughlan), New York, NY; **13.1** shutterstock (Monkey Business Images), New York, NY; **14.1** Fotolia.com (jackfrog), New York; **14.2** Corbis (237/Paul Bradbury/Ocean), Düsseldorf; **15.1** Corbis (GraphicaArtis), Düsseldorf; **15.2** shutterstock (Karen Grigoryan), New York, NY; **16.1** shutterstock (Lucky Business), New York, NY; **17.1** Thinkstock (ikick), München; **17.2** Corbis (Hero Images), Düsseldorf; **19.1** Corbis (Tetra Images), Düsseldorf; **21.1** Corbis (KidStock/Blend Images), Düsseldorf; **25.1–25.2** JDM Productions Inc., New York; **26.1** shutterstock (Veronica Louro), New York, NY; **26.2** Corbis (DreamPictures/ VStock/Blend Images/), Düsseldorf; **26.3** Corbis, Düsseldorf; **27.1** Getty Images (Vivien Killilea), München; **28.1** iStockphoto (wickedberlin), Calgary, Alberta; **28.2** Alamy Images (Vespasian), Abingdon, Oxon; **30.1** Fotolia.com (Monkey Business), New York; **30.2** shutterstock (JuliusKielaitis), New York, NY; **30.3** shutterstock (Palenque), New York, NY; **31.1** www.CartoonStock.com (Schwadron, Harley), Bath; **32.1** shutterstock (Gary Whitton), New York, NY; **32.2** shutterstock (Gimas), New York, NY; **32.3** iStockphoto (Pgiam), Calgary, Alberta; **33.1** Thinkstock (lisafx), München; **33.2** Picture-Alliance (Maja Hitij), Frankfurt; **33.3** Alamy Images (Jim West), Abingdon, Oxon; **33.4** shutterstock (ducu59us), New York, NY; **35.1** Thinkstock (darak77), München; **35.2** shutterstock (yurok), New York, NY; **35.3** Getty Images (fStop), München; **35.4** shutterstock (InesBazdar), New York, NY; **35.5** shutterstock (Fotoatelie), New York, NY; **35.6** Getty Images (Corbis), München; **36.1** Thinkstock (shironosov), München; **37.1** Getty Images (DEA/A. DAGLI ORTI/De Agostini), München; **37.2** shutterstock (Maridav), New York, NY; **37.3** shutterstock (Maridav), New York, NY; **38.1** JDM Productions Inc., New York; **39.1** shutterstock (HBRH), New York, NY; **40.1** shutterstock (Luciano Mortula), New York, NY; **41.1** Getty Images (Visions of America/UIG), München; **41.2** shutterstock (digishoots), New York, NY; **41.3** Thinkstock (stu99), München; **41.4** iStockphoto (carterdayne), Calgary, Alberta; **43.1** shutterstock (DrimaFilm), New York, NY; **45.1** shutterstock (Erika Cross), New York, NY; **45.2** shutterstock (martiapunts), New York, NY; **49.1** shutterstock (oneinchpunch), New York, NY; **49.2** shutterstock (FashionStock.com), New York, NY; **50.1–57.1** Stefani Kampmann/Morton Rhue: Asphalt Tribe ¿ Eine Graphic Novel © 2011 by Ravensburger Buchverlag Otto Maier GmbH, Ravensburg; **60.1** Alamy Images (Sean Pavone), Abingdon, Oxon; **61.1** JDM Productions Inc., New York; **61.2** JDM Productions Inc., New York; **62.1** shutterstock (Kamira), New York, NY; **64.1** iStockphoto (Jitalia17), Calgary, Alberta; **65.1** shutterstock (Vacclav), New York, NY; **65.2** shutterstock (Christopher Penler), New York, NY; **67.1** shutterstock (View Apart), New York, NY; **68.1** shutterstock (Kaesler Media), New York, NY; **69.1** akg-images (Jason Hook), Berlin; **69.2** Corbis (Matt Moyer), Düsseldorf; **69.3** shutterstock (pisaphotography), New York, NY; **70.1** Getty Images (Moviepix), München; **70.2** Getty Images (Hero Images), München; **71.1** NASA (PD), Washington , D.C.; **71.2** Getty Images (CBS Photo Archive), München; **72.1** Getty Images (Barry King/WireImage), München; **74.1** Getty Images (Moviepix), München; **74.2** ddp images GmbH (Capital Pictures), Hamburg; **76.1–77.1; 77.2** JDM Productions Inc., New York; **78.1** iStockphoto (Li Kim Goh), Calgary, Alberta; **78.2** Getty Images (Photolibrary/David H. Carriere), München; **78.3** iStockphoto (David Sucsy), Calgary, Alberta; **79.1** Thinkstock (Rawpixel Ltd), München; **80.1** Alamy Images (Stillman Rogers), Abingdon, Oxon; **80.2** shutterstock (wavebreakmedia), New York, NY; **81.1** Alamy Images (GREG RYAN), Abingdon, Oxon; **81.2** Getty Images (Ann Ronan Picture Library/Heritage Images), München; **84.1** shutterstock (Radoslaw Lecyk), New York, NY; **85.1** Klett-Archiv (©2016 The Statue of Liberty - Ellis Island Foundation), Stuttgart; **85.2** Klett-Archiv (United States Census Bureau), Stuttgart; **86.1** Alamy Images (Pictorial Press Ltd), Abingdon, Oxon; **88.1** Getty Images (Hulton Archive), München; **88.2** Ullstein Bild GmbH, Berlin; **88.3** Corbis (Bettmann), Düsseldorf; **88.4** Alamy Images (Arcaid Images/Hedrich Blessing/ Chicago Historical Society), Abingdon, Oxon; **88.5** Getty Images (SSPL/Science Museum), München; **88.6** Getty Images (AFP), München; **88.7** Alamy Images (M4OS Photos), Abingdon, Oxon; **89.1** shutterstock (Joseph Sohm), New York, NY; **91.1** Getty Images (Hero Images), München; **95.1–95.3** JDM Productions Inc., New York; **96.1** Alamy Images (Shotshop GmbH), Abingdon, Oxon; **96.2** Alamy Images (White Star/Monica Gumm), Abingdon, Oxon; **96.3** Ullstein Bild GmbH (Jazz Archiv Hamburg), Berlin; **97.1** Alamy Images (ClassicStock), Abingdon, Oxon; **98.1** Alamy Images (Aurora Photos), Abingdon, Oxon; **98.2** Mauritius Images (Jim West/ Alamy), Mittenwald; **101.1** Klett-Archiv (Study of Brookings Institution, 2013), Stuttgart; **102.1** shutterstock (Nagel Photography), New York, NY; **103.1** shutterstock (Galyna Andrushko), New York, NY; **103.2** shutterstock (Brenda Linskey), New York, NY; **103.3** shutterstock (Nick Fox), New York, NY; **105.1** © 2015 Matthew Karsten, Miami; **107.1** Mauritius Images (United Archives), Mittenwald; **107.2** Mauritius Images (SiliconValleyStock/Alamy), Mittenwald; **107.3** shutterstock (holbox), New York, NY; **108.1–108.4** JDM Productions Inc., New York; **109.1** iStockphoto (Elena Elisseeva), Calgary, Alberta; **109.2** iStockphoto (alexxx1981), Calgary, Alberta; **109.3** iStockphoto (AlexKozlov), Calgary, Alberta; **109.4** iStockphoto (wundervisuals), Calgary, Alberta; **110.1** Getty Images (Corbis Documentary), München; **111.1** shutterstock (Pavel L Photo and Video), New York, NY; **111.2** shutterstock (Monika Wieland), New York, NY;

111.3 Getty Images (Moment/Michael Lee), München; **111.4** shutterstock (Corepics VOF), New York, NY; **113.1** shutterstock (cdrin), New York, NY; **114.1** shutterstock (Philipe Ancheta), New York, NY; **114.2** Getty Images (Rob Carr), München; **114.3** Getty Images (Corbis), München; **114.4** laif (Lars Schneider/Aurora), Köln; **115.1** Picture-Alliance (Design Pics), Frankfurt; **116.1** iStockphoto (professorphotoshop), Calgary, Alberta; **116.2** shutterstock (Dan Breckwoldt), New York, NY; **117.1** Getty Images (National Geographic), München; **118.1** Getty Images (All Canada Photos), München; **118.2** Getty Images (Werner Forman/ Universal Images Group), München; **118.3** Okapia (Clark James Mishler/Alaska Stock), Frankfurt; **120.1** Getty Images (Science Source), München; **120.2** shutterstock (Galyna Andrushko), New York, NY; **121.1** Getty Images (Corbis Documentary), München; **121.2** shutterstock (M. Shcherbyna), New York, NY; **121.3** shutterstock (Kamira), New York, NY; **121.4** iStockphoto (David Sucsy), Calgary, Alberta; **121.5** shutterstock (Sean Pavone), New York, NY; **123.1; 125.1; 122.1; 124.1** The Absolutely True Diary of a Part-Time Indian, Author: Sherman Alexie, Illustrator: Ellen Forney, Andersen Press.; **126.1** Klett-Archiv, Stuttgart; **„127.1; 127.2** JDM Productions Inc., New York; **134.1** shutterstock (Northfoto), New York, NY; **137.1–137.3** Stefani Kampmann/Morton Rhue: Asphalt Tribe ¿ Eine Graphic Novel © 2011 by Ravensburger Buchverlag Otto Maier GmbH, Ravensburg; **139.1** Mauritius Images (colaimages/Alamy), Mittenwald; **140.1** Mauritius Images (JT Vintage/Keystone View Company), Mittenwald; **140.2** Mauritius Images (JT Vintage/F. Jay Haynes), Mittenwald; **141.1** Getty Images (LightRocket/Wolfgang Kaehler), München; **143.1** Getty Images (The Asahi Shimbun), München; **145.1** shutterstock (jadimages), New York, NY; **145.2** Getty Images (National Geographic), München; **146.1** shutterstock (Antonio Guillem), New York, NY; **155.1** Thinkstock (Comstock), München; **156.1** Thinkstock (Tom Ackerman), München; **157.1** iStockphoto (clu), Calgary, Alberta; **159.1** dreamstime.com (Edward Bartel), Brentwood, TN; **159.2** akg-images (Album), Berlin; **163.1** Fotolia.com (jackfrog), New York; **163.2** Corbis (237/Paul Bradbury/ Ocean), Düsseldorf; **165.1** Getty Images (Corbis), München; **165.2** Fotolia.com (jackfrog), New York; **168.1** Fotolia.com (jackfrog), New York; **168.2** Thinkstock (Wavebreakmedia Ltd), München; **170.1** Fotolia.com (Pierre brillot), New York; **178.1** Thinkstock (Brand X Pictures), München; **186.1** Thinkstock (LUNA-MARINA), München; **186.2** Fotolia. com (spiritofamerica), New York; **192.2** shutterstock (suicidecrew), New York, NY; **208.2** Thinkstock (Photos.com), München; **214.1** Thinkstock (stu99), München; **219.1** iStockphoto (Pgiam), Calgary, Alberta; **264.1** Thinkstock (Creatas Images), München; **269.1** Picture-Alliance (Design Pics), Frankfurt; **270.1** Klett-Archiv (DeutscheInDenUSA.com), Stuttgart; **271.1** shutterstock (Rainer Lesniewski), New York, NY; **272.1** shutterstock (Joseph Sohm), New York, NY; **273.1** shutterstock (Anton Foltin), New York, NY; **273.2** shutterstock (Zack Frank), New York, NY; **274.1** Getty Images (SuperStock), München; **274.2** Thinkstock (TenleyThompson), München; **274.3** Glow Images GmbH (Heritage Images RM), München; **275.1** Interfoto (Granger, NYC), München; **275.2** Getty Images (Bettmann), München; **275.3** Imago, Berlin; **275.4** Picture-Alliance (abaca), Frankfurt

Textquellen:

40 Song: "Empire State of Mind" Text: Carter, Shawn/ Hunte, Angela/Keyes, Bert/Keys, Alicia/Robinson, Sylvia/ Sewell, Janet Andrea/Shuckburgh, Alexander William, © Carter Boys Music/EMI April Music/Foray Music/Gambi Music Inc/Global Talent Publishing/J Sewell Publishing/ Lellow Productions Inc/Masani El Shabazz, EMI Music Publishing Germany GmbH, Berlin/Rolf Budde Musikverlag GmbH, Berlin/Neue Welt Musikverlag GmbH, Hamburg; **60** Reprinted with the permission of Simon & Schuster Books for Young Readers, an imprint of Simon & Schuster Children's Publishing Division, from CAN'T GET THERE FROM HERE by Todd Strasser. Copyright © 2004 by Todd Strasser. All rights reserved.; **66** http://www.twc.org/about-us/a-poem-as-big-as-nyc/a-poem-as-big-as-nyc-poems/; **89** Song: "Firework" Text: Dean, Esther/Eriksen, Mikkel Storleer/Hermansen, Tor Erik/Perry, Katy/Wilhelm, Sandy Julien, Verlag: Dat Damn Dean Music/Di Piu S.R.L./ EMI Music Publishing Ltd./Peermusic Ltd/When I'm rich You'll be my Bitch EMI Music Publishing Germany GmbH & Co. KG, Hamburg EMI Music Publishing Germany GmbH & Co. KG, Hamburg Peermusic (Germany) GmbH, Hamburg; **96** http:// www.balinstadt.de; **103** From *Rough Guides*, London, http:// www.roughguides.com; **105+106** © 2015 Matthew Karsten; **116** Adapted from the version of the legend by Joe Jack of the Cowichan Tribe, British Columbia; **122–125** *The Absolutely True Diary of a Part-Time Indian*, Sherman Alexie, Andersen Press.

Sollte es in einem Einzelfall nicht gelungen sein, den korrekten Rechteinhaber ausfindig zu machen, so werden berechtigte Ansprüche selbstverständlich im Rahmen der üblichen Regelungen abgegolten.

ALASKA
Denali
CANADA
CANADA
Seattle
Portland
WASHINGTON
OREGON
Rocky Mountains
MONTANA
NORTH DAKOTA
IDAHO
WYOMING
SOUTH DAKOTA
NEVADA
UTAH
NEBRASKA
San Francisco
Denver
CALIFORNIA
COLORADO
Las Vegas
HOLLYWOOD
ARIZONA
OKLAHO
Los Angeles
Pacific Ocean
San Diego
Phoenix
NEW MEXICO
TEXAS
HAWAII
MEXICO

THE UNITED STATES OF AMERICA